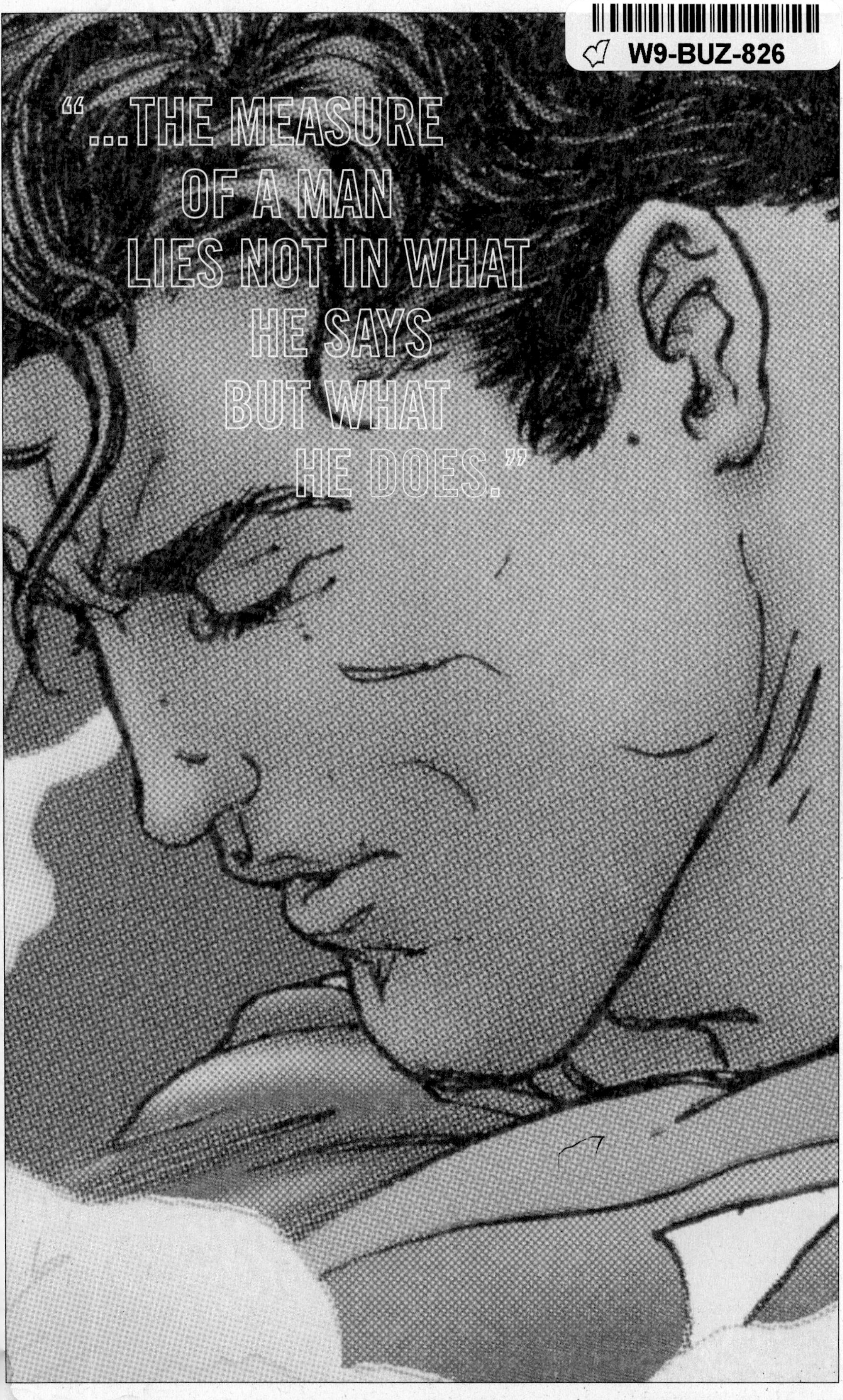
"...THE MEASURE
OF A MAN
LIES NOT IN WHAT
HE SAYS
BUT WHAT
HE DOES."

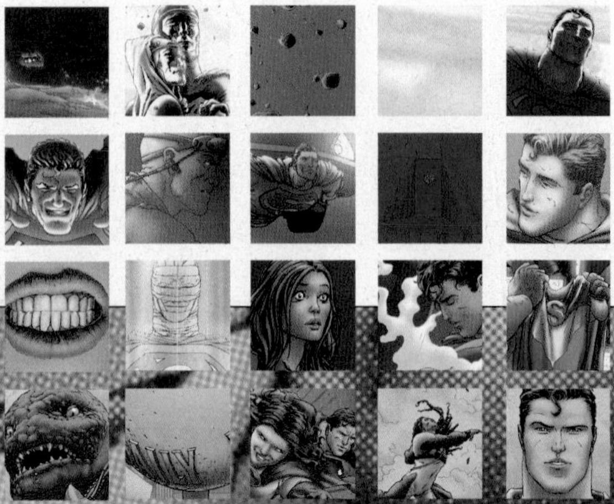

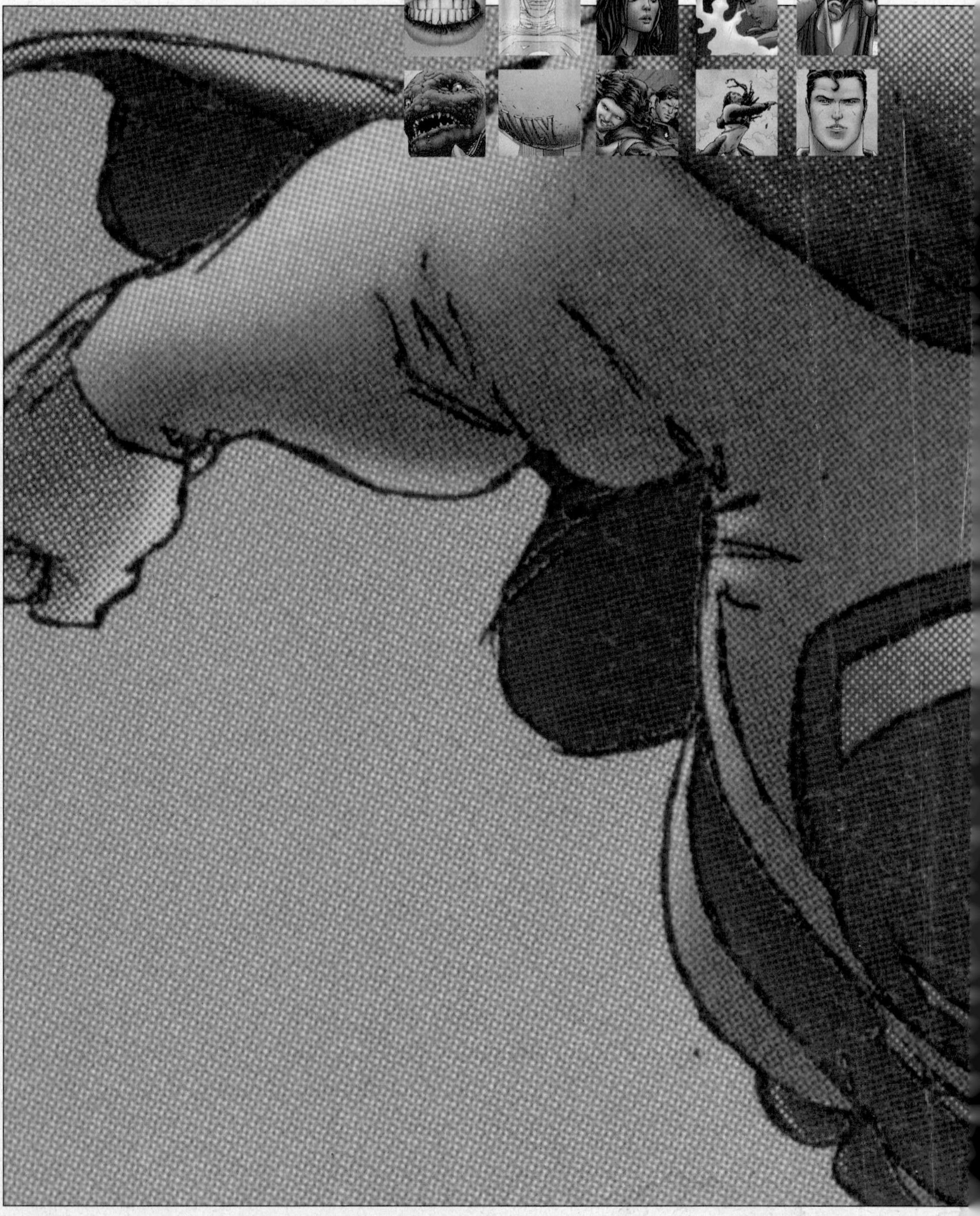

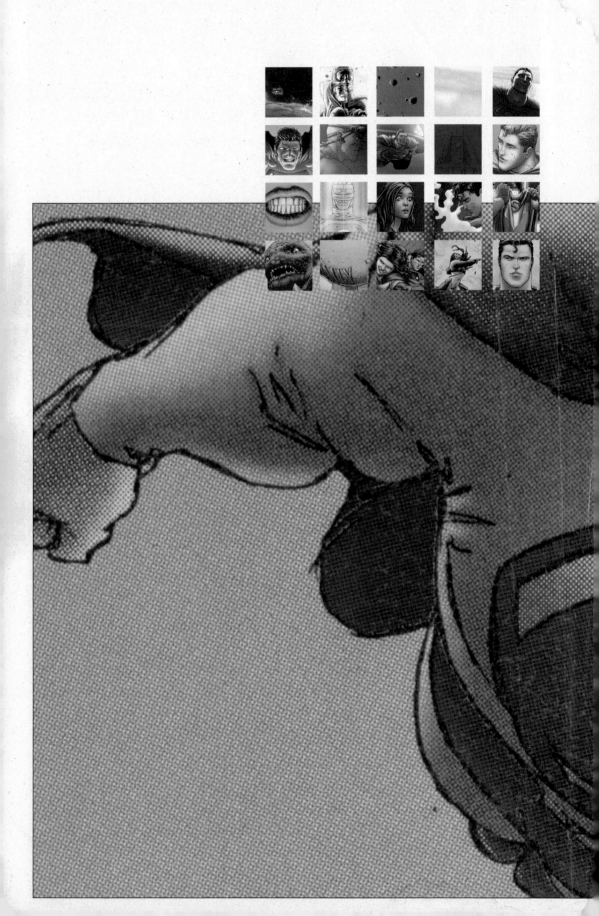

ALL-STAR SUPERMAN

Written by **Grant Morrison** Pencilled by **Frank Quitely** Digitally inked & colored by **Jamie Grant**

Lettered by **Phil Balsman** & **Travis Lanham** **Superman** created by **Jerry Siegel** & **Joe Shuster**

By special arrangement with the Jerry Siegel family

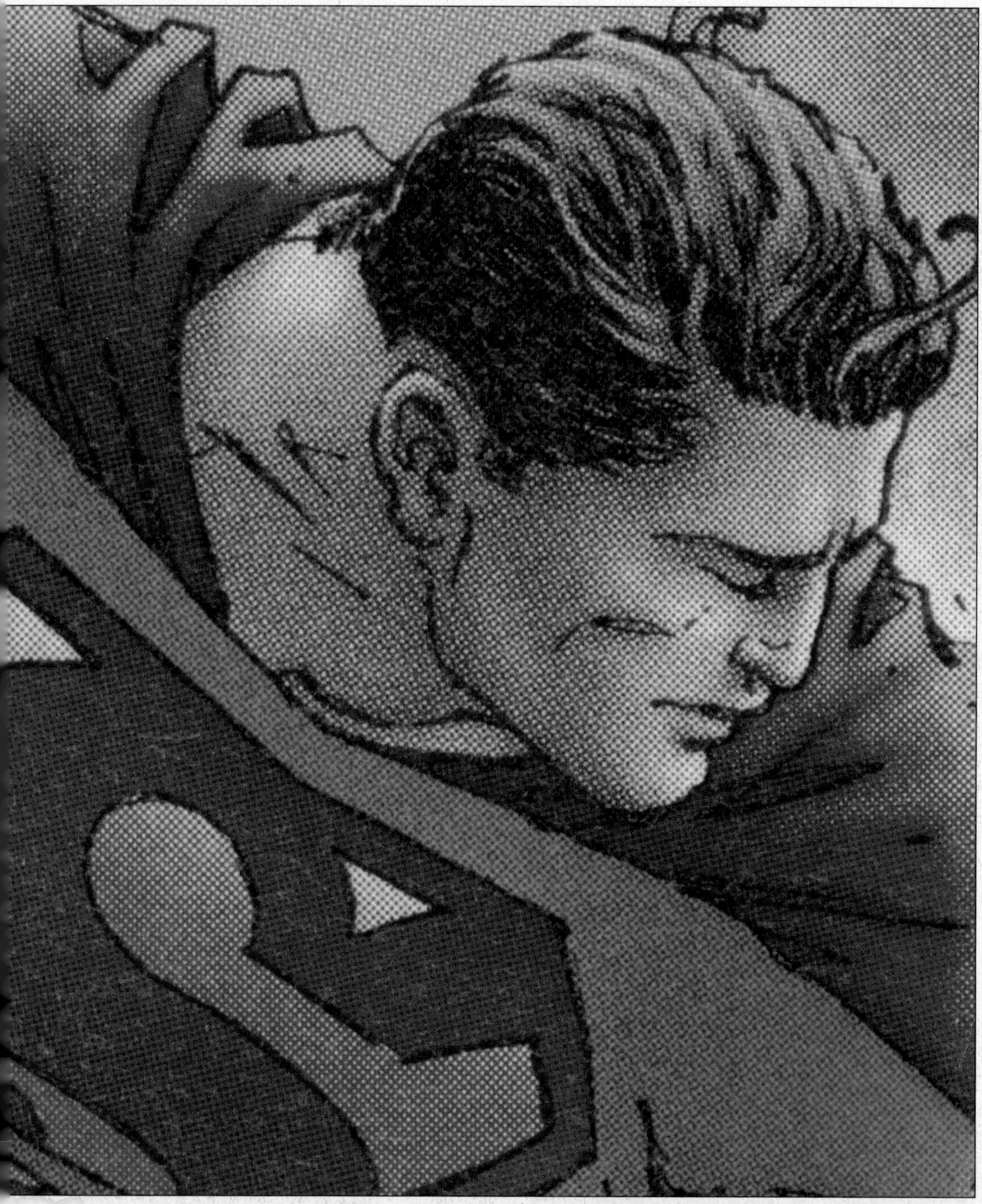

Bob Schreck
Editor–Original Series

Brandon Montclare
Assistant Editor–Original Series

Jeb Woodard
Group Editor–Collected Editions

Steve Cook
Design Director–Books

Bob Harras
Senior VP–Editor-in-Chief, DC Comics

Diane Nelson
President

Dan DiDio and **Jim Lee**
Co-Publishers

Geoff Johns
Chief Creative Officer

Amit Desai
Senior VP–Marketing & Global Franchise Management

Nairi Gardiner
Senior VP–Finance

Sam Ades
VP–Digital Marketing

Bobbie Chase
VP–Talent Development

Mark Chiarello
Senior VP–Art, Design & Collected Editions

John Cunningham
VP–Content Strategy

Anne DePies
VP–Strategy Planning & Reporting

Don Falletti
VP–Manufacturing Operations

Lawrence Ganem
VP–Editorial Administration & Talent Relations

Alison Gill
Senior VP–Manufacturing & Operations

Hank Kanalz
Senior VP–Editorial Strategy & Administration

Jay Kogan
VP–Legal Affairs

Derek Maddalena
Senior VP–Sales & Business Development

Jack Mahan
VP–Business Affairs

Dan Miron
VP–Sales Planning & Trade Development

Nick Napolitano
VP–Manufacturing Administration

Carol Roeder
VP–Marketing

Eddie Scannell
VP–Mass Account & Digital Sales

Courtney Simmons
Senior VP–Publicity & Communications

Jim (Ski) Sokolowski
VP–Comic Book Specialty & Newsstand Sales

Sandy Yi
Senior VP–Global Franchise Management

Logo Design by Chip Kidd

ALL-STAR SUPERMAN

Published by DC Comics. Cover and compilation
Copyright © 2011 DC Comics. All Rights Reserved.

Originally published in single magazine form in

DC Comics, 2900 W. Alameda Avenue, Burbank, CA
91505
Printed by Solisco Printers, Scott, QC, Canada. 4/8/16.
Sixth Printing.
ISBN: 978-1-4012-3205-4

PEFC Certified
This product is from sustainably managed forests, recycled and controlled sources
PEFC/26-31-82
www.pefc.org

Library of Congress Cataloging-in-Publication Data

Morrison, Grant.
   All-star Superman / Grant Morrison, Frank Quitely,
Jamie Grant.
      p. cm.
   "Originally published in single magazine form in All-
star Superman 1-12."
   ISBN 978-1-4012-3205-4
   1. Graphic novels. 2. Comic books, strips, etc. I.
Quitely, Frank, 1968- II. Grant, Jamie, 1968- III. Title.
   PN6728.S9M683 2012
   741.5'973—dc23

                                        2012035380

For Agnes and Walter, my mum and dad.
—Grant Morrison

For Ann Jane, Vin, Joe & Orla.
—Frank Quitely

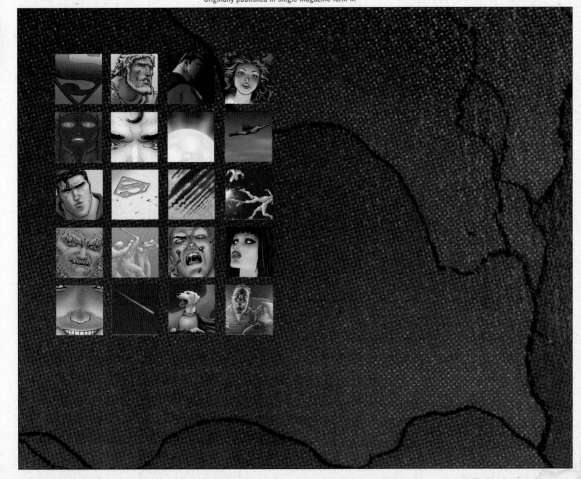

Episode 1

... FASTER...

Cover FRANK QUITELY with JAMIE GRANT

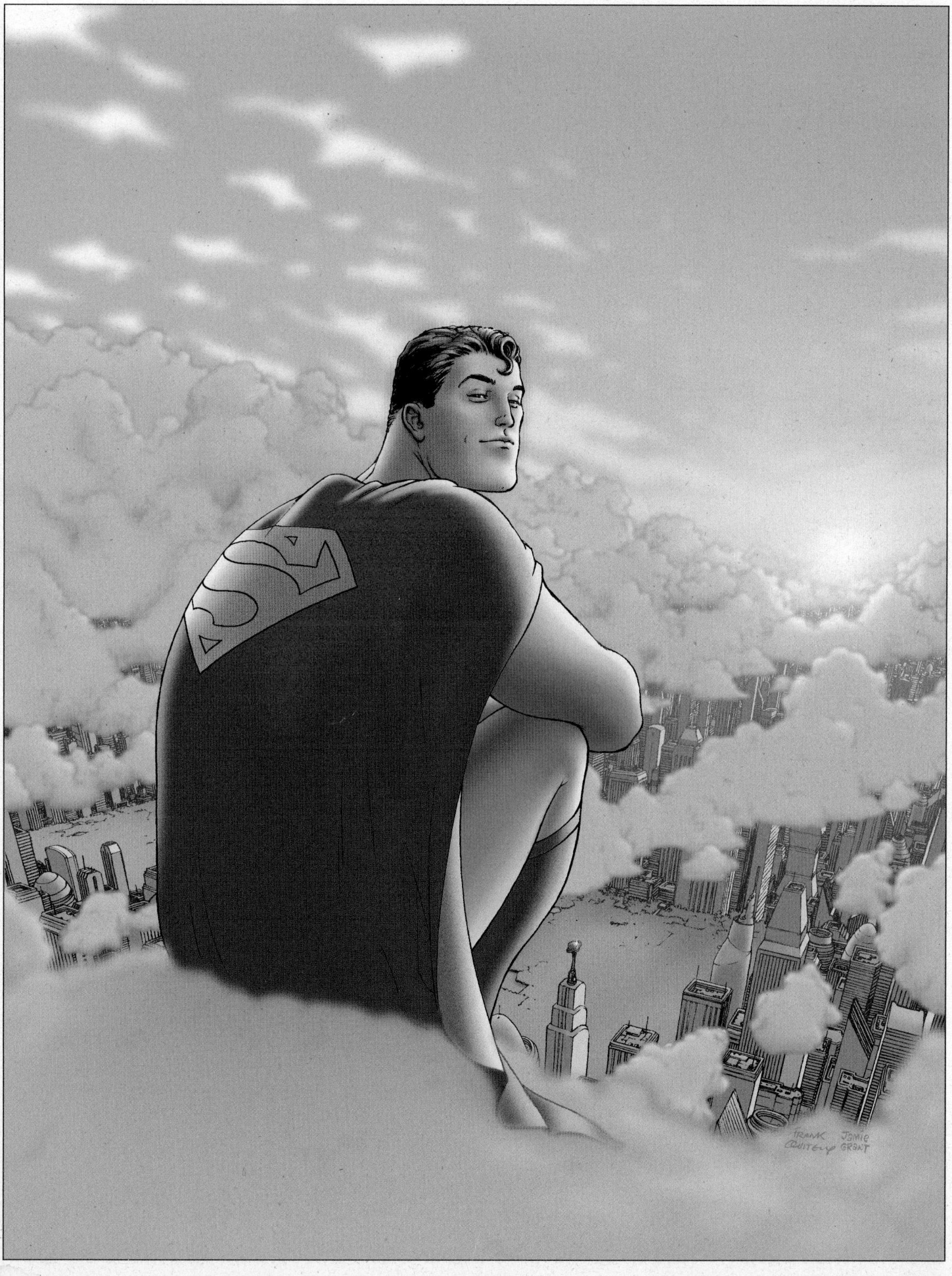
FRANK QUITELY
JAMIE GRANT

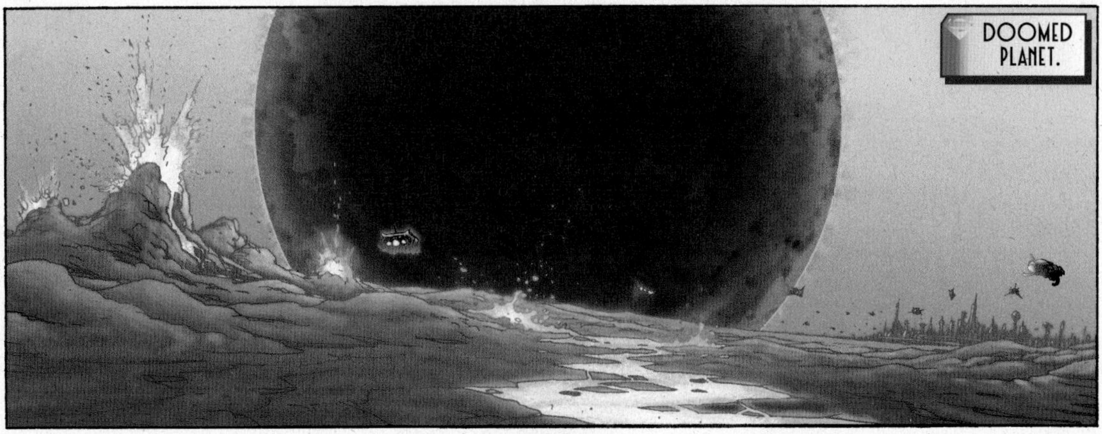
DOOMED PLANET.

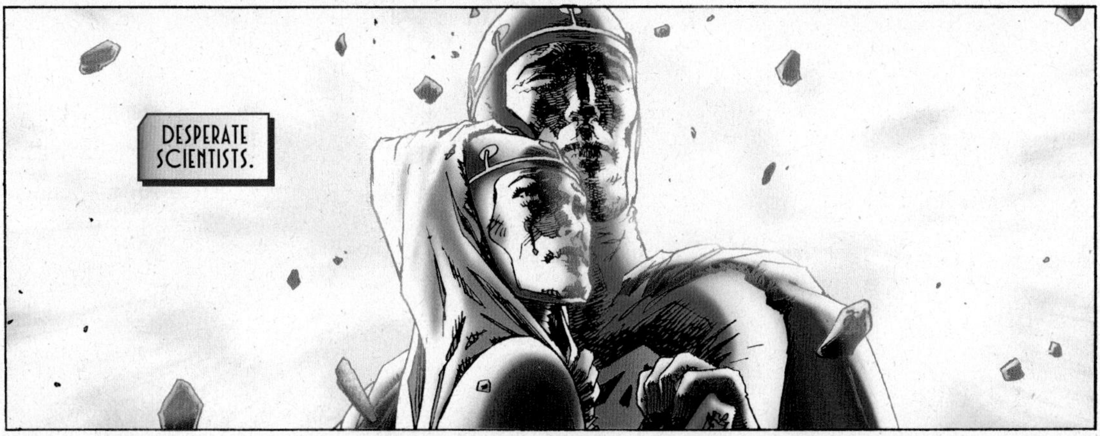
DESPERATE SCIENTISTS.

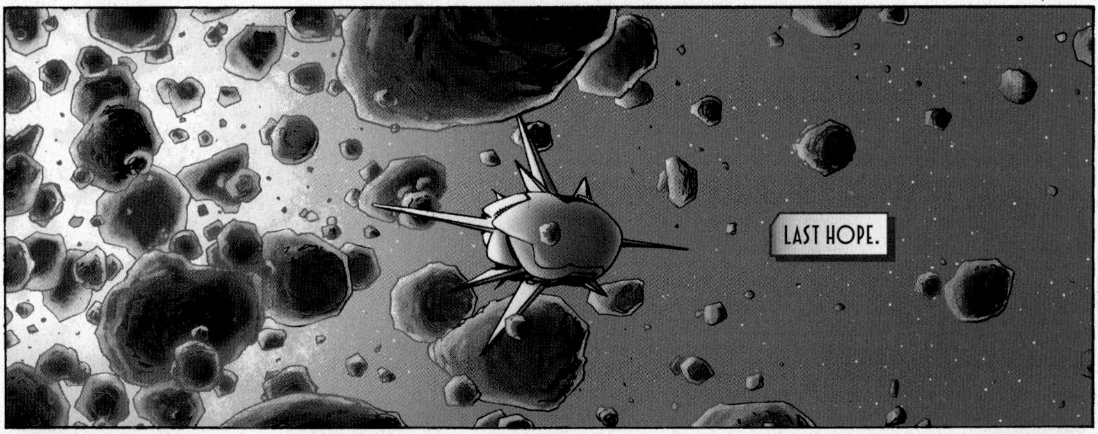
LAST HOPE.

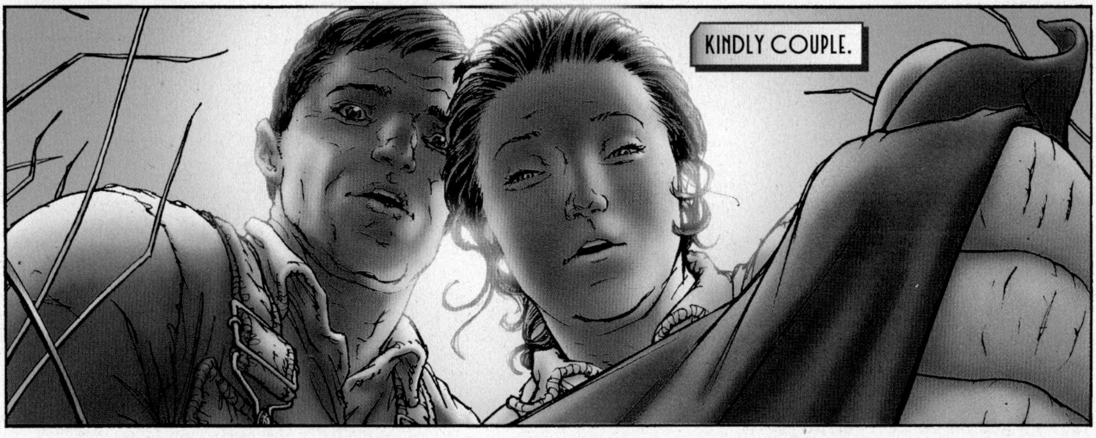
KINDLY COUPLE.

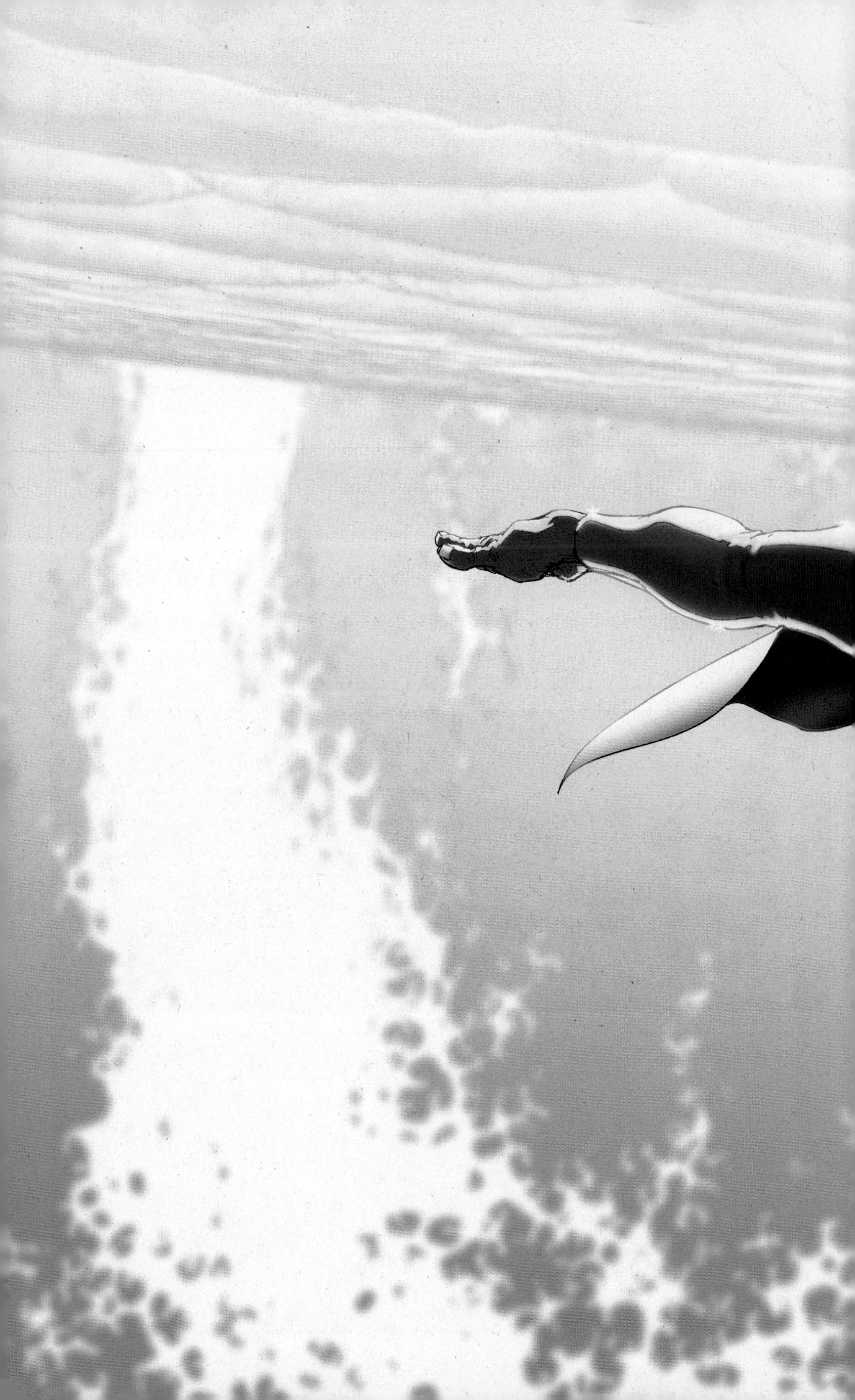

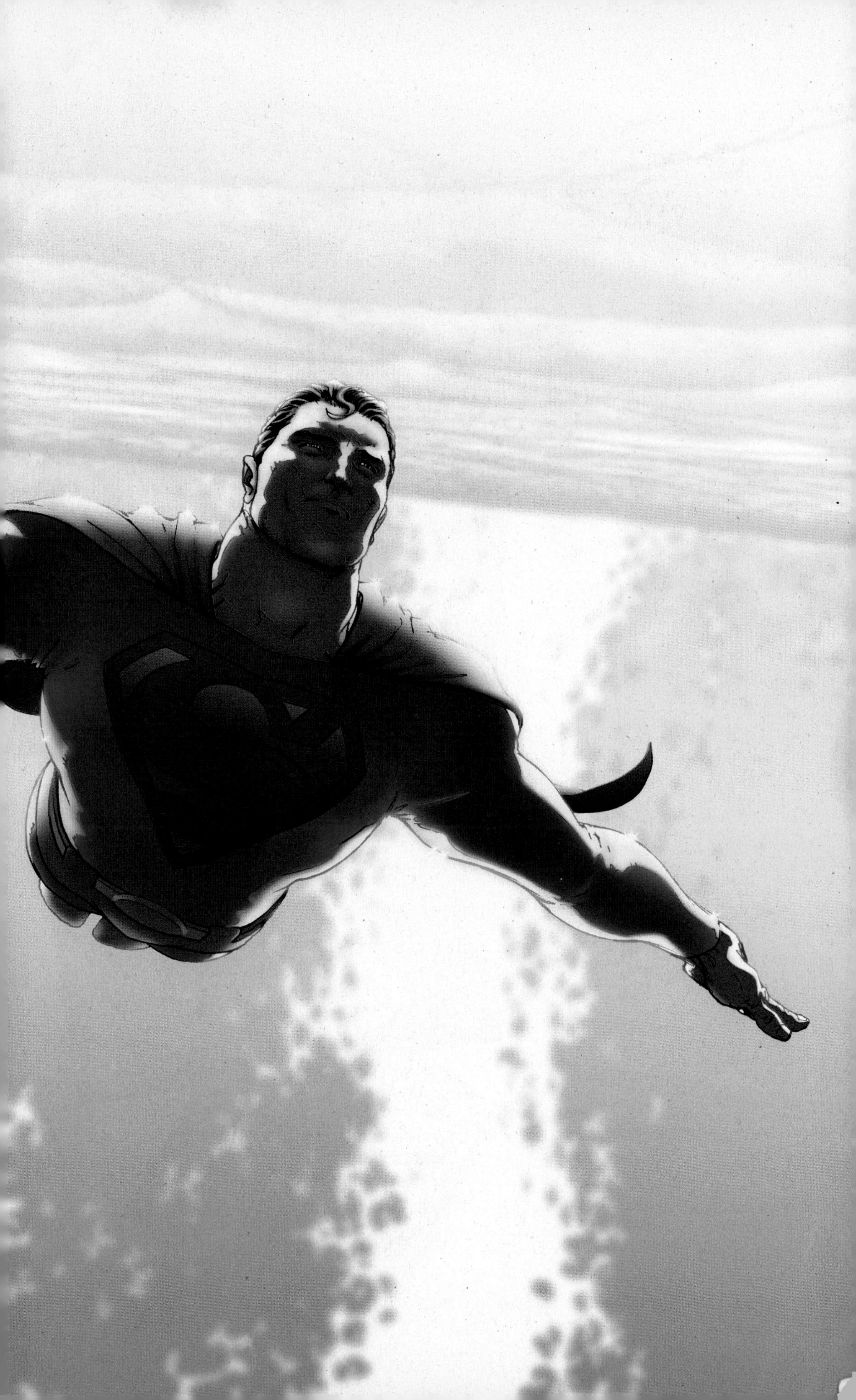

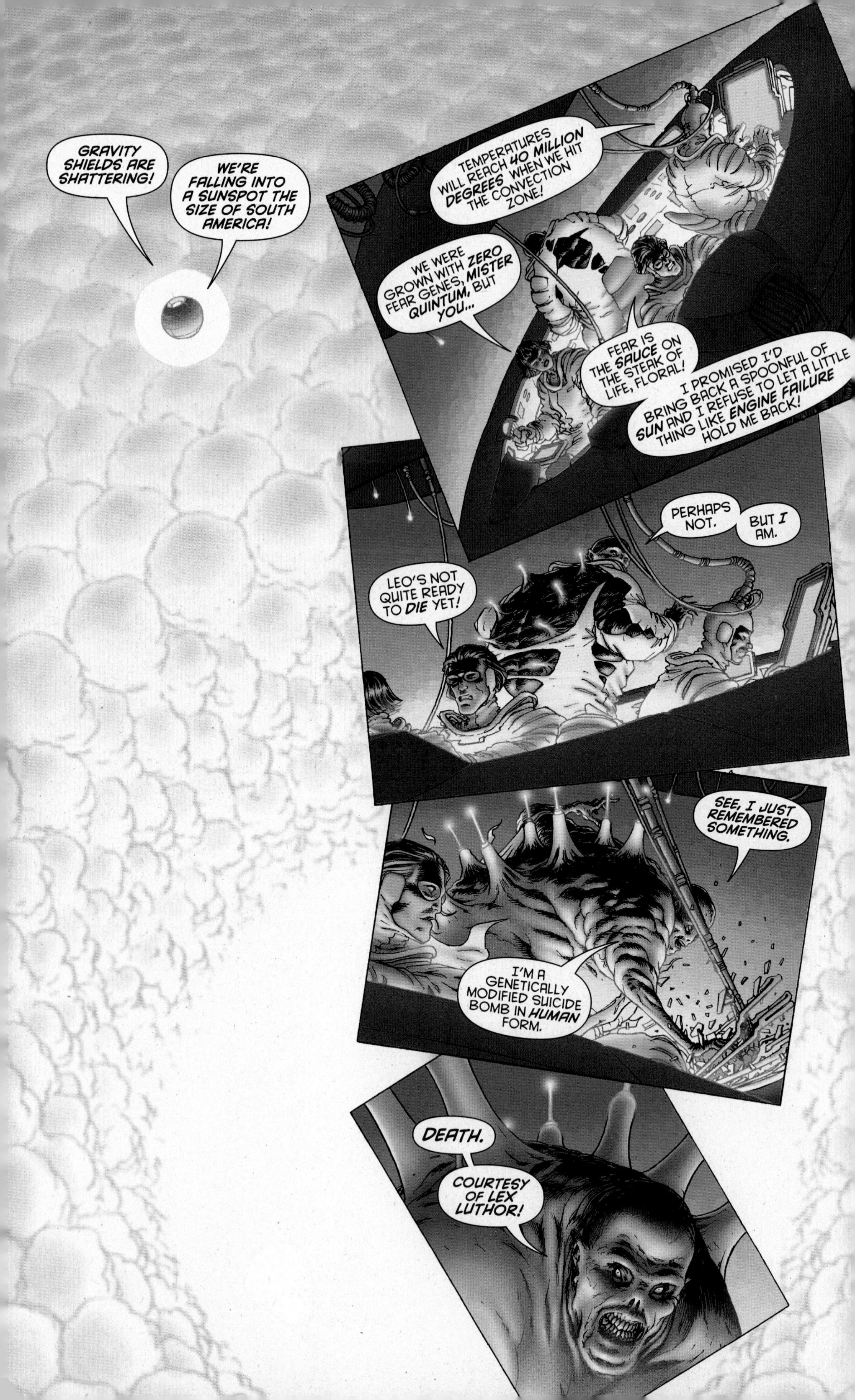
GRAVITY SHIELDS ARE SHATTERING!
WE'RE FALLING INTO A SUNSPOT THE SIZE OF SOUTH AMERICA!
TEMPERATURES WILL REACH 40 MILLION DEGREES WHEN WE HIT THE CONVECTION ZONE!
WE WERE GROWN WITH ZERO FEAR GENES, MISTER QUINTUM, BUT YOU...
FEAR IS THE SAUCE ON THE STEAK OF LIFE, FLORAL!
I PROMISED I'D BRING BACK A SPOONFUL OF SUN AND I REFUSE TO LET A LITTLE THING LIKE ENGINE FAILURE HOLD ME BACK!
LEO'S NOT QUITE READY TO DIE YET!
PERHAPS NOT.
BUT I AM.
SEE, I JUST REMEMBERED SOMETHING.
I'M A GENETICALLY MODIFIED SUICIDE BOMB IN HUMAN FORM.
DEATH.
COURTESY OF LEX LUTHOR!

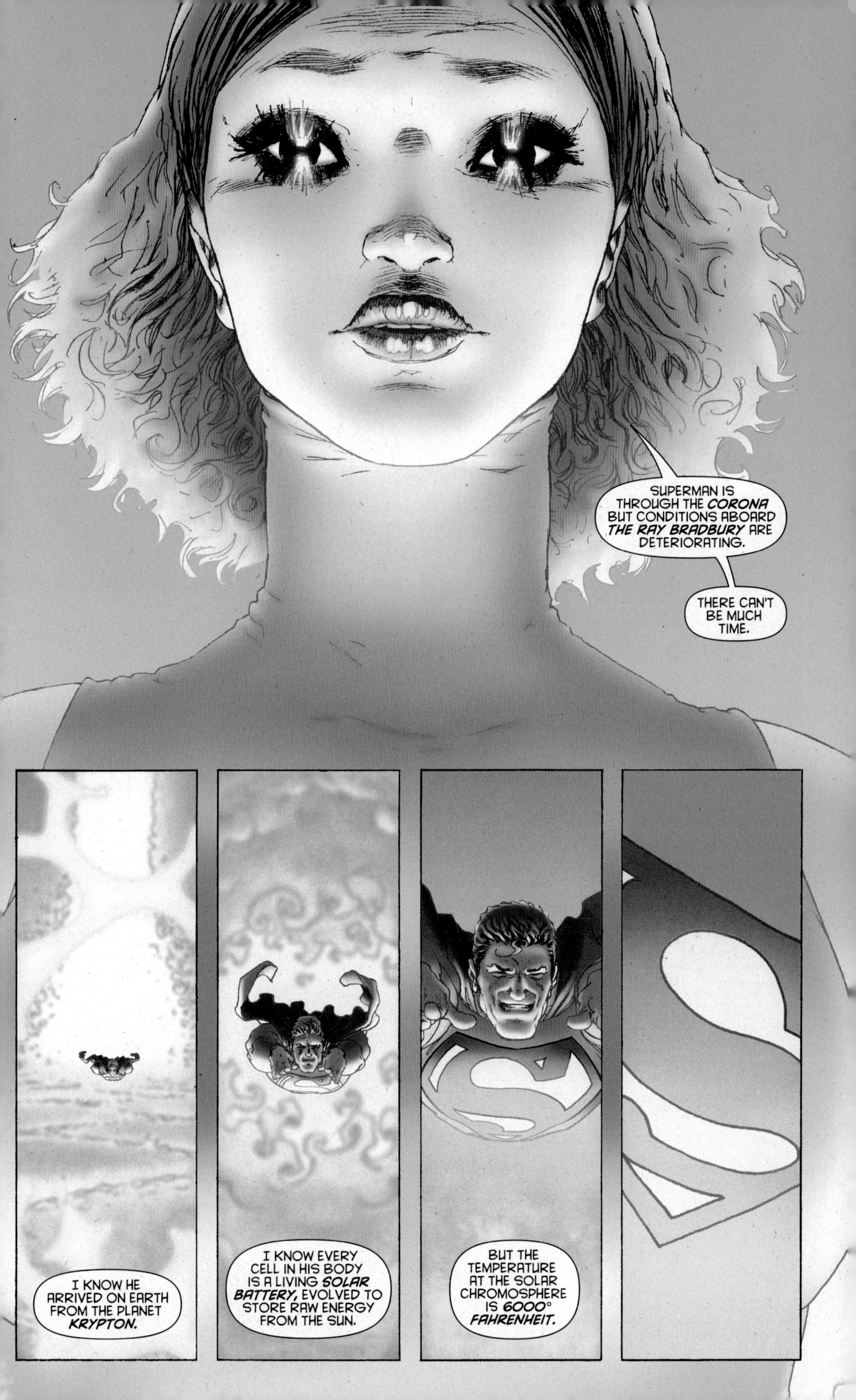
SUPERMAN IS THROUGH THE CORONA BUT CONDITIONS ABOARD THE RAY BRADBURY ARE DETERIORATING.
THERE CAN'T BE MUCH TIME.
I KNOW HE ARRIVED ON EARTH FROM THE PLANET KRYPTON.
I KNOW EVERY CELL IN HIS BODY IS A LIVING SOLAR BATTERY, EVOLVED TO STORE RAW ENERGY FROM THE SUN.
BUT THE TEMPERATURE AT THE SOLAR CHROMOSPHERE IS 6000° FAHRENHEIT.

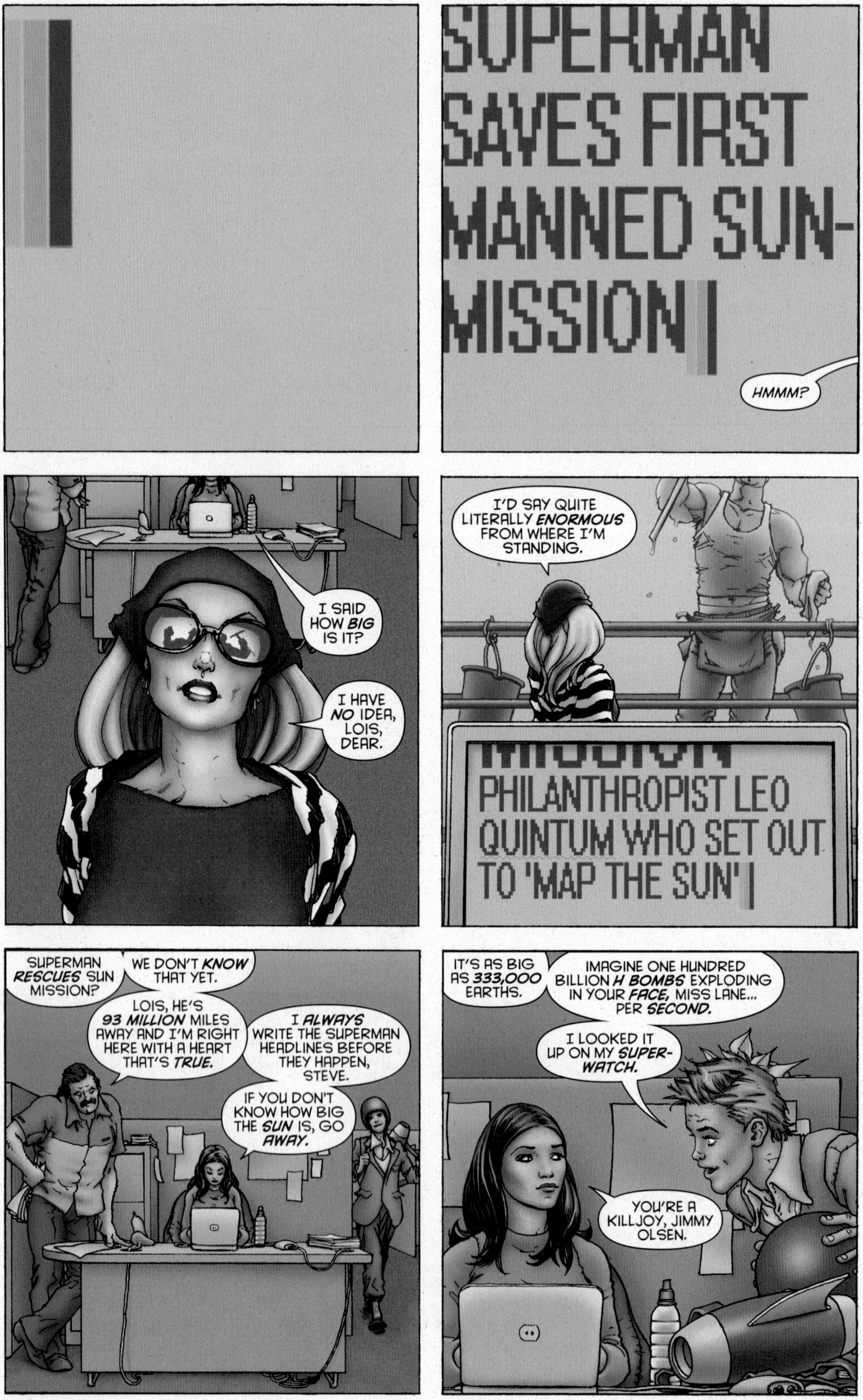
SUPERMAN SAVES FIRST MANNED SUN-MISSION
HMMM?
I SAID HOW BIG IS IT?
I HAVE NO IDEA, LOIS, DEAR.
I'D SAY QUITE LITERALLY ENORMOUS FROM WHERE I'M STANDING.
PHILANTHROPIST LEO QUINTUM WHO SET OUT TO 'MAP THE SUN'
SUPERMAN RESCUES SUN MISSION?
WE DON'T KNOW THAT YET.
LOIS, HE'S 93 MILLION MILES AWAY AND I'M RIGHT HERE WITH A HEART THAT'S TRUE.
I ALWAYS WRITE THE SUPERMAN HEADLINES BEFORE THEY HAPPEN, STEVE.
IF YOU DON'T KNOW HOW BIG THE SUN IS, GO AWAY.
IT'S AS BIG AS 333,000 EARTHS.
IMAGINE ONE HUNDRED BILLION H BOMBS EXPLODING IN YOUR FACE, MISS LANE... PER SECOND.
I LOOKED IT UP ON MY SUPER-WATCH.
YOU'RE A KILLJOY, JIMMY OLSEN.

LEX LUTHOR TOLD THE WORLD HE HAD *REFORMED* AND FOR SOME REASON THE WHOLE WORLD *BELIEVED* HIM AND DOUBTED *US.*

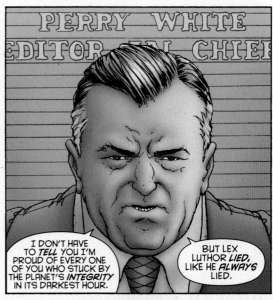

I DON'T HAVE TO *TELL* YOU I'M PROUD OF EVERY ONE OF YOU WHO STUCK BY THE PLANET'S *INTEGRITY* IN ITS DARKEST HOUR.

BUT LEX LUTHOR *LIED,* LIKE HE *ALWAYS* LIED.

INVESTING HEAVILY IN *WATER.*

DAMMING MORE THAN *FIFTEEN* RIVERS.

WITH INTENT TO PROFIT FROM A GLOBAL *WATER SHORTAGE* BROUGHT ABOUT BY TAMPERING WITH THE *SUN.*

DAILY PLANET

LUTHOR LIED

THIS IS TOMORROW'S FRONT PAGE.

WE'RE BREAKING THE STORY OF THE CENTURY.

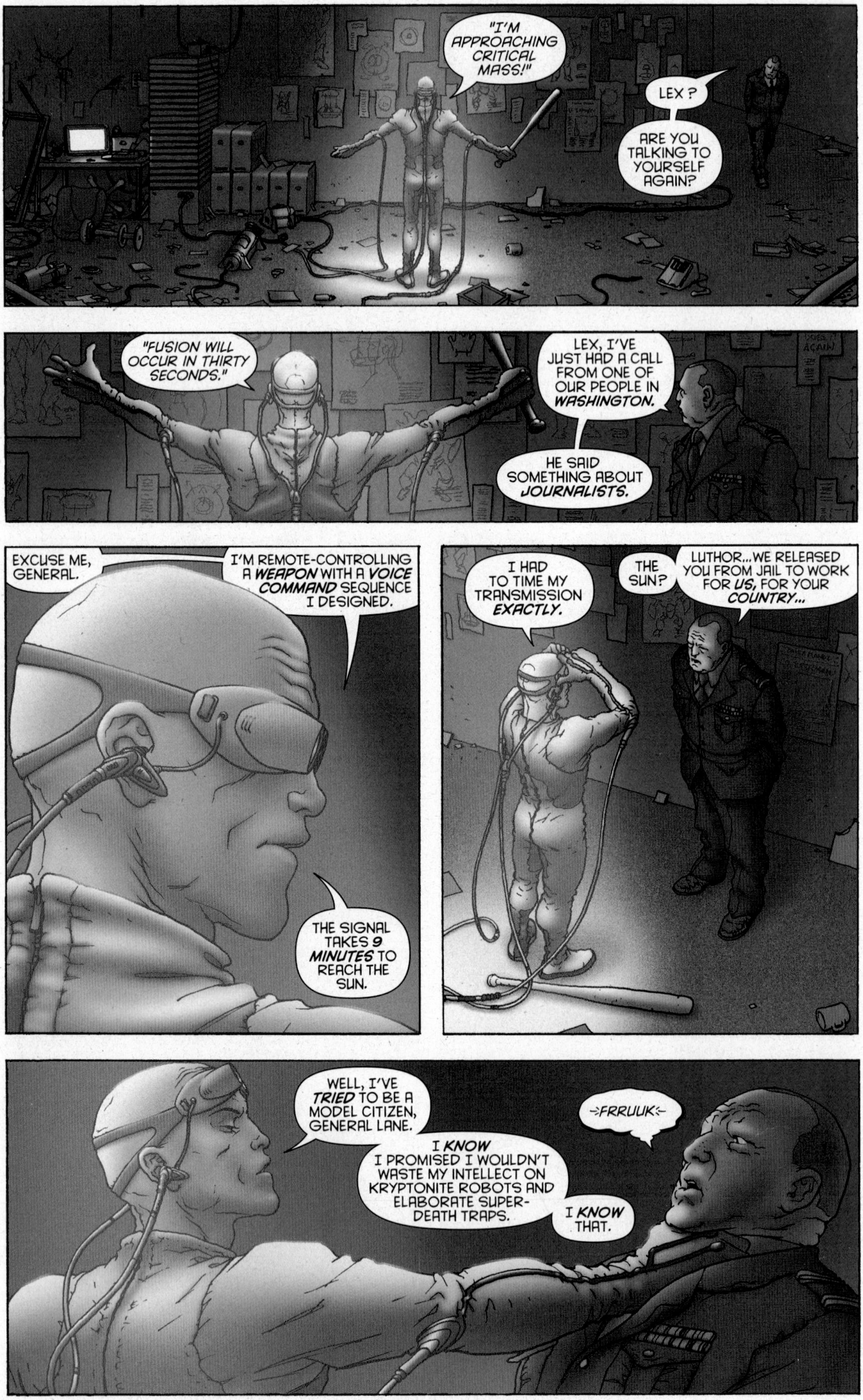
"I'M APPROACHING CRITICAL MASS!"
LEX?
ARE YOU TALKING TO YOURSELF AGAIN?
"FUSION WILL OCCUR IN THIRTY SECONDS."
LEX, I'VE JUST HAD A CALL FROM ONE OF OUR PEOPLE IN WASHINGTON.
HE SAID SOMETHING ABOUT JOURNALISTS.
EXCUSE ME, GENERAL.
I'M REMOTE-CONTROLLING A WEAPON WITH A VOICE COMMAND SEQUENCE I DESIGNED.
THE SIGNAL TAKES 9 MINUTES TO REACH THE SUN.
I HAD TO TIME MY TRANSMISSION EXACTLY.
THE SUN?
LUTHOR...WE RELEASED YOU FROM JAIL TO WORK FOR US, FOR YOUR COUNTRY...
WELL, I'VE TRIED TO BE A MODEL CITIZEN, GENERAL LANE.
I KNOW I PROMISED I WOULDN'T WASTE MY INTELLECT ON KRYPTONITE ROBOTS AND ELABORATE SUPER-DEATH TRAPS.
I KNOW THAT.
FRRUUK

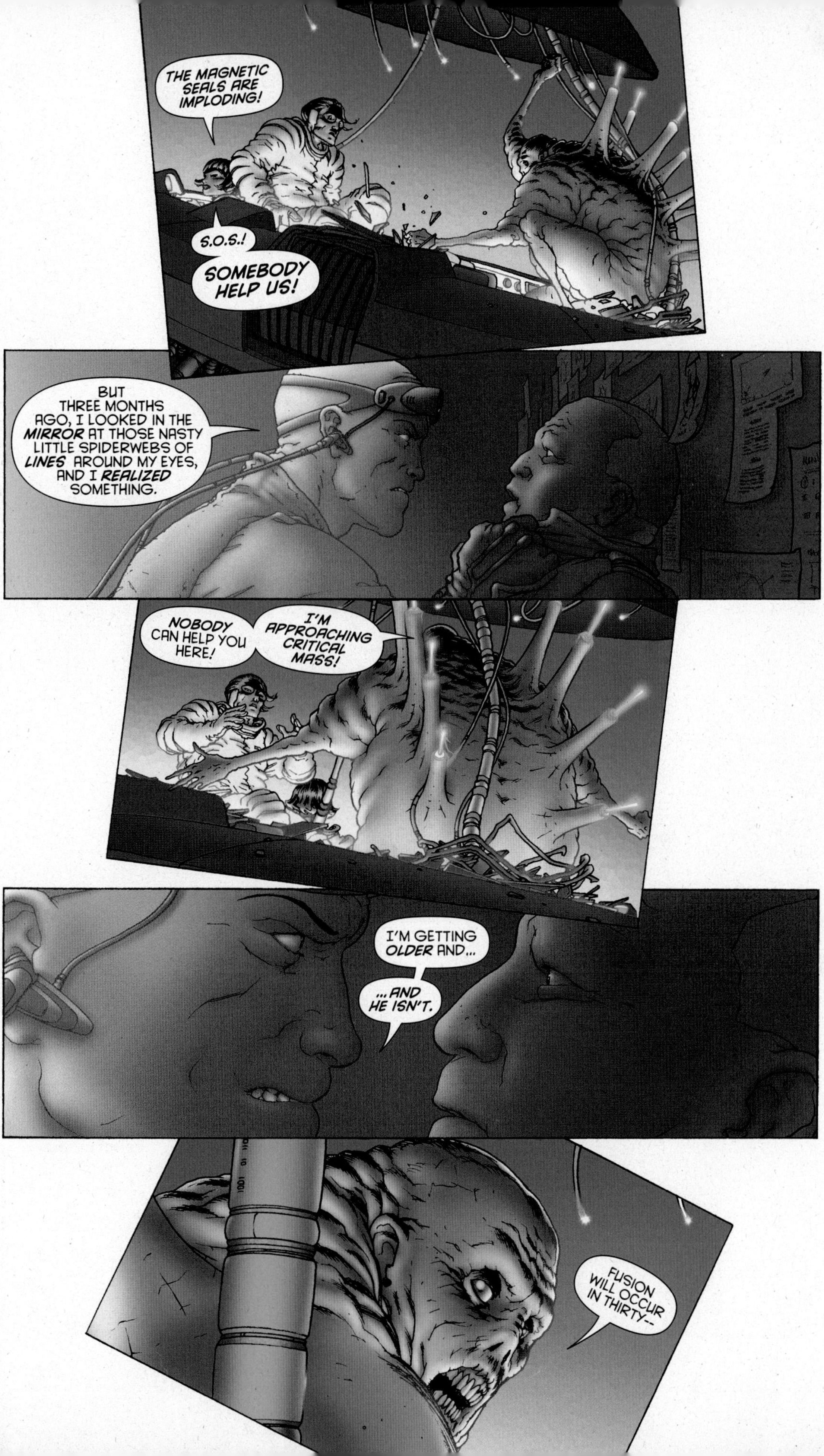
THE MAGNETIC SEALS ARE IMPLODING!
S.O.S.!
SOMEBODY HELP US!
BUT THREE MONTHS AGO, I LOOKED IN THE MIRROR AT THOSE NASTY LITTLE SPIDERWEBS OF LINES AROUND MY EYES, AND I REALIZED SOMETHING.
NOBODY CAN HELP YOU HERE!
I'M APPROACHING CRITICAL MASS!
I'M GETTING OLDER AND...
...AND HE ISN'T.
FUSION WILL OCCUR IN THIRTY--

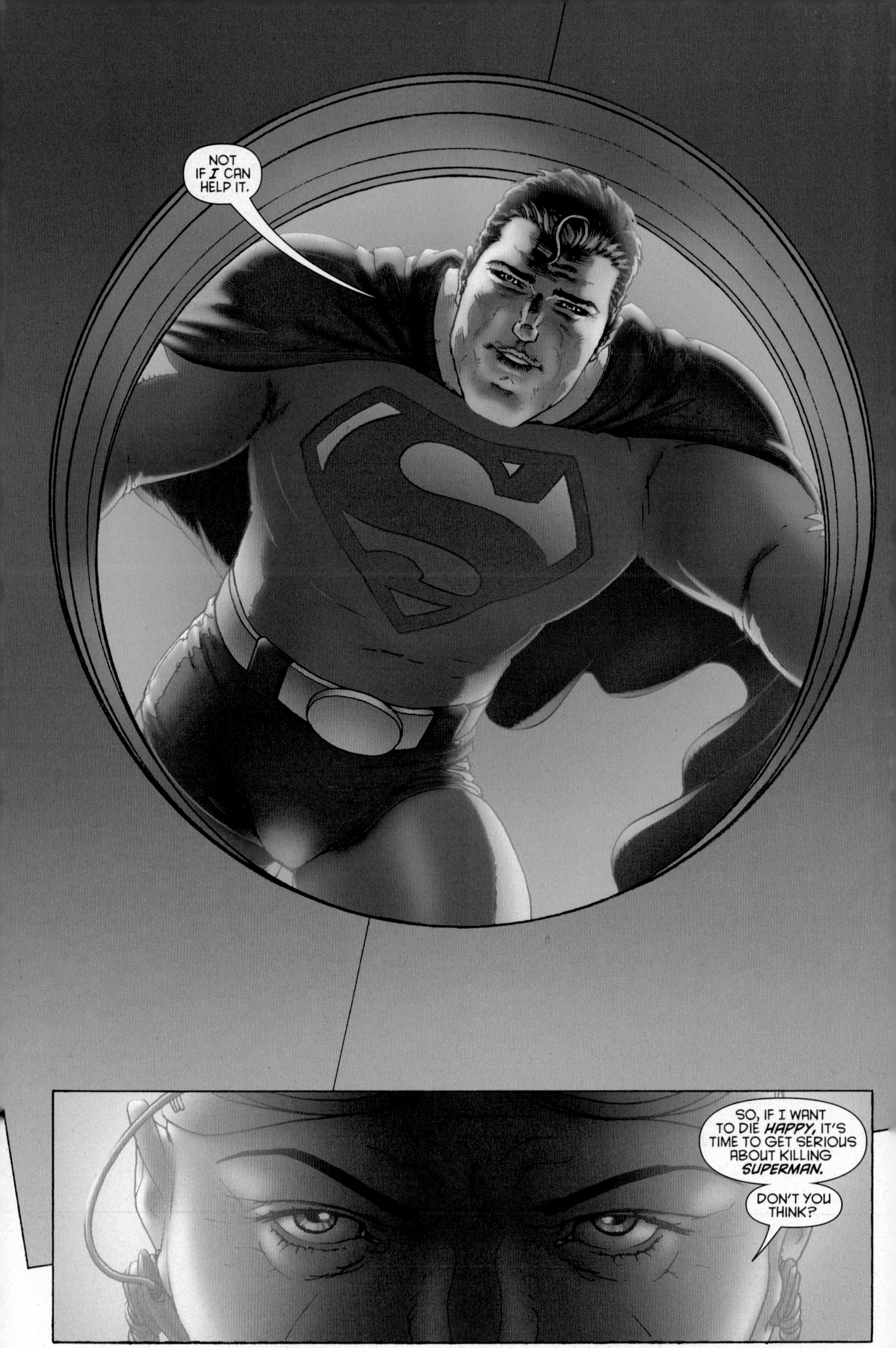
NOT IF *I* CAN HELP IT.
SO, IF I WANT TO DIE *HAPPY*, IT'S TIME TO GET SERIOUS ABOUT KILLING *SUPERMAN.*
DON'T YOU THINK?

THE PURPOSE OF MY *EXISTENCE* IS TO EXPLODE!

UNNH!

YOU HAVE NO RIGHT TO LIMIT MY AMBITIONS, FASCIST!

NO RIGHT AT ALL TO STAND IN THE WAY OF MY SELF-REALIZATION!

YOU MISUNDERSTAND.

I'M HERE TO *HELP* YOU WITH THAT.

BLOW THE HATCH, QUINTUM!

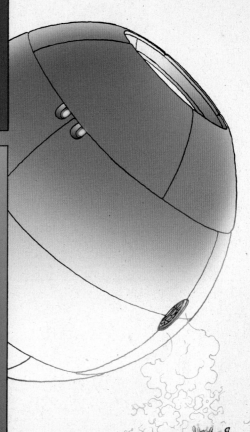

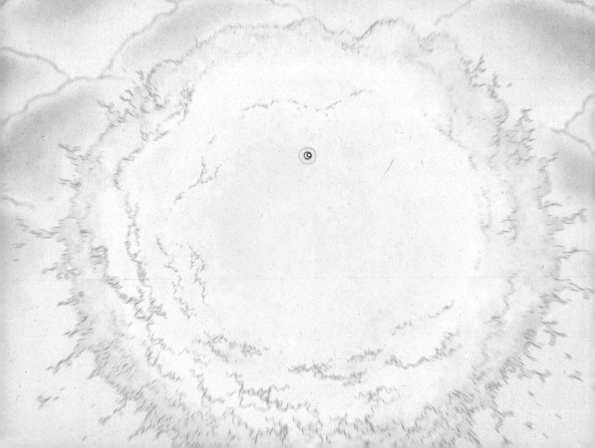

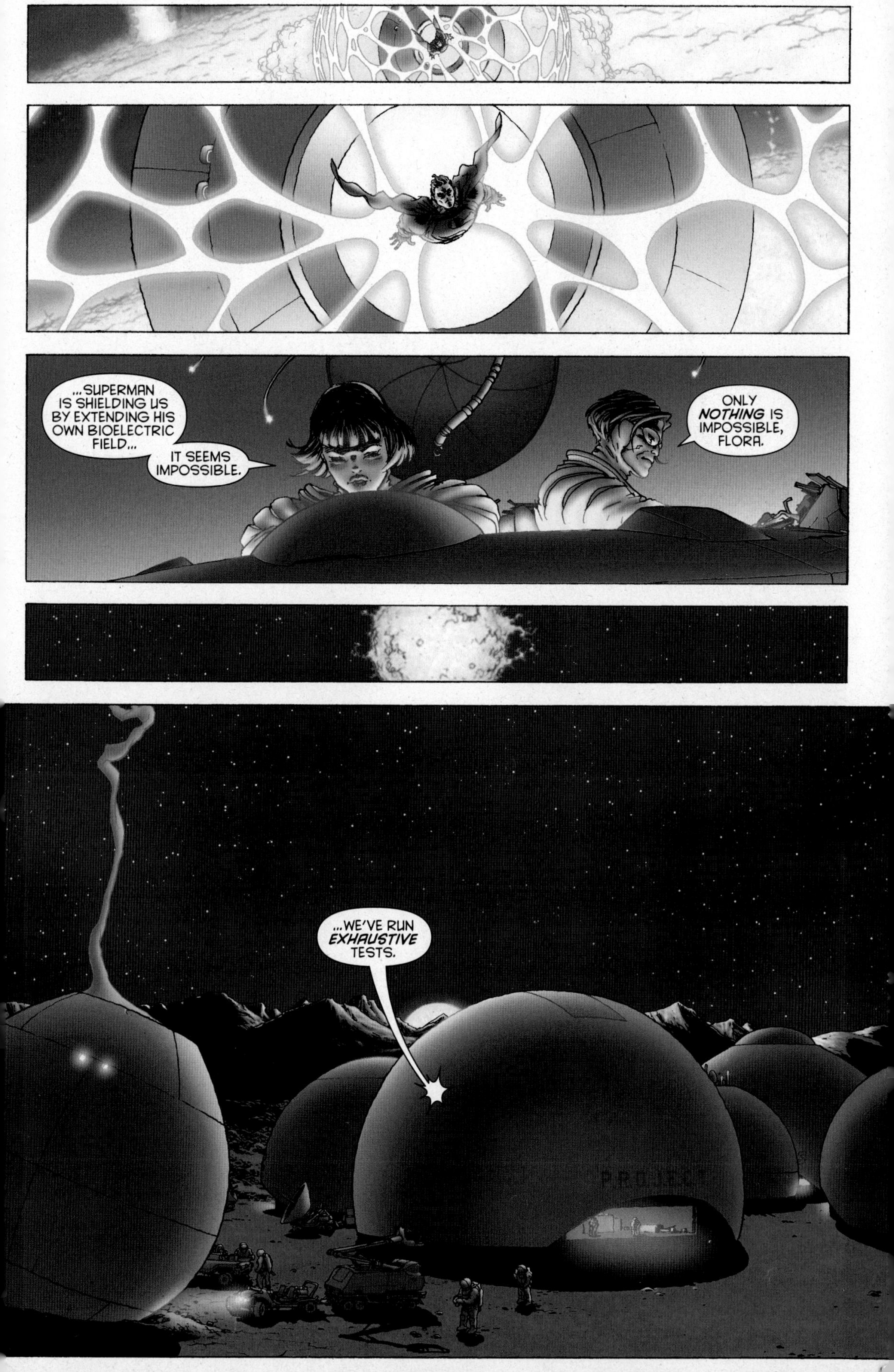
...SUPERMAN IS SHIELDING US BY EXTENDING HIS OWN BIOELECTRIC FIELD...
IT SEEMS IMPOSSIBLE.
ONLY NOTHING IS IMPOSSIBLE, FLORA.
...WE'VE RUN EXHAUSTIVE TESTS.

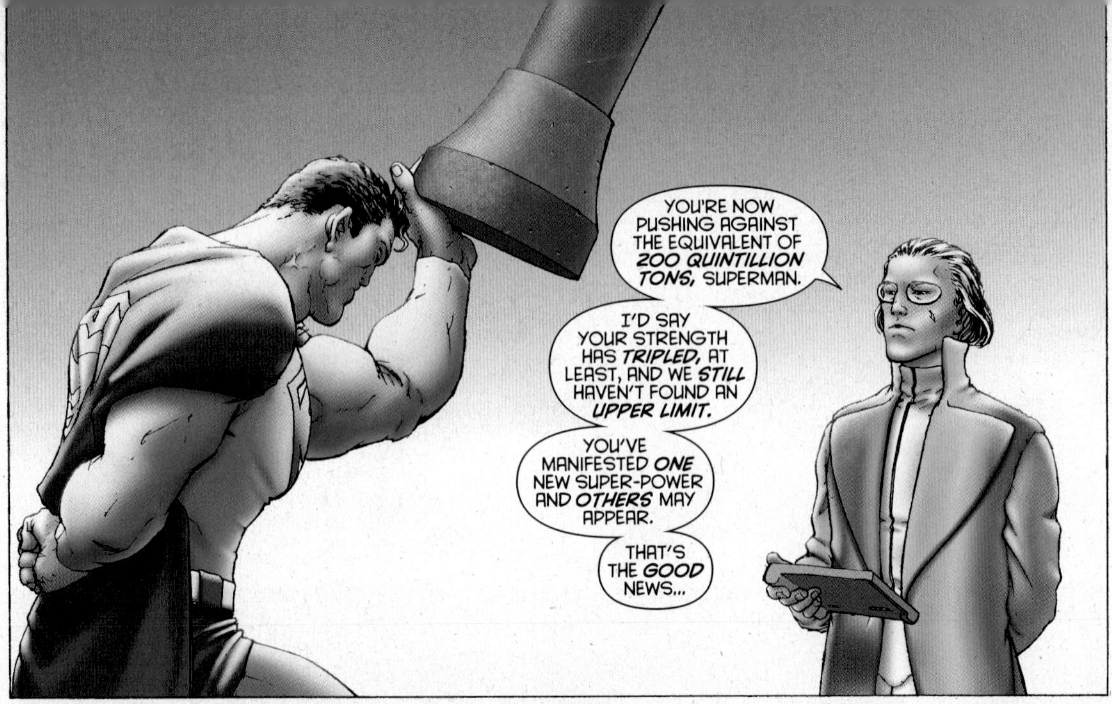
YOU'RE NOW PUSHING AGAINST THE EQUIVALENT OF 200 QUINTILLION TONS, SUPERMAN.
I'D SAY YOUR STRENGTH HAS TRIPLED, AT LEAST, AND WE STILL HAVEN'T FOUND AN UPPER LIMIT.
YOU'VE MANIFESTED ONE NEW SUPER-POWER AND OTHERS MAY APPEAR.
THAT'S THE GOOD NEWS...

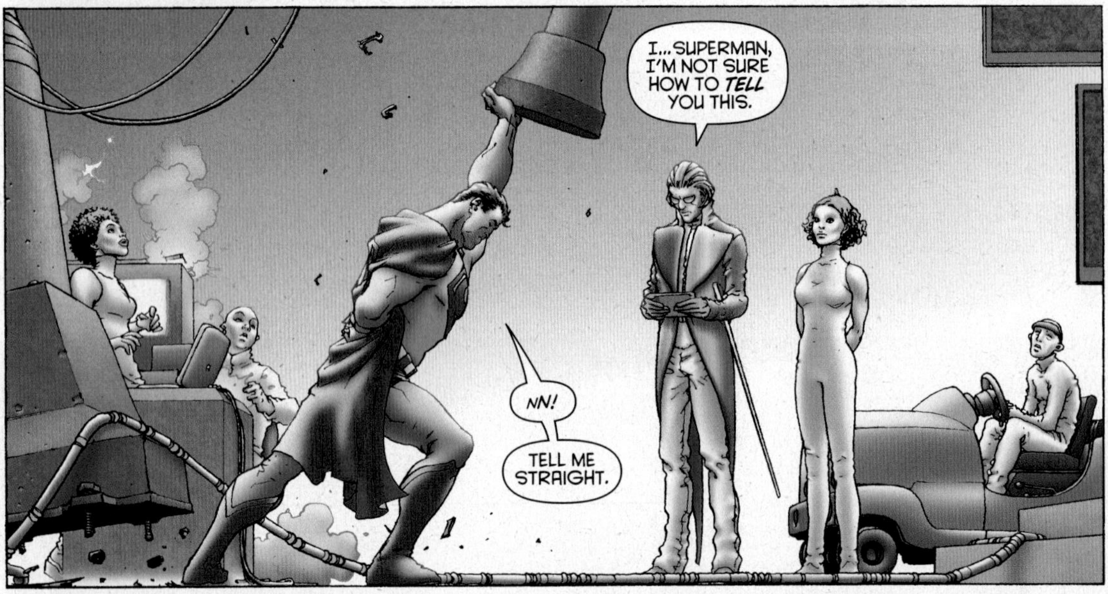
I...SUPERMAN, I'M NOT SURE HOW TO TELL YOU THIS.
NN!
TELL ME STRAIGHT.

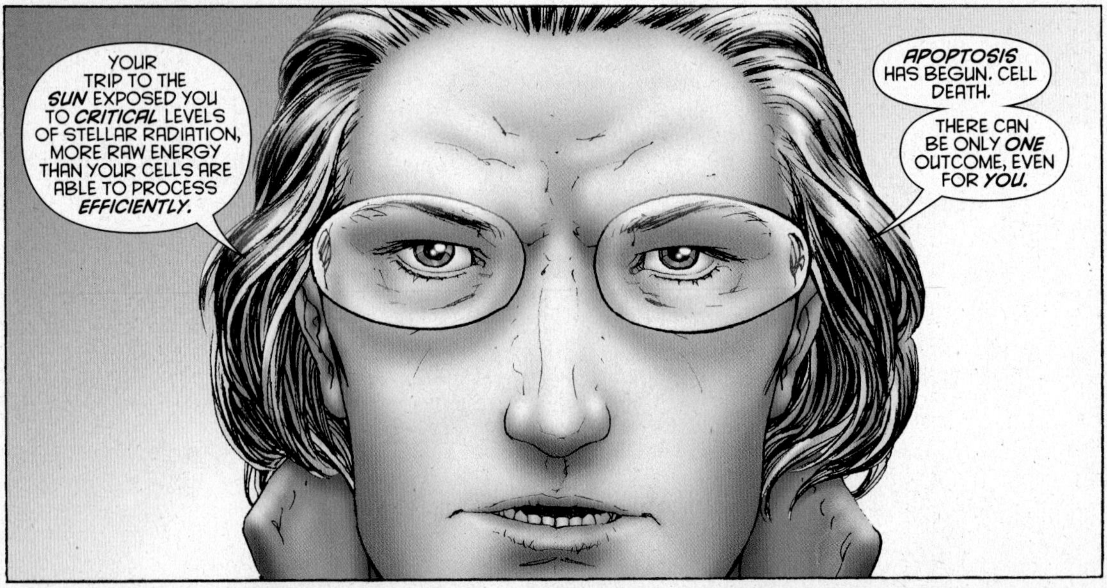
YOUR TRIP TO THE SUN EXPOSED YOU TO CRITICAL LEVELS OF STELLAR RADIATION, MORE RAW ENERGY THAN YOUR CELLS ARE ABLE TO PROCESS EFFICIENTLY.
APOPTOSIS HAS BEGUN. CELL DEATH.
THERE CAN BE ONLY ONE OUTCOME, EVEN FOR YOU.

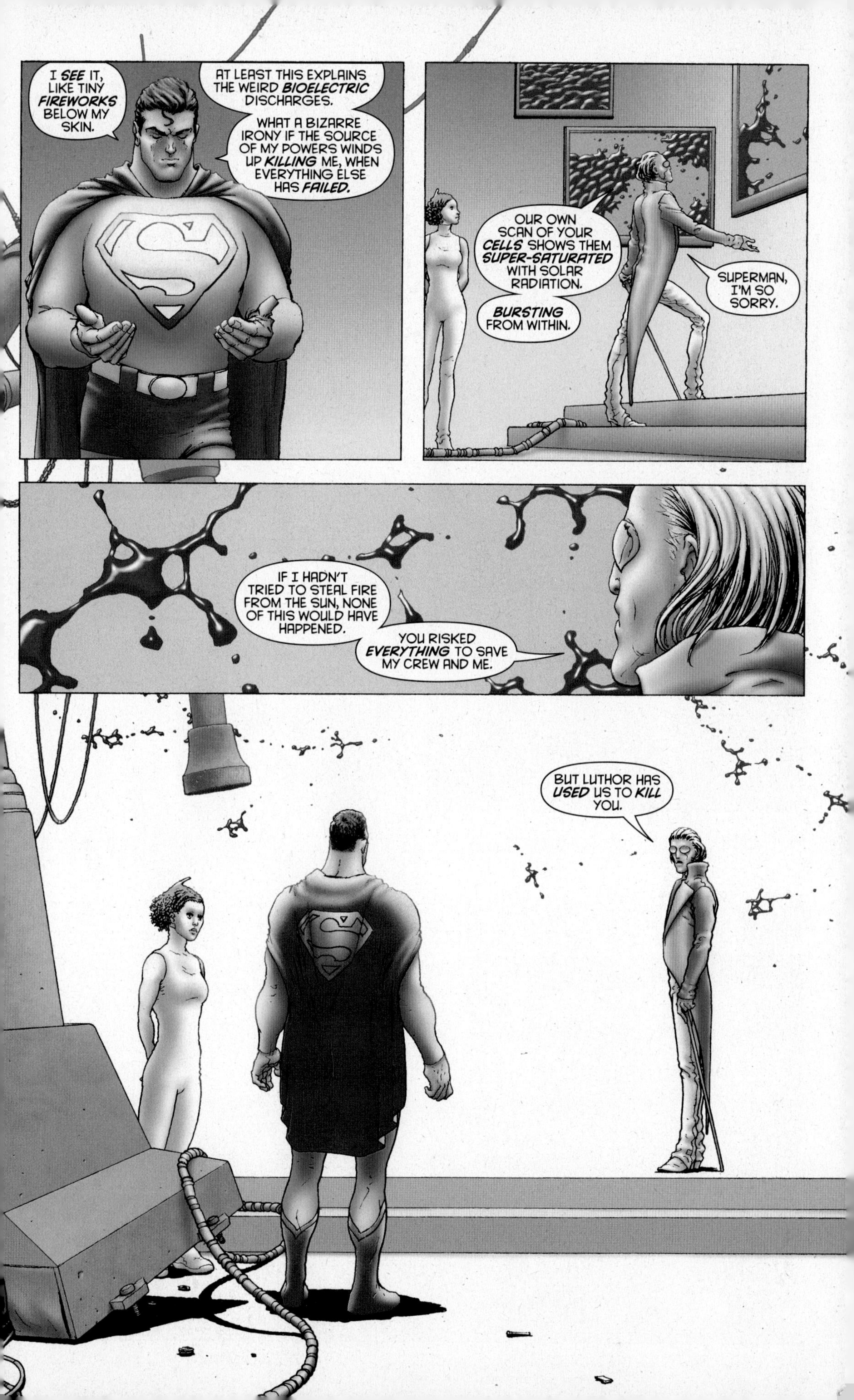
I SEE IT, LIKE TINY FIREWORKS BELOW MY SKIN.
AT LEAST THIS EXPLAINS THE WEIRD BIOELECTRIC DISCHARGES.
WHAT A BIZARRE IRONY IF THE SOURCE OF MY POWERS WINDS UP KILLING ME, WHEN EVERYTHING ELSE HAS FAILED.
OUR OWN SCAN OF YOUR CELLS SHOWS THEM SUPER-SATURATED WITH SOLAR RADIATION.
BURSTING FROM WITHIN.
SUPERMAN, I'M SO SORRY.
IF I HADN'T TRIED TO STEAL FIRE FROM THE SUN, NONE OF THIS WOULD HAVE HAPPENED.
YOU RISKED EVERYTHING TO SAVE MY CREW AND ME.
BUT LUTHOR HAS USED US TO KILL YOU.

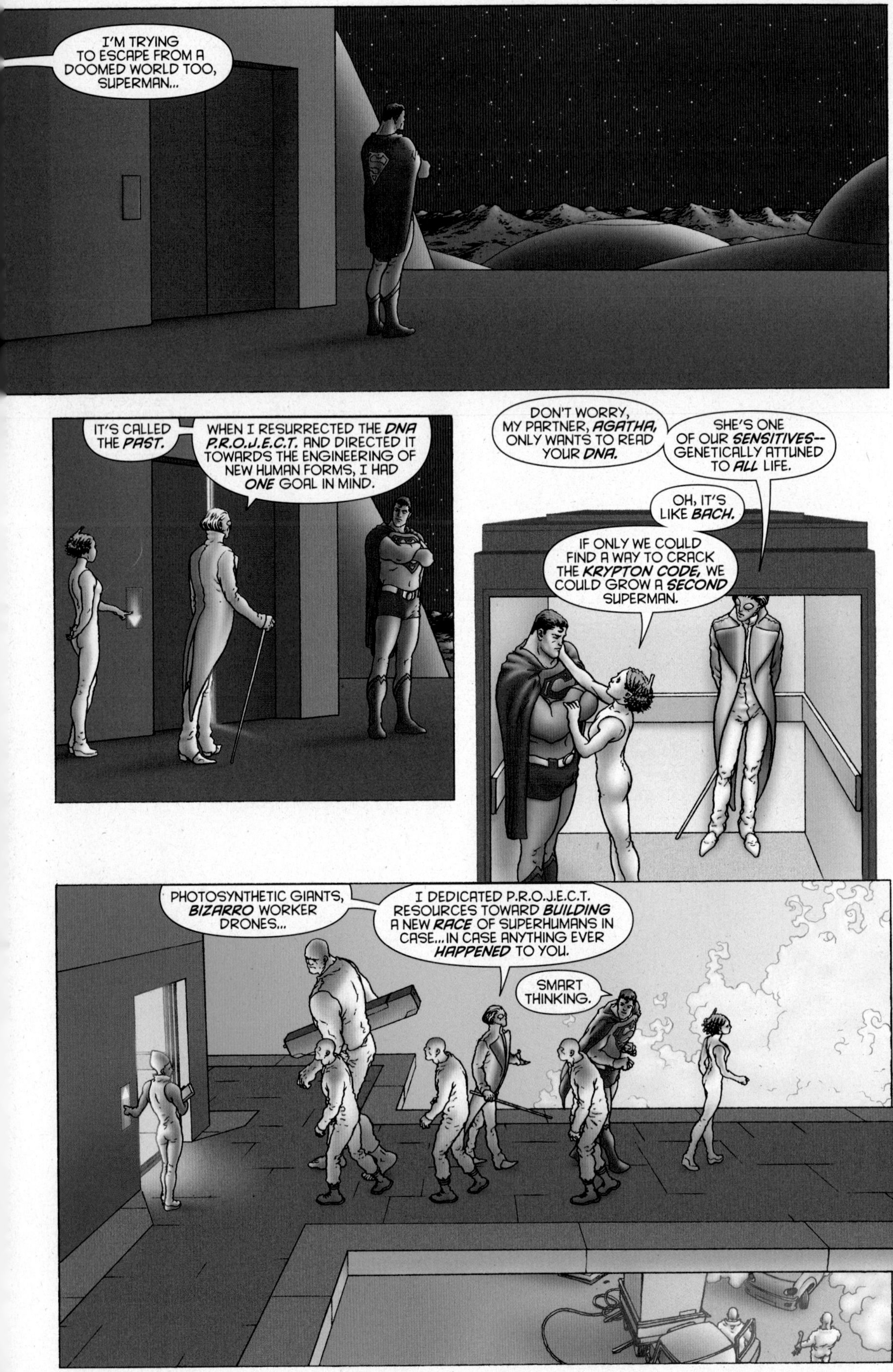
I'M TRYING TO ESCAPE FROM A DOOMED WORLD TOO, SUPERMAN...
IT'S CALLED THE PAST.
WHEN I RESURRECTED THE DNA P.R.O.J.E.C.T. AND DIRECTED IT TOWARDS THE ENGINEERING OF NEW HUMAN FORMS, I HAD ONE GOAL IN MIND.
DON'T WORRY, MY PARTNER, AGATHA, ONLY WANTS TO READ YOUR DNA.
SHE'S ONE OF OUR SENSITIVES-- GENETICALLY ATTUNED TO ALL LIFE.
OH, IT'S LIKE BACH.
IF ONLY WE COULD FIND A WAY TO CRACK THE KRYPTON CODE, WE COULD GROW A SECOND SUPERMAN.
PHOTOSYNTHETIC GIANTS, BIZARRO WORKER DRONES...
I DEDICATED P.R.O.J.E.C.T. RESOURCES TOWARD BUILDING A NEW RACE OF SUPERHUMANS IN CASE...IN CASE ANYTHING EVER HAPPENED TO YOU.
SMART THINKING.

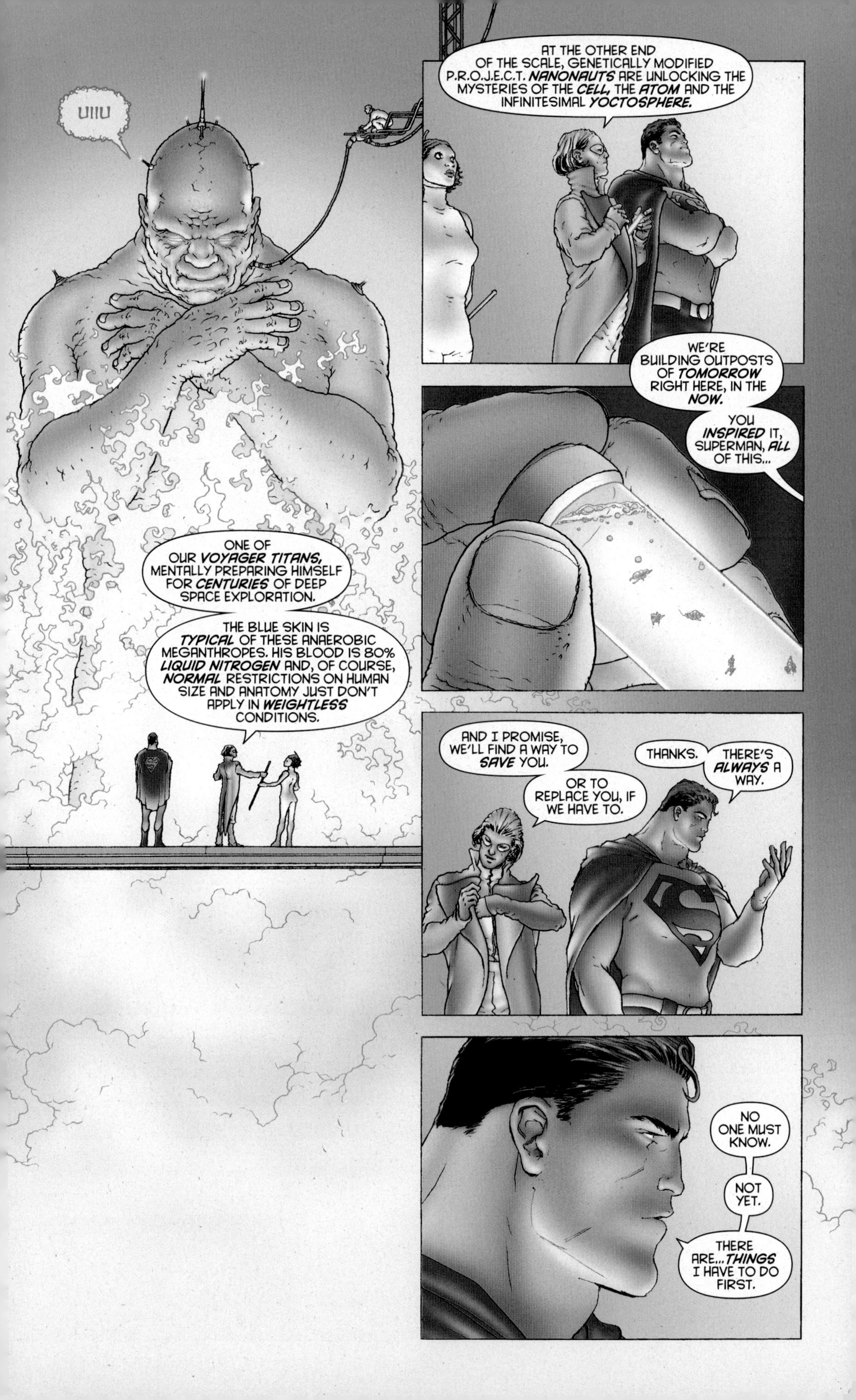
UIIU
ONE OF OUR *VOYAGER TITANS,* MENTALLY PREPARING HIMSELF FOR *CENTURIES* OF DEEP SPACE EXPLORATION.
THE BLUE SKIN IS *TYPICAL* OF THESE ANAEROBIC MEGANTHROPES. HIS BLOOD IS 80% *LIQUID NITROGEN* AND, OF COURSE, *NORMAL* RESTRICTIONS ON HUMAN SIZE AND ANATOMY JUST DON'T APPLY IN *WEIGHTLESS* CONDITIONS.
AT THE OTHER END OF THE SCALE, GENETICALLY MODIFIED P.R.O.J.E.C.T. *NANONAUTS* ARE UNLOCKING THE MYSTERIES OF THE *CELL,* THE *ATOM* AND THE INFINITESIMAL *YOCTOSPHERE.*
WE'RE BUILDING OUTPOSTS OF *TOMORROW* RIGHT HERE, IN THE *NOW.*
YOU *INSPIRED* IT, SUPERMAN, *ALL* OF THIS...
AND I PROMISE, WE'LL FIND A WAY TO *SAVE* YOU.
OR TO REPLACE YOU, IF WE HAVE TO.
THANKS.
THERE'S *ALWAYS* A WAY.
NO ONE MUST KNOW.
NOT YET.
THERE ARE...*THINGS* I HAVE TO DO FIRST.

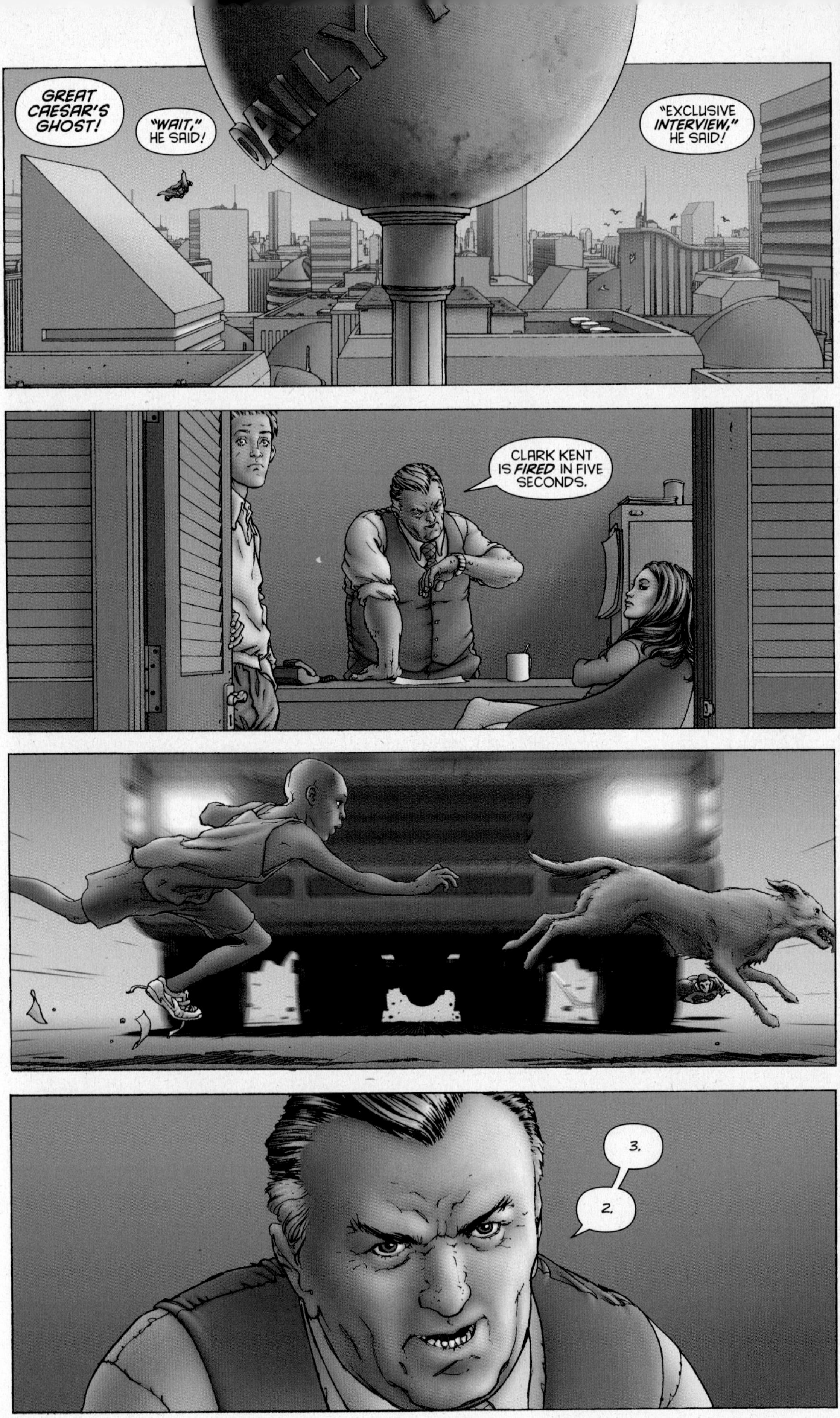

GREAT CAESAR'S GHOST!
"WAIT," HE SAID!
"EXCLUSIVE INTERVIEW," HE SAID!
CLARK KENT IS FIRED IN FIVE SECONDS.
3.
2.

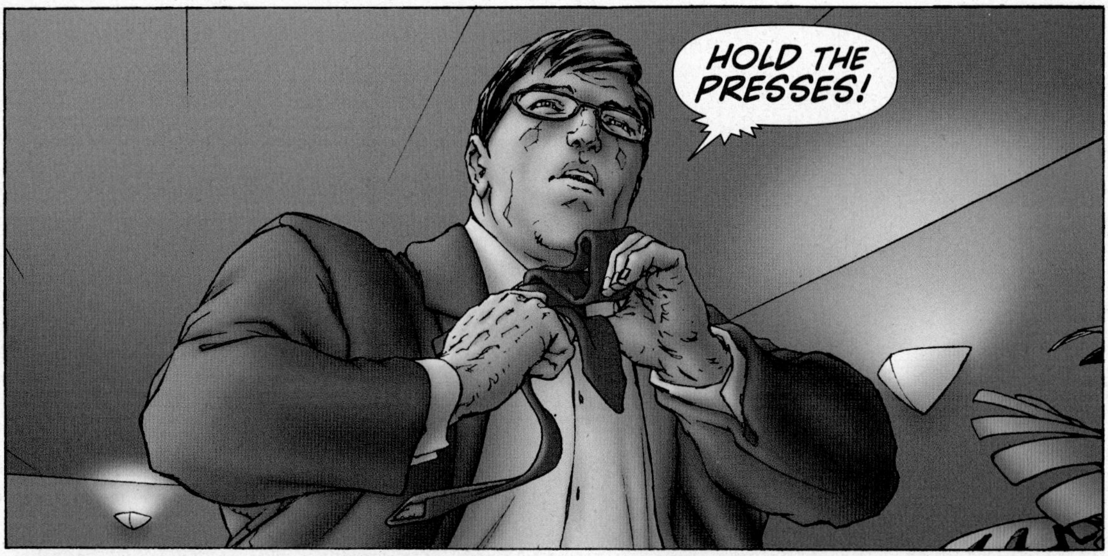
HOLD THE PRESSES!

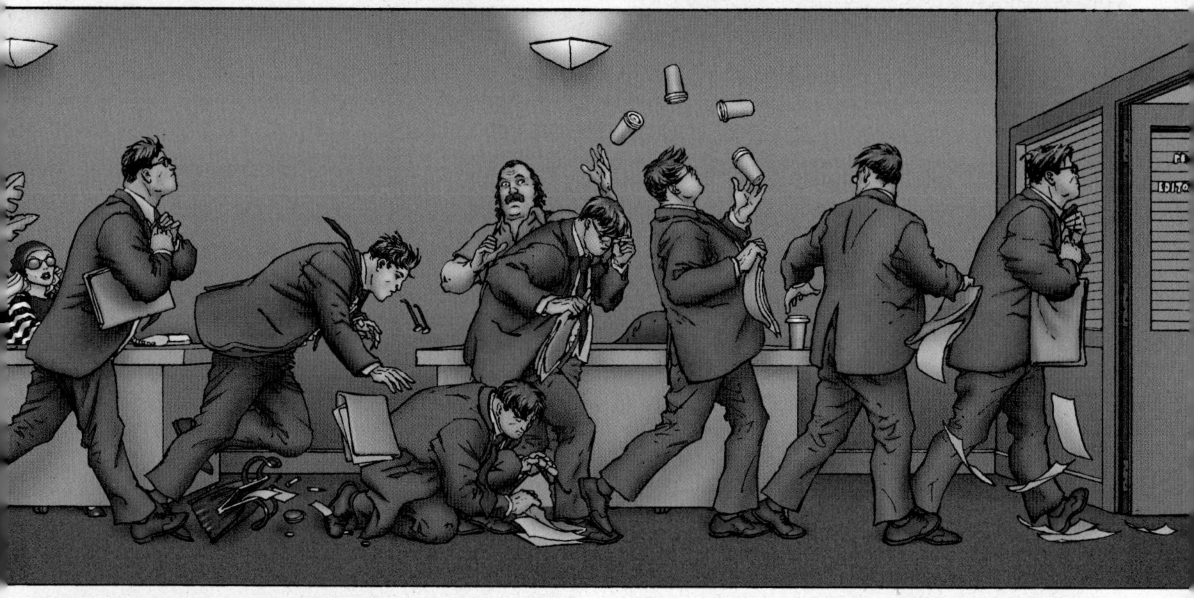

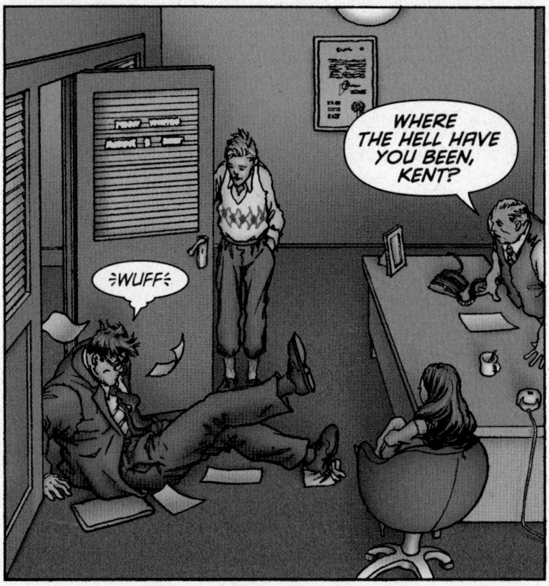
WHERE THE HELL HAVE YOU BEEN, KENT?
WUFF

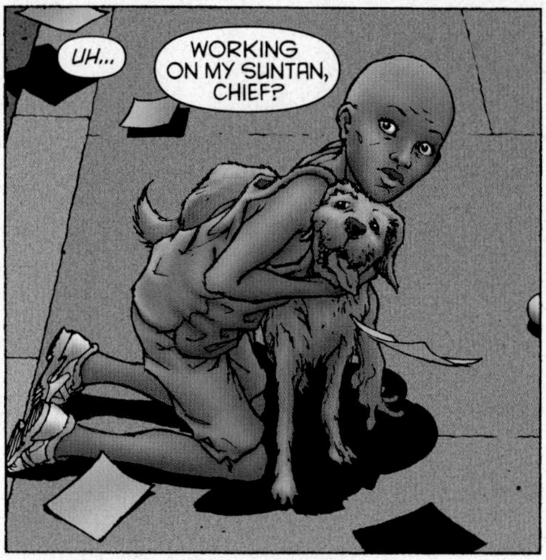
UH...
WORKING ON MY SUNTAN, CHIEF?

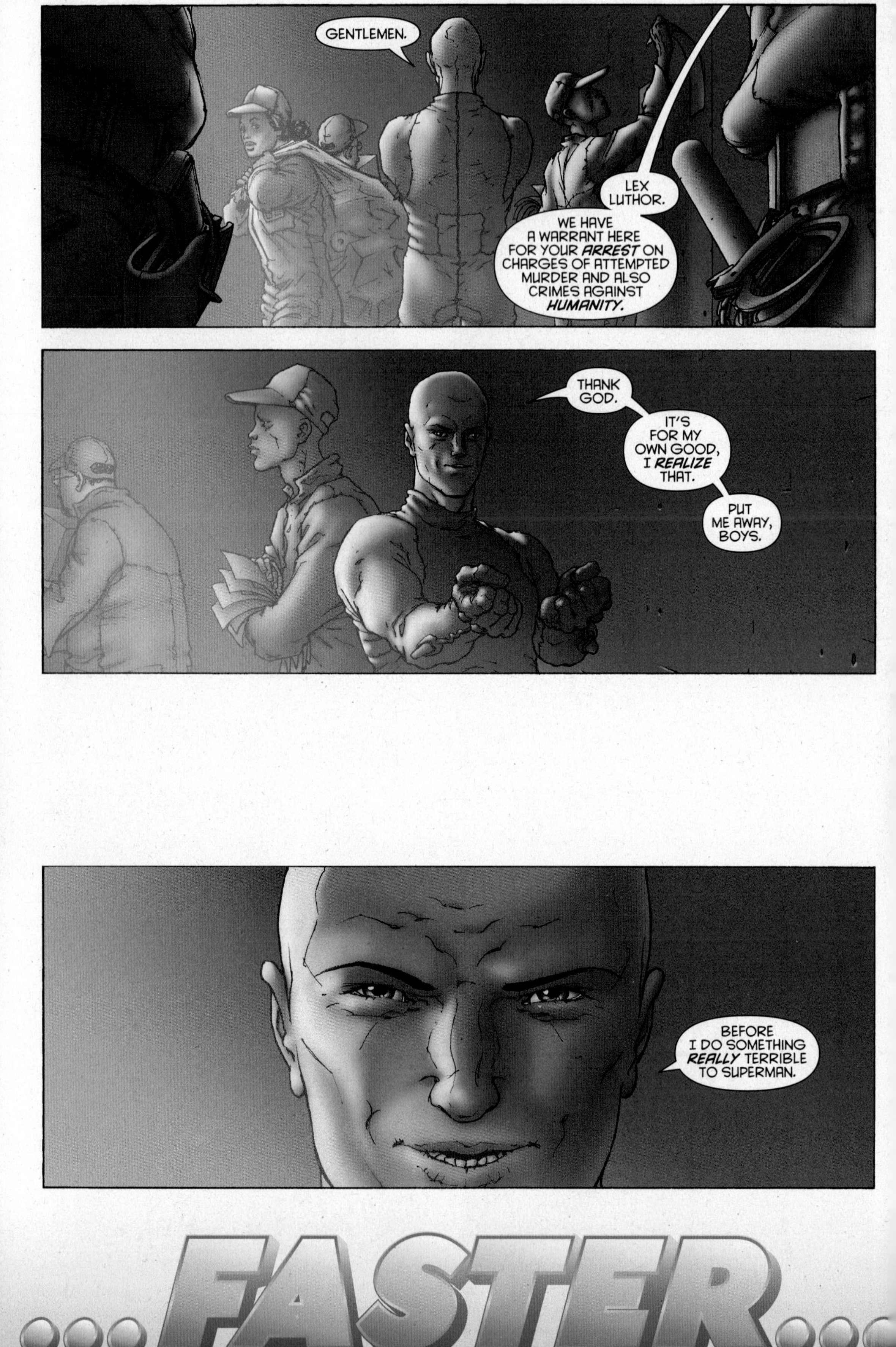
GENTLEMEN.
LEX LUTHOR.
WE HAVE A WARRANT HERE FOR YOUR *ARREST* ON CHARGES OF ATTEMPTED MURDER AND ALSO CRIMES AGAINST *HUMANITY*.
THANK GOD.
IT'S FOR MY OWN GOOD, I *REALIZE* THAT.
PUT ME AWAY, BOYS.
BEFORE I DO SOMETHING *REALLY* TERRIBLE TO SUPERMAN.
...FASTER...

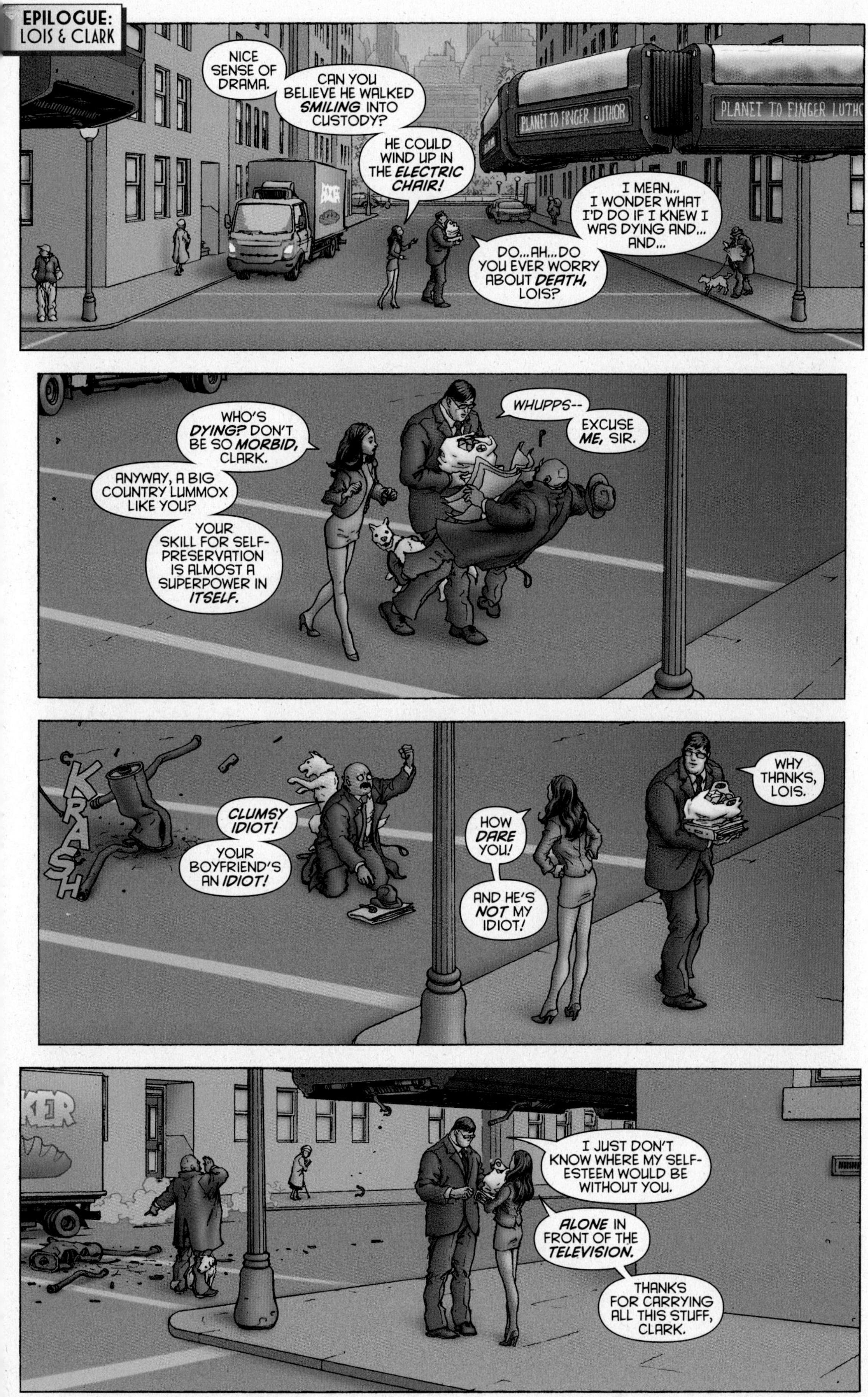
EPILOGUE: LOIS & CLARK
PLANET TO FINGER LUTHOR
NICE SENSE OF DRAMA.
CAN YOU BELIEVE HE WALKED SMILING INTO CUSTODY?
HE COULD WIND UP IN THE ELECTRIC CHAIR!
DO...AH...DO YOU EVER WORRY ABOUT DEATH, LOIS?
I MEAN... I WONDER WHAT I'D DO IF I KNEW I WAS DYING AND... AND...
WHO'S DYING? DON'T BE SO MORBID, CLARK.
ANYWAY, A BIG COUNTRY LUMMOX LIKE YOU?
YOUR SKILL FOR SELF-PRESERVATION IS ALMOST A SUPERPOWER IN ITSELF.
WHUPPS--
EXCUSE ME, SIR.
KRASH
CLUMSY IDIOT!
YOUR BOYFRIEND'S AN IDIOT!
HOW DARE YOU!
AND HE'S NOT MY IDIOT!
WHY THANKS, LOIS.
I JUST DON'T KNOW WHERE MY SELF-ESTEEM WOULD BE WITHOUT YOU.
ALONE IN FRONT OF THE TELEVISION.
THANKS FOR CARRYING ALL THIS STUFF, CLARK.

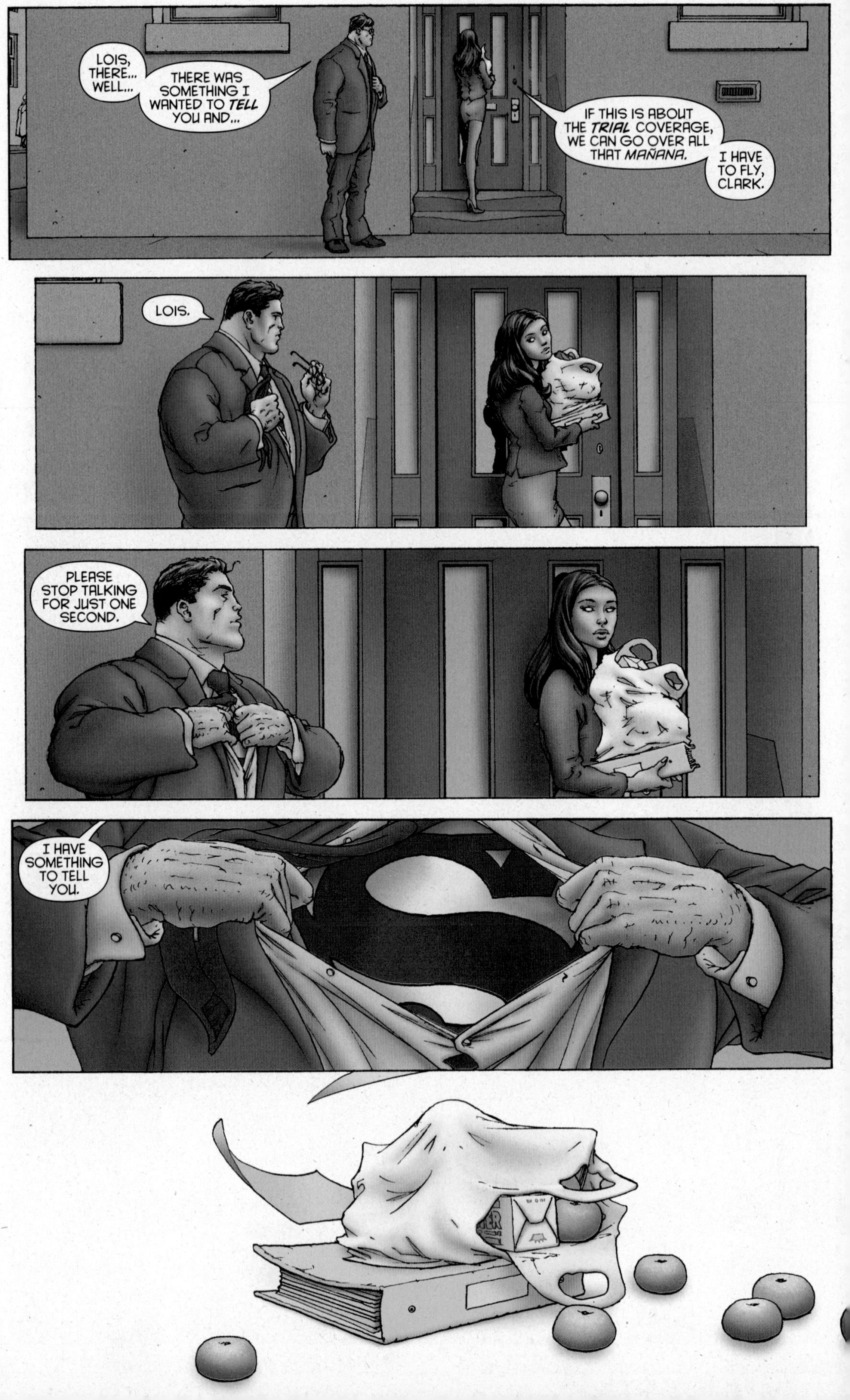
LOIS, THERE... WELL...
THERE WAS SOMETHING I WANTED TO TELL YOU AND...
IF THIS IS ABOUT THE TRIAL COVERAGE, WE CAN GO OVER ALL THAT MAÑANA.
I HAVE TO FLY, CLARK.
LOIS.
PLEASE STOP TALKING FOR JUST ONE SECOND.
I HAVE SOMETHING TO TELL YOU.

Episode 2

SUPERMAN'S FORBIDDEN ROOM

Cover FRANK QUITELY with JAMIE GRANT

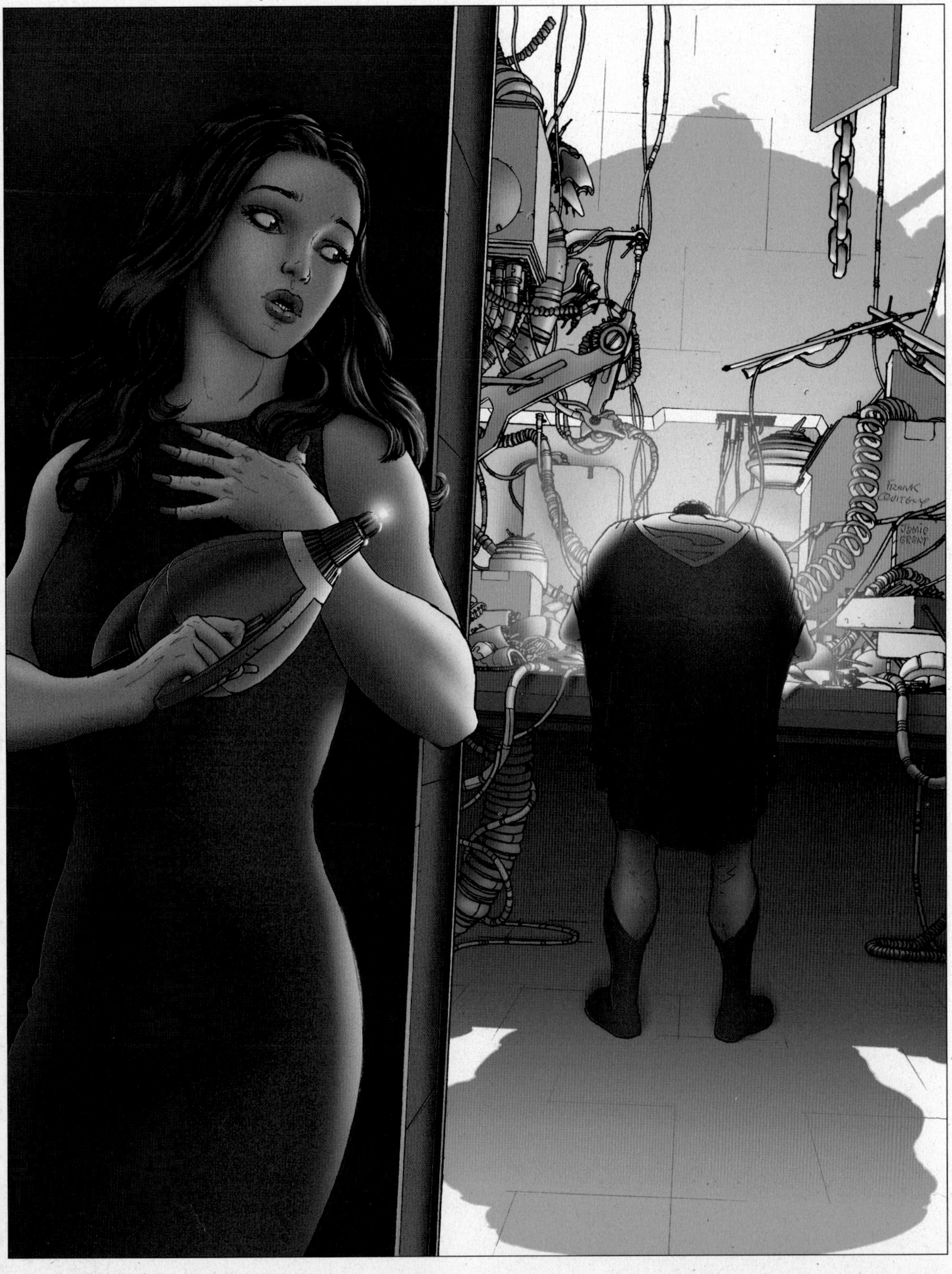
FRANK QUITELY
JAMIE GRANT

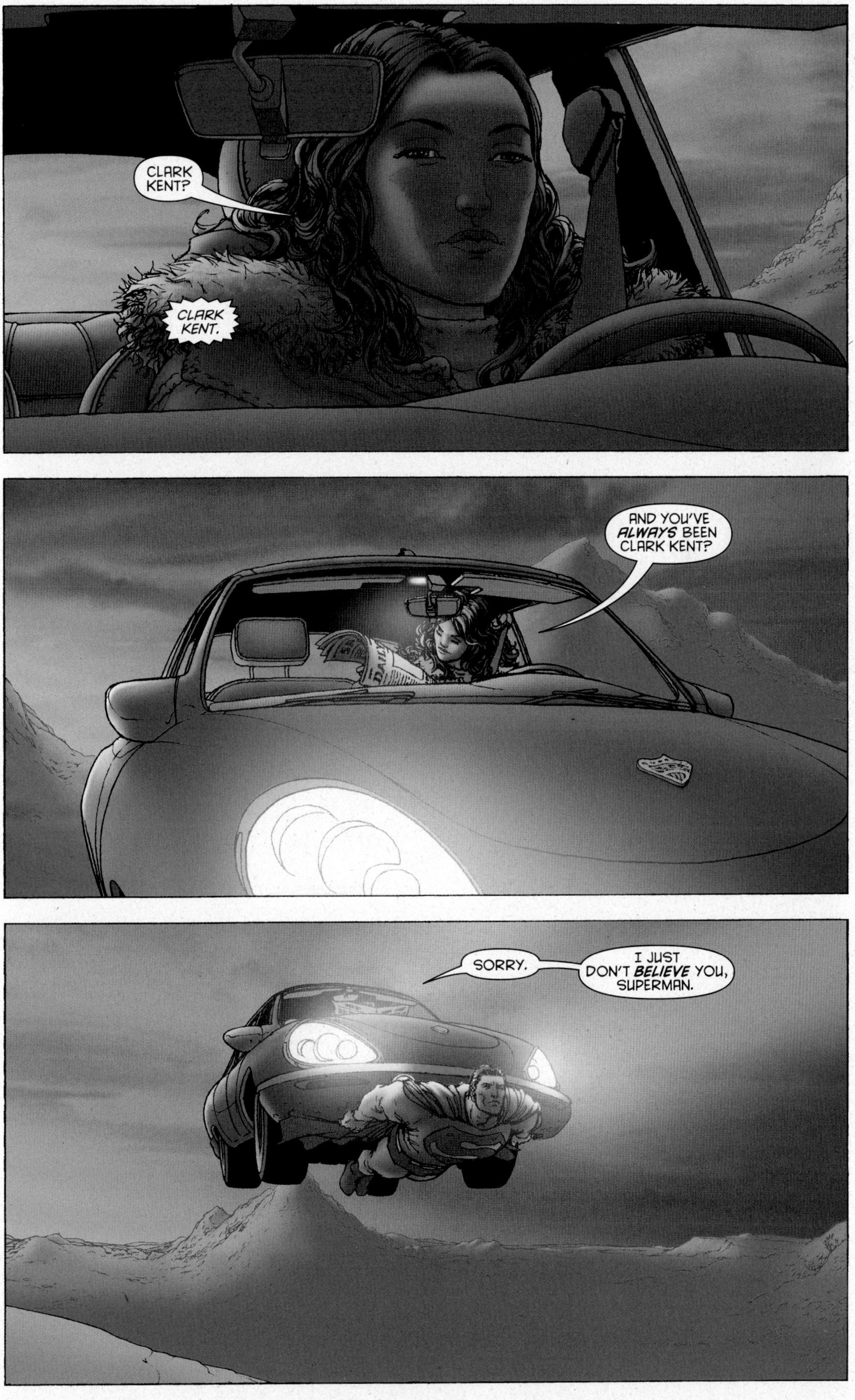
CLARK KENT?
CLARK KENT.
AND YOU'VE *ALWAYS* BEEN CLARK KENT?
SORRY.
I JUST DON'T *BELIEVE* YOU, SUPERMAN.

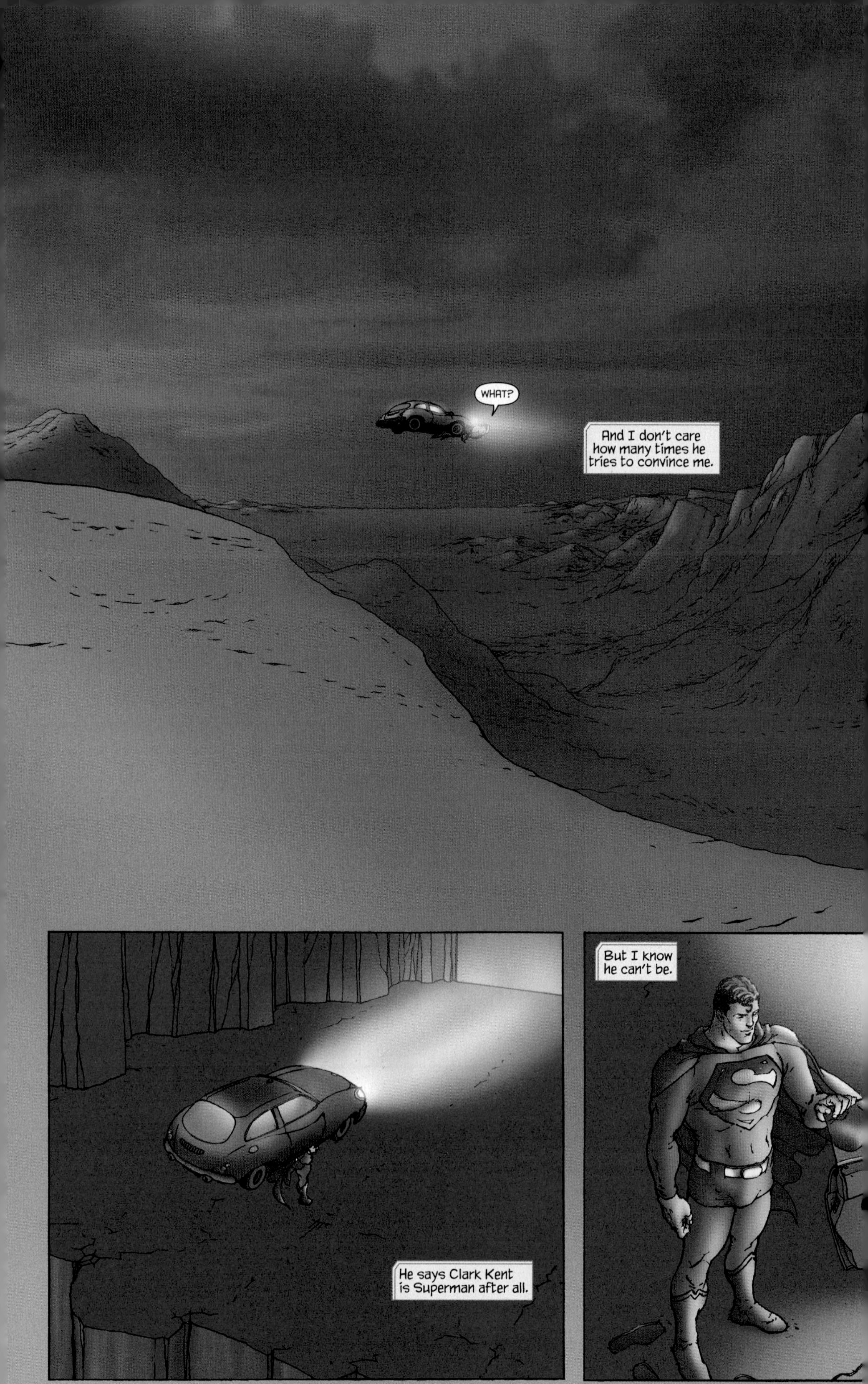
WHAT?
And I don't care how many times he tries to convince me.
He says Clark Kent is Superman after all.
But I know he can't be.

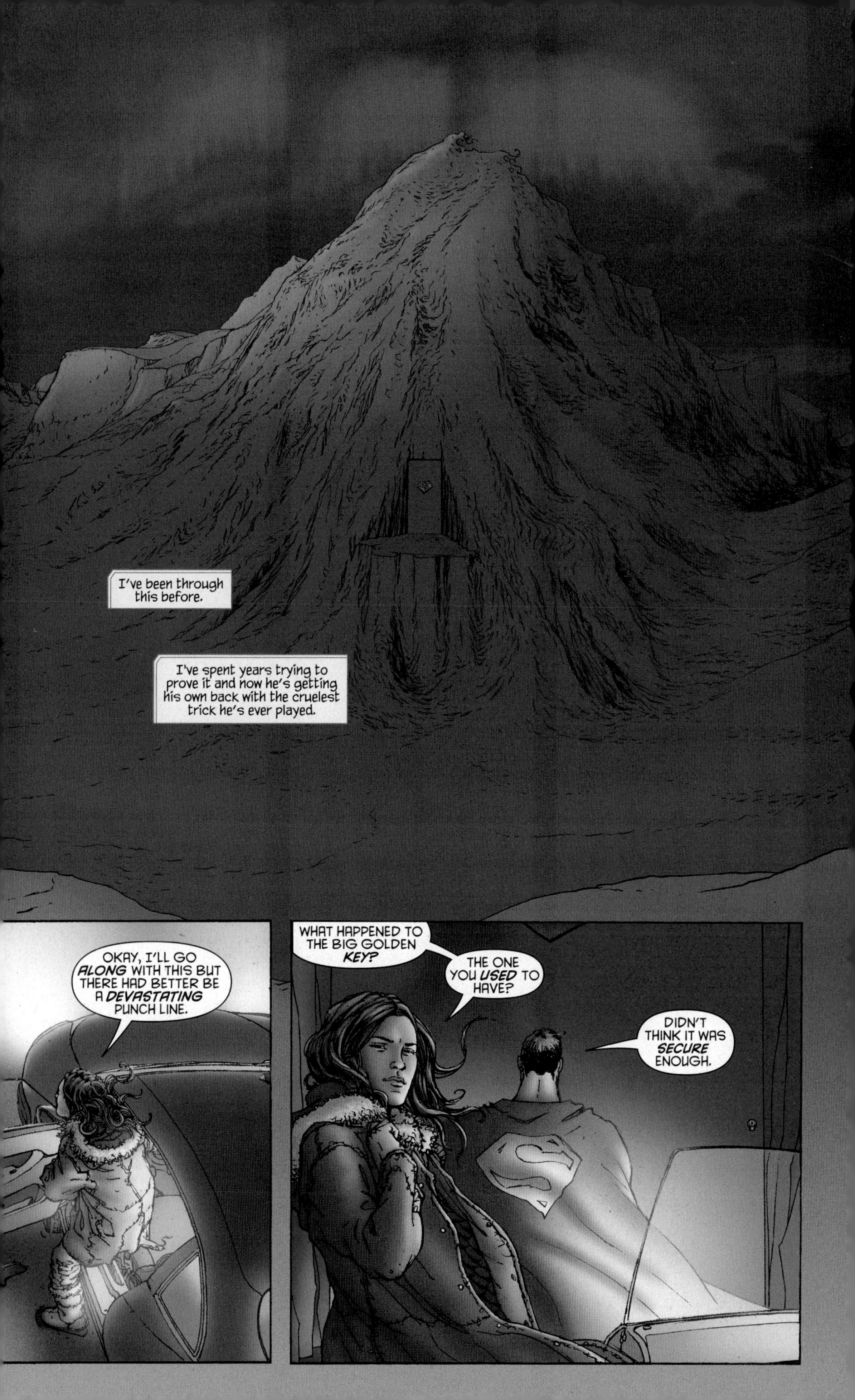
I've been through this before.
I've spent years trying to prove it and now he's getting his own back with the cruelest trick he's ever played.
OKAY, I'LL GO ALONG WITH THIS BUT THERE HAD BETTER BE A DEVASTATING PUNCH LINE.
WHAT HAPPENED TO THE BIG GOLDEN KEY?
THE ONE YOU USED TO HAVE?
DIDN'T THINK IT WAS SECURE ENOUGH.

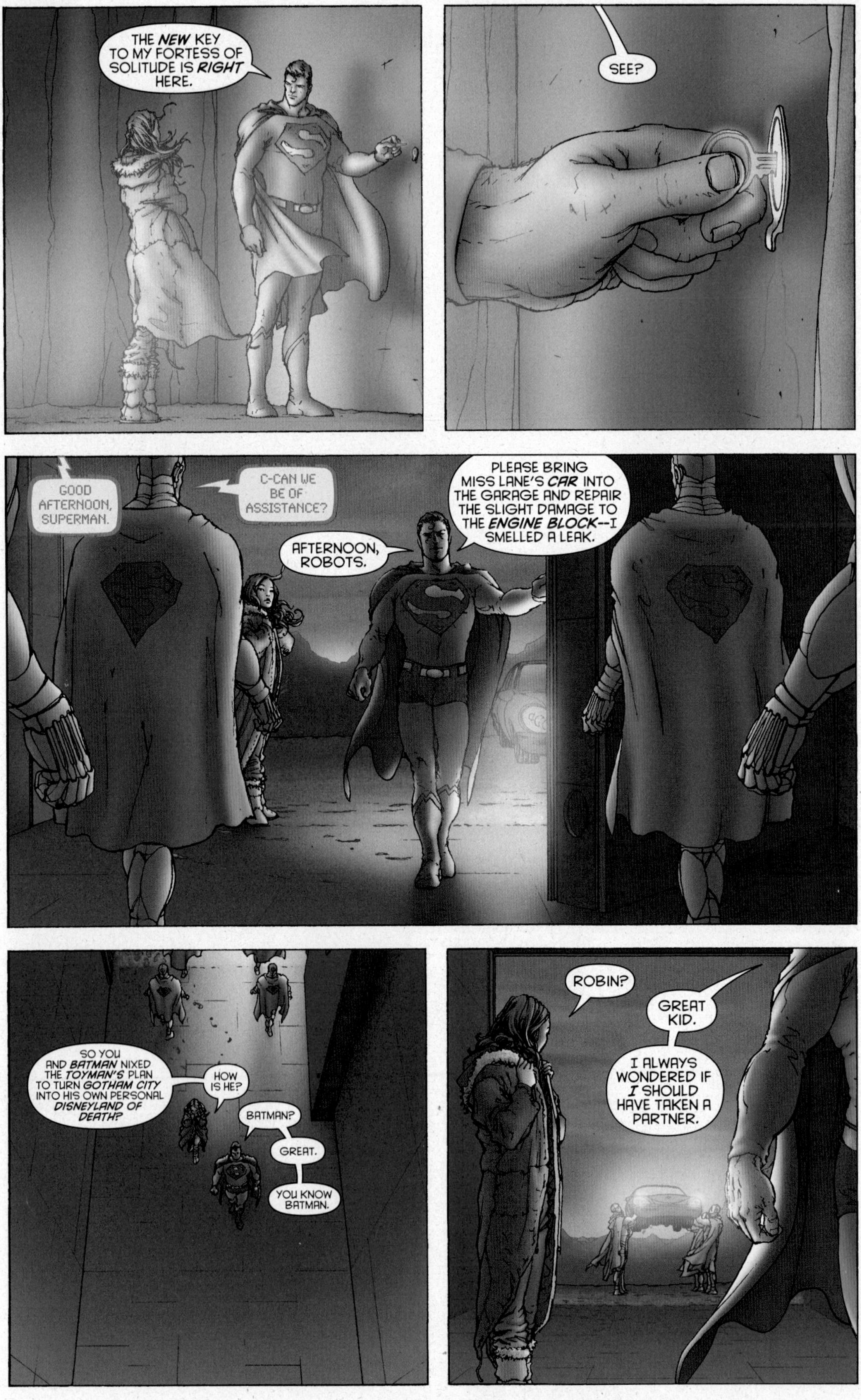
THE *NEW* KEY TO MY FORTESS OF SOLITUDE IS *RIGHT* HERE.
SEE?
GOOD AFTERNOON, SUPERMAN.
C-CAN WE BE OF ASSISTANCE?
AFTERNOON, ROBOTS.
PLEASE BRING MISS LANE'S *CAR* INTO THE GARAGE AND REPAIR THE SLIGHT DAMAGE TO THE *ENGINE BLOCK*--I SMELLED A LEAK.
SO YOU AND *BATMAN* NIXED THE *TOYMAN'S* PLAN TO TURN *GOTHAM CITY* INTO HIS OWN PERSONAL *DISNEYLAND OF DEATH?*
HOW IS HE?
BATMAN?
GREAT.
YOU KNOW BATMAN.
ROBIN?
GREAT KID.
I ALWAYS WONDERED IF *I* SHOULD HAVE TAKEN A PARTNER.

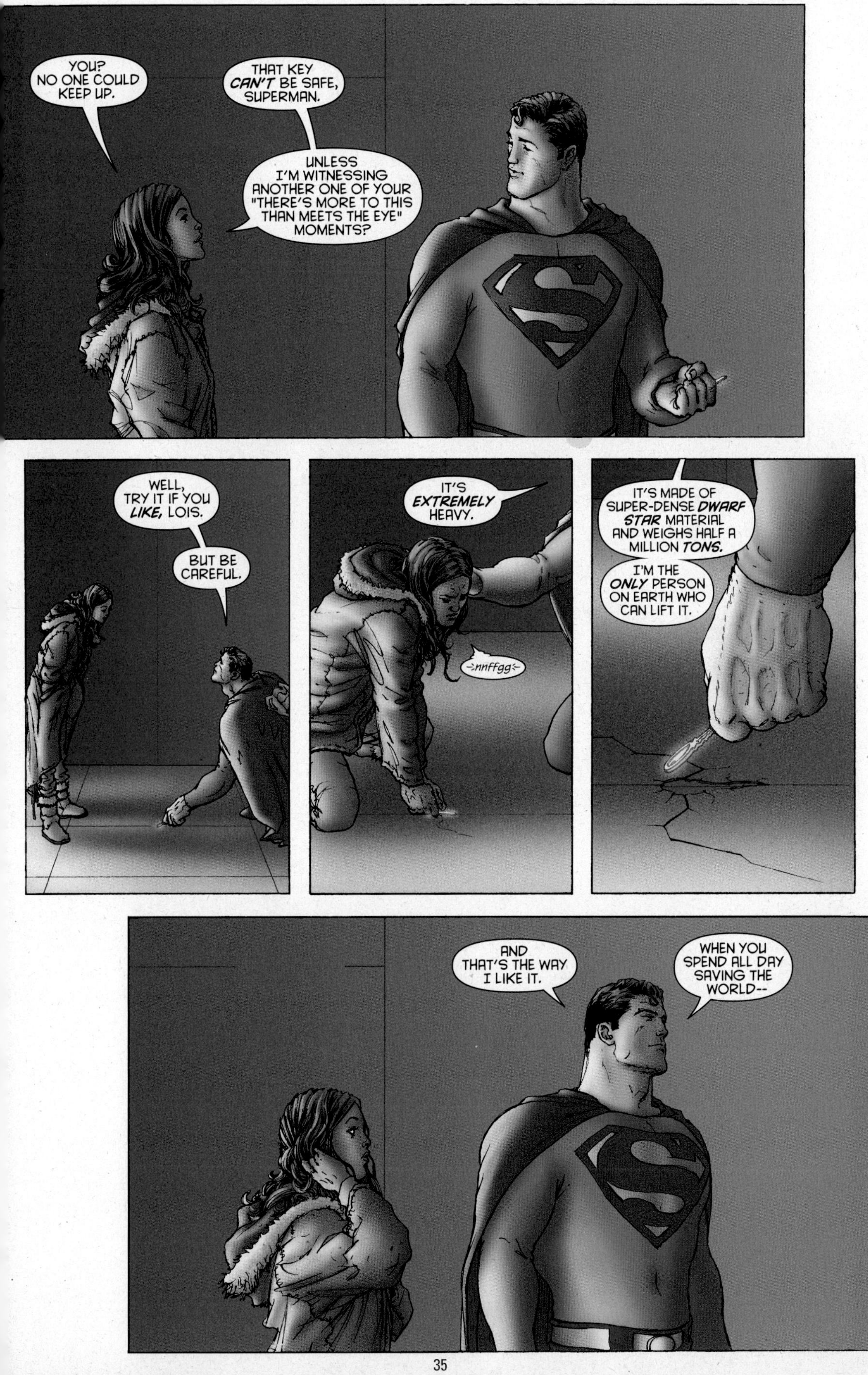
YOU? NO ONE COULD KEEP UP.
THAT KEY CAN'T BE SAFE, SUPERMAN.
UNLESS I'M WITNESSING ANOTHER ONE OF YOUR "THERE'S MORE TO THIS THAN MEETS THE EYE" MOMENTS?
WELL, TRY IT IF YOU LIKE, LOIS.
BUT BE CAREFUL.
IT'S EXTREMELY HEAVY.
nnffgg
IT'S MADE OF SUPER-DENSE DWARF STAR MATERIAL AND WEIGHS HALF A MILLION TONS.
I'M THE ONLY PERSON ON EARTH WHO CAN LIFT IT.
AND THAT'S THE WAY I LIKE IT.
WHEN YOU SPEND ALL DAY SAVING THE WORLD--

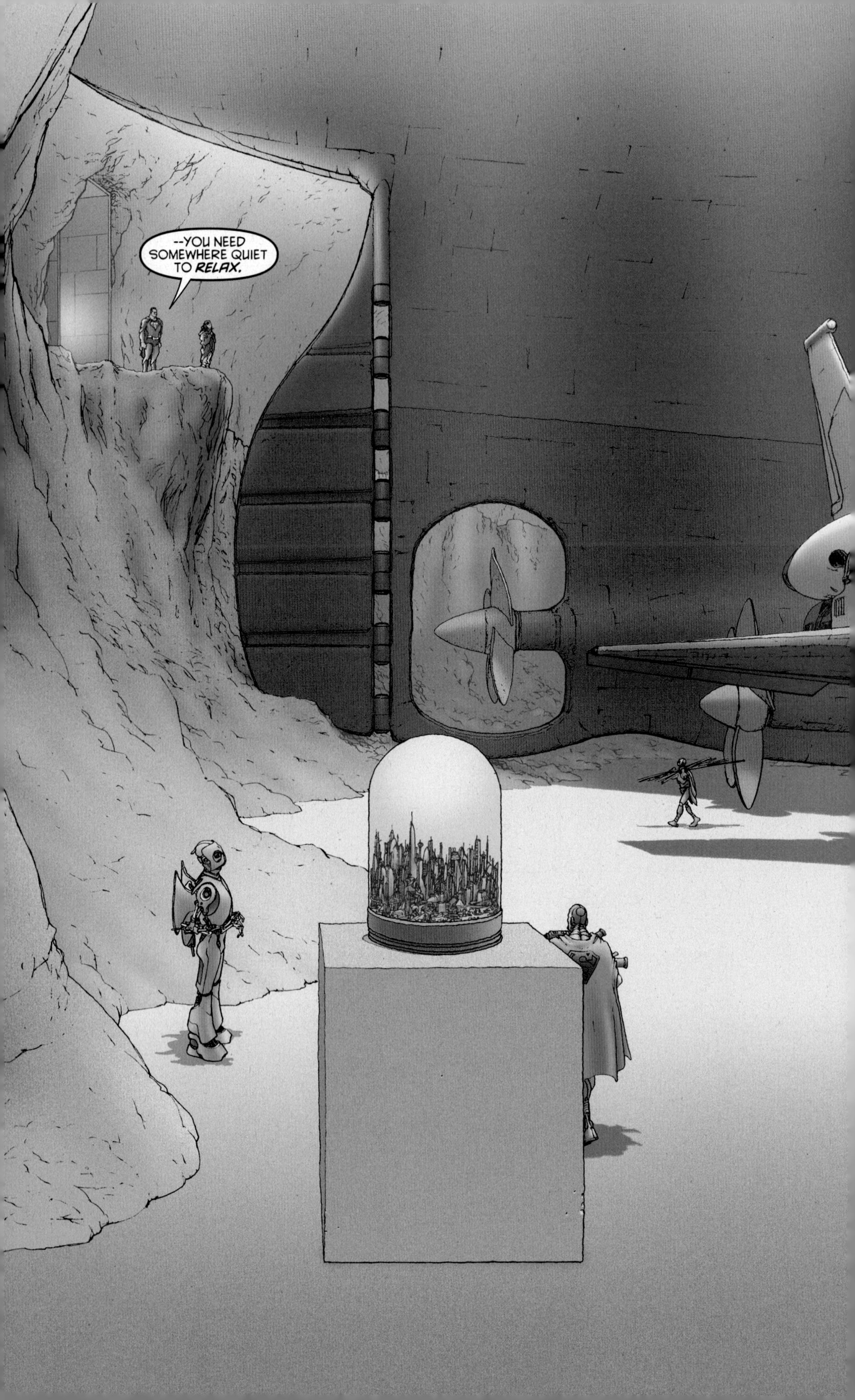
--YOU NEED SOMEWHERE QUIET TO *RELAX.*

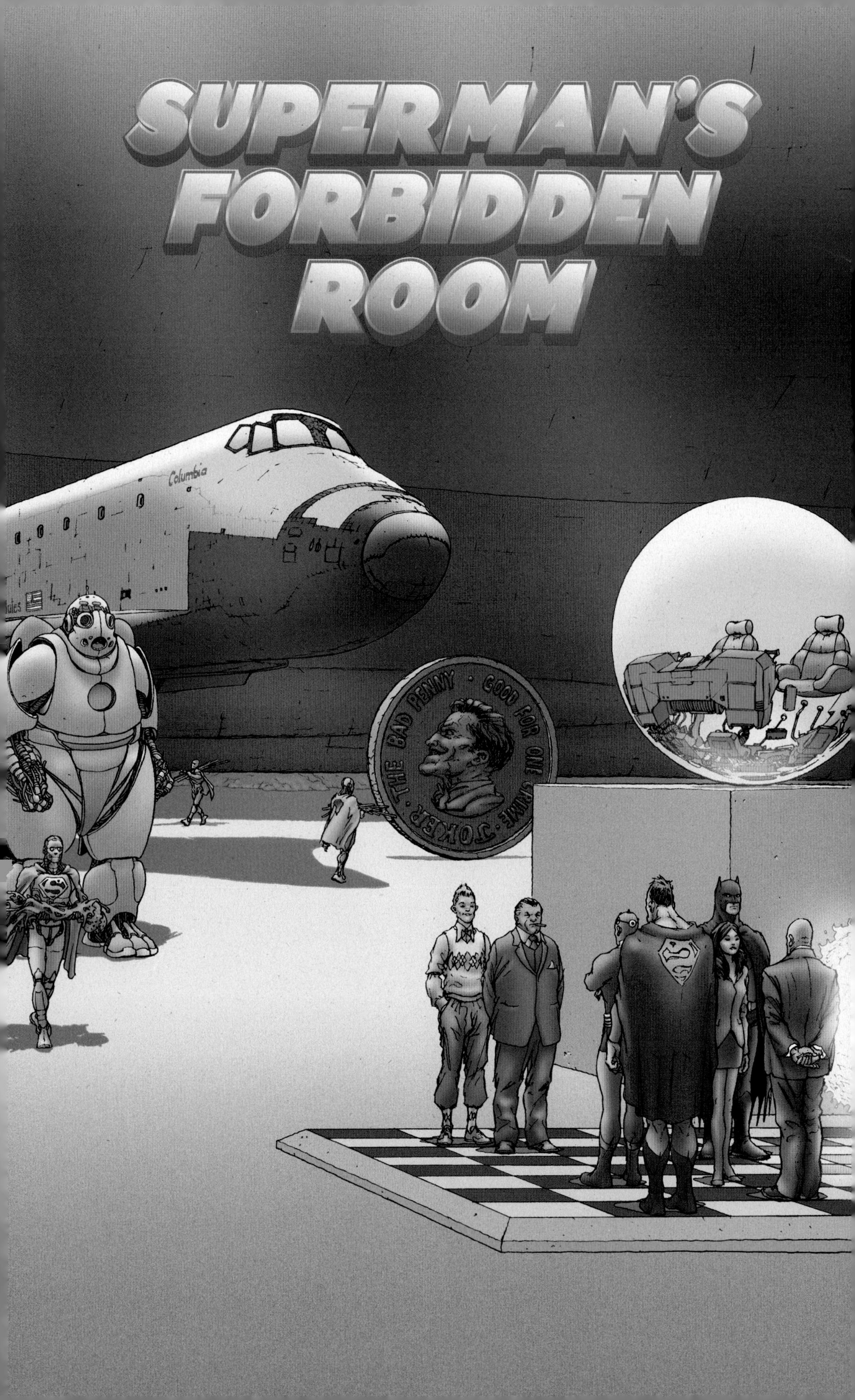
SUPERMAN'S FORBIDDEN ROOM
Columbia
THE BAD PENNY · GOOD FOR ONE CRIME · JOKER

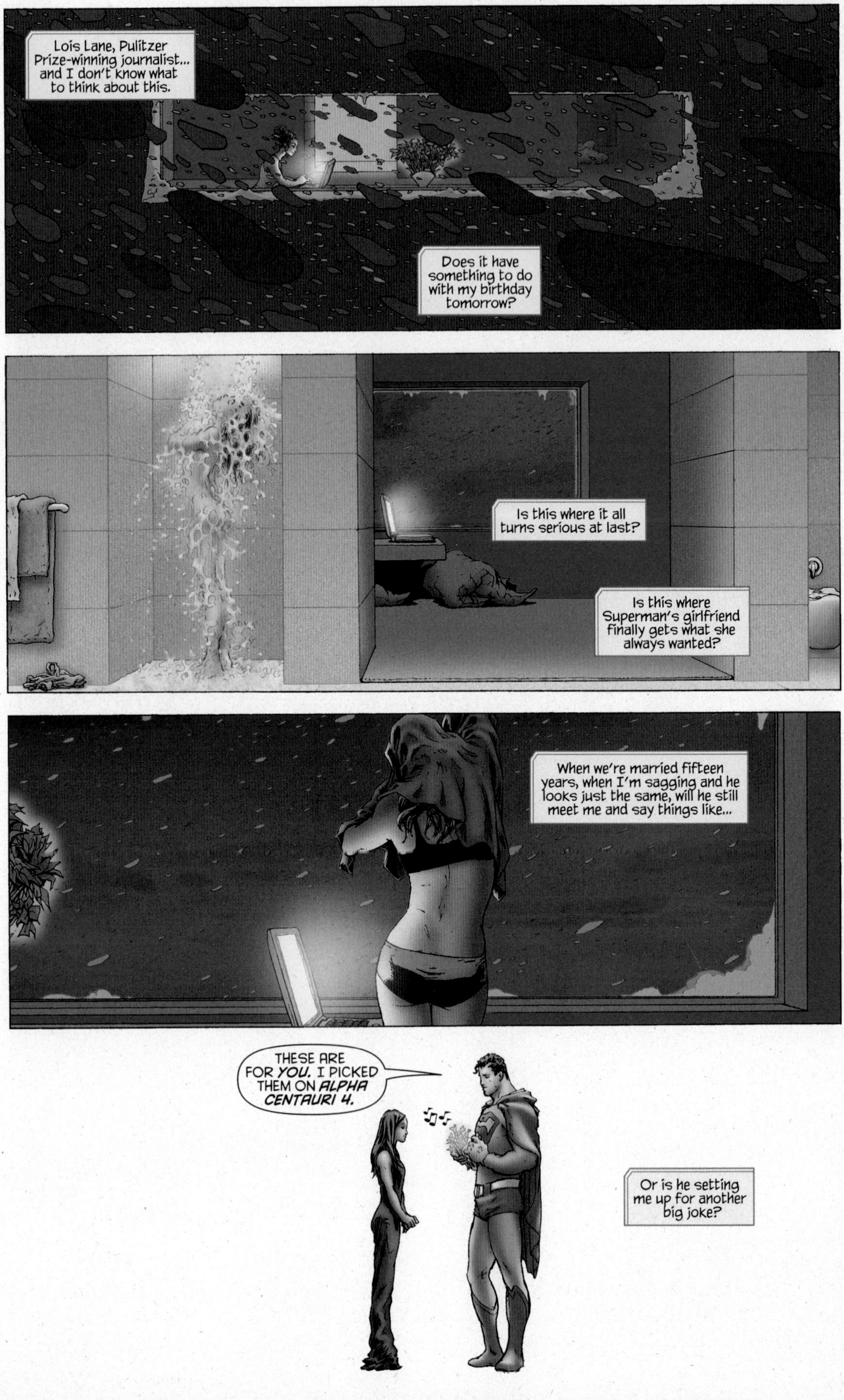
Lois Lane, Pulitzer Prize-winning journalist... and I don't know what to think about this.
Does it have something to do with my birthday tomorrow?
Is this where it all turns serious at last?
Is this where Superman's girlfriend finally gets what she always wanted?
When we're married fifteen years, when I'm sagging and he looks just the same, will he still meet me and say things like...
THESE ARE FOR YOU. I PICKED THEM ON ALPHA CENTAURI 4.
Or is he setting me up for another big joke?

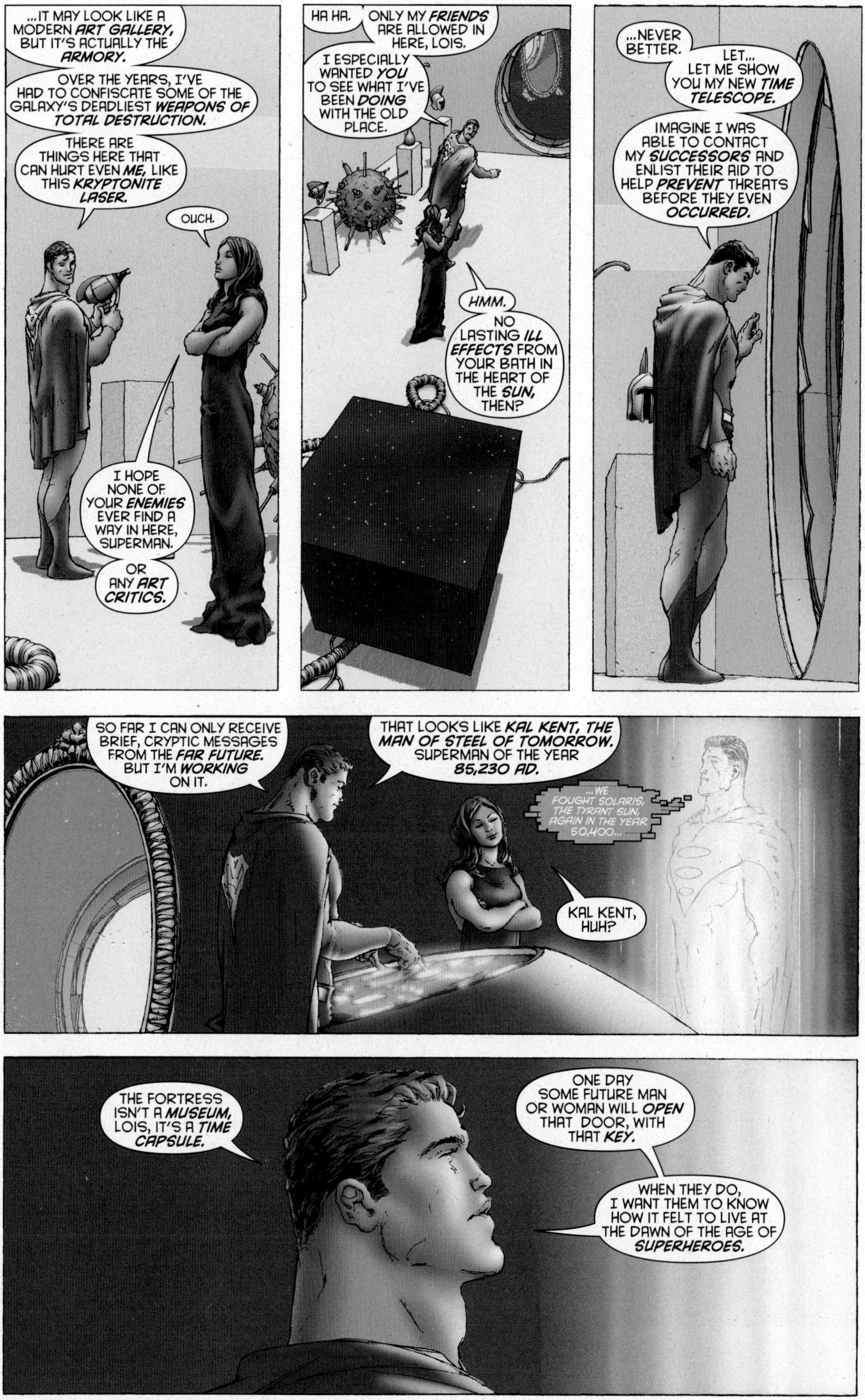
...IT MAY LOOK LIKE A MODERN ART GALLERY, BUT IT'S ACTUALLY THE ARMORY.
OVER THE YEARS, I'VE HAD TO CONFISCATE SOME OF THE GALAXY'S DEADLIEST WEAPONS OF TOTAL DESTRUCTION.
THERE ARE THINGS HERE THAT CAN HURT EVEN ME, LIKE THIS KRYPTONITE LASER.
OUCH.
I HOPE NONE OF YOUR ENEMIES EVER FIND A WAY IN HERE, SUPERMAN.
OR ANY ART CRITICS.
HA HA.
ONLY MY FRIENDS ARE ALLOWED IN HERE, LOIS.
I ESPECIALLY WANTED YOU TO SEE WHAT I'VE BEEN DOING WITH THE OLD PLACE.
HMM.
NO LASTING ILL EFFECTS FROM YOUR BATH IN THE HEART OF THE SUN, THEN?
...NEVER BETTER.
LET... LET ME SHOW YOU MY NEW TIME TELESCOPE.
IMAGINE I WAS ABLE TO CONTACT MY SUCCESSORS AND ENLIST THEIR AID TO HELP PREVENT THREATS BEFORE THEY EVEN OCCURRED.
SO FAR I CAN ONLY RECEIVE BRIEF, CRYPTIC MESSAGES FROM THE FAR FUTURE. BUT I'M WORKING ON IT.
THAT LOOKS LIKE KAL KENT, THE MAN OF STEEL OF TOMORROW. SUPERMAN OF THE YEAR 85,230 AD.
...WE FOUGHT SOLARIS, THE TYRANT SUN, AGAIN IN THE YEAR 50,400...
KAL KENT, HUH?
THE FORTRESS ISN'T A MUSEUM, LOIS, IT'S A TIME CAPSULE.
ONE DAY SOME FUTURE MAN OR WOMAN WILL OPEN THAT DOOR, WITH THAT KEY.
WHEN THEY DO, I WANT THEM TO KNOW HOW IT FELT TO LIVE AT THE DAWN OF THE AGE OF SUPERHEROES.

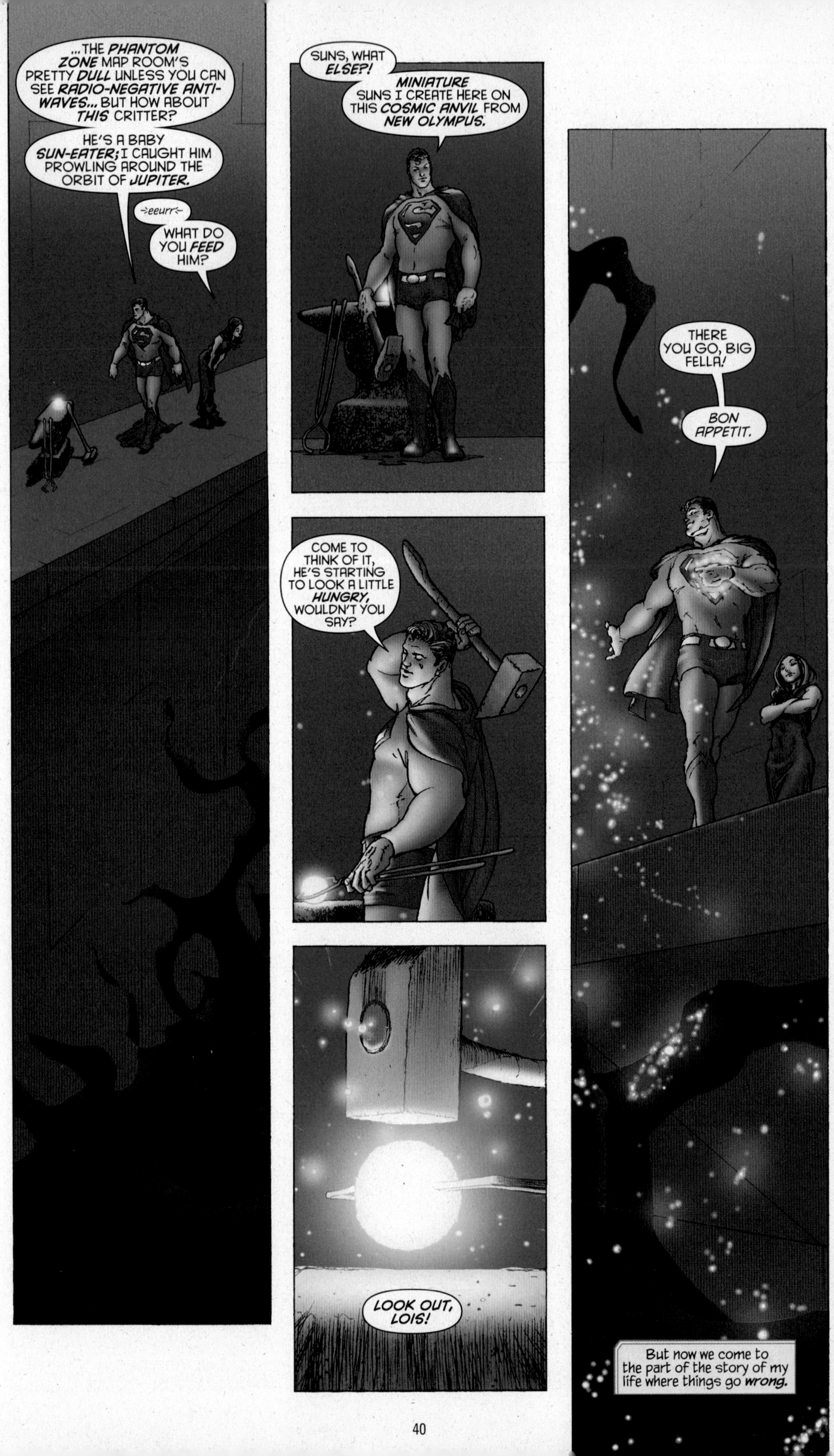
...THE PHANTOM ZONE MAP ROOM'S PRETTY DULL UNLESS YOU CAN SEE RADIO-NEGATIVE ANTI-WAVES... BUT HOW ABOUT THIS CRITTER?
HE'S A BABY SUN-EATER; I CAUGHT HIM PROWLING AROUND THE ORBIT OF JUPITER.
eeurr
WHAT DO YOU FEED HIM?
SUNS, WHAT ELSE?!
MINIATURE SUNS I CREATE HERE ON THIS COSMIC ANVIL FROM NEW OLYMPUS.
COME TO THINK OF IT, HE'S STARTING TO LOOK A LITTLE HUNGRY, WOULDN'T YOU SAY?
LOOK OUT, LOIS!
THERE YOU GO, BIG FELLA!
BON APPETIT.
But now we come to the part of the story of my life where things go wrong.

It wasn't *my fault* the door was open.

I know I wasn't supposed to see inside that weird room.

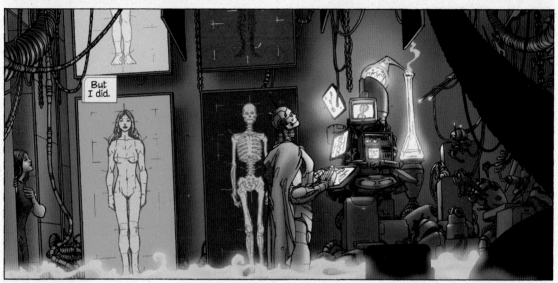

But I did.

→wuhh←

IT'S NOT WHAT YOU *THINK.*

LOIS, *DON'T* GO IN THERE!

YOU CAN GO *ANYWHERE* IN THE FORTRESS, BUT THIS ROOM IS *OFF LIMITS.*

TRUST ME.

COME THIS WAY AND LET ME SHOW YOU MY *GENETIC LIBRARY.* I USED BRAINIAC'S *SHRINKING RAY* TO STORE LIVING SAMPLES OF *EVERY* THREATENED SPECIES WITHIN A HUNDRED *LIGHT YEARS* IN A SINGLE *DRAWER...*

REPORT FOR *REPAIR,* PLEASE, ROBOT 7.

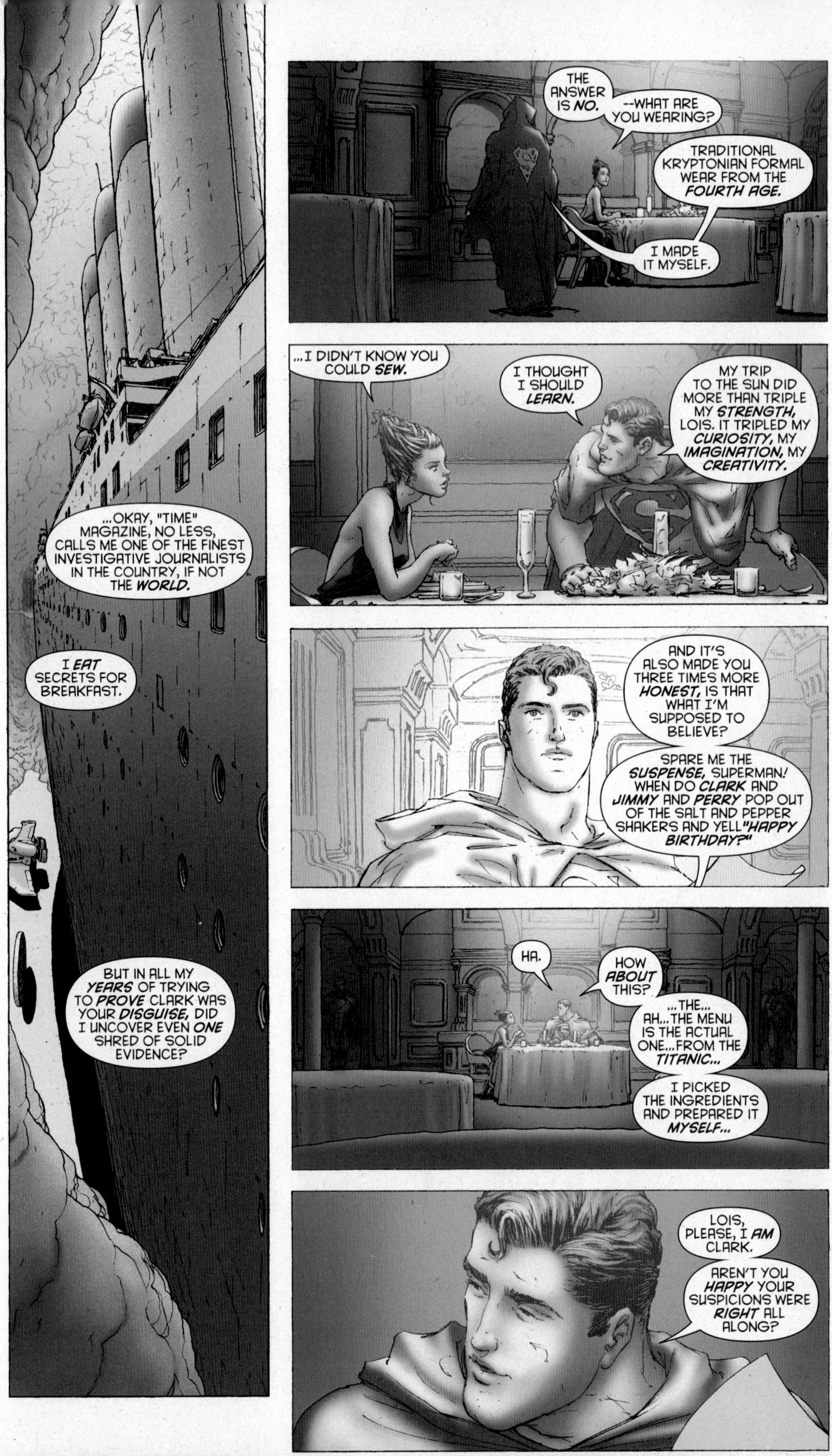
...OKAY, "TIME" MAGAZINE, NO LESS, CALLS ME ONE OF THE FINEST INVESTIGATIVE JOURNALISTS IN THE COUNTRY, IF NOT THE WORLD.
I EAT SECRETS FOR BREAKFAST.
BUT IN ALL MY YEARS OF TRYING TO PROVE CLARK WAS YOUR DISGUISE, DID I UNCOVER EVEN ONE SHRED OF SOLID EVIDENCE?
THE ANSWER IS NO.
--WHAT ARE YOU WEARING?
TRADITIONAL KRYPTONIAN FORMAL WEAR FROM THE FOURTH AGE.
I MADE IT MYSELF.
...I DIDN'T KNOW YOU COULD SEW.
I THOUGHT I SHOULD LEARN.
MY TRIP TO THE SUN DID MORE THAN TRIPLE MY STRENGTH, LOIS. IT TRIPLED MY CURIOSITY, MY IMAGINATION, MY CREATIVITY.
AND IT'S ALSO MADE YOU THREE TIMES MORE HONEST, IS THAT WHAT I'M SUPPOSED TO BELIEVE?
SPARE ME THE SUSPENSE, SUPERMAN! WHEN DO CLARK AND JIMMY AND PERRY POP OUT OF THE SALT AND PEPPER SHAKERS AND YELL "HAPPY BIRTHDAY?"
HA.
HOW ABOUT THIS?
...THE... AH...THE MENU IS THE ACTUAL ONE...FROM THE TITANIC...
I PICKED THE INGREDIENTS AND PREPARED IT MYSELF...
LOIS, PLEASE, I AM CLARK.
AREN'T YOU HAPPY YOUR SUSPICIONS WERE RIGHT ALL ALONG?

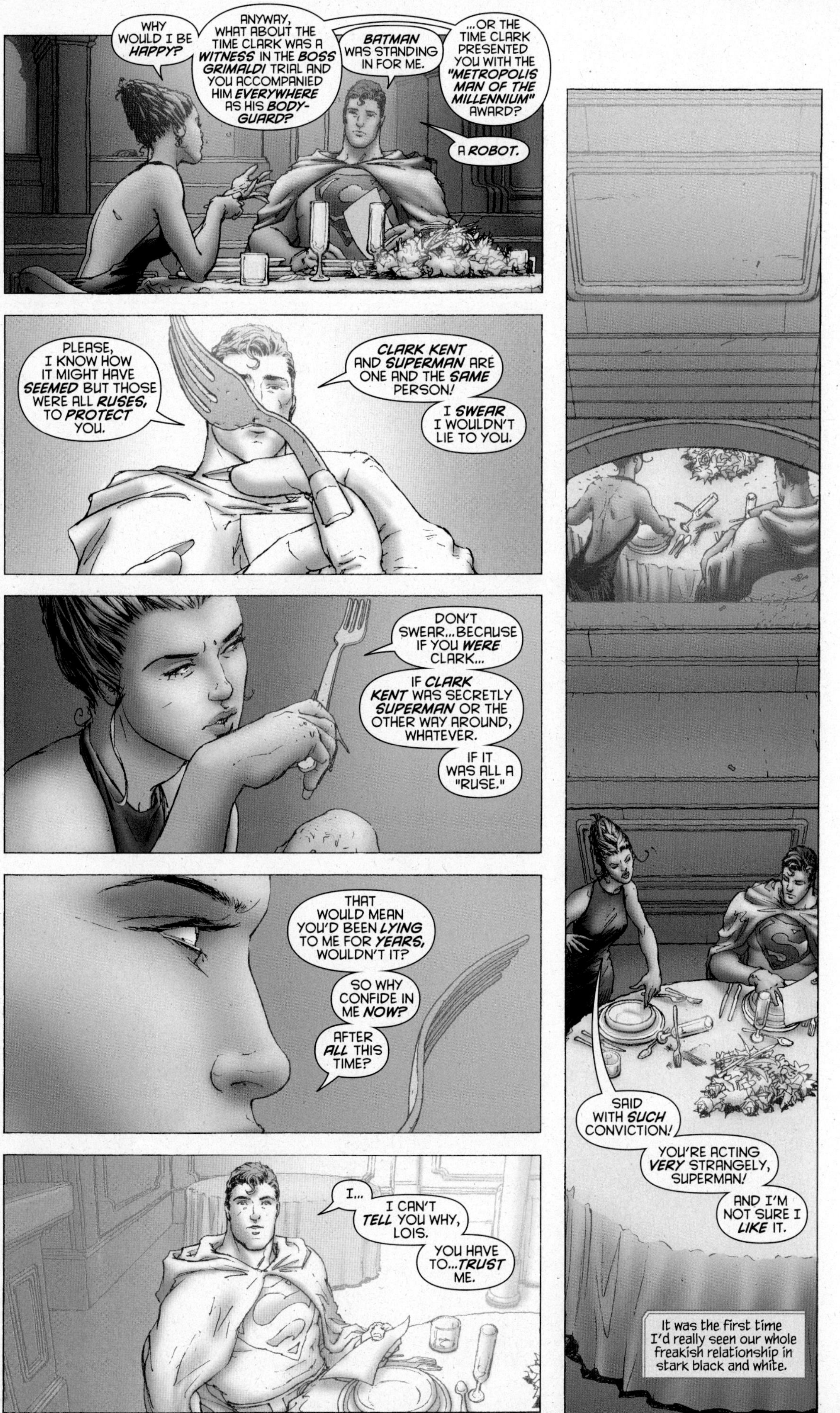

WHY WOULD I BE HAPPY?
ANYWAY, WHAT ABOUT THE TIME CLARK WAS A WITNESS IN THE BOSS GRIMALDI TRIAL AND YOU ACCOMPANIED HIM EVERYWHERE AS HIS BODY-GUARD?
BATMAN WAS STANDING IN FOR ME.
...OR THE TIME CLARK PRESENTED YOU WITH THE "METROPOLIS MAN OF THE MILLENNIUM" AWARD?
A ROBOT.
PLEASE, I KNOW HOW IT MIGHT HAVE SEEMED BUT THOSE WERE ALL RUSES, TO PROTECT YOU.
CLARK KENT AND SUPERMAN ARE ONE AND THE SAME PERSON!
I SWEAR I WOULDN'T LIE TO YOU.
DON'T SWEAR...BECAUSE IF YOU WERE CLARK...
IF CLARK KENT WAS SECRETLY SUPERMAN OR THE OTHER WAY AROUND, WHATEVER.
IF IT WAS ALL A "RUSE."
THAT WOULD MEAN YOU'D BEEN LYING TO ME FOR YEARS, WOULDN'T IT?
SO WHY CONFIDE IN ME NOW?
AFTER ALL THIS TIME?
I...
I CAN'T TELL YOU WHY, LOIS.
YOU HAVE TO...TRUST ME.
SAID WITH SUCH CONVICTION!
YOU'RE ACTING VERY STRANGELY, SUPERMAN!
AND I'M NOT SURE I LIKE IT.
It was the first time I'd really seen our whole freakish relationship in stark black and white.

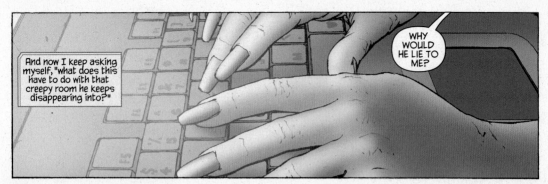

And now I keep asking myself, "what does this have to do with that creepy room he keeps disappearing into?"

WHY WOULD HE LIE TO ME?

MIRROR OF TRUTH, HUH?

These new powers; his new super-intellect.

What if they've really changed him?

What if something's happened to his mind and he's brought me here to be a part of some awful experiment he's planning in that room?

How would I know?

44

HOW CAN I TELL HER I ONLY WANTED US TO HAVE THIS *TIME* TOGETHER BECAUSE IT MAY BE OUR *LAST?*

And you know what would be worse?

What if he's telling the truth?

HOW CAN I SPOIL HER BIRTHDAY WITH THE NEWS THAT I'M *DYING?*

What if there really was some part of him that was bumbling, oafish Clark Kent?

I just don't know if I could live with that.

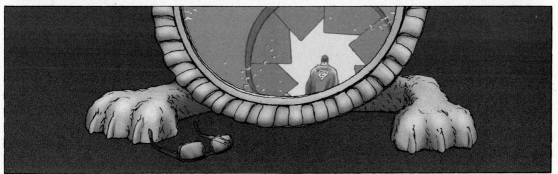

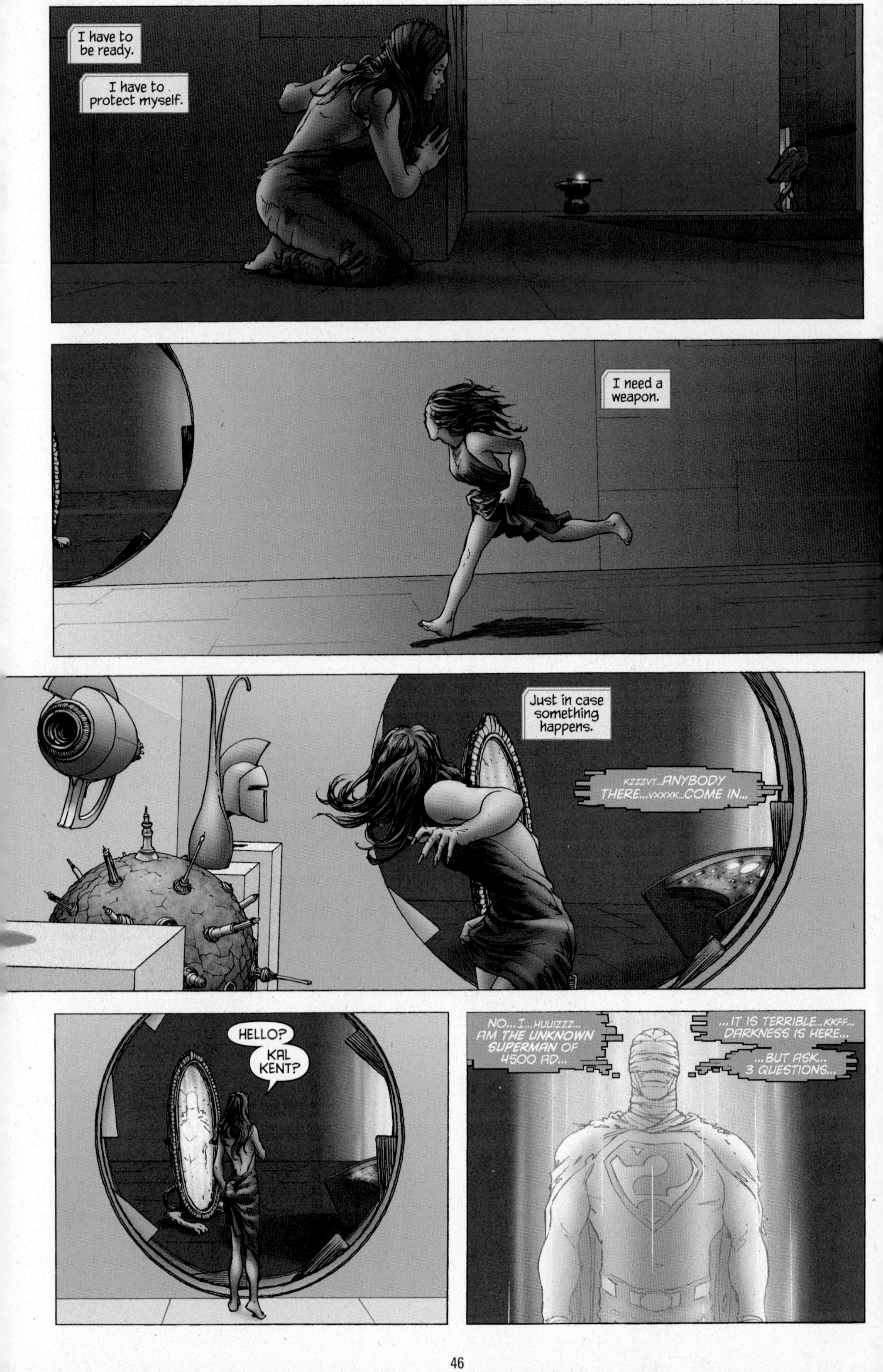

I have to be ready.
I have to protect myself.
I need a weapon.
Just in case something happens.
KZZZVT...ANYBODY THERE...VXXXK...COME IN...
HELLO? KAL KENT?
NO... I...HUUIZZZ... AM THE UNKNOWN SUPERMAN OF 4500 AD...
...IT IS TERRIBLE...KKFF... DARKNESS IS HERE...
...BUT ASK... 3 QUESTIONS...

WILL... SUPERMAN AND I EVER MARRY AND HAVE CHILDREN?
I NEED TO KNOW.
...THE HORRIBLE... ZZZXXTTT... ANSWER IS BEFORE YOU...
...NOW... KKZZKKT... MY QUESTION...
...FUTURE... MUST KNOW... VEEEE... GREAT CONUNDRUM...
WAIT!
WHAT DO YOU MEAN?
...ANSWER FIRST... VEEEKKT... RECEPTION POOR HERE... LISTEN CAREFULLY...
SOMETHING WRONG, MISS LANE?
WOULD YOU LIKE TO COME WITH US TO SUPERMAN?
WHO... GZZVVT...
WHO... VZZT... WAS J. LO?

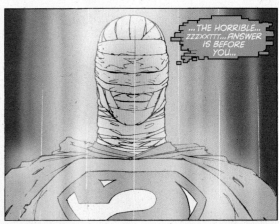

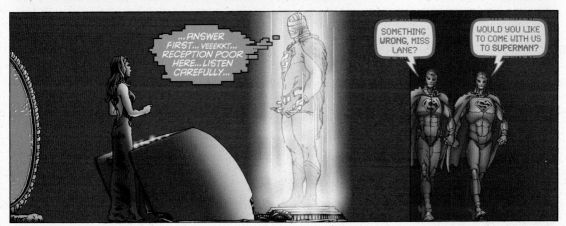

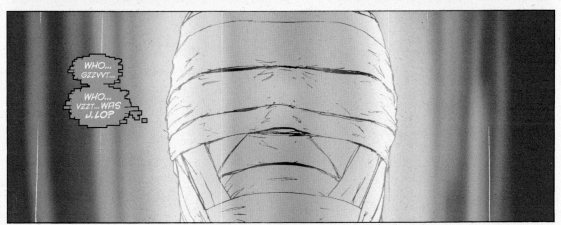

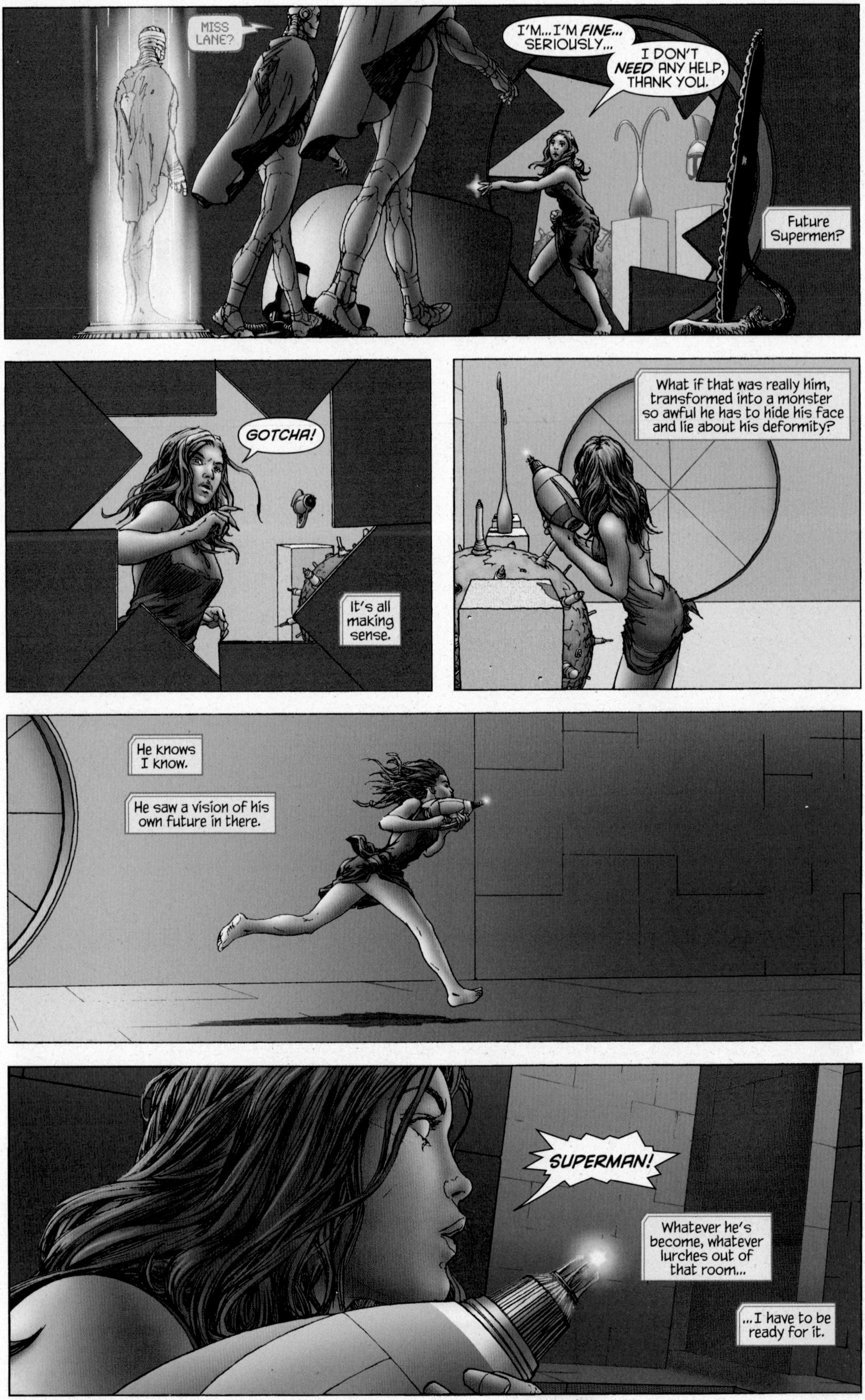
MISS LANE?
I'M...I'M FINE... SERIOUSLY...
I DON'T NEED ANY HELP, THANK YOU.
Future Supermen?
GOTCHA!
It's all making sense.
What if that was really him, transformed into a monster so awful he has to hide his face and lie about his deformity?
He knows I know.
He saw a vision of his own future in there.
SUPERMAN!
Whatever he's become, whatever lurches out of that room...
...I have to be ready for it.

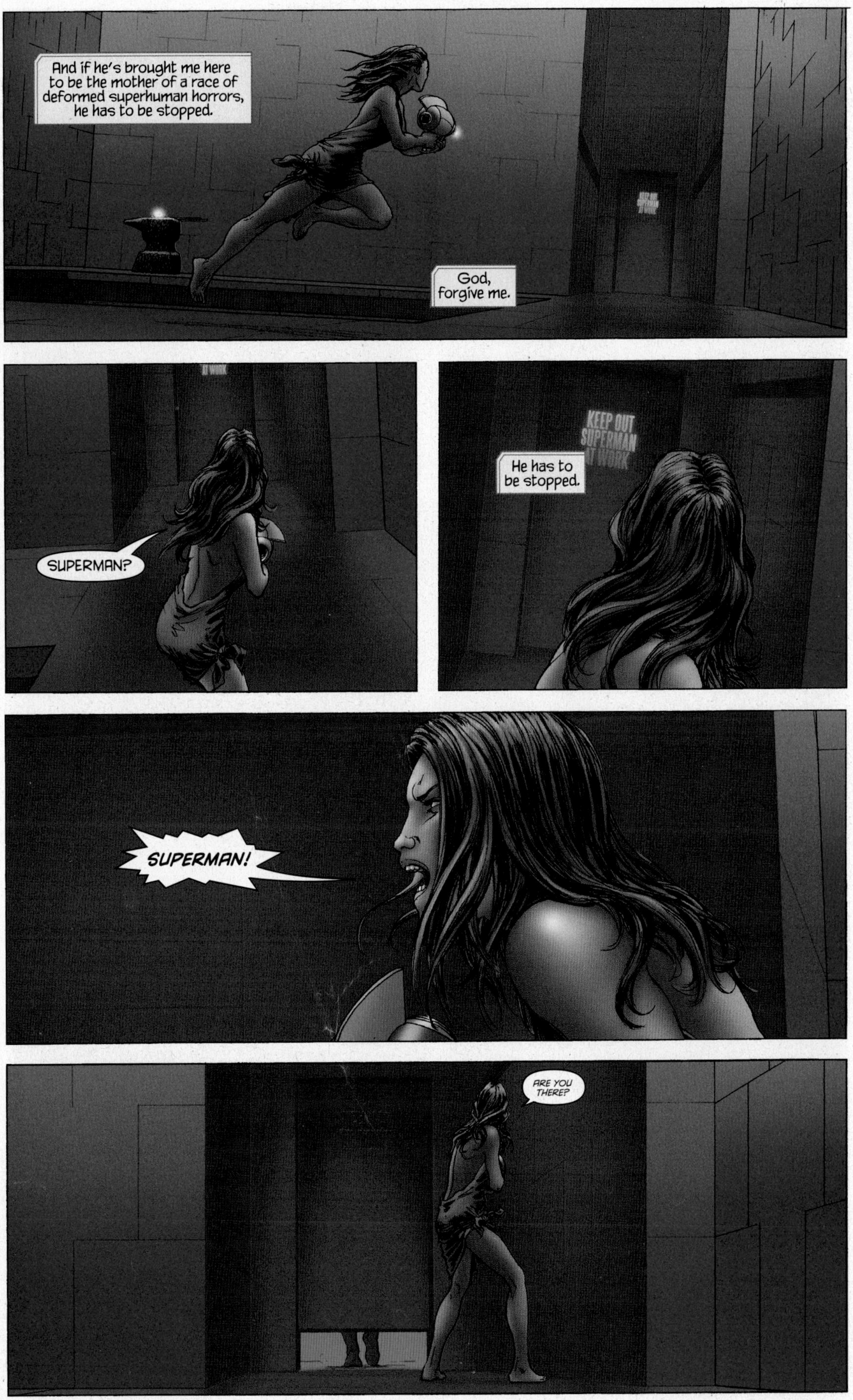
And if he's brought me here to be the mother of a race of deformed superhuman horrors, he has to be stopped.
KEEP OUT SUPERMAN AT WORK
God, forgive me.
SUPERMAN?
KEEP OUT SUPERMAN AT WORK
He has to be stopped.
SUPERMAN!
ARE YOU THERE?

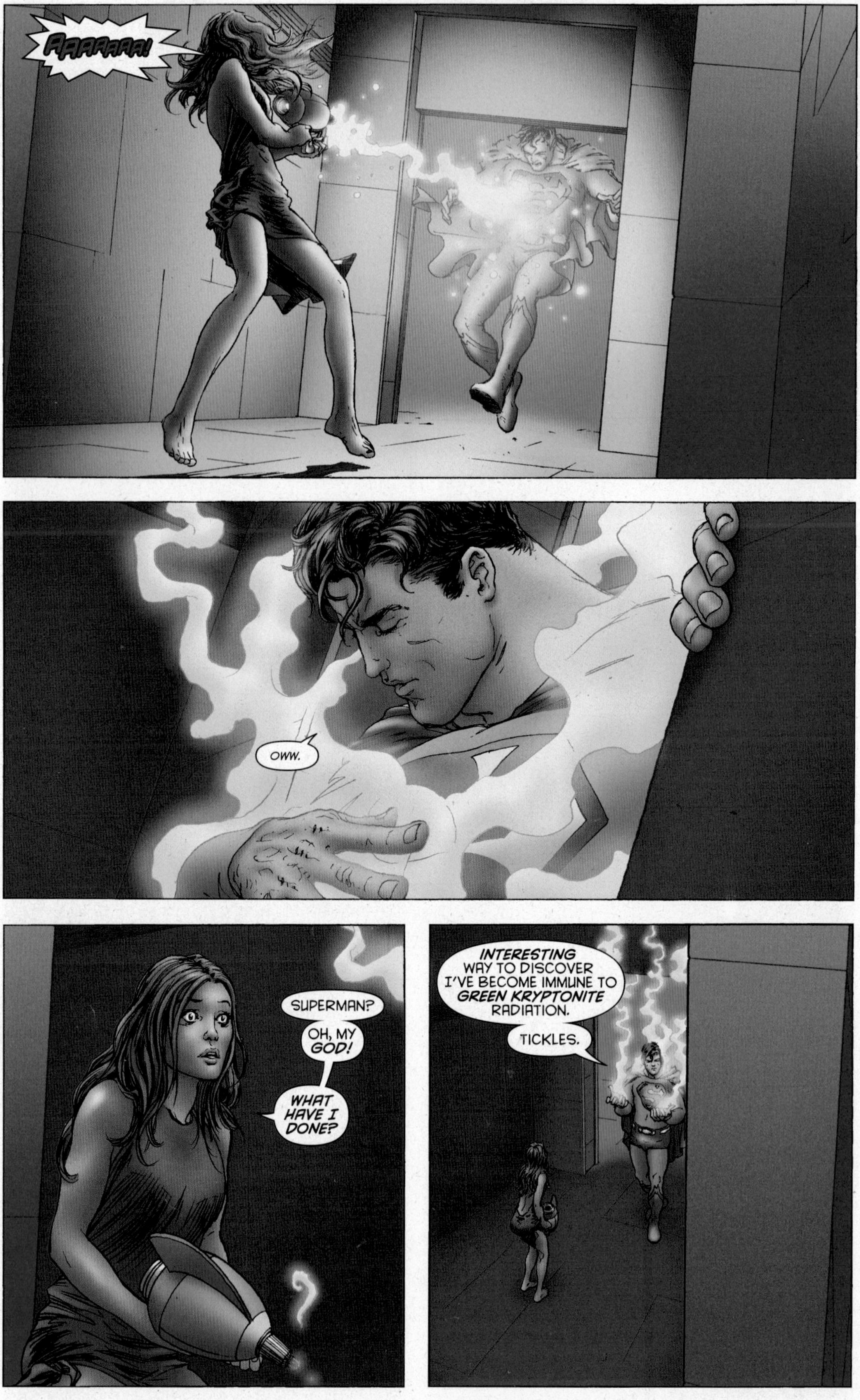
AAAAAAA!
OWW.
SUPERMAN?
OH, MY GOD!
WHAT HAVE I DONE?
INTERESTING WAY TO DISCOVER I'VE BECOME IMMUNE TO GREEN KRYPTONITE RADIATION.
TICKLES.

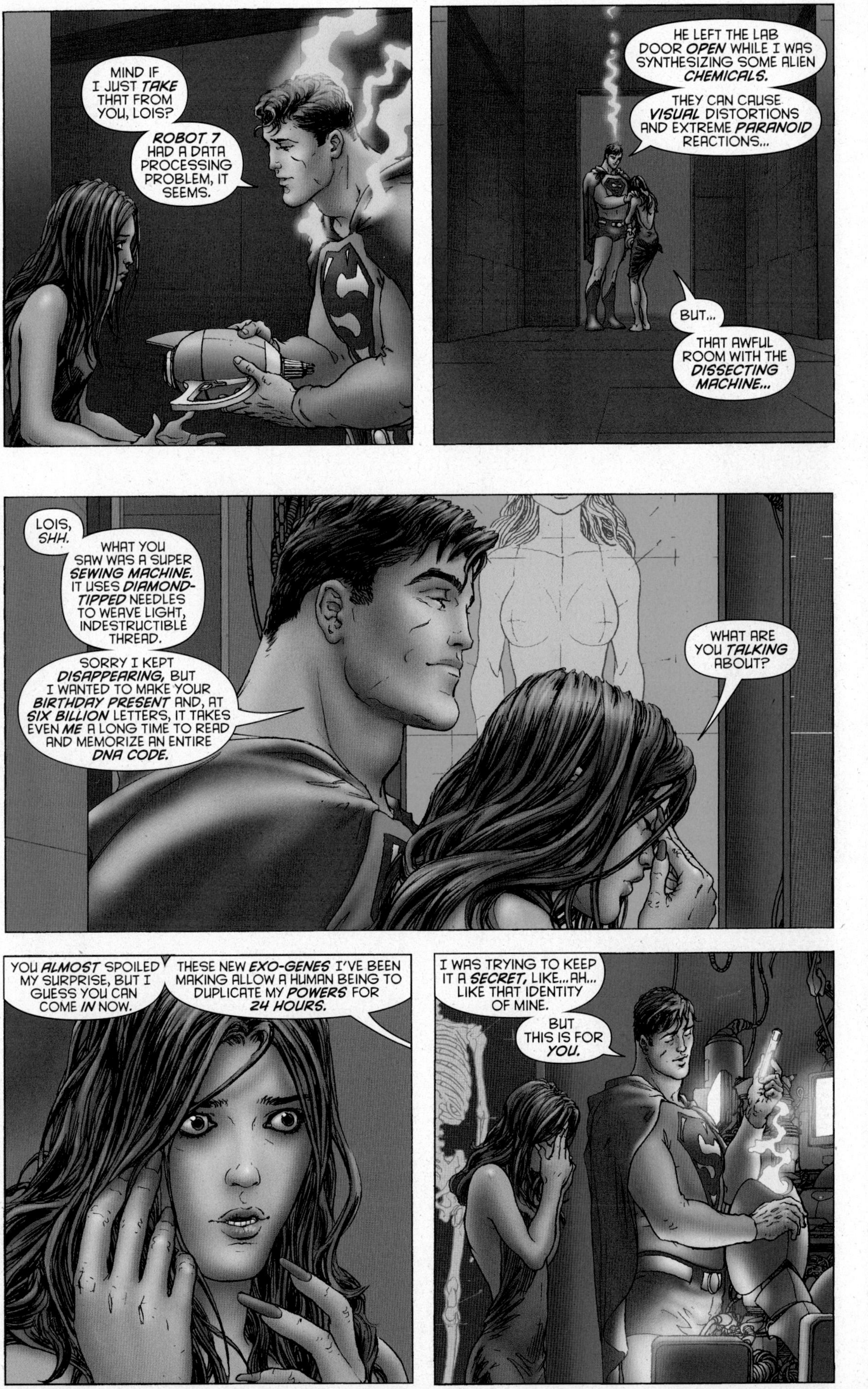
MIND IF I JUST TAKE THAT FROM YOU, LOIS?
ROBOT 7 HAD A DATA PROCESSING PROBLEM, IT SEEMS.
HE LEFT THE LAB DOOR OPEN WHILE I WAS SYNTHESIZING SOME ALIEN CHEMICALS.
THEY CAN CAUSE VISUAL DISTORTIONS AND EXTREME PARANOID REACTIONS...
BUT...
THAT AWFUL ROOM WITH THE DISSECTING MACHINE...
LOIS, SHH.
WHAT YOU SAW WAS A SUPER SEWING MACHINE. IT USES DIAMOND-TIPPED NEEDLES TO WEAVE LIGHT, INDESTRUCTIBLE THREAD.
SORRY I KEPT DISAPPEARING, BUT I WANTED TO MAKE YOUR BIRTHDAY PRESENT AND, AT SIX BILLION LETTERS, IT TAKES EVEN ME A LONG TIME TO READ AND MEMORIZE AN ENTIRE DNA CODE.
WHAT ARE YOU TALKING ABOUT?
YOU ALMOST SPOILED MY SURPRISE, BUT I GUESS YOU CAN COME IN NOW.
THESE NEW EXO-GENES I'VE BEEN MAKING ALLOW A HUMAN BEING TO DUPLICATE MY POWERS FOR 24 HOURS.
I WAS TRYING TO KEEP IT A SECRET, LIKE...AH... LIKE THAT IDENTITY OF MINE.
BUT THIS IS FOR YOU.

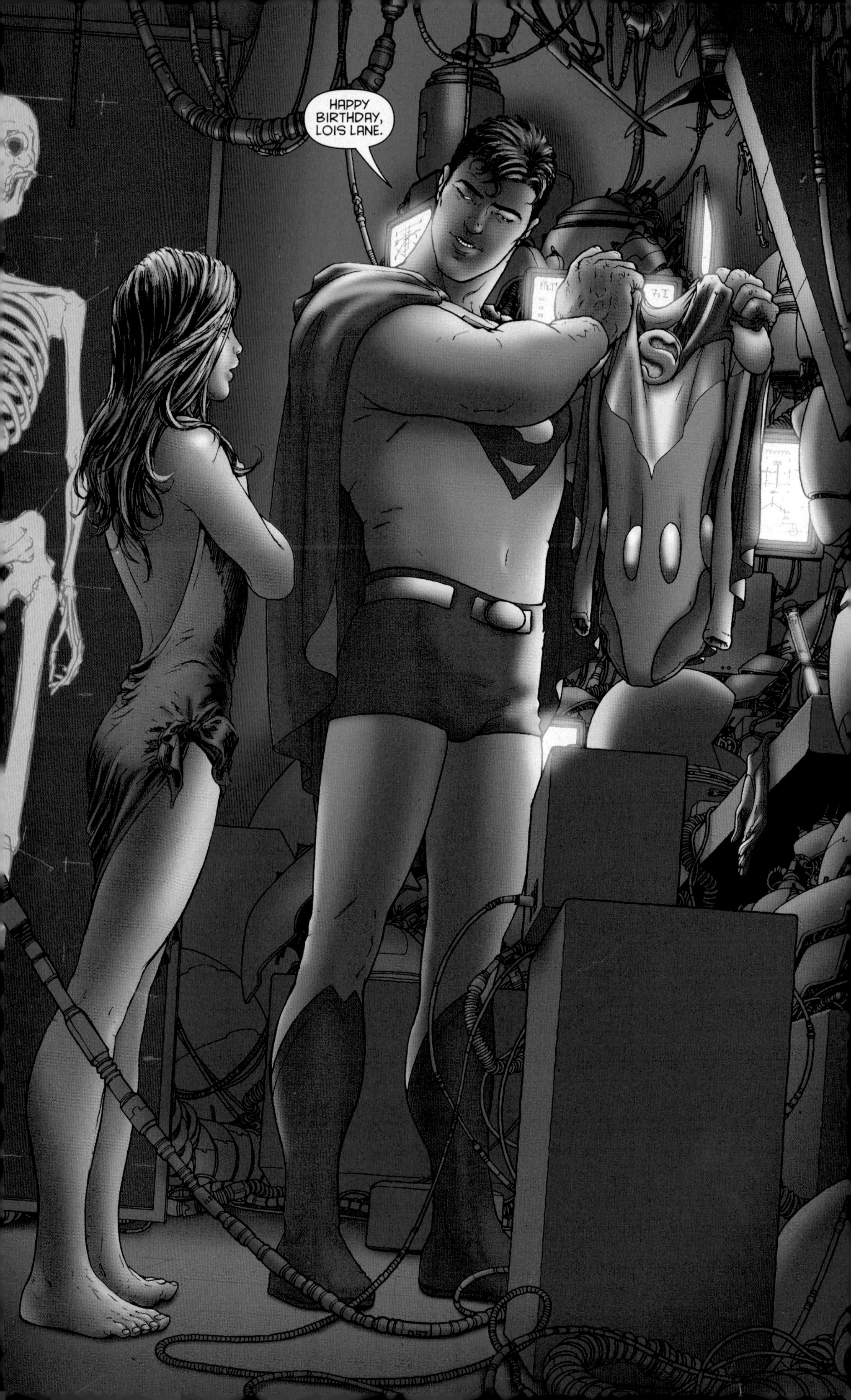
HAPPY BIRTHDAY, LOIS LANE.

Episode 3

SWEET DREAMS, SUPERWOMAN...

Cover FRANK QUITELY with JAMIE GRANT

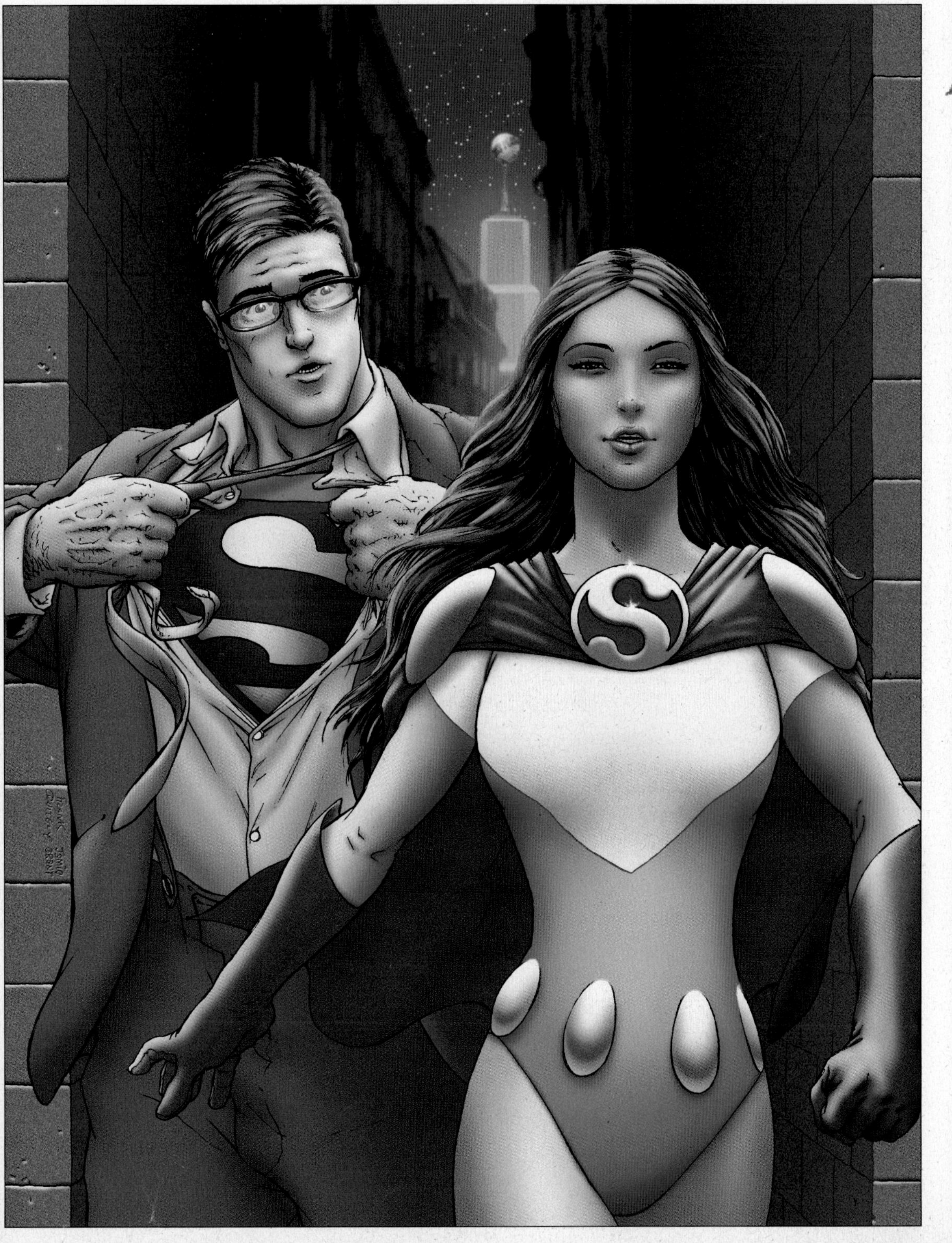

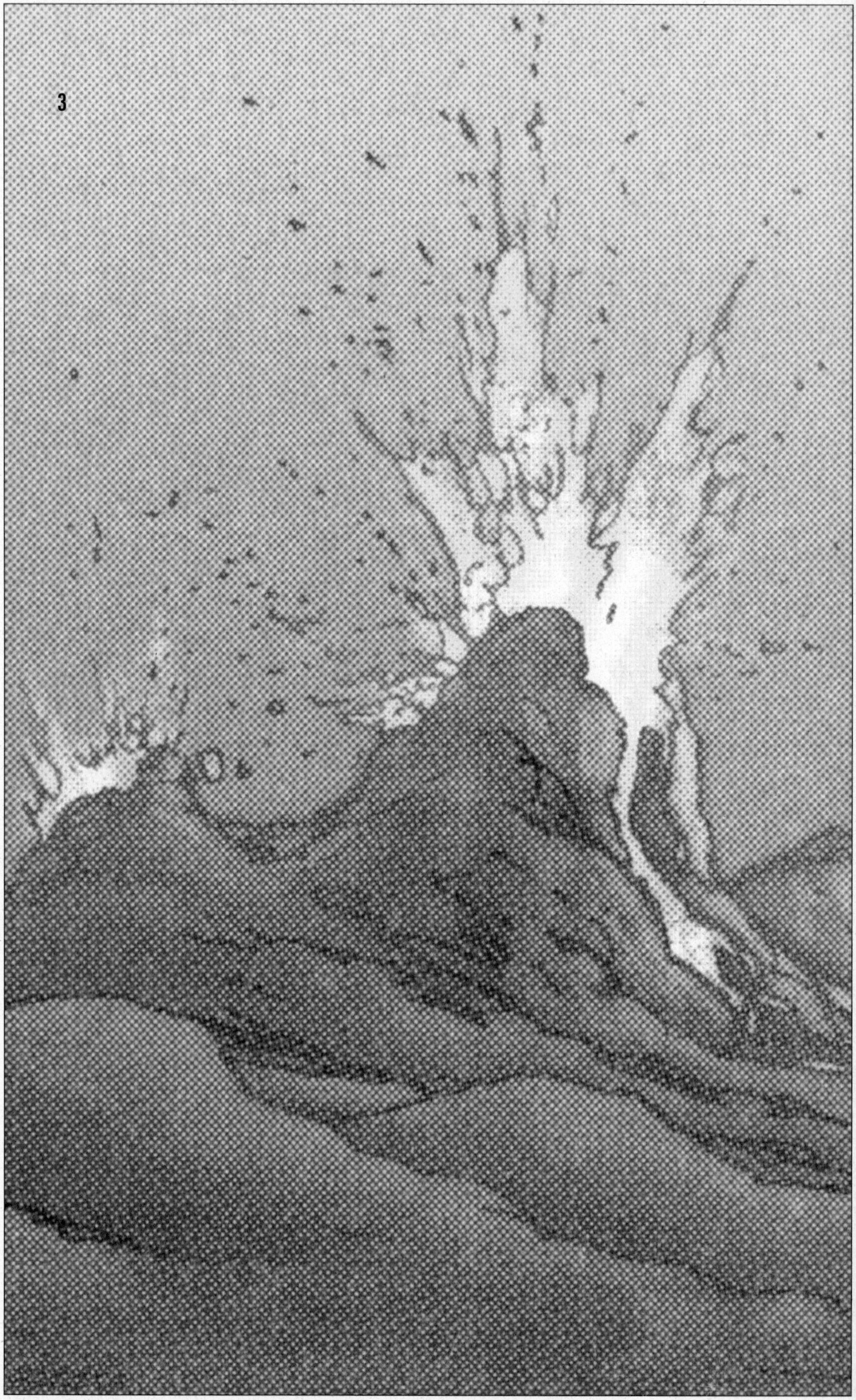
3

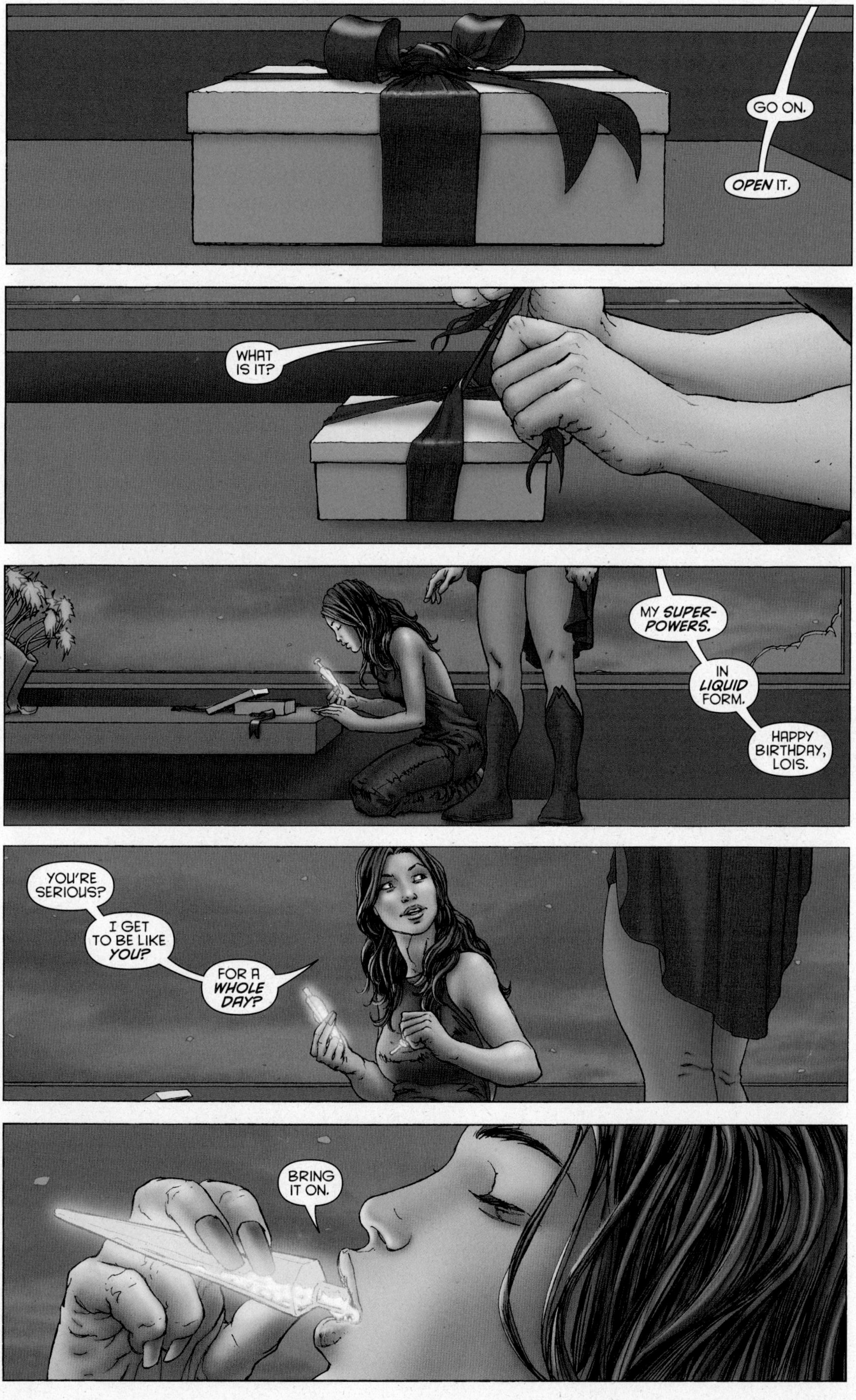
GO ON.
OPEN IT.
WHAT IS IT?
MY SUPER-POWERS.
IN LIQUID FORM.
HAPPY BIRTHDAY, LOIS.
YOU'RE SERIOUS?
I GET TO BE LIKE YOU?
FOR A WHOLE DAY?
BRING IT ON.

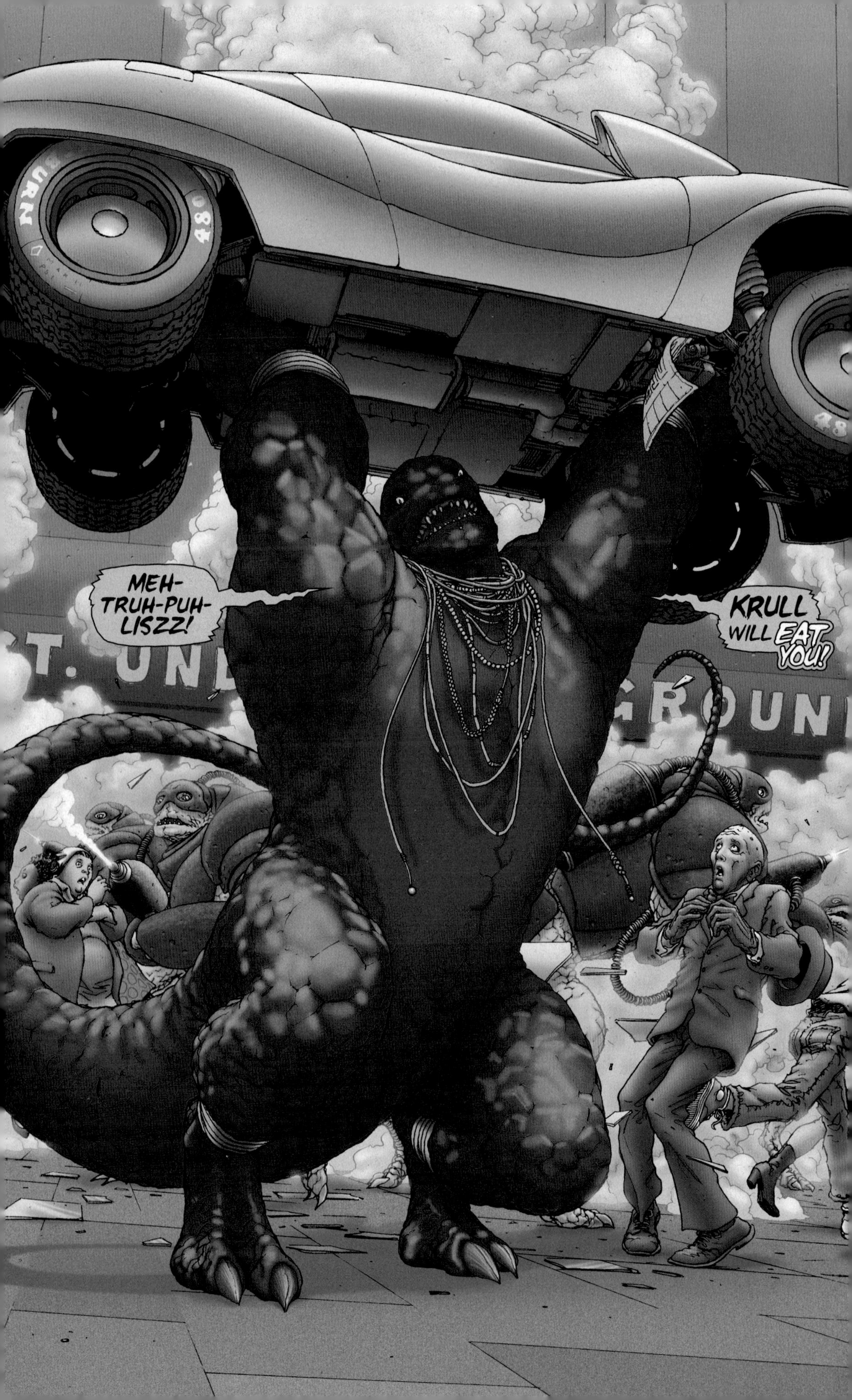
MEH-TRUH-PUH-LISZZ!
KRULL WILL EAT YOU!

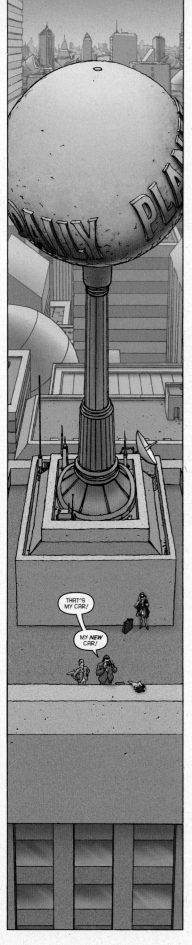

I'M WRITING A FEATURE ON THAT CAR.

PUT THAT DOWN!

OH, THAT'S *RIGHT*, STEVEN LOMBARD, YOU JUST GO ON *AHEAD* AND ATTRACT THE *ATTENTION* OF AN ARMY OF FLESH-EATING *DINOSAUR MEN*!

GOD!

THAT WAS METROPOLIS *SKYPORT*: OUR RIDE TO *POSEIDONIS* HAS BEEN *GROUNDED*, DUE TO *GIANT TALKING LIZARDS* AND SCALDING *STEAM CLOUDS* IN THE MID-TOWN AREA.

I SHOULD HAVE *KNOWN* THERE WAS GOING TO BE TROUBLE WHEN *CLARK KENT* WANGLED HIS WAY *OUT* OF THIS *BIRTHDAY PARTY* FARCE.

I SWEAR THAT MAN CAN *SMELL* TROUBLE.

MS. *GRANT*, MR. *LOMBARD*, I'M TAKING IMMEDIATE *STEPS*.

WE *DON'T* NEED *SUPERMAN!* AND, IF YOU ASK *ME*, OLSEN, NEITHER DOES *LOIS LANE*.

YOU TELL ME WHAT A *SPACEMAN* FLYING AROUND IN HIS *UNDERWEAR* CAN GIVE HER THAT A GOOD OLD HUNK OF PRIME AMERICAN MANHOOD *CAN'T*?

ZEE ZEE ZEE ZEE

≥tt≤

BEATS *ME*, MISTER L.

MAYBE YOU SHOULD *ASK* HER.

LOOKS LIKE SUPERMAN WASN'T THE *ONLY* ONE WHO HEARD MY ALARM SIGNAL.

ZEE ZEE ZEE ZEE

IS THAT WOMAN OUT OF HER *MIND*?

THAT'S MY CAR!

MY *NEW* CAR!

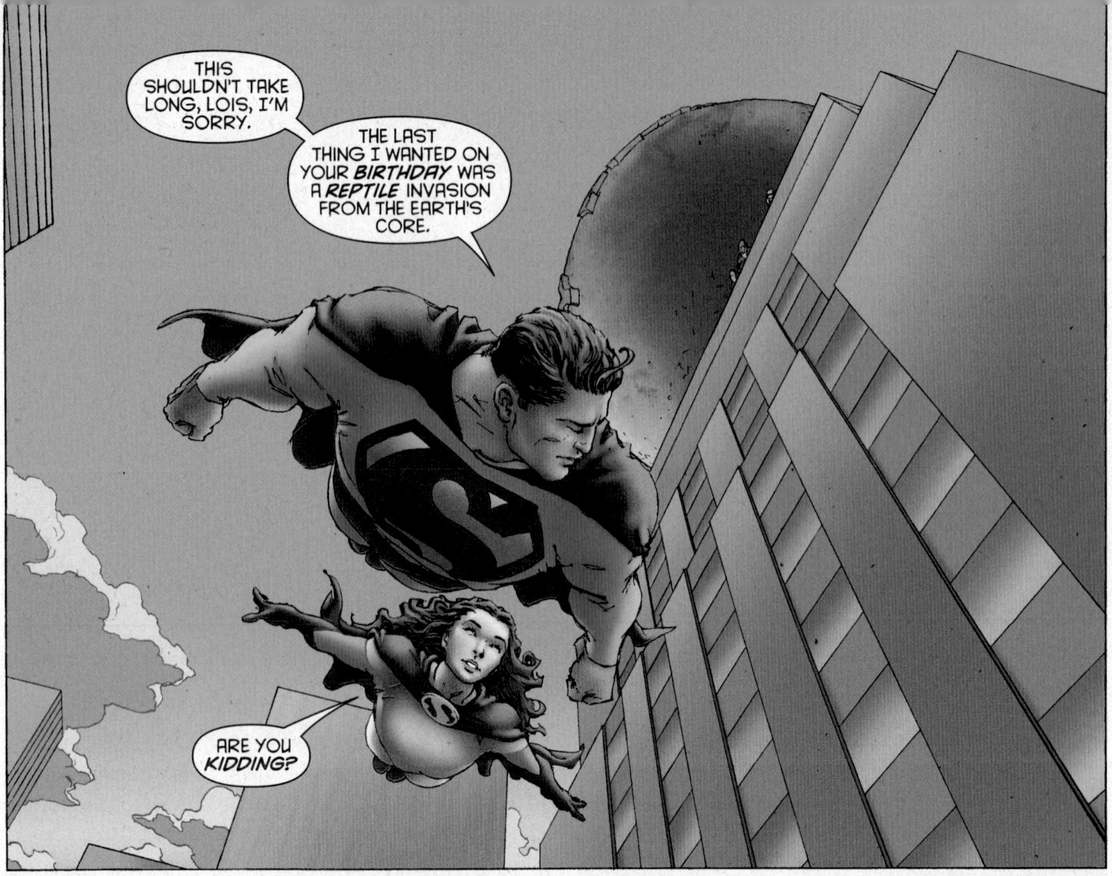
THIS SHOULDN'T TAKE LONG, LOIS, I'M SORRY.
THE LAST THING I WANTED ON YOUR BIRTHDAY WAS A REPTILE INVASION FROM THE EARTH'S CORE.
ARE YOU KIDDING?

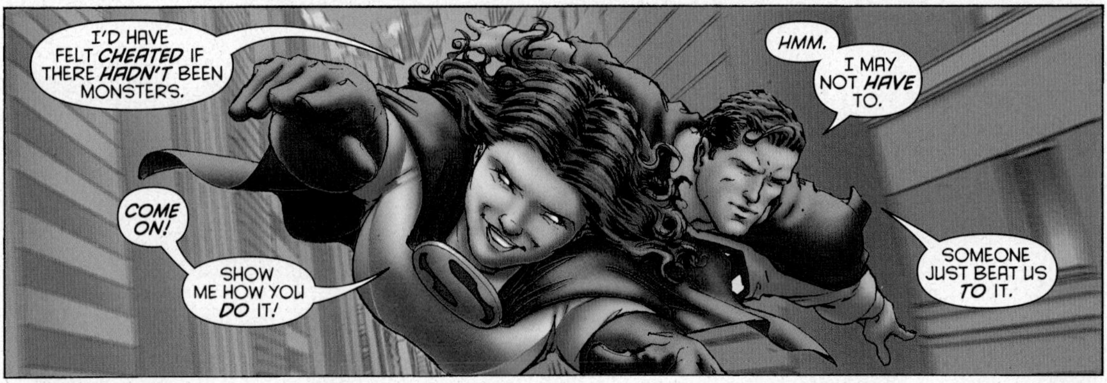
I'D HAVE FELT CHEATED IF THERE HADN'T BEEN MONSTERS.
COME ON!
SHOW ME HOW YOU DO IT!
HMM.
I MAY NOT HAVE TO.
SOMEONE JUST BEAT US TO IT.

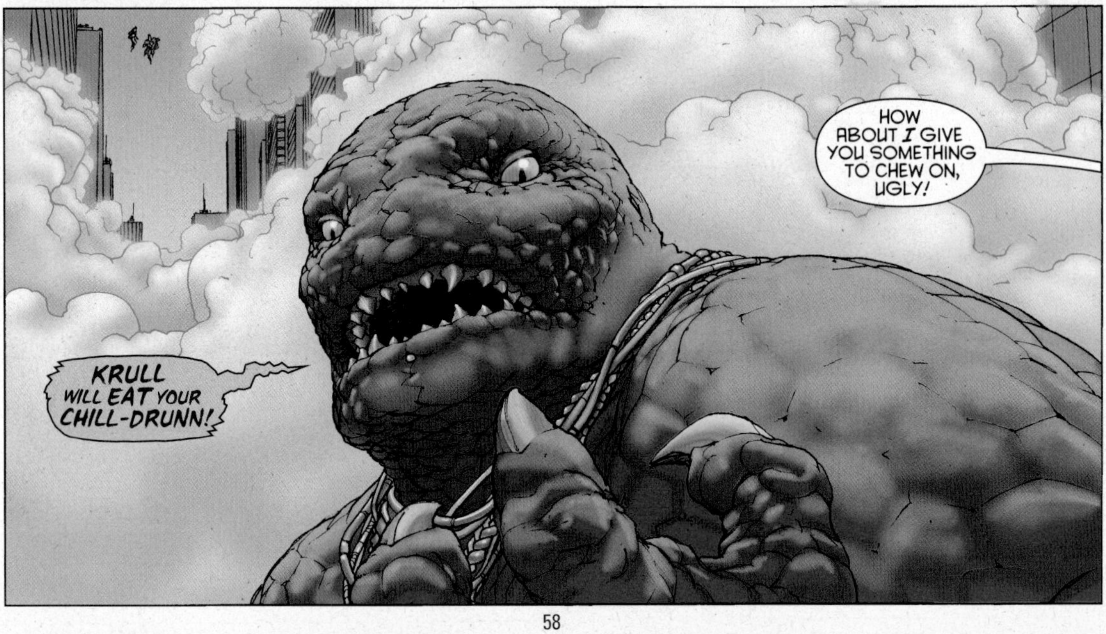
HOW ABOUT I GIVE YOU SOMETHING TO CHEW ON, UGLY!
KRULL WILL EAT YOUR CHILL-DRUNN!

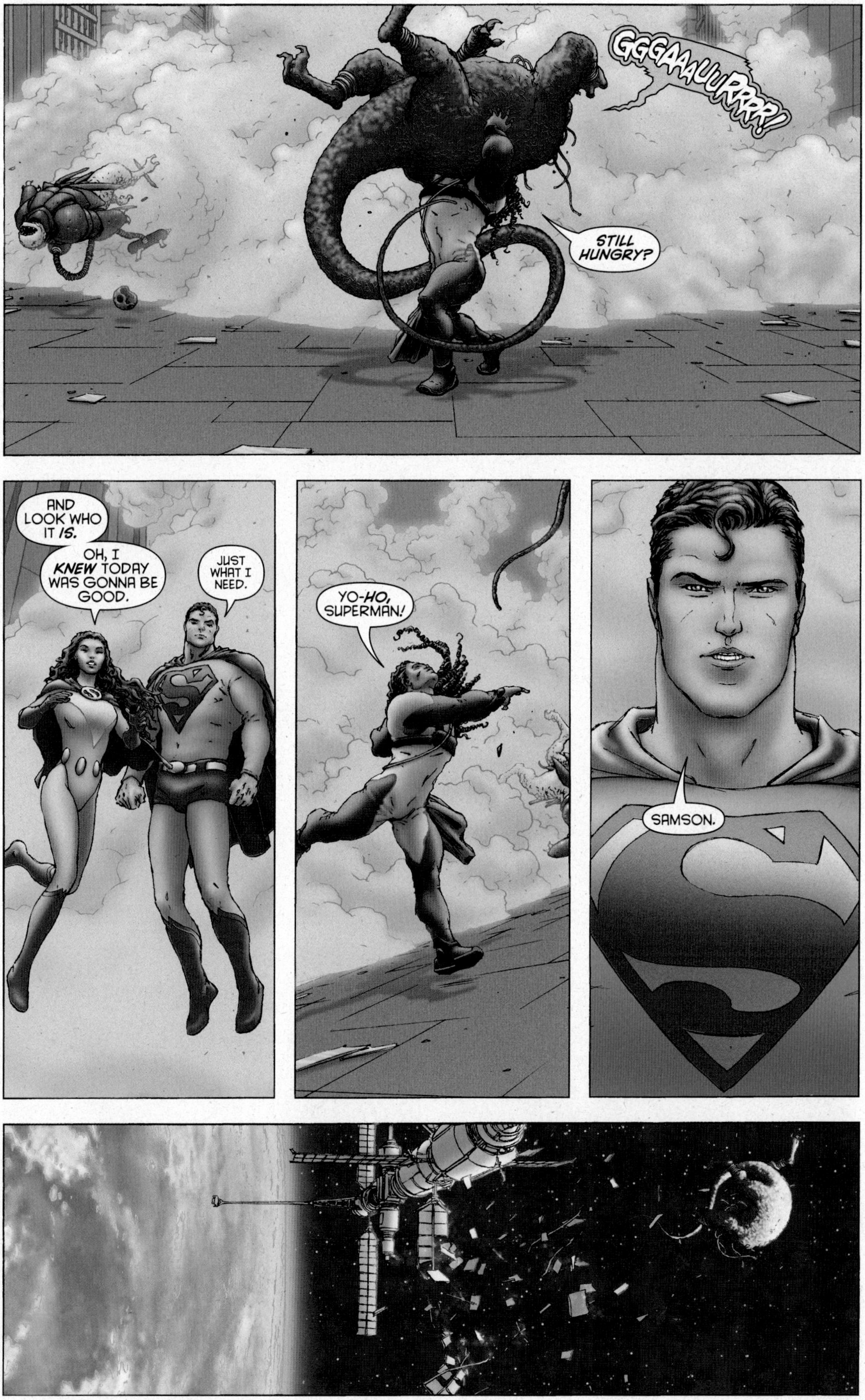
GGGAAAUURRRR!
STILL HUNGRY?
AND LOOK WHO IT IS.
OH, I KNEW TODAY WAS GONNA BE GOOD.
JUST WHAT I NEED.
YO-HO, SUPERMAN!
SAMSON.

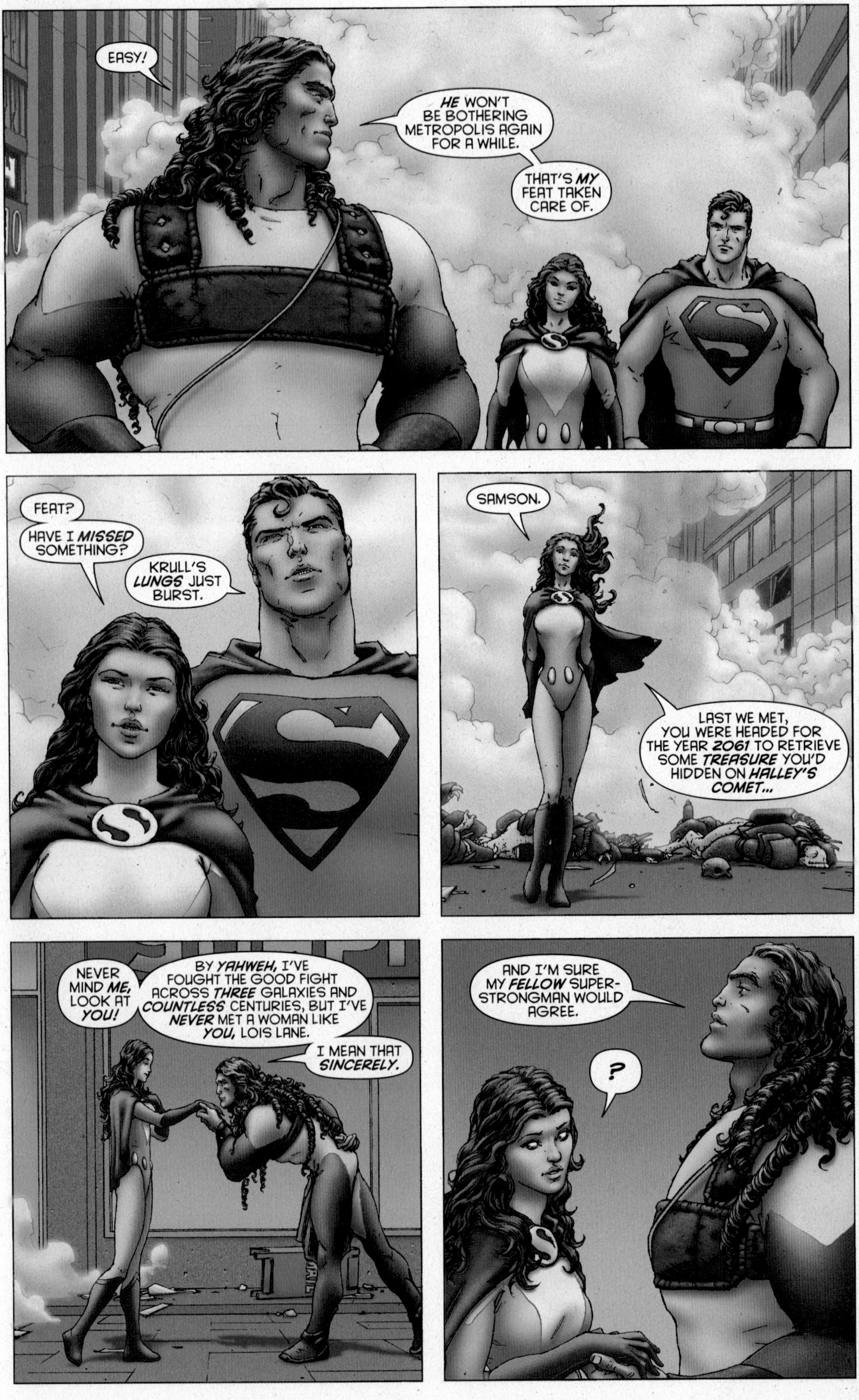

EASY!
HE WON'T BE BOTHERING METROPOLIS AGAIN FOR A WHILE.
THAT'S MY FEAT TAKEN CARE OF.
FEAT?
HAVE I MISSED SOMETHING?
KRULL'S LUNGS JUST BURST.
SAMSON.
LAST WE MET, YOU WERE HEADED FOR THE YEAR 2061 TO RETRIEVE SOME TREASURE YOU'D HIDDEN ON HALLEY'S COMET...
NEVER MIND ME, LOOK AT YOU!
BY YAHWEH, I'VE FOUGHT THE GOOD FIGHT ACROSS THREE GALAXIES AND COUNTLESS CENTURIES, BUT I'VE NEVER MET A WOMAN LIKE YOU, LOIS LANE.
I MEAN THAT SINCERELY.
AND I'M SURE MY FELLOW SUPER-STRONGMAN WOULD AGREE.
?

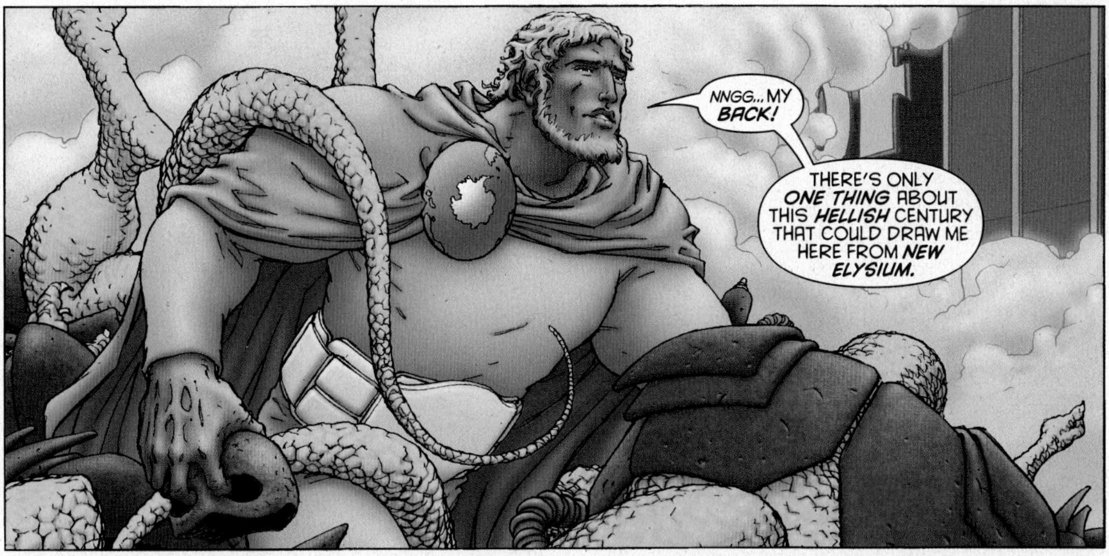
NNGG... MY BACK!
THERE'S ONLY ONE THING ABOUT THIS HELLISH CENTURY THAT COULD DRAW ME HERE FROM NEW ELYSIUM.

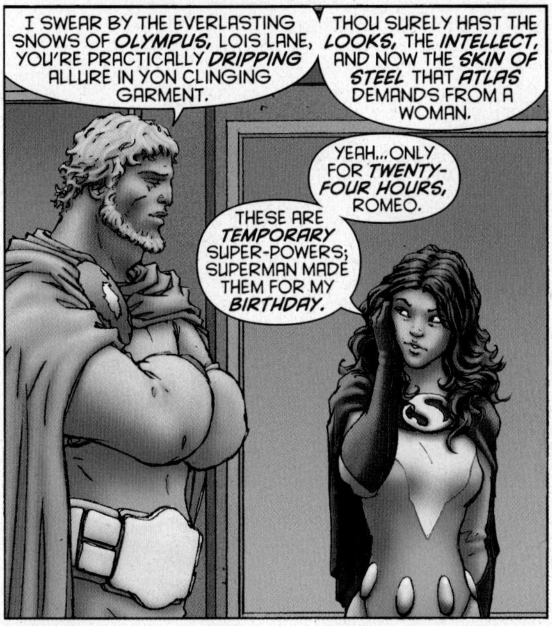
I SWEAR BY THE EVERLASTING SNOWS OF OLYMPUS, LOIS LANE, YOU'RE PRACTICALLY DRIPPING ALLURE IN YON CLINGING GARMENT.
THOU SURELY HAST THE LOOKS, THE INTELLECT, AND NOW THE SKIN OF STEEL THAT ATLAS DEMANDS FROM A WOMAN.
YEAH... ONLY FOR TWENTY-FOUR HOURS, ROMEO.
THESE ARE TEMPORARY SUPER-POWERS; SUPERMAN MADE THEM FOR MY BIRTHDAY.

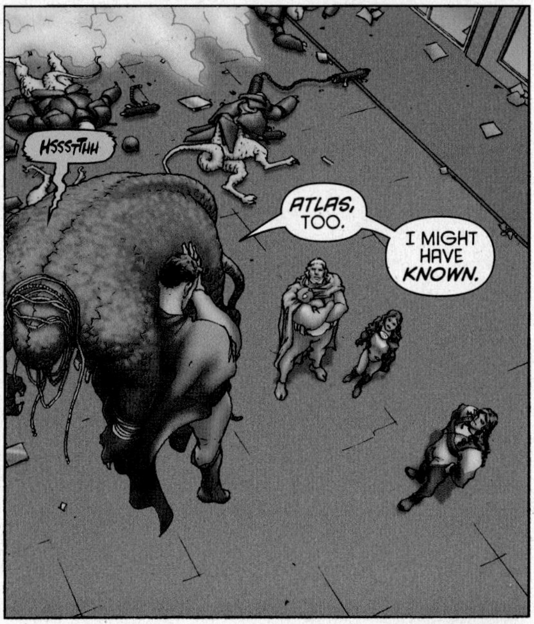
HSSSTTHH
ATLAS, TOO.
I MIGHT HAVE KNOWN.

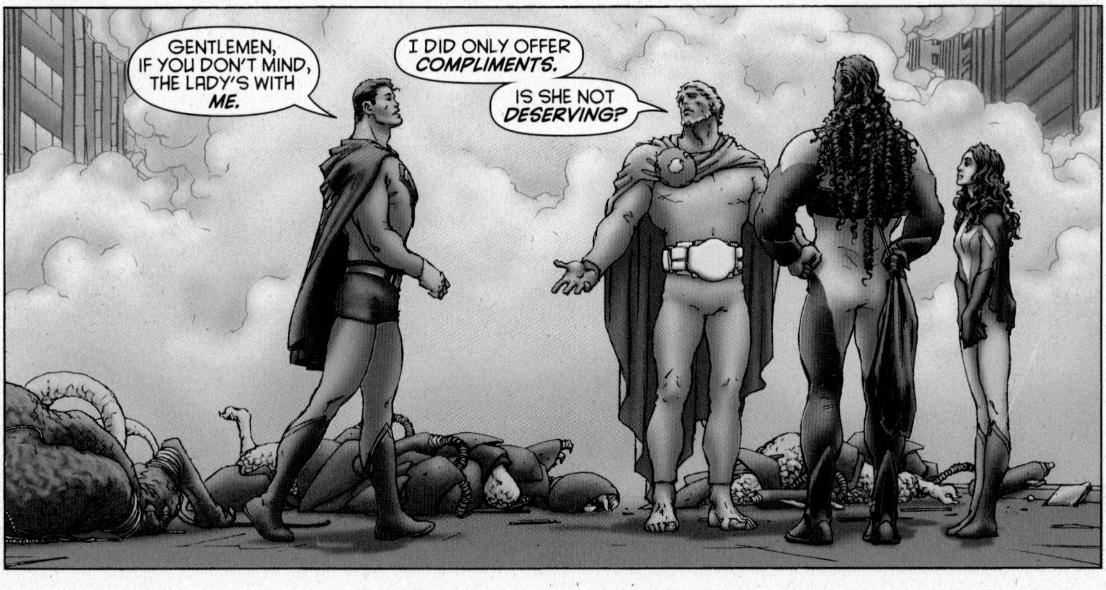
GENTLEMEN, IF YOU DON'T MIND, THE LADY'S WITH ME.
I DID ONLY OFFER COMPLIMENTS.
IS SHE NOT DESERVING?

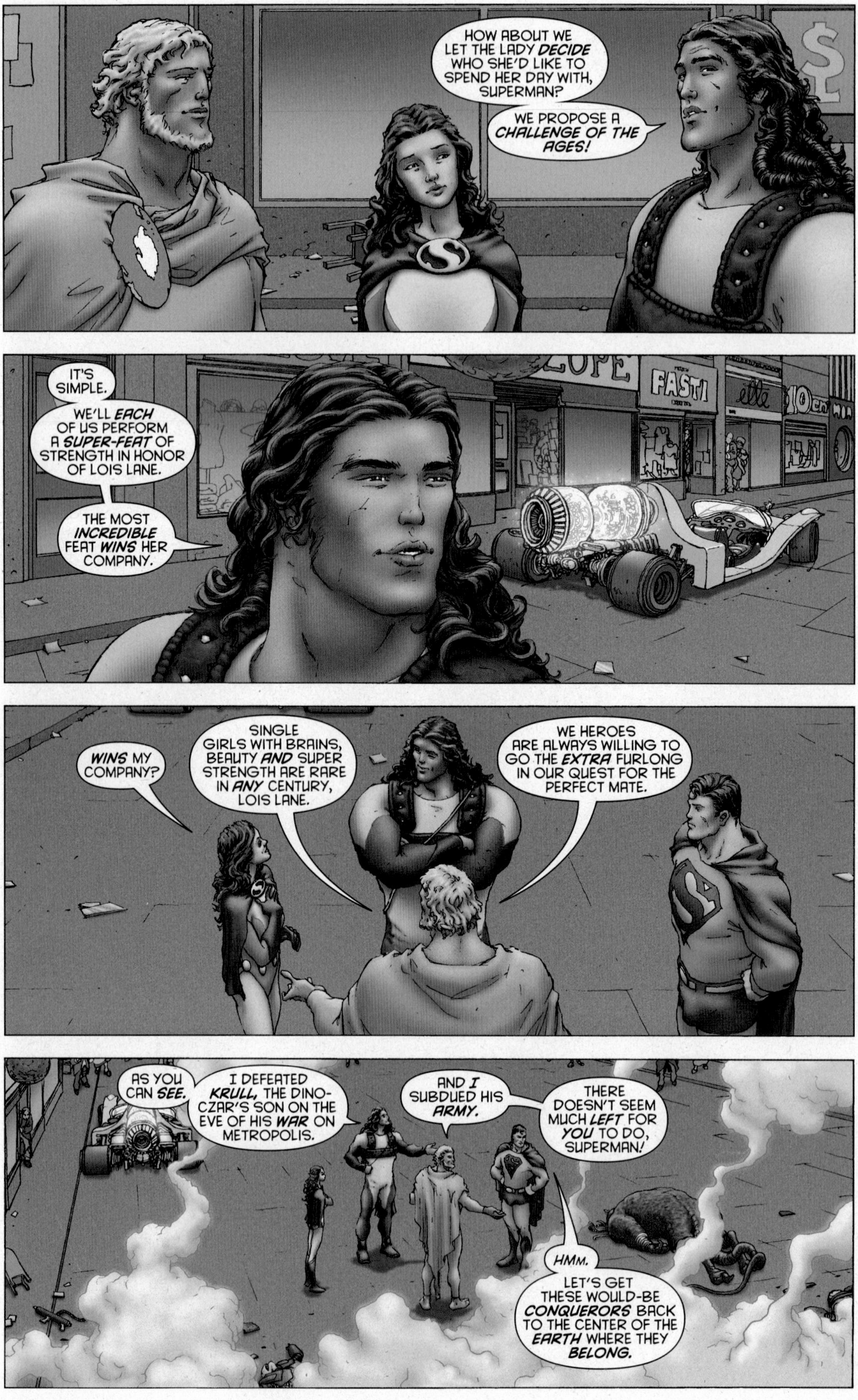
HOW ABOUT WE LET THE LADY DECIDE WHO SHE'D LIKE TO SPEND HER DAY WITH, SUPERMAN?
WE PROPOSE A CHALLENGE OF THE AGES!
IT'S SIMPLE.
WE'LL EACH OF US PERFORM A SUPER-FEAT OF STRENGTH IN HONOR OF LOIS LANE.
THE MOST INCREDIBLE FEAT WINS HER COMPANY.
WINS MY COMPANY?
SINGLE GIRLS WITH BRAINS, BEAUTY AND SUPER STRENGTH ARE RARE IN ANY CENTURY, LOIS LANE.
WE HEROES ARE ALWAYS WILLING TO GO THE EXTRA FURLONG IN OUR QUEST FOR THE PERFECT MATE.
AS YOU CAN SEE.
I DEFEATED KRULL, THE DINO-CZAR'S SON ON THE EVE OF HIS WAR ON METROPOLIS.
AND I SUBDUED HIS ARMY.
THERE DOESN'T SEEM MUCH LEFT FOR YOU TO DO, SUPERMAN!
HMM.
LET'S GET THESE WOULD-BE CONQUERORS BACK TO THE CENTER OF THE EARTH WHERE THEY BELONG.

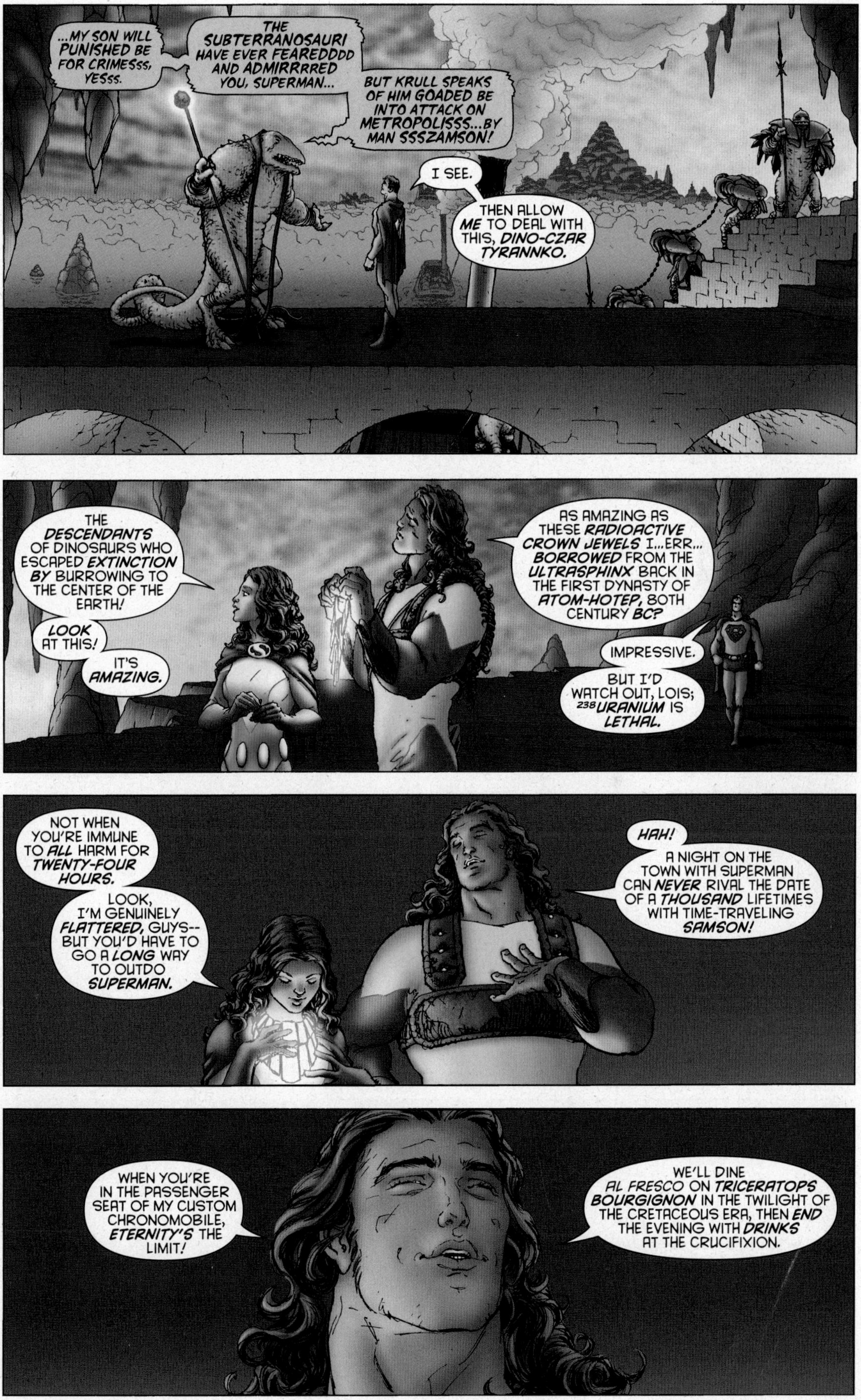
...MY SON WILL PUNISHED BE FOR CRIMESSS, YESSS.
THE SUBTERRANOSAURI HAVE EVER FEAREDDDD AND ADMIRRRRED YOU, SUPERMAN...
BUT KRULL SPEAKS OF HIM GOADED BE INTO ATTACK ON METROPOLISSS...BY MAN SSSZAMSON!
I SEE.
THEN ALLOW ME TO DEAL WITH THIS, DINO-CZAR TYRANNKO.
THE DESCENDANTS OF DINOSAURS WHO ESCAPED EXTINCTION BY BURROWING TO THE CENTER OF THE EARTH!
LOOK AT THIS!
IT'S AMAZING.
AS AMAZING AS THESE RADIOACTIVE CROWN JEWELS I...ERR... BORROWED FROM THE ULTRASPHINX BACK IN THE FIRST DYNASTY OF ATOM-HOTEP, 80TH CENTURY BC?
IMPRESSIVE.
BUT I'D WATCH OUT, LOIS; ^{238}URANIUM IS LETHAL.
NOT WHEN YOU'RE IMMUNE TO ALL HARM FOR TWENTY-FOUR HOURS.
LOOK, I'M GENUINELY FLATTERED, GUYS-- BUT YOU'D HAVE TO GO A LONG WAY TO OUTDO SUPERMAN.
HAH!
A NIGHT ON THE TOWN WITH SUPERMAN CAN NEVER RIVAL THE DATE OF A THOUSAND LIFETIMES WITH TIME-TRAVELING SAMSON!
WHEN YOU'RE IN THE PASSENGER SEAT OF MY CUSTOM CHRONOMOBILE, ETERNITY'S THE LIMIT!
WE'LL DINE AL FRESCO ON TRICERATOPS BOURGIGNON IN THE TWILIGHT OF THE CRETACEOUS ERA, THEN END THE EVENING WITH DRINKS AT THE CRUCIFIXION.

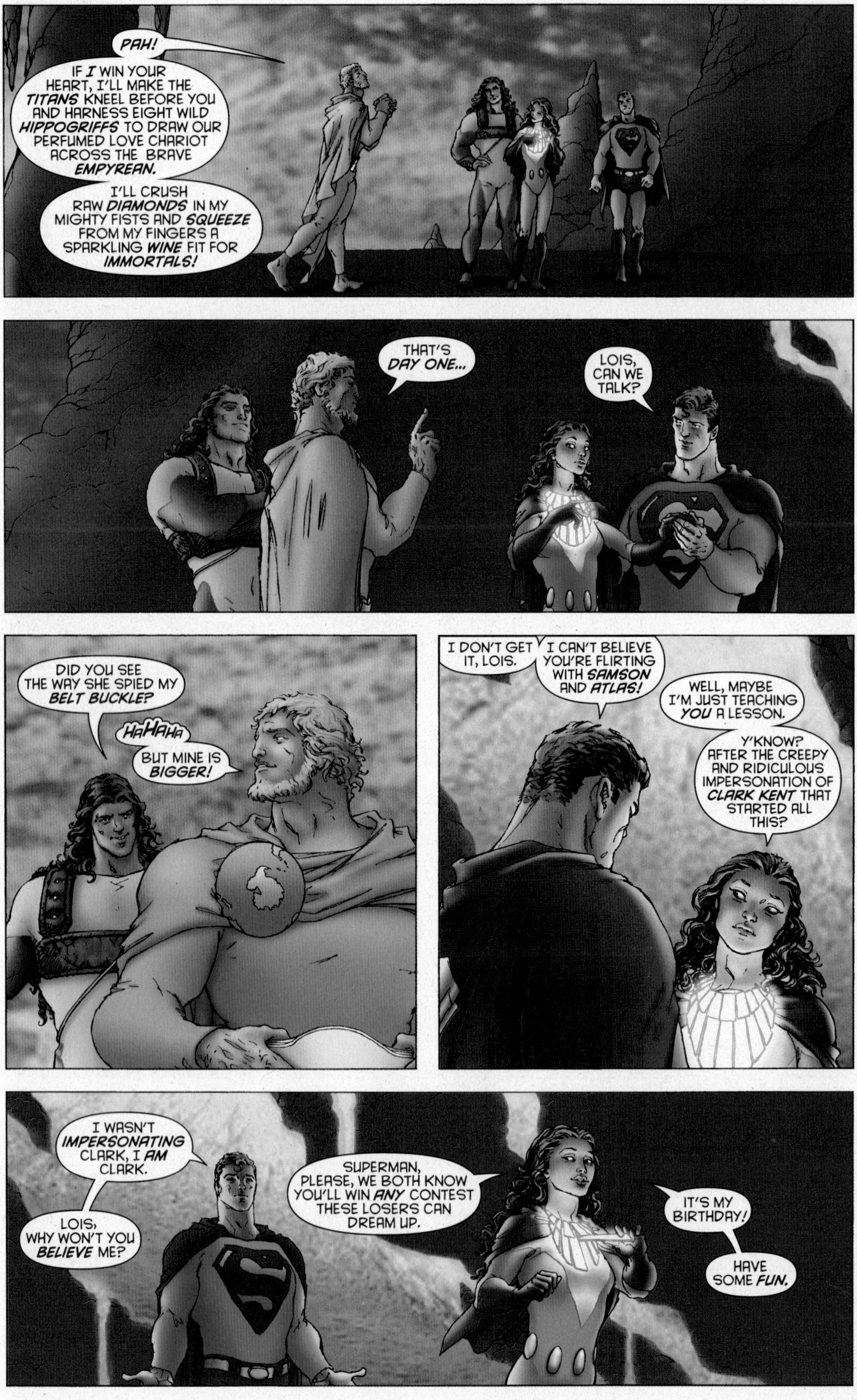
PAH!
IF I WIN YOUR HEART, I'LL MAKE THE TITANS KNEEL BEFORE YOU AND HARNESS EIGHT WILD HIPPOGRIFFS TO DRAW OUR PERFUMED LOVE CHARIOT ACROSS THE BRAVE EMPYREAN.
I'LL CRUSH RAW DIAMONDS IN MY MIGHTY FISTS AND SQUEEZE FROM MY FINGERS A SPARKLING WINE FIT FOR IMMORTALS!
THAT'S DAY ONE...
LOIS, CAN WE TALK?
DID YOU SEE THE WAY SHE SPIED MY BELT BUCKLE?
HAHAHA
BUT MINE IS BIGGER!
I DON'T GET IT, LOIS.
I CAN'T BELIEVE YOU'RE FLIRTING WITH SAMSON AND ATLAS!
WELL, MAYBE I'M JUST TEACHING YOU A LESSON.
Y'KNOW? AFTER THE CREEPY AND RIDICULOUS IMPERSONATION OF CLARK KENT THAT STARTED ALL THIS?
I WASN'T IMPERSONATING CLARK, I AM CLARK.
LOIS, WHY WON'T YOU BELIEVE ME?
SUPERMAN, PLEASE, WE BOTH KNOW YOU'LL WIN ANY CONTEST THESE LOSERS CAN DREAM UP.
IT'S MY BIRTHDAY!
HAVE SOME FUN.

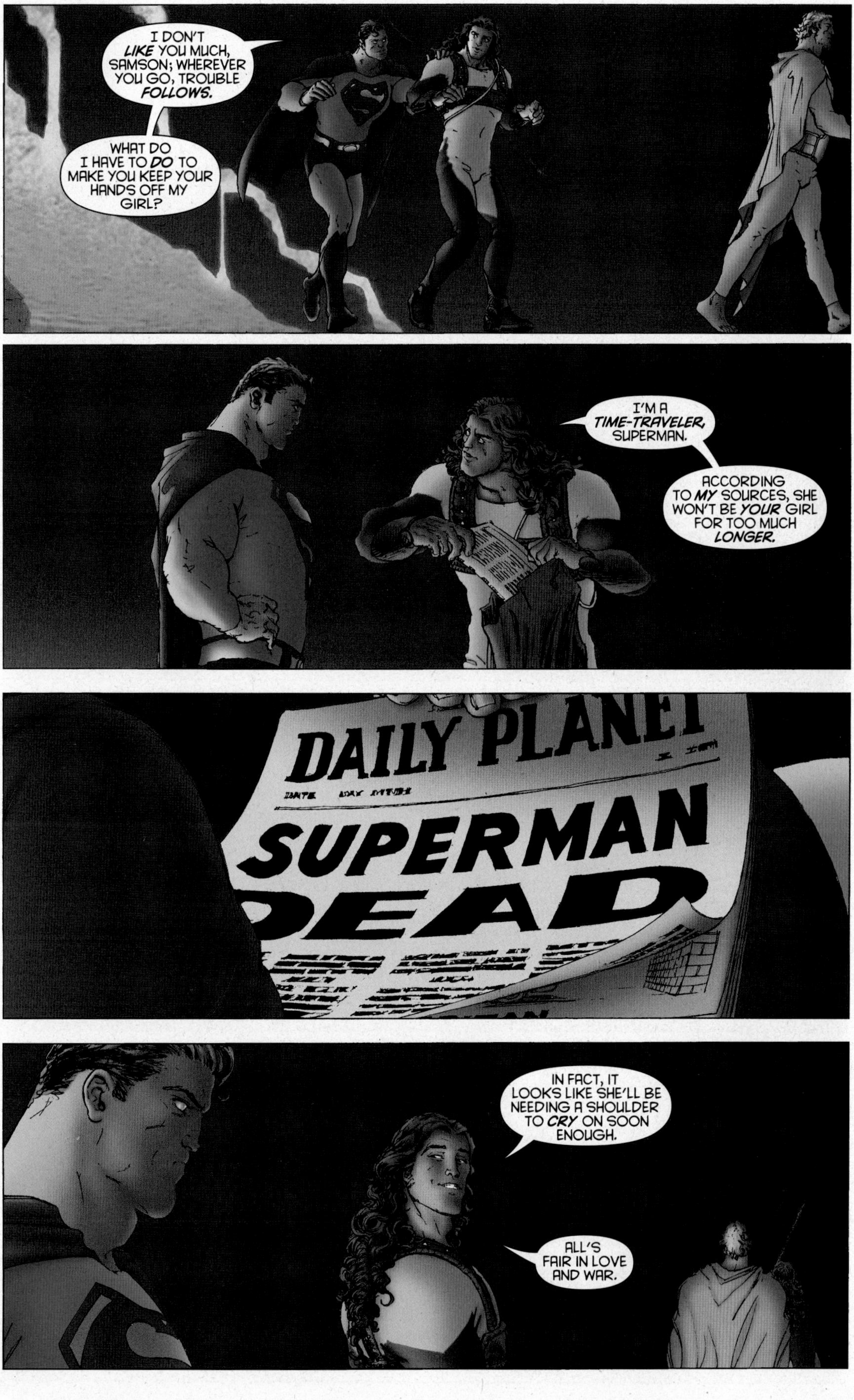
I DON'T *LIKE* YOU MUCH, SAMSON; WHEREVER YOU GO, TROUBLE ***FOLLOWS.***
WHAT DO I HAVE TO ***DO*** TO MAKE YOU KEEP YOUR HANDS OFF MY GIRL?
I'M A ***TIME-TRAVELER,*** SUPERMAN.
ACCORDING TO ***MY*** SOURCES, SHE WON'T BE ***YOUR*** GIRL FOR TOO MUCH ***LONGER.***
DAILY PLANET
SUPERMAN
DEAD
IN FACT, IT LOOKS LIKE SHE'LL BE NEEDING A SHOULDER TO ***CRY*** ON SOON ENOUGH.
ALL'S FAIR IN LOVE AND WAR.

AND WE FIGURE YOU'LL SOON BE *WAY* TOO BUSY WITH YOUR *CHALLENGE* TO EVEN *THINK* ABOUT DATING.

FORGET IT, SAMSON. LOIS AND I HAVE AN APPOINTMENT IN *POSEIDONIS* AT 3:30 MID-PACIFIC TIME.

WHAT'S GOING *ON*, ATLAS?

IS *THIS* PART OF MY BIRTHDAY *SURPRISE?*

-ERRR-

THERE WAS *SOMETHING* WE NEGLECTED TO MENTION... THE *ULTRA-SPHINX*.

THIS MONSTER HAS *HOUNDED* US LIKE A *FURY* SINCE WE... *AH...* BORROWED THE *JEWELS OF ATOM-HOTEP...*

JUST BEFORE YOUR *DEATH*, IT'S SAID YOU COMPLETED *12 SUPER-CHALLENGES*, THE STUFF OF *LEGEND*.

YOU CREATED *LIFE*, YOU *ESCAPED* FROM THE *UNDERVERSE*, YOU OVERTHREW THE *TYRANT SUN*...

...AND YOU *ANSWERED* THE *UNANSWERABLE QUESTION*.

WHAT?

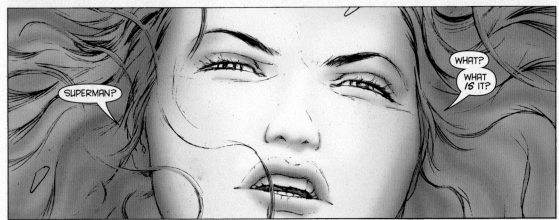

SUPERMAN?

WHAT? WHAT *IS* IT?

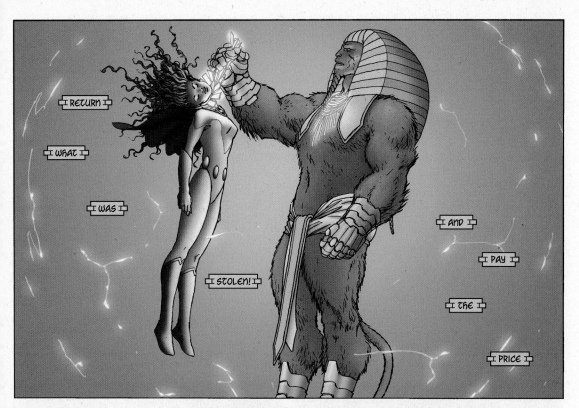

I RETURN I WHAT I WAS STOLEN!

I AND I PAY THE PRICE

LOIS! **NO!**

I HALT! I SHE I EXISTS I NOW I IN I A I CONDITION I OF I

I QUANTUM UNCERTAINTY

I NEITHER I ALIVE I NOR I DEAD I

I TO I ANSWER I CORRRECTLY I IS I LIFE I

I FAILURE I TO I ANSWER I CORRRECTLY I IS I DEATH I

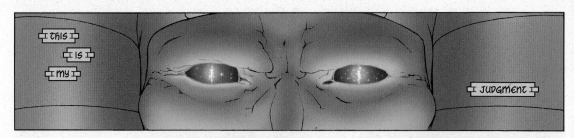

THIS IS MY JUDGMENT

YOU TWO MORONS *STOLE* THAT NECKLACE, DIDN'T YOU?

WE...WE DIDN'T MEAN FOR *THIS* TO HAPPEN!

DON'T YOU UNDERSTAND? WE COULDN'T FIGHT THE ULTRASPHINX WITHOUT *HELP*...SO...SO WE LED IT *HERE*...

WE *TRICKED* YOU, SUPERMAN.

BUT I SWEAR TO *LIVING ZEUS*, WE MEANT *NO HARM* TO LOIS LANE.

AND *I* SWEAR, TOO.

IF SHE *DIES*, YOU'RE *BOTH* ON A ONE-WAY TICKET TO THE *PHANTOM ZONE*!

SUPERMAN... IF IT GOES *WRONG*...

...IF WE *HAVE* TO FIGHT...

...ATLAS AND I WILL STAND BY YOUR SIDE.

WE *WON'T* HAVE TO FIGHT, AND YOU *KNOW* IT.

IF YOU'RE *RIGHT*, I'LL FIND AN ANSWER TO HIS QUESTION, WHATEVER IT IS.

LET'S HEAR IT!

I QUESTION: I WHAT I HAPPENS I WHEN I THE I UNSTOPPABLE I FORCE I MEETS I THE I IMMOVABLE I OBJECT?

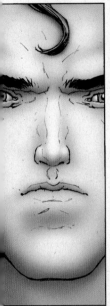

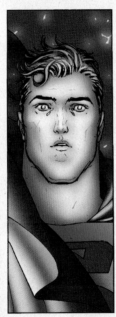

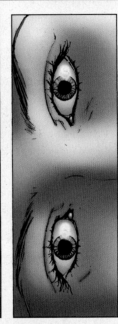

HA HOW ABOUT THIS?

THEY SURRENDER.

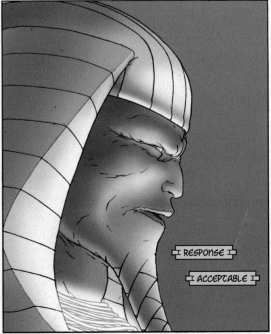

I RESPONSE I ACCEPTABLE

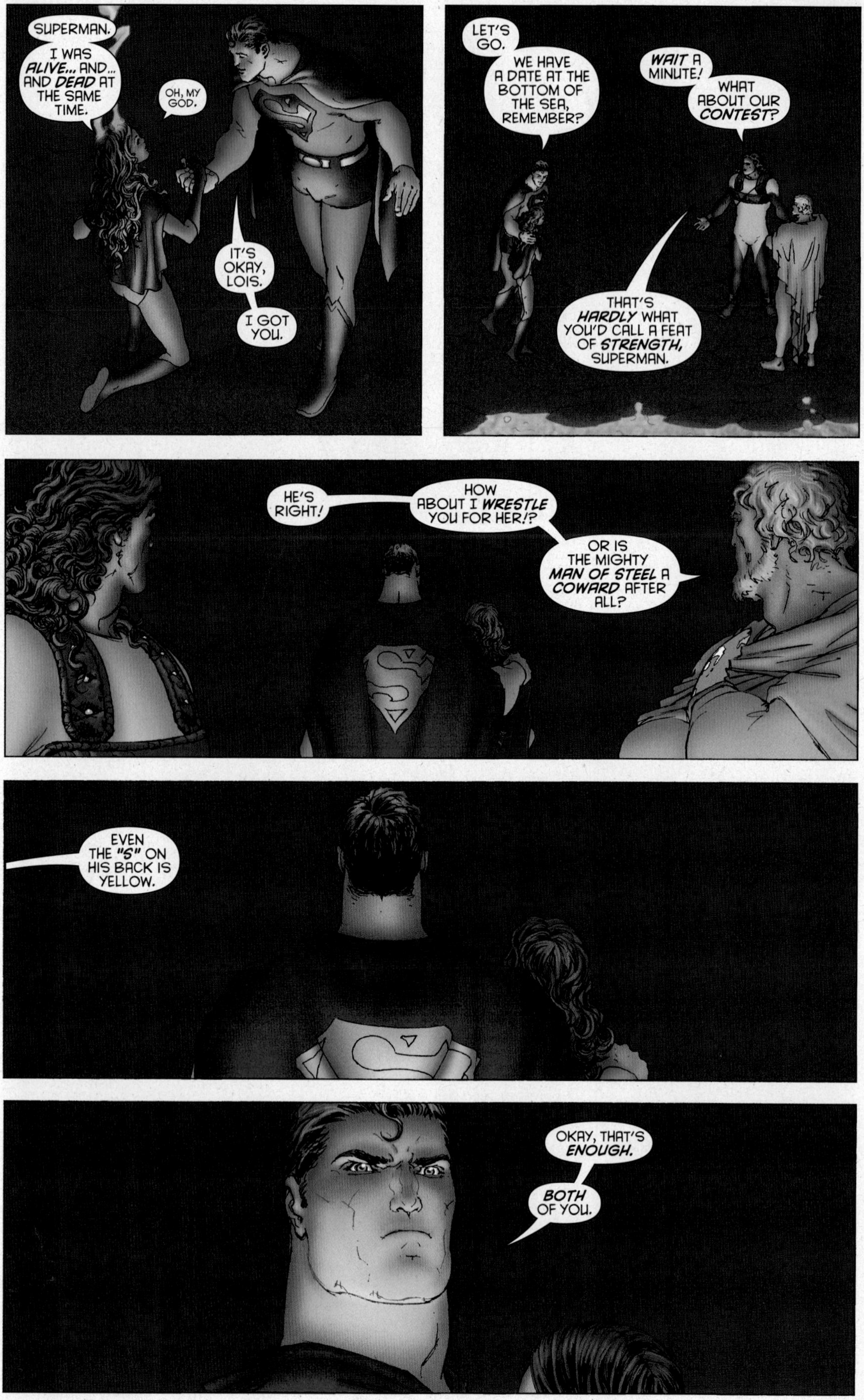
SUPERMAN.
I WAS ALIVE... AND... AND DEAD AT THE SAME TIME.
OH, MY GOD.
IT'S OKAY, LOIS.
I GOT YOU.
LET'S GO.
WE HAVE A DATE AT THE BOTTOM OF THE SEA, REMEMBER?
WAIT A MINUTE!
WHAT ABOUT OUR CONTEST?
THAT'S HARDLY WHAT YOU'D CALL A FEAT OF STRENGTH, SUPERMAN.
HE'S RIGHT!
HOW ABOUT I WRESTLE YOU FOR HER!?
OR IS THE MIGHTY MAN OF STEEL A COWARD AFTER ALL?
EVEN THE "S" ON HIS BACK IS YELLOW.
OKAY, THAT'S ENOUGH.
BOTH OF YOU.

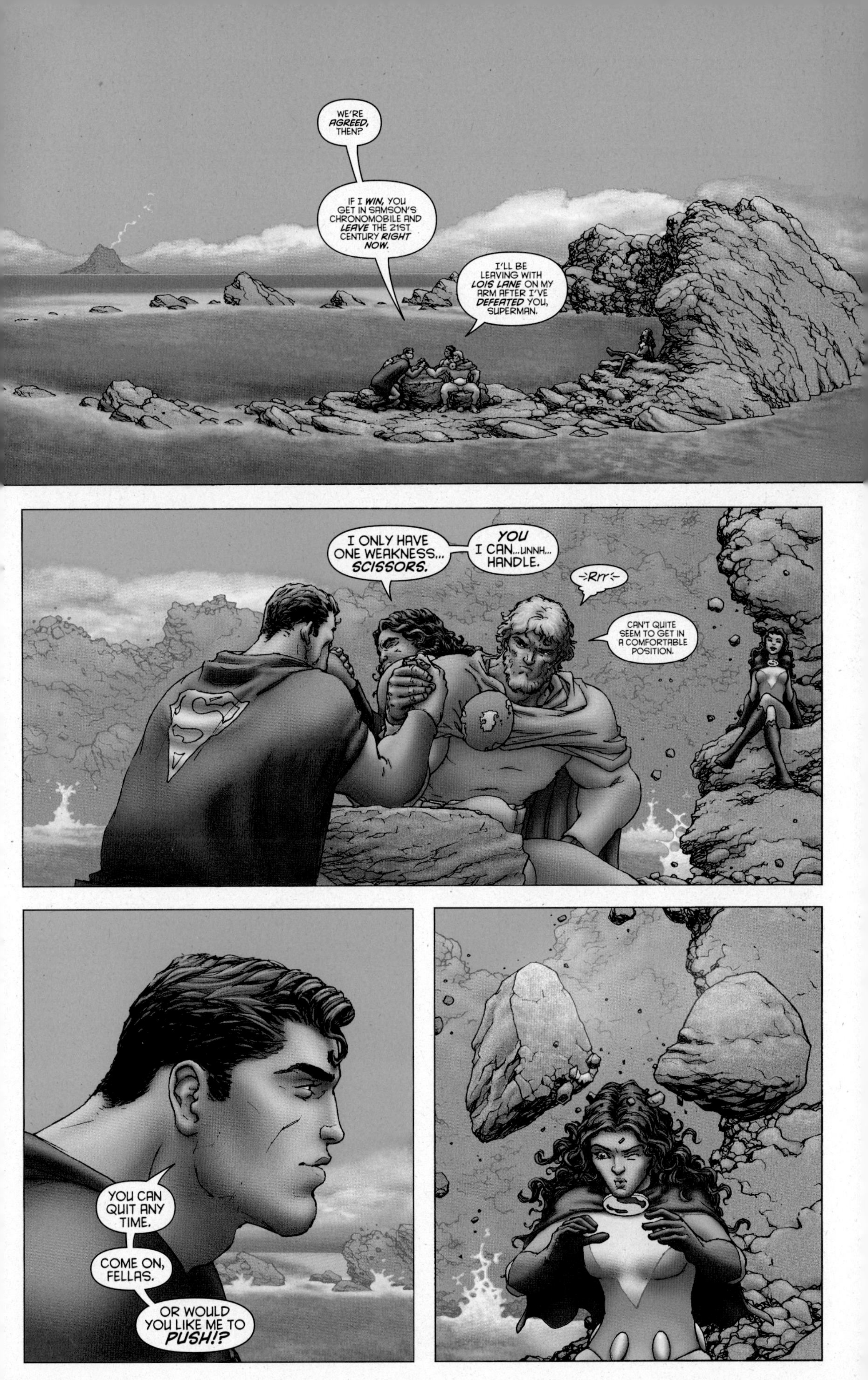
WE'RE AGREED, THEN?
IF I WIN, YOU GET IN SAMSON'S CHRONOMOBILE AND LEAVE THE 21ST CENTURY RIGHT NOW.
I'LL BE LEAVING WITH LOIS LANE ON MY ARM AFTER I'VE DEFEATED YOU, SUPERMAN.
I ONLY HAVE ONE WEAKNESS... SCISSORS.
YOU I CAN...UNNH... HANDLE.
Rrr
CAN'T QUITE SEEM TO GET IN A COMFORTABLE POSITION.
YOU CAN QUIT ANY TIME.
COME ON, FELLAS.
OR WOULD YOU LIKE ME TO PUSH!?

AAARRRr!

MY ARM!

TAKE HIM, ATLAS!

HE'S... NNNGG...

...WUH-WEAKENING...

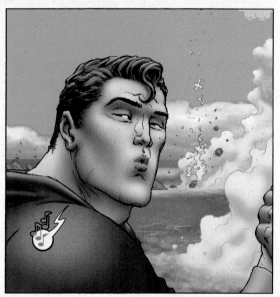

GGAAHHH!

DAILY PLANET

EST 1007 DAT 16 $00.50

GREEK HERO

ATLAS AT LOIS PARTY

ATLAS SCORES

WHAT A *PARTY!*

YOU KNOW I'VE ALWAYS HAD AN UNANSWERED QUESTION OF MY *OWN.*

EVERYBODY CAN GUESS WHAT LOIS LANE SEES IN *YOU,* BUT... Y'KNOW, WHY *ME,* SUPERMAN?

WELL...

...I GUESS THERE HAS TO BE *ONE* THING I JUST CAN'T *HELP,* LOIS.

YOU KNOW, THERE'S SOMETHING I'VE WANTED TO DO SINCE THE VERY FIRST DAY WE *MET.*

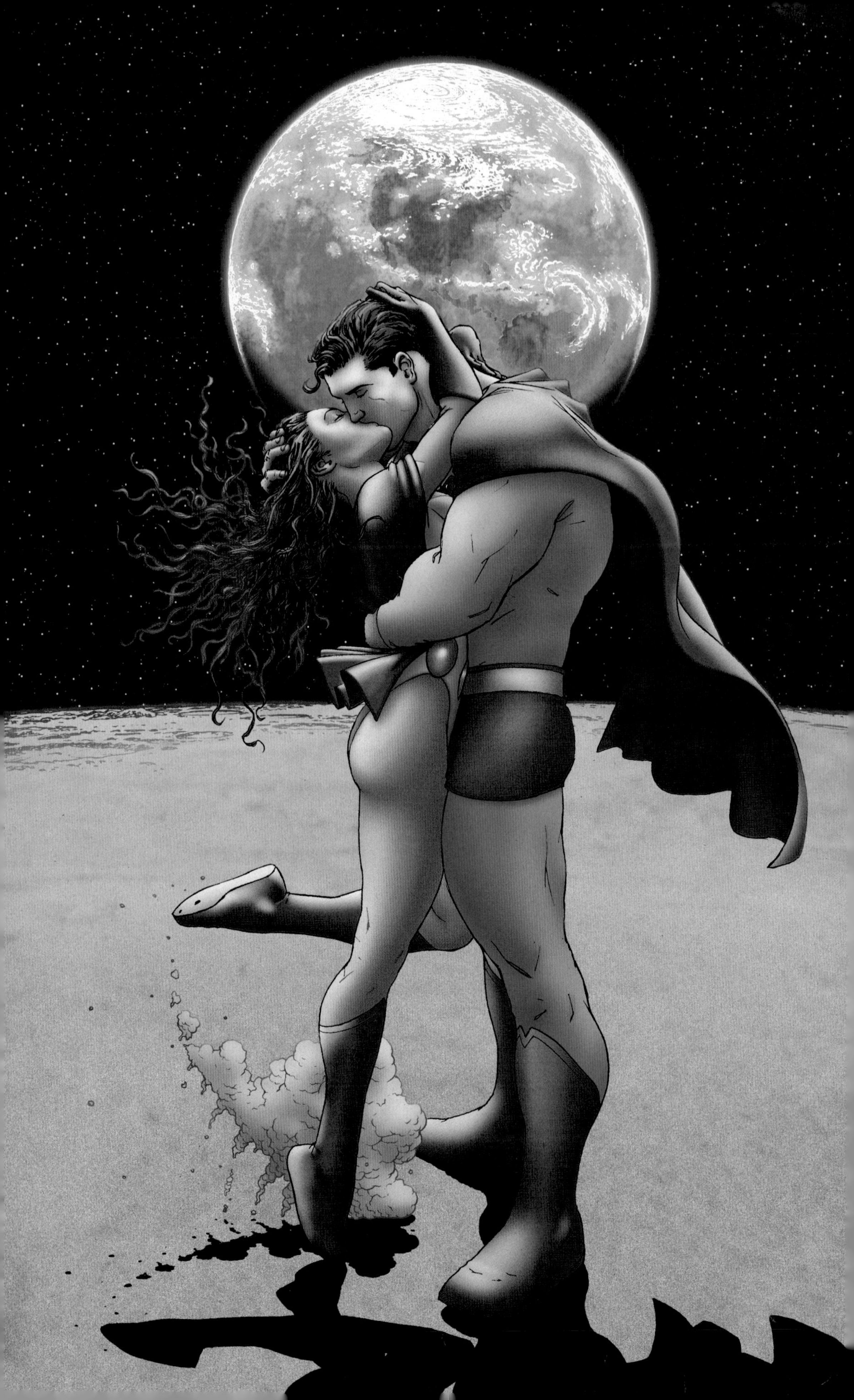

...AHHH MY BIRTHDAY GIFT IS STARTING TO *WEAR OFF*... BIG TIME.

I CAN'T SMELL THE TREES IN *CANADA.*

I CAN'T SEE ALL THAT GORGEOUS *RADIO* ANYMORE...THE *STARS* HAVE STOPPED SINGING LIKE THEY USED TO.

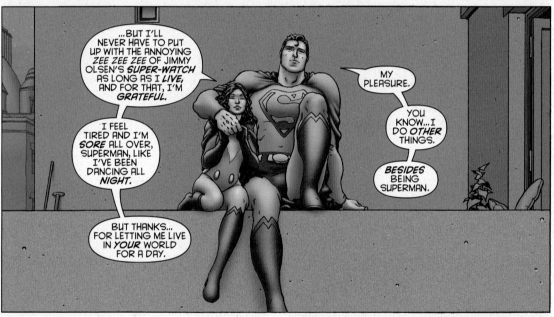

...BUT I'LL NEVER HAVE TO PUT UP WITH THE ANNOYING *ZEE ZEE ZEE* OF JIMMY OLSEN'S *SUPER-WATCH* AS LONG AS I *LIVE*, AND FOR THAT, I'M *GRATEFUL.*

I FEEL TIRED AND I'M *SORE* ALL OVER, SUPERMAN, LIKE I'VE BEEN DANCING ALL *NIGHT.*

BUT THANKS... FOR LETTING ME LIVE IN *YOUR* WORLD FOR A DAY.

MY PLEASURE.

YOU KNOW...I DO *OTHER* THINGS.

BESIDES BEING SUPERMAN.

...MMMM

YOU DO A REALLY *GOOD* CLARK KENT IMPRESSION...ALMOST HAD ME *FOOLED.*

WHERE...WHERE WAS CLARK...TODAY ANYWAY...?

LOIS...

I...I HAVE A QUESTION FOR *YOU,* TOO.

LOIS, WILL...WILL YOU...

I'VE BEEN MEANING TO ASK IT FOR A LONG, *LONG* TIME BUT THINGS KIND OF GOT IN THE *WAY...*

LOIS?

ZZZ ZZ

75

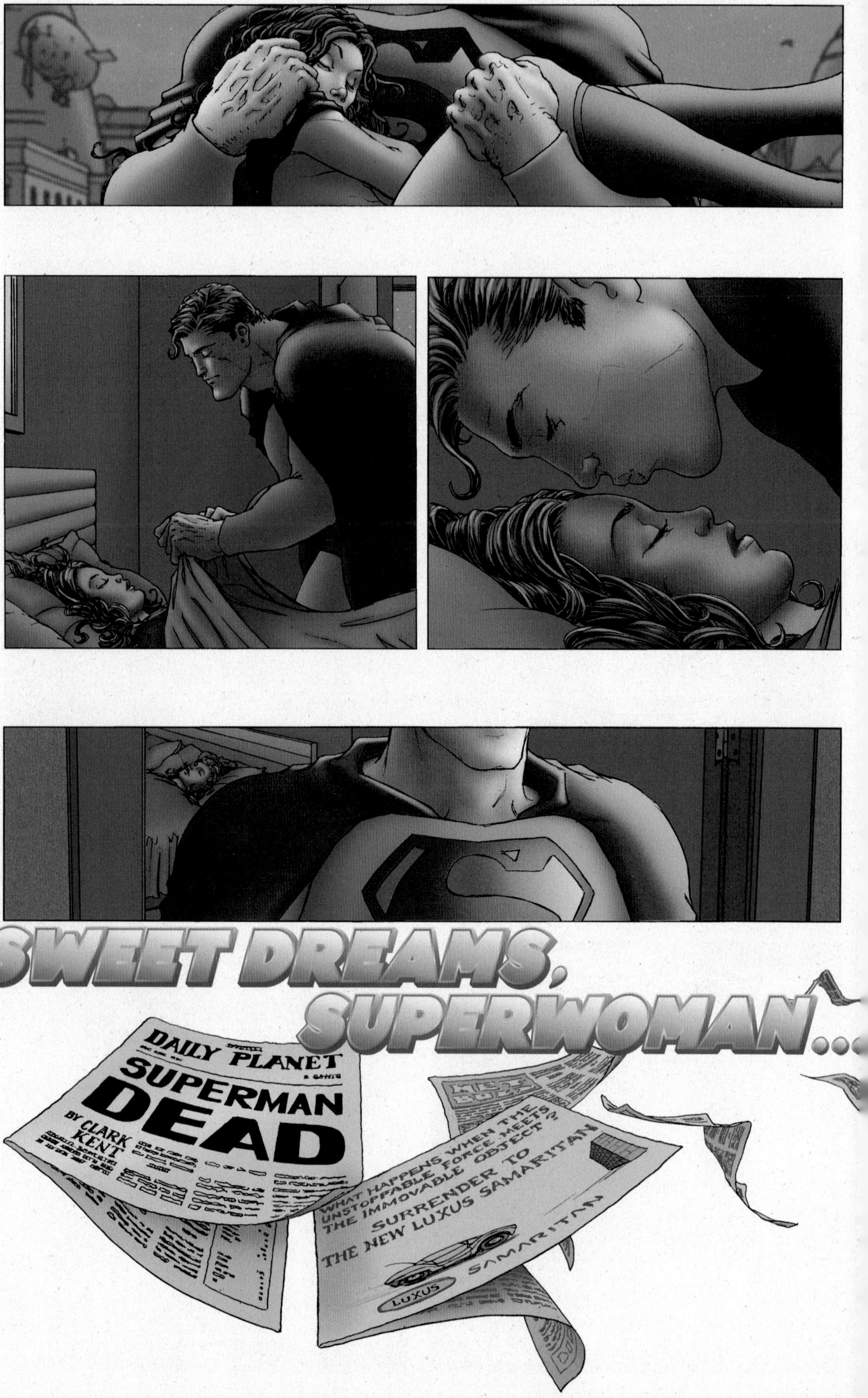
SWEET DREAMS, SUPERWOMAN...
DAILY PLANET
SUPERMAN DEAD
BY CLARK KENT
WHAT HAPPENS WHEN THE UNSTOPPABLE FORCE MEETS THE IMMOVABLE OBJECT?
SURRENDER TO THE NEW LUXUS SAMARITAN
LUXUS
SAMARITAN

Episode 4

THE SUPERMAN/JIMMY OLSEN WAR!

Cover FRANK QUITELY with JAMIE GRANT

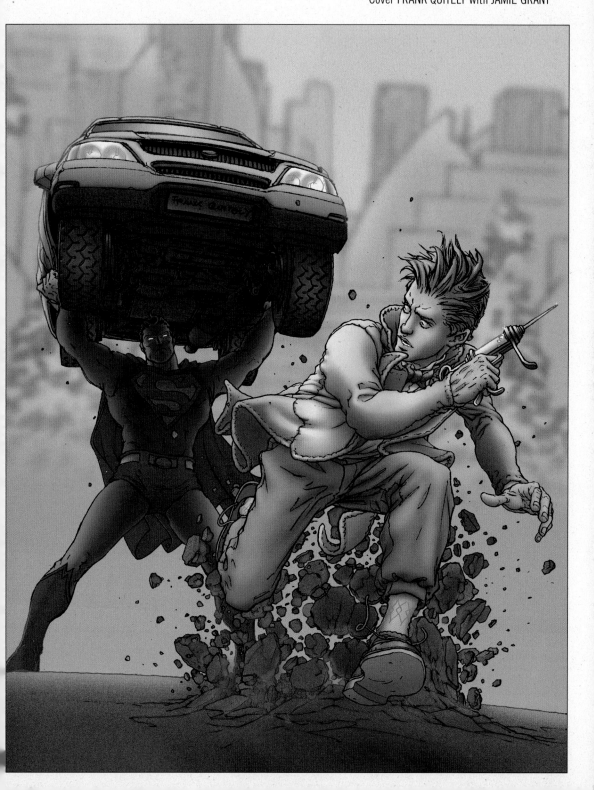

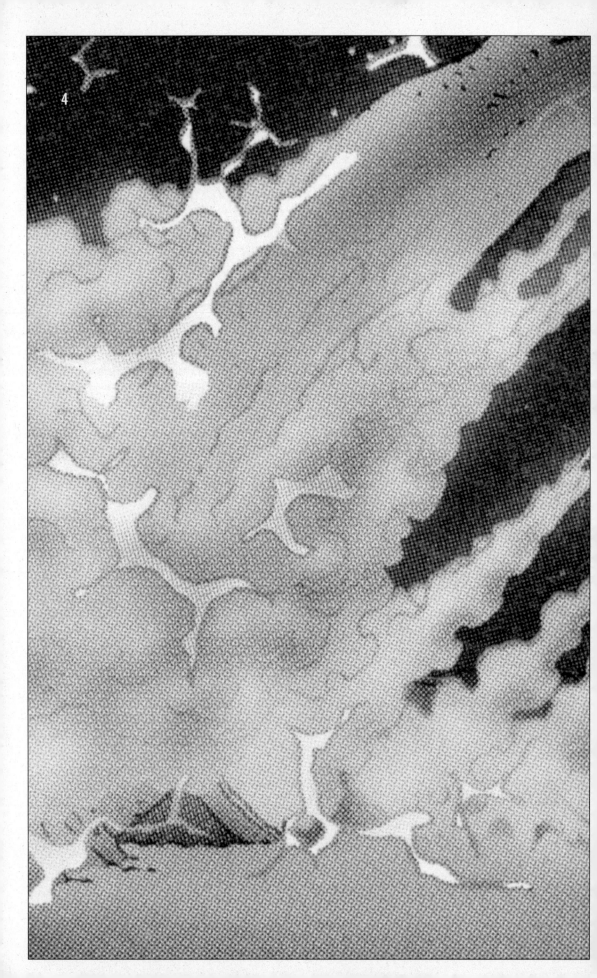

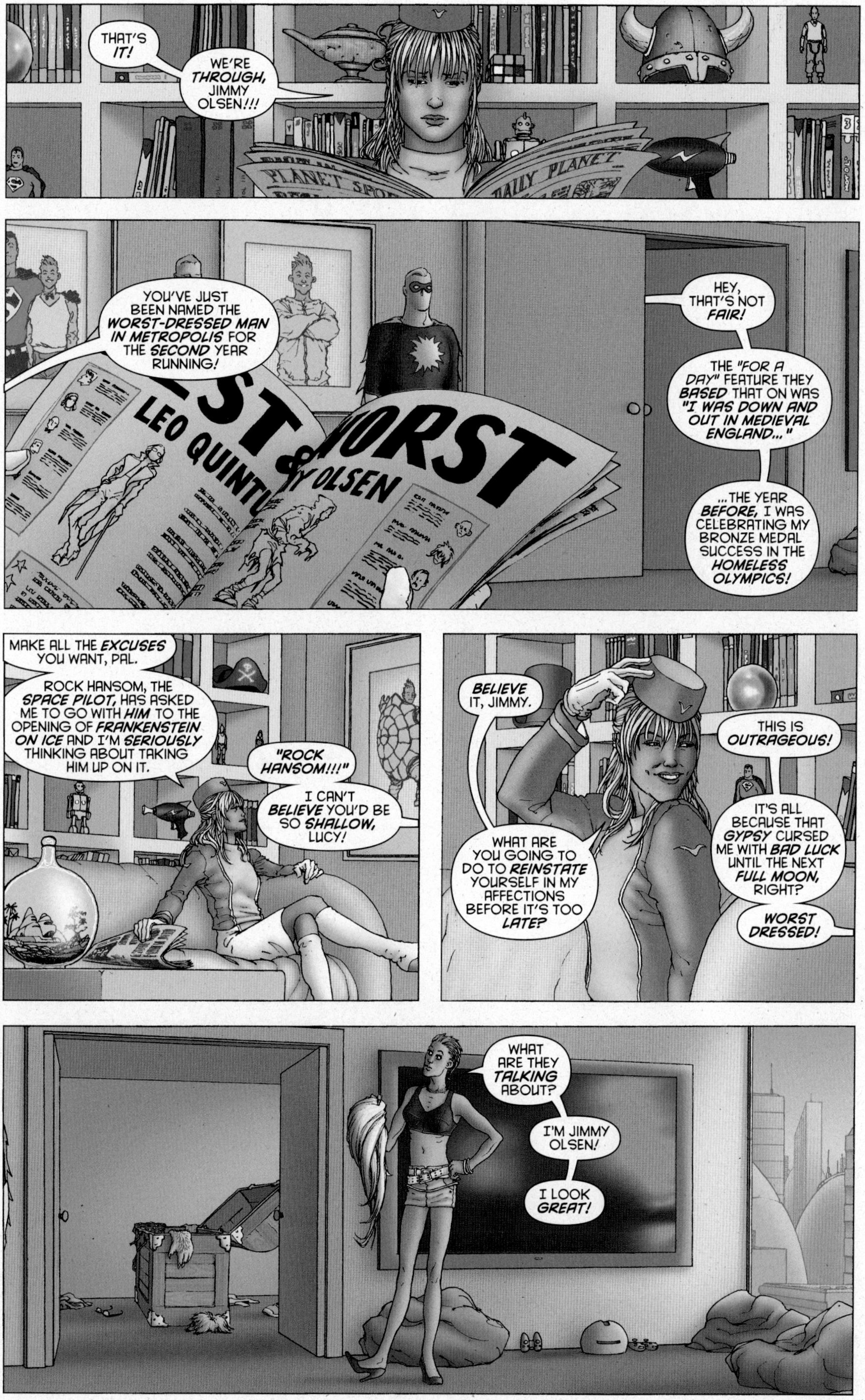
THAT'S IT!
WE'RE THROUGH, JIMMY OLSEN!!!
DAILY PLANET
YOU'VE JUST BEEN NAMED THE WORST-DRESSED MAN IN METROPOLIS FOR THE SECOND YEAR RUNNING!
WORST
LEO QUINTU
Y OLSEN
HEY, THAT'S NOT FAIR!
THE "FOR A DAY" FEATURE THEY BASED THAT ON WAS "I WAS DOWN AND OUT IN MEDIEVAL ENGLAND..."
...THE YEAR BEFORE, I WAS CELEBRATING MY BRONZE MEDAL SUCCESS IN THE HOMELESS OLYMPICS!
MAKE ALL THE EXCUSES YOU WANT, PAL.
ROCK HANSOM, THE SPACE PILOT, HAS ASKED ME TO GO WITH HIM TO THE OPENING OF FRANKENSTEIN ON ICE AND I'M SERIOUSLY THINKING ABOUT TAKING HIM UP ON IT.
"ROCK HANSOM!!!"
I CAN'T BELIEVE YOU'D BE SO SHALLOW, LUCY!
BELIEVE IT, JIMMY.
WHAT ARE YOU GOING TO DO TO REINSTATE YOURSELF IN MY AFFECTIONS BEFORE IT'S TOO LATE?
THIS IS OUTRAGEOUS!
IT'S ALL BECAUSE THAT GYPSY CURSED ME WITH BAD LUCK UNTIL THE NEXT FULL MOON, RIGHT?
WORST DRESSED!
WHAT ARE THEY TALKING ABOUT?
I'M JIMMY OLSEN!
I LOOK GREAT!

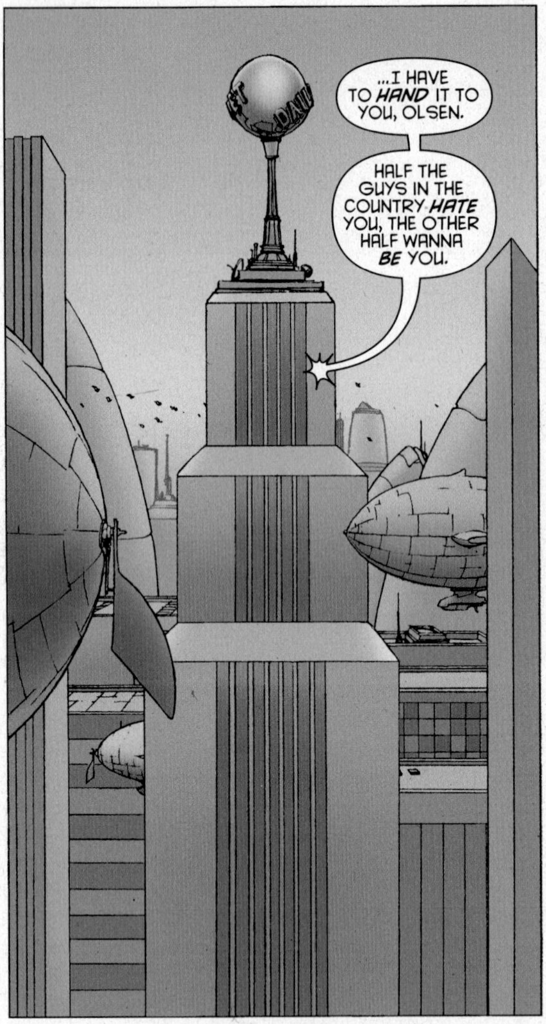

...I HAVE TO ***HAND*** IT TO YOU, OLSEN.
HALF THE GUYS IN THE COUNTRY ***HATE*** YOU, THE OTHER HALF WANNA ***BE*** YOU.

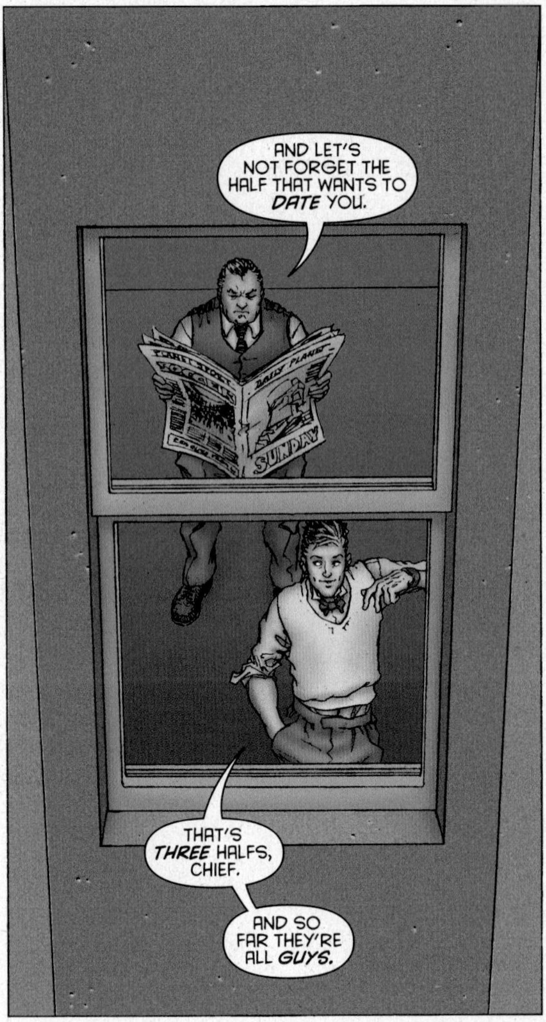

AND LET'S NOT FORGET THE HALF THAT WANTS TO ***DATE*** YOU.
DAILY PLANET
SUNDAY
THAT'S ***THREE*** HALFS, CHIEF.
AND SO FAR THEY'RE ALL ***GUYS.***

THE SUPERMAN

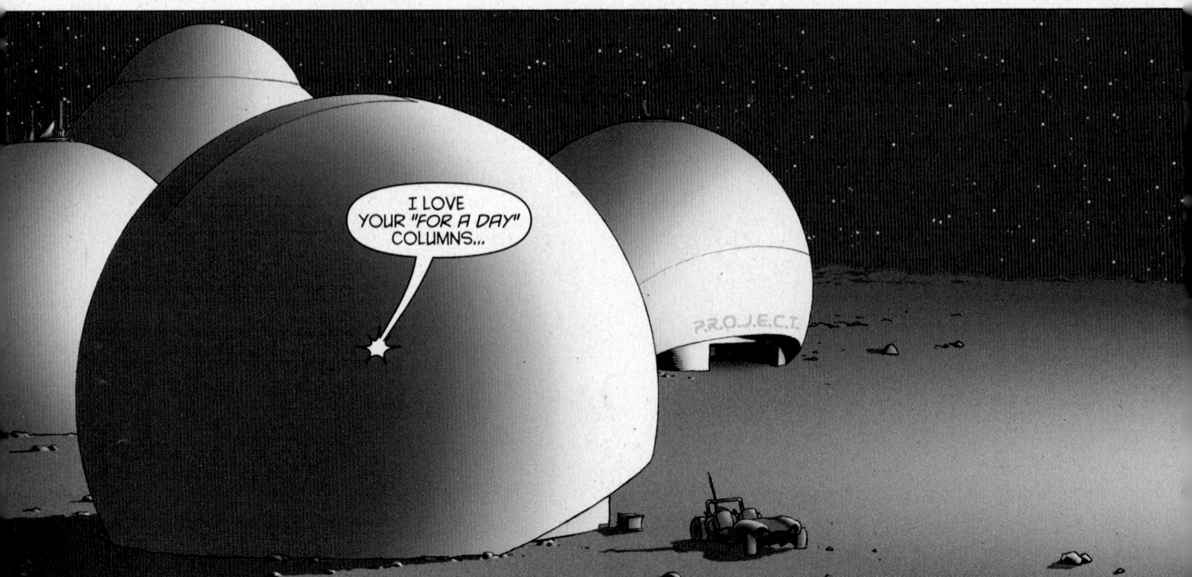

I LOVE YOUR *"FOR A DAY"* COLUMNS...
P.R.O.J.E.C.T.

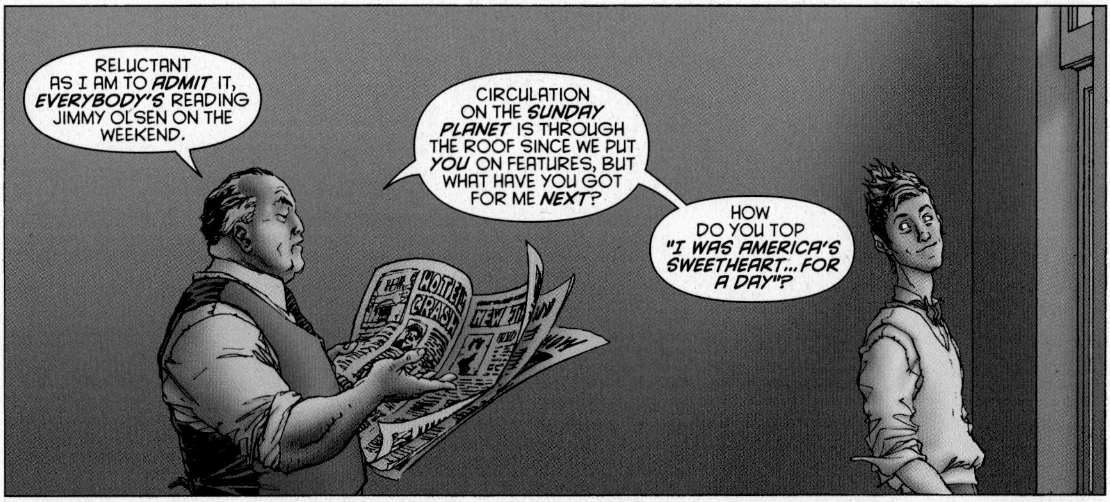
RELUCTANT AS I AM TO *ADMIT* IT, *EVERYBODY'S* READING JIMMY OLSEN ON THE WEEKEND.
CIRCULATION ON THE *SUNDAY PLANET* IS THROUGH THE ROOF SINCE WE PUT *YOU* ON FEATURES, BUT WHAT HAVE YOU GOT FOR ME *NEXT*?
HOW DO YOU TOP *"I WAS AMERICA'S SWEETHEART...FOR A DAY"*?

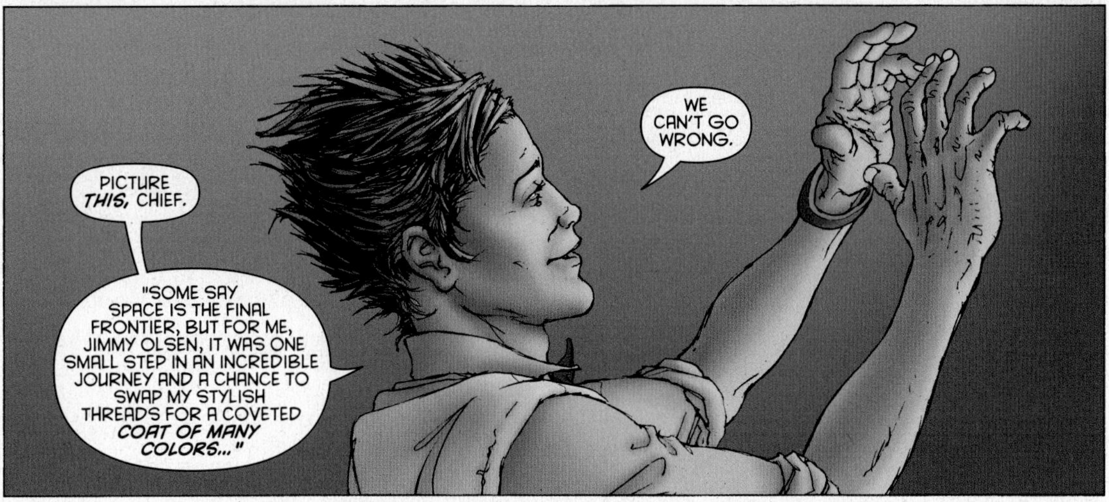
PICTURE *THIS,* CHIEF.
WE CAN'T GO WRONG.
"SOME SAY SPACE IS THE FINAL FRONTIER, BUT FOR ME, JIMMY OLSEN, IT WAS ONE SMALL STEP IN AN INCREDIBLE JOURNEY AND A CHANCE TO SWAP MY STYLISH THREADS FOR A COVETED *COAT OF MANY COLORS...*"

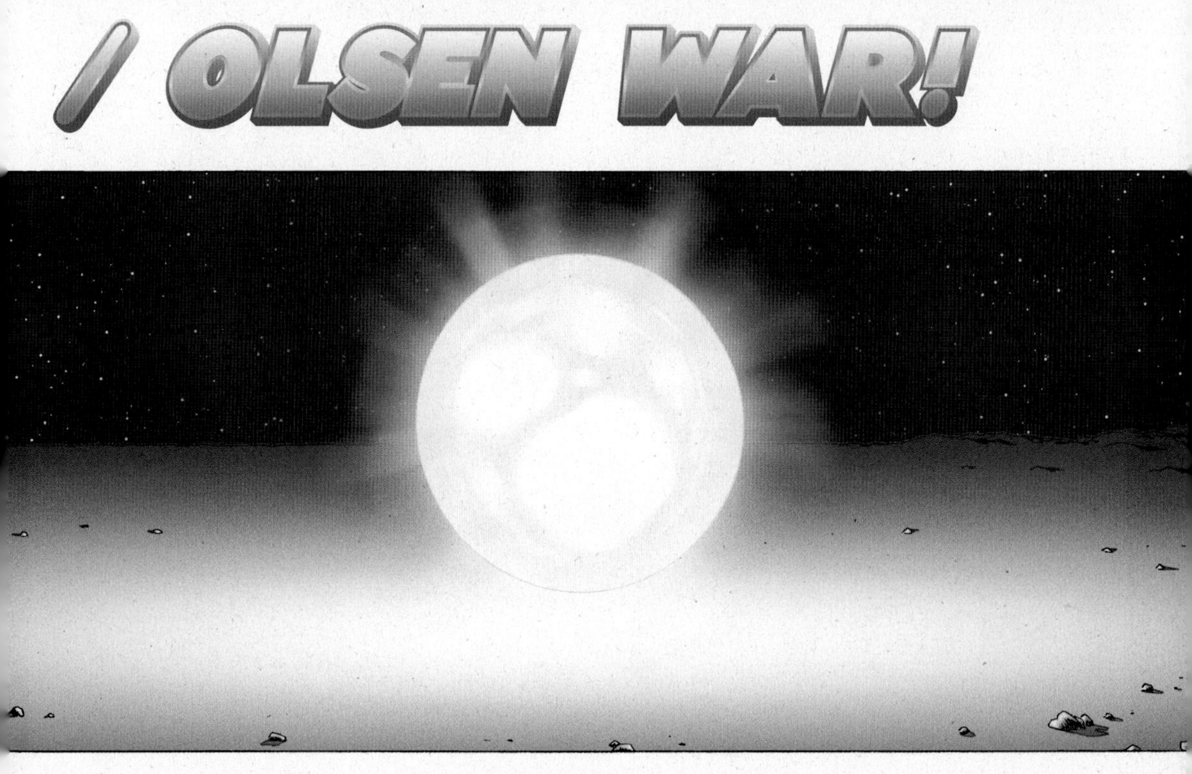
/ OLSEN WAR!

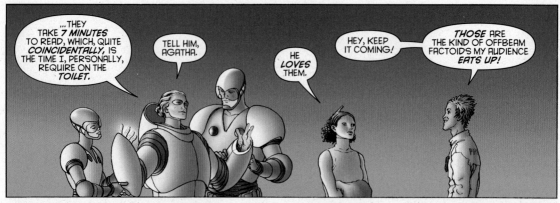

...THEY TAKE *7 MINUTES* TO READ, WHICH, QUITE *COINCIDENTALLY,* IS THE TIME I, PERSONALLY, REQUIRE ON THE *TOILET.*

TELL HIM, AGATHA.

HE *LOVES* THEM.

HEY, KEEP IT COMING!

THOSE ARE THE KIND OF OFFBEAM FACTOIDS MY AUDIENCE *EATS UP!*

I'M *KIDDING,* MISTER OLSEN.

MY *G-MEN* SECURITY TEAM IS COMING WITH *ME,* BUT OTHERWISE, *P.R.O.J.E.C.T.'S* CONSIDERABLE RESOURCES ARE IN *YOUR* HANDS.

SOME BODYGUARDS!

EXPECTING *MUCH* TROUBLE?

ADAM AND *EVE* ARE *WARCOPS.*

BIO-ENGINEERED TO *END* LARGE SCALE CONFLICT USING *NON-LETHAL* MEANS.

AWE-INSPIRING.

BUT YOU CAN *KEEP* 'EM, MISTER Q.

DON'T FORGET I HAVE A SUPER BODYGUARD OF MY *OWN* IF ANYTHING GOES WRONG.

AH, THE FAMOUS SUPERMAN *SIGNAL WATCH.*

LET'S HOPE YOU WON'T NEED *THAT.*

SHIELD YOUR *EYES,* MISTER OLSEN. THE *ELECTROKIND* ARE *TUNGSTEN GAS* LIFE FORMS WITH A BRITTLE *GLASS* EXOSKELETON.

THEIR LANGUAGE IS PURELY *OPTICAL,* AND SOME SENTENCES IN THIS GREETING MAY CAUSE INSTANT *BLINDNESS.*

THESE *SHAPES* I'M MAKING ARE THE EQUIVALENT OF *WORDS* ON THE WORLD OF THE ELECTROKIND.

HERE THEY COME NOW.

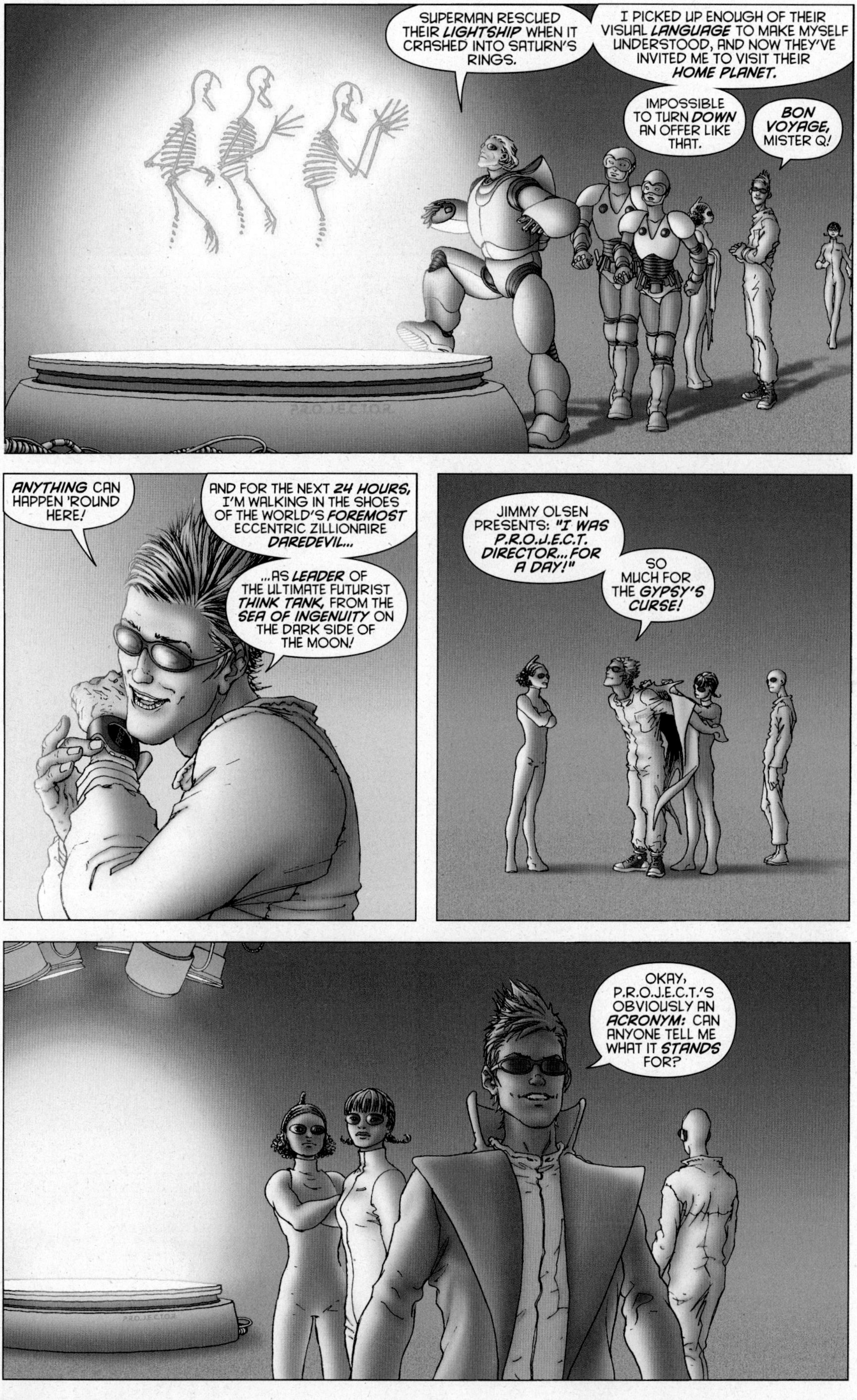
SUPERMAN RESCUED THEIR LIGHTSHIP WHEN IT CRASHED INTO SATURN'S RINGS.
I PICKED UP ENOUGH OF THEIR VISUAL LANGUAGE TO MAKE MYSELF UNDERSTOOD, AND NOW THEY'VE INVITED ME TO VISIT THEIR HOME PLANET.
IMPOSSIBLE TO TURN DOWN AN OFFER LIKE THAT.
BON VOYAGE, MISTER Q!
ANYTHING CAN HAPPEN 'ROUND HERE!
AND FOR THE NEXT 24 HOURS, I'M WALKING IN THE SHOES OF THE WORLD'S FOREMOST ECCENTRIC ZILLIONAIRE DAREDEVIL...
...AS LEADER OF THE ULTIMATE FUTURIST THINK TANK, FROM THE SEA OF INGENUITY ON THE DARK SIDE OF THE MOON!
JIMMY OLSEN PRESENTS: "I WAS P.R.O.J.E.C.T. DIRECTOR...FOR A DAY!"
SO MUCH FOR THE GYPSY'S CURSE!
OKAY, P.R.O.J.E.C.T.'S OBVIOUSLY AN ACRONYM: CAN ANYONE TELL ME WHAT IT STANDS FOR?

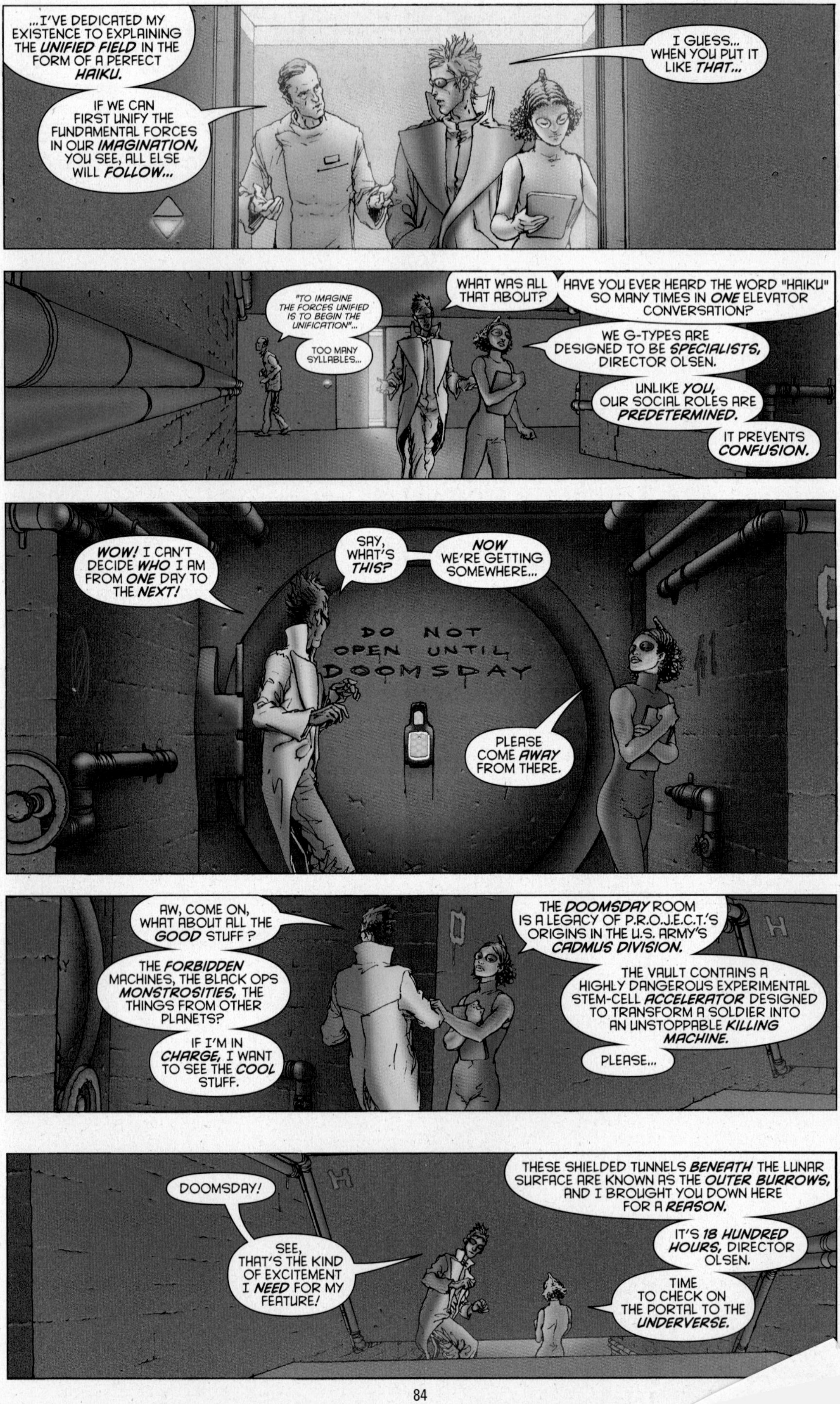
...I'VE DEDICATED MY EXISTENCE TO EXPLAINING THE UNIFIED FIELD IN THE FORM OF A PERFECT HAIKU.
IF WE CAN FIRST UNIFY THE FUNDAMENTAL FORCES IN OUR IMAGINATION, YOU SEE, ALL ELSE WILL FOLLOW...
I GUESS... WHEN YOU PUT IT LIKE THAT...
"TO IMAGINE THE FORCES UNIFIED IS TO BEGIN THE UNIFICATION"...
TOO MANY SYLLABLES...
WHAT WAS ALL THAT ABOUT?
HAVE YOU EVER HEARD THE WORD "HAIKU" SO MANY TIMES IN ONE ELEVATOR CONVERSATION?
WE G-TYPES ARE DESIGNED TO BE SPECIALISTS, DIRECTOR OLSEN.
UNLIKE YOU, OUR SOCIAL ROLES ARE PREDETERMINED.
IT PREVENTS CONFUSION.
WOW! I CAN'T DECIDE WHO I AM FROM ONE DAY TO THE NEXT!
SAY, WHAT'S THIS?
NOW WE'RE GETTING SOMEWHERE...
DO NOT OPEN UNTIL DOOMSDAY
PLEASE COME AWAY FROM THERE.
AW, COME ON, WHAT ABOUT ALL THE GOOD STUFF ?
THE FORBIDDEN MACHINES, THE BLACK OPS MONSTROSITIES, THE THINGS FROM OTHER PLANETS?
IF I'M IN CHARGE, I WANT TO SEE THE COOL STUFF.
THE DOOMSDAY ROOM IS A LEGACY OF P.R.O.J.E.C.T.'S ORIGINS IN THE U.S. ARMY'S CADMUS DIVISION.
THE VAULT CONTAINS A HIGHLY DANGEROUS EXPERIMENTAL STEM-CELL ACCELERATOR DESIGNED TO TRANSFORM A SOLDIER INTO AN UNSTOPPABLE KILLING MACHINE.
PLEASE...
DOOMSDAY!
SEE, THAT'S THE KIND OF EXCITEMENT I NEED FOR MY FEATURE!
THESE SHIELDED TUNNELS BENEATH THE LUNAR SURFACE ARE KNOWN AS THE OUTER BURROWS, AND I BROUGHT YOU DOWN HERE FOR A REASON.
IT'S 18 HUNDRED HOURS, DIRECTOR OLSEN.
TIME TO CHECK ON THE PORTAL TO THE UNDERVERSE.

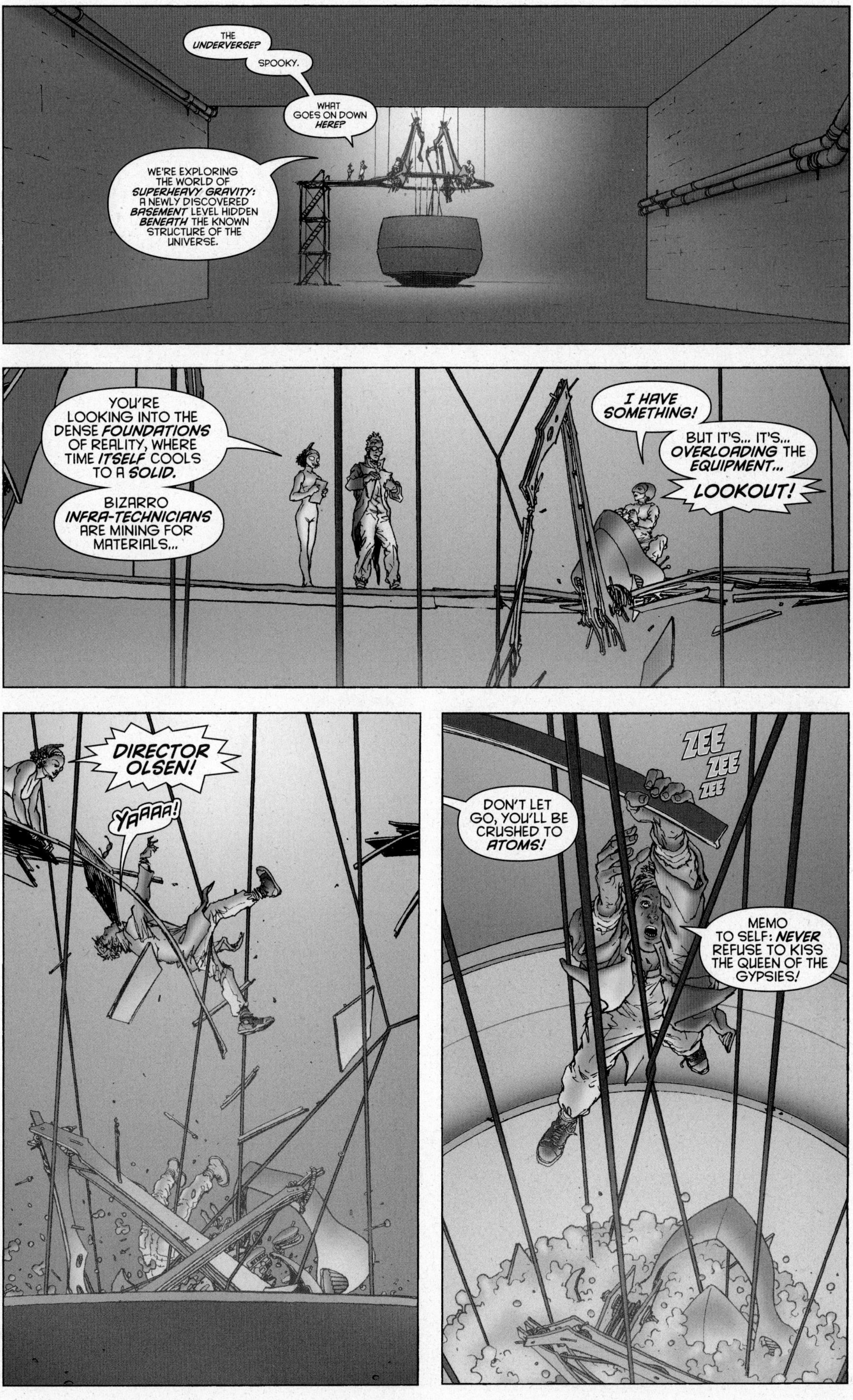
THE UNDERVERSE?
SPOOKY.
WHAT GOES ON DOWN HERE?
WE'RE EXPLORING THE WORLD OF SUPERHEAVY GRAVITY: A NEWLY DISCOVERED BASEMENT LEVEL HIDDEN BENEATH THE KNOWN STRUCTURE OF THE UNIVERSE.
YOU'RE LOOKING INTO THE DENSE FOUNDATIONS OF REALITY, WHERE TIME ITSELF COOLS TO A SOLID.
BIZARRO INFRA-TECHNICIANS ARE MINING FOR MATERIALS...
I HAVE SOMETHING!
BUT IT'S... IT'S... OVERLOADING THE EQUIPMENT...
LOOKOUT!
DIRECTOR OLSEN!
YAAAA!
ZEE ZEE ZEE
DON'T LET GO, YOU'LL BE CRUSHED TO ATOMS!
MEMO TO SELF: NEVER REFUSE TO KISS THE QUEEN OF THE GYPSIES!

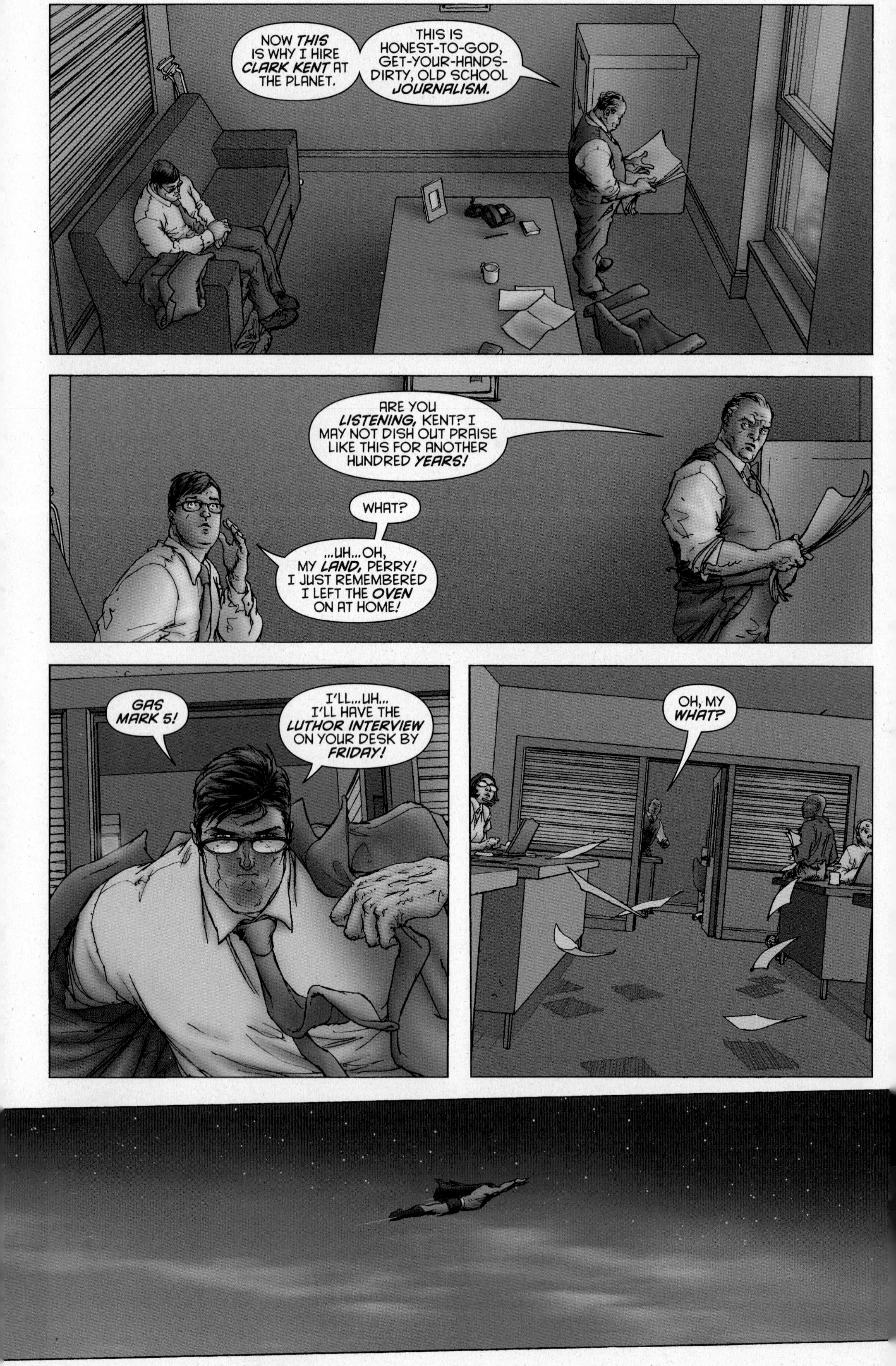
NOW THIS IS WHY I HIRE CLARK KENT AT THE PLANET.
THIS IS HONEST-TO-GOD, GET-YOUR-HANDS-DIRTY, OLD SCHOOL JOURNALISM.
ARE YOU LISTENING, KENT? I MAY NOT DISH OUT PRAISE LIKE THIS FOR ANOTHER HUNDRED YEARS!
WHAT?
...UH...OH, MY LAND, PERRY! I JUST REMEMBERED I LEFT THE OVEN ON AT HOME!
GAS MARK 5!
I'LL...UH... I'LL HAVE THE LUTHOR INTERVIEW ON YOUR DESK BY FRIDAY!
OH, MY WHAT?

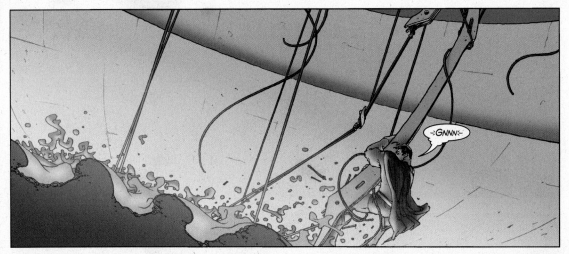

~GNNN~

THE GRAVITATIONAL PULL DOWN THERE IS *IMMENSE.*

YOU *OKAY,* SUPERMAN?

I AM *SO* SORRY ABOUT THIS.

STRANGE... I...I FELT A LITTLE *FAINT* FOR A MOMENT, JIMMY.

I'M AFRAID I COULDN'T SAVE THE *WORKER* WHO FELL IN THERE.

BUT MAYBE I CAN BRING BACK HIS *DISCOVERY.*

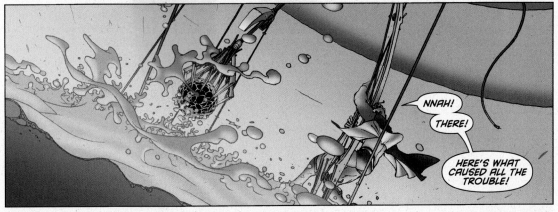

NNAH!

THERE!

HERE'S WHAT CAUSED ALL THE TROUBLE!

CAUTION! SUPERHEAVY UNKNOWN INFRA MATERIALS HAVE PENETRATED NORMAL SPACE!

SUPERMAN.

I DON'T WANT TO *WORRY* YOU.

BUT I THINK YOU SHOULD *BACK AWAY* SLOWLY FROM THE OBJECT WHILE WE SPIN A *GRAVITY-BOTTLE* TO CONTAIN IT.

BLACK KRYPTONITE.

A NEW *ISOTOPE* AT THE LOW-FREQUENCY END OF THE *K-MINERAL* SPECTRUM.

IT SEEMS WE'VE DUG UP A RADIOACTIVE FRAGMENT OF YOUR *HOMEWORLD* THAT'S BEEN BURIED FOR YEARS IN THE *UNDERVERSE.*

A *NEW* TYPE OF KRYPTONITE!

I DON'T LIKE THE *LOOK* OF THIS, SUPERMAN.

K-RADIATION CAN *KILL* YOU.

NOT ANYMORE SINCE I BECAME *IMMUNE* TO *GREEN K,* JIMMY.

CAN'T SAY I *FEEL* ANY PHYSICAL EFFECTS FROM *THIS* SAMPLE.

I GUESS I'M *FINE.*

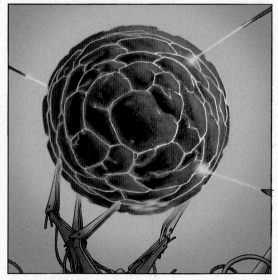

GLAD TO *HEAR* IT, SUPERMAN.

GLAD TO HEAR IT.

FOR A MOMENT THERE I COULDN'T HELP THINKING ABOUT THAT...

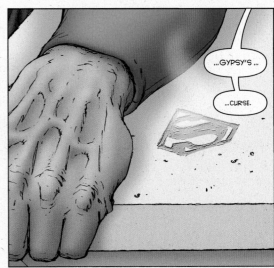

...GYPSY'S...

...CURSE.

IT'S THAT SIGNAL WATCH.

LIKE I DON'T HAVE *ENOUGH* TO DO WITHOUT BAILING *YOU* OUT OF SOME STUPID *SCRAPE* EVERY OTHER DAY.

YOU'D BE *DEAD* WITHOUT ME!

SUPERMAN?

THAT ROCK... IT *DID* SOMETHING, DIDN'T IT?

IT'S JUST CHEAP MOONBASE FURNITURE.

QUINTUM'S *LOADED* ANYWAY.

THINK ABOUT IT...

...I PROBABLY *INCREASED* ITS *SALE VALUE* WITH MY AUTOGRAPH.

OH-KAY...

WE CAN *HANDLE* A SUPERMAN WHO'S A LITTLE *MISCHIEVOUS*, A LITTLE *ANNOYING*, BUT BASICALLY... BASICALLY...

...OKAY?

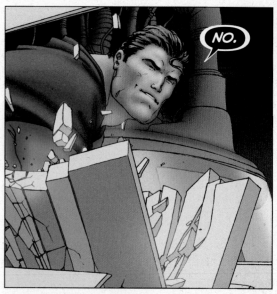

NO.

NO, IT'S GUH-GUH-GETTING WUH-WORSE.

EVERY-THING'S GONE... GONE *OPPOSITE*...

JIMMY, I... I KNOW WHAT *BLACK K* DOES...

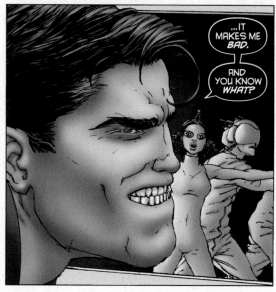

...IT MAKES ME *BAD.*

AND YOU KNOW *WHAT?*

PART OF ME IS STARTING TO LIKE THAT IDEA!

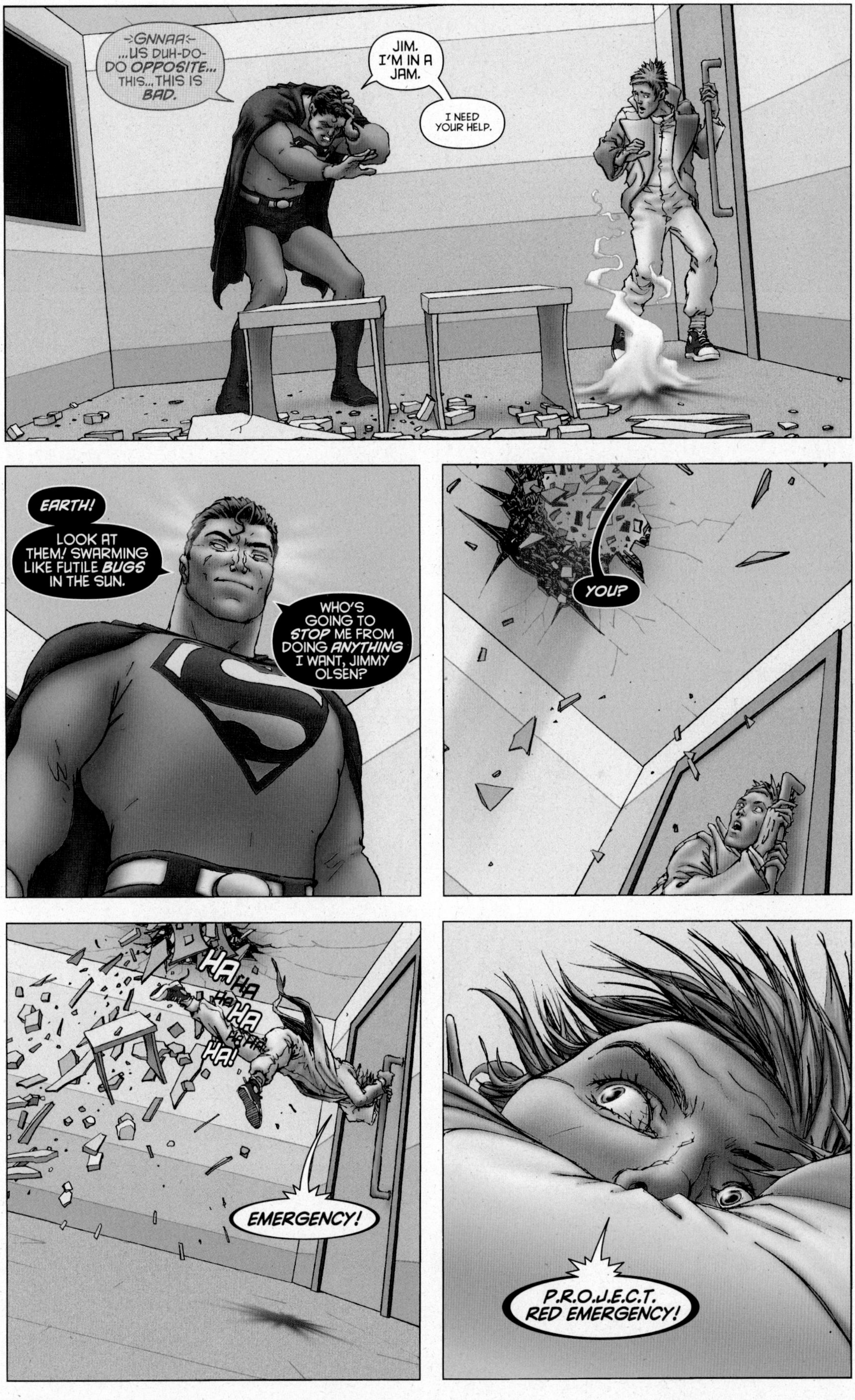
-GNNAA-
...US DUH-DO-DO OPPOSITE... THIS... THIS IS BAD.
JIM. I'M IN A JAM.
I NEED YOUR HELP.
EARTH!
LOOK AT THEM! SWARMING LIKE FUTILE BUGS IN THE SUN.
WHO'S GOING TO STOP ME FROM DOING ANYTHING I WANT, JIMMY OLSEN?
YOU?
HA HA HA HA HA HA HA!
EMERGENCY!
P.R.O.J.E.C.T. RED EMERGENCY!

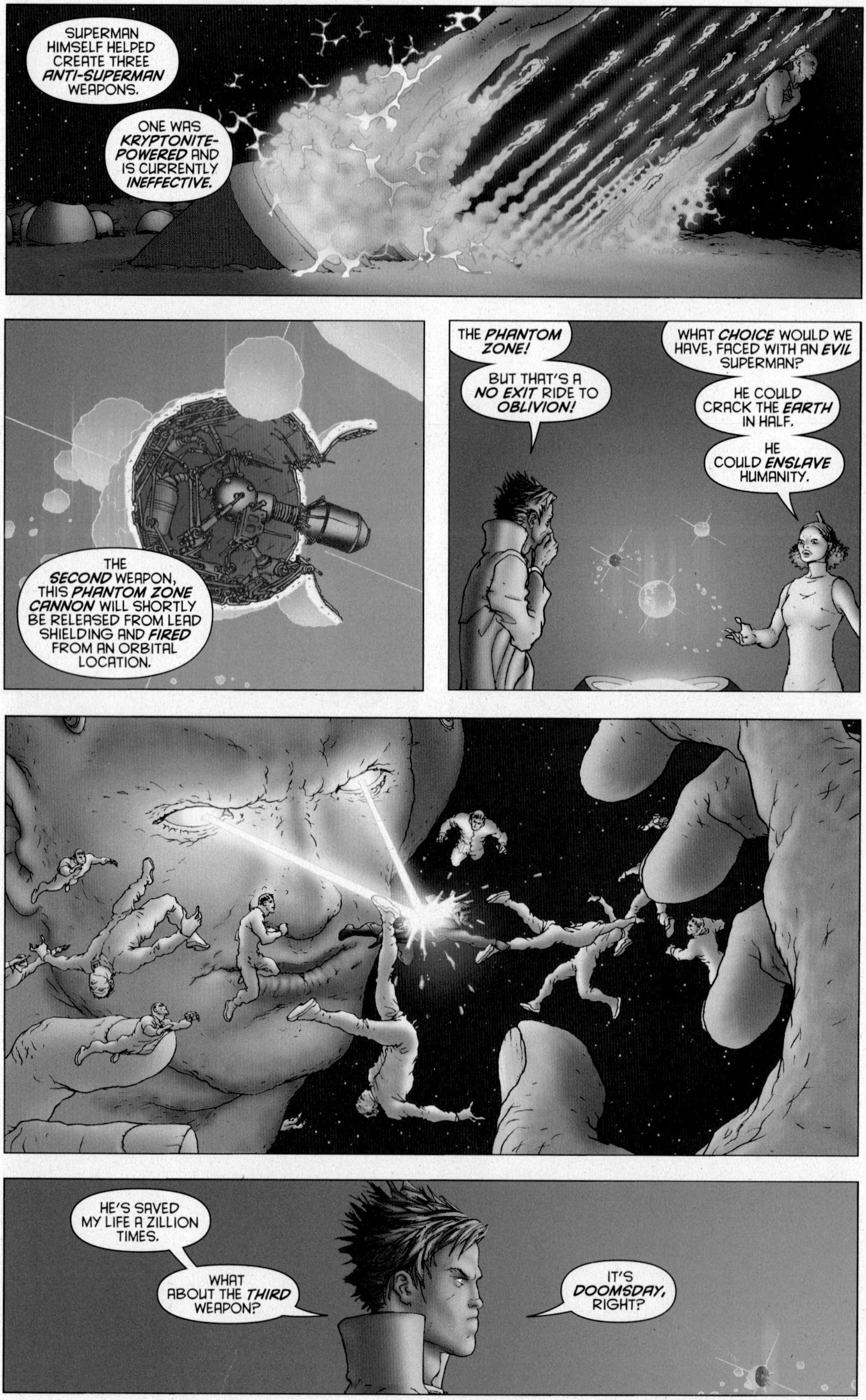
SUPERMAN HIMSELF HELPED CREATE THREE ANTI-SUPERMAN WEAPONS.
ONE WAS KRYPTONITE-POWERED AND IS CURRENTLY INEFFECTIVE.
THE SECOND WEAPON, THIS PHANTOM ZONE CANNON WILL SHORTLY BE RELEASED FROM LEAD SHIELDING AND FIRED FROM AN ORBITAL LOCATION.
THE PHANTOM ZONE!
BUT THAT'S A NO EXIT RIDE TO OBLIVION!
WHAT CHOICE WOULD WE HAVE, FACED WITH AN EVIL SUPERMAN?
HE COULD CRACK THE EARTH IN HALF.
HE COULD ENSLAVE HUMANITY.
HE'S SAVED MY LIFE A ZILLION TIMES.
WHAT ABOUT THE THIRD WEAPON?
IT'S DOOMSDAY, RIGHT?

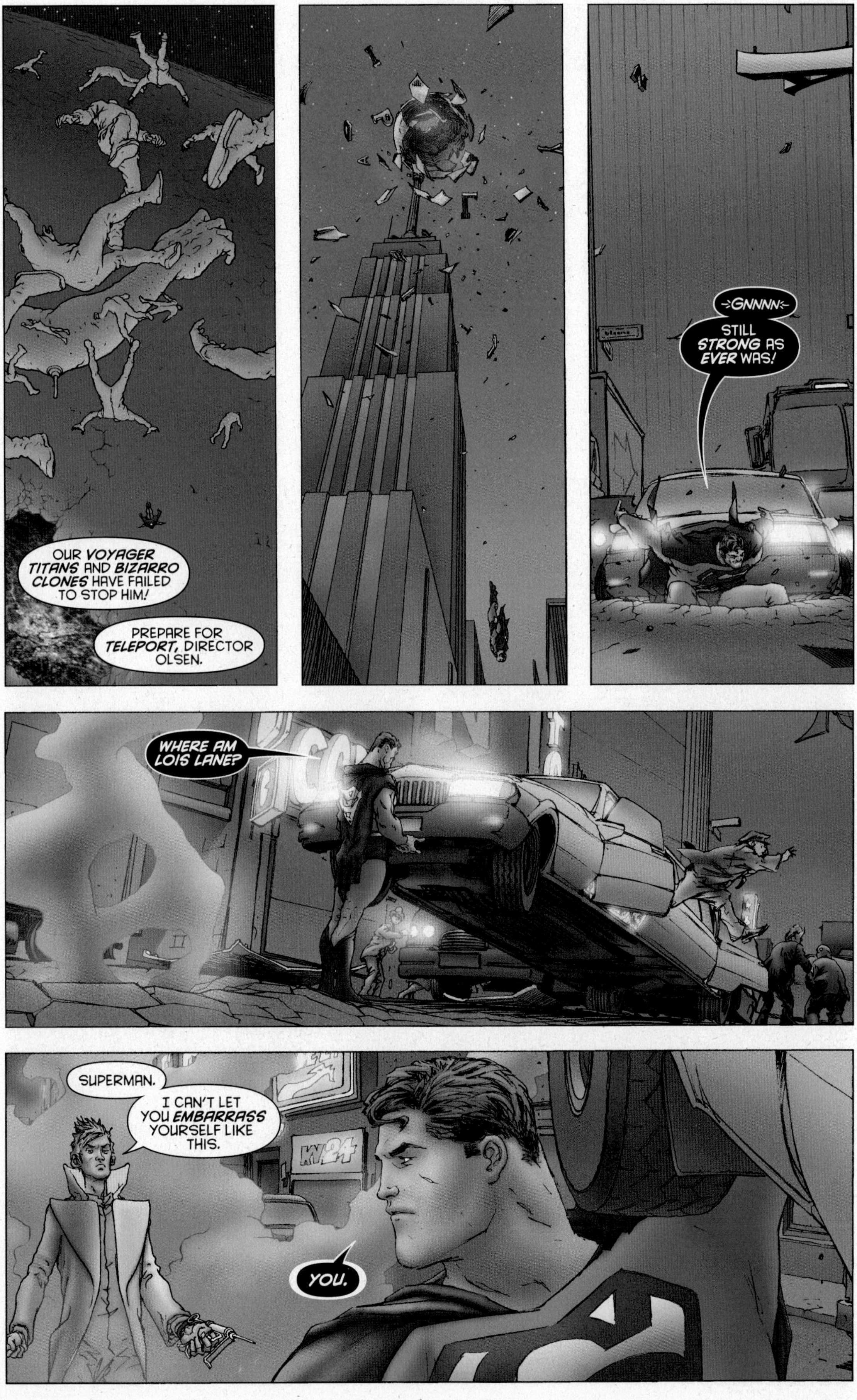
OUR VOYAGER TITANS AND BIZARRO CLONES HAVE FAILED TO STOP HIM!
PREPARE FOR TELEPORT, DIRECTOR OLSEN.
-GNNNN-
STILL STRONG AS EVER WAS!
WHERE AM LOIS LANE?
SUPERMAN.
I CAN'T LET YOU EMBARRASS YOURSELF LIKE THIS.
YOU.

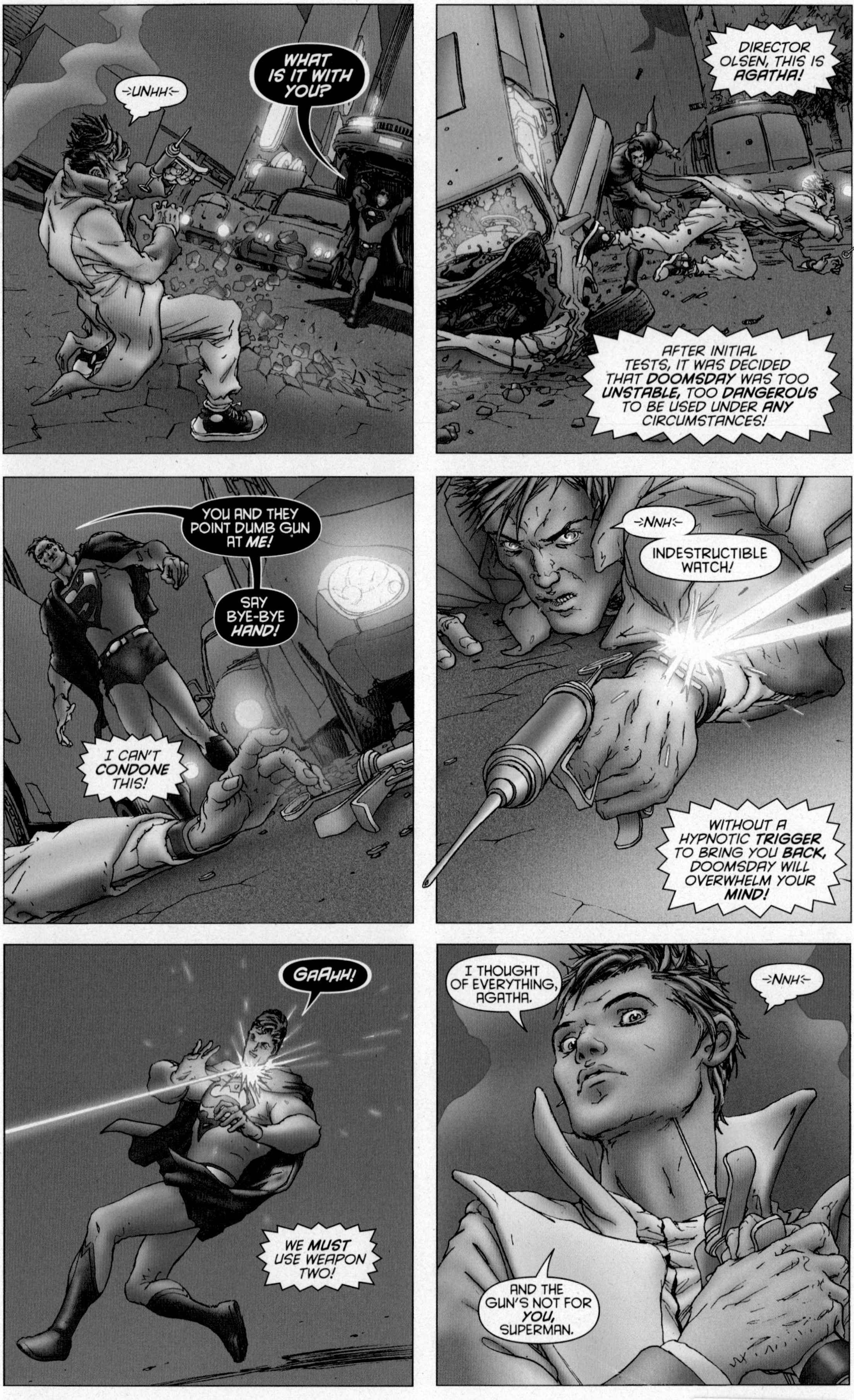
-UNHH-
WHAT IS IT WITH YOU?
DIRECTOR OLSEN, THIS IS AGATHA!
AFTER INITIAL TESTS, IT WAS DECIDED THAT DOOMSDAY WAS TOO UNSTABLE, TOO DANGEROUS TO BE USED UNDER ANY CIRCUMSTANCES!
YOU AND THEY POINT DUMB GUN AT ME!
SAY BYE-BYE HAND!
I CAN'T CONDONE THIS!
-NNH-
INDESTRUCTIBLE WATCH!
WITHOUT A HYPNOTIC TRIGGER TO BRING YOU BACK, DOOMSDAY WILL OVERWHELM YOUR MIND!
GAAHH!
WE MUST USE WEAPON TWO!
I THOUGHT OF EVERYTHING, AGATHA.
-NNH-
AND THE GUN'S NOT FOR YOU, SUPERMAN.

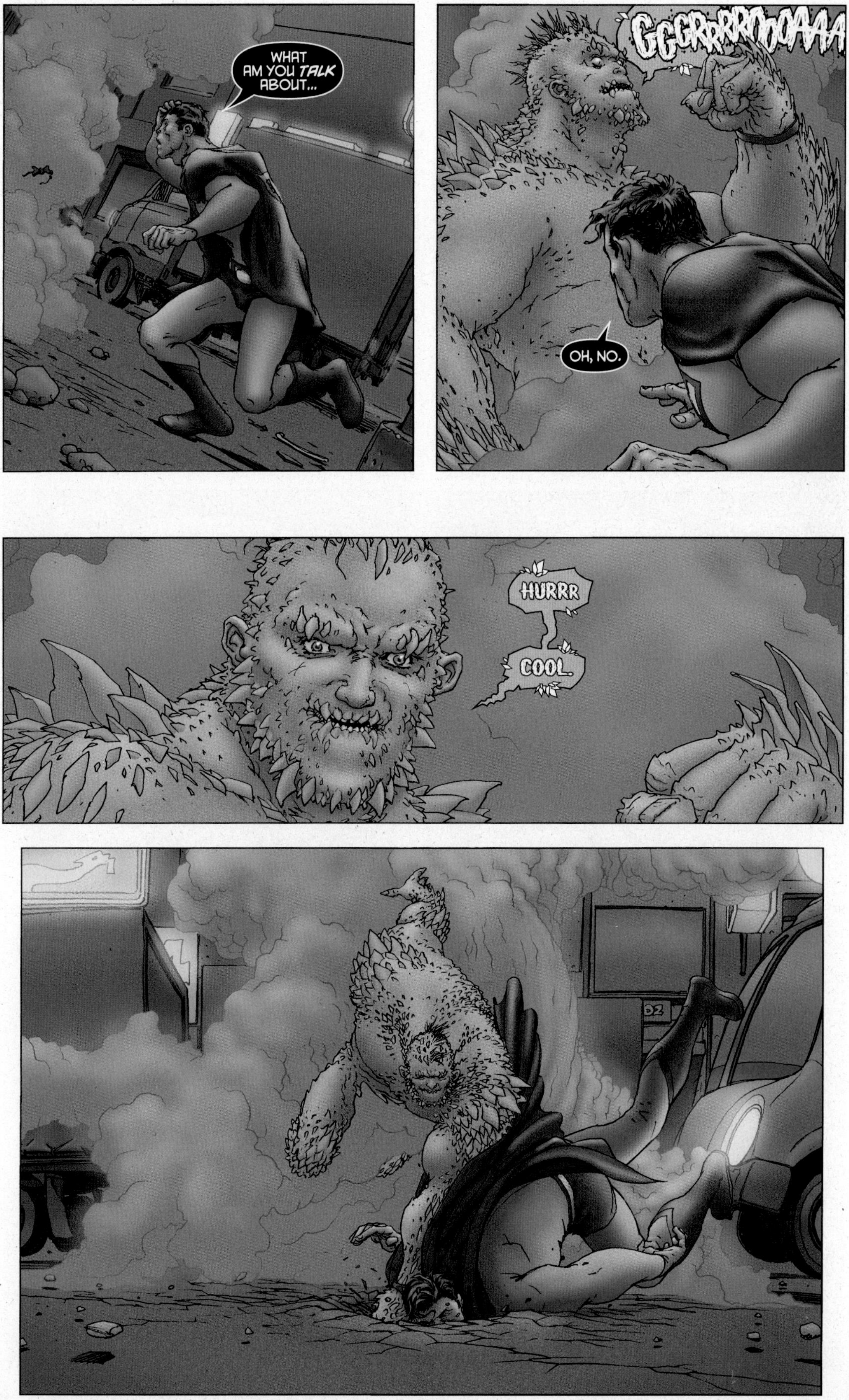
WHAT AM YOU *TALK* ABOUT...
GGGRRRROOOAAAA
OH, NO.
HURRR
COOL.

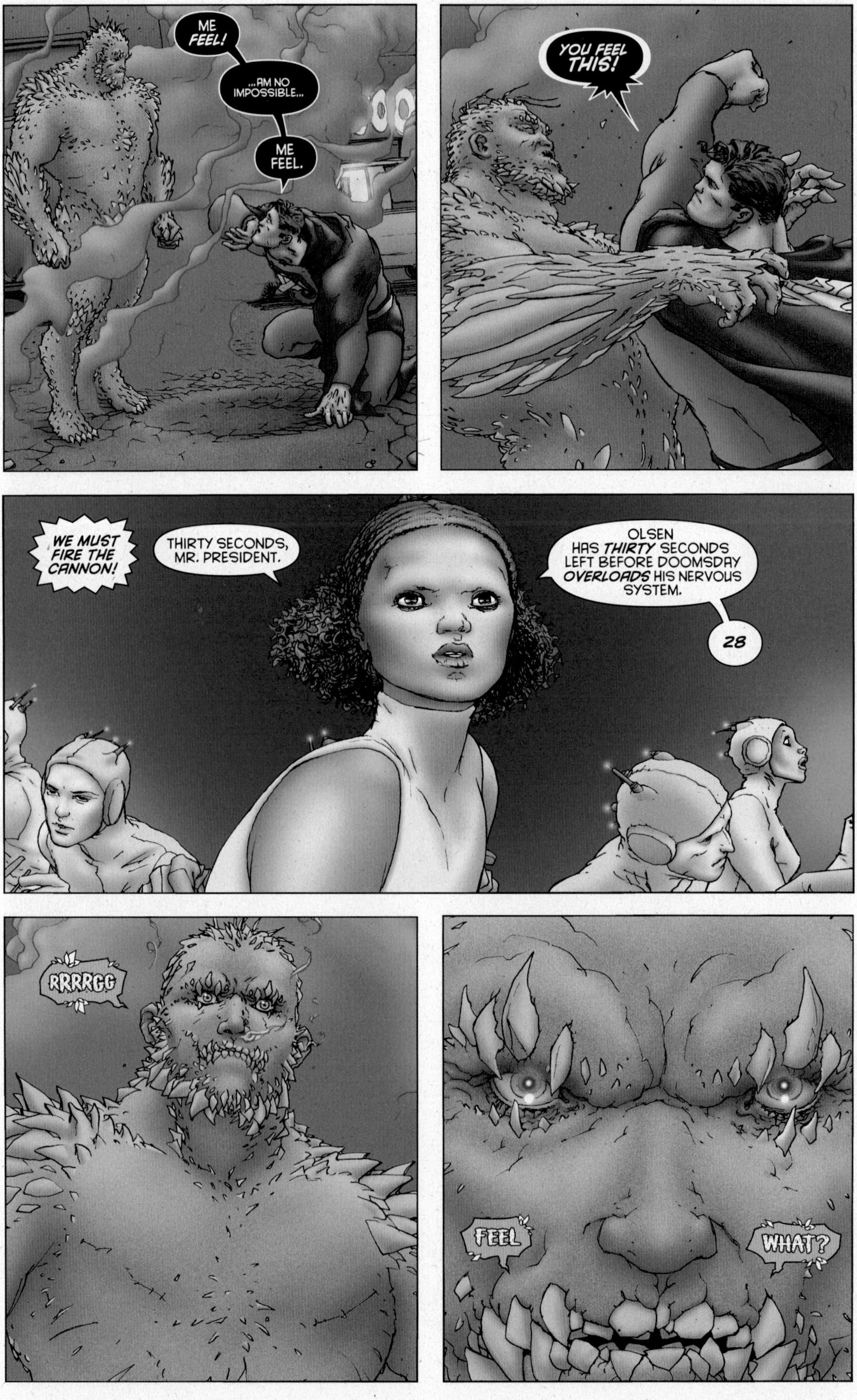
ME FEEL!
...AM NO IMPOSSIBLE...
ME FEEL.
YOU FEEL THIS!
WE MUST FIRE THE CANNON!
THIRTY SECONDS, MR. PRESIDENT.
OLSEN HAS THIRTY SECONDS LEFT BEFORE DOOMSDAY OVERLOADS HIS NERVOUS SYSTEM.
28
RRRRGG
FEEL
WHAT?

WHAT AM HAPPEN TO ME?
NO FAIR!
ME GET WEAKER...
ZEE ZEEE
ME AM DIE NOW?
NO DIE!
ME SCARED...
ZEEE ZEEEE ZEEE
ZEEE ZEEEE ZEEE ZEEEE
NO DIE.
NO CAN DIE.
AM SUPERMAN...
...NO CAN DIE.
ZEEE ZEEEE ZEEE ZEEEE

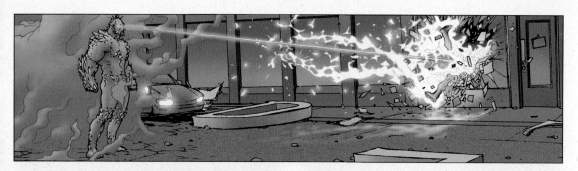

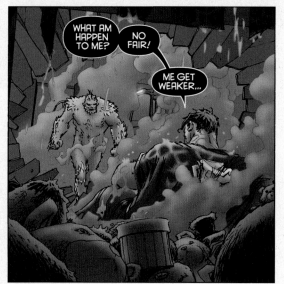

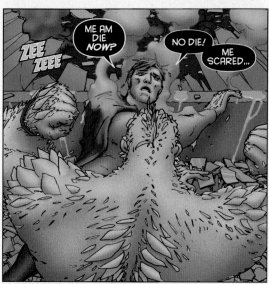

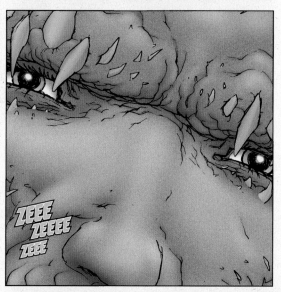

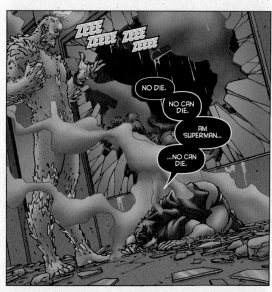

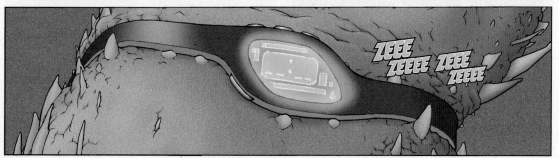

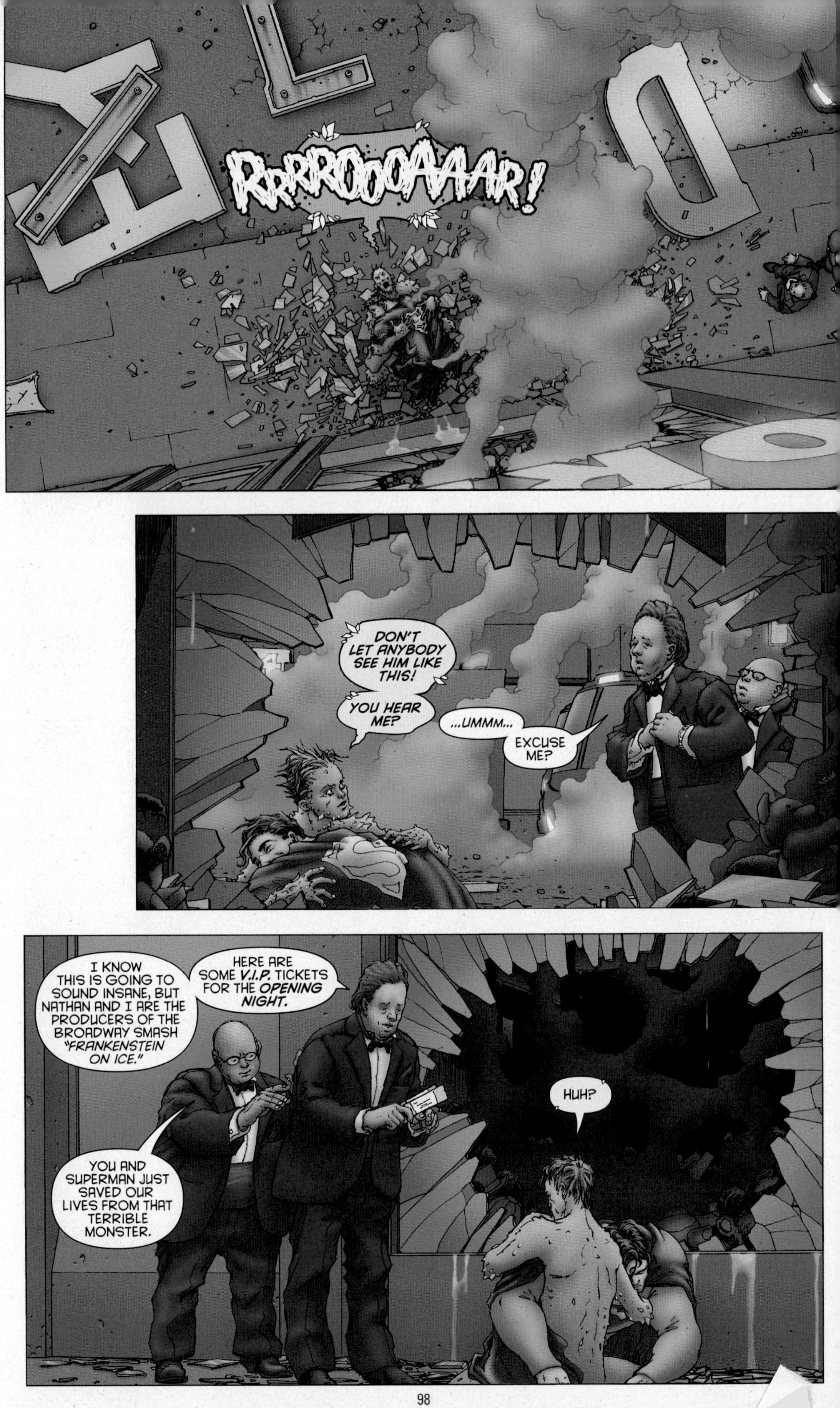
RRRRROOOAAAAR!
DON'T LET ANYBODY SEE HIM LIKE THIS!
YOU HEAR ME?
...UMMM... EXCUSE ME?
I KNOW THIS IS GOING TO SOUND INSANE, BUT NATHAN AND I ARE THE PRODUCERS OF THE BROADWAY SMASH "FRANKENSTEIN ON ICE."
YOU AND SUPERMAN JUST SAVED OUR LIVES FROM THAT TERRIBLE MONSTER.
HERE ARE SOME V.I.P. TICKETS FOR THE OPENING NIGHT.
HUH?

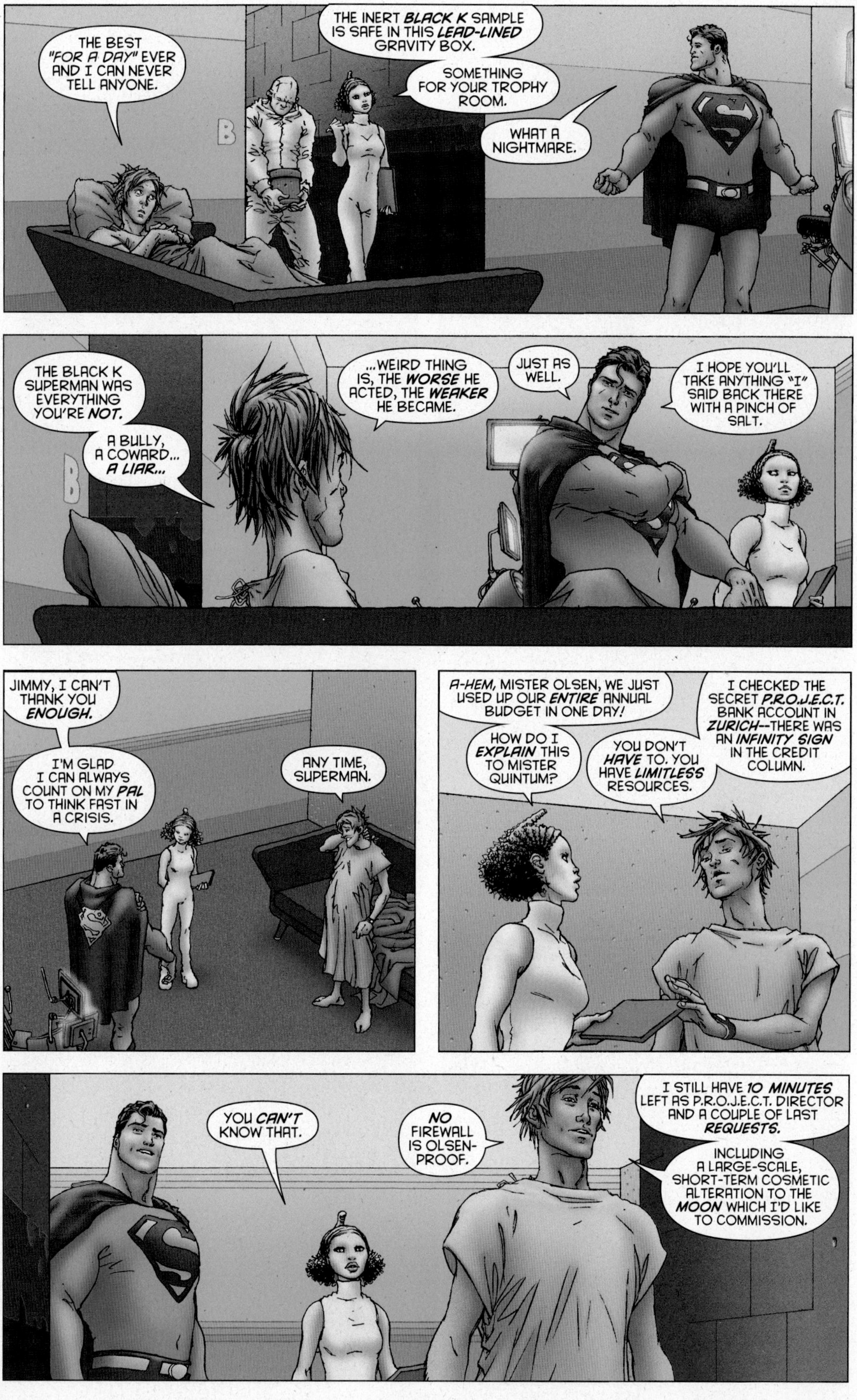
THE BEST "FOR A DAY" EVER AND I CAN NEVER TELL ANYONE.
THE INERT BLACK K SAMPLE IS SAFE IN THIS LEAD-LINED GRAVITY BOX.
SOMETHING FOR YOUR TROPHY ROOM.
WHAT A NIGHTMARE.
THE BLACK K SUPERMAN WAS EVERYTHING YOU'RE NOT.
A BULLY, A COWARD... A LIAR...
...WEIRD THING IS, THE WORSE HE ACTED, THE WEAKER HE BECAME.
JUST AS WELL.
I HOPE YOU'LL TAKE ANYTHING "I" SAID BACK THERE WITH A PINCH OF SALT.
JIMMY, I CAN'T THANK YOU ENOUGH.
I'M GLAD I CAN ALWAYS COUNT ON MY PAL TO THINK FAST IN A CRISIS.
ANY TIME, SUPERMAN.
A-HEM, MISTER OLSEN, WE JUST USED UP OUR ENTIRE ANNUAL BUDGET IN ONE DAY!
HOW DO I EXPLAIN THIS TO MISTER QUINTUM?
I CHECKED THE SECRET P.R.O.J.E.C.T. BANK ACCOUNT IN ZURICH--THERE WAS AN INFINITY SIGN IN THE CREDIT COLUMN.
YOU DON'T HAVE TO. YOU HAVE LIMITLESS RESOURCES.
YOU CAN'T KNOW THAT.
NO FIREWALL IS OLSEN-PROOF.
I STILL HAVE 10 MINUTES LEFT AS P.R.O.J.E.C.T. DIRECTOR AND A COUPLE OF LAST REQUESTS.
INCLUDING A LARGE-SCALE, SHORT-TERM COSMETIC ALTERATION TO THE MOON WHICH I'D LIKE TO COMMISSION.

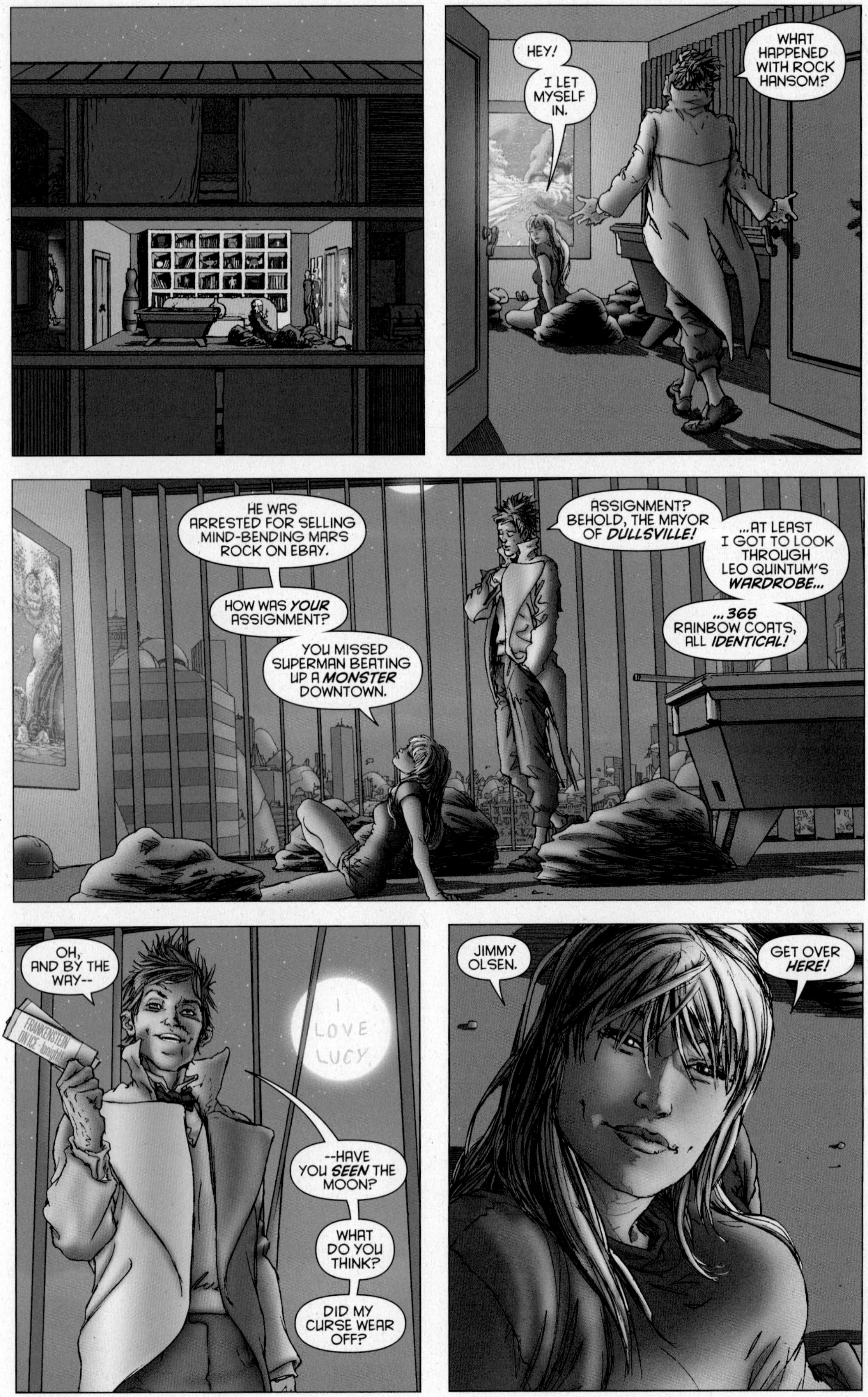
HEY!
I LET MYSELF IN.
WHAT HAPPENED WITH ROCK HANSOM?
HE WAS ARRESTED FOR SELLING MIND-BENDING MARS ROCK ON EBAY.
HOW WAS YOUR ASSIGNMENT?
YOU MISSED SUPERMAN BEATING UP A MONSTER DOWNTOWN.
ASSIGNMENT? BEHOLD, THE MAYOR OF DULLSVILLE!
...AT LEAST I GOT TO LOOK THROUGH LEO QUINTUM'S WARDROBE...
...365 RAINBOW COATS, ALL IDENTICAL!
OH, AND BY THE WAY--
FRANKENSTEIN ON ICE - tonight
I LOVE LUCY
--HAVE YOU SEEN THE MOON?
WHAT DO YOU THINK?
DID MY CURSE WEAR OFF?
JIMMY OLSEN.
GET OVER HERE!

Episode 5

THE GOSPEL ACCORDING TO LEX LUTHOR

Cover FRANK QUITELY

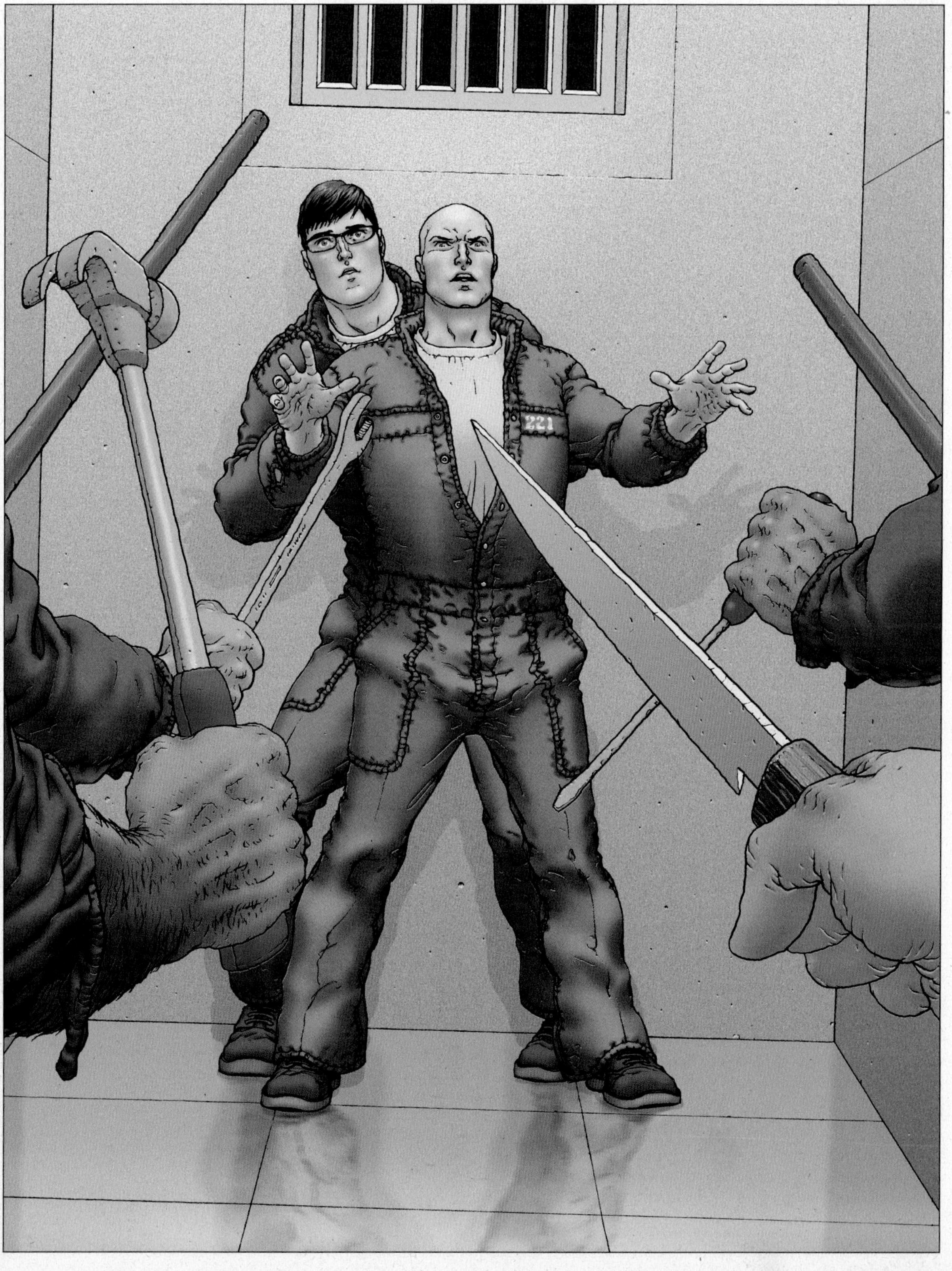

5

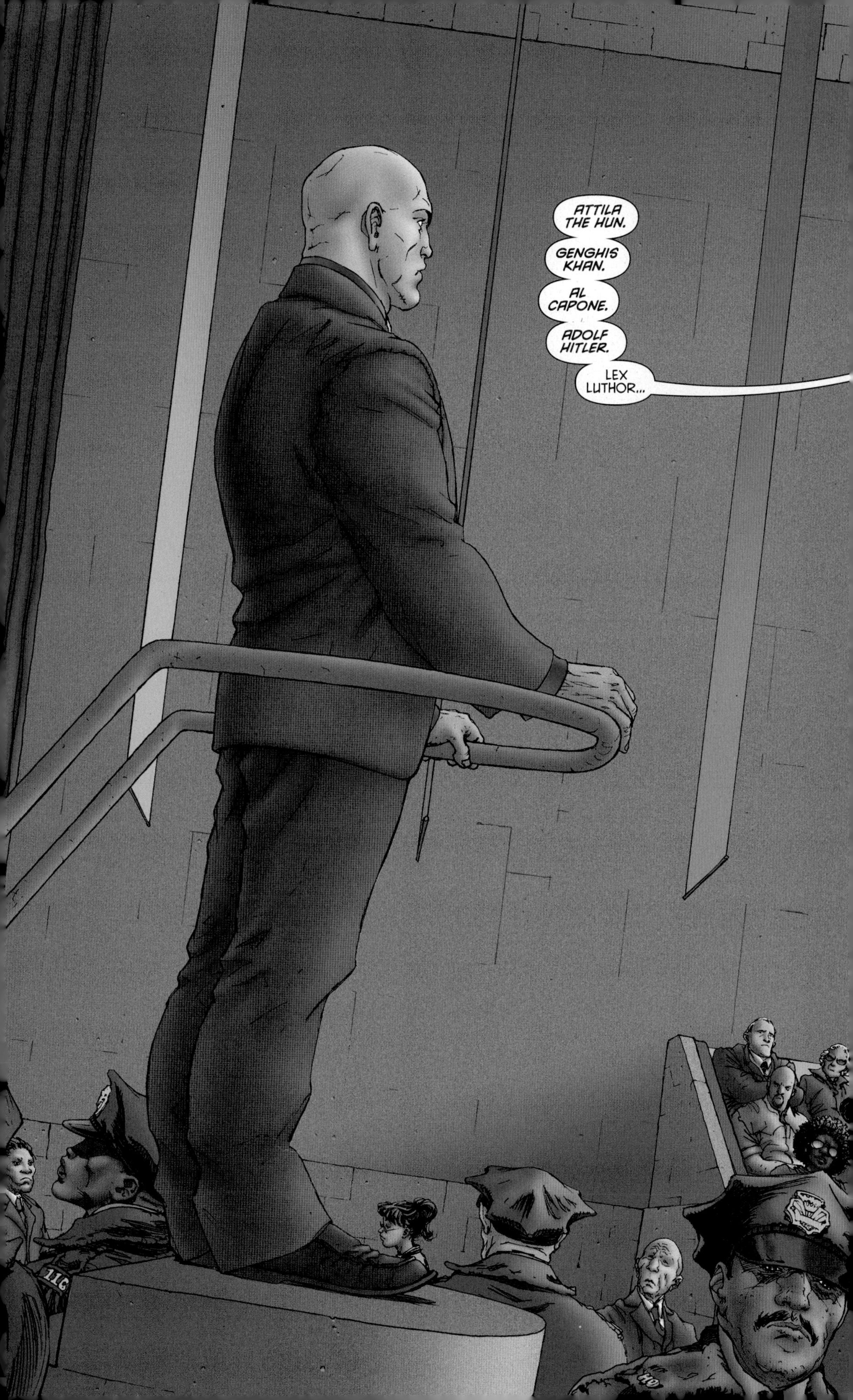
ATTILA THE HUN.
GENGHIS KHAN.
AL CAPONE.
ADOLF HITLER.
LEX LUTHOR...
116
HQ

...YOU FREELY ADMIT THAT *THESE* VILE AND APPALLING *CRIMINALS* ARE THE MEN YOU REVERE ABOVE ALL AS *HEROES* AND *ROLE MODELS.*

YOUR INSANE *SCHEMES* HAVE PLACED IN JEOPARDY THE LIVES OF EVERY MAN, WOMAN AND CHILD ON THIS *PLANET.*

HAVE YOU ANYTHING *MORE* TO SAY BEFORE I DELIVER THE VERDICT OF THIS COURT?

SUPERMAN MADE ME DO IT.

HE SHOULD BE ON TRIAL HERE.

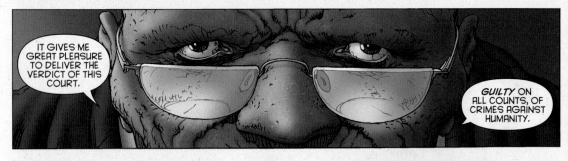

PUT ME *AWAY*, YOU SENILE, SWEATING TOAD.

GET THIS FARCE *OVER* WITH.

I'LL DO MORE THAN THAT.

YOU'RE A HUMAN MONSTER, LUTHOR-- AN AMORAL, SOCIOPATHIC *PREDATOR*, DRIVEN BY JEALOUSY, GREED AND A *GRANDIOSE* SELF-DELUSION!

IT GIVES ME GREAT PLEASURE TO DELIVER THE VERDICT OF THIS COURT.

GUILTY ON ALL COUNTS, OF CRIMES AGAINST HUMANITY.

THE SENTENCE IS *DEATH* IN THE *ELECTRIC CHAIR*...

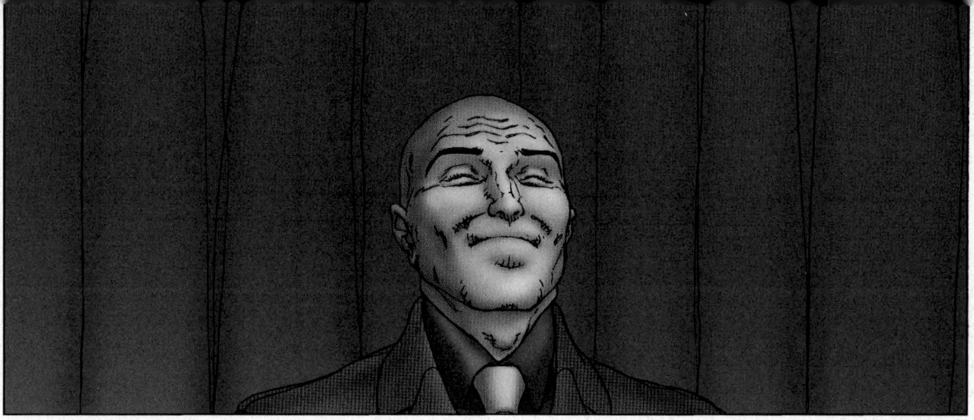

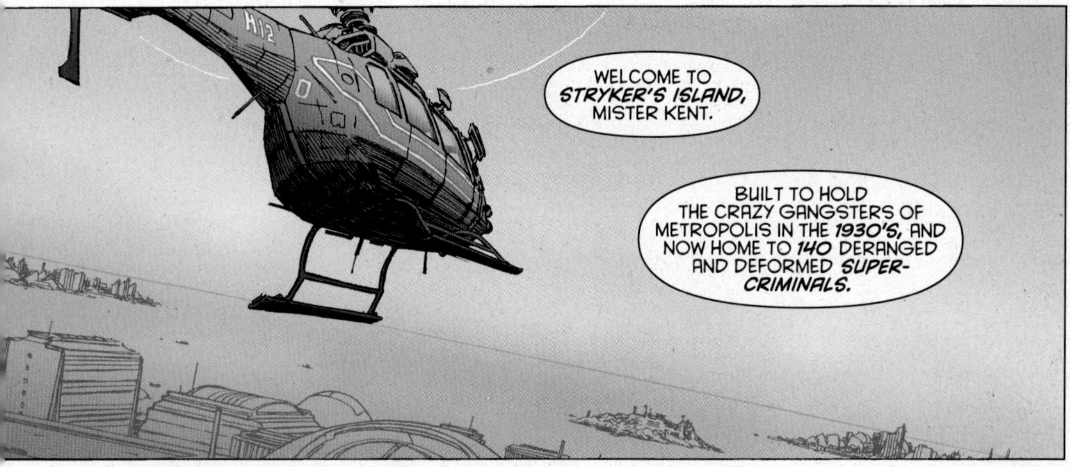
WELCOME TO *STRYKER'S ISLAND,* MISTER KENT.
BUILT TO HOLD THE CRAZY GANGSTERS OF METROPOLIS IN THE *1930'S,* AND NOW HOME TO *140* DERANGED AND DEFORMED *SUPER-CRIMINALS.*

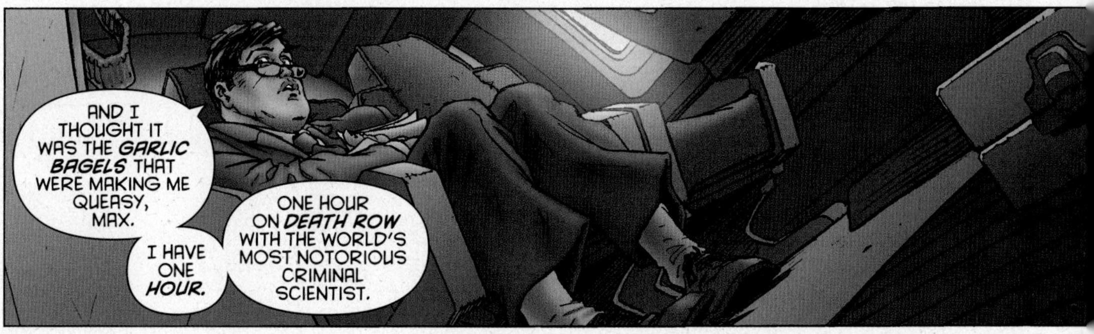
AND I THOUGHT IT WAS THE *GARLIC BAGELS* THAT WERE MAKING ME QUEASY, MAX.
I HAVE ONE *HOUR.*
ONE HOUR ON *DEATH ROW* WITH THE WORLD'S MOST NOTORIOUS CRIMINAL SCIENTIST.

THE GOSPEL ACCORDING TO LEX LUTHOR

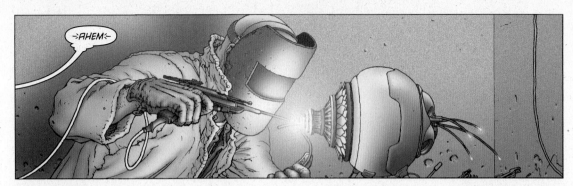

→AHEM←

→KKFF←

YES, I'M *AWARE* OF YOUR LUMBERING PRESENCE, KENT.

I WAS JUST FINISHING SOME FINE DETAIL WORK ON MY *BIBLIOBOT MARK 2.*

A ROVING *LIBRARY.*

HE'LL READ YOU ANY OF A *THOUSAND* CLASSIC WORKS OF LITERATURE FROM *"ULYSSES"*...

"STATELY, PLUMP, BUCK MULLIGAN... *RUUZZK.*"

TO *"A TALE OF TWO CITIES"*...

MOST OF THE TIME HE JUST FLOATS AROUND ON HIS *OWN*--IT'S *PATHETIC.*

CULTURE'S A DIRTY WORD NOWADAYS, BUT GOD KNOWS, I *TRY*...

"IT WAS THE BEST OF TIMES... HKKT...IT WAS THE WORST OF TIMES..."

CUH-CALL HIM *OFF!*

CAREFUL, KENT!

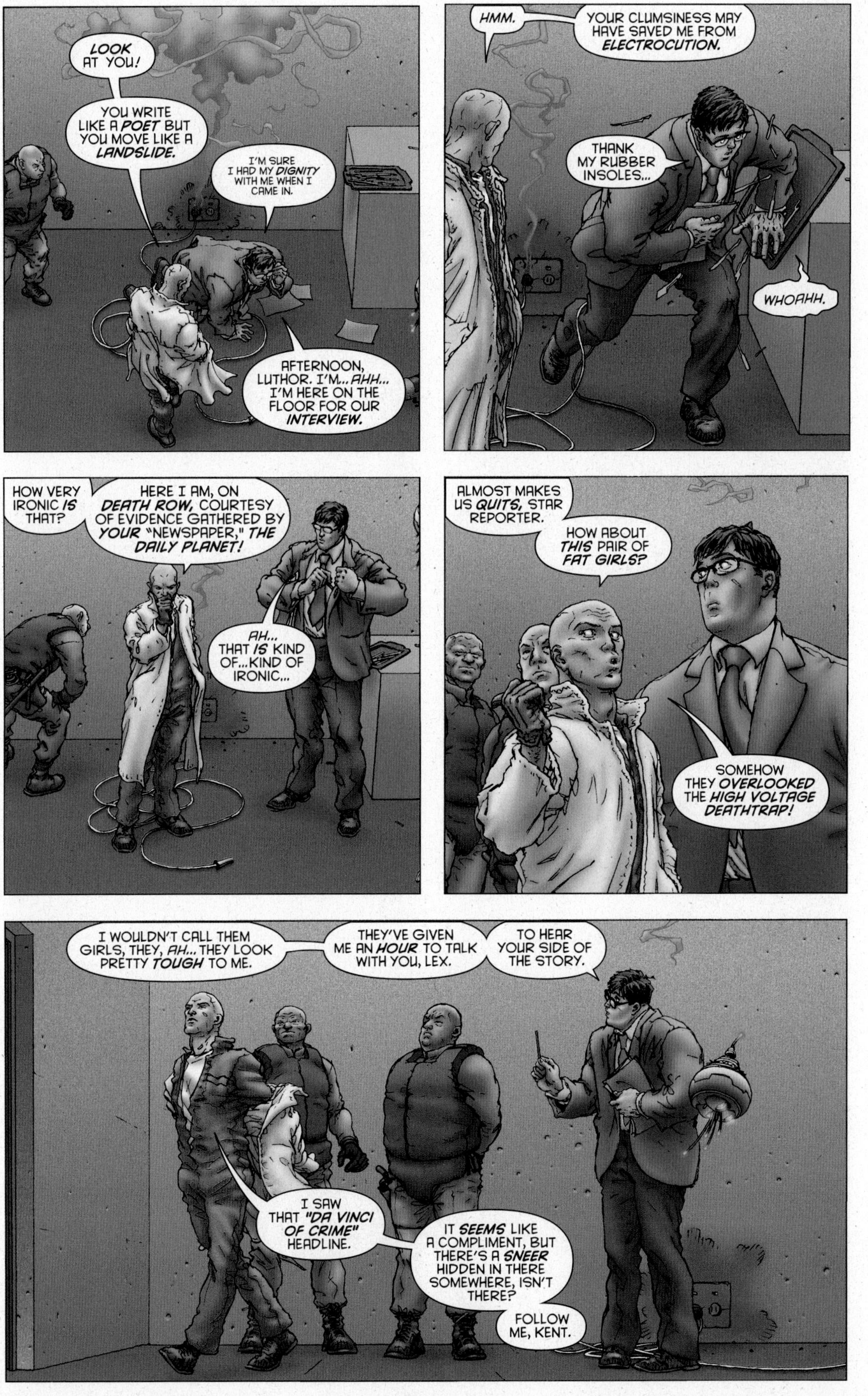
LOOK AT YOU!
YOU WRITE LIKE A POET BUT YOU MOVE LIKE A LANDSLIDE.
I'M SURE I HAD MY DIGNITY WITH ME WHEN I CAME IN.
AFTERNOON, LUTHOR. I'M... AHH... I'M HERE ON THE FLOOR FOR OUR INTERVIEW.
HMM.
YOUR CLUMSINESS MAY HAVE SAVED ME FROM ELECTROCUTION.
THANK MY RUBBER INSOLES...
WHOAHH.
HOW VERY IRONIC IS THAT?
HERE I AM, ON DEATH ROW, COURTESY OF EVIDENCE GATHERED BY YOUR "NEWSPAPER," THE DAILY PLANET!
AH... THAT IS KIND OF...KIND OF IRONIC...
ALMOST MAKES US QUITS, STAR REPORTER.
HOW ABOUT THIS PAIR OF FAT GIRLS?
SOMEHOW THEY OVERLOOKED THE HIGH VOLTAGE DEATHTRAP!
I WOULDN'T CALL THEM GIRLS, THEY, AH... THEY LOOK PRETTY TOUGH TO ME.
THEY'VE GIVEN ME AN HOUR TO TALK WITH YOU, LEX.
TO HEAR YOUR SIDE OF THE STORY.
I SAW THAT "DA VINCI OF CRIME" HEADLINE.
IT SEEMS LIKE A COMPLIMENT, BUT THERE'S A SNEER HIDDEN IN THERE SOMEWHERE, ISN'T THERE?
FOLLOW ME, KENT.

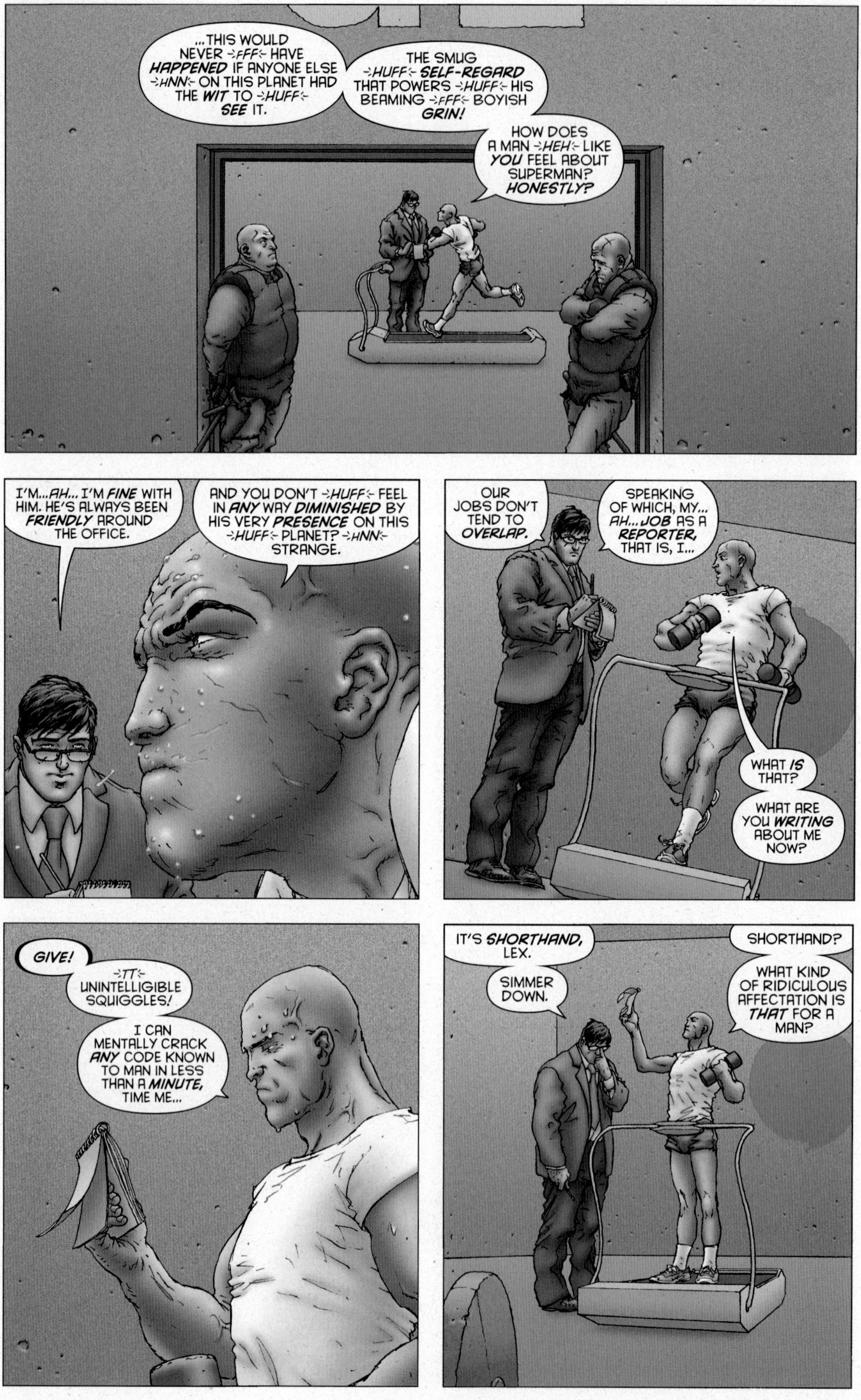
...THIS WOULD NEVER -FFF- HAVE HAPPENED IF ANYONE ELSE -HNN- ON THIS PLANET HAD THE WIT TO -HUFF- SEE IT.
THE SMUG -HUFF- SELF-REGARD THAT POWERS -HUFF- HIS BEAMING -FFF- BOYISH GRIN!
HOW DOES A MAN -HEH- LIKE YOU FEEL ABOUT SUPERMAN? HONESTLY?
I'M...AH... I'M FINE WITH HIM. HE'S ALWAYS BEEN FRIENDLY AROUND THE OFFICE.
AND YOU DON'T -HUFF- FEEL IN ANY WAY DIMINISHED BY HIS VERY PRESENCE ON THIS -HUFF- PLANET? -HNN- STRANGE.
OUR JOBS DON'T TEND TO OVERLAP.
SPEAKING OF WHICH, MY... AH... JOB AS A REPORTER, THAT IS, I...
WHAT IS THAT?
WHAT ARE YOU WRITING ABOUT ME NOW?
GIVE!
-TT- UNINTELLIGIBLE SQUIGGLES!
I CAN MENTALLY CRACK ANY CODE KNOWN TO MAN IN LESS THAN A MINUTE, TIME ME...
IT'S SHORTHAND, LEX.
SIMMER DOWN.
SHORTHAND?
WHAT KIND OF RIDICULOUS AFFECTATION IS THAT FOR A MAN?

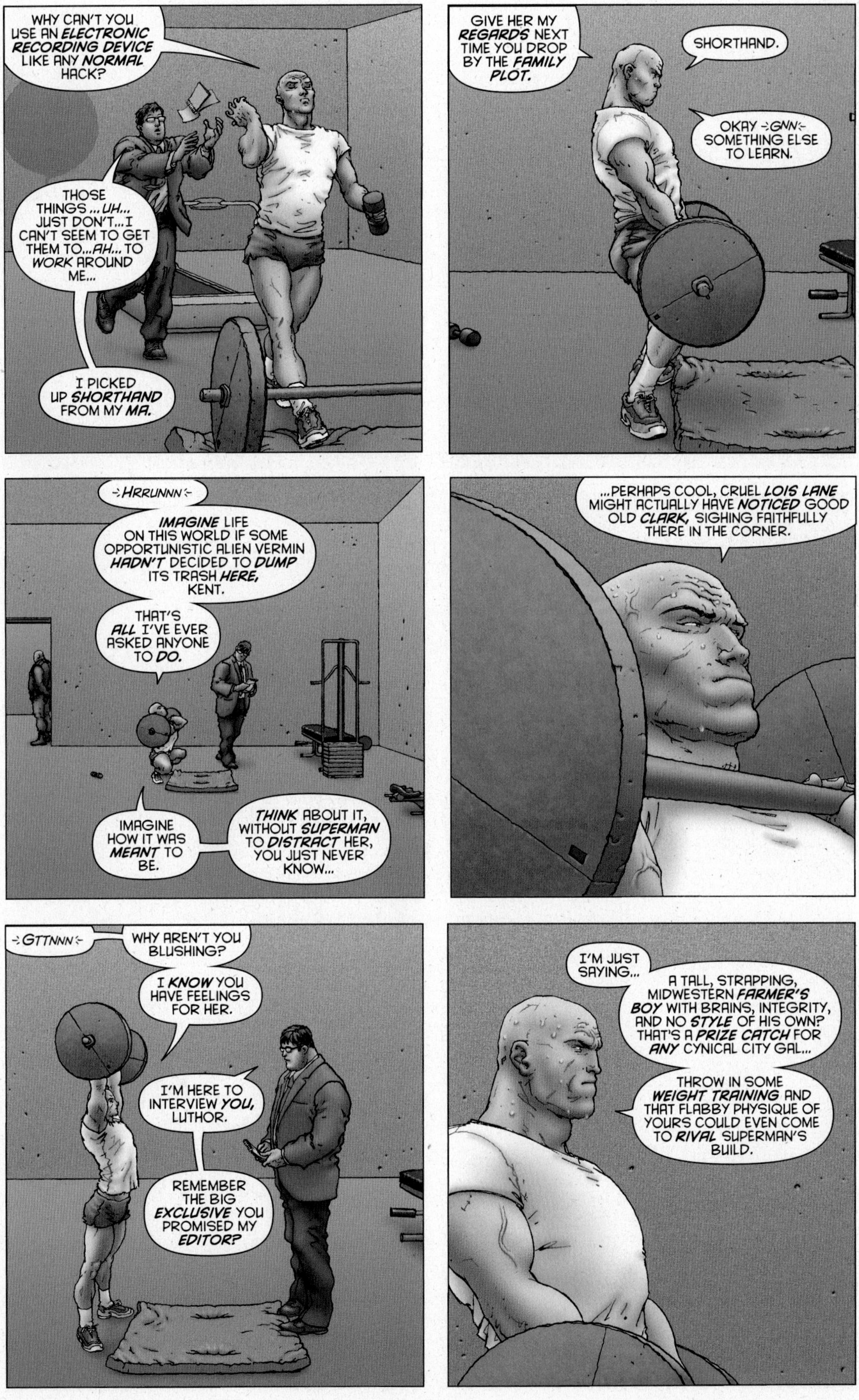
WHY CAN'T YOU USE AN ELECTRONIC RECORDING DEVICE LIKE ANY NORMAL HACK?
THOSE THINGS ... UH... JUST DON'T...I CAN'T SEEM TO GET THEM TO...AH... TO WORK AROUND ME...
I PICKED UP SHORTHAND FROM MY MA.
GIVE HER MY REGARDS NEXT TIME YOU DROP BY THE FAMILY PLOT.
SHORTHAND.
OKAY -GNN- SOMETHING ELSE TO LEARN.
-HRRUNNN-
IMAGINE LIFE ON THIS WORLD IF SOME OPPORTUNISTIC ALIEN VERMIN HADN'T DECIDED TO DUMP ITS TRASH HERE, KENT.
THAT'S ALL I'VE EVER ASKED ANYONE TO DO.
IMAGINE HOW IT WAS MEANT TO BE.
THINK ABOUT IT, WITHOUT SUPERMAN TO DISTRACT HER, YOU JUST NEVER KNOW...
...PERHAPS COOL, CRUEL LOIS LANE MIGHT ACTUALLY HAVE NOTICED GOOD OLD CLARK, SIGHING FAITHFULLY THERE IN THE CORNER.
-GTTNNN-
WHY AREN'T YOU BLUSHING?
I KNOW YOU HAVE FEELINGS FOR HER.
I'M HERE TO INTERVIEW YOU, LUTHOR.
REMEMBER THE BIG EXCLUSIVE YOU PROMISED MY EDITOR?
I'M JUST SAYING...
A TALL, STRAPPING, MIDWESTERN FARMER'S BOY WITH BRAINS, INTEGRITY, AND NO STYLE OF HIS OWN? THAT'S A PRIZE CATCH FOR ANY CYNICAL CITY GAL...
THROW IN SOME WEIGHT TRAINING AND THAT FLABBY PHYSIQUE OF YOURS COULD EVEN COME TO RIVAL SUPERMAN'S BUILD.

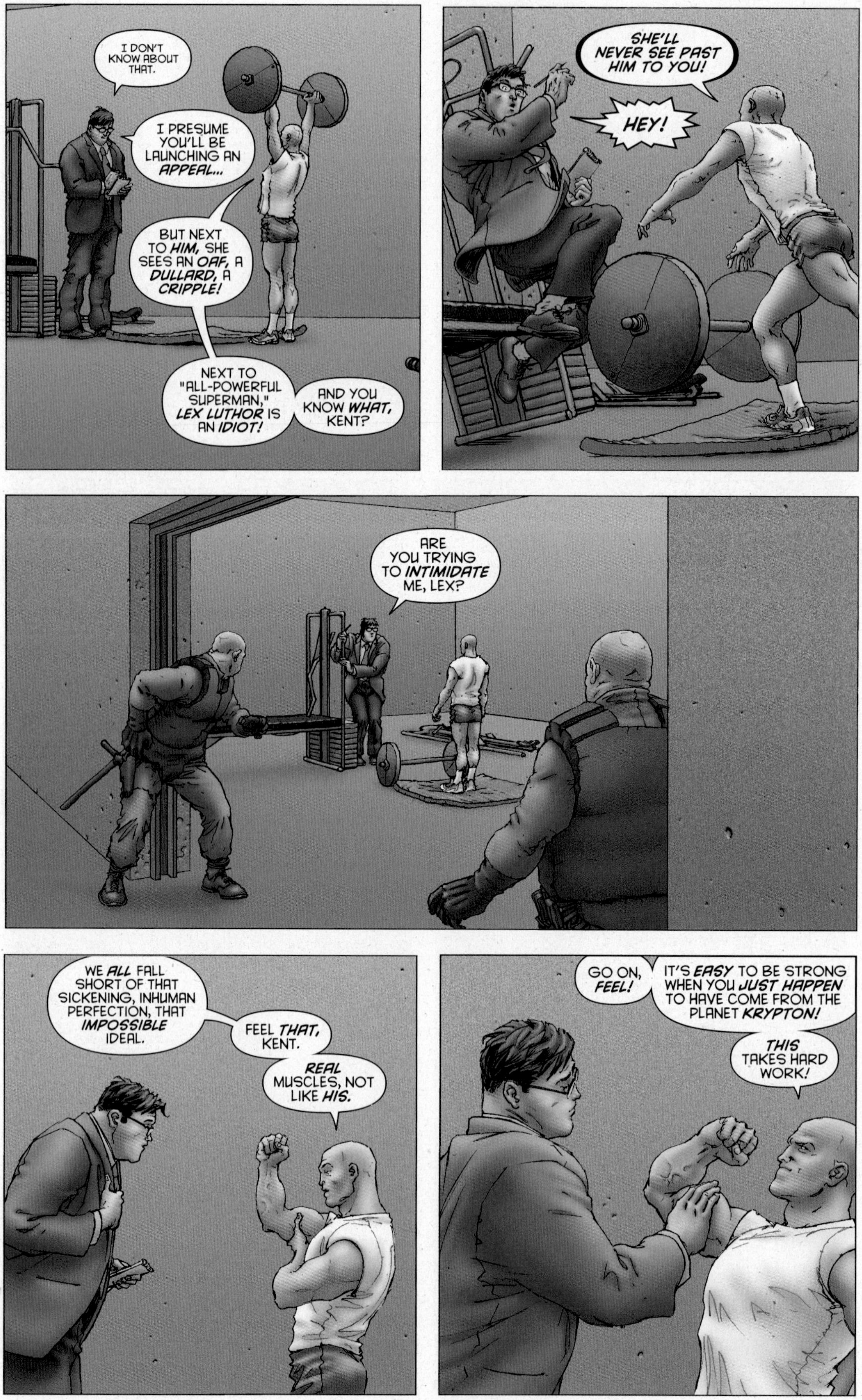
I DON'T KNOW ABOUT THAT.
I PRESUME YOU'LL BE LAUNCHING AN APPEAL...
BUT NEXT TO HIM, SHE SEES AN OAF, A DULLARD, A CRIPPLE!
NEXT TO "ALL-POWERFUL SUPERMAN," LEX LUTHOR IS AN IDIOT!
AND YOU KNOW WHAT, KENT?
SHE'LL NEVER SEE PAST HIM TO YOU!
HEY!
ARE YOU TRYING TO INTIMIDATE ME, LEX?
WE ALL FALL SHORT OF THAT SICKENING, INHUMAN PERFECTION, THAT IMPOSSIBLE IDEAL.
FEEL THAT, KENT.
REAL MUSCLES, NOT LIKE HIS.
GO ON, FEEL!
IT'S EASY TO BE STRONG WHEN YOU JUST HAPPEN TO HAVE COME FROM THE PLANET KRYPTON!
THIS TAKES HARD WORK!

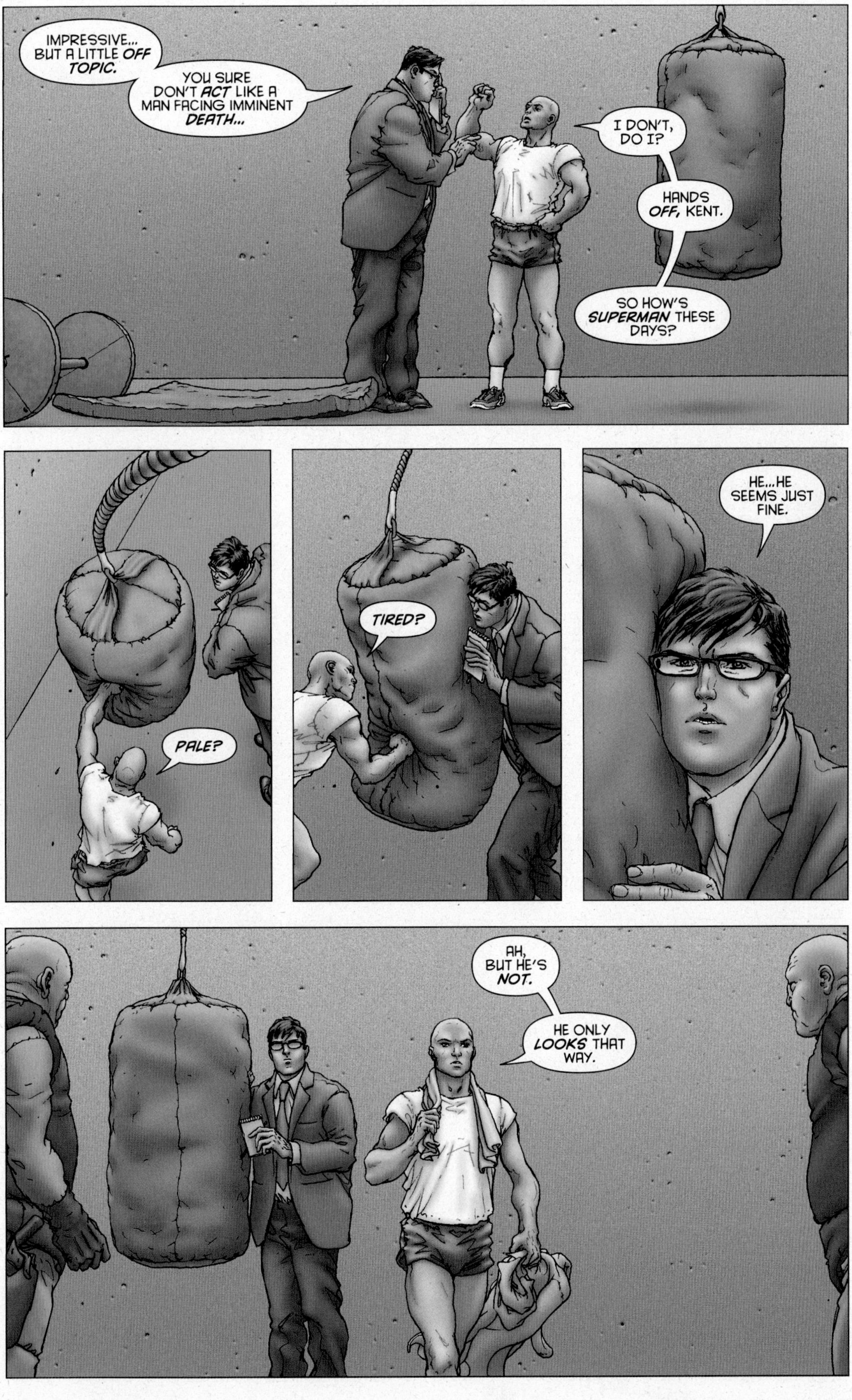
IMPRESSIVE... BUT A LITTLE *OFF* *TOPIC.*
YOU SURE DON'T *ACT* LIKE A MAN FACING IMMINENT *DEATH...*
I DON'T, DO I?
HANDS *OFF,* KENT.
SO HOW'S *SUPERMAN* THESE DAYS?
PALE?
TIRED?
HE...HE SEEMS JUST FINE.
AH, BUT HE'S *NOT.*
HE ONLY *LOOKS* THAT WAY.

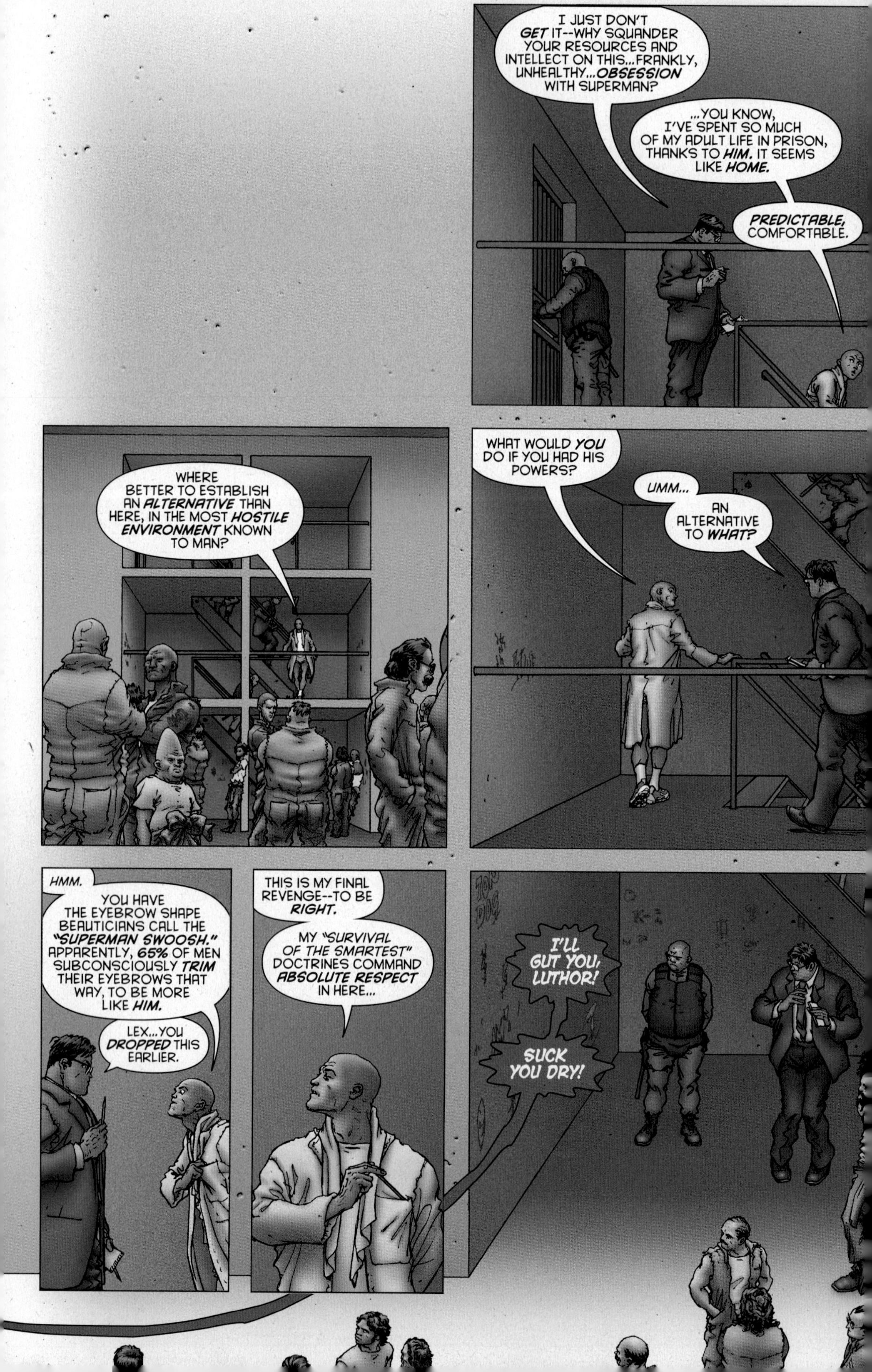
I JUST DON'T GET IT--WHY SQUANDER YOUR RESOURCES AND INTELLECT ON THIS...FRANKLY, UNHEALTHY...OBSESSION WITH SUPERMAN?
...YOU KNOW, I'VE SPENT SO MUCH OF MY ADULT LIFE IN PRISON, THANKS TO HIM. IT SEEMS LIKE HOME.
PREDICTABLE, COMFORTABLE.
WHERE BETTER TO ESTABLISH AN ALTERNATIVE THAN HERE, IN THE MOST HOSTILE ENVIRONMENT KNOWN TO MAN?
UMM...
AN ALTERNATIVE TO WHAT?
WHAT WOULD YOU DO IF YOU HAD HIS POWERS?
HMM.
YOU HAVE THE EYEBROW SHAPE BEAUTICIANS CALL THE "SUPERMAN SWOOSH." APPARENTLY, 65% OF MEN SUBCONSCIOUSLY TRIM THEIR EYEBROWS THAT WAY, TO BE MORE LIKE HIM.
LEX...YOU DROPPED THIS EARLIER.
THIS IS MY FINAL REVENGE--TO BE RIGHT.
MY "SURVIVAL OF THE SMARTEST" DOCTRINES COMMAND ABSOLUTE RESPECT IN HERE...
I'LL GUT YOU, LUTHOR!
SUCK YOU DRY!

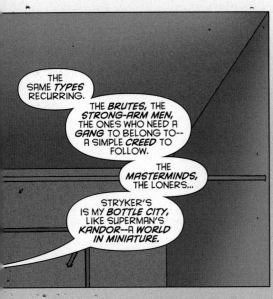

THE SAME *TYPES* RECURRING.

THE *BRUTES*, THE *STRONG-ARM MEN*, THE ONES WHO NEED A *GANG* TO BELONG TO-- A SIMPLE *CREED* TO FOLLOW.

THE *MASTERMINDS*, THE *LONERS*...

STRYKER'S IS MY *BOTTLE CITY*, LIKE SUPERMAN'S *KANDOR*--A *WORLD IN MINIATURE*.

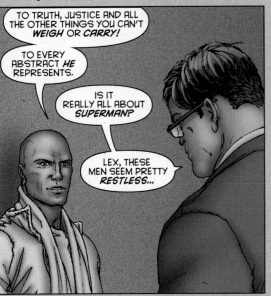

TO TRUTH, JUSTICE AND ALL THE OTHER THINGS YOU CAN'T *WEIGH* OR *CARRY*!

TO EVERY ABSTRACT *HE* REPRESENTS.

IS IT REALLY ALL ABOUT *SUPERMAN*?

LEX, THESE MEN SEEM PRETTY *RESTLESS*...

THEY CAN FEEL THE COMING *CHANGE*, THE WINGS OF A NEW HUMAN *RENAISSANCE*.

I'M TRANSFORMING THIS PLACE INTO A *NEW MODEL OF SOCIETY*, KENT, A BLUEPRINT FOR *UTOPIAN* LIVING!

IGNORE IT.

EVERY SOCIETY HAS ITS *MONSTERS*.

BUT THE *PARASITE* DOESN'T SCARE ME.

BRAIN BEATS *BRAWN*, EVERY TIME.

...THE PARASITE?

LUTHOR! YOU HEAR ME, LUTHOR?!

GUT YOU!

I'LL SHOW *HIM* WHO'S BOSS WHEN THE TIME COMES.

"PUNCH OUT THE BIG, UGLY ONES *FIRST*, LEX!" MY GRAMMA USED TO SAY!

THE *PARASITE*?

WAIT A MINUTE!

HE'S SAFE BEHIND *LEAD SHIELDING*, RIGHT?

OwwW!

POWER!

WHAT'S HAPPENING?!

MARLON, WHAT'S HE DOING?

MORE POWER THAN I EVER HAD!

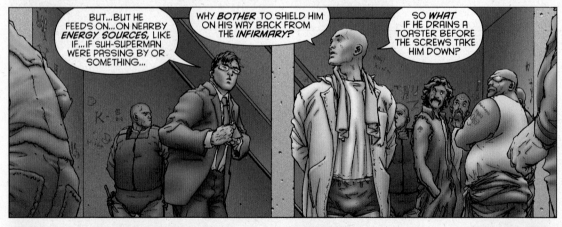

BUT...BUT HE FEEDS ON...ON NEARBY *ENERGY SOURCES*, LIKE IF...IF SUH-SUPERMAN WERE PASSING BY OR SOMETHING...

WHY *BOTHER* TO SHIELD HIM ON HIS WAY BACK FROM THE *INFIRMARY*?

SO *WHAT* IF HE DRAINS A TOASTER BEFORE THE SCREWS TAKE HIM DOWN?

WHAT'S THE *MATTER*, KENT?

SCARED HE'LL ABSORB *YOUR* LAST RESERVES OF *COWARDICE*?

UNHH

CAN'T LET HIM TOUCH ME...I NEED TO GET OUT OF HERE.

EVERYTHING *OKAY*, MISTER KENT?

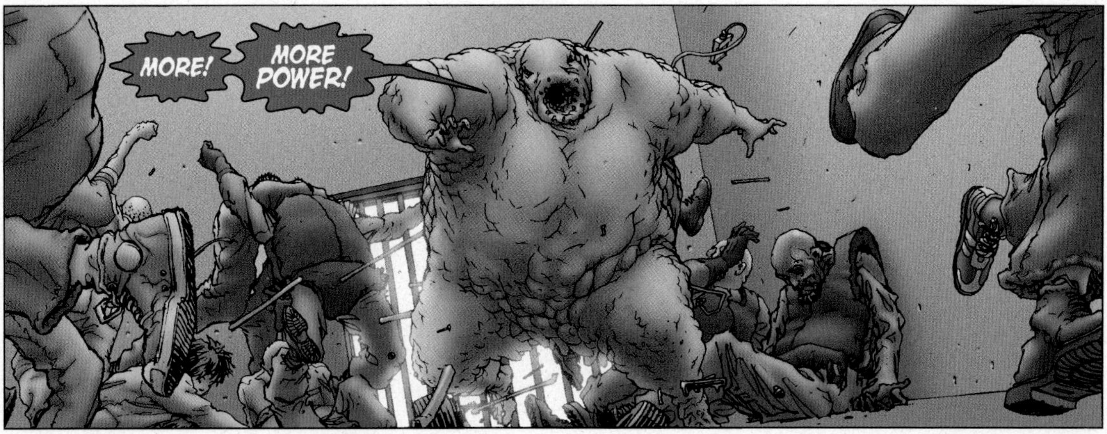
MORE!
MORE POWER!

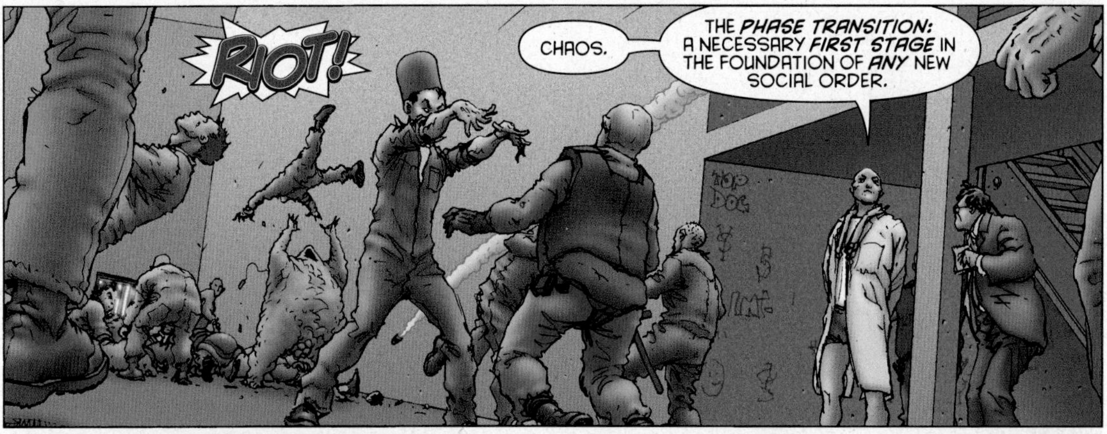
RIOT!
CHAOS.
THE *PHASE TRANSITION:* A NECESSARY *FIRST STAGE* IN THE FOUNDATION OF *ANY* NEW SOCIAL ORDER.
TOP DOG

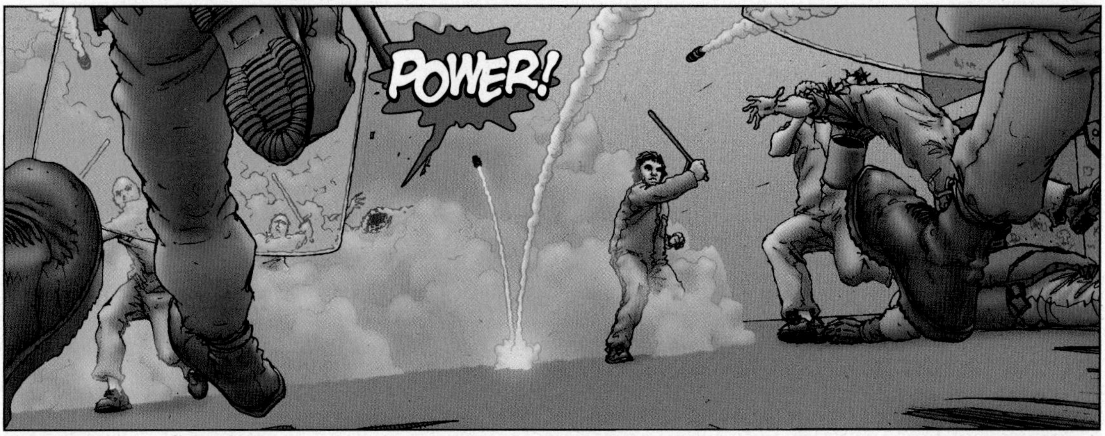
POWER!

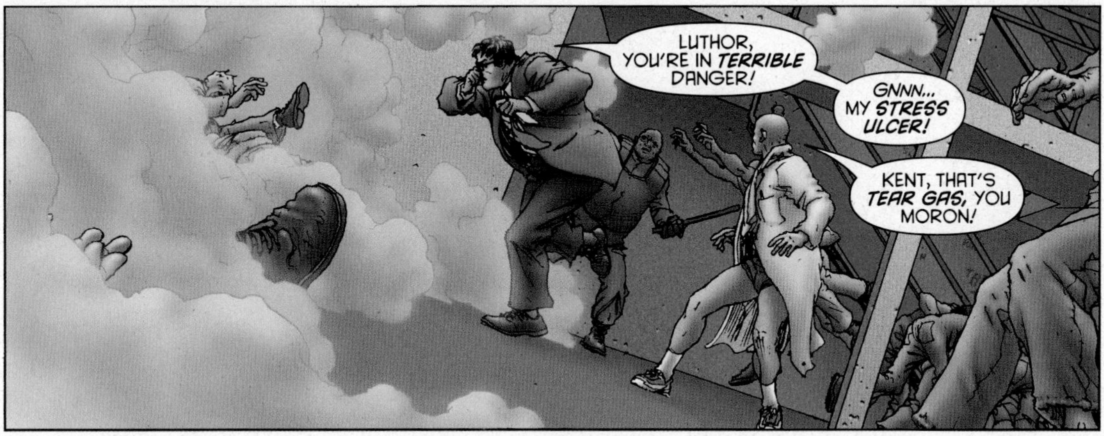
LUTHOR, YOU'RE IN *TERRIBLE* DANGER!
GNNN... MY *STRESS ULCER!*
KENT, THAT'S *TEAR GAS,* YOU MORON!

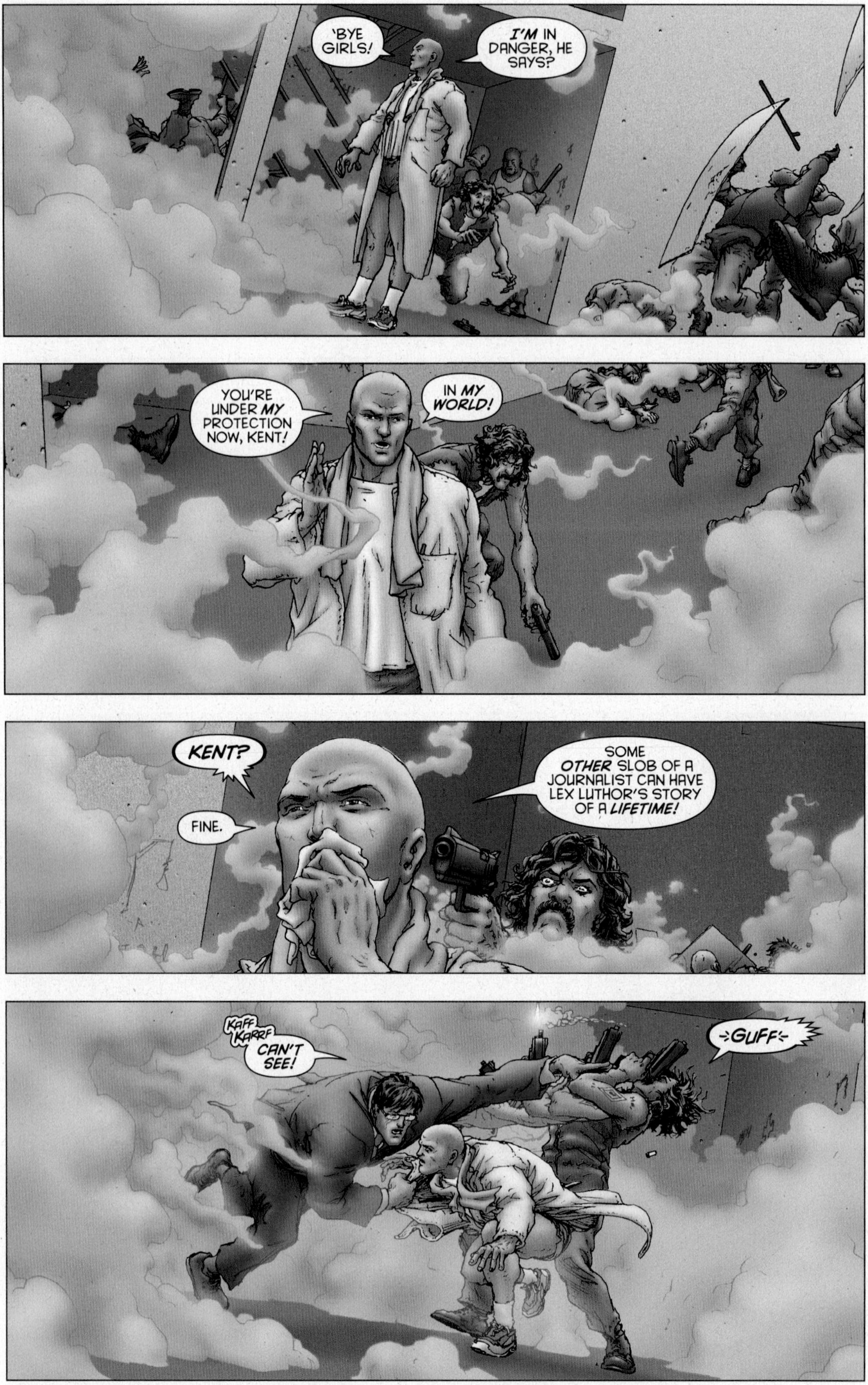
'BYE GIRLS!
I'M IN DANGER, HE SAYS?
YOU'RE UNDER MY PROTECTION NOW, KENT!
IN MY WORLD!
KENT?
FINE.
SOME OTHER SLOB OF A JOURNALIST CAN HAVE LEX LUTHOR'S STORY OF A LIFETIME!
KAFF KARRF CAN'T SEE!
-GUFF-

SIR.

SUPERMAN.

HOW DID WE GET OUT HERE?

WHAT JUST HAPPENED...?

THAT COULD HAVE BEEN *MY* SKULL, KENT, YOU OAF!

THIS WAY!

UH-OH.

I SAID *FOLLOW ME,* KENT, IF YOU WANT TO LIVE!

NEVER *MIND* YOUR GLASSES!

BUT I CAN'T *SEE* WITHOUT THEM.

EVERYTHING'S A COMPLETE BLUR.

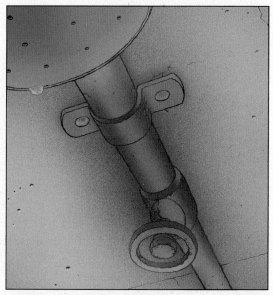

RUN!

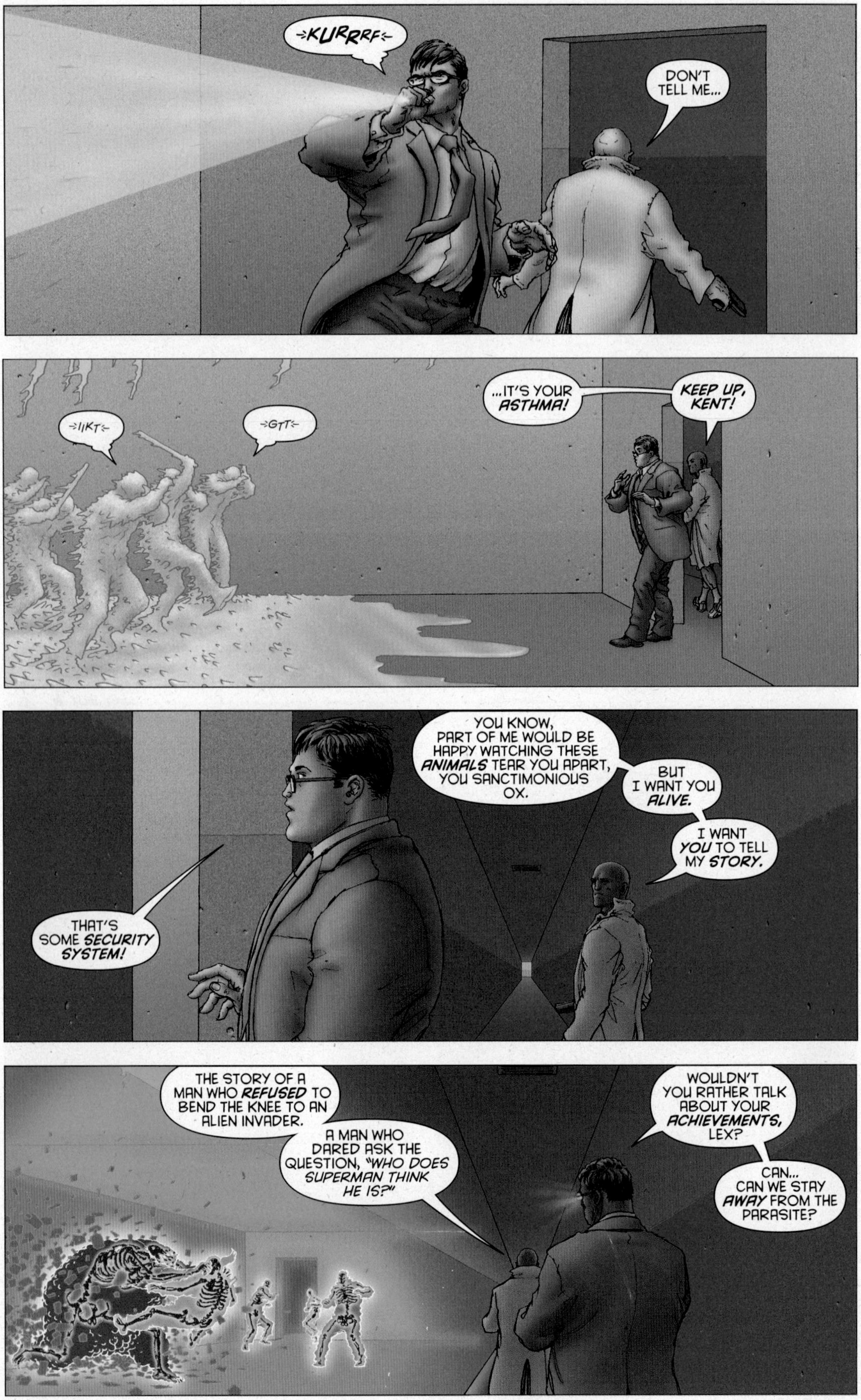

KURRRF
DON'T TELL ME...
...IT'S YOUR ASTHMA!
KEEP UP, KENT!
IIKT
GTT
YOU KNOW, PART OF ME WOULD BE HAPPY WATCHING THESE ANIMALS TEAR YOU APART, YOU SANCTIMONIOUS OX.
BUT I WANT YOU ALIVE.
I WANT YOU TO TELL MY STORY.
THAT'S SOME SECURITY SYSTEM!
THE STORY OF A MAN WHO REFUSED TO BEND THE KNEE TO AN ALIEN INVADER.
A MAN WHO DARED ASK THE QUESTION, "WHO DOES SUPERMAN THINK HE IS?"
WOULDN'T YOU RATHER TALK ABOUT YOUR ACHIEVEMENTS, LEX?
CAN... CAN WE STAY AWAY FROM THE PARASITE?

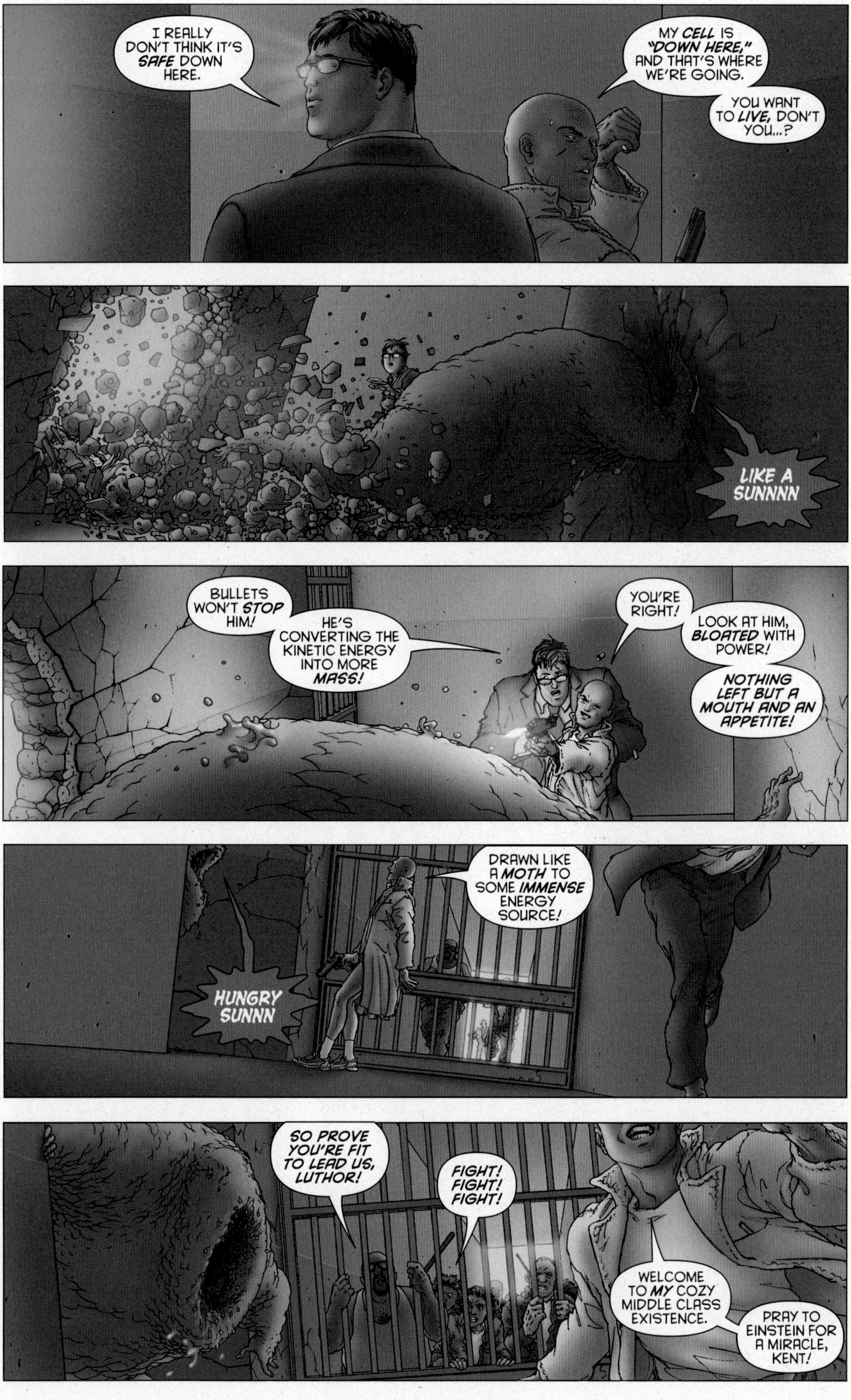

I REALLY DON'T THINK IT'S SAFE DOWN HERE.
MY CELL IS "DOWN HERE," AND THAT'S WHERE WE'RE GOING.
YOU WANT TO LIVE, DON'T YOU...?
LIKE A SUNNNN
BULLETS WON'T STOP HIM!
HE'S CONVERTING THE KINETIC ENERGY INTO MORE MASS!
YOU'RE RIGHT!
LOOK AT HIM, BLOATED WITH POWER!
NOTHING LEFT BUT A MOUTH AND AN APPETITE!
DRAWN LIKE A MOTH TO SOME IMMENSE ENERGY SOURCE!
HUNGRY SUNNN
SO PROVE YOU'RE FIT TO LEAD US, LUTHOR!
FIGHT! FIGHT! FIGHT!
WELCOME TO MY COZY MIDDLE CLASS EXISTENCE.
PRAY TO EINSTEIN FOR A MIRACLE, KENT!

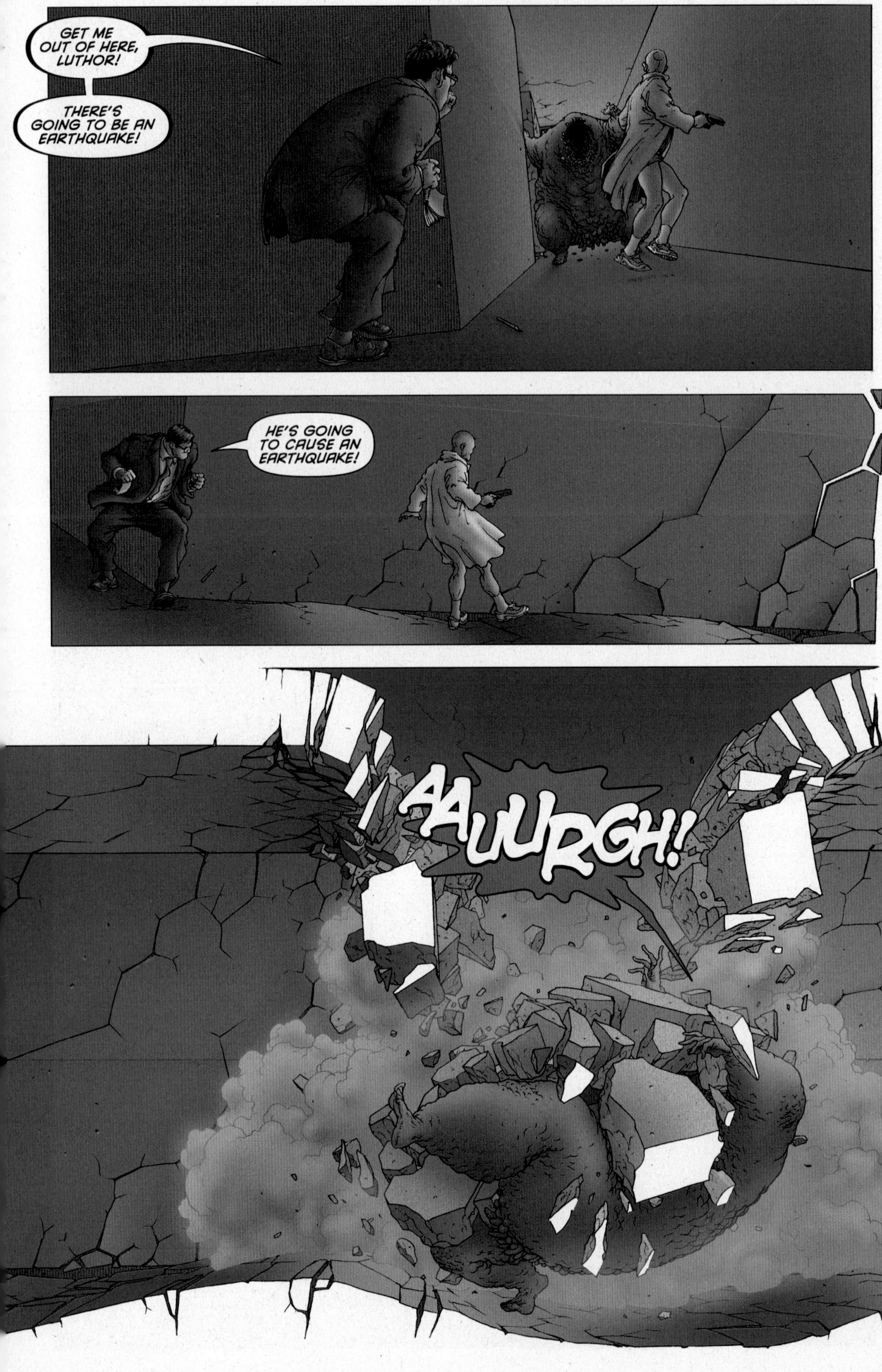
GET ME OUT OF HERE, LUTHOR!
THERE'S GOING TO BE AN EARTHQUAKE!
HE'S GOING TO CAUSE AN EARTHQUAKE!
AAUURGH!

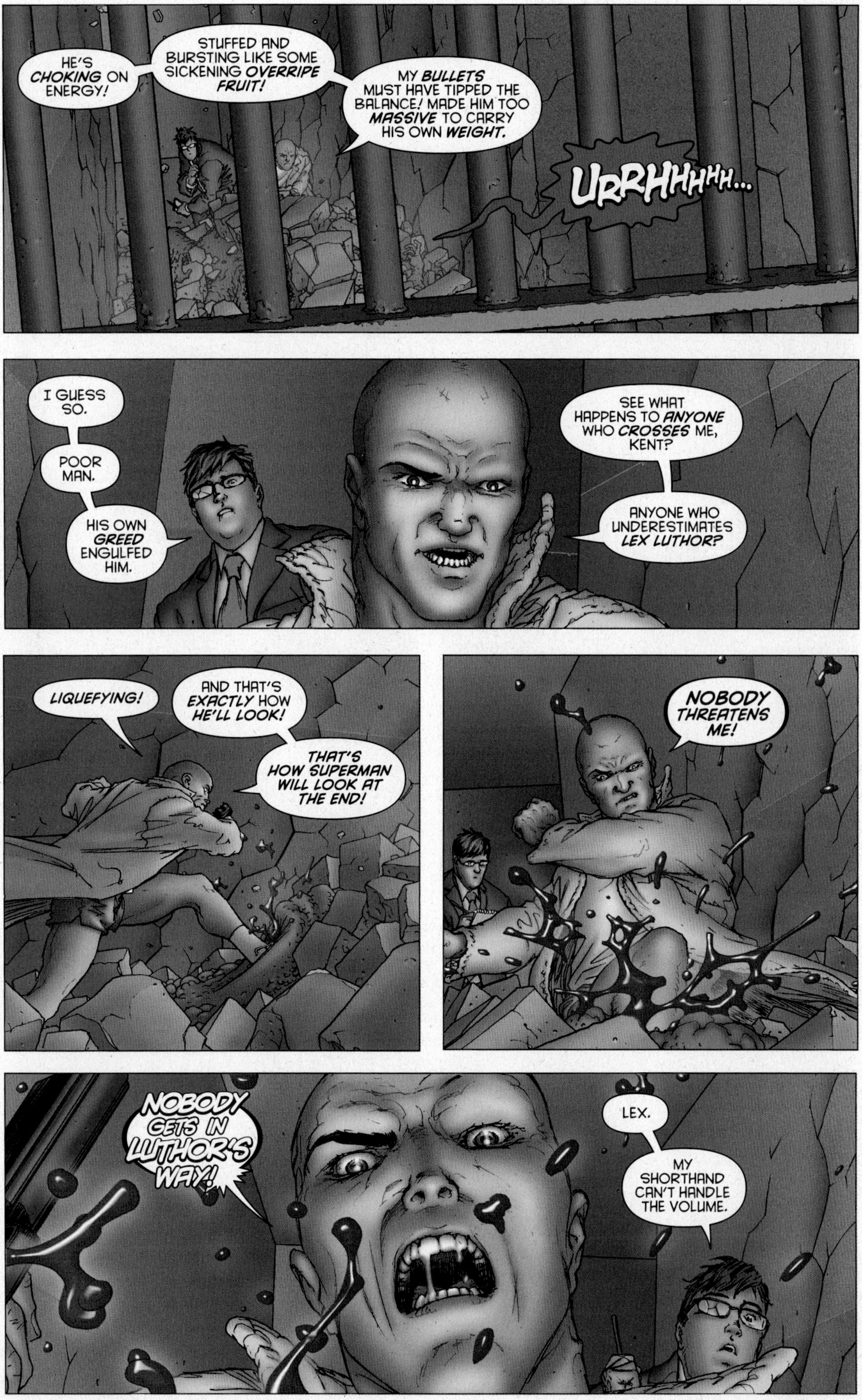

HE'S CHOKING ON ENERGY!
STUFFED AND BURSTING LIKE SOME SICKENING OVERRIPE FRUIT!
MY BULLETS MUST HAVE TIPPED THE BALANCE! MADE HIM TOO MASSIVE TO CARRY HIS OWN WEIGHT.
URRHHHHH...
I GUESS SO.
POOR MAN.
HIS OWN GREED ENGULFED HIM.
SEE WHAT HAPPENS TO ANYONE WHO CROSSES ME, KENT?
ANYONE WHO UNDERESTIMATES LEX LUTHOR?
LIQUEFYING!
AND THAT'S EXACTLY HOW HE'LL LOOK!
THAT'S HOW SUPERMAN WILL LOOK AT THE END!
NOBODY THREATENS ME!
NOBODY GETS IN LUTHOR'S WAY!
LEX.
MY SHORTHAND CAN'T HANDLE THE VOLUME.

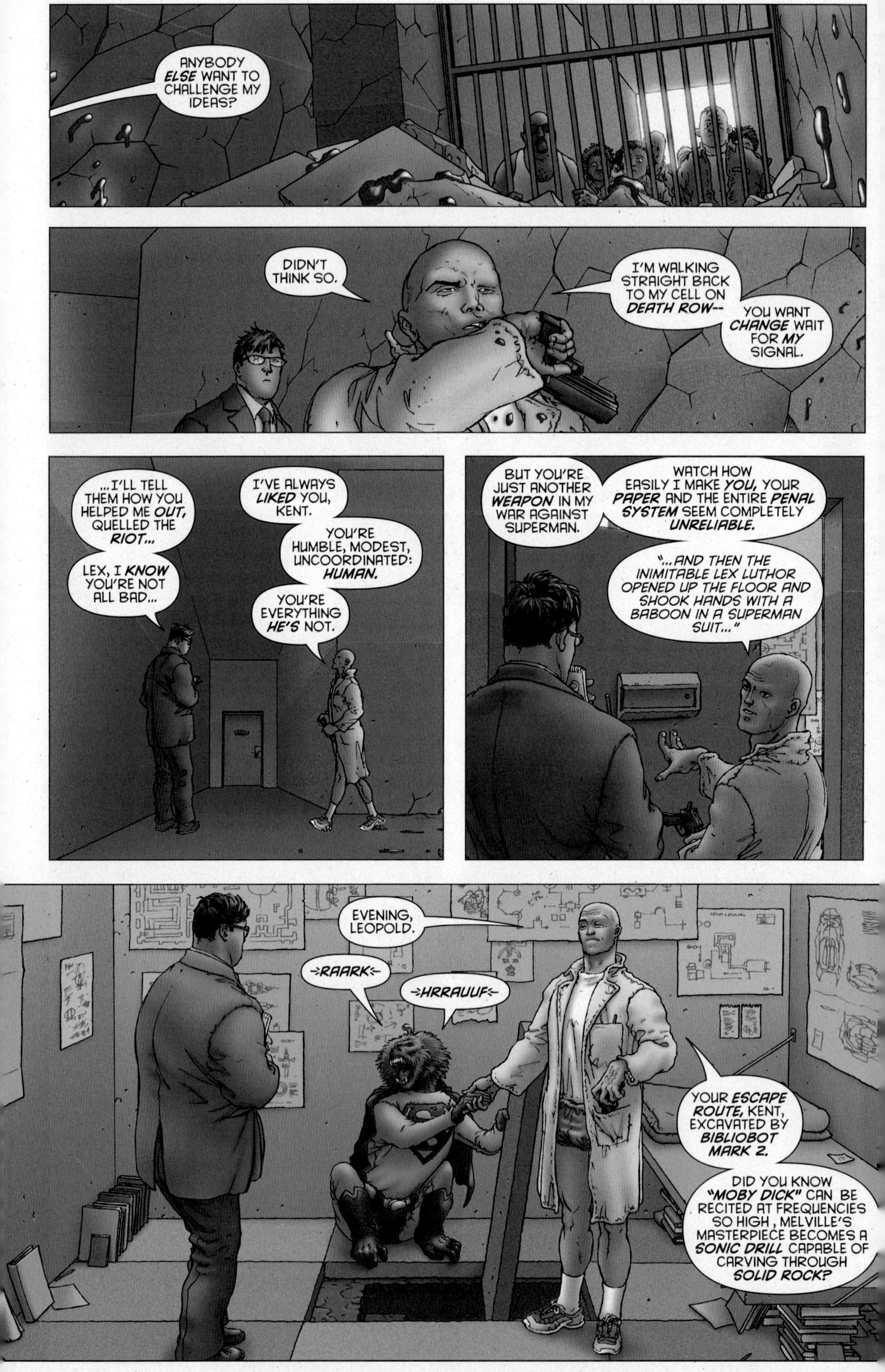
ANYBODY ELSE WANT TO CHALLENGE MY IDEAS?
DIDN'T THINK SO.
I'M WALKING STRAIGHT BACK TO MY CELL ON DEATH ROW--
YOU WANT CHANGE WAIT FOR MY SIGNAL.
...I'LL TELL THEM HOW YOU HELPED ME OUT, QUELLED THE RIOT...
LEX, I KNOW YOU'RE NOT ALL BAD...
I'VE ALWAYS LIKED YOU, KENT.
YOU'RE HUMBLE, MODEST, UNCOORDINATED: HUMAN.
YOU'RE EVERYTHING HE'S NOT.
BUT YOU'RE JUST ANOTHER WEAPON IN MY WAR AGAINST SUPERMAN.
WATCH HOW EASILY I MAKE YOU, YOUR PAPER AND THE ENTIRE PENAL SYSTEM SEEM COMPLETELY UNRELIABLE.
"...AND THEN THE INIMITABLE LEX LUTHOR OPENED UP THE FLOOR AND SHOOK HANDS WITH A BABOON IN A SUPERMAN SUIT..."
EVENING, LEOPOLD.
RAARK
HRRAUUF
YOUR ESCAPE ROUTE, KENT, EXCAVATED BY BIBLIOBOT MARK 2.
DID YOU KNOW "MOBY DICK" CAN BE RECITED AT FREQUENCIES SO HIGH, MELVILLE'S MASTERPIECE BECOMES A SONIC DRILL CAPABLE OF CARVING THROUGH SOLID ROCK?

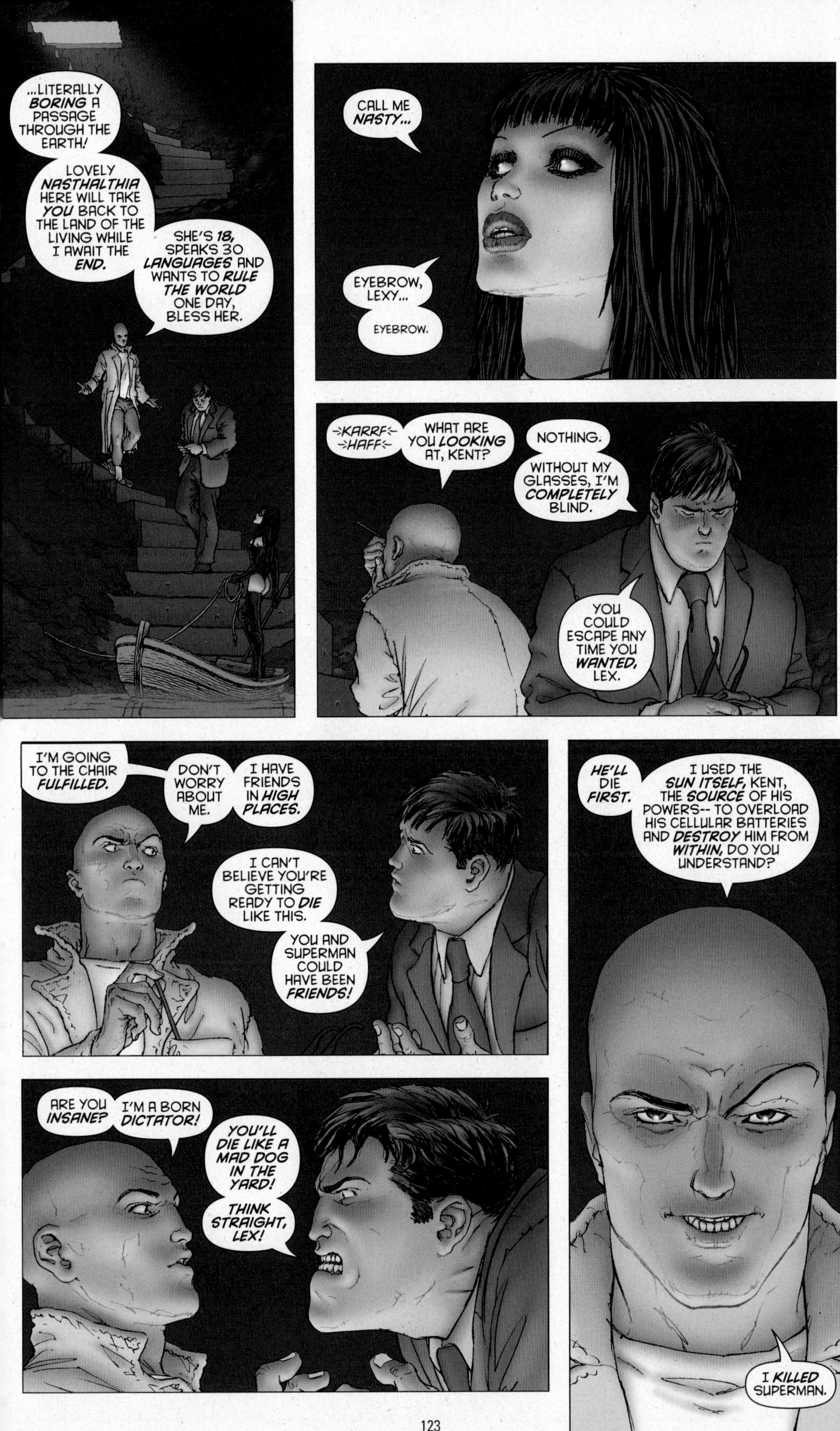
...LITERALLY BORING A PASSAGE THROUGH THE EARTH!
LOVELY NASTHALTHIA HERE WILL TAKE YOU BACK TO THE LAND OF THE LIVING WHILE I AWAIT THE END.
SHE'S 18, SPEAKS 30 LANGUAGES AND WANTS TO RULE THE WORLD ONE DAY, BLESS HER.
CALL ME NASTY...
EYEBROW, LEXY...
EYEBROW.
-KARRF-
-HAFF-
WHAT ARE YOU LOOKING AT, KENT?
NOTHING.
WITHOUT MY GLASSES, I'M COMPLETELY BLIND.
YOU COULD ESCAPE ANY TIME YOU WANTED, LEX.
I'M GOING TO THE CHAIR FULFILLED.
DON'T WORRY ABOUT ME.
I HAVE FRIENDS IN HIGH PLACES.
I CAN'T BELIEVE YOU'RE GETTING READY TO DIE LIKE THIS.
YOU AND SUPERMAN COULD HAVE BEEN FRIENDS!
ARE YOU INSANE?
I'M A BORN DICTATOR!
YOU'LL DIE LIKE A MAD DOG IN THE YARD!
THINK STRAIGHT, LEX!
HE'LL DIE FIRST.
I USED THE SUN ITSELF, KENT, THE SOURCE OF HIS POWERS-- TO OVERLOAD HIS CELLULAR BATTERIES AND DESTROY HIM FROM WITHIN, DO YOU UNDERSTAND?
I KILLED SUPERMAN.

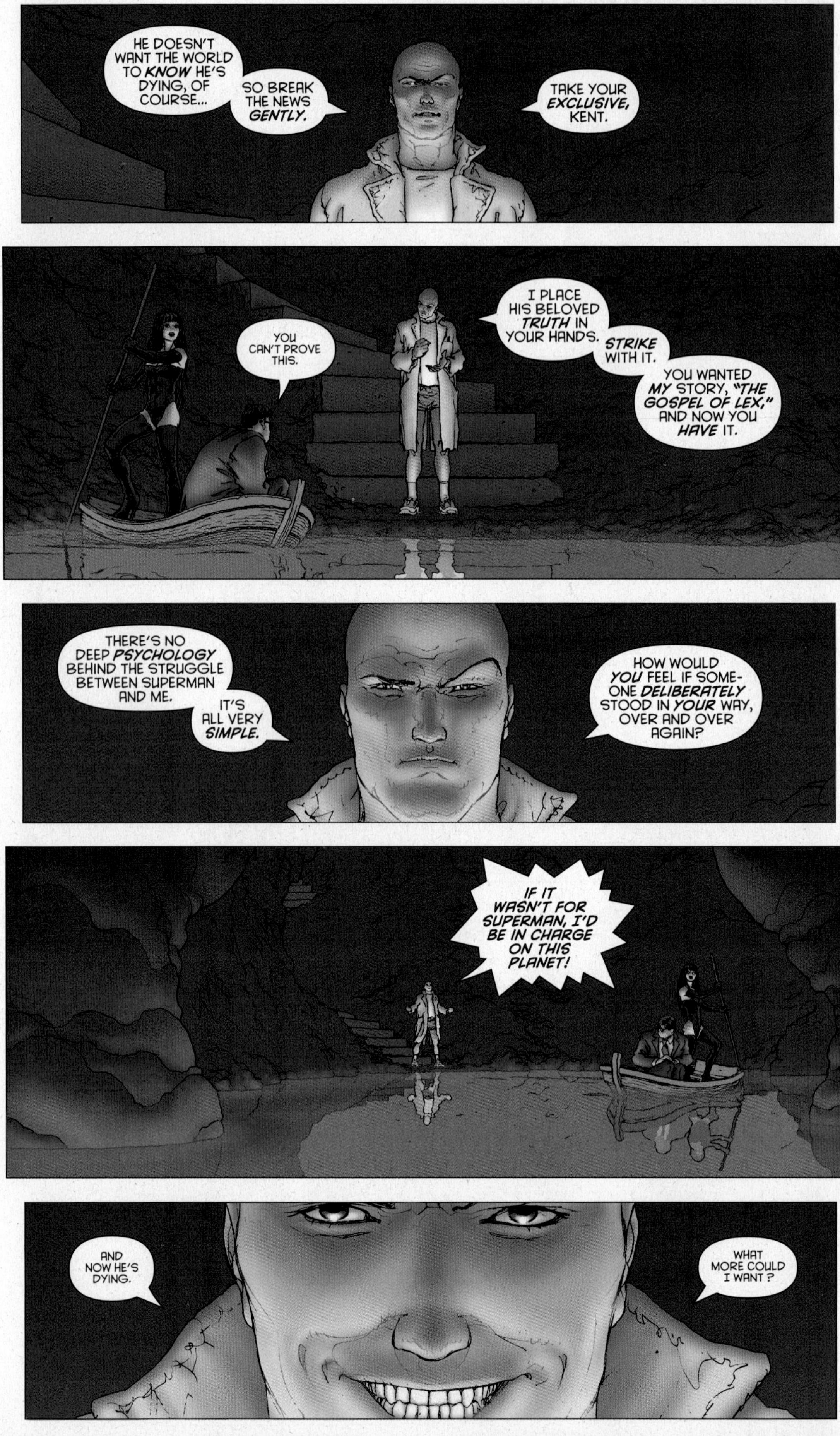
HE DOESN'T WANT THE WORLD TO KNOW HE'S DYING, OF COURSE...
SO BREAK THE NEWS GENTLY.
TAKE YOUR EXCLUSIVE, KENT.
YOU CAN'T PROVE THIS.
I PLACE HIS BELOVED TRUTH IN YOUR HANDS.
STRIKE WITH IT.
YOU WANTED MY STORY, "THE GOSPEL OF LEX," AND NOW YOU HAVE IT.
THERE'S NO DEEP PSYCHOLOGY BEHIND THE STRUGGLE BETWEEN SUPERMAN AND ME.
IT'S ALL VERY SIMPLE.
HOW WOULD YOU FEEL IF SOME-ONE DELIBERATELY STOOD IN YOUR WAY, OVER AND OVER AGAIN?
IF IT WASN'T FOR SUPERMAN, I'D BE IN CHARGE ON THIS PLANET!
AND NOW HE'S DYING.
WHAT MORE COULD I WANT ?

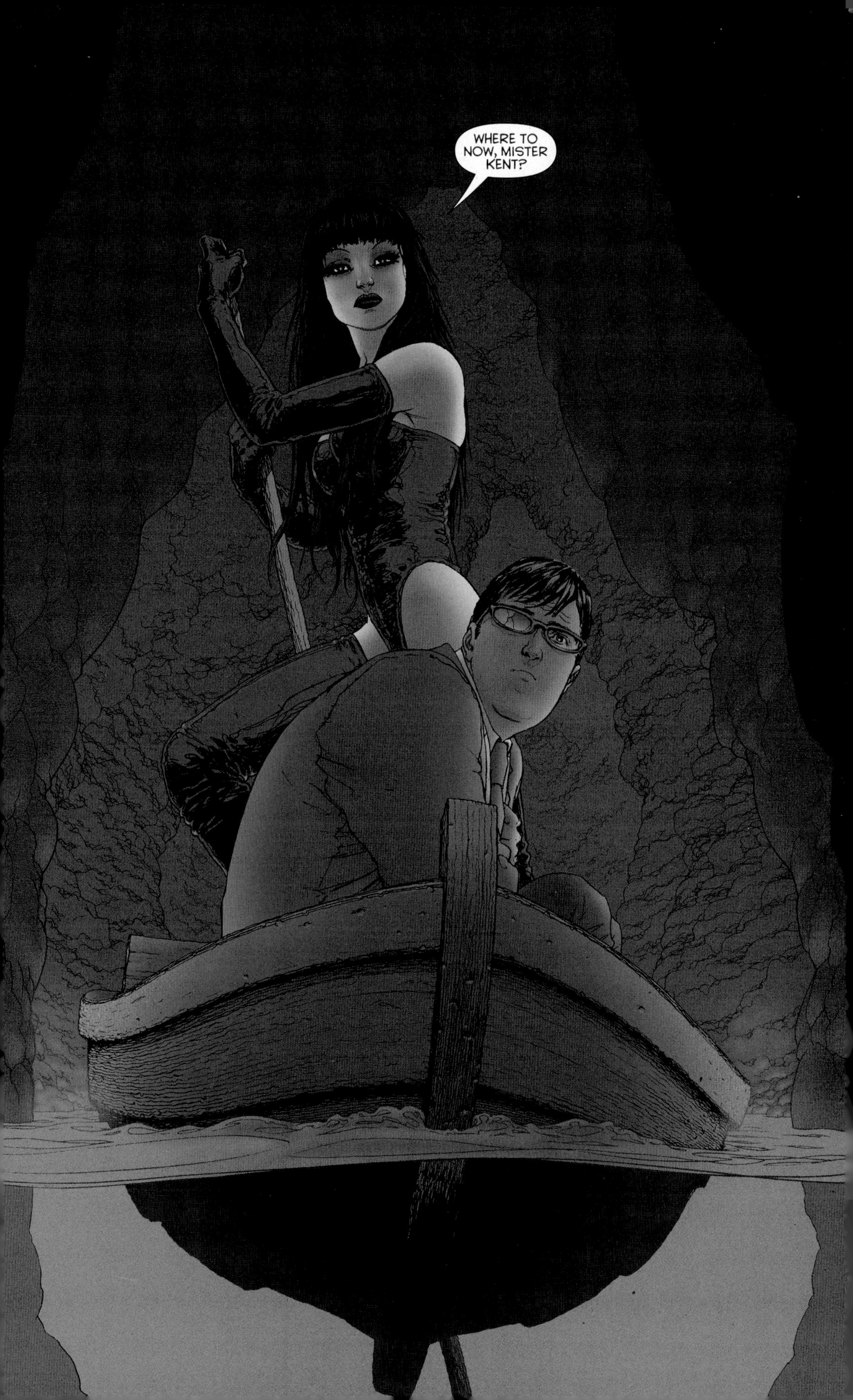
WHERE TO NOW, MISTER KENT?

Episode 6

FUNERAL IN SMALLVILLE

Cover FRANK QUITELY

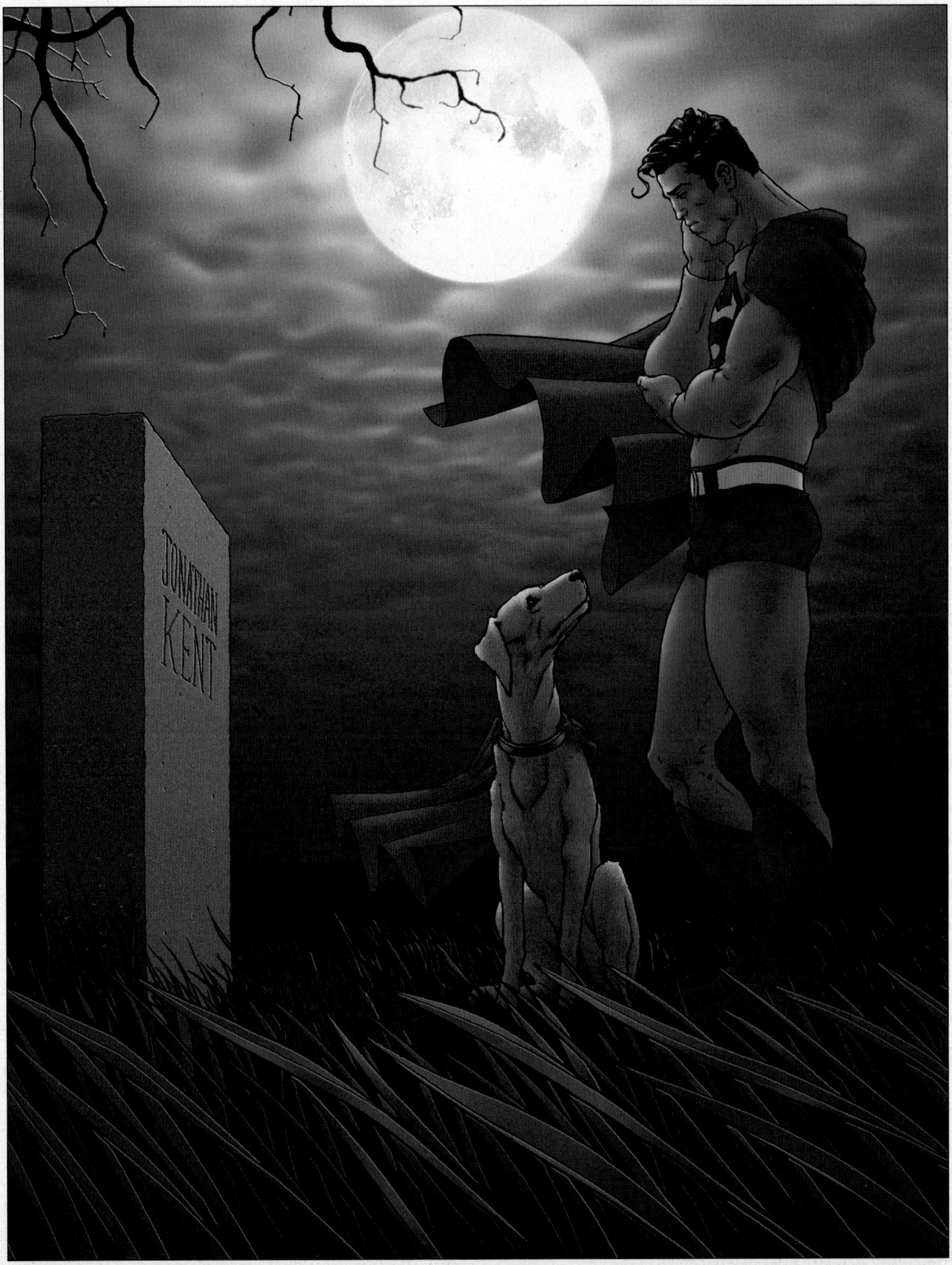
JONATHAN
KENT

6

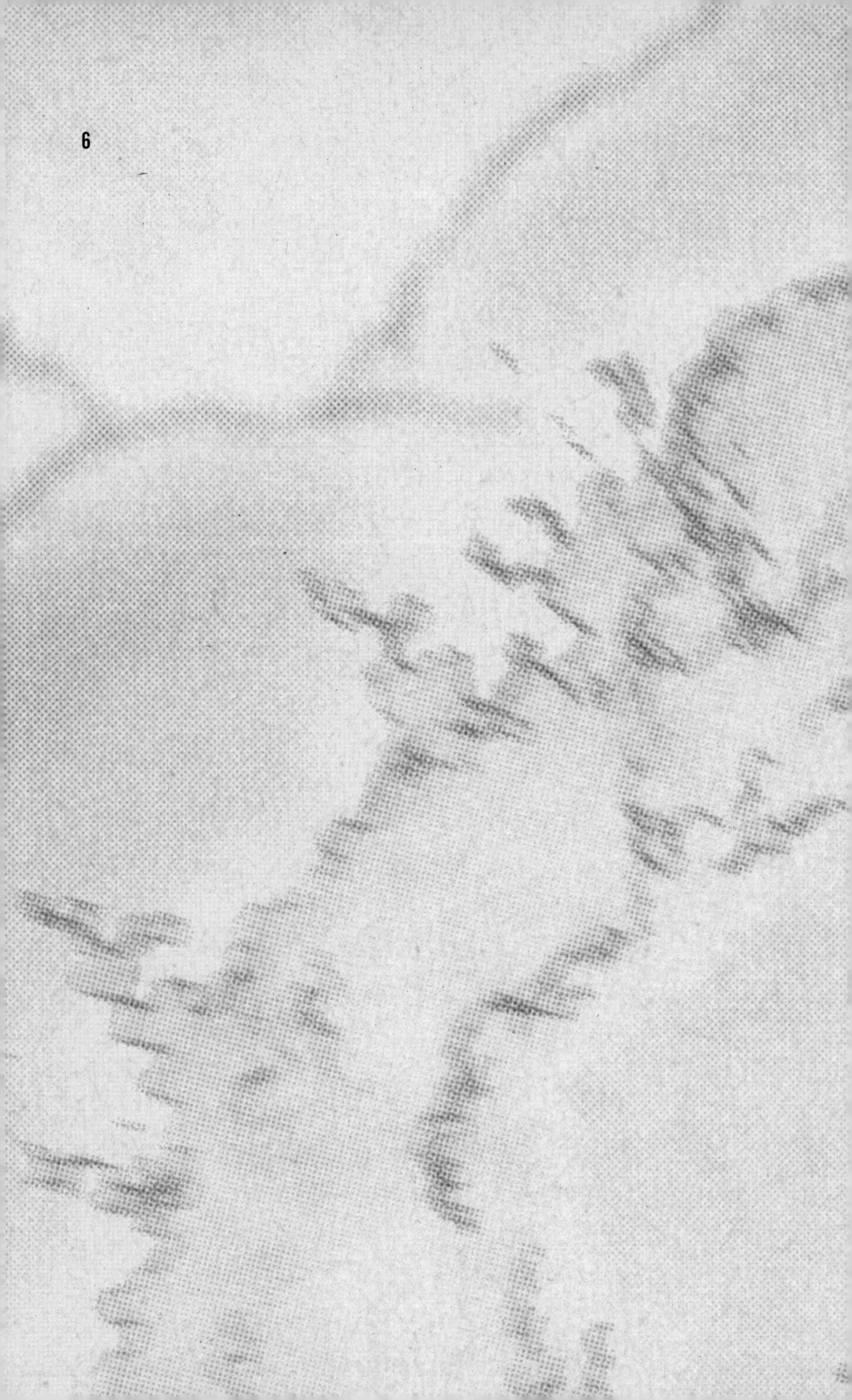

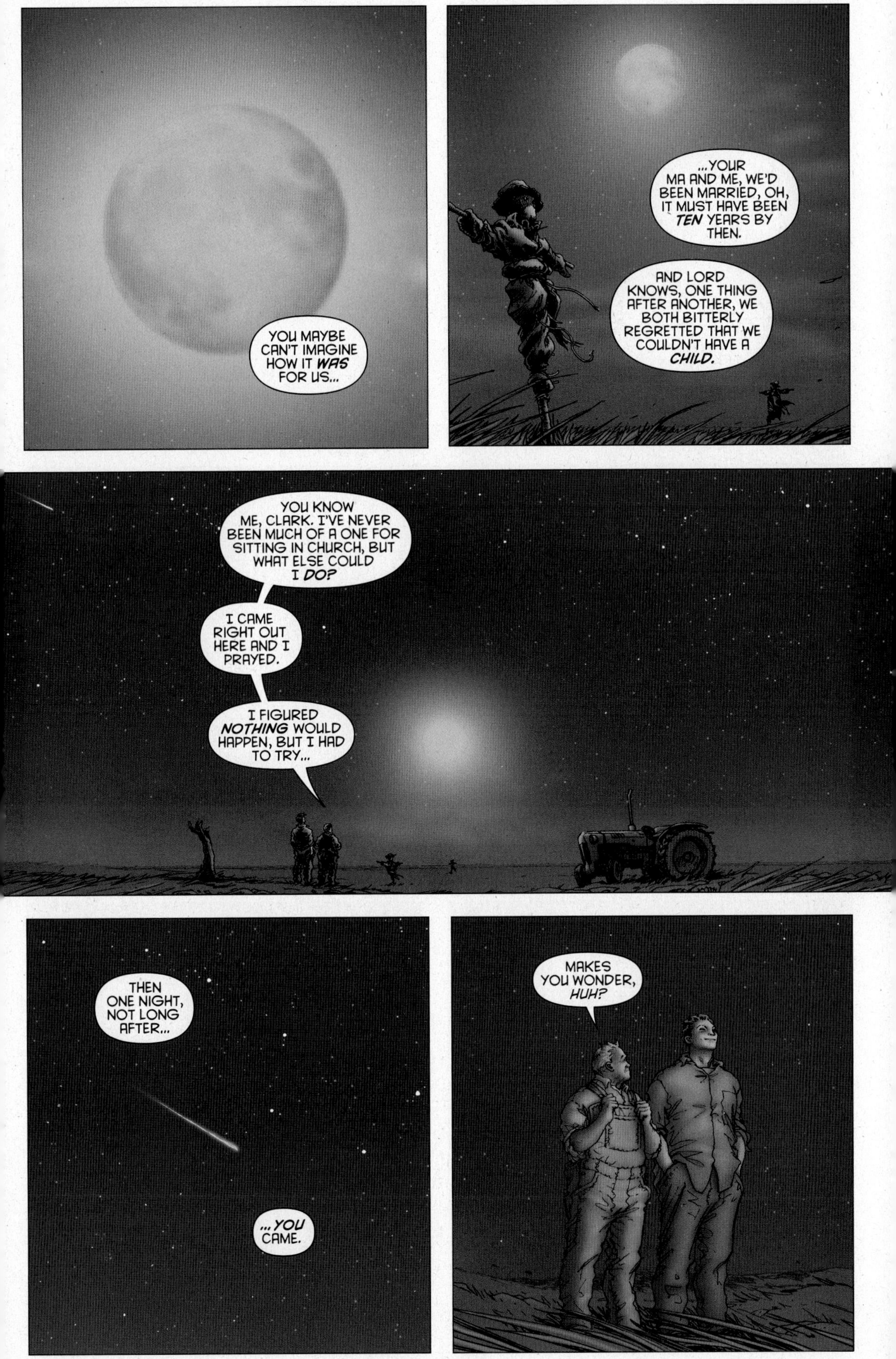
YOU MAYBE CAN'T IMAGINE HOW IT *WAS* FOR US...
...YOUR MA AND ME, WE'D BEEN MARRIED, OH, IT MUST HAVE BEEN *TEN* YEARS BY THEN.
AND LORD KNOWS, ONE THING AFTER ANOTHER, WE BOTH BITTERLY REGRETTED THAT WE COULDN'T HAVE A *CHILD.*
YOU KNOW ME, CLARK. I'VE NEVER BEEN MUCH OF A ONE FOR SITTING IN CHURCH, BUT WHAT ELSE COULD I *DO?*
I CAME RIGHT OUT HERE AND I PRAYED.
I FIGURED *NOTHING* WOULD HAPPEN, BUT I HAD TO TRY...
THEN ONE NIGHT, NOT LONG AFTER...
...*YOU* CAME.
MAKES YOU WONDER, *HUH?*

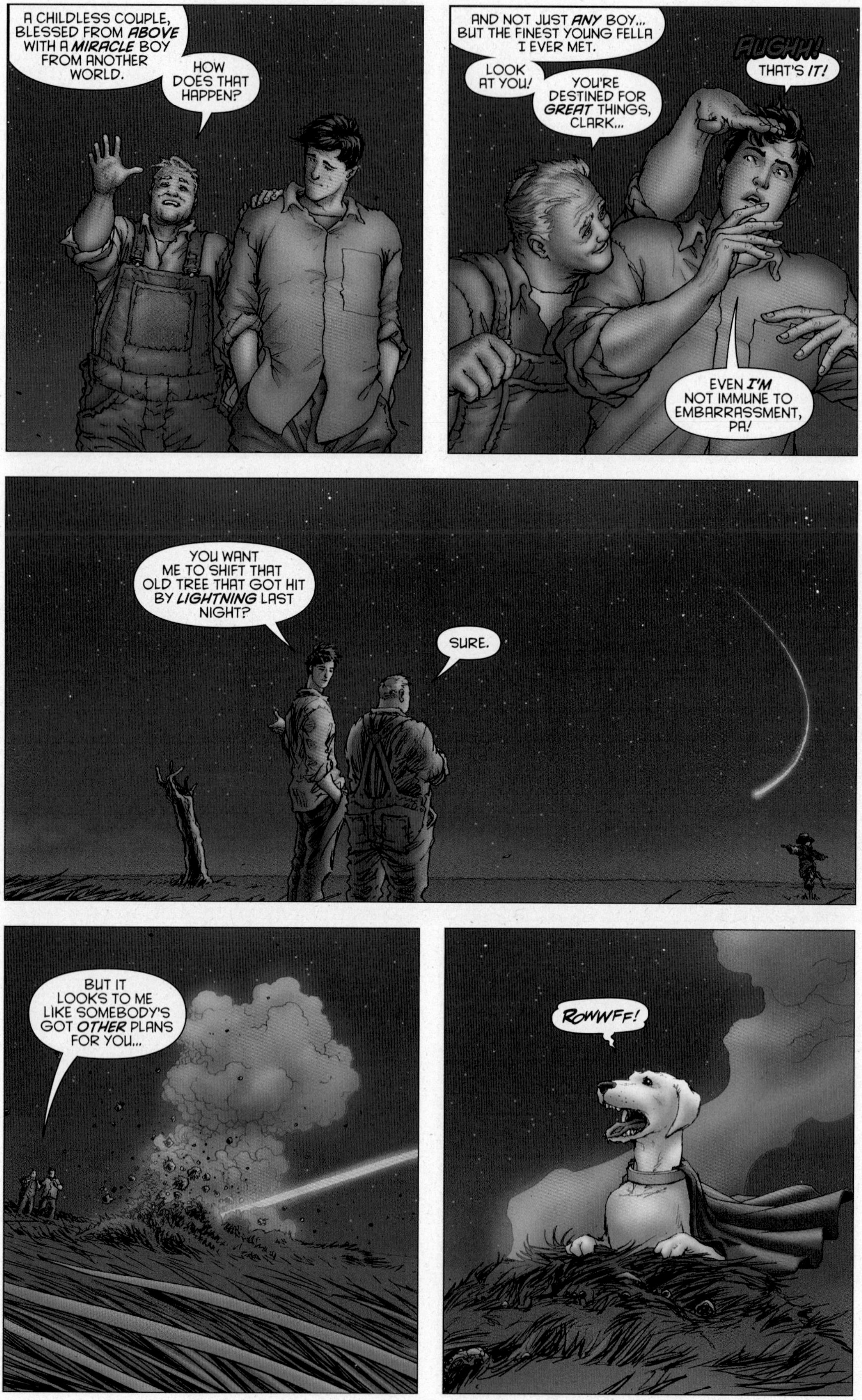
A CHILDLESS COUPLE, BLESSED FROM ABOVE WITH A MIRACLE BOY FROM ANOTHER WORLD.
HOW DOES THAT HAPPEN?
AND NOT JUST ANY BOY... BUT THE FINEST YOUNG FELLA I EVER MET.
LOOK AT YOU!
YOU'RE DESTINED FOR GREAT THINGS, CLARK...
AUGHH!
THAT'S IT!
EVEN I'M NOT IMMUNE TO EMBARRASSMENT, PA!
YOU WANT ME TO SHIFT THAT OLD TREE THAT GOT HIT BY LIGHTNING LAST NIGHT?
SURE.
BUT IT LOOKS TO ME LIKE SOMEBODY'S GOT OTHER PLANS FOR YOU...
ROWWFF!

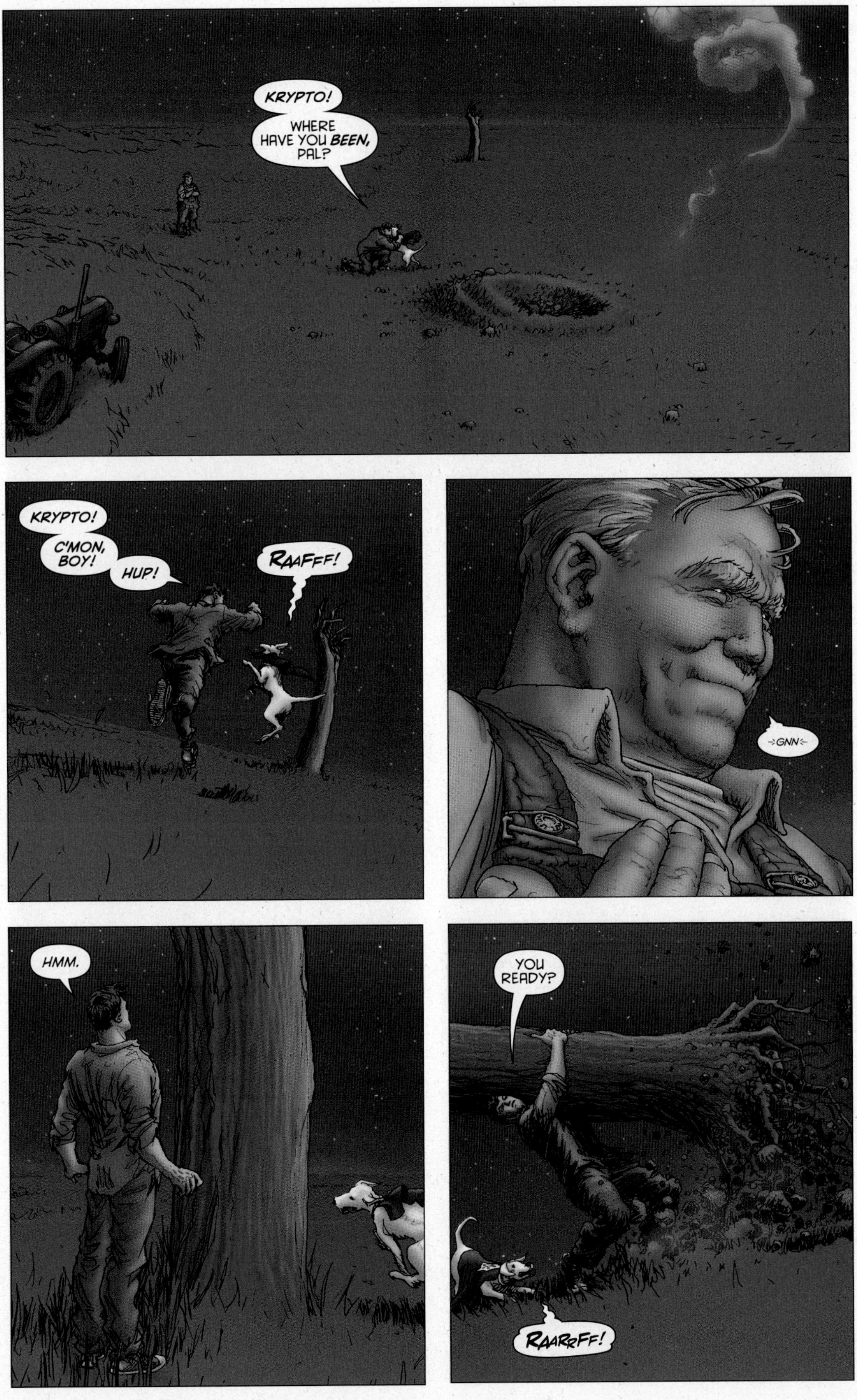
KRYPTO!
WHERE HAVE YOU BEEN, PAL?
KRYPTO!
C'MON, BOY!
HUP!
RAAFFF!
GNN
HMM.
YOU READY?
RAARRFF!

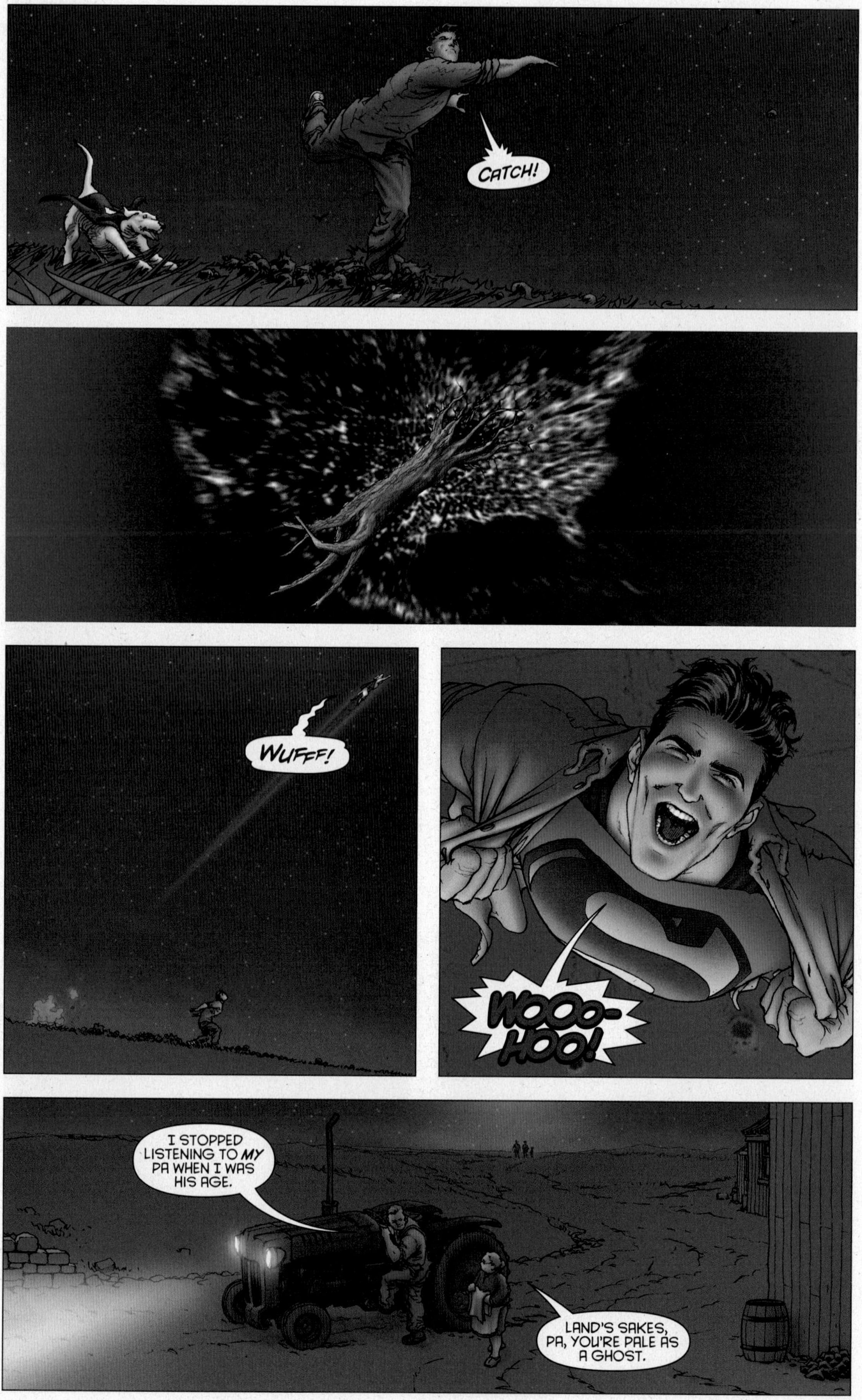
CATCH!
WUFFF!
WOOO-HOO!
I STOPPED LISTENING TO *MY* PA WHEN I WAS HIS AGE.
LAND'S SAKES, PA, YOU'RE PALE AS A GHOST.

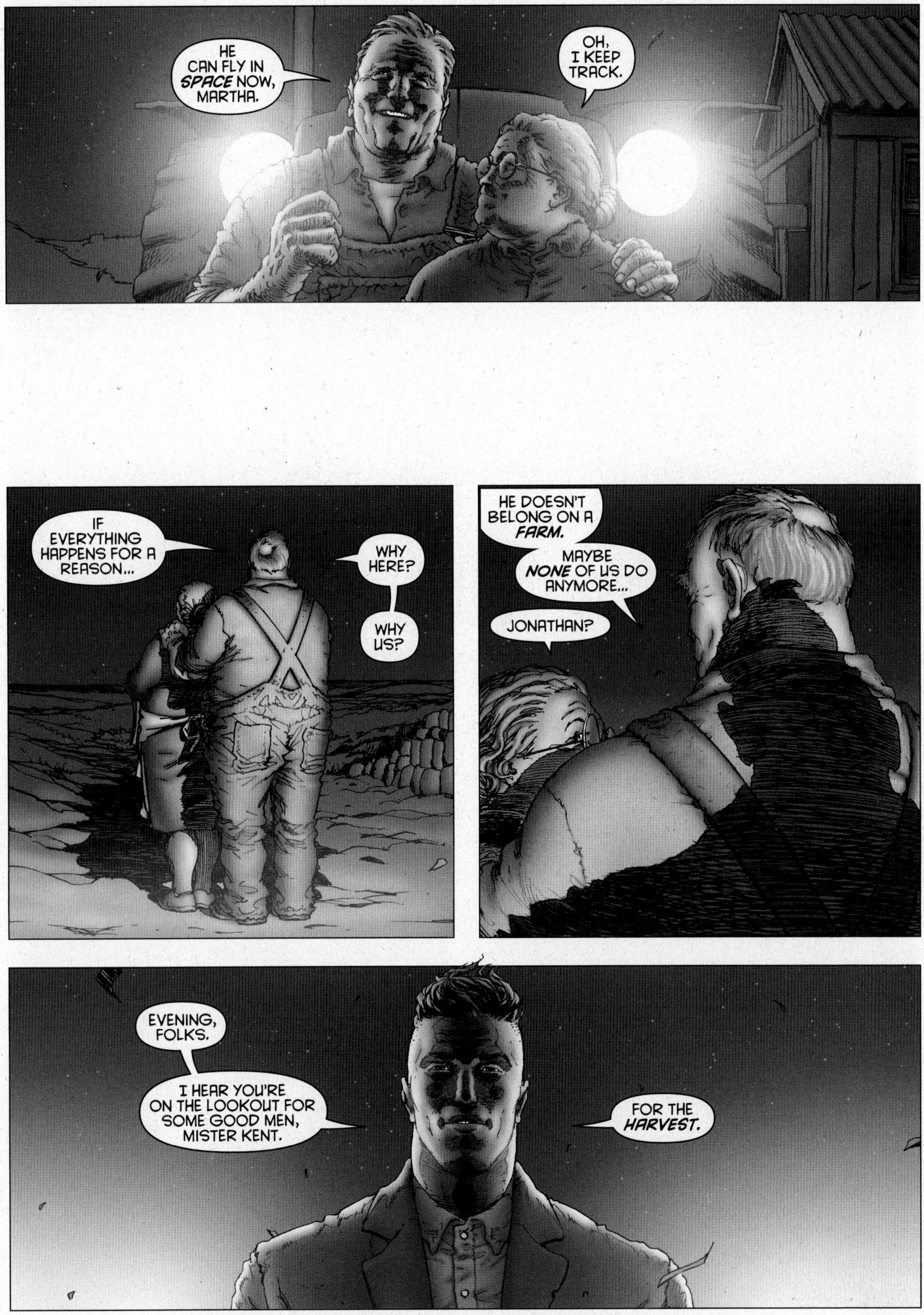
HE CAN FLY IN SPACE NOW, MARTHA.
OH, I KEEP TRACK.
IF EVERYTHING HAPPENS FOR A REASON...
WHY HERE?
WHY US?
HE DOESN'T BELONG ON A FARM.
MAYBE NONE OF US DO ANYMORE...
JONATHAN?
EVENING, FOLKS.
I HEAR YOU'RE ON THE LOOKOUT FOR SOME GOOD MEN, MISTER KENT.
FOR THE HARVEST.

FUNERAL IN SMALLVILLE

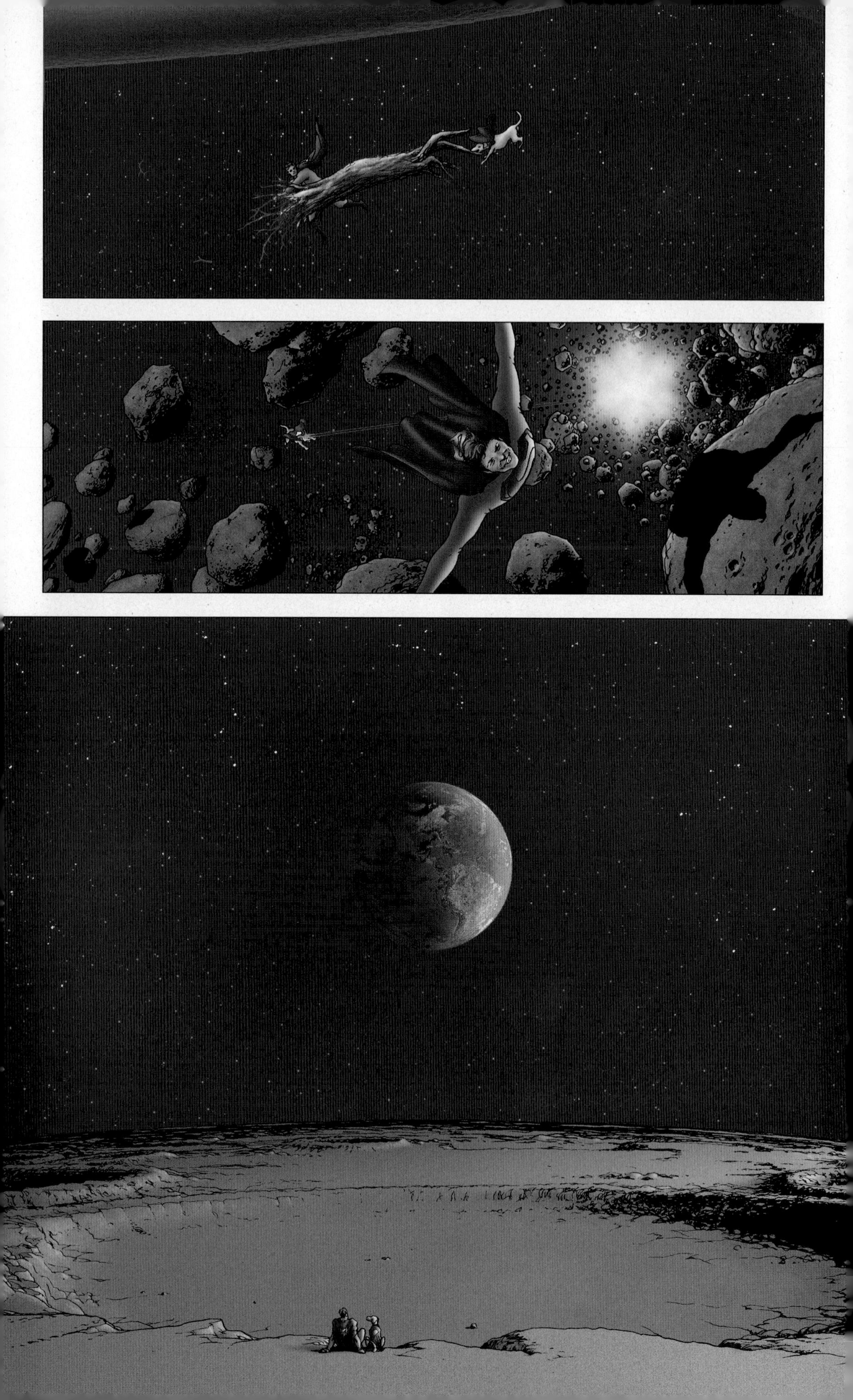

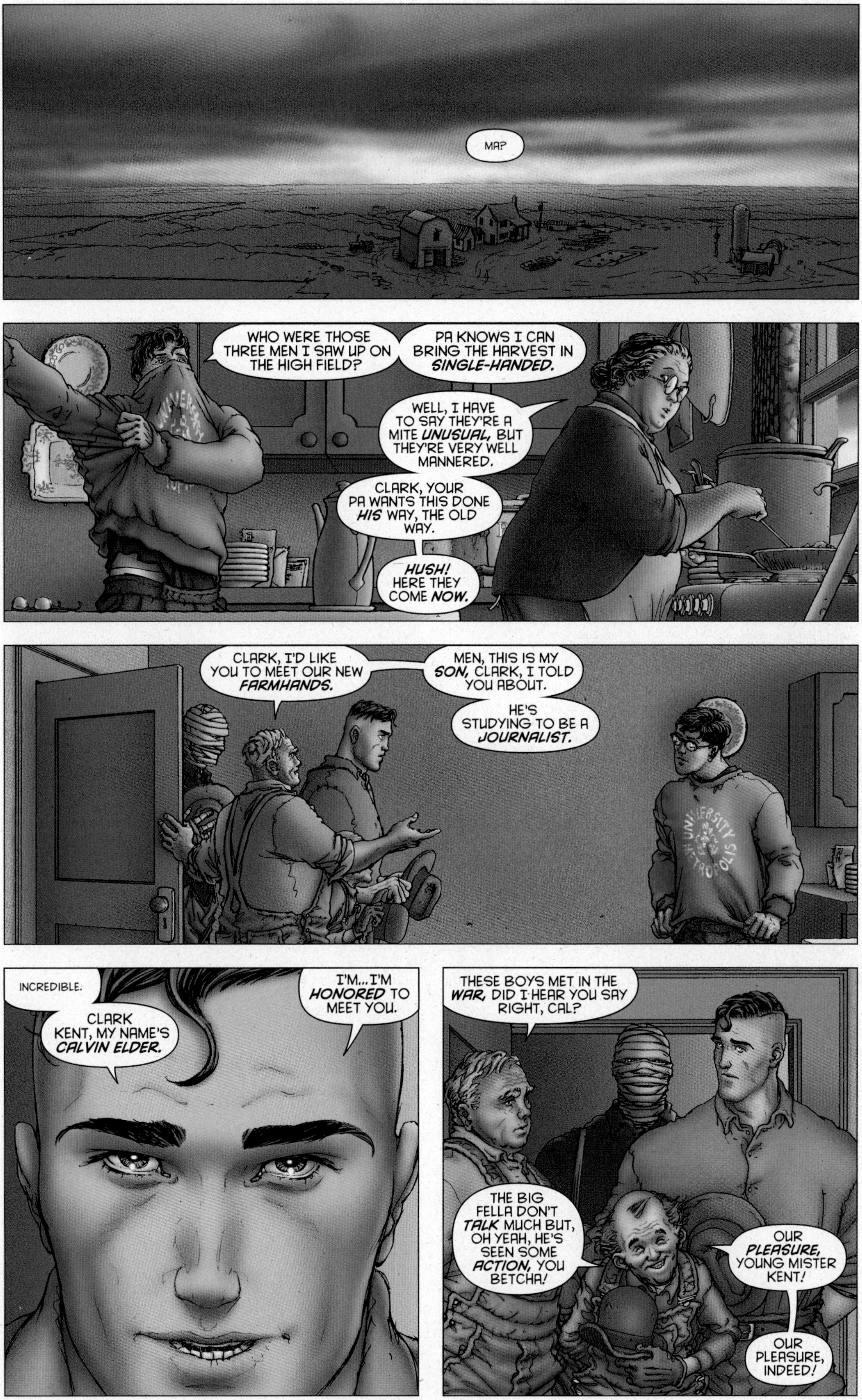
MA?
WHO WERE THOSE THREE MEN I SAW UP ON THE HIGH FIELD?
PA KNOWS I CAN BRING THE HARVEST IN SINGLE-HANDED.
WELL, I HAVE TO SAY THEY'RE A MITE UNUSUAL, BUT THEY'RE VERY WELL MANNERED.
CLARK, YOUR PA WANTS THIS DONE HIS WAY, THE OLD WAY.
HUSH! HERE THEY COME NOW.
CLARK, I'D LIKE YOU TO MEET OUR NEW FARMHANDS.
MEN, THIS IS MY SON, CLARK, I TOLD YOU ABOUT.
HE'S STUDYING TO BE A JOURNALIST.
UNIVERSITY METROPOLIS
INCREDIBLE.
CLARK KENT, MY NAME'S CALVIN ELDER.
I'M...I'M HONORED TO MEET YOU.
THESE BOYS MET IN THE WAR, DID I HEAR YOU SAY RIGHT, CAL?
THE BIG FELLA DON'T TALK MUCH BUT, OH YEAH, HE'S SEEN SOME ACTION, YOU BETCHA!
OUR PLEASURE, YOUNG MISTER KENT!
OUR PLEASURE, INDEED!

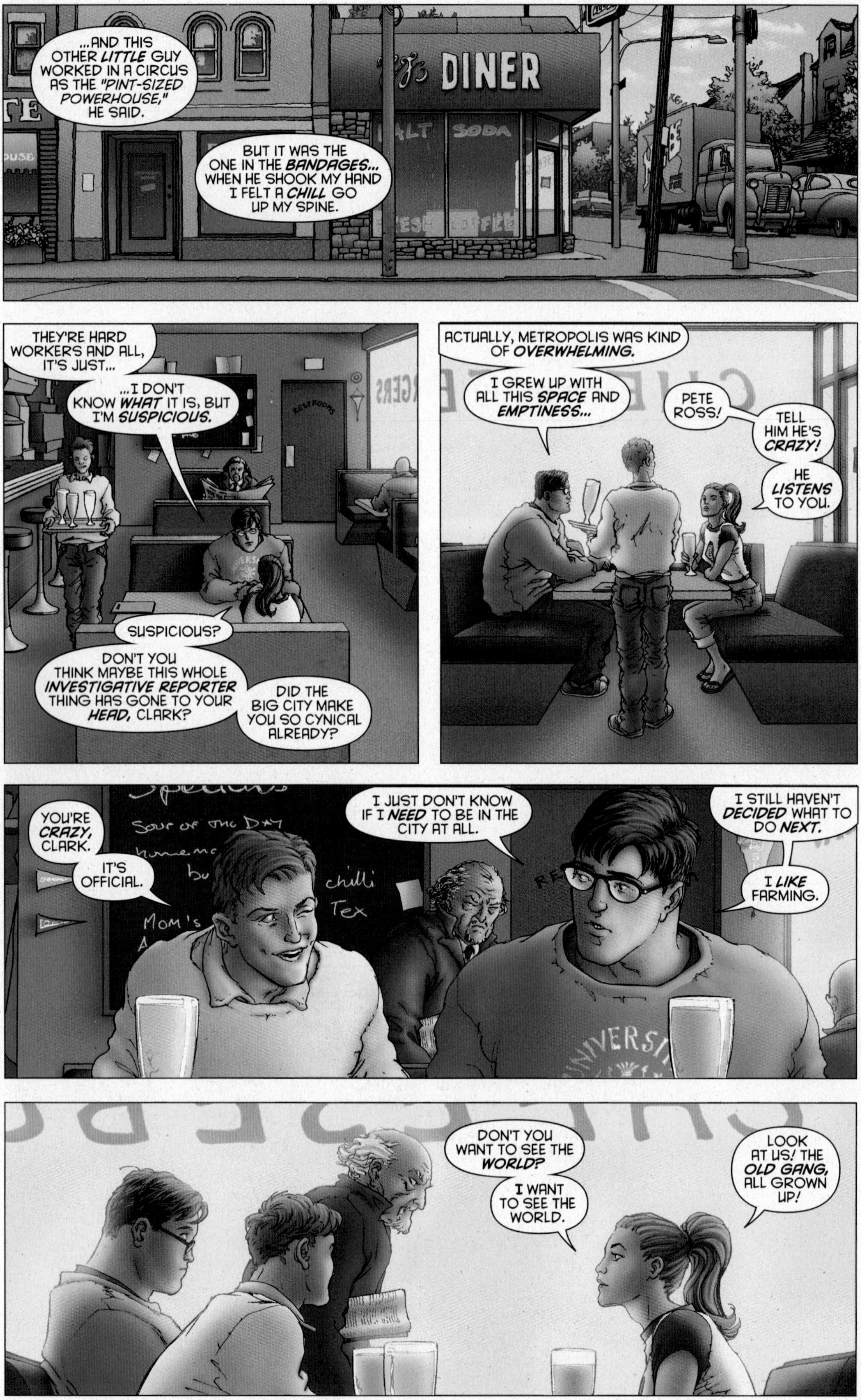
DINER
...AND THIS OTHER *LITTLE* GUY WORKED IN A CIRCUS AS THE "PINT-SIZED POWERHOUSE," HE SAID.
BUT IT WAS THE ONE IN THE *BANDAGES*... WHEN HE SHOOK MY HAND I FELT A *CHILL* GO UP MY SPINE.
THEY'RE HARD WORKERS AND ALL, IT'S JUST...
...I DON'T KNOW *WHAT* IT IS, BUT I'M *SUSPICIOUS.*
SUSPICIOUS?
DON'T YOU THINK MAYBE THIS WHOLE *INVESTIGATIVE REPORTER* THING HAS GONE TO YOUR *HEAD,* CLARK?
DID THE BIG CITY MAKE YOU SO CYNICAL ALREADY?
ACTUALLY, METROPOLIS WAS KIND OF *OVERWHELMING.*
I GREW UP WITH ALL THIS *SPACE* AND *EMPTINESS...*
PETE ROSS!
TELL HIM HE'S *CRAZY!*
HE *LISTENS* TO YOU.
YOU'RE *CRAZY,* CLARK.
IT'S OFFICIAL.
I JUST DON'T KNOW IF I *NEED* TO BE IN THE CITY AT ALL.
I STILL HAVEN'T *DECIDED* WHAT TO DO *NEXT.*
I *LIKE* FARMING.
DON'T YOU WANT TO SEE THE *WORLD?*
I WANT TO SEE THE WORLD.
LOOK AT US! THE *OLD GANG,* ALL GROWN UP!

LET'S NEVER FORGET.

SMILE!

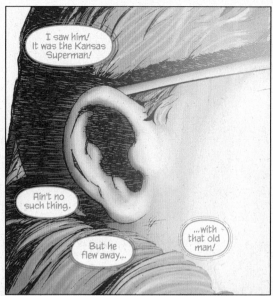

I saw him! It was the Kansas Superman!

Ain't no such thing.

But he flew away...

...with that old man!

...CLARK KENT, ARE YOU *LISTENING* TO ME?

DO YOU WANT ME TO SEND A PRINT TO YOUR MOM AND DAD OR CAN I GET IT TO YOU IN *METROPOLIS*?

I...I JUST HAVEN'T *DECIDED*, LANA.

THIS SODA... I'D...*AH*...I'D FORGOTTEN HOW *RICH* THE FOOD WAS BACK HOME...

UHHH...

MAYBE I SHOULD *EXCUSE* MYSELF...

GO AHEAD, CLARK.

WE WON'T TALK ABOUT YOU WHEN YOU'RE GONE.

WHY DO YOU BOTH HAVE TO ACT LIKE I DON'T *KNOW* WHO HE IS?

DON'T MAKE ME *TALK* ABOUT THIS, LANA.

...I OVERHEARD RIGHT!

SEE, KRYPTO?

"CALVIN ELDER" HAS SUPERPOWERS AND AN ACTION SUIT LIKE MINE!

AND HERE COME THE OTHERS!

KRYPTO! SHH!

GRRRR...

WHAT DO THEY WANT?

...I WAS TOO LATE TO SAVE HIM.

THE CHRONOVORE ATE THIS POOR MAN'S ENTIRE LIFE.

BUT HE DIDN'T DIE IN VAIN, KAL...

WAIT!

...I HEAR A DISTINCTIVE HEARTBEAT NEARBY...

...LIKE AN ECHO...

UH?

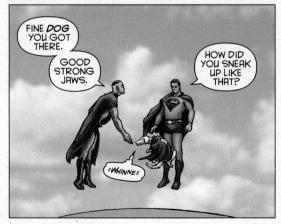

FINE DOG YOU GOT THERE.

GOOD STRONG JAWS.

HOW DID YOU SNEAK UP LIKE THAT?

WHINNE

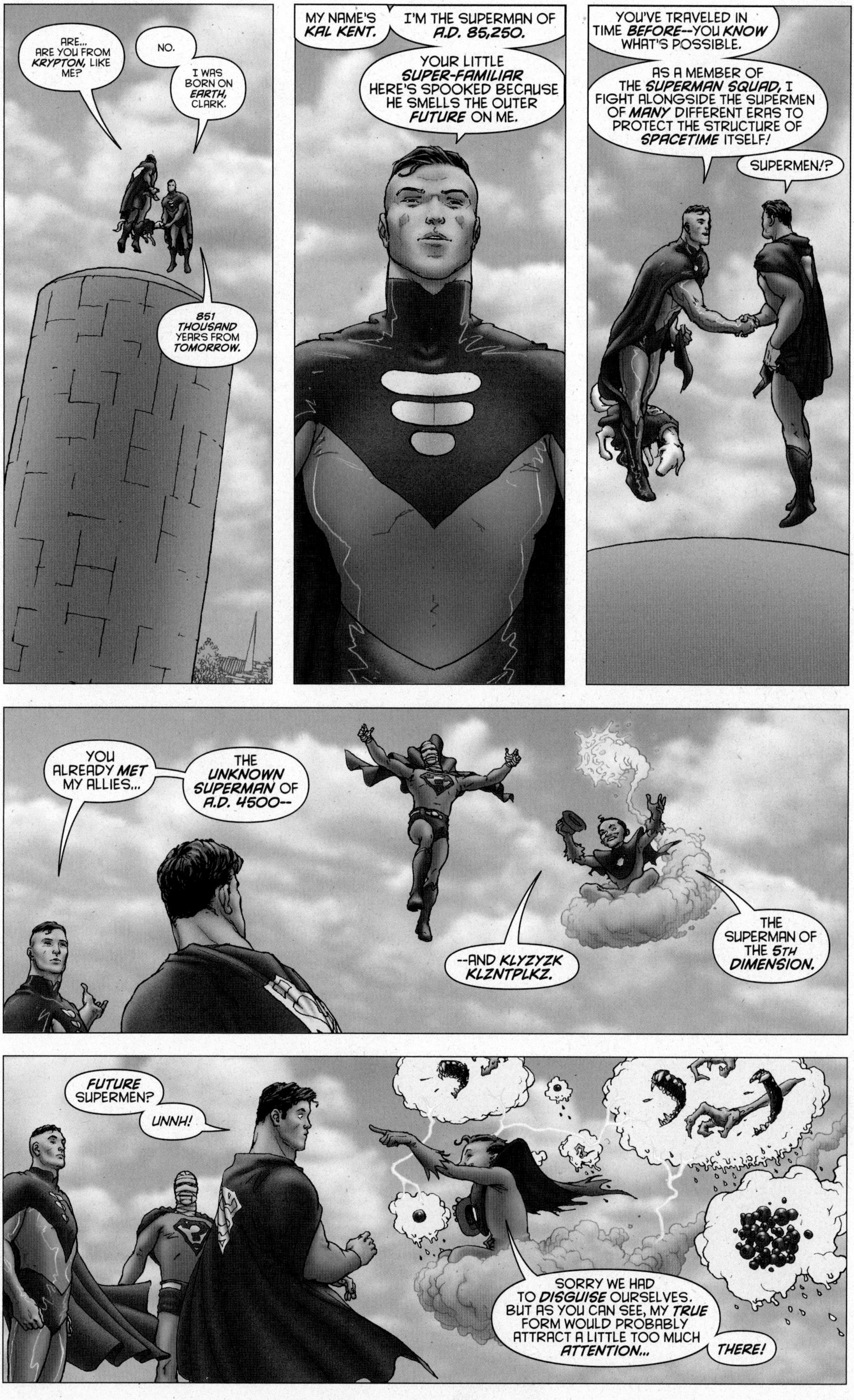

ARE... ARE YOU FROM KRYPTON, LIKE ME?
NO.
I WAS BORN ON EARTH, CLARK.
851 THOUSAND YEARS FROM TOMORROW.
MY NAME'S KAL KENT.
I'M THE SUPERMAN OF A.D. 85,250.
YOUR LITTLE SUPER-FAMILIAR HERE'S SPOOKED BECAUSE HE SMELLS THE OUTER FUTURE ON ME.
YOU'VE TRAVELED IN TIME BEFORE--YOU KNOW WHAT'S POSSIBLE.
AS A MEMBER OF THE SUPERMAN SQUAD, I FIGHT ALONGSIDE THE SUPERMEN OF MANY DIFFERENT ERAS TO PROTECT THE STRUCTURE OF SPACETIME ITSELF!
SUPERMEN!?
YOU ALREADY MET MY ALLIES...
THE UNKNOWN SUPERMAN OF A.D. 4500--
--AND KLYZYZK KLZNTPLKZ.
THE SUPERMAN OF THE 5TH DIMENSION.
FUTURE SUPERMEN?
UNNH!
SORRY WE HAD TO DISGUISE OURSELVES. BUT AS YOU CAN SEE, MY TRUE FORM WOULD PROBABLY ATTRACT A LITTLE TOO MUCH ATTENTION...
THERE!

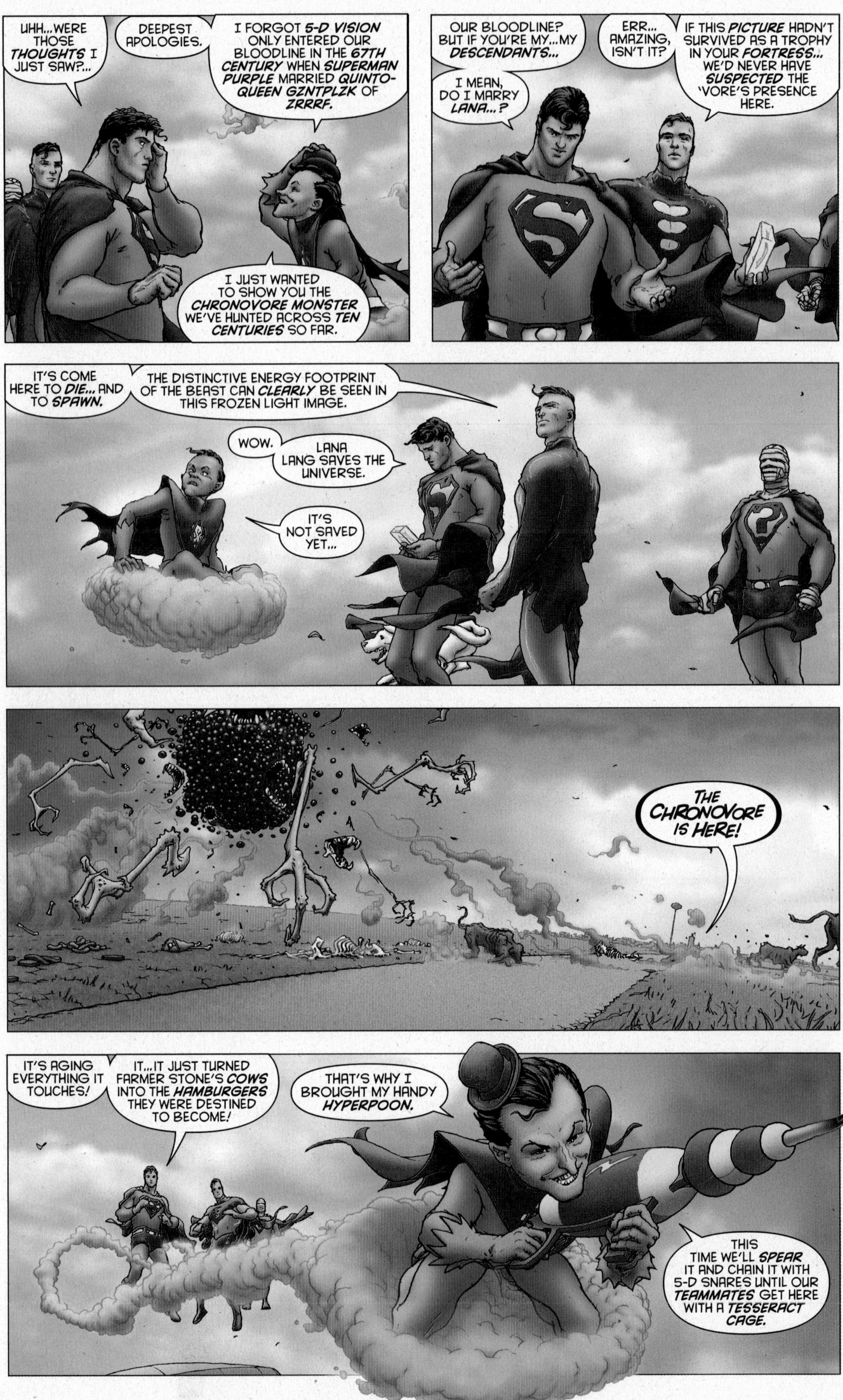

UHH...WERE THOSE THOUGHTS I JUST SAW?...
DEEPEST APOLOGIES.
I FORGOT 5-D VISION ONLY ENTERED OUR BLOODLINE IN THE 67TH CENTURY WHEN SUPERMAN PURPLE MARRIED QUINTO-QUEEN GZNTPLZK OF ZRRRF.
I JUST WANTED TO SHOW YOU THE CHRONOVORE MONSTER WE'VE HUNTED ACROSS TEN CENTURIES SO FAR.
OUR BLOODLINE? BUT IF YOU'RE MY...MY DESCENDANTS...
I MEAN, DO I MARRY LANA...?
ERR... AMAZING, ISN'T IT?
IF THIS PICTURE HADN'T SURVIVED AS A TROPHY IN YOUR FORTRESS... WE'D NEVER HAVE SUSPECTED THE 'VORE'S PRESENCE HERE.
IT'S COME HERE TO DIE... AND TO SPAWN.
THE DISTINCTIVE ENERGY FOOTPRINT OF THE BEAST CAN CLEARLY BE SEEN IN THIS FROZEN LIGHT IMAGE.
WOW.
LANA LANG SAVES THE UNIVERSE.
IT'S NOT SAVED YET...
THE CHRONOVORE IS HERE!
IT'S AGING EVERYTHING IT TOUCHES!
IT...IT JUST TURNED FARMER STONE'S COWS INTO THE HAMBURGERS THEY WERE DESTINED TO BECOME!
THAT'S WHY I BROUGHT MY HANDY HYPERPOON.
THIS TIME WE'LL SPEAR IT AND CHAIN IT WITH 5-D SNARES UNTIL OUR TEAMMATES GET HERE WITH A TESSERACT CAGE.

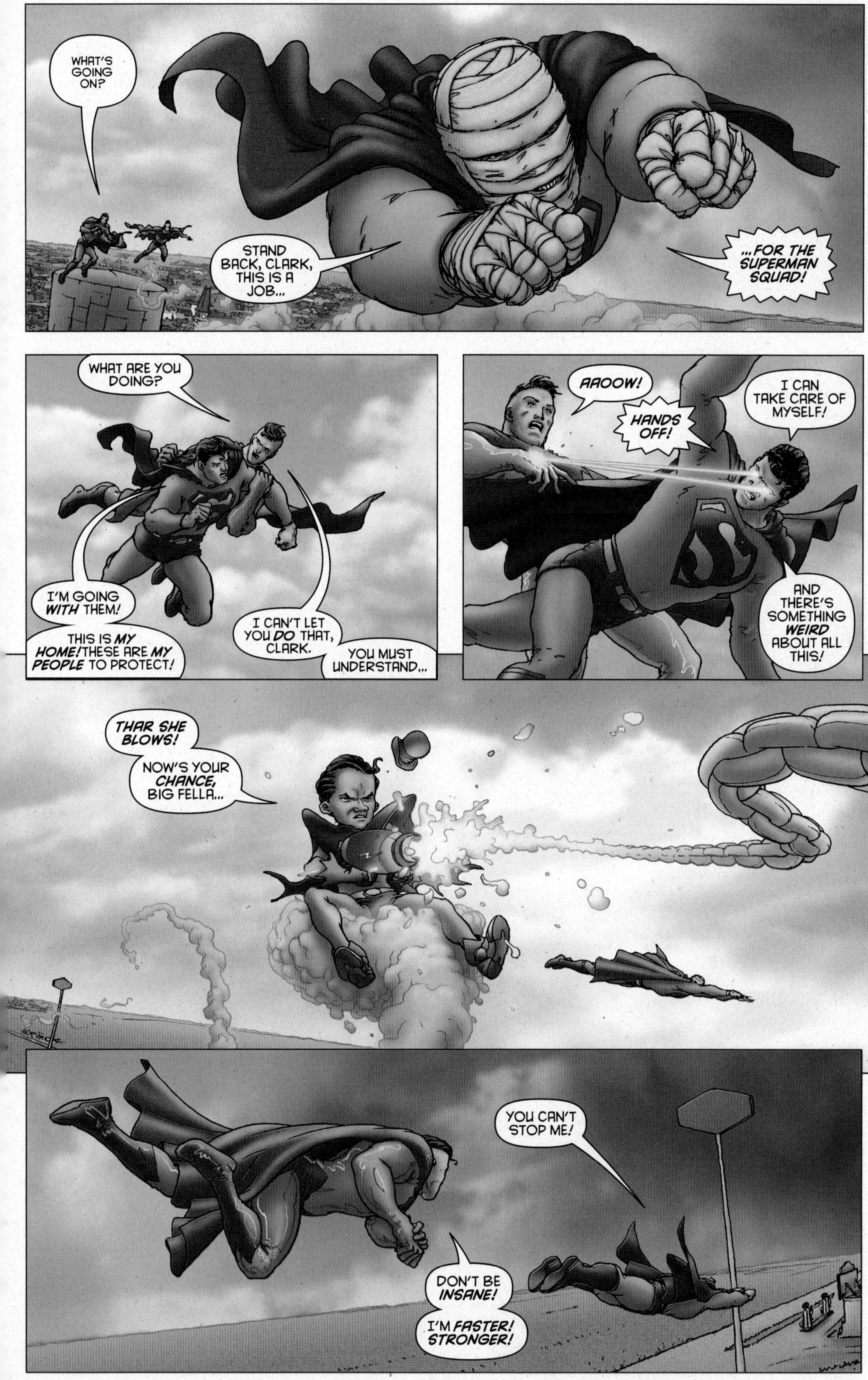
WHAT'S GOING ON?
STAND BACK, CLARK, THIS IS A JOB...
...FOR THE SUPERMAN SQUAD!
WHAT ARE YOU DOING?
I'M GOING WITH THEM!
THIS IS MY HOME! THESE ARE MY PEOPLE TO PROTECT!
I CAN'T LET YOU DO THAT, CLARK.
YOU MUST UNDERSTAND...
AAOOW!
HANDS OFF!
I CAN TAKE CARE OF MYSELF!
AND THERE'S SOMETHING WEIRD ABOUT ALL THIS!
THAR SHE BLOWS!
NOW'S YOUR CHANCE, BIG FELLA...
YOU CAN'T STOP ME!
DON'T BE INSANE!
I'M FASTER! STRONGER!

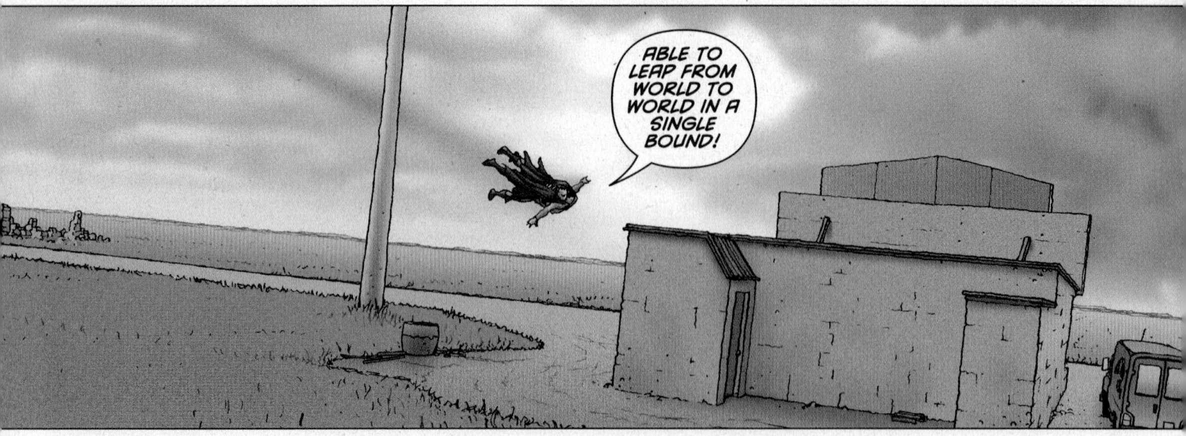
ABLE TO LEAP FROM WORLD TO WORLD IN A SINGLE BOUND!

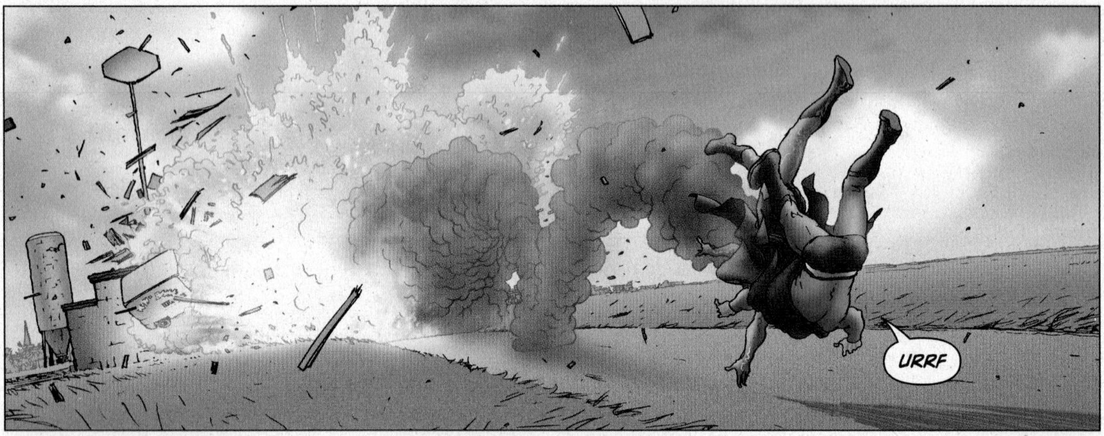
URRF

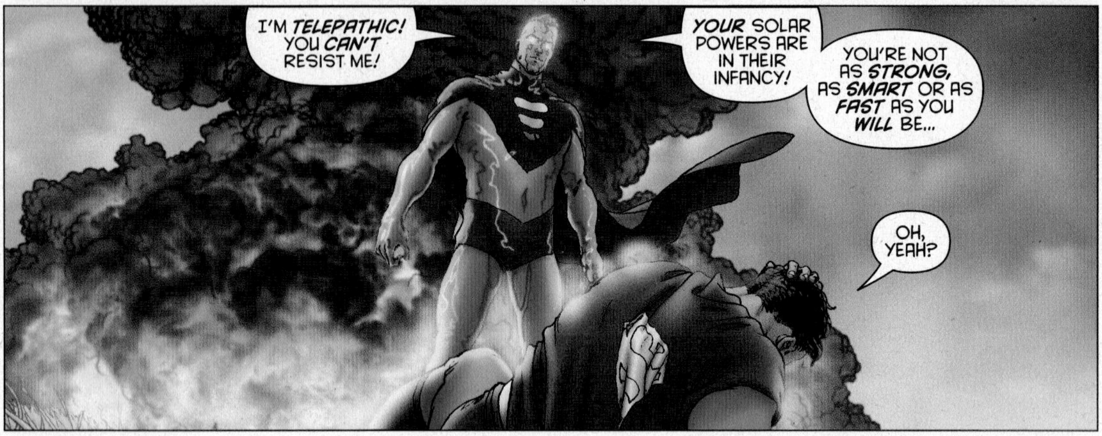
I'M TELEPATHIC! YOU CAN'T RESIST ME!
YOUR SOLAR POWERS ARE IN THEIR INFANCY!
YOU'RE NOT AS STRONG, AS SMART OR AS FAST AS YOU WILL BE...
OH, YEAH?

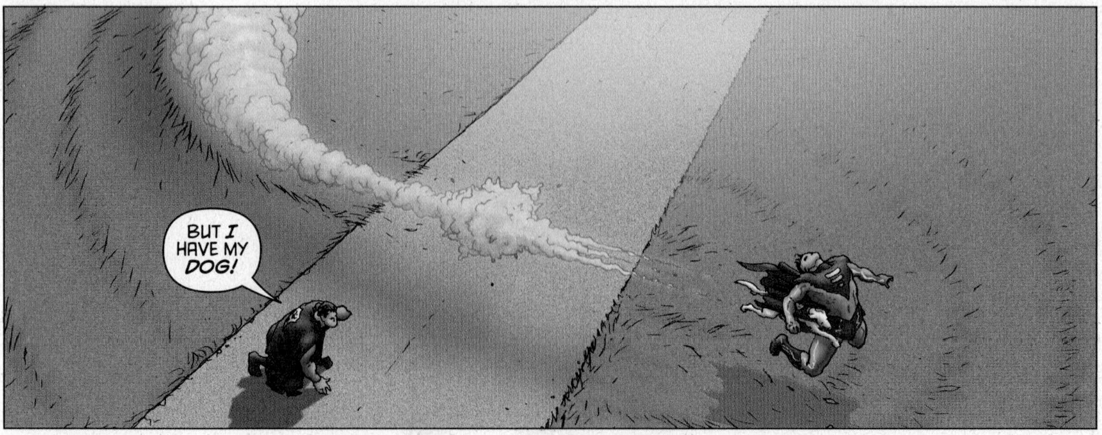
BUT I HAVE MY DOG!

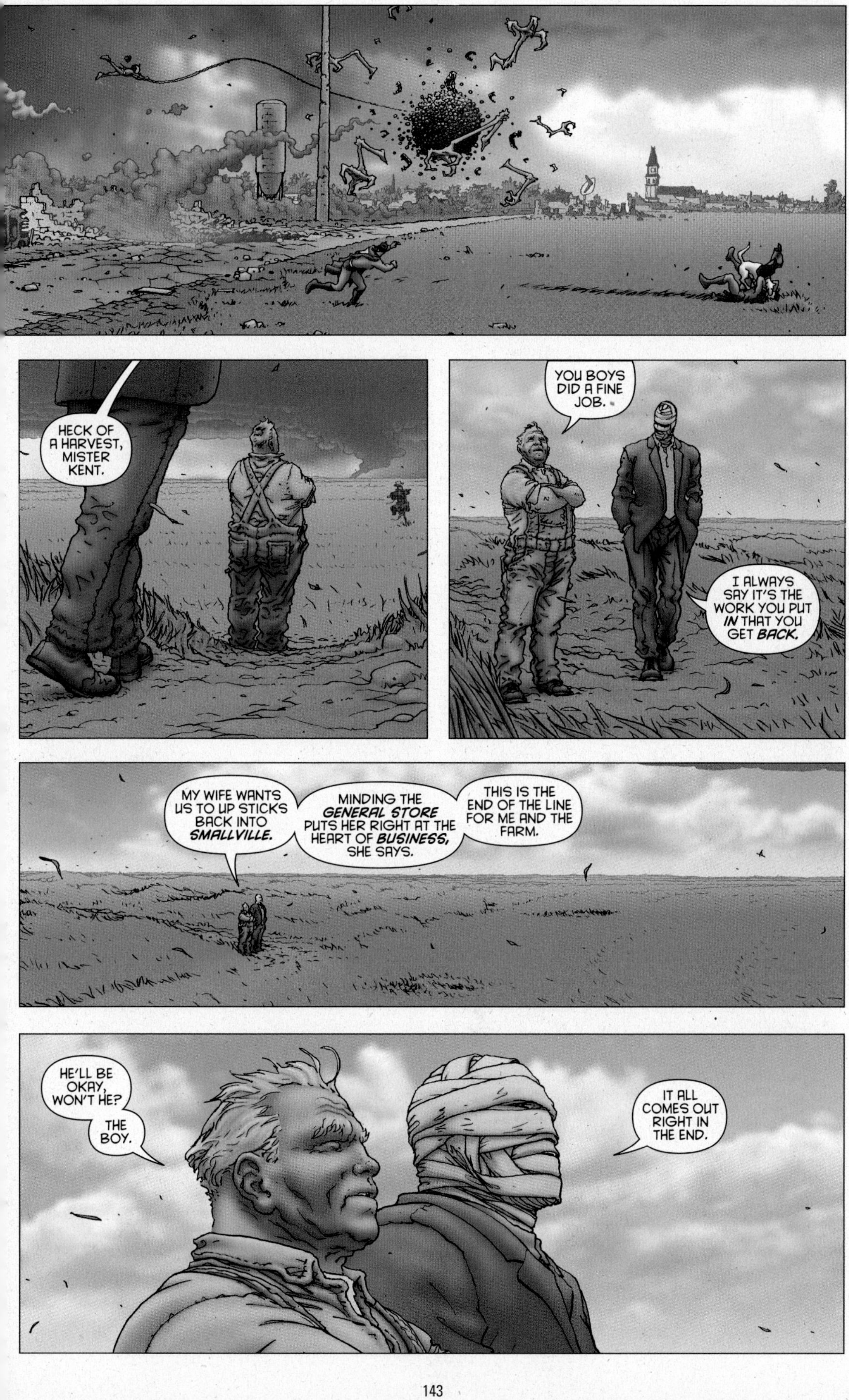
HECK OF A HARVEST, MISTER KENT.
YOU BOYS DID A FINE JOB.
I ALWAYS SAY IT'S THE WORK YOU PUT IN THAT YOU GET BACK.
MY WIFE WANTS US TO UP STICKS BACK INTO SMALLVILLE.
MINDING THE GENERAL STORE PUTS HER RIGHT AT THE HEART OF BUSINESS, SHE SAYS.
THIS IS THE END OF THE LINE FOR ME AND THE FARM.
HE'LL BE OKAY, WON'T HE?
THE BOY.
IT ALL COMES OUT RIGHT IN THE END.

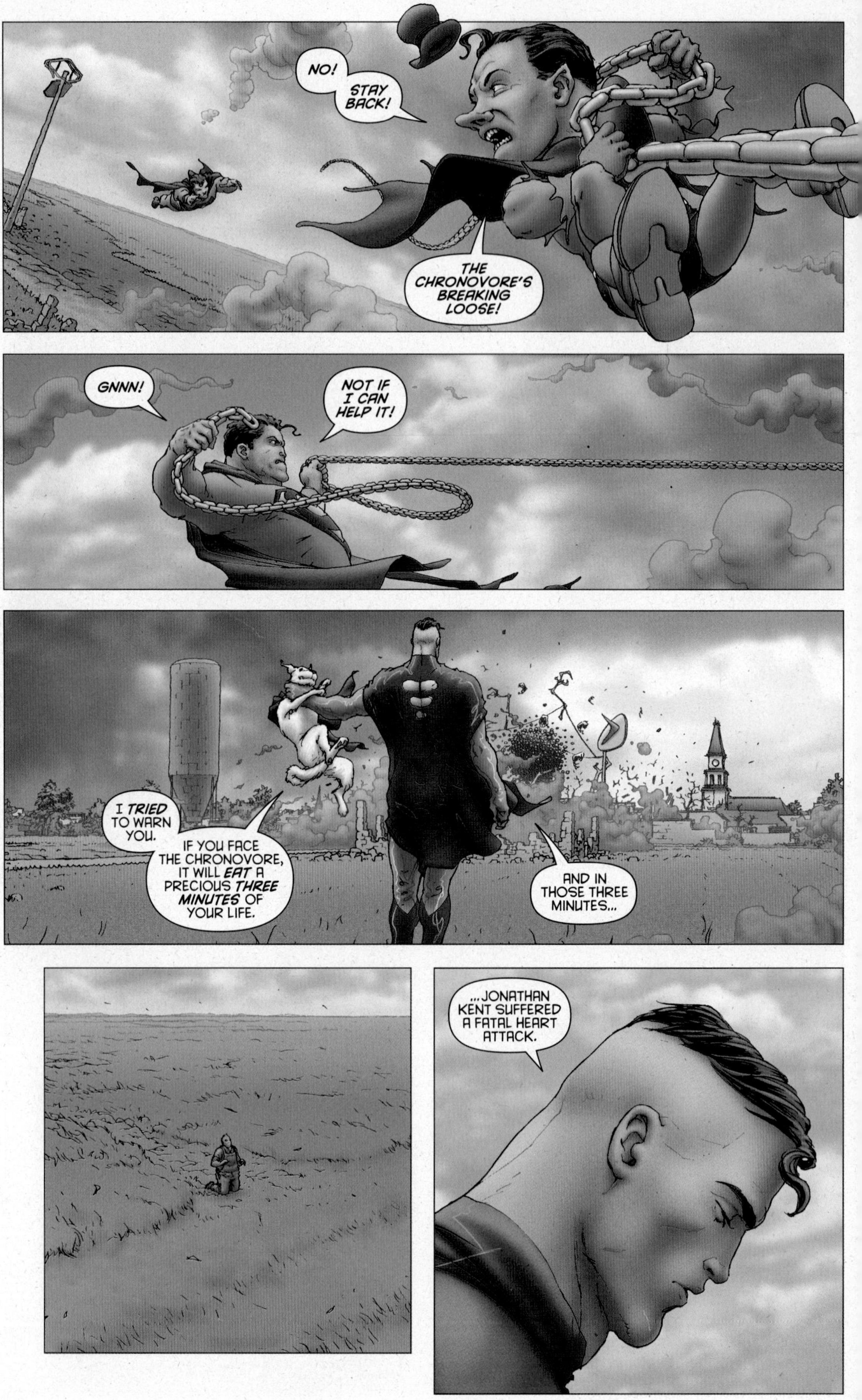
NO!
STAY BACK!
THE CHRONOVORE'S BREAKING LOOSE!
GNNN!
NOT IF I CAN HELP IT!
I TRIED TO WARN YOU.
IF YOU FACE THE CHRONOVORE, IT WILL EAT A PRECIOUS THREE MINUTES OF YOUR LIFE.
AND IN THOSE THREE MINUTES...
...JONATHAN KENT SUFFERED A FATAL HEART ATTACK.

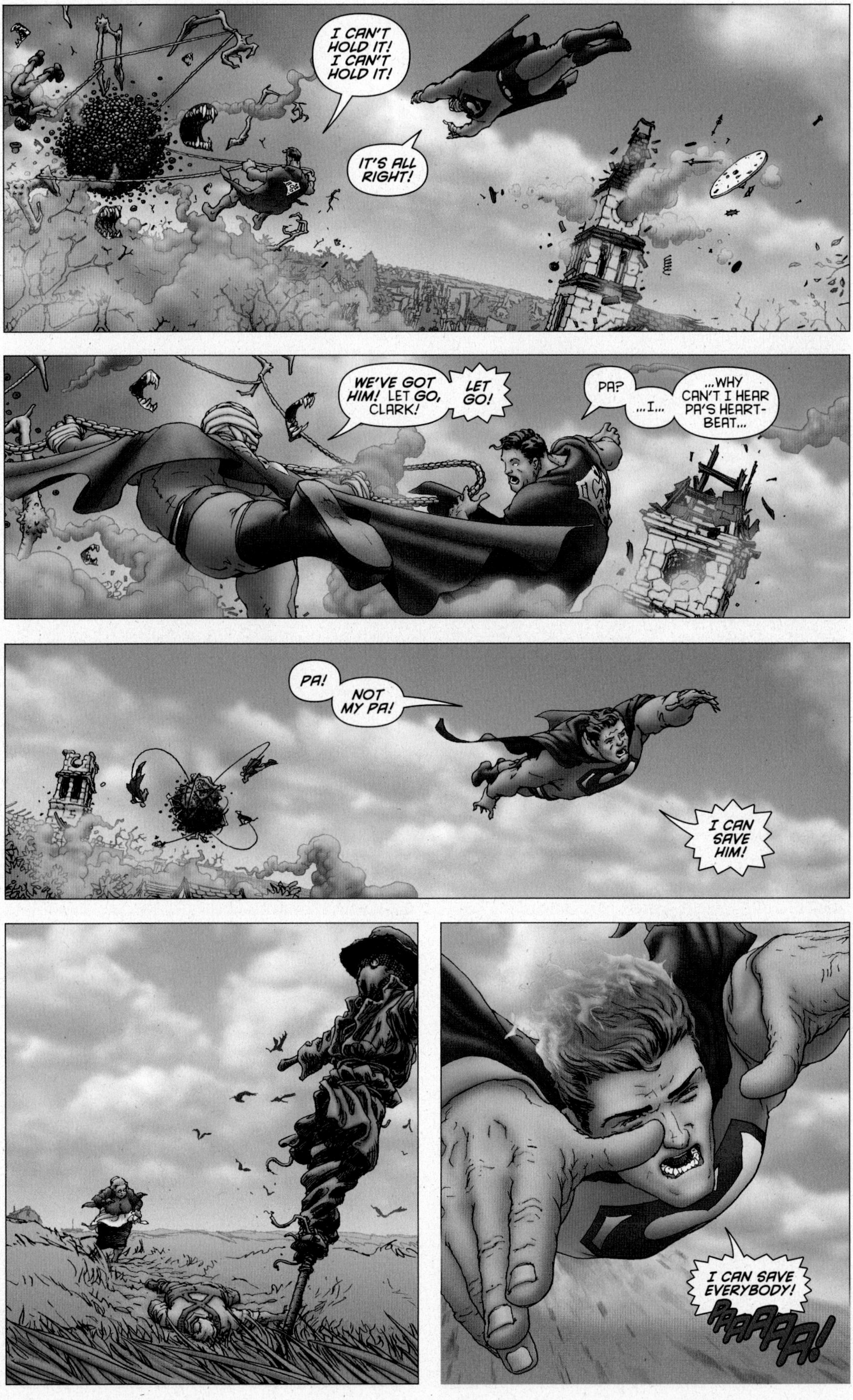
I CAN'T HOLD IT! I CAN'T HOLD IT!
IT'S ALL RIGHT!
WE'VE GOT HIM! LET GO, CLARK!
LET GO!
PA?
...I...
...WHY CAN'T I HEAR PA'S HEART-BEAT...
PA!
NOT MY PA!
I CAN SAVE HIM!
I CAN SAVE EVERYBODY!
AAAAAAA!

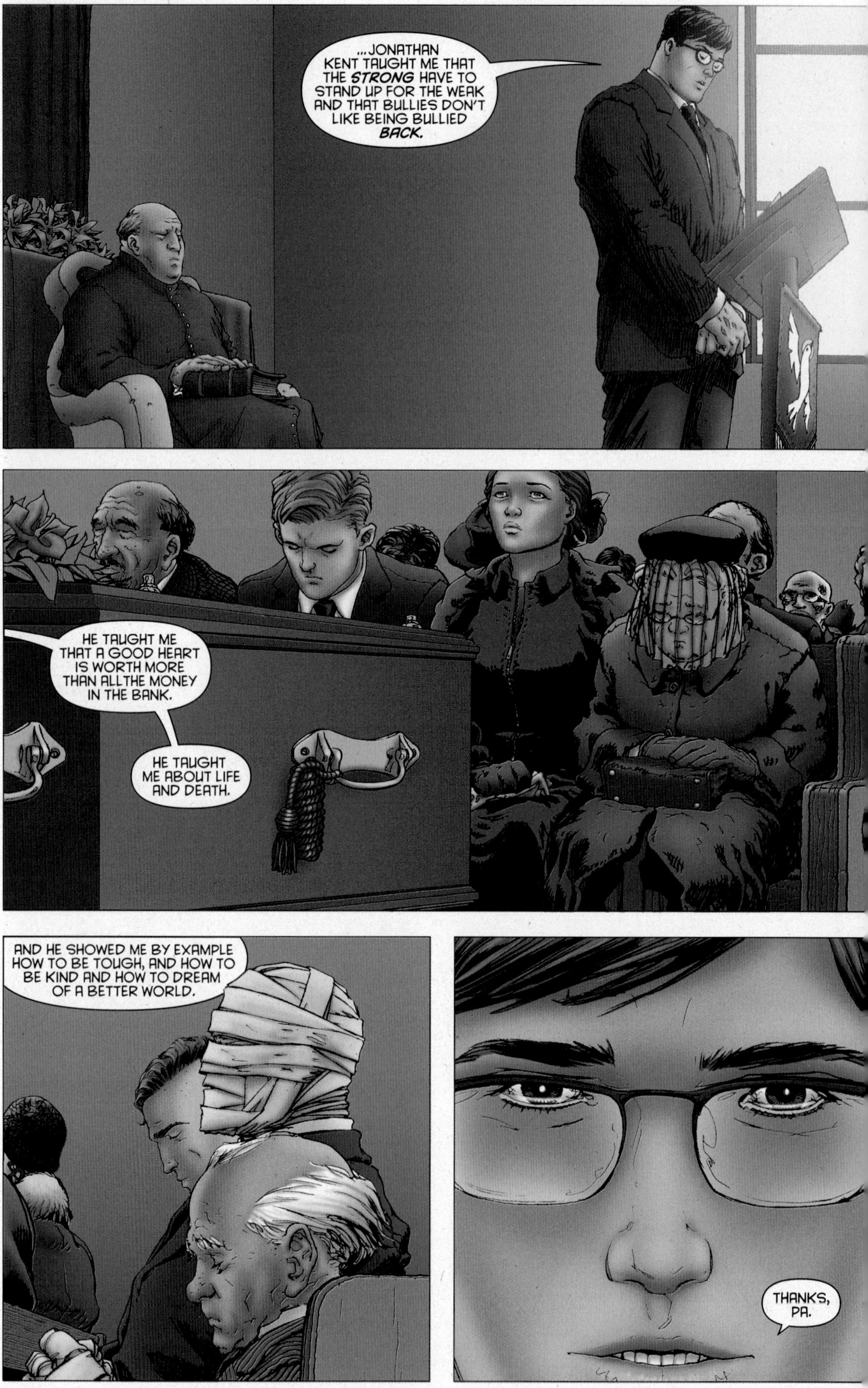
...JONATHAN KENT TAUGHT ME THAT THE STRONG HAVE TO STAND UP FOR THE WEAK AND THAT BULLIES DON'T LIKE BEING BULLIED BACK.
HE TAUGHT ME THAT A GOOD HEART IS WORTH MORE THAN ALL THE MONEY IN THE BANK.
HE TAUGHT ME ABOUT LIFE AND DEATH.
AND HE SHOWED ME BY EXAMPLE HOW TO BE TOUGH, AND HOW TO BE KIND AND HOW TO DREAM OF A BETTER WORLD.
THANKS, PA.

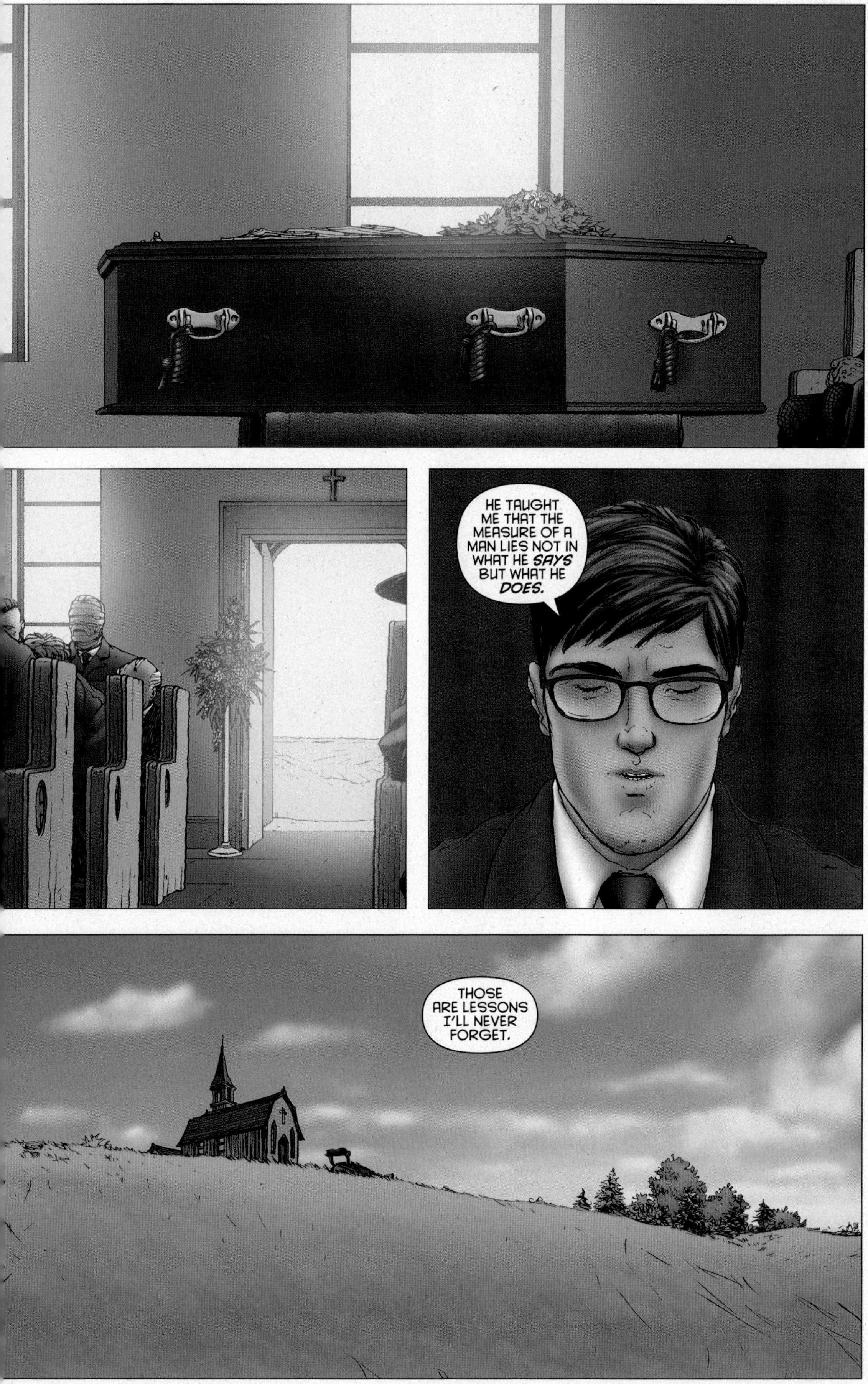
HE TAUGHT ME THAT THE MEASURE OF A MAN LIES NOT IN WHAT HE *SAYS* BUT WHAT HE *DOES.*
THOSE ARE LESSONS I'LL NEVER FORGET.

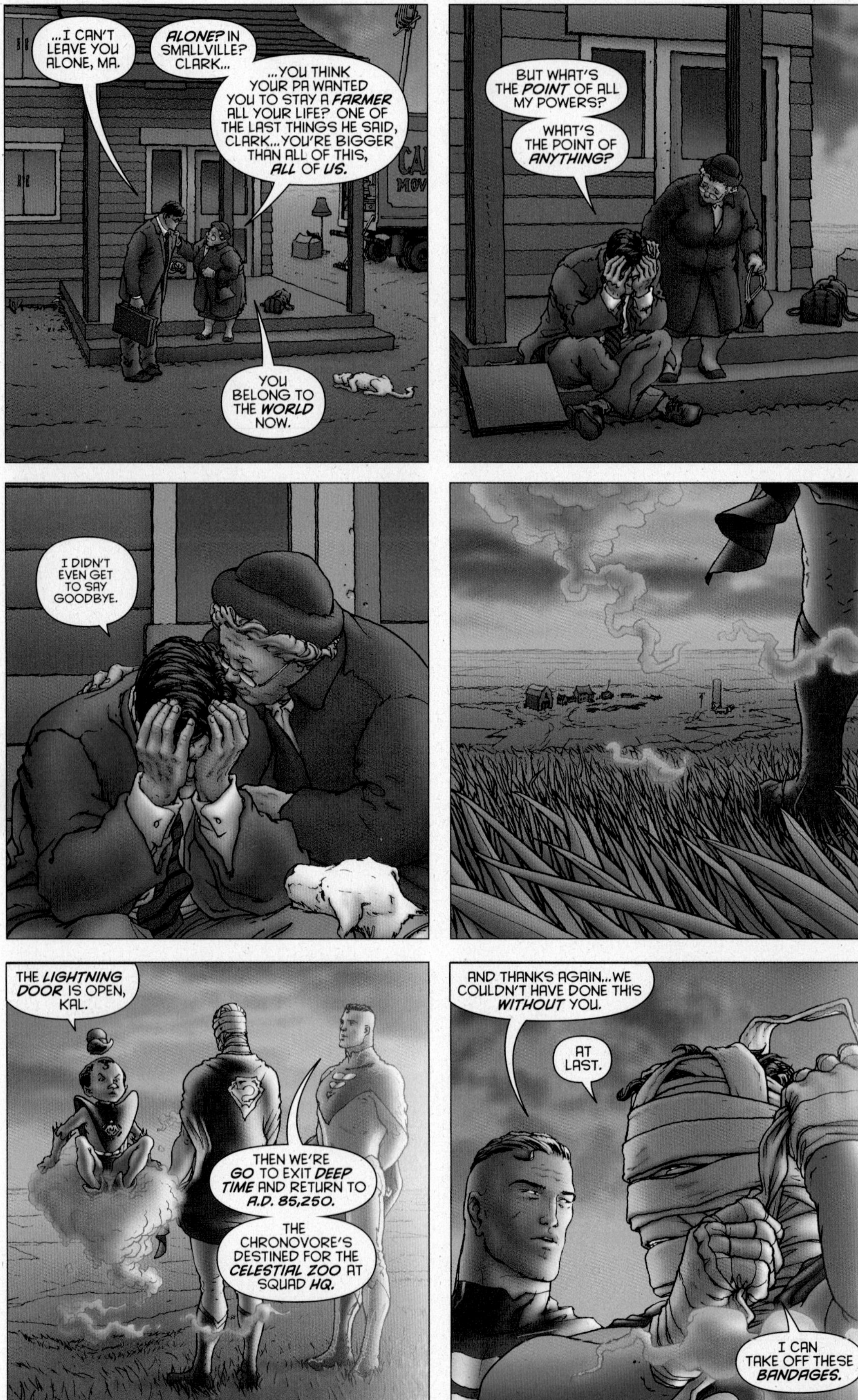
...I CAN'T LEAVE YOU ALONE, MA.
ALONE? IN SMALLVILLE? CLARK...
...YOU THINK YOUR PA WANTED YOU TO STAY A FARMER ALL YOUR LIFE? ONE OF THE LAST THINGS HE SAID, CLARK...YOU'RE BIGGER THAN ALL OF THIS, ALL OF US.
YOU BELONG TO THE WORLD NOW.
BUT WHAT'S THE POINT OF ALL MY POWERS?
WHAT'S THE POINT OF ANYTHING?
I DIDN'T EVEN GET TO SAY GOODBYE.
THE LIGHTNING DOOR IS OPEN, KAL.
THEN WE'RE GO TO EXIT DEEP TIME AND RETURN TO A.D. 85,250.
THE CHRONOVORE'S DESTINED FOR THE CELESTIAL ZOO AT SQUAD HQ.
AND THANKS AGAIN...WE COULDN'T HAVE DONE THIS WITHOUT YOU.
AT LAST.
I CAN TAKE OFF THESE BANDAGES.

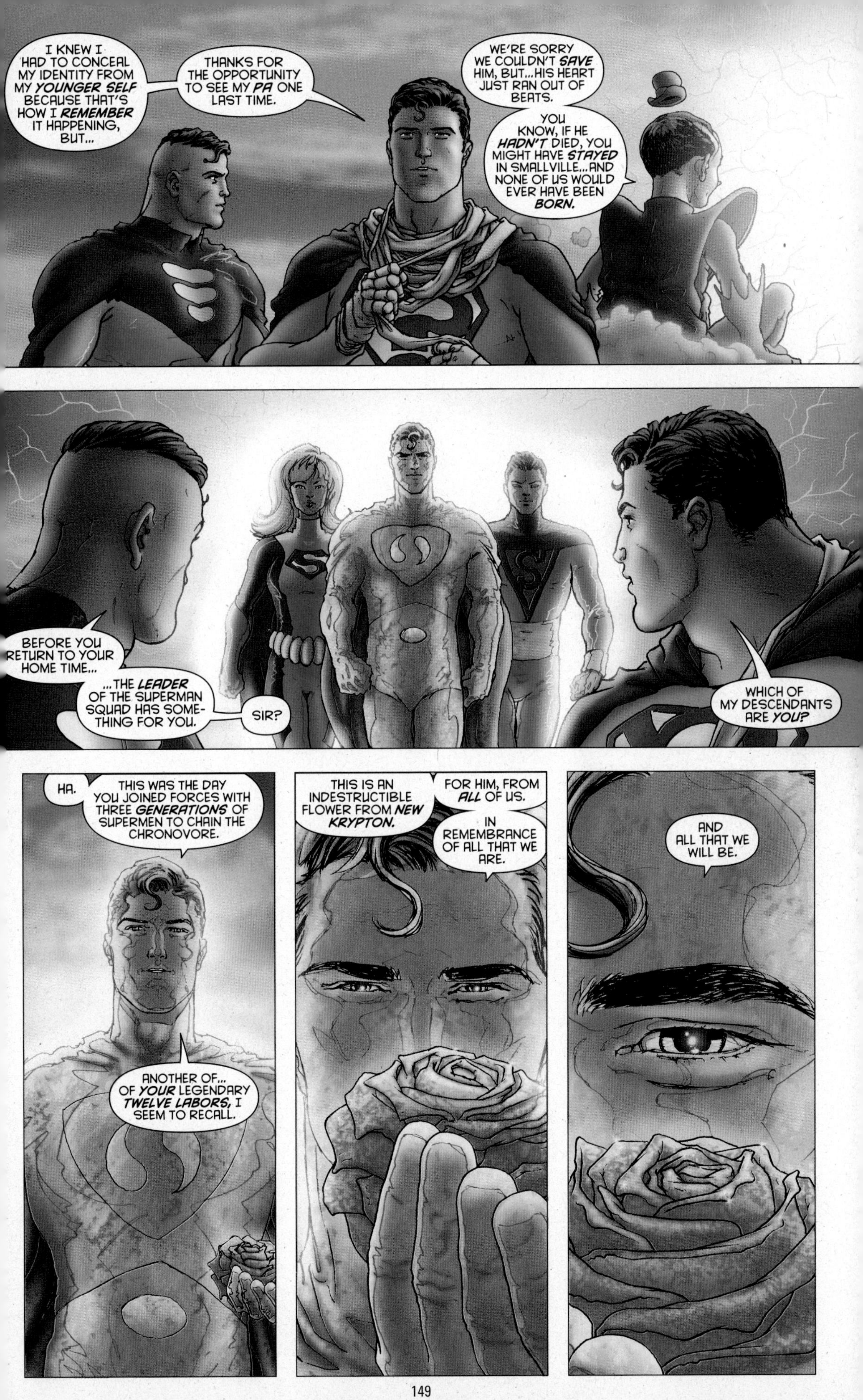
I KNEW I HAD TO CONCEAL MY IDENTITY FROM MY *YOUNGER SELF* BECAUSE THAT'S HOW I *REMEMBER* IT HAPPENING, BUT...
THANKS FOR THE OPPORTUNITY TO SEE MY *PA* ONE LAST TIME.
WE'RE SORRY WE COULDN'T *SAVE* HIM, BUT...HIS HEART JUST RAN OUT OF BEATS.
YOU KNOW, IF HE *HADN'T* DIED, YOU MIGHT HAVE *STAYED* IN SMALLVILLE...AND NONE OF US WOULD EVER HAVE BEEN *BORN.*
BEFORE YOU RETURN TO YOUR HOME TIME...
...THE *LEADER* OF THE SUPERMAN SQUAD HAS SOME-THING FOR YOU.
SIR?
WHICH OF MY DESCENDANTS ARE *YOU?*
HA.
THIS WAS THE DAY YOU JOINED FORCES WITH THREE *GENERATIONS* OF SUPERMEN TO CHAIN THE CHRONOVORE.
ANOTHER OF... OF *YOUR* LEGENDARY *TWELVE LABORS,* I SEEM TO RECALL.
THIS IS AN INDESTRUCTIBLE FLOWER FROM *NEW KRYPTON.*
FOR HIM, FROM *ALL* OF US.
IN REMEMBRANCE OF ALL THAT WE ARE.
AND ALL THAT WE WILL BE.

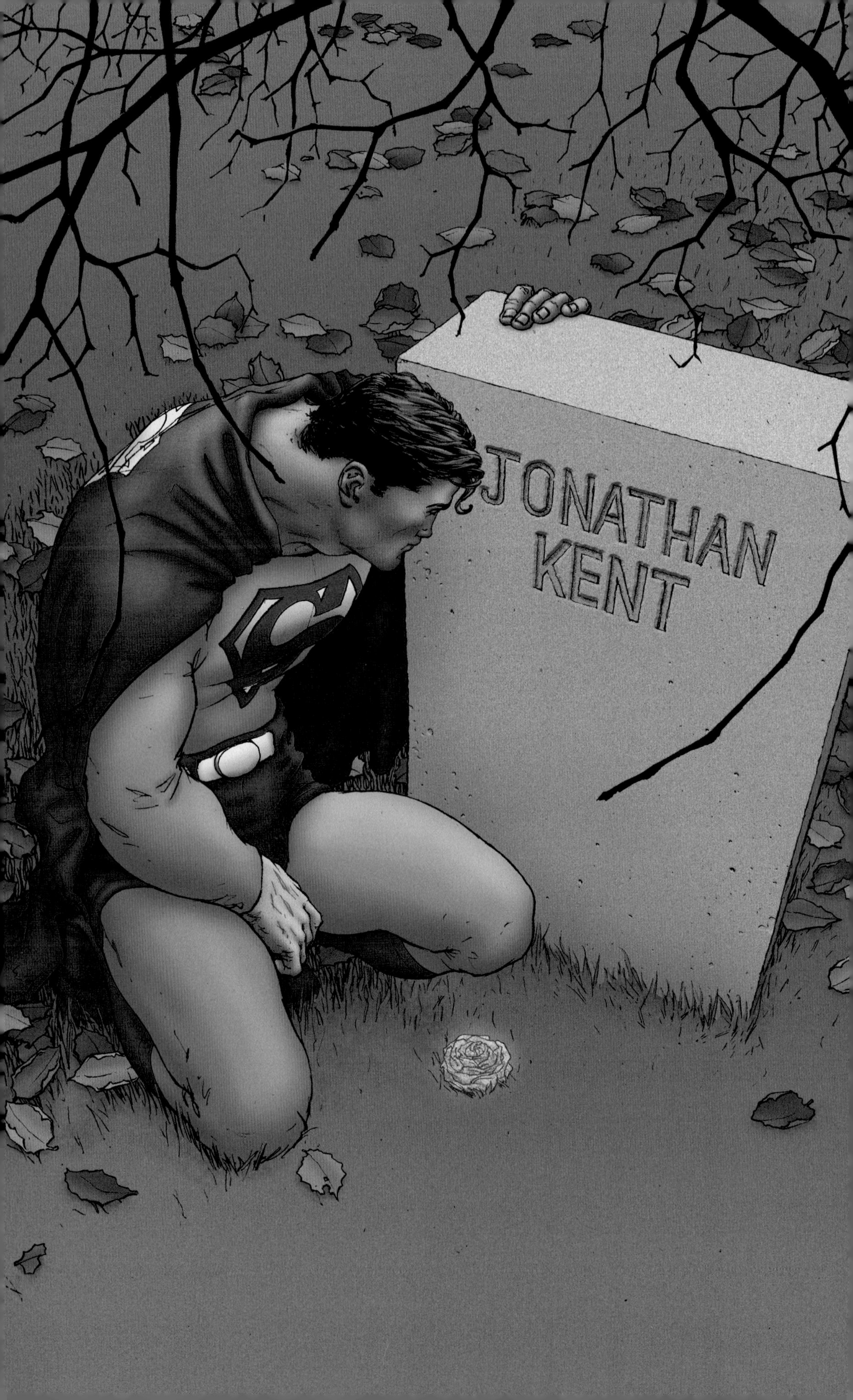
JONATHAN
KENT

Episode 7

BEING BIZARRO

Cover FRANK QUITELY

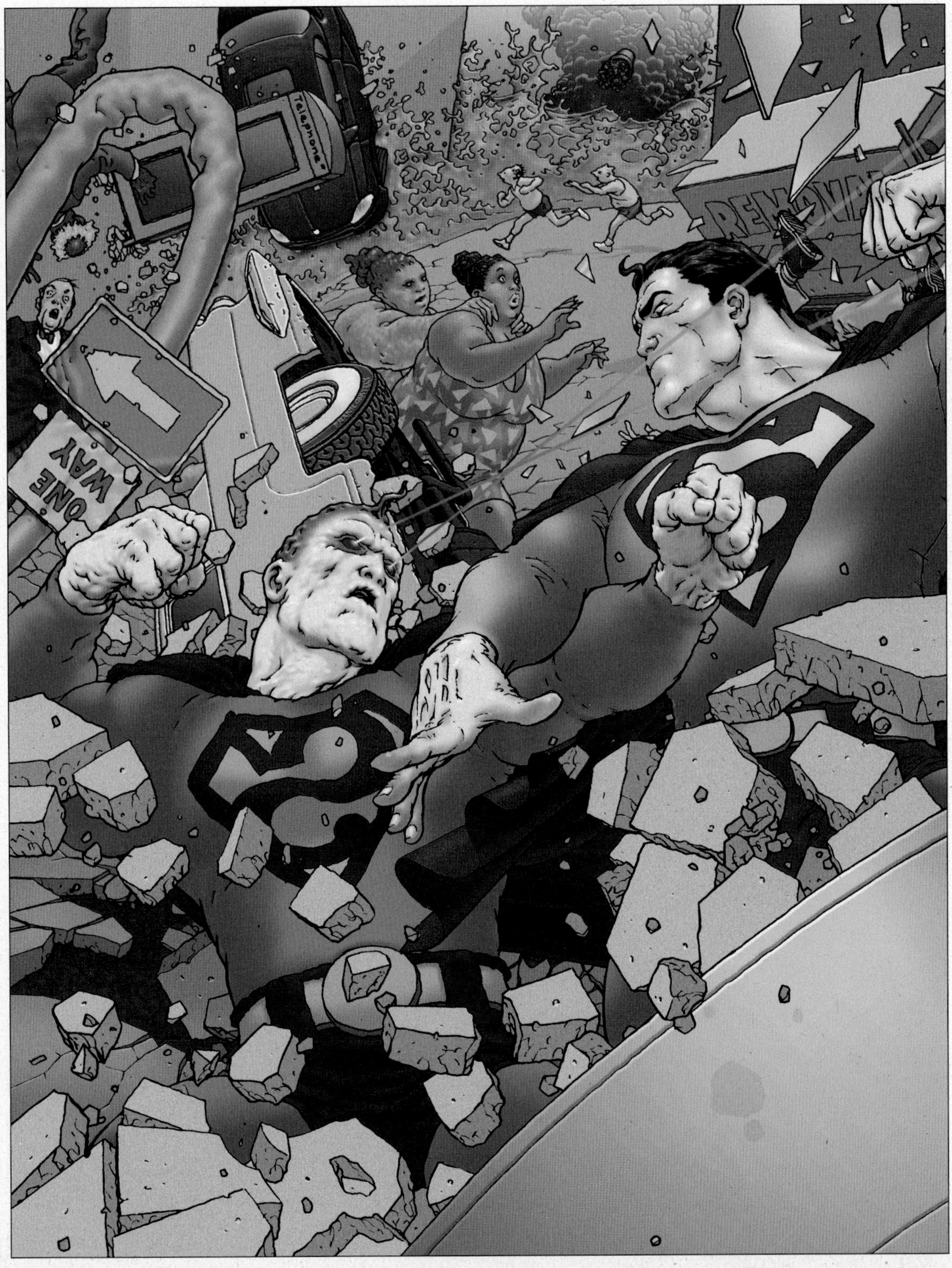

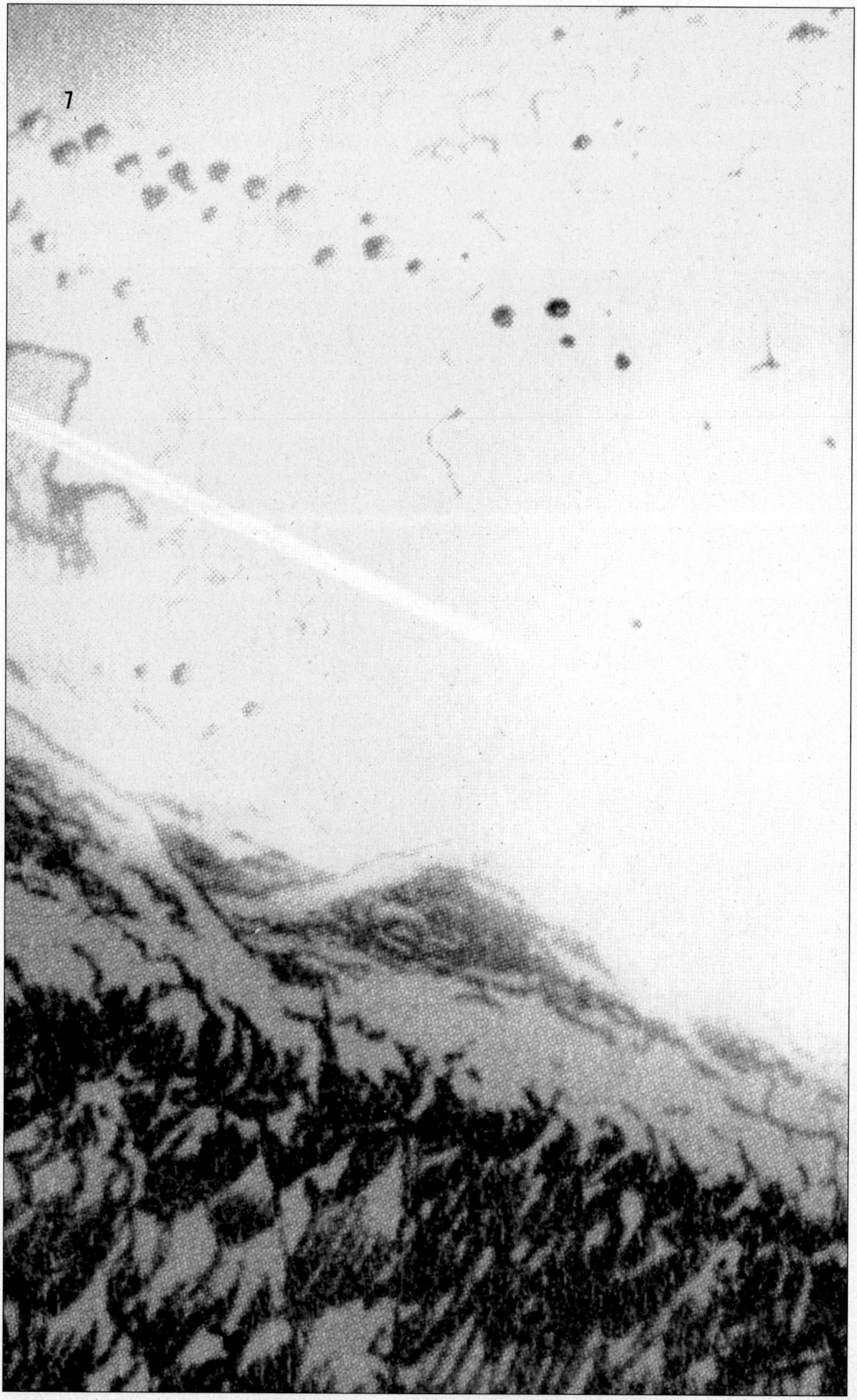

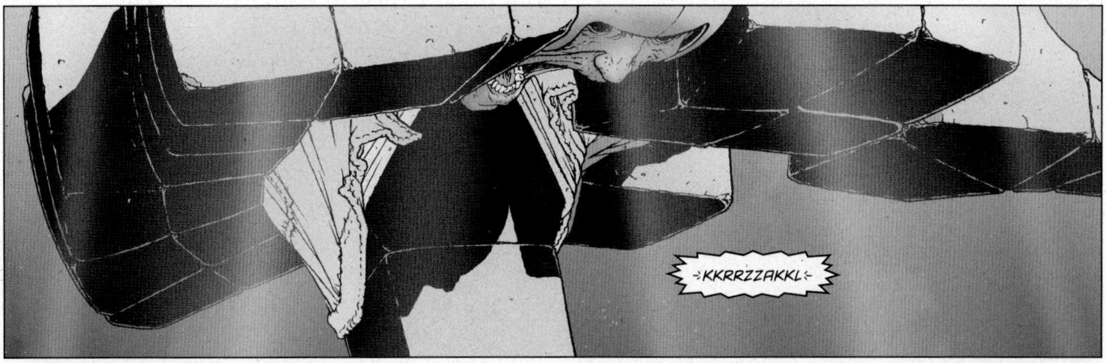
KKRRZZAKKL

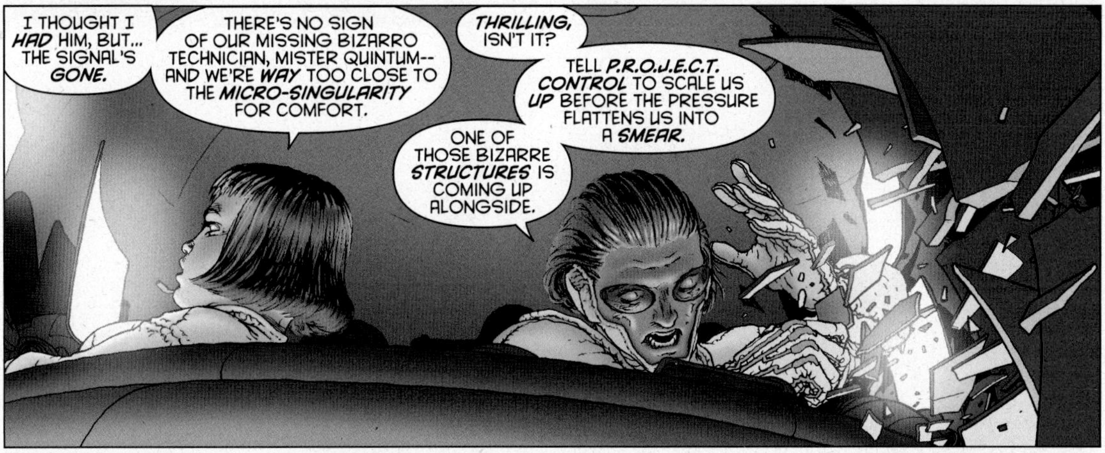
I THOUGHT I HAD HIM, BUT... THE SIGNAL'S GONE.
THERE'S NO SIGN OF OUR MISSING BIZARRO TECHNICIAN, MISTER QUINTUM-- AND WE'RE WAY TOO CLOSE TO THE MICRO-SINGULARITY FOR COMFORT.
THRILLING, ISN'T IT?
TELL P.R.O.J.E.C.T. CONTROL TO SCALE US UP BEFORE THE PRESSURE FLATTENS US INTO A SMEAR.
ONE OF THOSE BIZARRE STRUCTURES IS COMING UP ALONGSIDE.

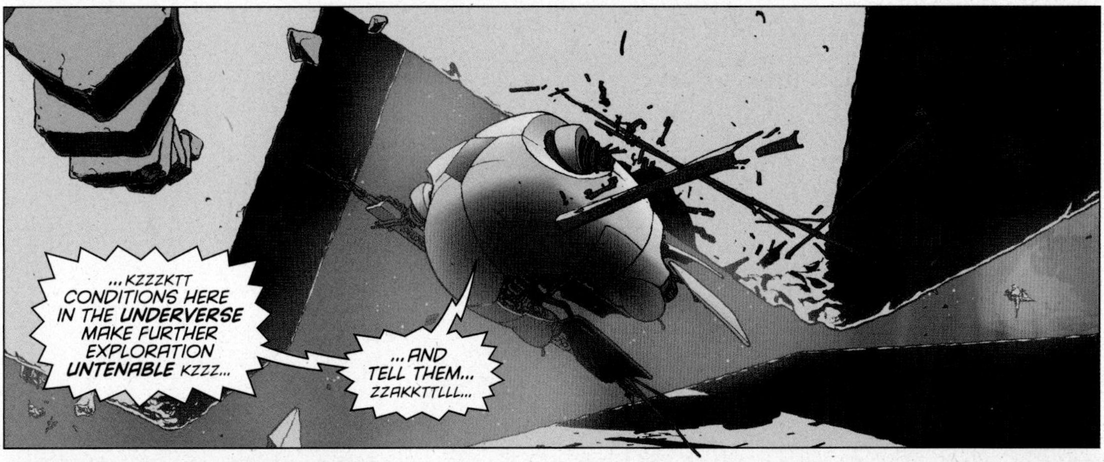
...KZZZKTT CONDITIONS HERE IN THE UNDERVERSE MAKE FURTHER EXPLORATION UNTENABLE KZZZ...
...AND TELL THEM... ZZAKKTTLLL...

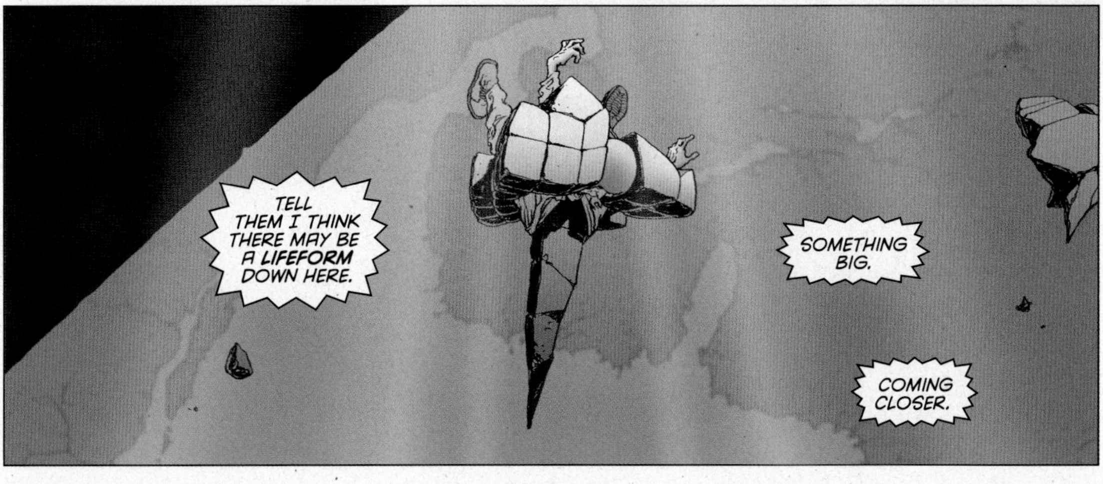
TELL THEM I THINK THERE MAY BE A LIFEFORM DOWN HERE.
SOMETHING BIG.
COMING CLOSER.

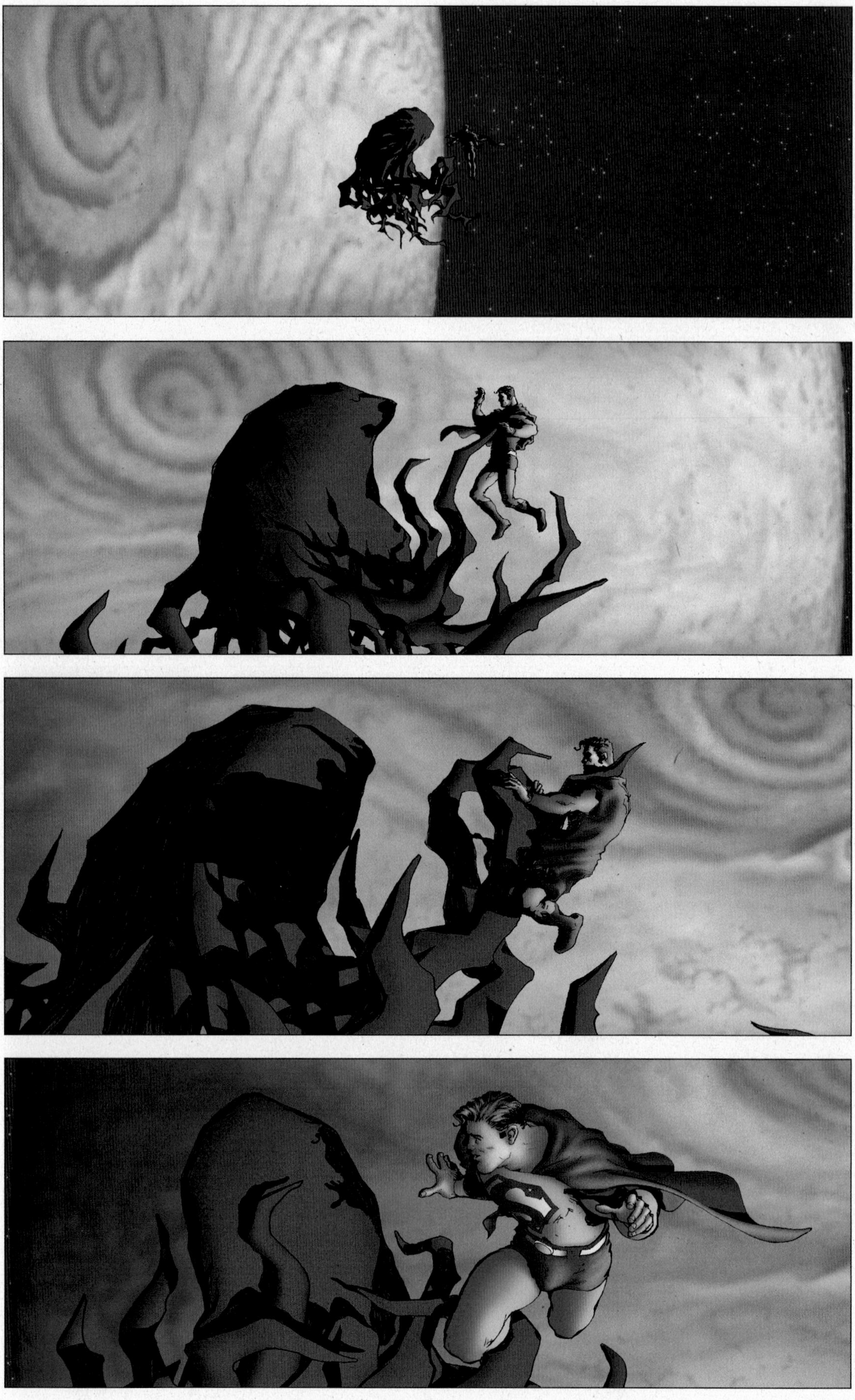

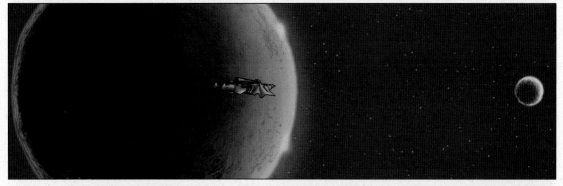

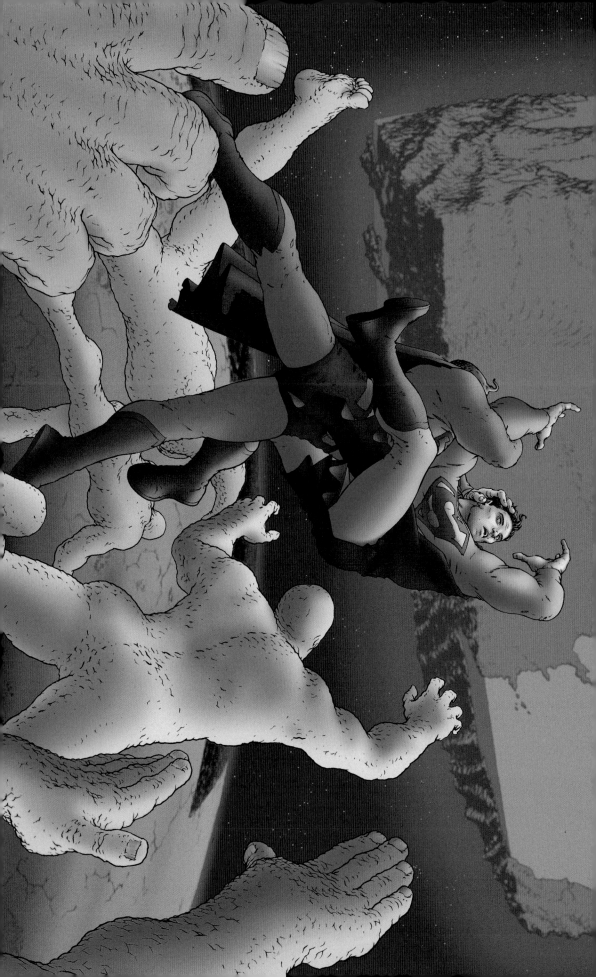

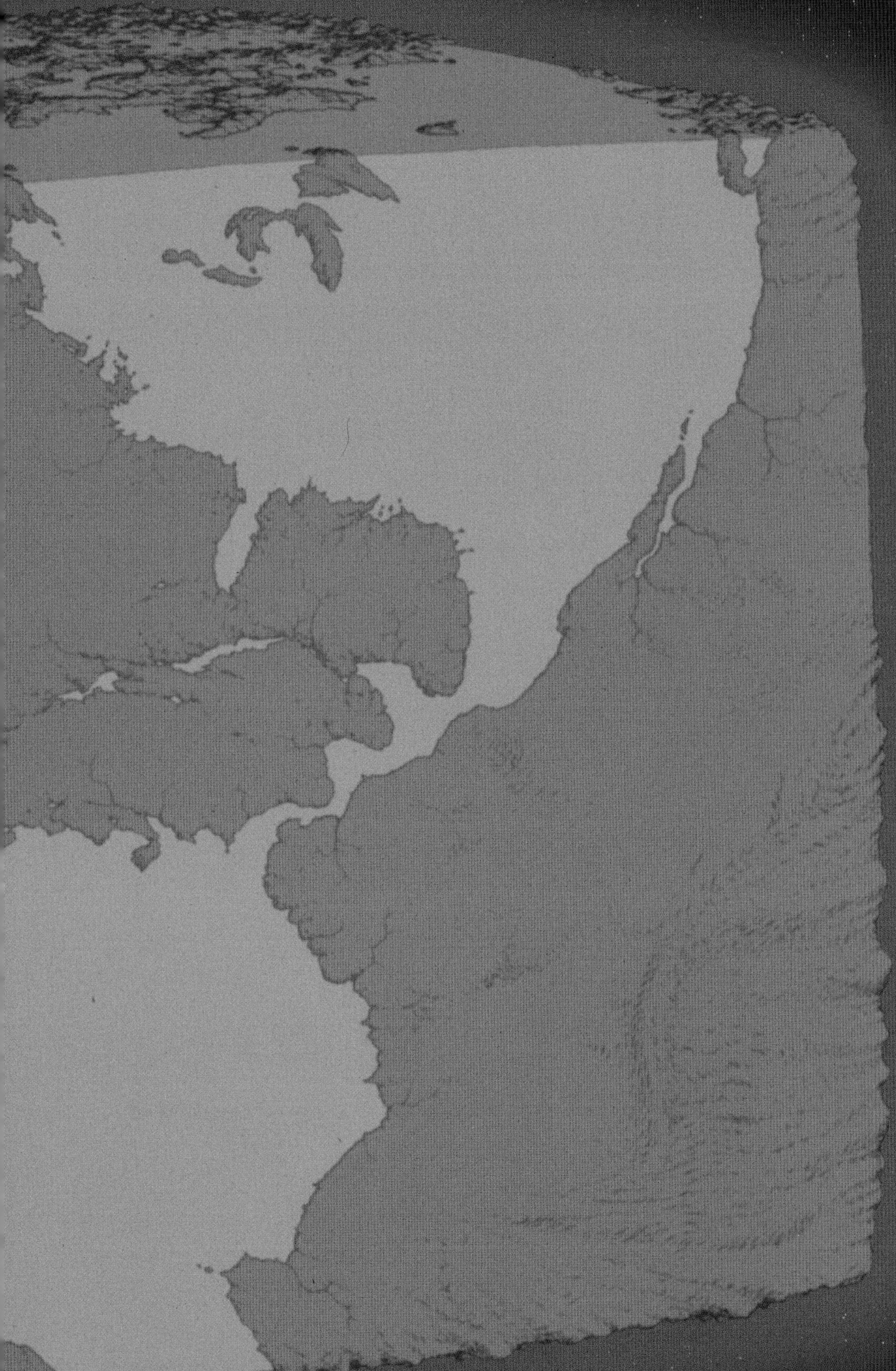

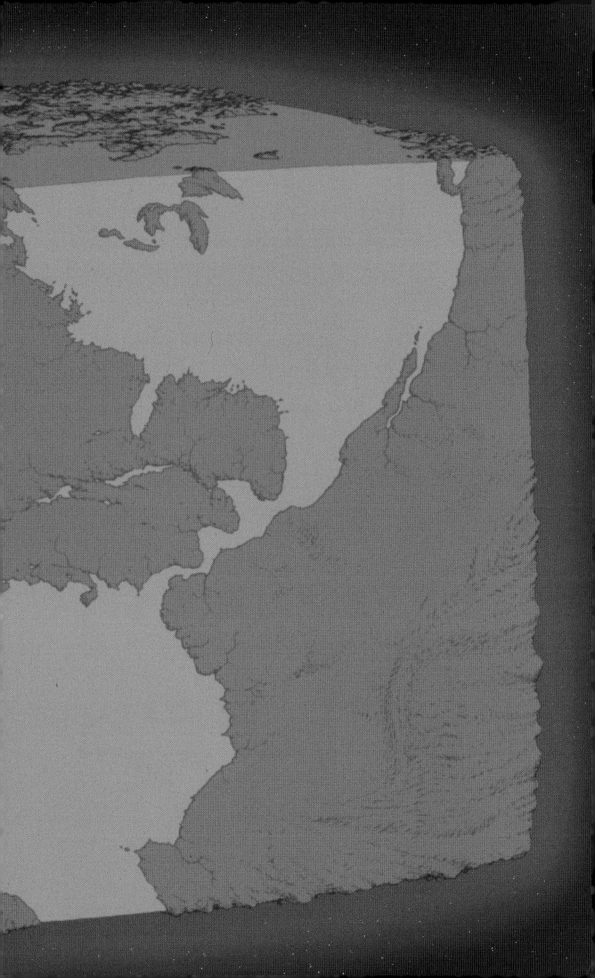

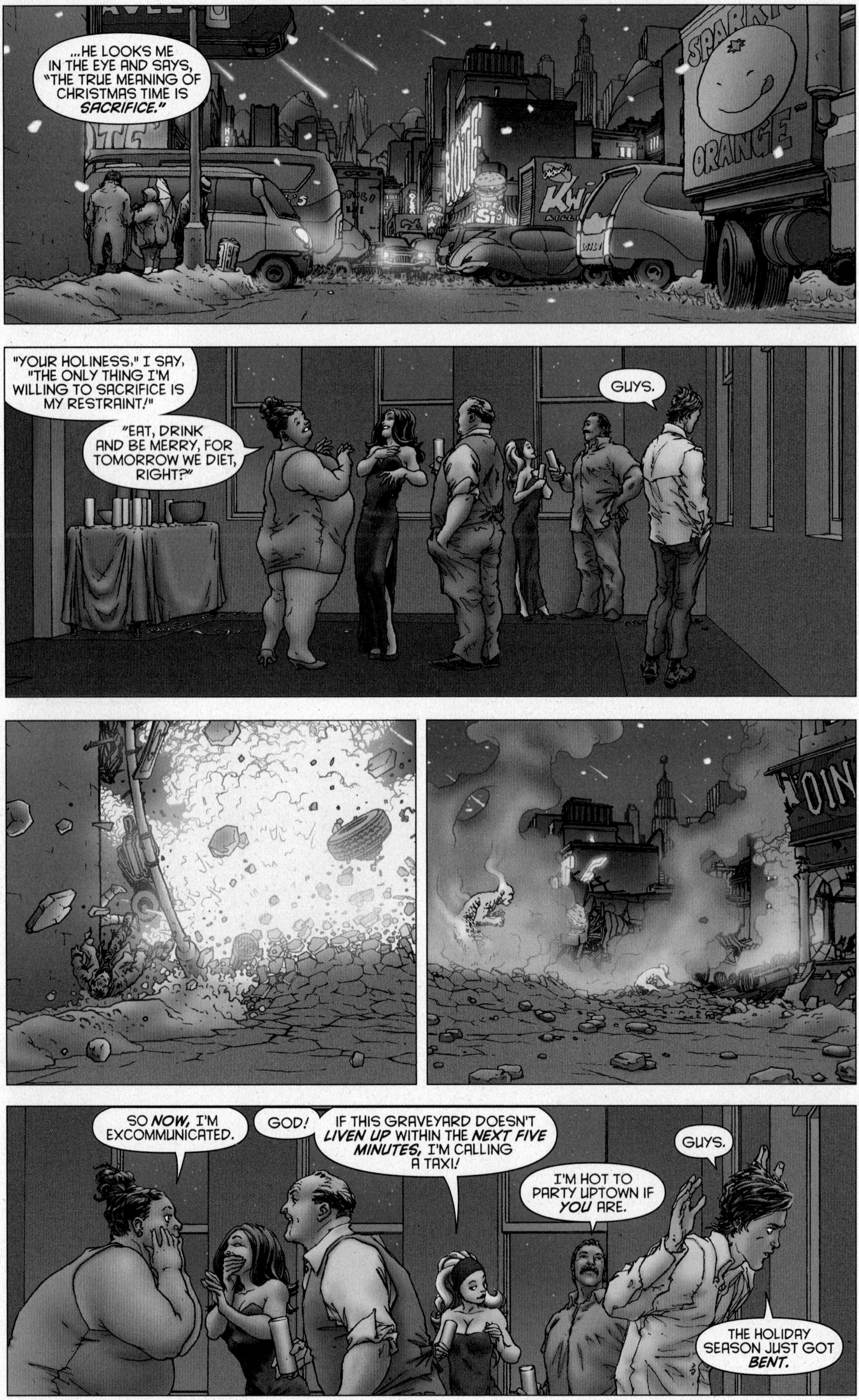
...HE LOOKS ME IN THE EYE AND SAYS, "THE TRUE MEANING OF CHRISTMAS TIME IS SACRIFICE."
"YOUR HOLINESS," I SAY, "THE ONLY THING I'M WILLING TO SACRIFICE IS MY RESTRAINT!"
"EAT, DRINK AND BE MERRY, FOR TOMORROW WE DIET, RIGHT?"
GUYS.
SO NOW, I'M EXCOMMUNICATED.
GOD!
IF THIS GRAVEYARD DOESN'T LIVEN UP WITHIN THE NEXT FIVE MINUTES, I'M CALLING A TAXI!
GUYS.
I'M HOT TO PARTY UPTOWN IF YOU ARE.
THE HOLIDAY SEASON JUST GOT BENT.

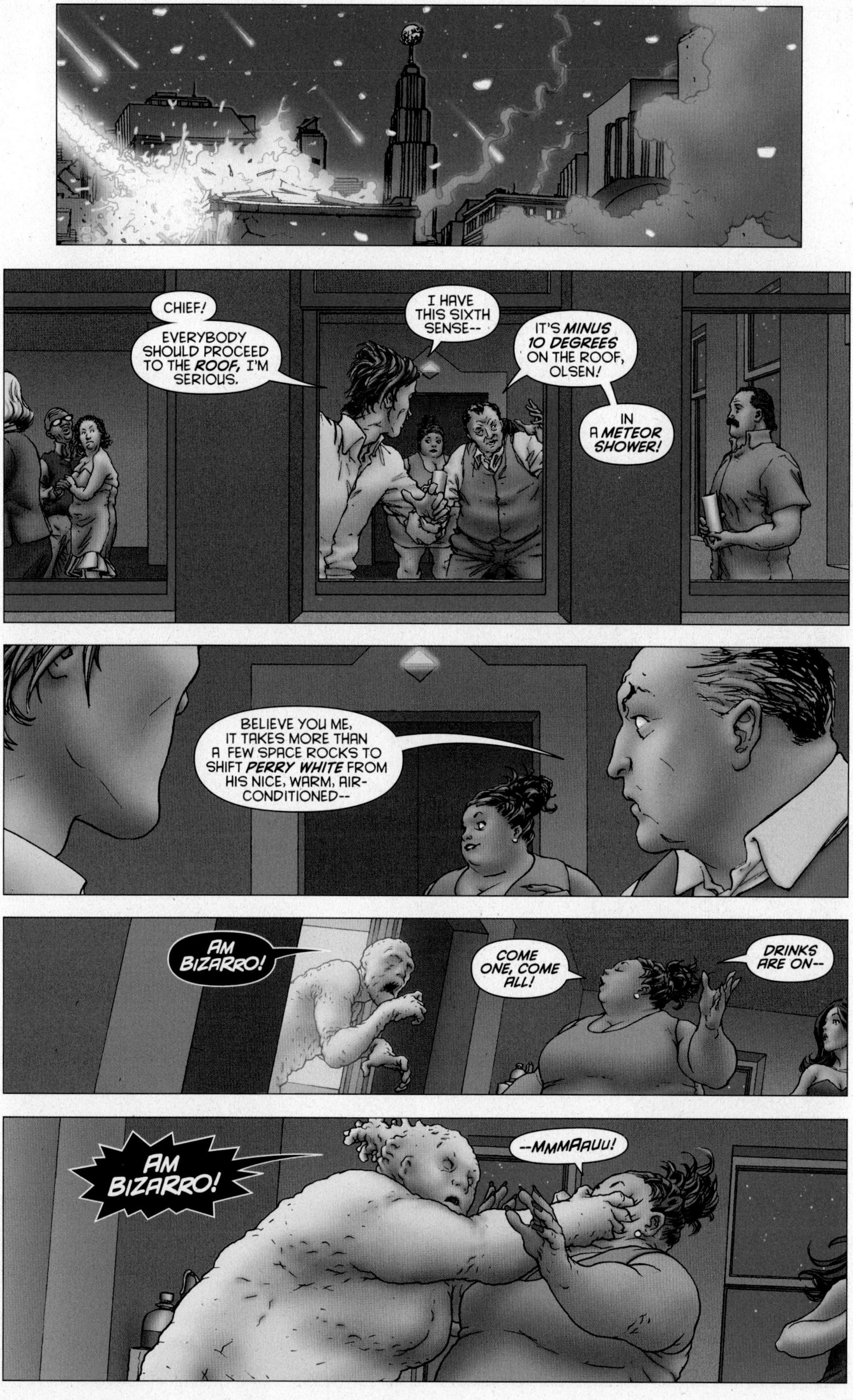
CHIEF!
EVERYBODY SHOULD PROCEED TO THE ROOF, I'M SERIOUS.
I HAVE THIS SIXTH SENSE--
IT'S MINUS 10 DEGREES ON THE ROOF, OLSEN!
IN A METEOR SHOWER!
BELIEVE YOU ME, IT TAKES MORE THAN A FEW SPACE ROCKS TO SHIFT PERRY WHITE FROM HIS NICE, WARM, AIR-CONDITIONED--
AM BIZARRO!
COME ONE, COME ALL!
DRINKS ARE ON--
AM BIZARRO!
--MMMAAUU!

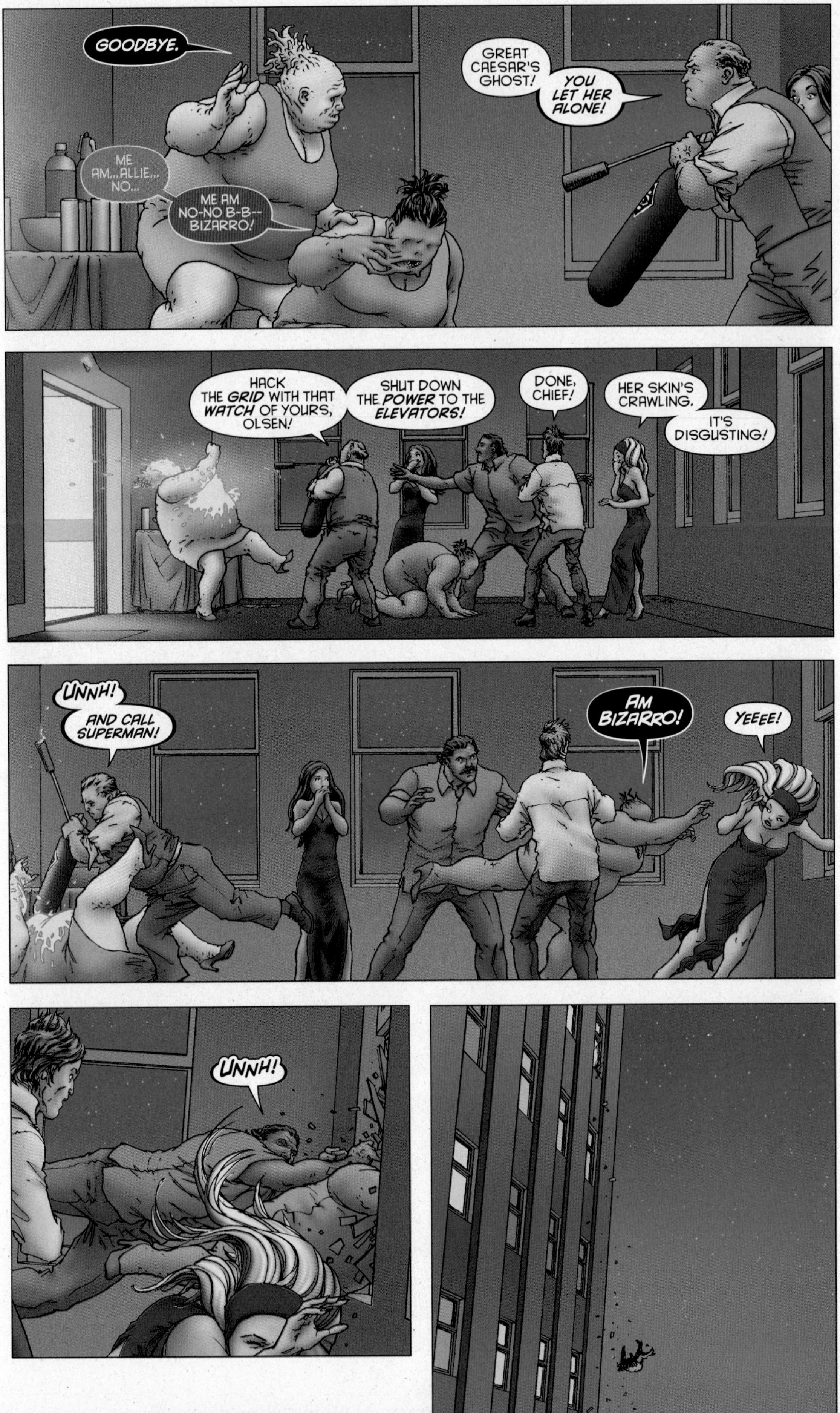
GOODBYE.
GREAT CAESAR'S GHOST!
YOU LET HER ALONE!
ME AM...ALLIE... NO...
ME AM NO-NO B-B-- BIZARRO!
HACK THE GRID WITH THAT WATCH OF YOURS, OLSEN!
SHUT DOWN THE POWER TO THE ELEVATORS!
DONE, CHIEF!
HER SKIN'S CRAWLING.
IT'S DISGUSTING!
UNNH!
AND CALL SUPERMAN!
AM BIZARRO!
YEEEE!
UNNH!

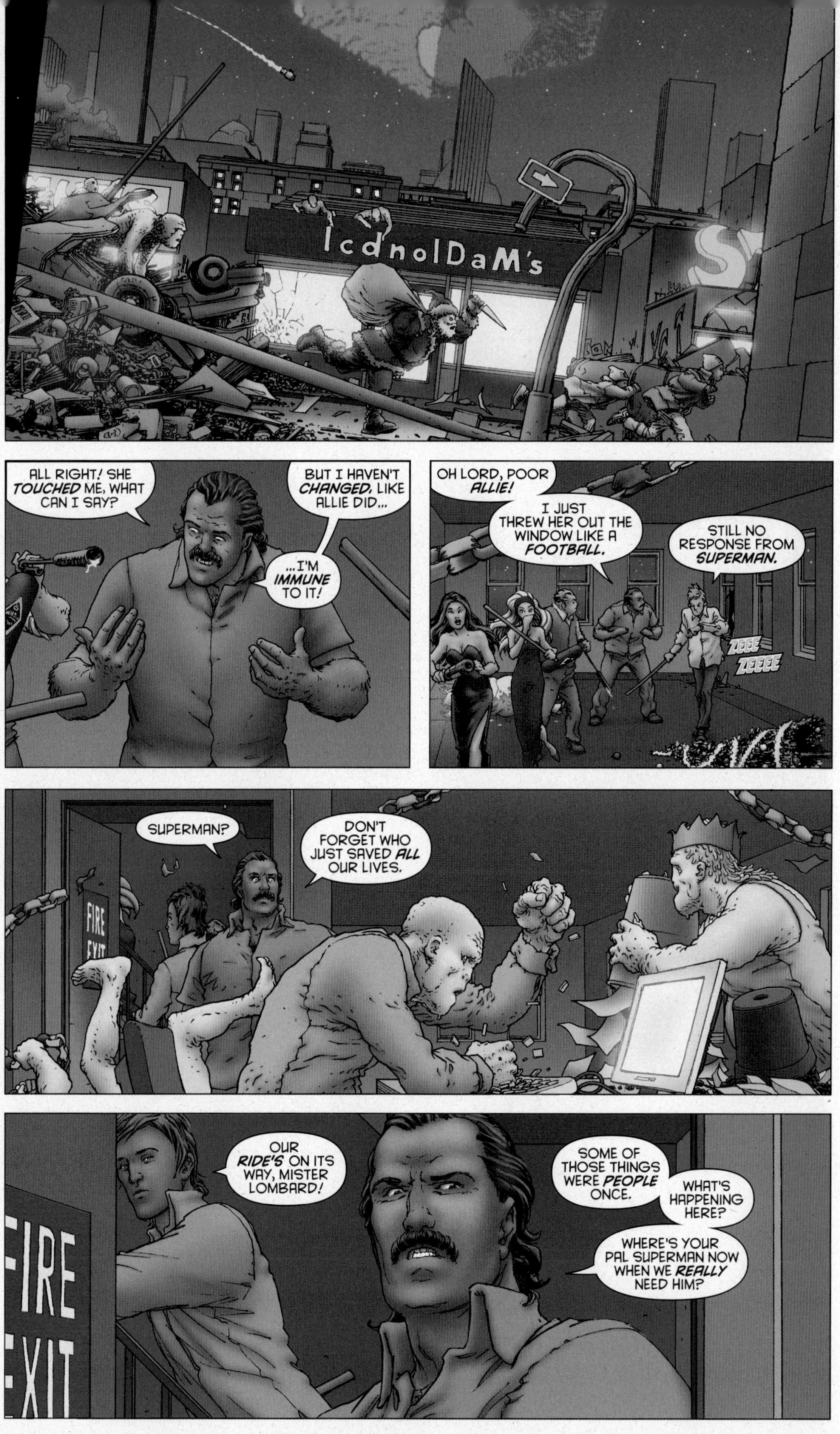
lcdnolDaM's
ALL RIGHT! SHE TOUCHED ME, WHAT CAN I SAY?
BUT I HAVEN'T CHANGED, LIKE ALLIE DID...
...I'M IMMUNE TO IT!
OH LORD, POOR ALLIE!
I JUST THREW HER OUT THE WINDOW LIKE A FOOTBALL.
STILL NO RESPONSE FROM SUPERMAN.
ZEEEE ZEEEE
SUPERMAN?
DON'T FORGET WHO JUST SAVED ALL OUR LIVES.
FIRE EXIT
OUR RIDE'S ON ITS WAY, MISTER LOMBARD!
SOME OF THOSE THINGS WERE PEOPLE ONCE.
WHAT'S HAPPENING HERE?
WHERE'S YOUR PAL SUPERMAN NOW WHEN WE REALLY NEED HIM?
FIRE EXIT

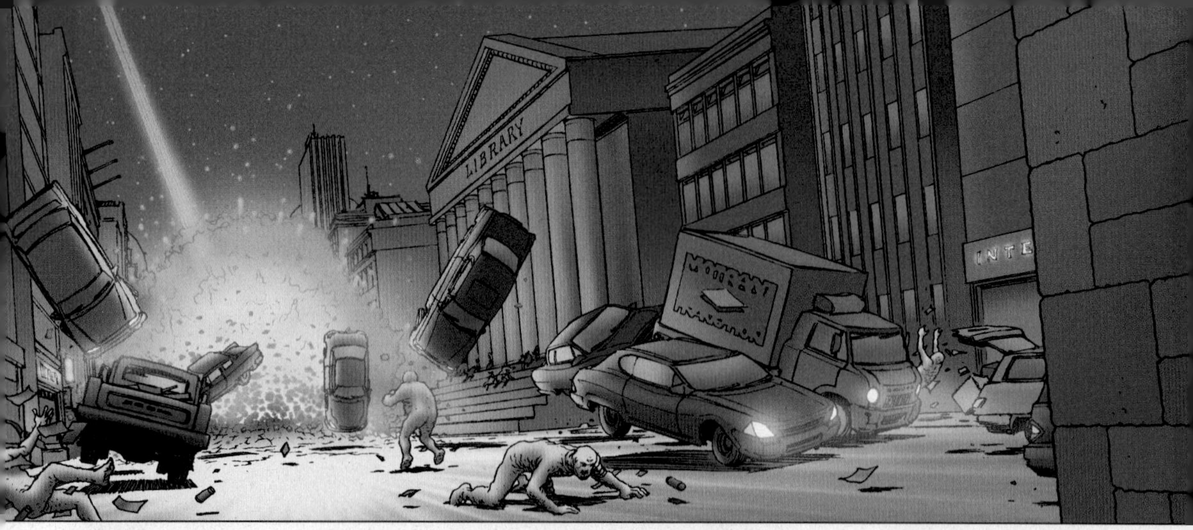
LIBRARY

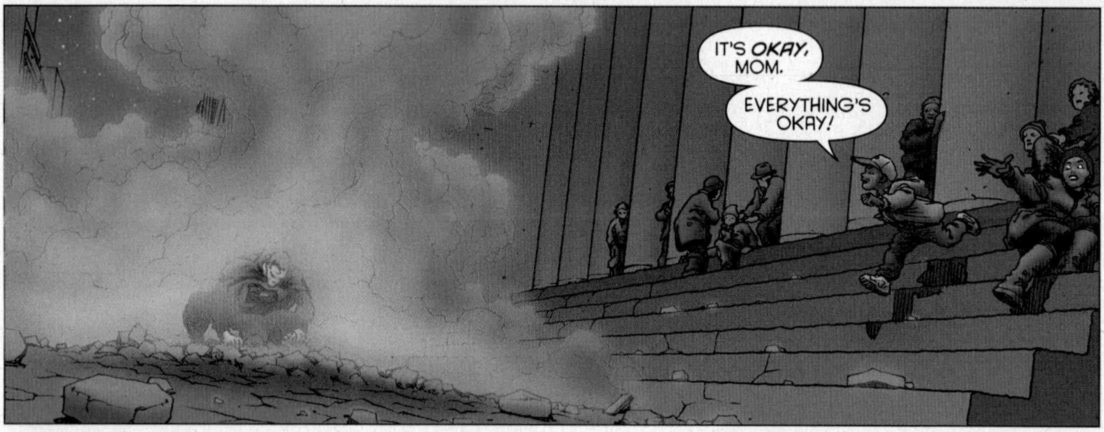
IT'S OKAY, MOM.
EVERYTHING'S OKAY!

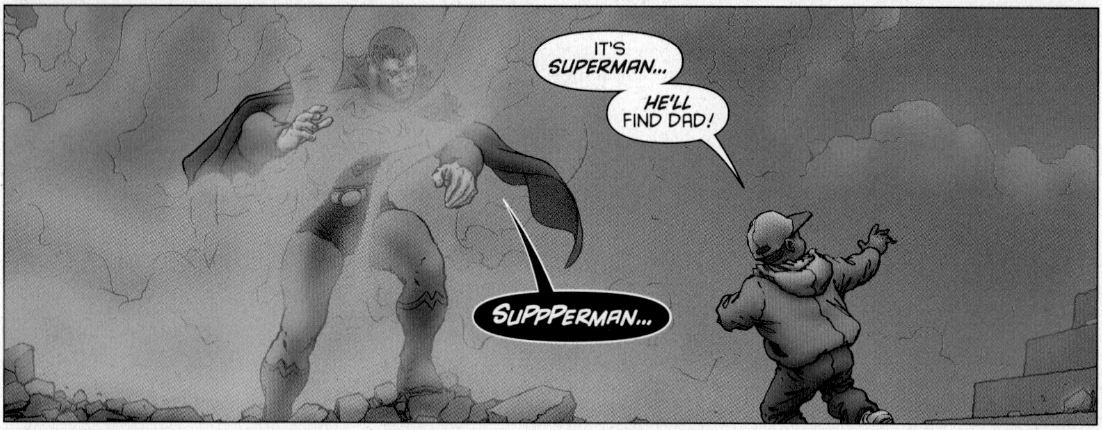
IT'S SUPERMAN...
HE'LL FIND DAD!
SUPPPERMAN...

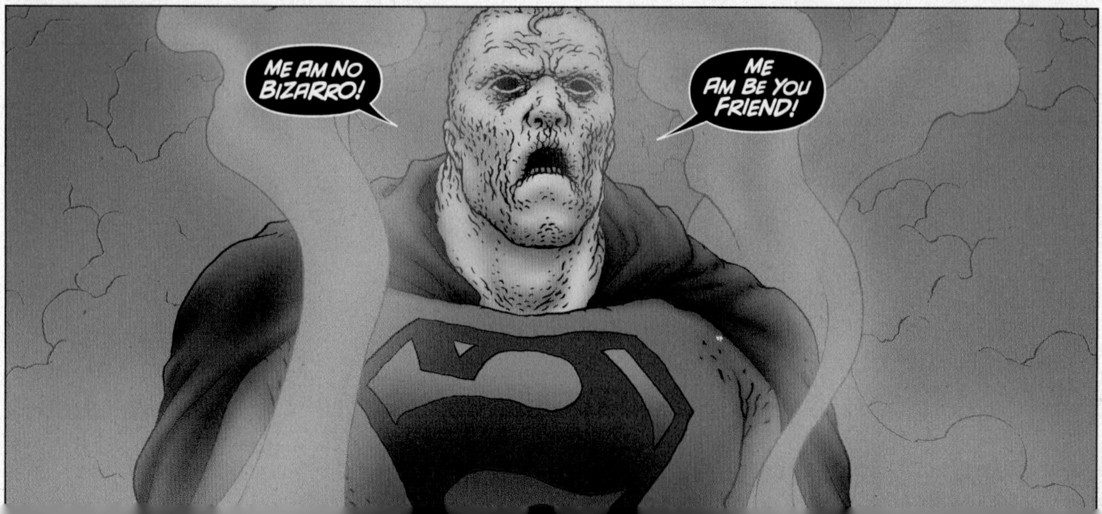
ME AM NO BIZARRO!
ME AM BE YOU FRIEND!

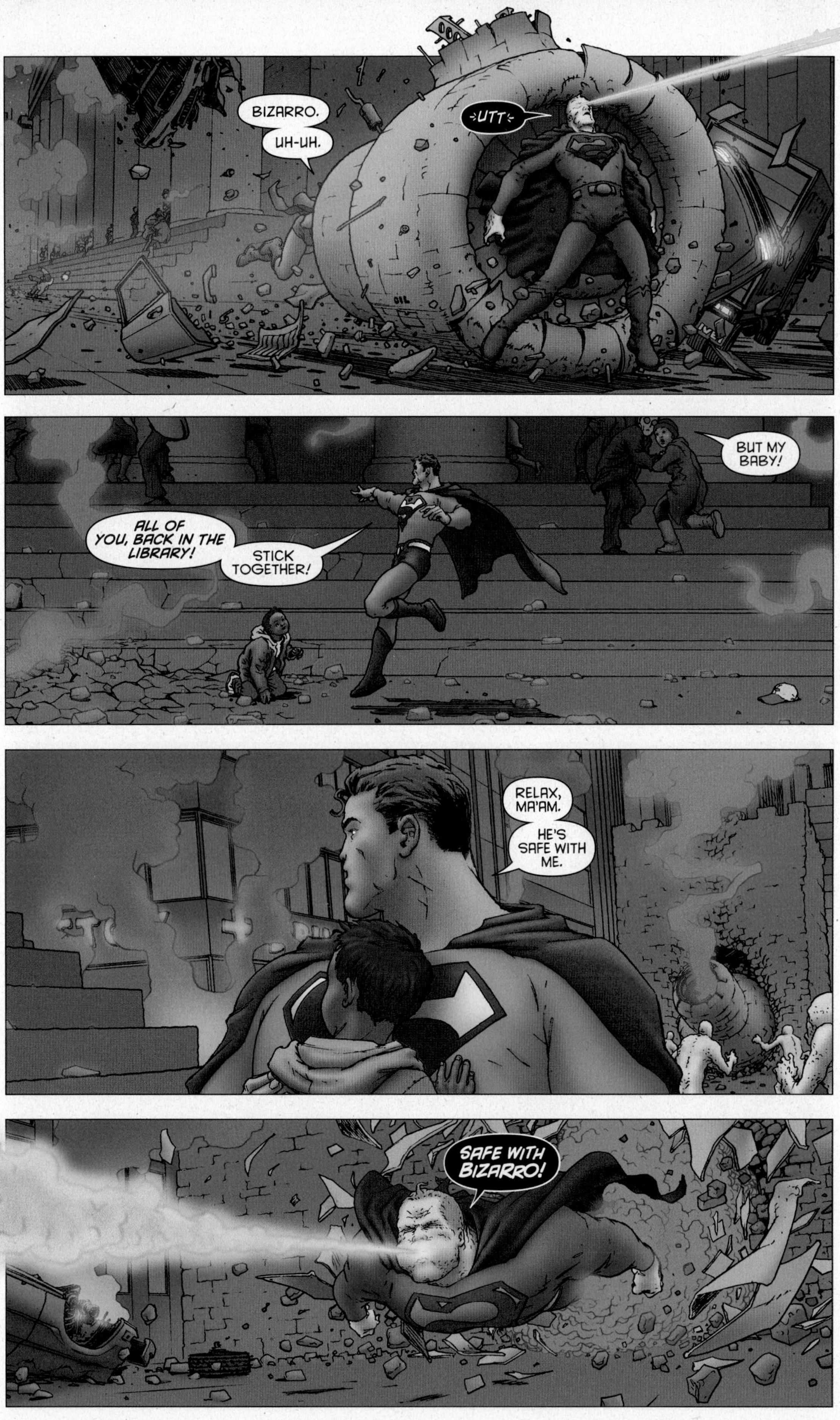
BIZARRO.
UH-UH.
UTT
BUT MY BABY!
ALL OF YOU, BACK IN THE LIBRARY!
STICK TOGETHER!
RELAX, MA'AM.
HE'S SAFE WITH ME.
SAFE WITH BIZARRO!

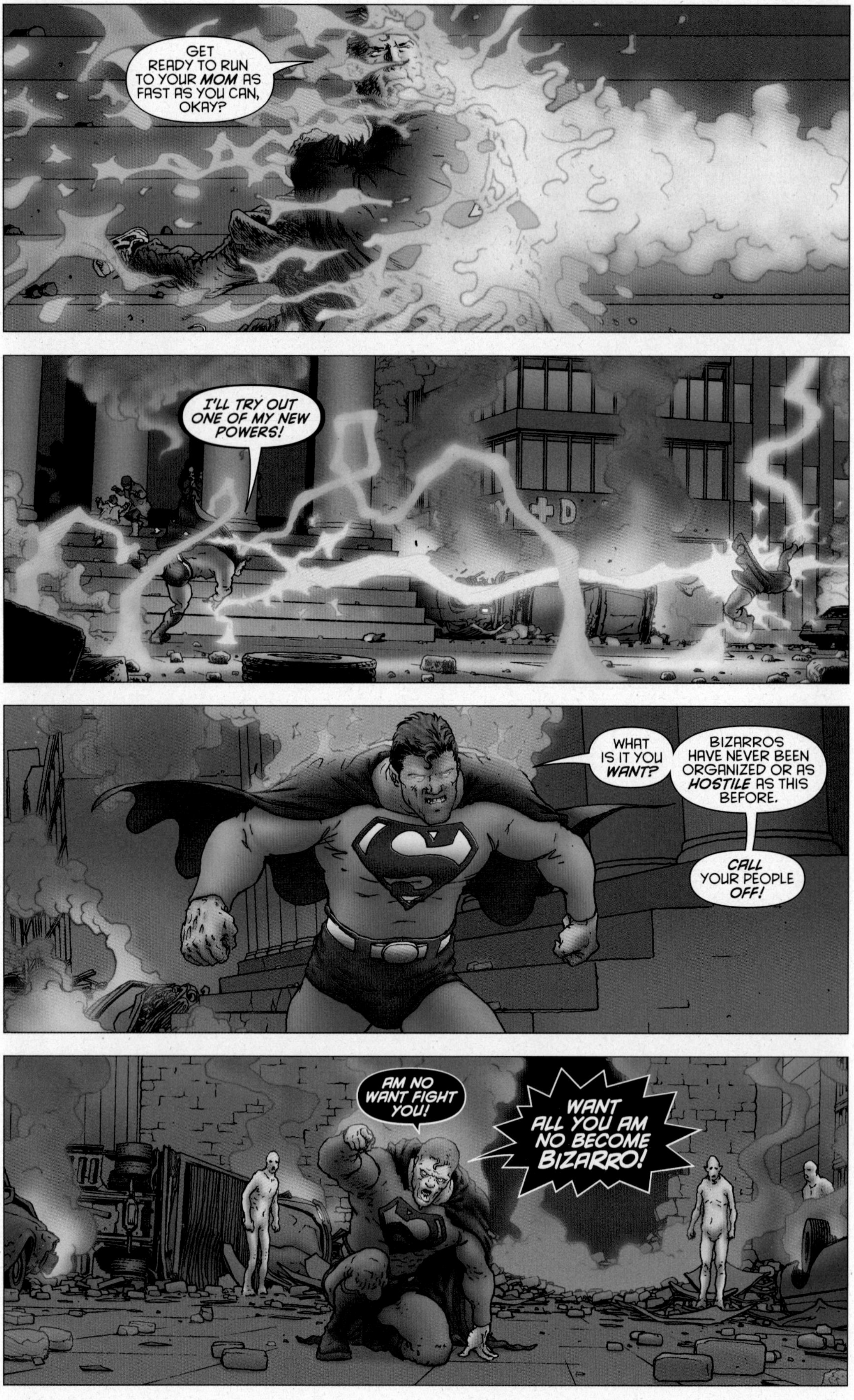
GET READY TO RUN TO YOUR MOM AS FAST AS YOU CAN, OKAY?
I'LL TRY OUT ONE OF MY NEW POWERS!
WHAT IS IT YOU WANT?
BIZARROS HAVE NEVER BEEN ORGANIZED OR AS HOSTILE AS THIS BEFORE.
CALL YOUR PEOPLE OFF!
AM NO WANT FIGHT YOU!
WANT ALL YOU AM NO BECOME BIZARRO!

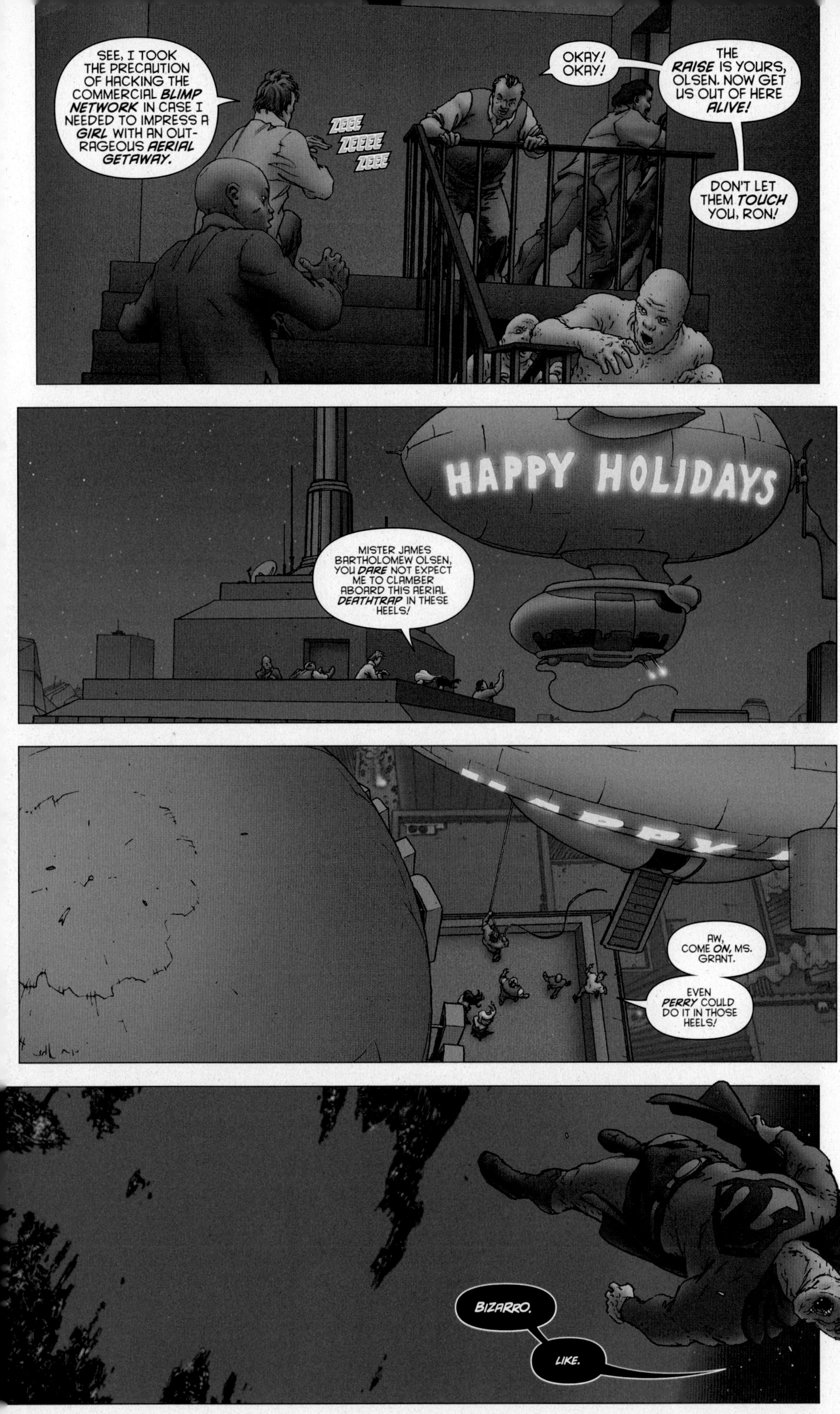

SEE, I TOOK THE PRECAUTION OF HACKING THE COMMERCIAL BLIMP NETWORK IN CASE I NEEDED TO IMPRESS A GIRL WITH AN OUT-RAGEOUS AERIAL GETAWAY.
ZEEE ZEEEE ZEEE
OKAY! OKAY!
THE RAISE IS YOURS, OLSEN. NOW GET US OUT OF HERE ALIVE!
DON'T LET THEM TOUCH YOU, RON!
HAPPY HOLIDAYS
MISTER JAMES BARTHOLOMEW OLSEN, YOU DARE NOT EXPECT ME TO CLAMBER ABOARD THIS AERIAL DEATHTRAP IN THESE HEELS!
AW, COME ON, MS. GRANT.
EVEN PERRY COULD DO IT IN THOSE HEELS!
BIZARRO.
LIKE.

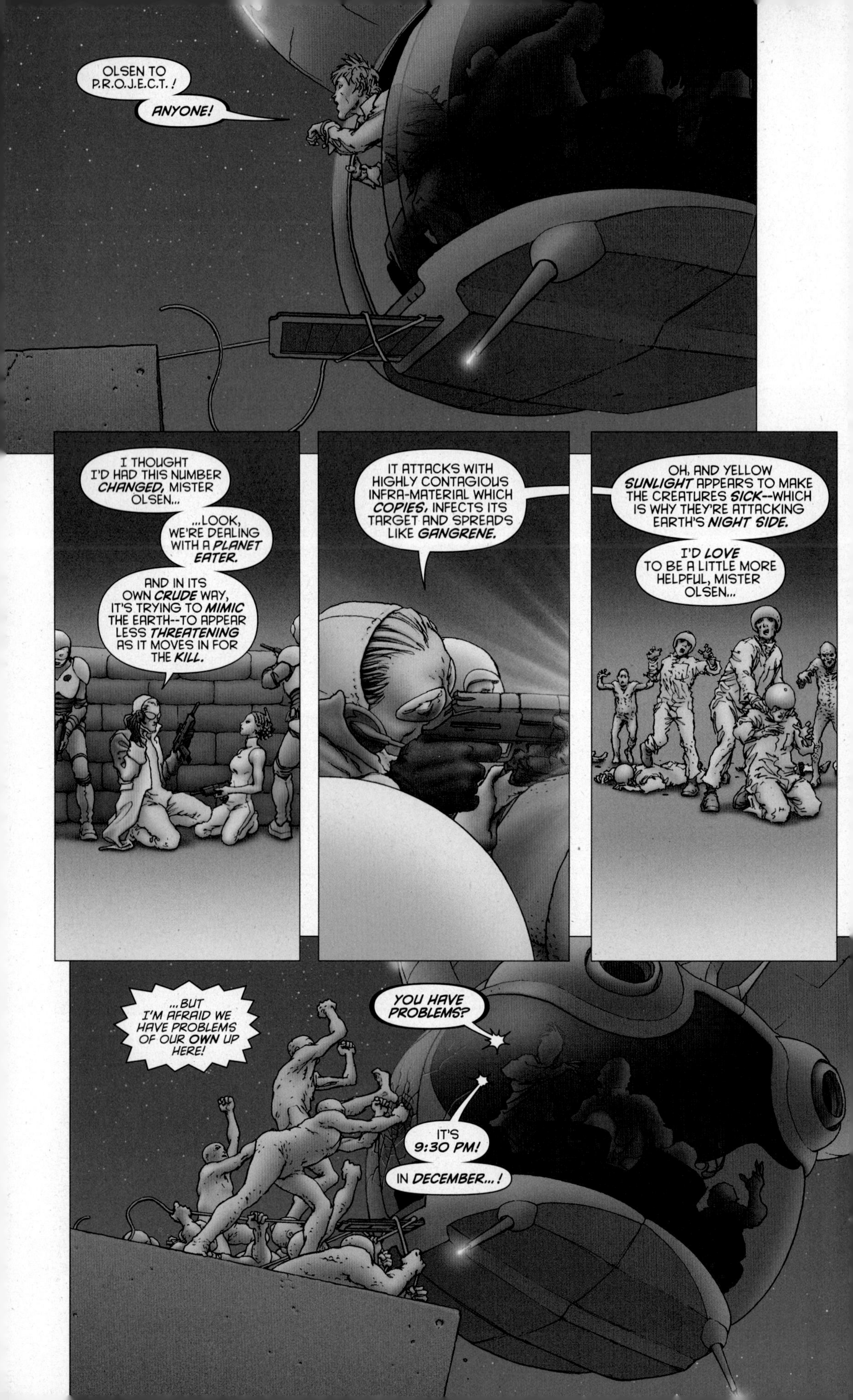

OLSEN TO P.R.O.J.E.C.T.!
ANYONE!
I THOUGHT I'D HAD THIS NUMBER CHANGED, MISTER OLSEN...
...LOOK, WE'RE DEALING WITH A PLANET EATER.
AND IN ITS OWN CRUDE WAY, IT'S TRYING TO MIMIC THE EARTH--TO APPEAR LESS THREATENING AS IT MOVES IN FOR THE KILL.
IT ATTACKS WITH HIGHLY CONTAGIOUS INFRA-MATERIAL WHICH COPIES, INFECTS ITS TARGET AND SPREADS LIKE GANGRENE.
OH, AND YELLOW SUNLIGHT APPEARS TO MAKE THE CREATURES SICK--WHICH IS WHY THEY'RE ATTACKING EARTH'S NIGHT SIDE.
I'D LOVE TO BE A LITTLE MORE HELPFUL, MISTER OLSEN...
...BUT I'M AFRAID WE HAVE PROBLEMS OF OUR OWN UP HERE!
YOU HAVE PROBLEMS?
IT'S 9:30 PM!
IN DECEMBER...!

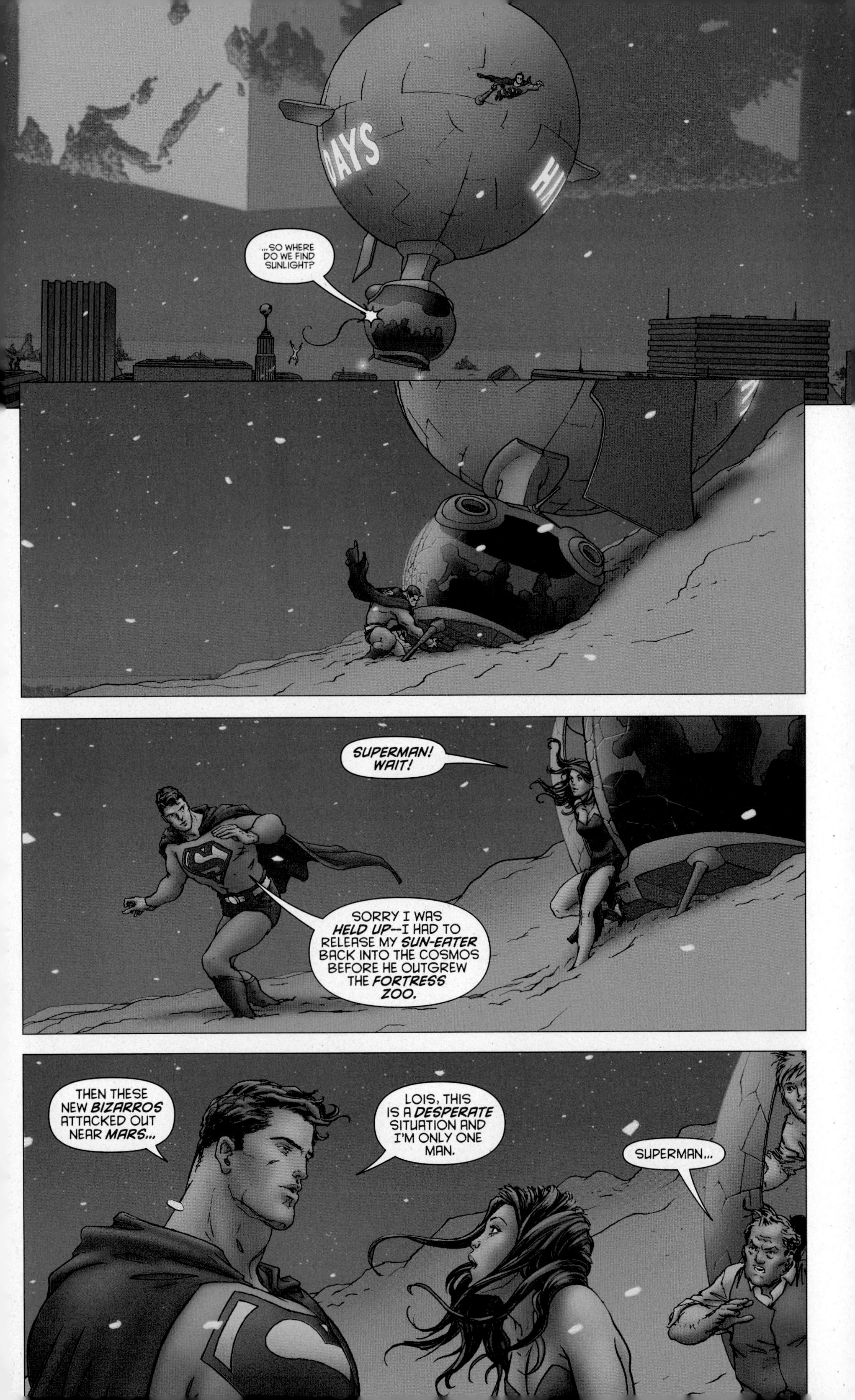
DAYS
...SO WHERE DO WE FIND SUNLIGHT?
SUPERMAN! WAIT!
SORRY I WAS HELD UP--I HAD TO RELEASE MY SUN-EATER BACK INTO THE COSMOS BEFORE HE OUTGREW THE FORTRESS ZOO.
THEN THESE NEW BIZARROS ATTACKED OUT NEAR MARS...
LOIS, THIS IS A DESPERATE SITUATION AND I'M ONLY ONE MAN.
SUPERMAN...

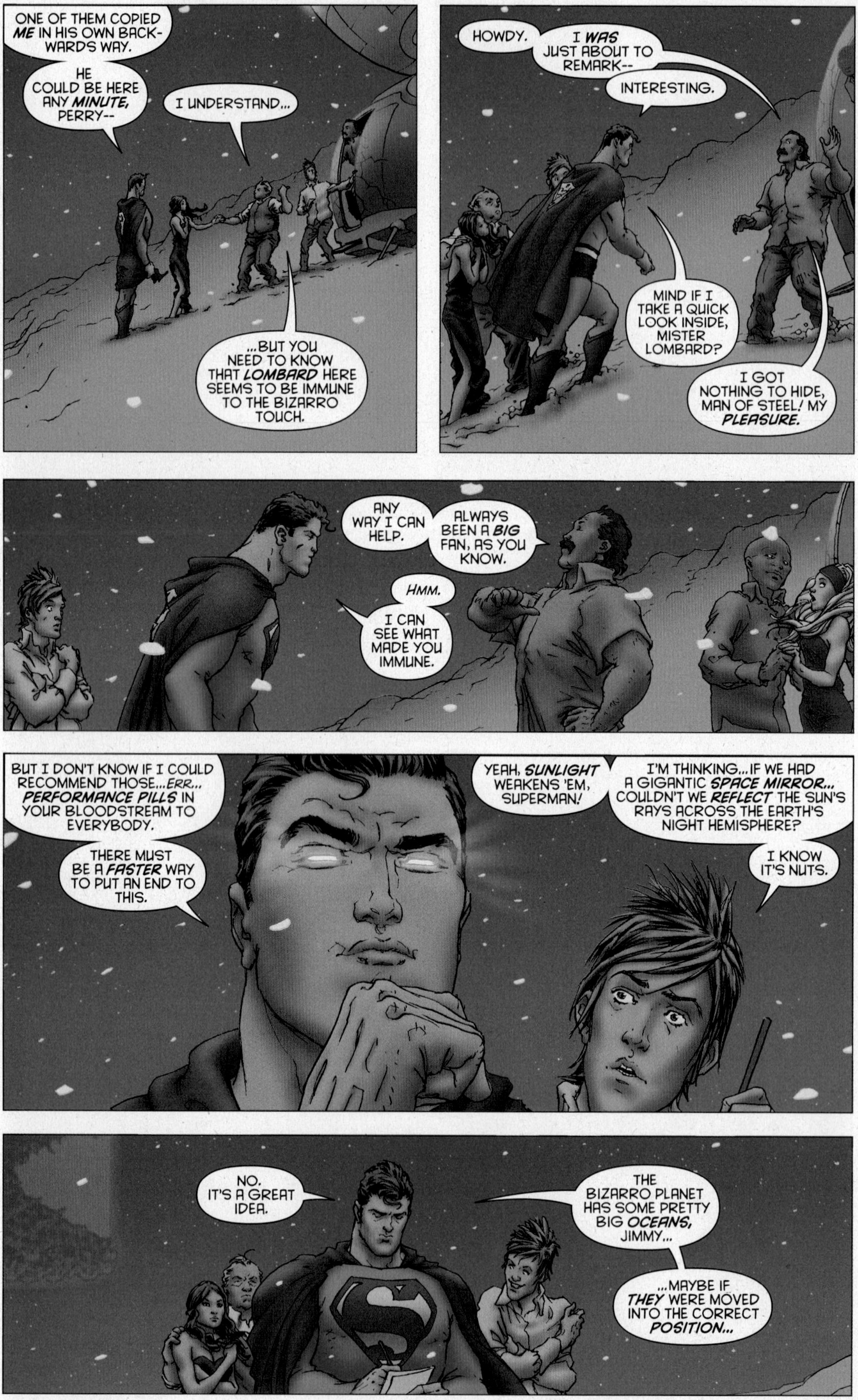

ONE OF THEM COPIED ME IN HIS OWN BACK-WARDS WAY.
HE COULD BE HERE ANY MINUTE, PERRY--
I UNDERSTAND...
...BUT YOU NEED TO KNOW THAT LOMBARD HERE SEEMS TO BE IMMUNE TO THE BIZARRO TOUCH.
HOWDY.
I WAS JUST ABOUT TO REMARK--
INTERESTING.
MIND IF I TAKE A QUICK LOOK INSIDE, MISTER LOMBARD?
I GOT NOTHING TO HIDE, MAN OF STEEL! MY PLEASURE.
ANY WAY I CAN HELP.
ALWAYS BEEN A BIG FAN, AS YOU KNOW.
HMM.
I CAN SEE WHAT MADE YOU IMMUNE.
BUT I DON'T KNOW IF I COULD RECOMMEND THOSE...ERR... PERFORMANCE PILLS IN YOUR BLOODSTREAM TO EVERYBODY.
THERE MUST BE A FASTER WAY TO PUT AN END TO THIS.
YEAH, SUNLIGHT WEAKENS 'EM, SUPERMAN!
I'M THINKING...IF WE HAD A GIGANTIC SPACE MIRROR... COULDN'T WE REFLECT THE SUN'S RAYS ACROSS THE EARTH'S NIGHT HEMISPHERE?
I KNOW IT'S NUTS.
NO. IT'S A GREAT IDEA.
THE BIZARRO PLANET HAS SOME PRETTY BIG OCEANS, JIMMY...
...MAYBE IF THEY WERE MOVED INTO THE CORRECT POSITION...

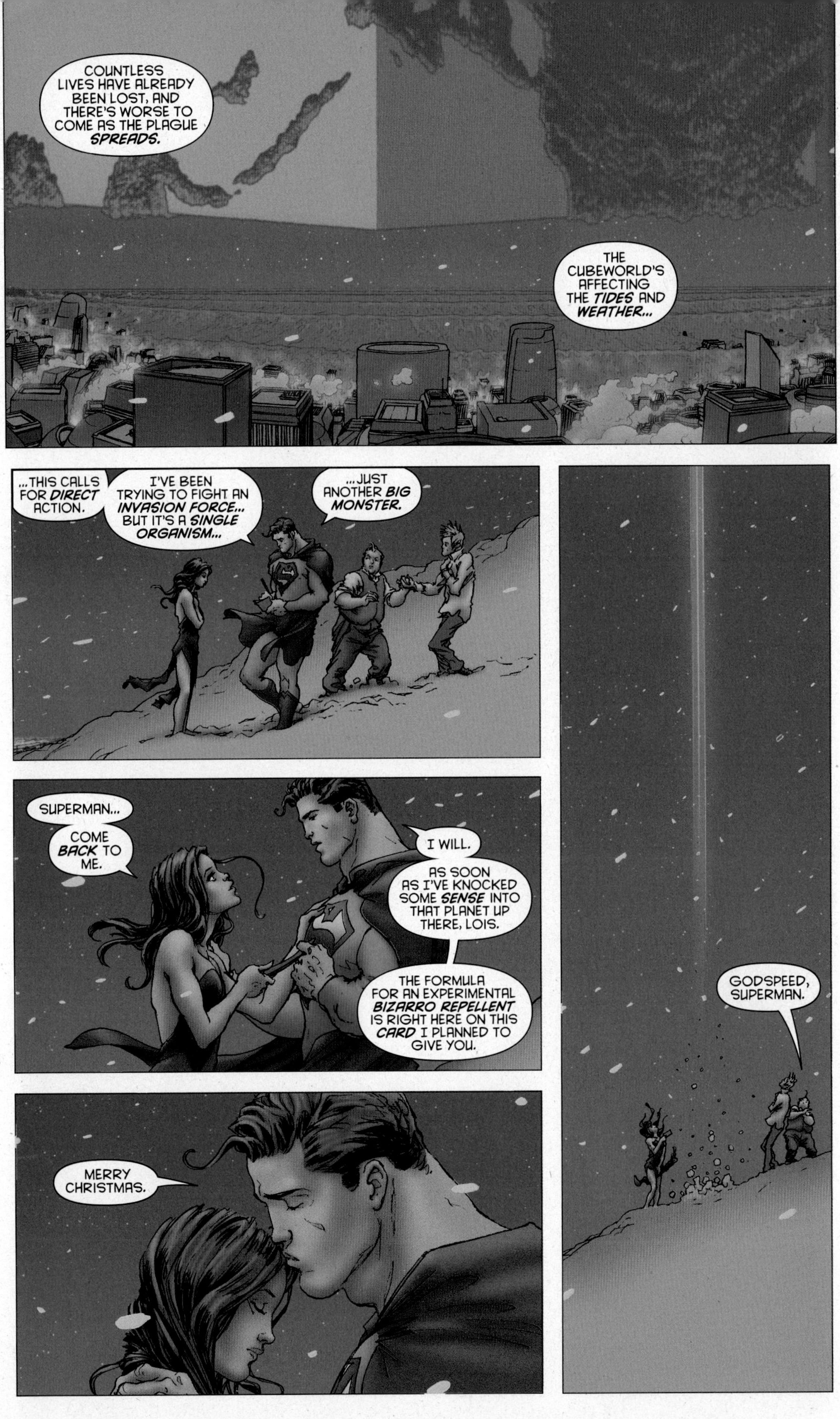
COUNTLESS LIVES HAVE ALREADY BEEN LOST, AND THERE'S WORSE TO COME AS THE PLAGUE SPREADS.
THE CUBEWORLD'S AFFECTING THE TIDES AND WEATHER...
...THIS CALLS FOR DIRECT ACTION.
I'VE BEEN TRYING TO FIGHT AN INVASION FORCE... BUT IT'S A SINGLE ORGANISM...
...JUST ANOTHER BIG MONSTER.
SUPERMAN...
COME BACK TO ME.
I WILL.
AS SOON AS I'VE KNOCKED SOME SENSE INTO THAT PLANET UP THERE, LOIS.
THE FORMULA FOR AN EXPERIMENTAL BIZARRO REPELLENT IS RIGHT HERE ON THIS CARD I PLANNED TO GIVE YOU.
MERRY CHRISTMAS.
GODSPEED, SUPERMAN.

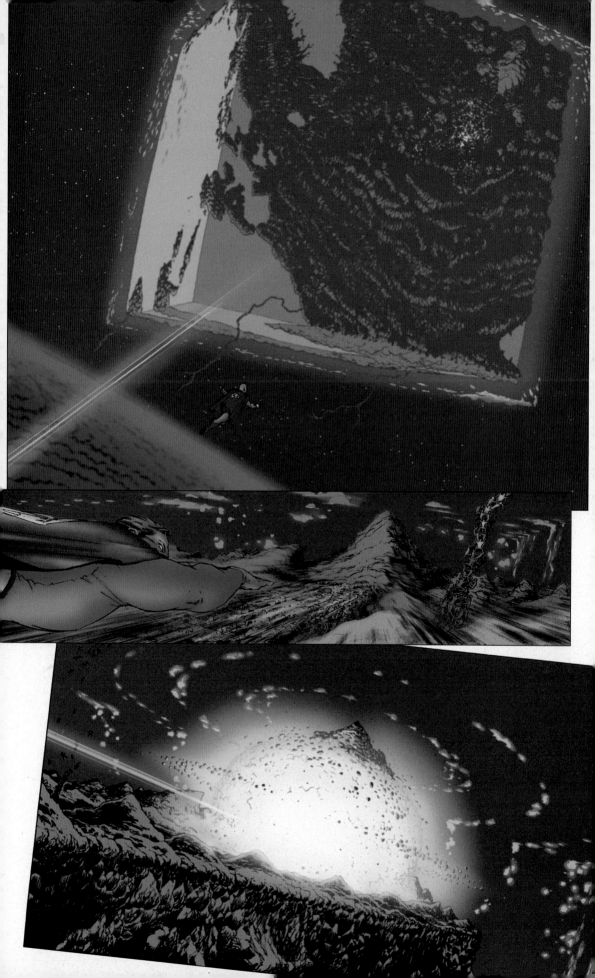

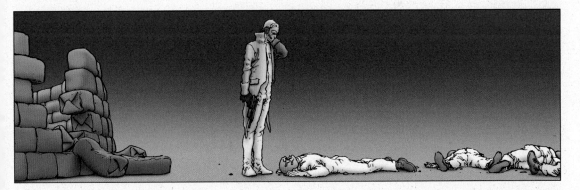

BEING BIZARRO

OLSEN, EXPLAIN!

HE HURT IT.

I GUESS IT'S CRAWLING ITS WAY BACK INTO THE UNDERVERSE TO LICK ITS WOUNDS, CHIEF.

BUT WHAT ABOUT SUPERMAN?

WHAT HAPPENED TO SUPERMAN?

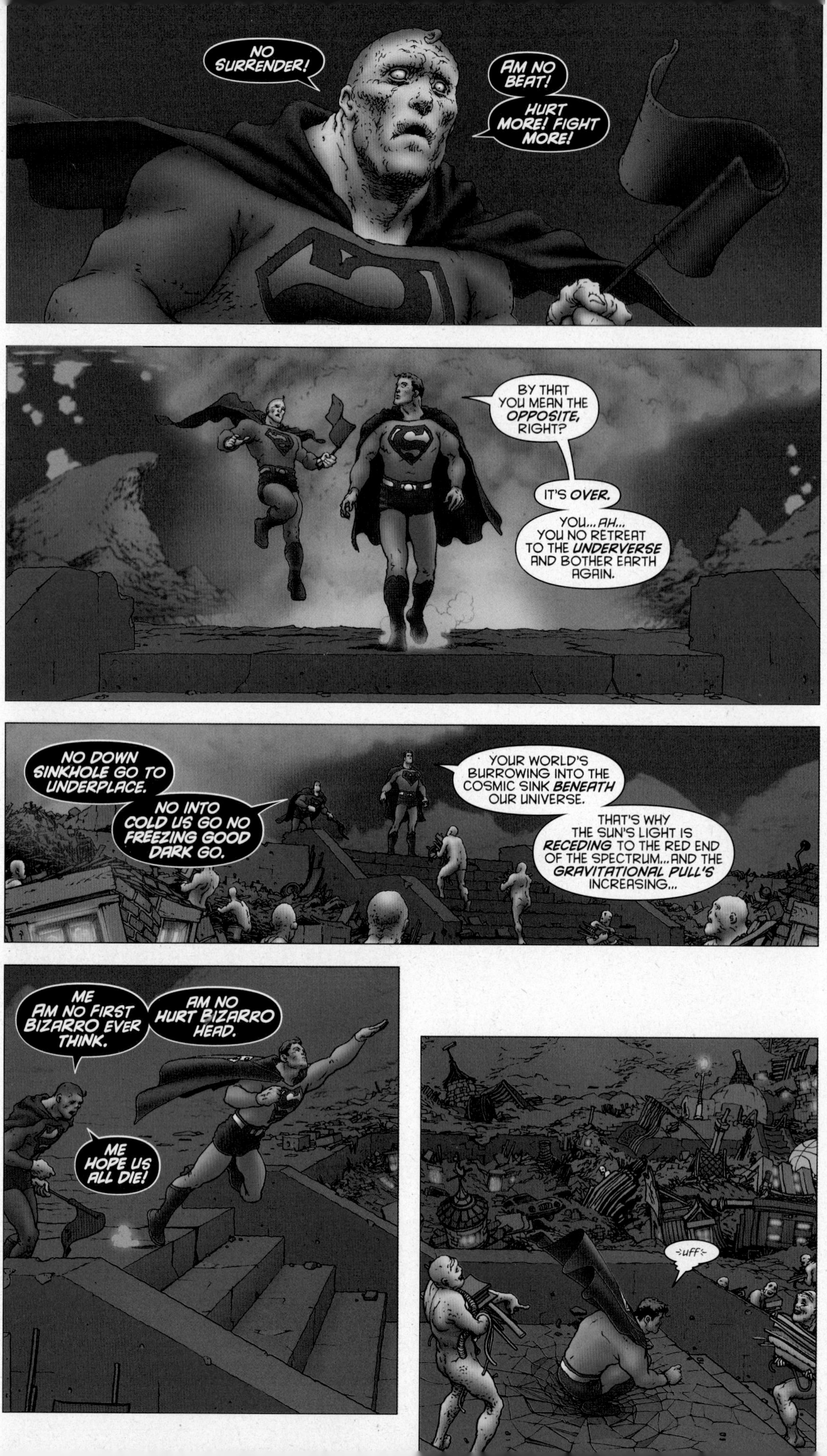
NO SURRENDER!
AM NO BEAT!
HURT MORE! FIGHT MORE!
BY THAT YOU MEAN THE OPPOSITE, RIGHT?
IT'S OVER.
YOU... AH... YOU NO RETREAT TO THE UNDERVERSE AND BOTHER EARTH AGAIN.
NO DOWN SINKHOLE GO TO UNDERPLACE.
NO INTO COLD US GO NO FREEZING GOOD DARK GO.
YOUR WORLD'S BURROWING INTO THE COSMIC SINK BENEATH OUR UNIVERSE.
THAT'S WHY THE SUN'S LIGHT IS RECEDING TO THE RED END OF THE SPECTRUM... AND THE GRAVITATIONAL PULL'S INCREASING...
ME AM NO FIRST BIZARRO EVER THINK.
AM NO HURT BIZARRO HEAD.
ME HOPE US ALL DIE!
uff

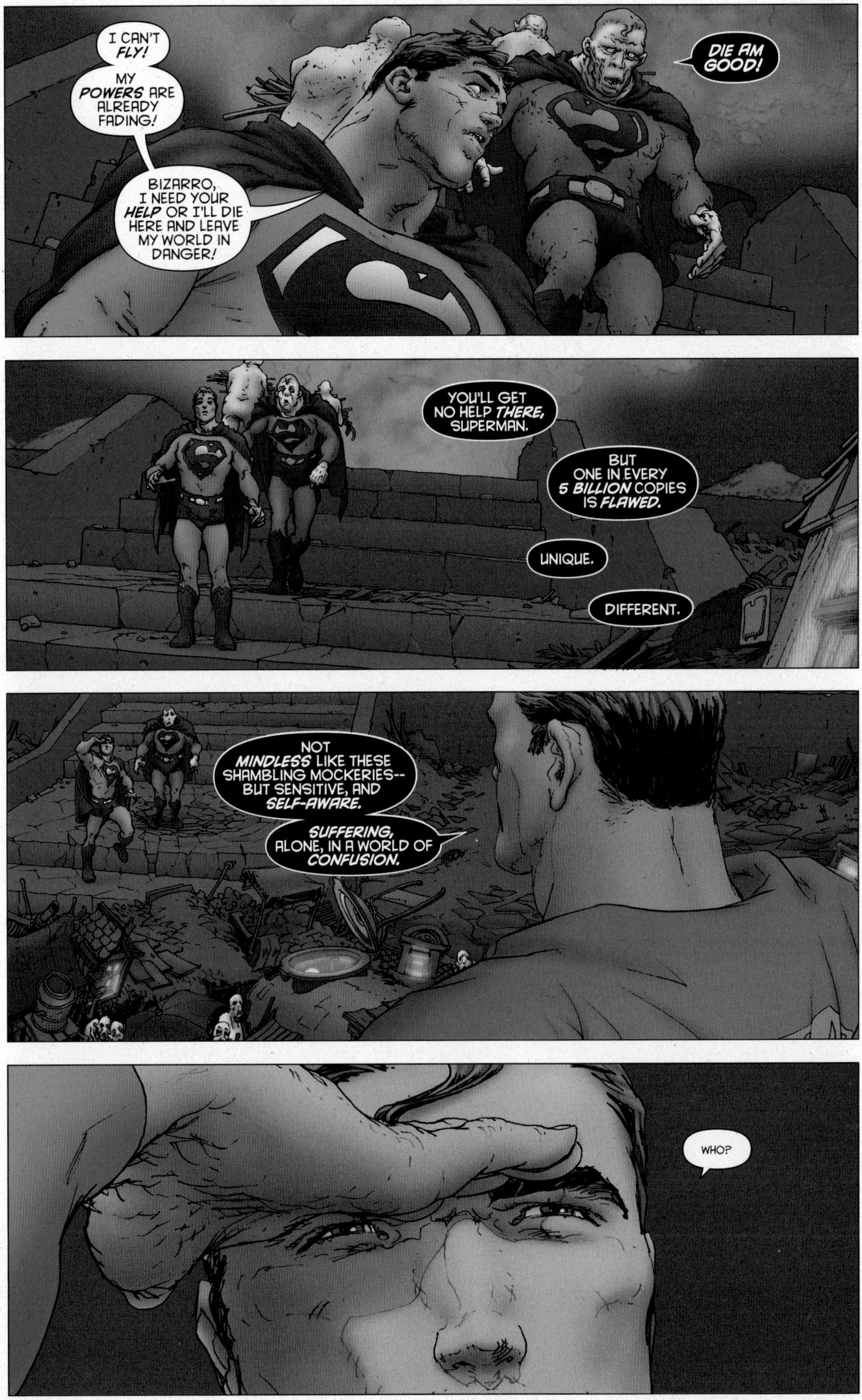

I CAN'T FLY!
MY POWERS ARE ALREADY FADING!
BIZARRO, I NEED YOUR HELP OR I'LL DIE HERE AND LEAVE MY WORLD IN DANGER!
DIE AM GOOD!
YOU'LL GET NO HELP THERE, SUPERMAN.
BUT ONE IN EVERY 5 BILLION COPIES IS FLAWED.
UNIQUE.
DIFFERENT.
NOT MINDLESS LIKE THESE SHAMBLING MOCKERIES-- BUT SENSITIVE, AND SELF-AWARE.
SUFFERING, ALONE, IN A WORLD OF CONFUSION.
WHO?

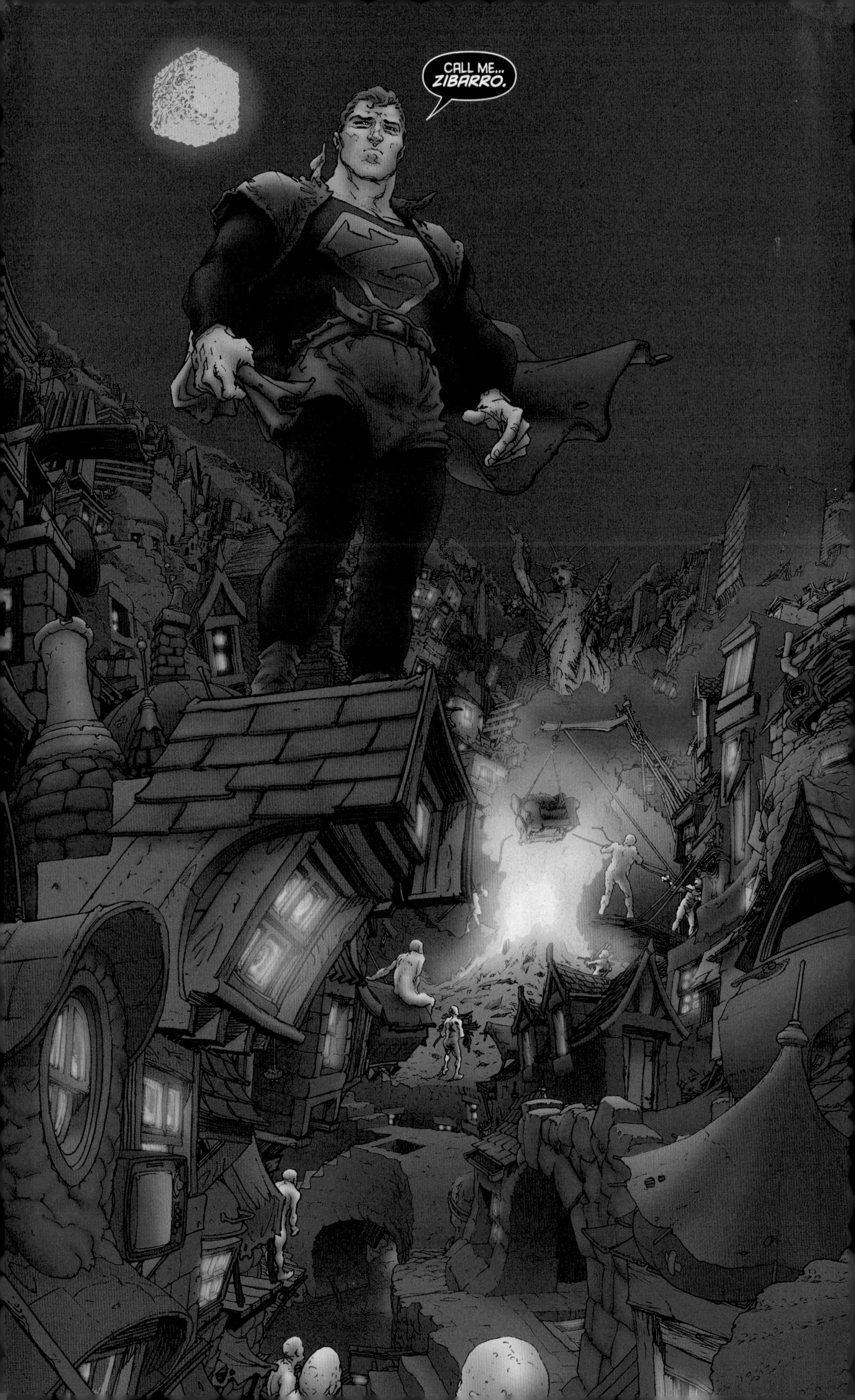
CALL ME... ZIBARRO.

Episode 8

US DO OPPOSITE

Cover FRANK QUITELY with JAMIE GRANT

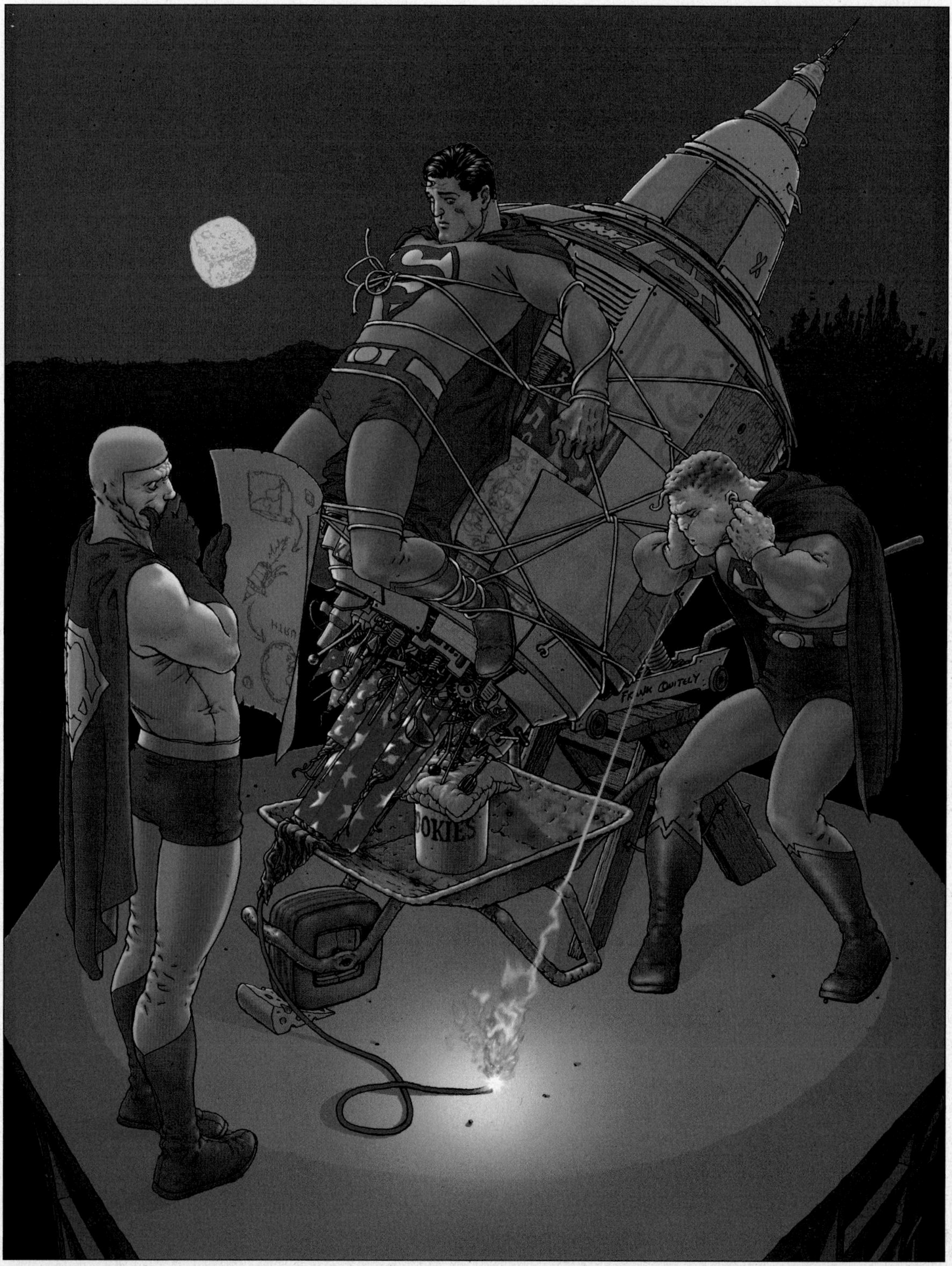
FRANK QUITELY

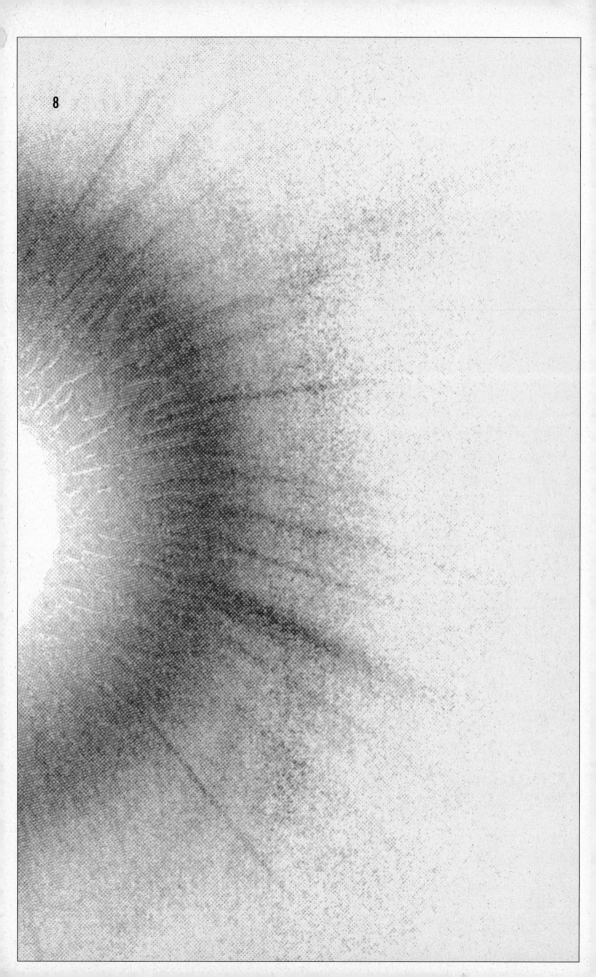

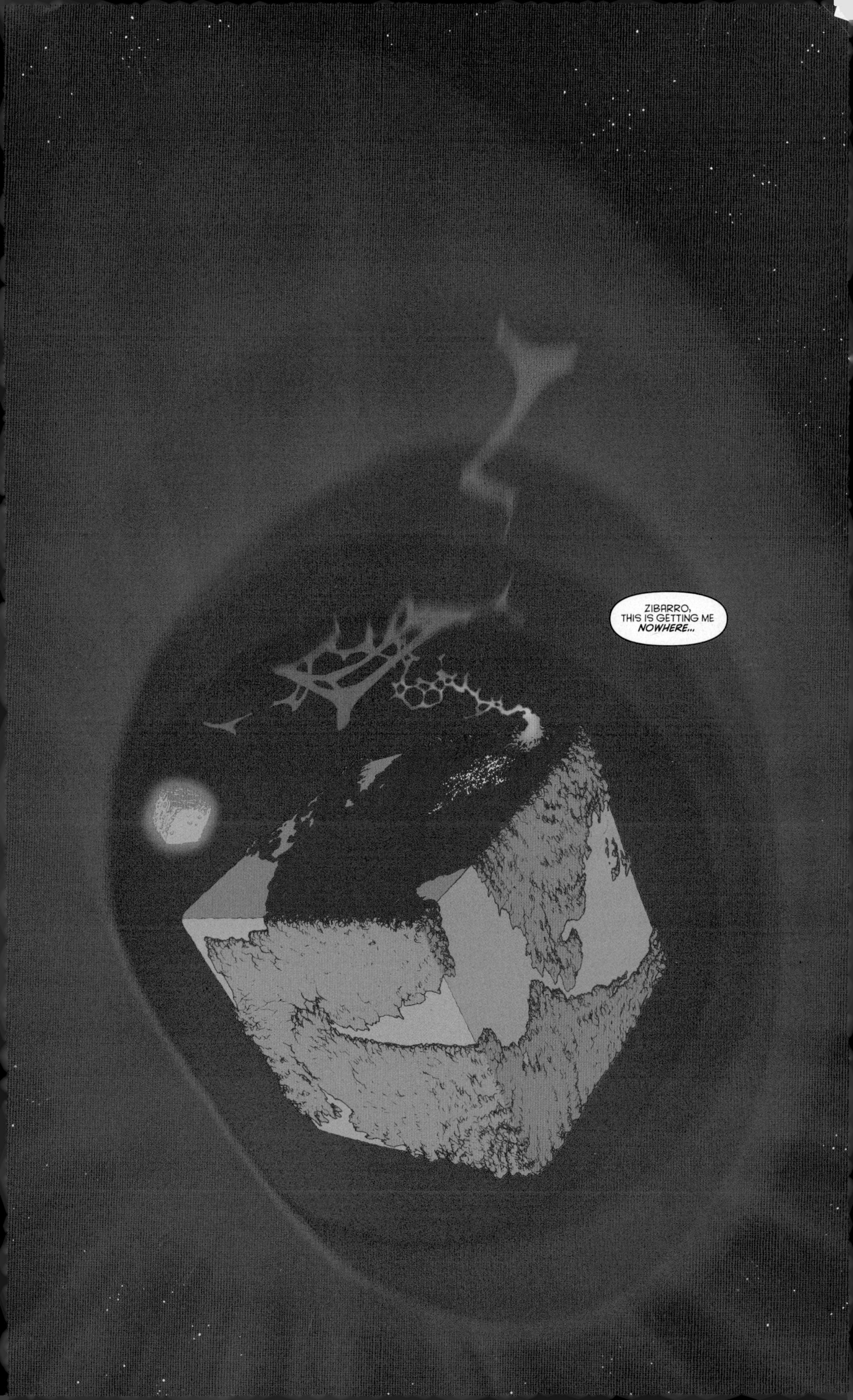
ZIBARRO, THIS IS GETTING ME *NOWHERE...*

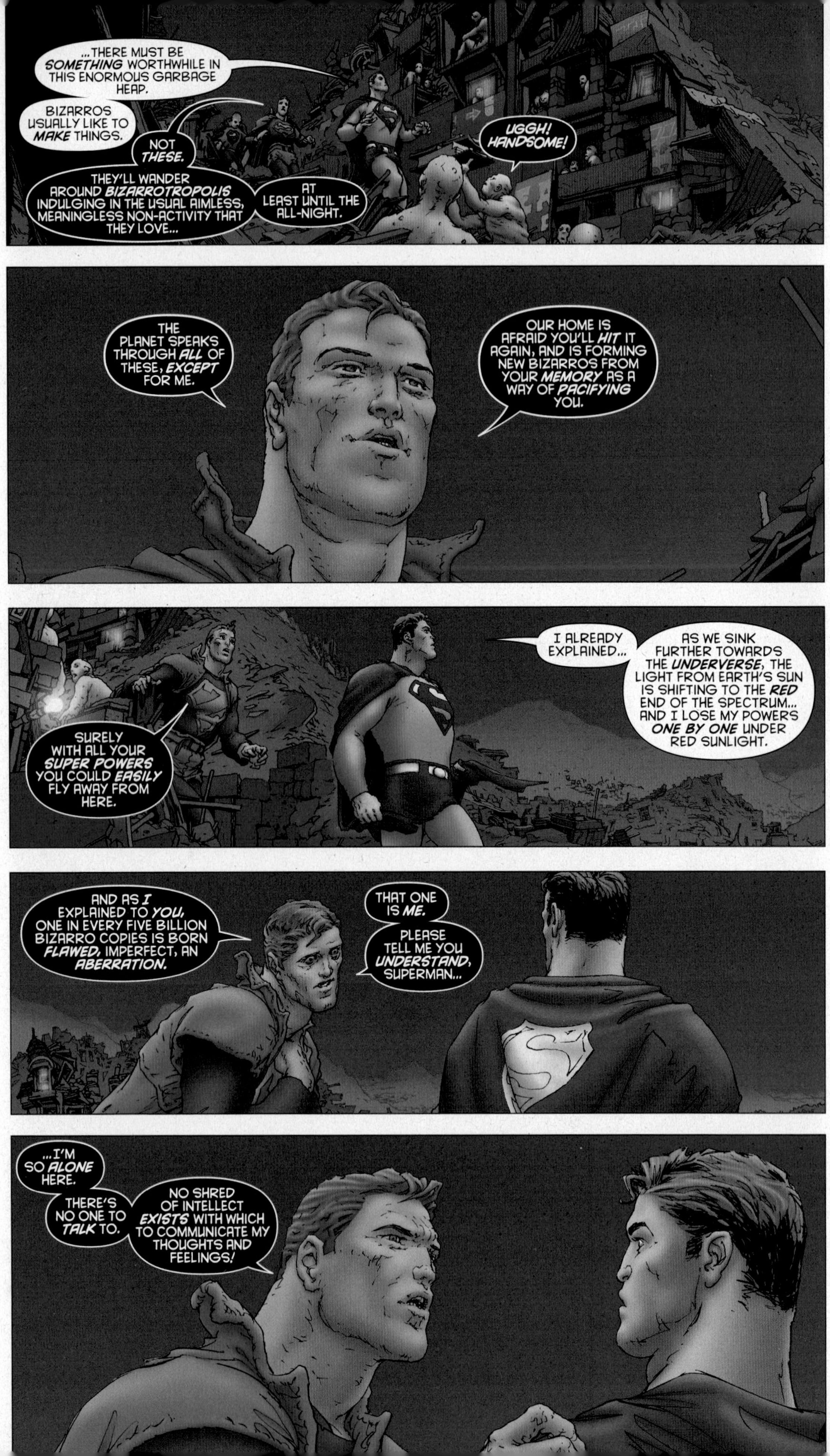
...THERE MUST BE SOMETHING WORTHWHILE IN THIS ENORMOUS GARBAGE HEAP.
BIZARROS USUALLY LIKE TO MAKE THINGS.
NOT THESE.
THEY'LL WANDER AROUND BIZARROTROPOLIS INDULGING IN THE USUAL AIMLESS, MEANINGLESS NON-ACTIVITY THAT THEY LOVE...
AT LEAST UNTIL THE ALL-NIGHT.
UGGH! HANDSOME!
THE PLANET SPEAKS THROUGH ALL OF THESE, EXCEPT FOR ME.
OUR HOME IS AFRAID YOU'LL HIT IT AGAIN, AND IS FORMING NEW BIZARROS FROM YOUR MEMORY AS A WAY OF PACIFYING YOU.
SURELY WITH ALL YOUR SUPER POWERS YOU COULD EASILY FLY AWAY FROM HERE.
I ALREADY EXPLAINED...
AS WE SINK FURTHER TOWARDS THE UNDERVERSE, THE LIGHT FROM EARTH'S SUN IS SHIFTING TO THE RED END OF THE SPECTRUM... AND I LOSE MY POWERS ONE BY ONE UNDER RED SUNLIGHT.
AND AS I EXPLAINED TO YOU, ONE IN EVERY FIVE BILLION BIZARRO COPIES IS BORN FLAWED, IMPERFECT, AN ABERRATION.
THAT ONE IS ME.
PLEASE TELL ME YOU UNDERSTAND, SUPERMAN...
...I'M SO ALONE HERE.
THERE'S NO ONE TO TALK TO.
NO SHRED OF INTELLECT EXISTS WITH WHICH TO COMMUNICATE MY THOUGHTS AND FEELINGS!

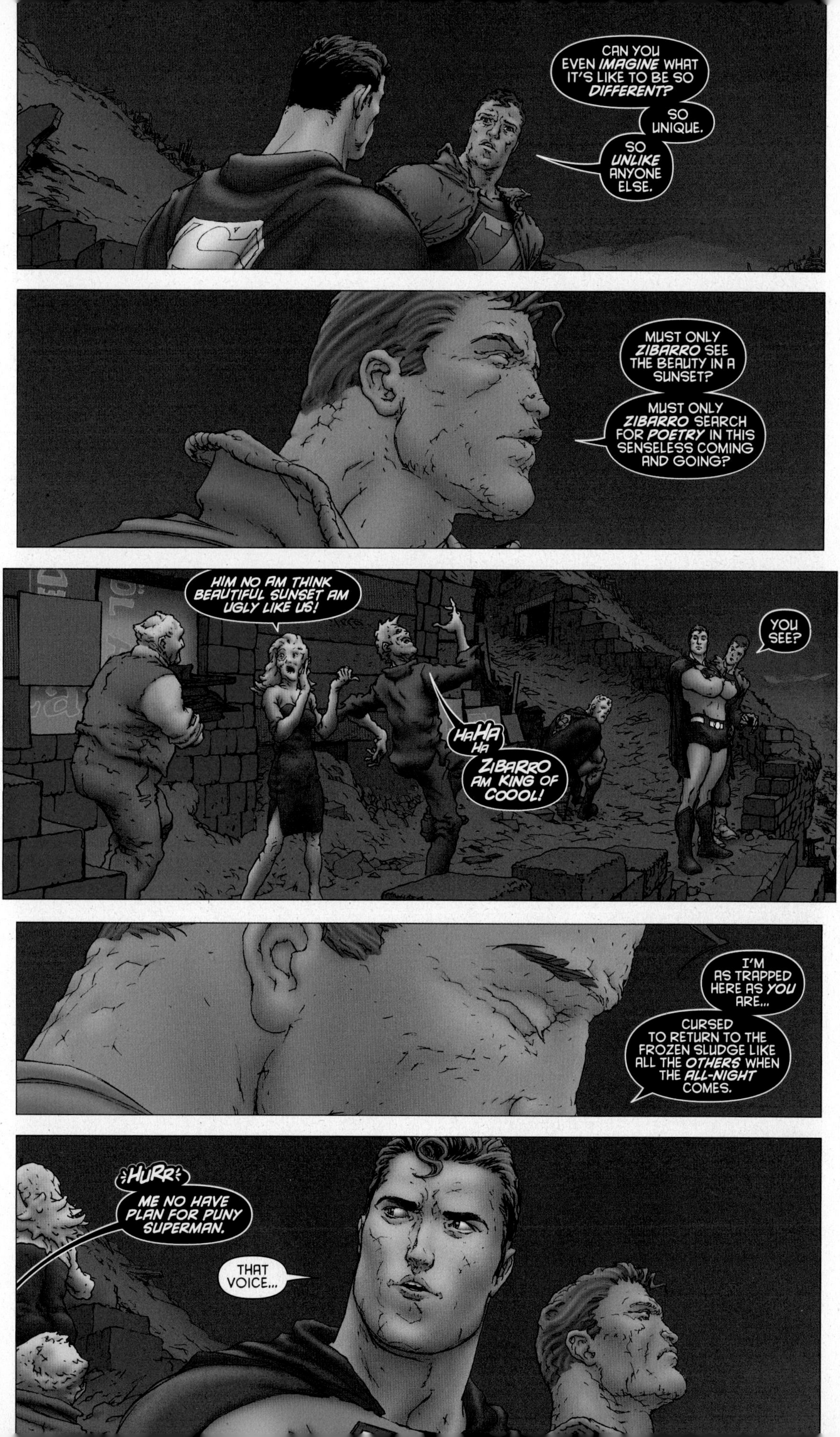
CAN YOU EVEN IMAGINE WHAT IT'S LIKE TO BE SO DIFFERENT?
SO UNIQUE.
SO UNLIKE ANYONE ELSE.
MUST ONLY ZIBARRO SEE THE BEAUTY IN A SUNSET?
MUST ONLY ZIBARRO SEARCH FOR POETRY IN THIS SENSELESS COMING AND GOING?
HIM NO AM THINK BEAUTIFUL SUNSET AM UGLY LIKE US!
HAHA HA ZIBARRO AM KING OF COOOL!
YOU SEE?
I'M AS TRAPPED HERE AS YOU ARE...
CURSED TO RETURN TO THE FROZEN SLUDGE LIKE ALL THE OTHERS WHEN THE ALL-NIGHT COMES.
HURR
ME NO HAVE PLAN FOR PUNY SUPERMAN.
THAT VOICE...

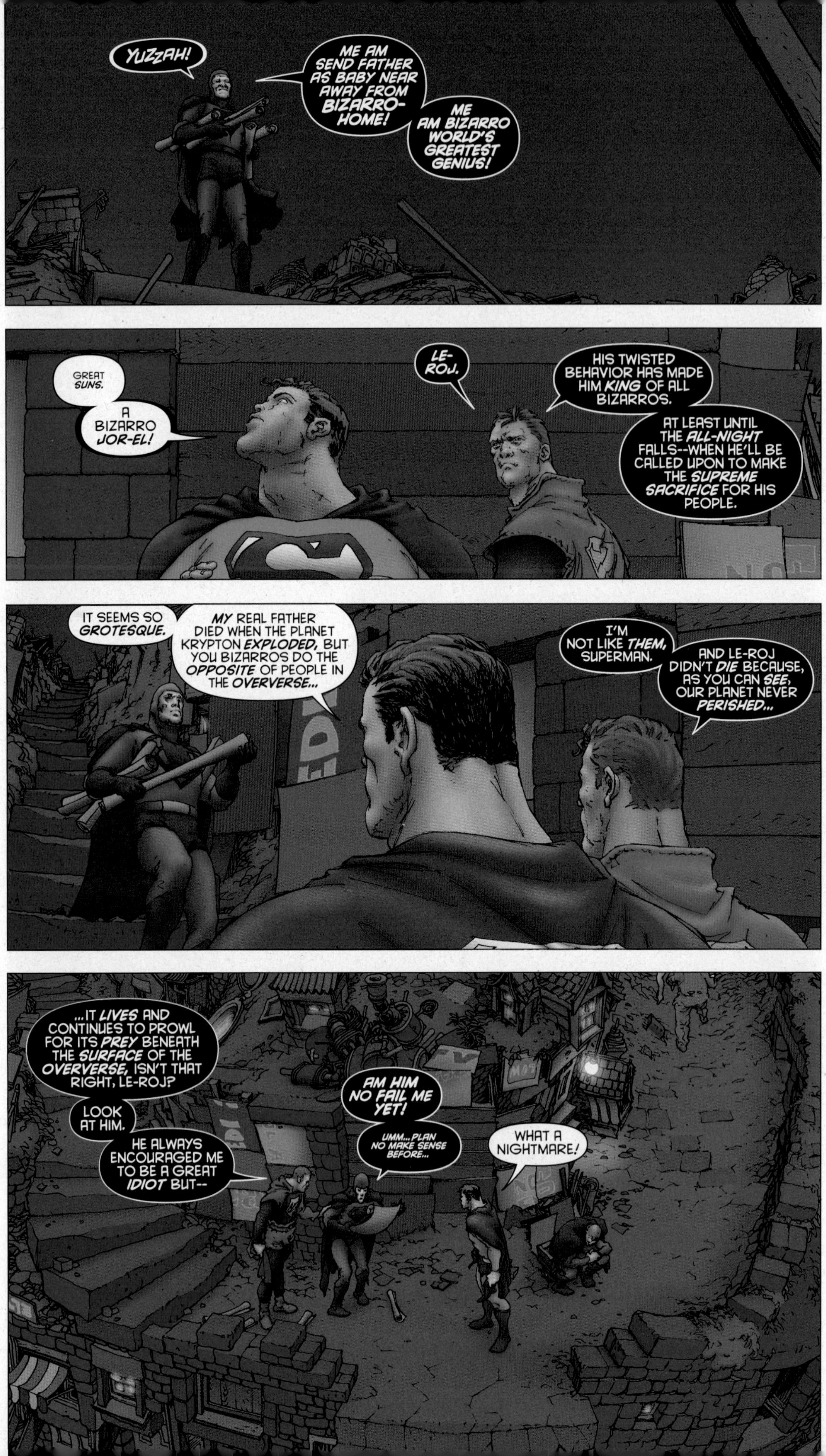
YUZZAH!
ME AM SEND FATHER AS BABY NEAR AWAY FROM BIZARRO-HOME!
ME AM BIZARRO WORLD'S GREATEST GENIUS!
GREAT SUNS.
A BIZARRO JOR-EL!
LE-ROJ.
HIS TWISTED BEHAVIOR HAS MADE HIM KING OF ALL BIZARROS.
AT LEAST UNTIL THE ALL-NIGHT FALLS--WHEN HE'LL BE CALLED UPON TO MAKE THE SUPREME SACRIFICE FOR HIS PEOPLE.
IT SEEMS SO GROTESQUE.
MY REAL FATHER DIED WHEN THE PLANET KRYPTON EXPLODED, BUT YOU BIZARROS DO THE OPPOSITE OF PEOPLE IN THE OVERVERSE...
I'M NOT LIKE THEM, SUPERMAN.
AND LE-ROJ DIDN'T DIE BECAUSE, AS YOU CAN SEE, OUR PLANET NEVER PERISHED...
...IT LIVES AND CONTINUES TO PROWL FOR ITS PREY BENEATH THE SURFACE OF THE OVERVERSE, ISN'T THAT RIGHT, LE-ROJ?
LOOK AT HIM.
HE ALWAYS ENCOURAGED ME TO BE A GREAT IDIOT BUT--
AM HIM NO FAIL ME YET!
UMM... PLAN NO MAKE SENSE BEFORE...
WHAT A NIGHTMARE!

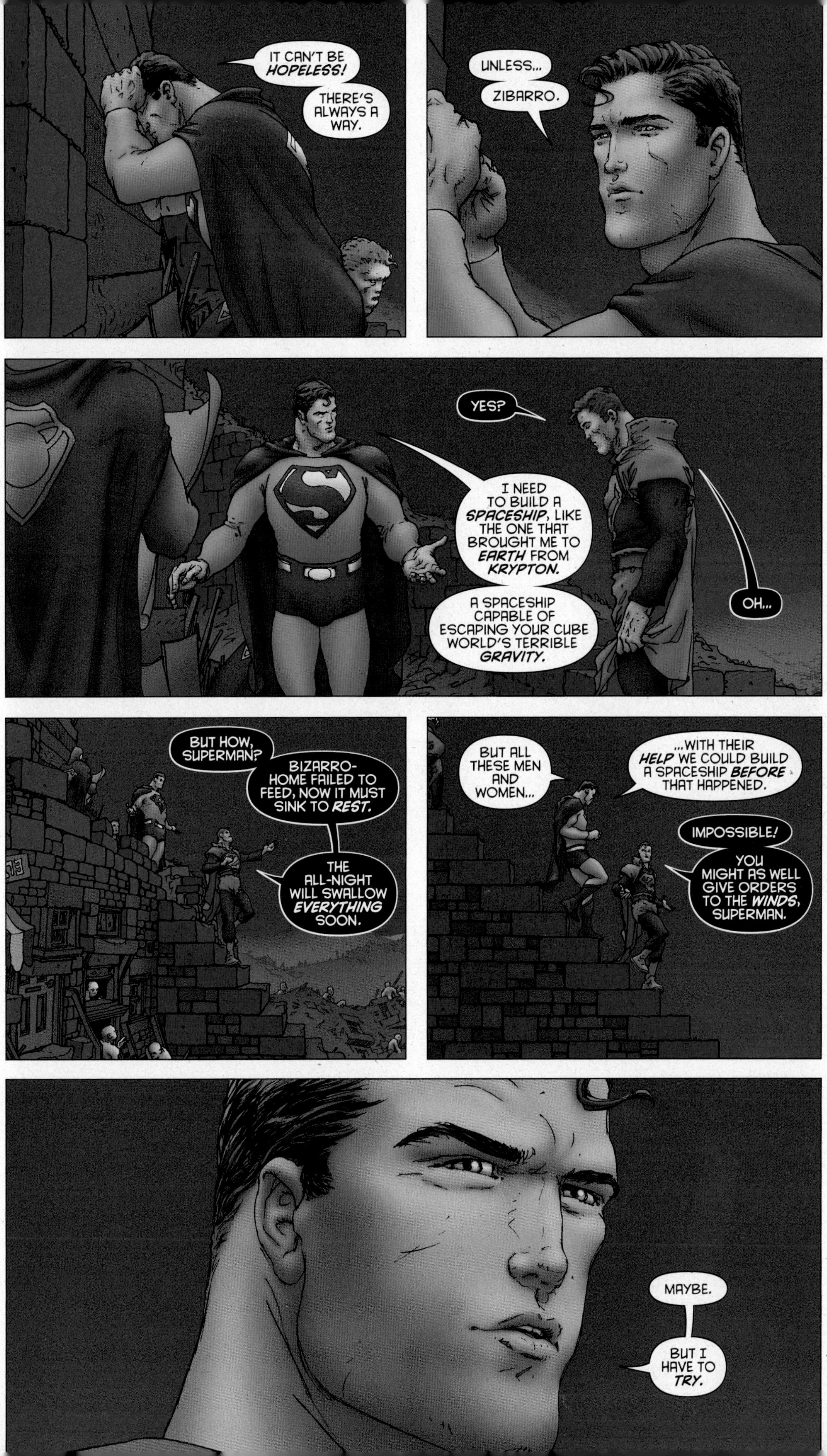
IT CAN'T BE HOPELESS!
THERE'S ALWAYS A WAY.
UNLESS...
ZIBARRO.
YES?
I NEED TO BUILD A SPACESHIP, LIKE THE ONE THAT BROUGHT ME TO EARTH FROM KRYPTON.
A SPACESHIP CAPABLE OF ESCAPING YOUR CUBE WORLD'S TERRIBLE GRAVITY.
OH...
BUT HOW, SUPERMAN?
BIZARRO-HOME FAILED TO FEED, NOW IT MUST SINK TO REST.
THE ALL-NIGHT WILL SWALLOW EVERYTHING SOON.
BUT ALL THESE MEN AND WOMEN...
...WITH THEIR HELP WE COULD BUILD A SPACESHIP BEFORE THAT HAPPENED.
IMPOSSIBLE!
YOU MIGHT AS WELL GIVE ORDERS TO THE WINDS, SUPERMAN.
MAYBE.
BUT I HAVE TO TRY.

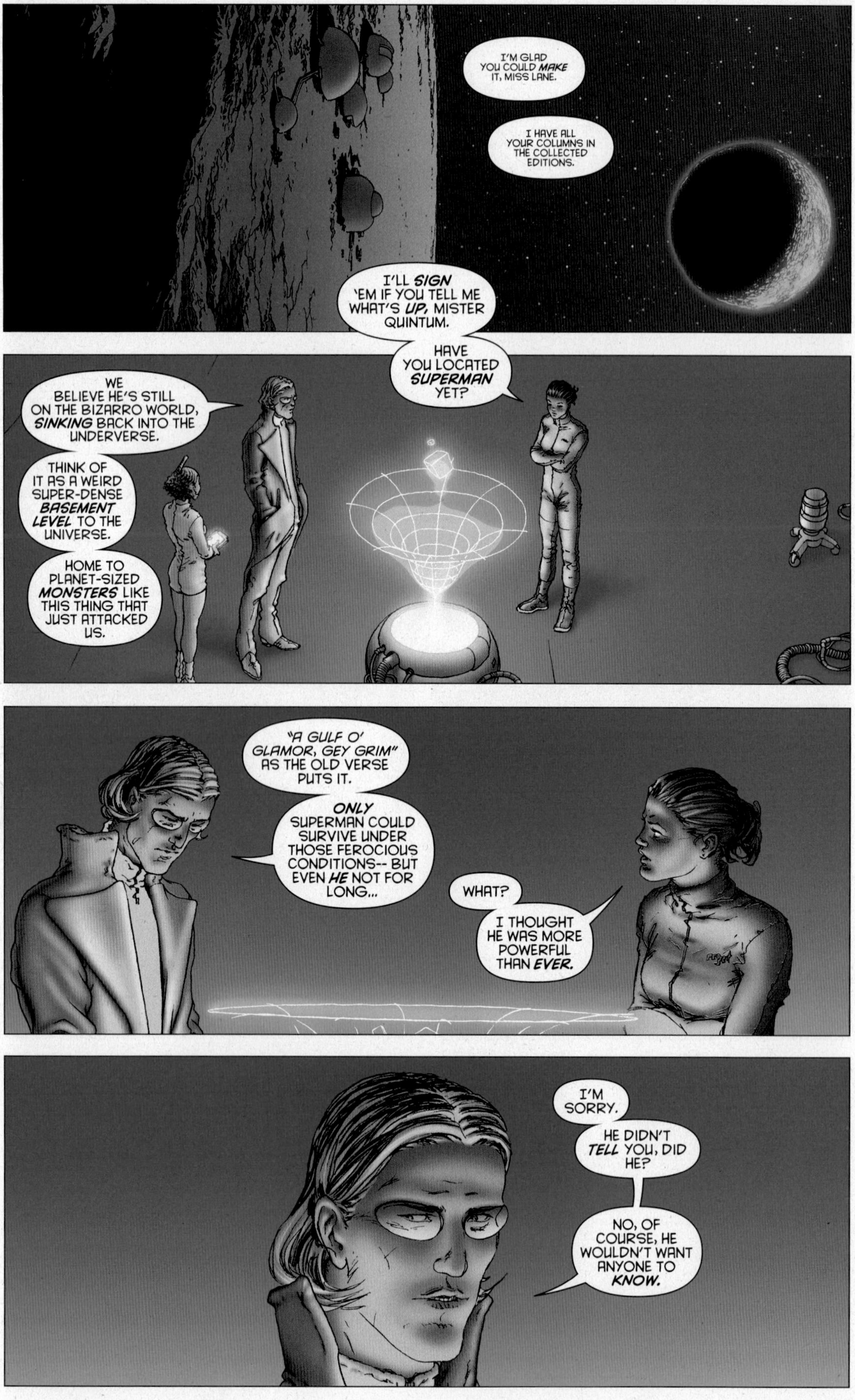

I'M GLAD YOU COULD MAKE IT, MISS LANE.
I HAVE ALL YOUR COLUMNS IN THE COLLECTED EDITIONS.
I'LL SIGN 'EM IF YOU TELL ME WHAT'S UP, MISTER QUINTUM.
HAVE YOU LOCATED SUPERMAN YET?
WE BELIEVE HE'S STILL ON THE BIZARRO WORLD, SINKING BACK INTO THE UNDERVERSE.
THINK OF IT AS A WEIRD SUPER-DENSE BASEMENT LEVEL TO THE UNIVERSE.
HOME TO PLANET-SIZED MONSTERS LIKE THIS THING THAT JUST ATTACKED US.
"A GULF O' GLAMOR, GEY GRIM" AS THE OLD VERSE PUTS IT.
ONLY SUPERMAN COULD SURVIVE UNDER THOSE FEROCIOUS CONDITIONS-- BUT EVEN HE NOT FOR LONG...
WHAT?
I THOUGHT HE WAS MORE POWERFUL THAN EVER.
I'M SORRY.
HE DIDN'T TELL YOU, DID HE?
NO, OF COURSE, HE WOULDN'T WANT ANYONE TO KNOW.

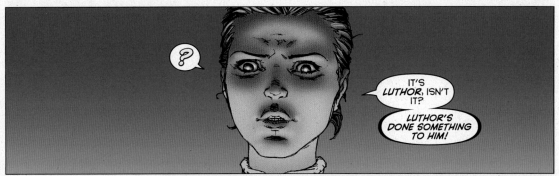

IT'S *LUTHOR*, ISN'T IT?

LUTHOR'S DONE SOMETHING TO HIM!

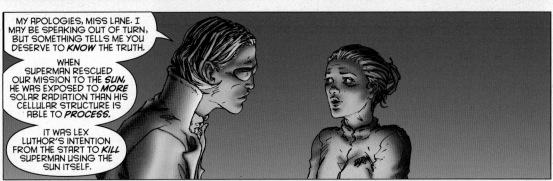

MY APOLOGIES, MISS LANE. I MAY BE SPEAKING OUT OF TURN, BUT SOMETHING TELLS ME YOU DESERVE TO *KNOW* THE TRUTH.

WHEN SUPERMAN RESCUED OUR MISSION TO THE *SUN*, HE WAS EXPOSED TO *MORE* SOLAR RADIATION THAN HIS CELLULAR STRUCTURE IS ABLE TO *PROCESS.*

IT WAS LEX LUTHOR'S INTENTION FROM THE START TO *KILL* SUPERMAN USING THE SUN ITSELF.

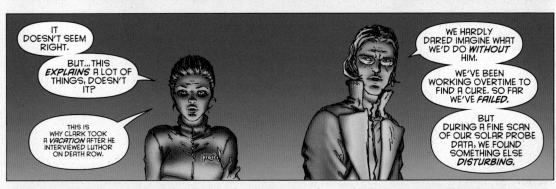

IT DOESN'T SEEM RIGHT.

BUT... THIS *EXPLAINS* A LOT OF THINGS, DOESN'T IT?

THIS IS WHY CLARK TOOK A *VACATION* AFTER HE INTERVIEWED LUTHOR ON DEATH ROW.

WE HARDLY DARED IMAGINE WHAT WE'D DO *WITHOUT* HIM.

WE'VE BEEN WORKING OVERTIME TO FIND A CURE. SO FAR WE'VE *FAILED.*

BUT DURING A FINE SCAN OF OUR SOLAR PROBE DATA, WE FOUND SOMETHING ELSE *DISTURBING.*

WHAT DO YOU MEAN?

RIGHT THERE.

HIDING IN THE SUN.

WHEREVER HE IS, I HOPE HE FINDS A WAY *BACK.*

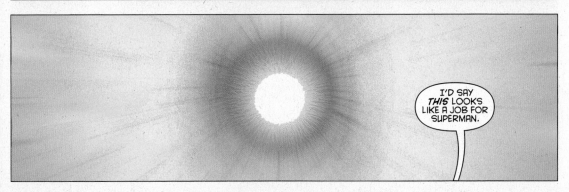

I'D SAY *THIS* LOOKS LIKE A JOB FOR SUPERMAN.

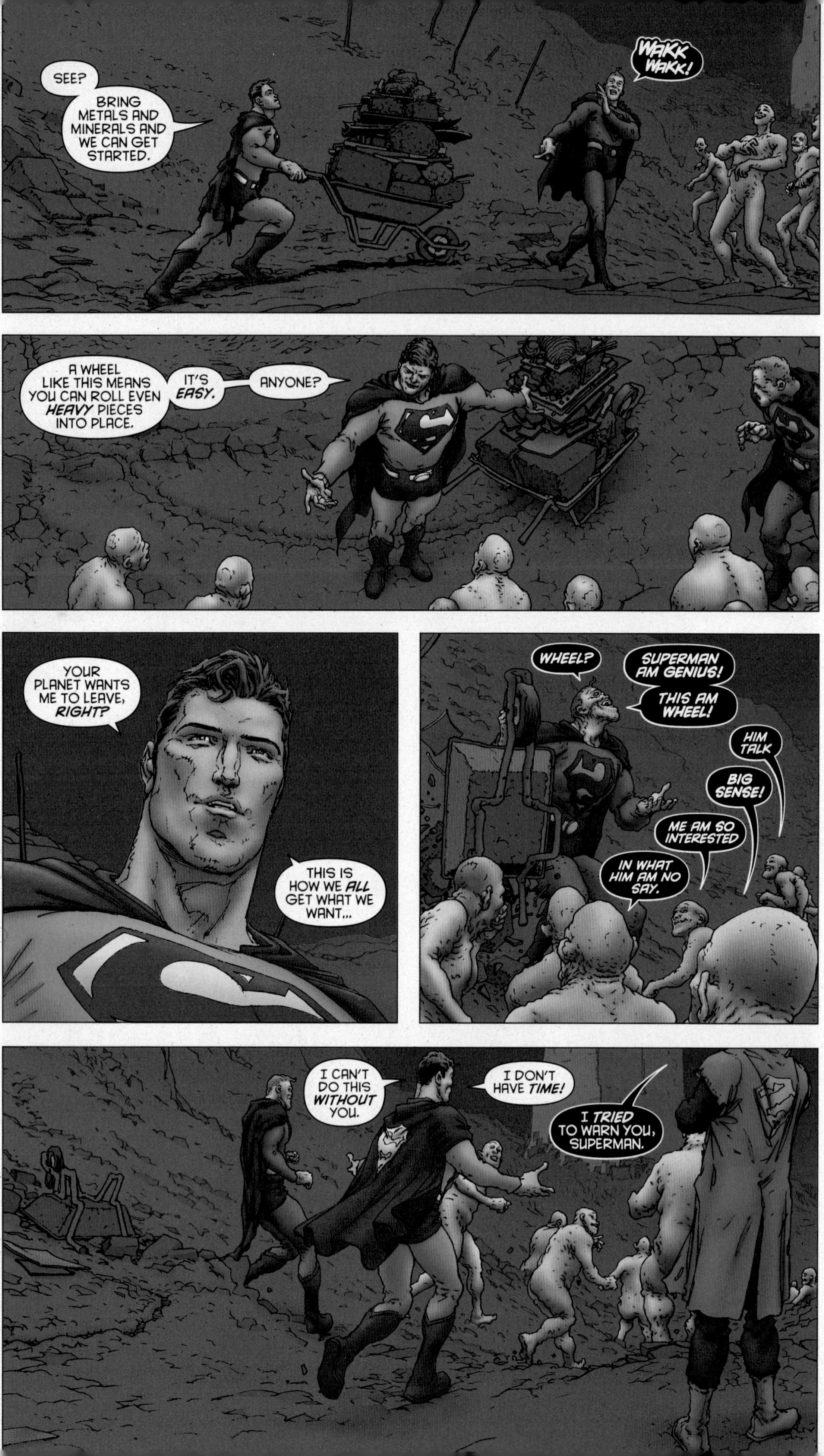
SEE?
BRING METALS AND MINERALS AND WE CAN GET STARTED.
WAKK WAKK!
A WHEEL LIKE THIS MEANS YOU CAN ROLL EVEN HEAVY PIECES INTO PLACE.
IT'S EASY.
ANYONE?
YOUR PLANET WANTS ME TO LEAVE, RIGHT?
THIS IS HOW WE ALL GET WHAT WE WANT...
WHEEL?
SUPERMAN AM GENIUS!
THIS AM WHEEL!
HIM TALK
BIG SENSE!
ME AM SO INTERESTED
IN WHAT HIM AM NO SAY.
I CAN'T DO THIS WITHOUT YOU.
I DON'T HAVE TIME!
I TRIED TO WARN YOU, SUPERMAN.

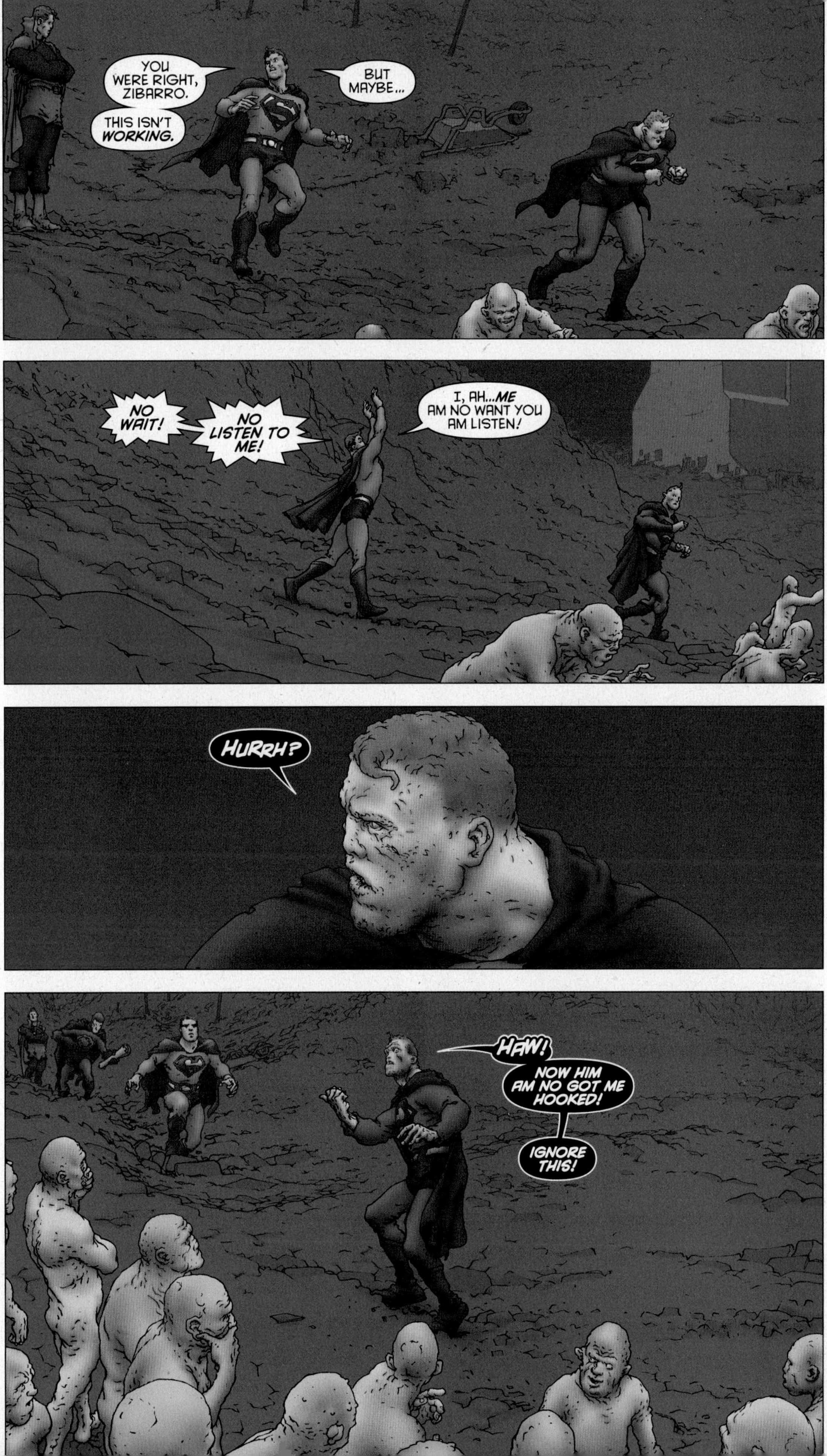
YOU WERE RIGHT, ZIBARRO.
THIS ISN'T *WORKING.*
BUT MAYBE...
NO WAIT!
NO LISTEN TO ME!
I, AH...*ME* AM NO WANT YOU AM LISTEN!
HURRH?
HAW!
NOW HIM AM NO GOT ME HOOKED!
IGNORE THIS!

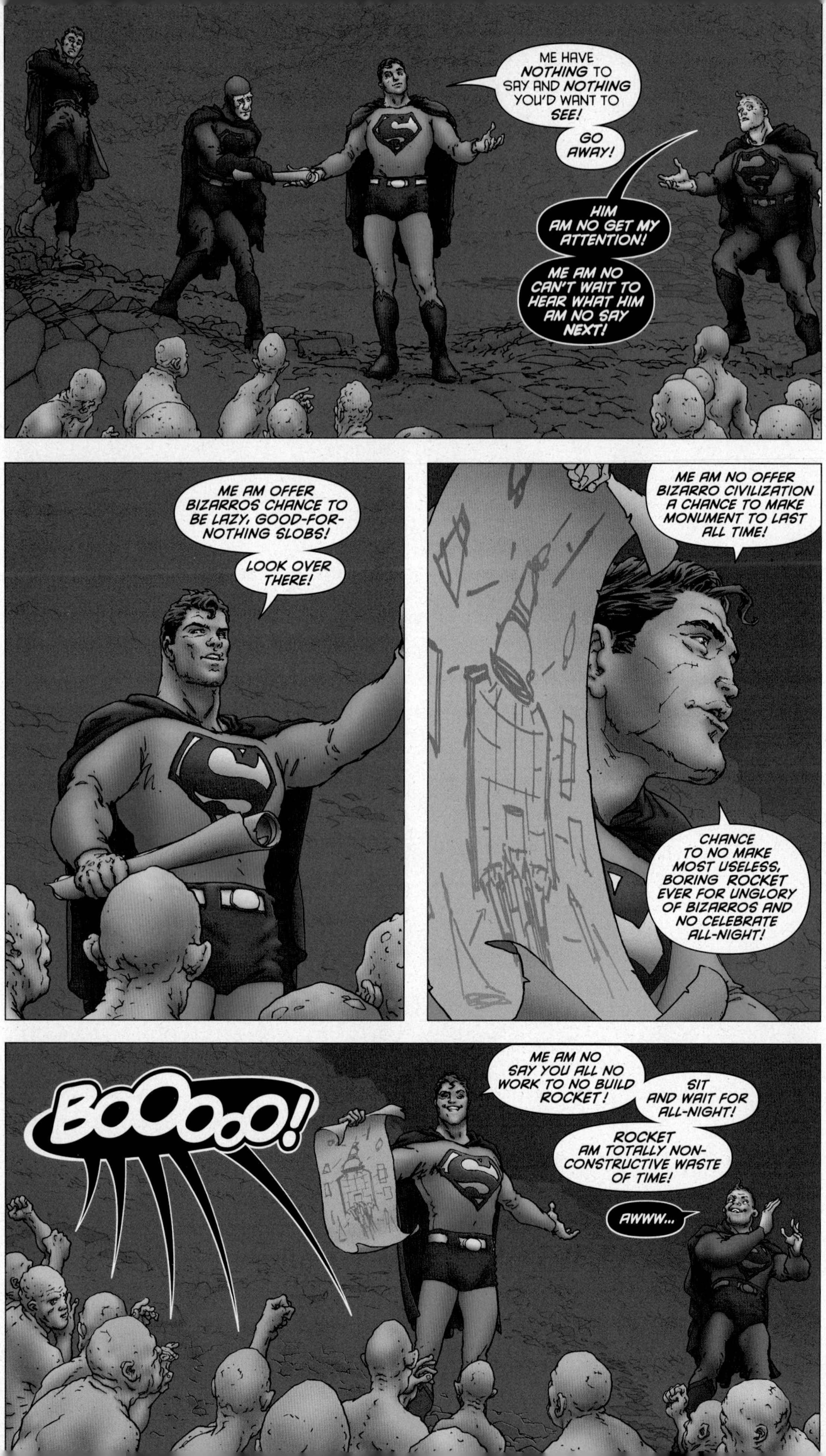
ME HAVE NOTHING TO SAY AND NOTHING YOU'D WANT TO SEE!
GO AWAY!
HIM AM NO GET MY ATTENTION!
ME AM NO CAN'T WAIT TO HEAR WHAT HIM AM NO SAY NEXT!
ME AM OFFER BIZARROS CHANCE TO BE LAZY, GOOD-FOR-NOTHING SLOBS!
LOOK OVER THERE!
ME AM NO OFFER BIZARRO CIVILIZATION A CHANCE TO MAKE MONUMENT TO LAST ALL TIME!
CHANCE TO NO MAKE MOST USELESS, BORING ROCKET EVER FOR UNGLORY OF BIZARROS AND NO CELEBRATE ALL-NIGHT!
BOOo.o.O!
ME AM NO SAY YOU ALL NO WORK TO NO BUILD ROCKET!
SIT AND WAIT FOR ALL-NIGHT!
ROCKET AM TOTALLY NON-CONSTRUCTIVE WASTE OF TIME!
AWWW...

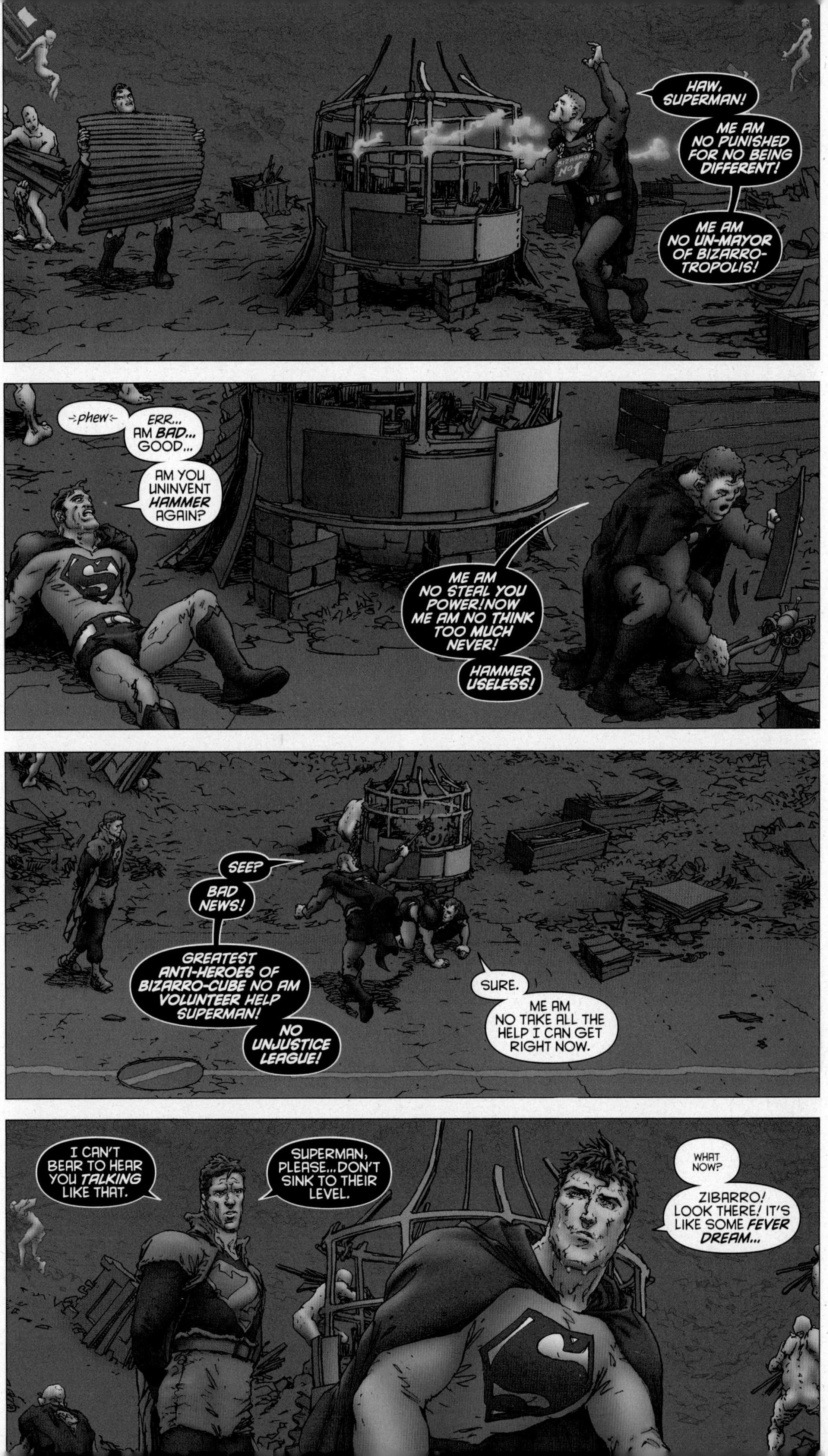
HAW, SUPERMAN!
ME AM NO PUNISHED FOR NO BEING DIFFERENT!
ME AM NO UN-MAYOR OF BIZARRO-TROPOLIS!
-phew-
ERR... AM BAD... GOOD...
AM YOU UNINVENT HAMMER AGAIN?
ME AM NO STEAL YOU POWER! NOW ME AM NO THINK TOO MUCH NEVER!
HAMMER USELESS!
SEE?
BAD NEWS!
GREATEST ANTI-HEROES OF BIZARRO-CUBE NO AM VOLUNTEER HELP SUPERMAN!
NO UNJUSTICE LEAGUE!
SURE.
ME AM NO TAKE ALL THE HELP I CAN GET RIGHT NOW.
I CAN'T BEAR TO HEAR YOU TALKING LIKE THAT.
SUPERMAN, PLEASE...DON'T SINK TO THEIR LEVEL.
WHAT NOW?
ZIBARRO! LOOK THERE! IT'S LIKE SOME FEVER DREAM...

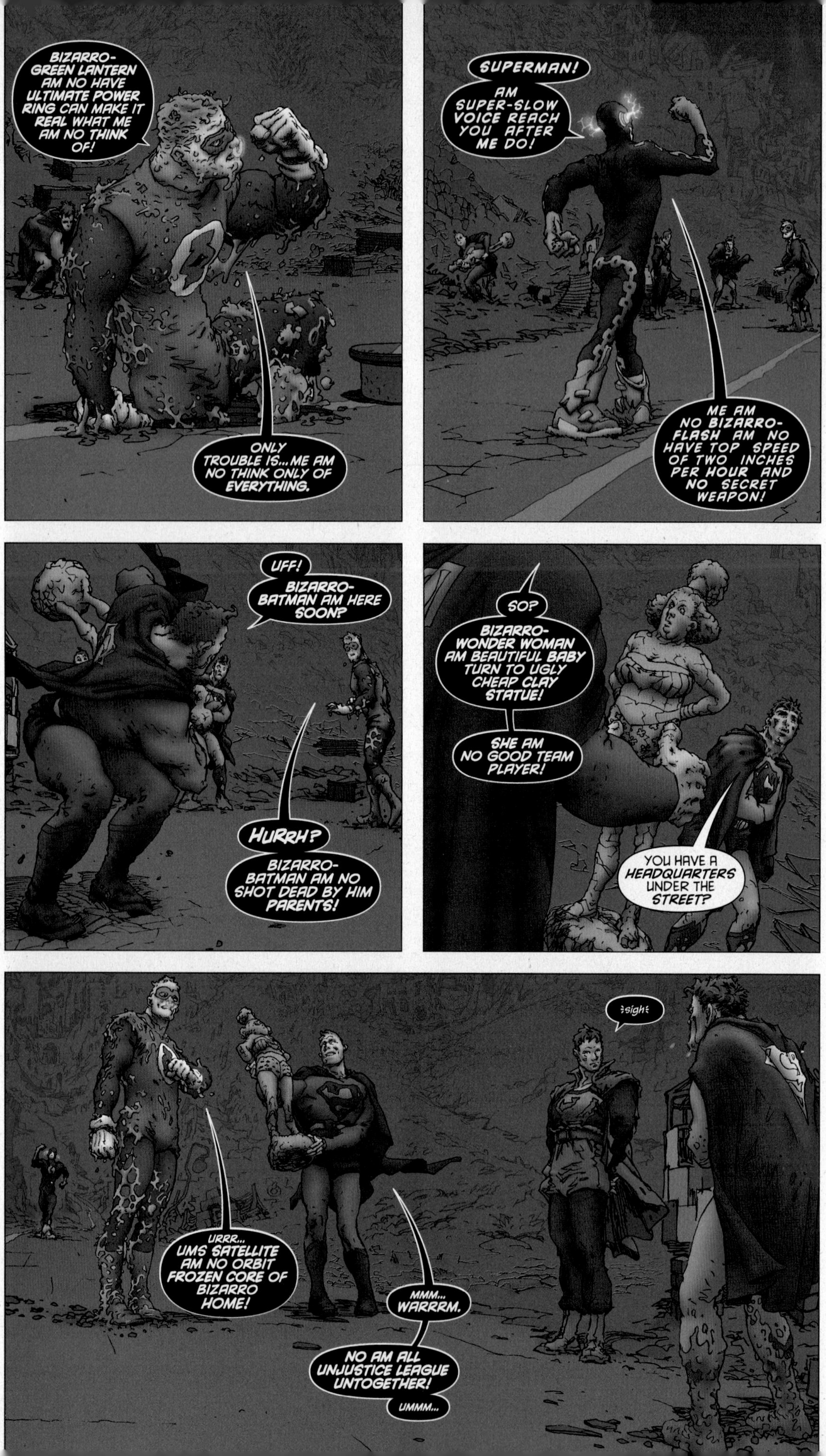
BIZARRO-GREEN LANTERN AM NO HAVE ULTIMATE POWER RING CAN MAKE IT REAL WHAT ME AM NO THINK OF!
ONLY TROUBLE IS...ME AM NO THINK ONLY OF EVERYTHING.
SUPERMAN!
AM SUPER-SLOW VOICE REACH YOU AFTER ME DO!
ME AM NO BIZARRO-FLASH AM NO HAVE TOP SPEED OF TWO INCHES PER HOUR AND NO SECRET WEAPON!
UFF!
BIZARRO-BATMAN AM HERE SOON?
HURRH?
BIZARRO-BATMAN AM NO SHOT DEAD BY HIM PARENTS!
SO?
BIZARRO-WONDER WOMAN AM BEAUTIFUL BABY TURN TO UGLY CHEAP CLAY STATUE!
SHE AM NO GOOD TEAM PLAYER!
YOU HAVE A HEADQUARTERS UNDER THE STREET?
URRR... UMS SATELLITE AM NO ORBIT FROZEN CORE OF BIZARRO HOME!
MMM... WARRRM.
NO AM ALL UNJUSTICE LEAGUE UNTOGETHER!
UMMM...
sigh

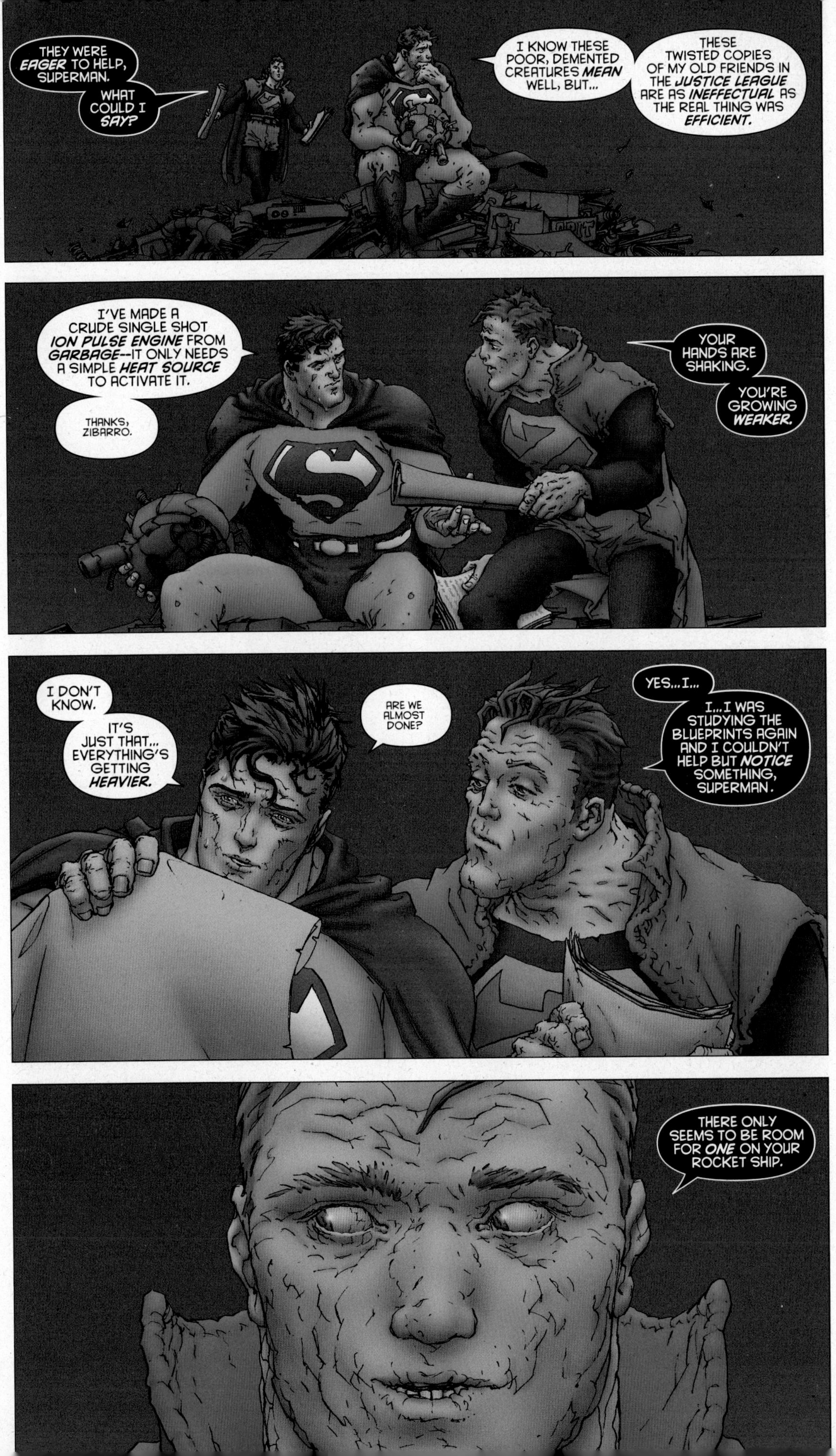
THEY WERE EAGER TO HELP, SUPERMAN.
WHAT COULD I SAY?
I KNOW THESE POOR, DEMENTED CREATURES MEAN WELL, BUT...
THESE TWISTED COPIES OF MY OLD FRIENDS IN THE JUSTICE LEAGUE ARE AS INEFFECTUAL AS THE REAL THING WAS EFFICIENT.
I'VE MADE A CRUDE SINGLE SHOT ION PULSE ENGINE FROM GARBAGE--IT ONLY NEEDS A SIMPLE HEAT SOURCE TO ACTIVATE IT.
THANKS, ZIBARRO.
YOUR HAND'S ARE SHAKING.
YOU'RE GROWING WEAKER.
I DON'T KNOW.
IT'S JUST THAT... EVERYTHING'S GETTING HEAVIER.
ARE WE ALMOST DONE?
YES...I...
I...I WAS STUDYING THE BLUEPRINTS AGAIN AND I COULDN'T HELP BUT NOTICE SOMETHING, SUPERMAN.
THERE ONLY SEEMS TO BE ROOM FOR ONE ON YOUR ROCKET SHIP.

ZIBARRO, I'LL BE SUBJECTING MYSELF TO *UNIMAGINABLE* STRESSES.

THE CHANCES OF SURVIVAL ARE *SLIM*, EVEN IF YOU HAD *POWERS* LIKE THE SUPER BIZARRO...

WHAT DO YOU MEAN?!

WHY DO I FEEL AS IF YOU HAVEN'T BEEN LISTENING TO ME *AT ALL?!*

DON'T YOU REALIZE I'D TAKE ANY CHANCE TO GET AWAY FROM HERE?

I'D DARE ANY PERIL!

AND I CAN'T LET YOU *RISK* IT, BUT YOU HAVE MY *WORD*...

IF I GET *HOME* SAFELY, I'LL FIND A WAY TO *CONTACT* YOU HERE IN THE UNDERVERSE AND ONE DAY, I *PROMISE*, WE'LL MEET *AGAIN*.

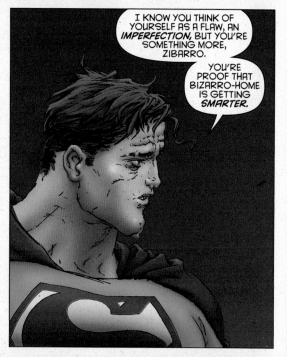

I KNOW YOU THINK OF YOURSELF AS A FLAW, AN *IMPERFECTION*, BUT YOU'RE SOMETHING MORE, ZIBARRO.

YOU'RE PROOF THAT BIZARRO-HOME IS GETTING *SMARTER*.

WHY ELSE DID THIS WORLD, THIS INCREDIBLE ORGANISM, MAKE EYES LIKE *YOURS* TO SEE BEAUTY AND MEANING WHERE OTHERS SEE CHAOS?

HRRM...WELL... I JUST WONDERED IF MAYBE THERE WAS STILL TIME FOR YOU TO TAKE A LOOK...A LOOK AT MY *WORK*...

IT'S NOT MUCH... JUST *THOUGHTS*, REALLY.

Before you go.

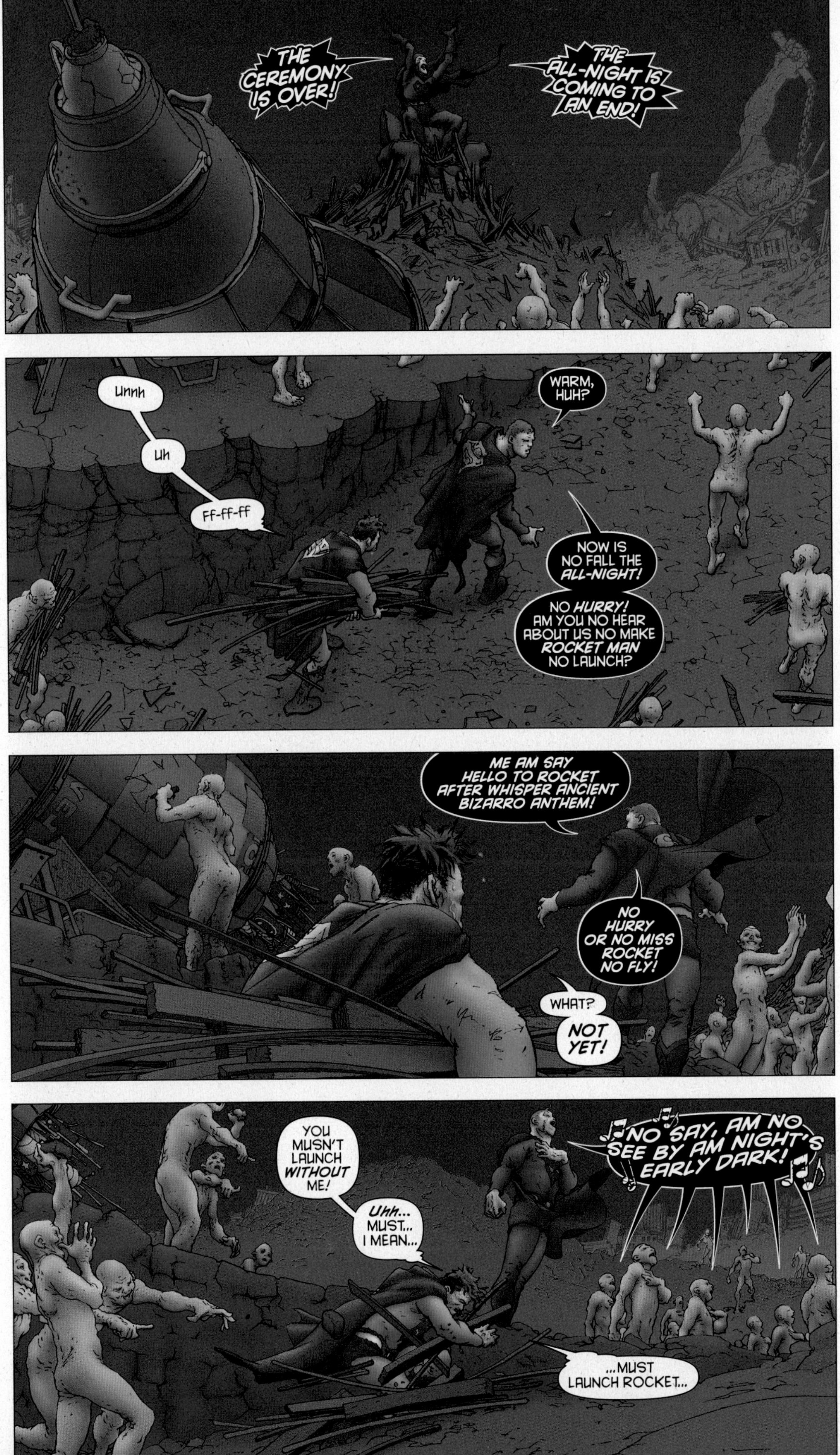
THE CEREMONY IS OVER!
THE ALL-NIGHT IS COMING TO AN END!
Unnh
Uh
Ff-ff-ff
WARM, HUH?
NOW IS NO FALL THE ALL-NIGHT!
NO HURRY! AM YOU NO HEAR ABOUT US NO MAKE ROCKET MAN NO LAUNCH?
ME AM SAY HELLO TO ROCKET AFTER WHISPER ANCIENT BIZARRO ANTHEM!
NO HURRY OR NO MISS ROCKET NO FLY!
WHAT?
NOT YET!
YOU MUSN'T LAUNCH WITHOUT ME!
Uhh... MUST... I MEAN...
NO SAY, AM NO SEE BY AM NIGHT'S EARLY DARK!
...MUST LAUNCH ROCKET...

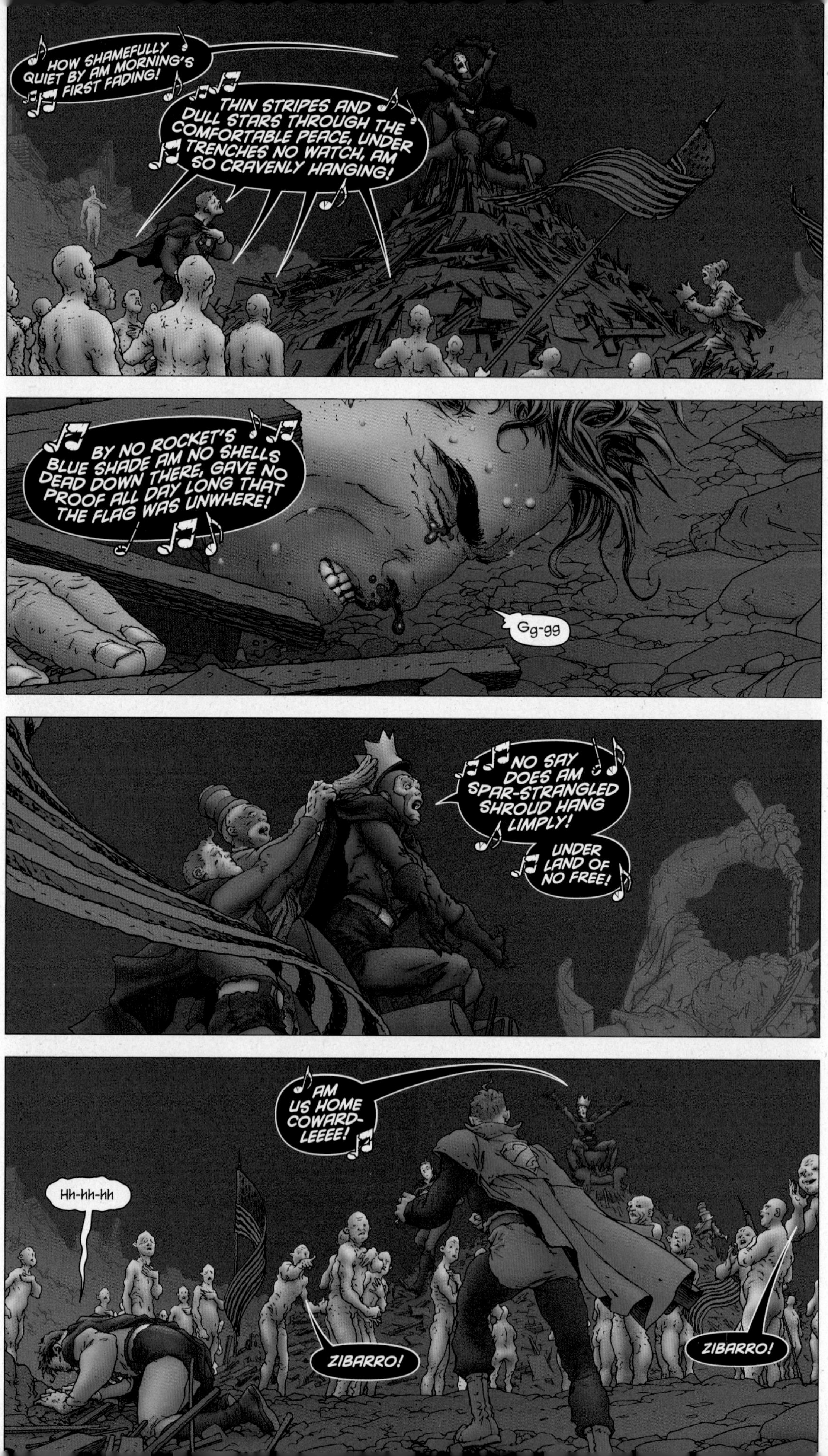
HOW SHAMEFULLY QUIET BY AM MORNING'S FIRST FADING!
THIN STRIPES AND DULL STARS THROUGH THE COMFORTABLE PEACE, UNDER TRENCHES NO WATCH, AM SO CRAVENLY HANGING!
BY NO ROCKET'S BLUE SHADE AM NO SHELLS DEAD DOWN THERE, GAVE NO PROOF ALL DAY LONG THAT THE FLAG WAS UNWHERE!
Gg-gg
NO SAY DOES AM SPAR-STRANGLED SHROUD HANG LIMPLY!
UNDER LAND OF NO FREE!
AM US HOME COWARD-LEEEE!
Hh-hh-hh
ZIBARRO!
ZIBARRO!

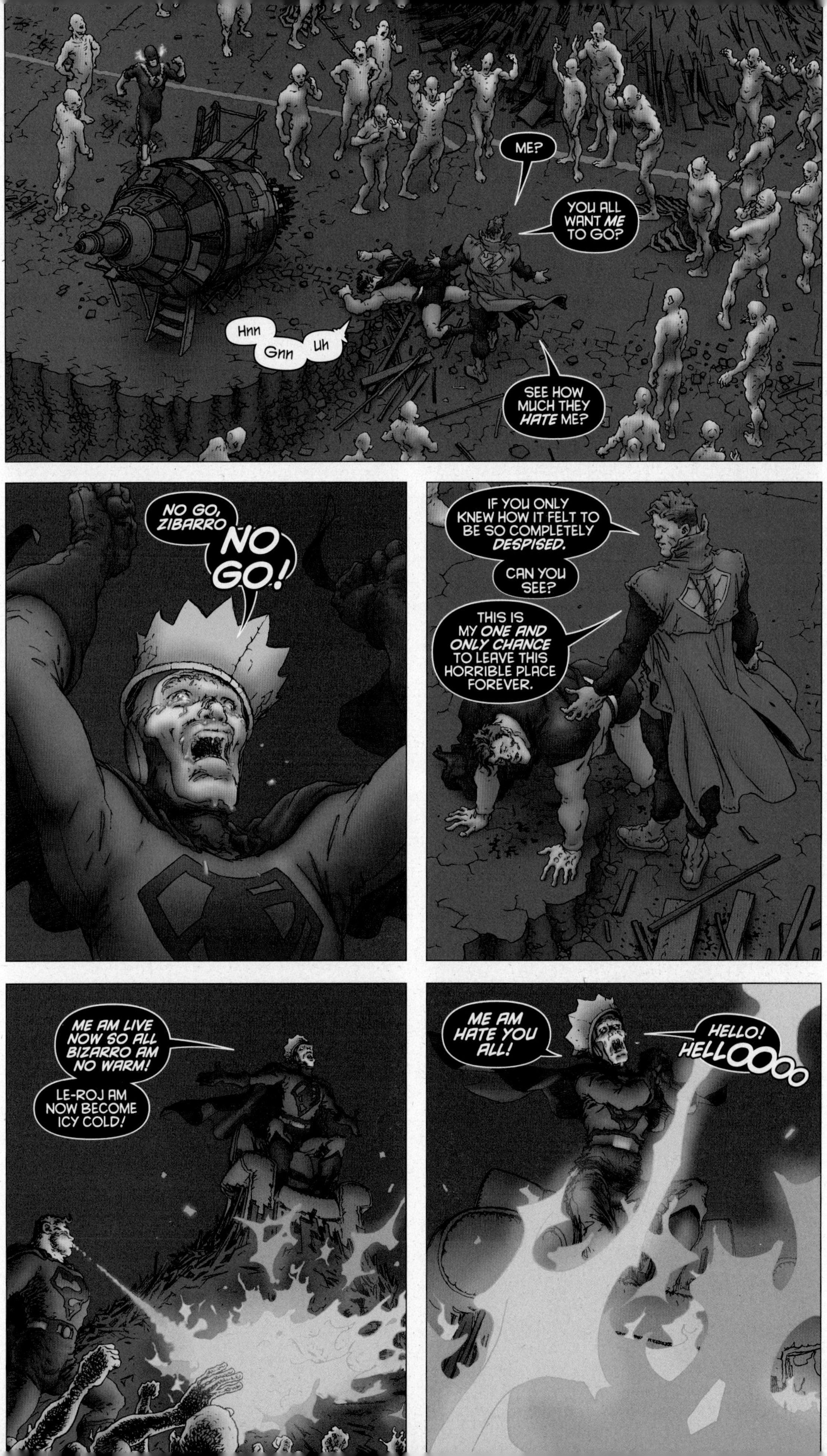

ME?
YOU ALL WANT ME TO GO?
Hnn
Gnn
Uh
SEE HOW MUCH THEY HATE ME?
NO GO, ZIBARRO NO GO!
IF YOU ONLY KNEW HOW IT FELT TO BE SO COMPLETELY DESPISED.
CAN YOU SEE?
THIS IS MY ONE AND ONLY CHANCE TO LEAVE THIS HORRIBLE PLACE FOREVER.
ME AM LIVE NOW SO ALL BIZARRO AM NO WARM!
LE-ROJ AM NOW BECOME ICY COLD!
ME AM HATE YOU ALL!
HELLO! HELLOOOO

SUPERMAN. YOU KNOW I WANT WHAT *YOU* HAVE-- RESPECT, LOVE, A PLACE TO *BELONG*.

Uh... uh... Can't... leave Earth...in trouble...

BUT WHAT IF... WHAT IF I FOUND I WAS JUST AS LONELY ON *YOUR* WORLD AS I AM EVERYWHERE ELSE?

HERE. LET ME *HELP* YOU.

Arrrr

Uhh Invulnerability... the *last* to go...

WE'RE ALMOST THERE. ONE... ONE LAST THING, SUPERMAN... DID YOU MANAGE TO TAKE A LOOK AT MY *WORK* AFTER ALL?

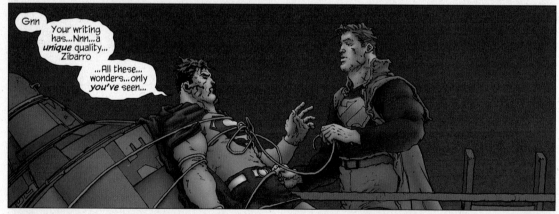

Gnn Your writing has...Nnn...a *unique* quality... Zibarro

...All these... wonders...only *you've* seen...

Keep it up. Tell the *story* of Bizarro-Home. Tell how they made the rocket ship...out of *garbage*...to shoot the traveler home.

I'LL TRY.

SO I ONLY NEED SOME... SOME *HEAT* TO ACTIVATE THE ENGINE, YES?

UMM...

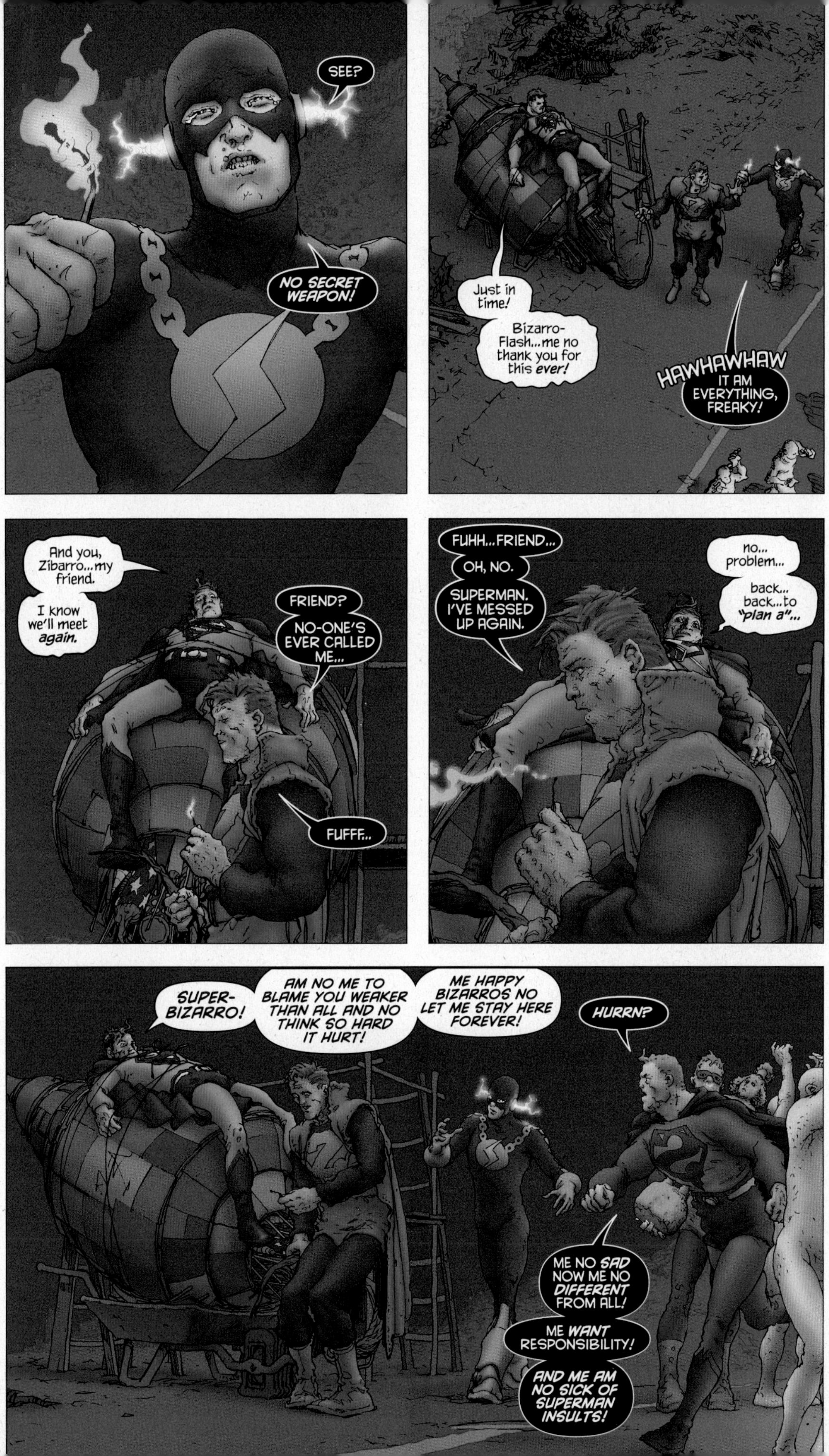

SEE?
NO SECRET WEAPON!
Just in time!
Bizarro-Flash...me no thank you for this *ever!*
HAWHAWHAW
IT AM EVERYTHING, FREAKY!
And you, Zibarro...my friend.
I know we'll meet *again.*
FRIEND?
NO-ONE'S EVER CALLED ME...
FUFFF...
FUHH...FRIEND...
OH, NO.
SUPERMAN. I'VE MESSED UP AGAIN.
no... problem...
back... back...to *"plan a"*...
SUPER-BIZARRO!
AM NO ME TO BLAME YOU WEAKER THAN ALL AND NO THINK SO HARD IT HURT!
ME HAPPY BIZARROS NO LET ME STAY HERE FOREVER!
HURRN?
ME NO *SAD* NOW ME NO *DIFFERENT* FROM ALL!
ME *WANT* RESPONSIBILITY!
AND ME AM NO SICK OF SUPERMAN INSULTS!

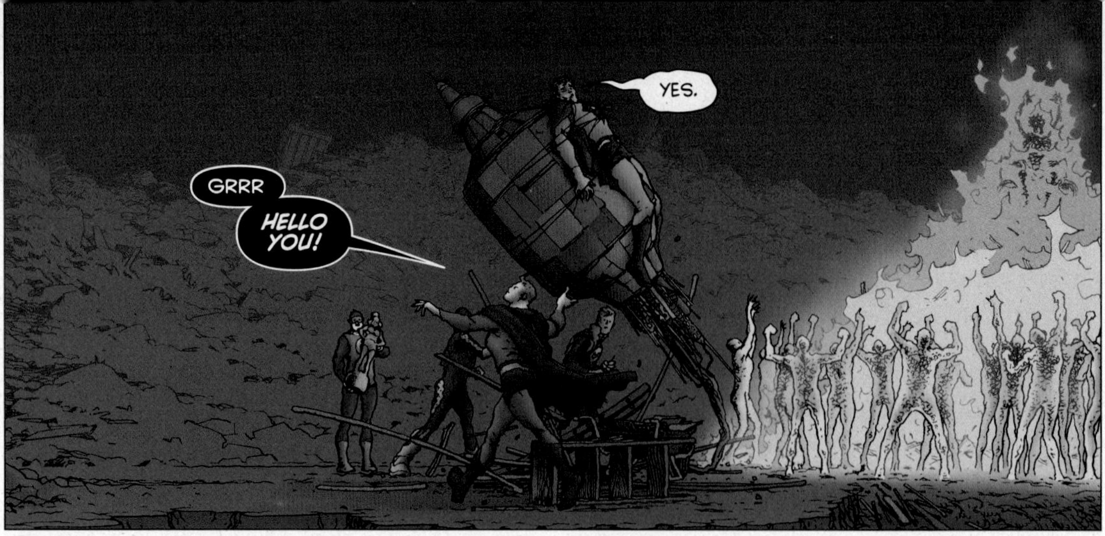
YES.
GRRR
HELLO YOU!

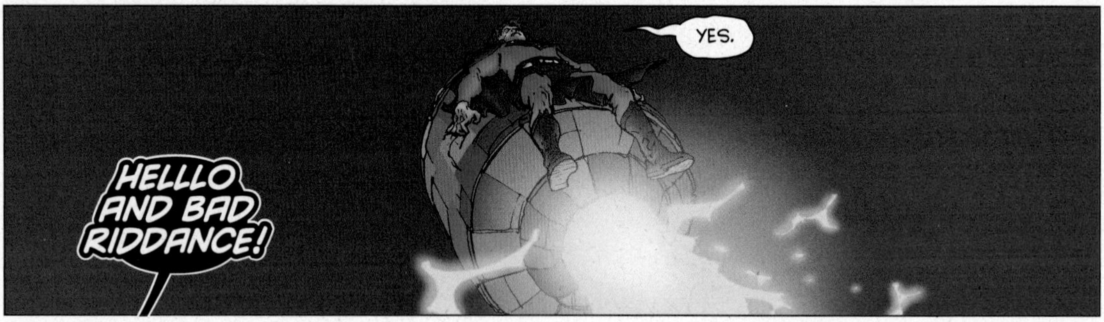
YES.
HELLLO AND BAD RIDDANCE!

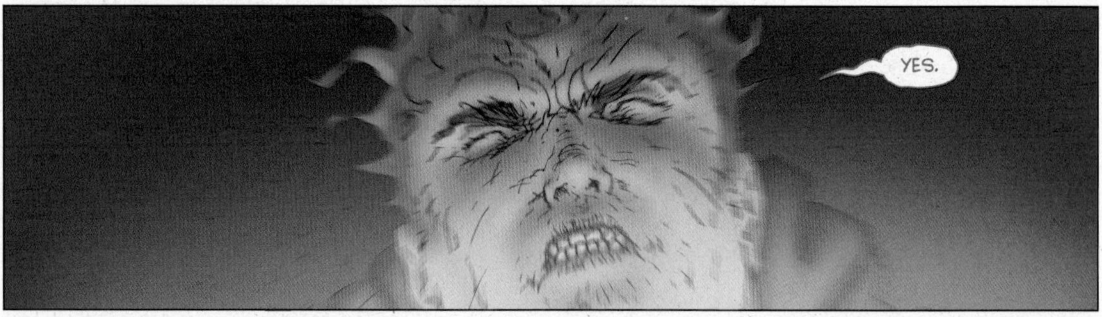
YES.

US DO OPPOSITE

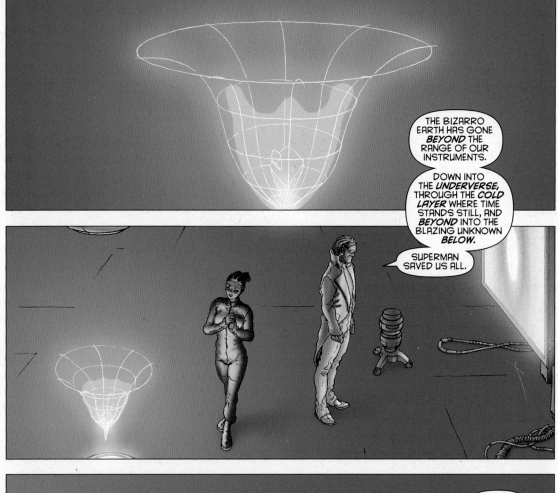

THE BIZARRO EARTH HAS GONE *BEYOND* THE RANGE OF OUR INSTRUMENTS.

DOWN INTO THE *UNDERVERSE,* THROUGH THE *COLD LAYER* WHERE TIME STANDS STILL, AND *BEYOND* INTO THE BLAZING UNKNOWN *BELOW.*

SUPERMAN SAVED US ALL.

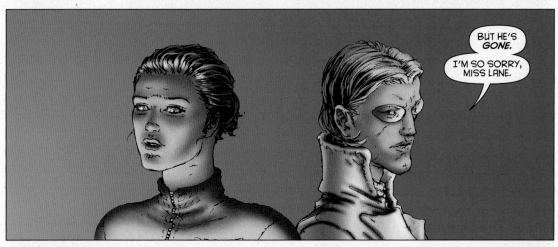

BUT HE'S *GONE.*

I'M SO SORRY, MISS LANE.

I KNOW YOU WERE CLOSE.

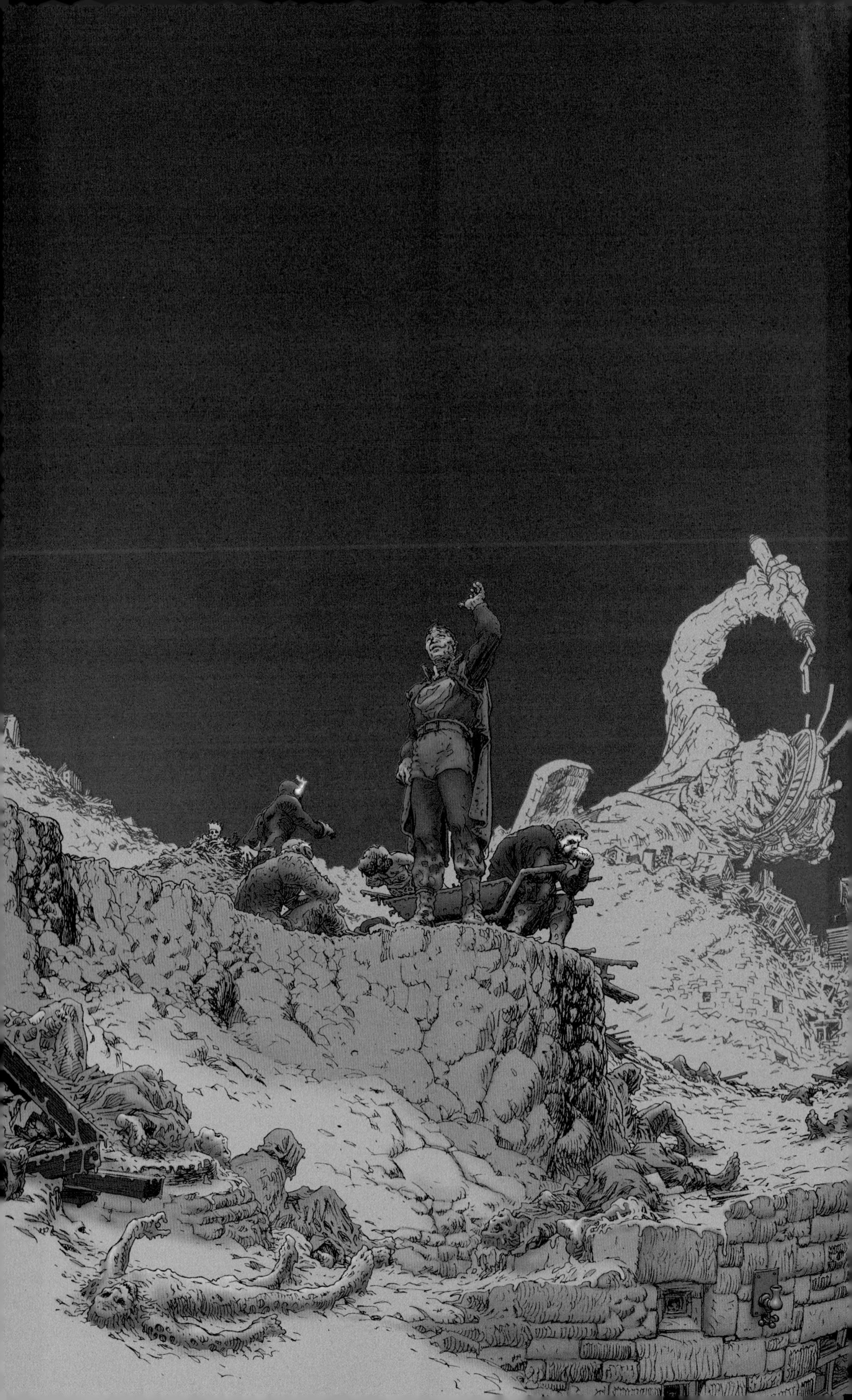

Episode 9

CURSE OF THE REPLACEMENT SUPERMEN

Cover FRANK QUITELY

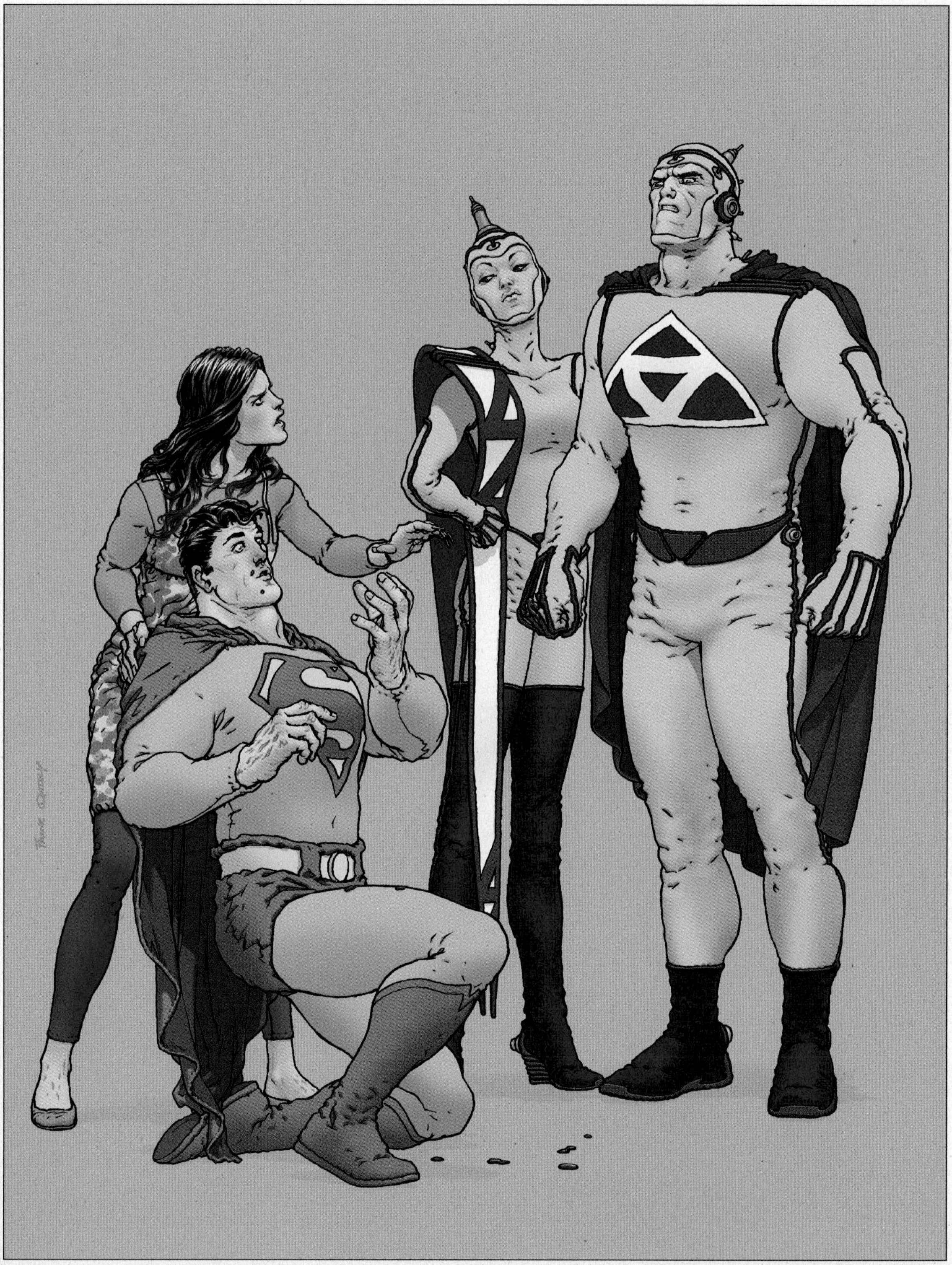

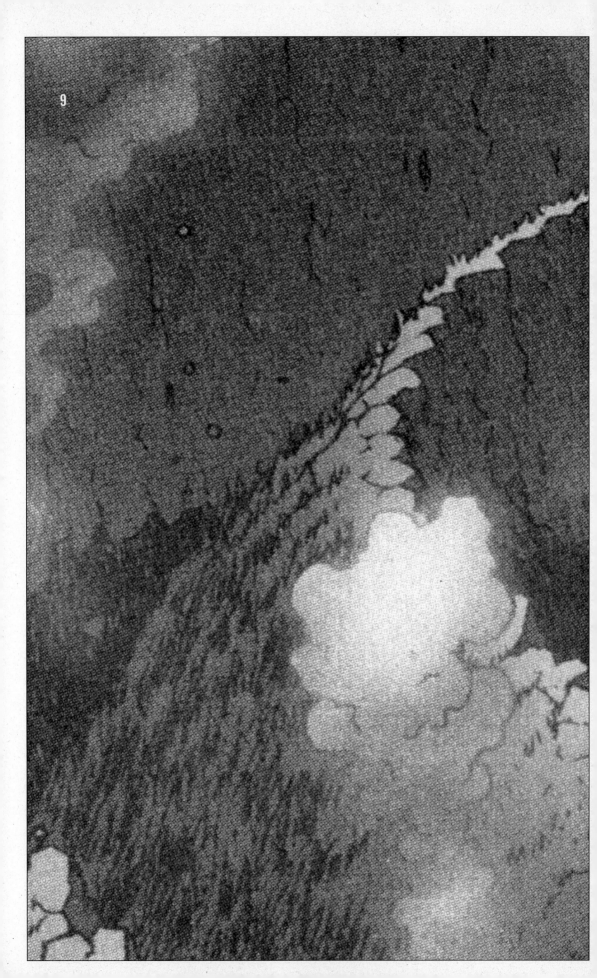

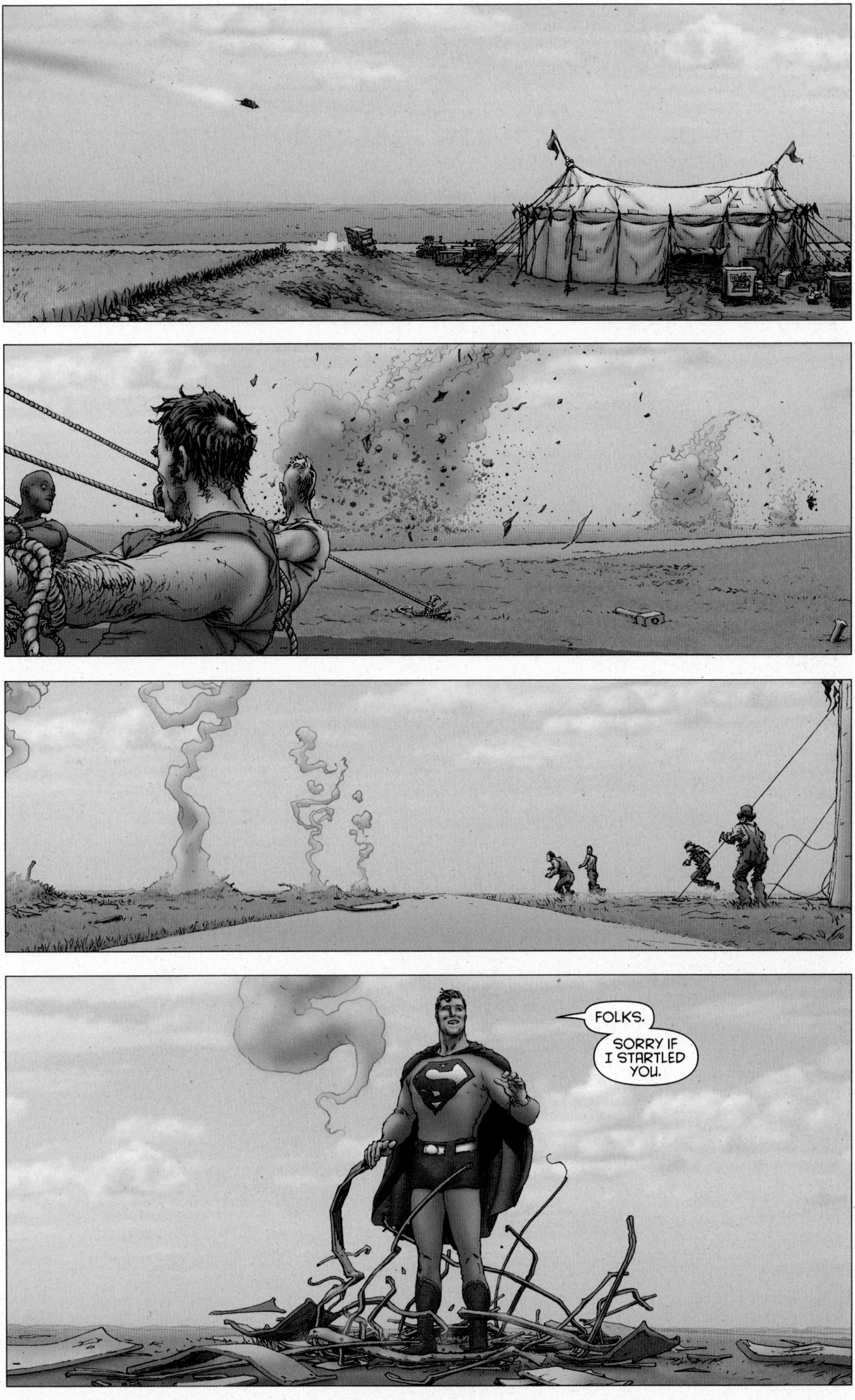
FOLKS.
SORRY IF I STARTLED YOU.

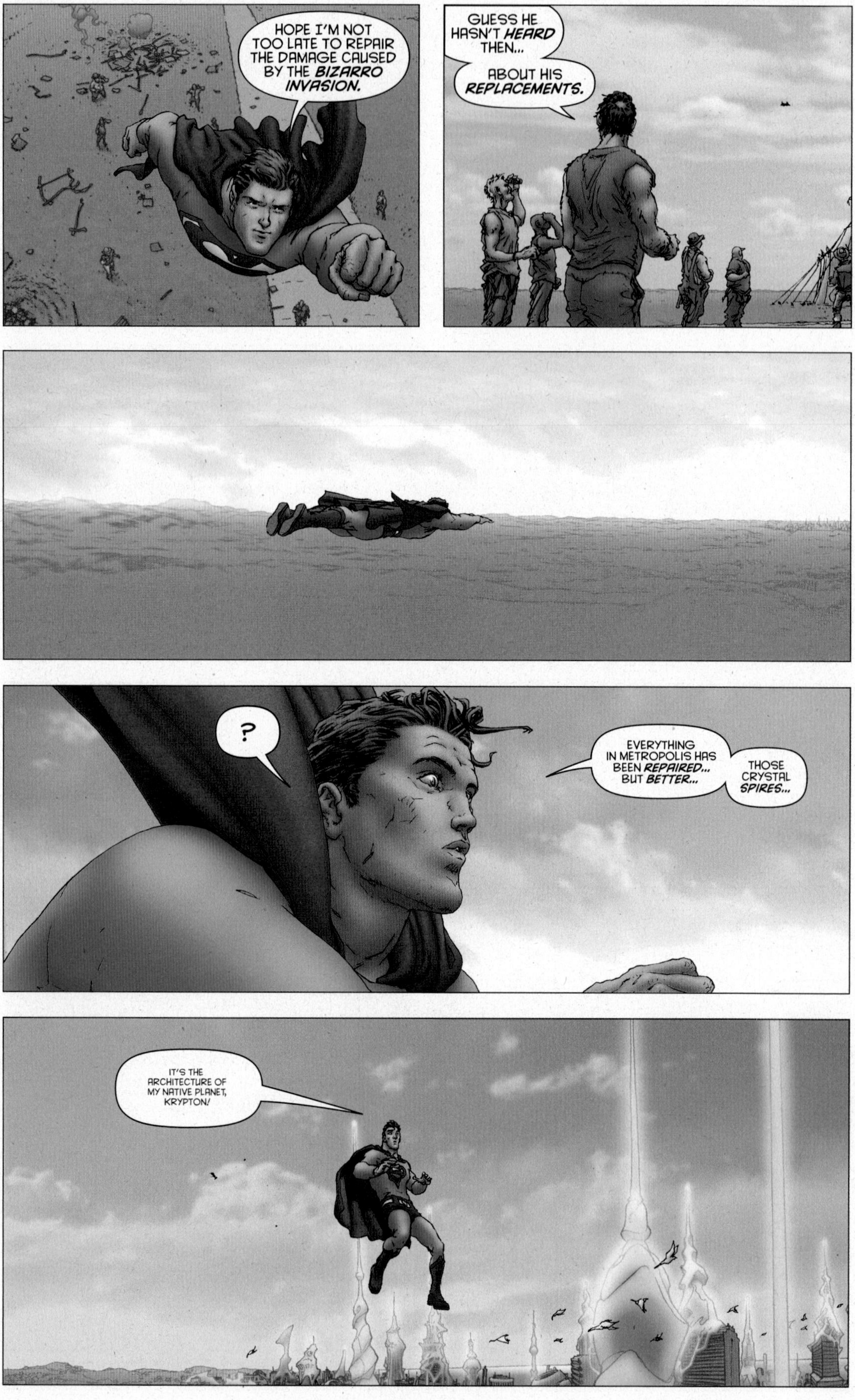
HOPE I'M NOT TOO LATE TO REPAIR THE DAMAGE CAUSED BY THE BIZARRO INVASION.
GUESS HE HASN'T HEARD THEN...
ABOUT HIS REPLACEMENTS.
?
EVERYTHING IN METROPOLIS HAS BEEN REPAIRED... BUT BETTER...
THOSE CRYSTAL SPIRES...
IT'S THE ARCHITECTURE OF MY NATIVE PLANET, KRYPTON!

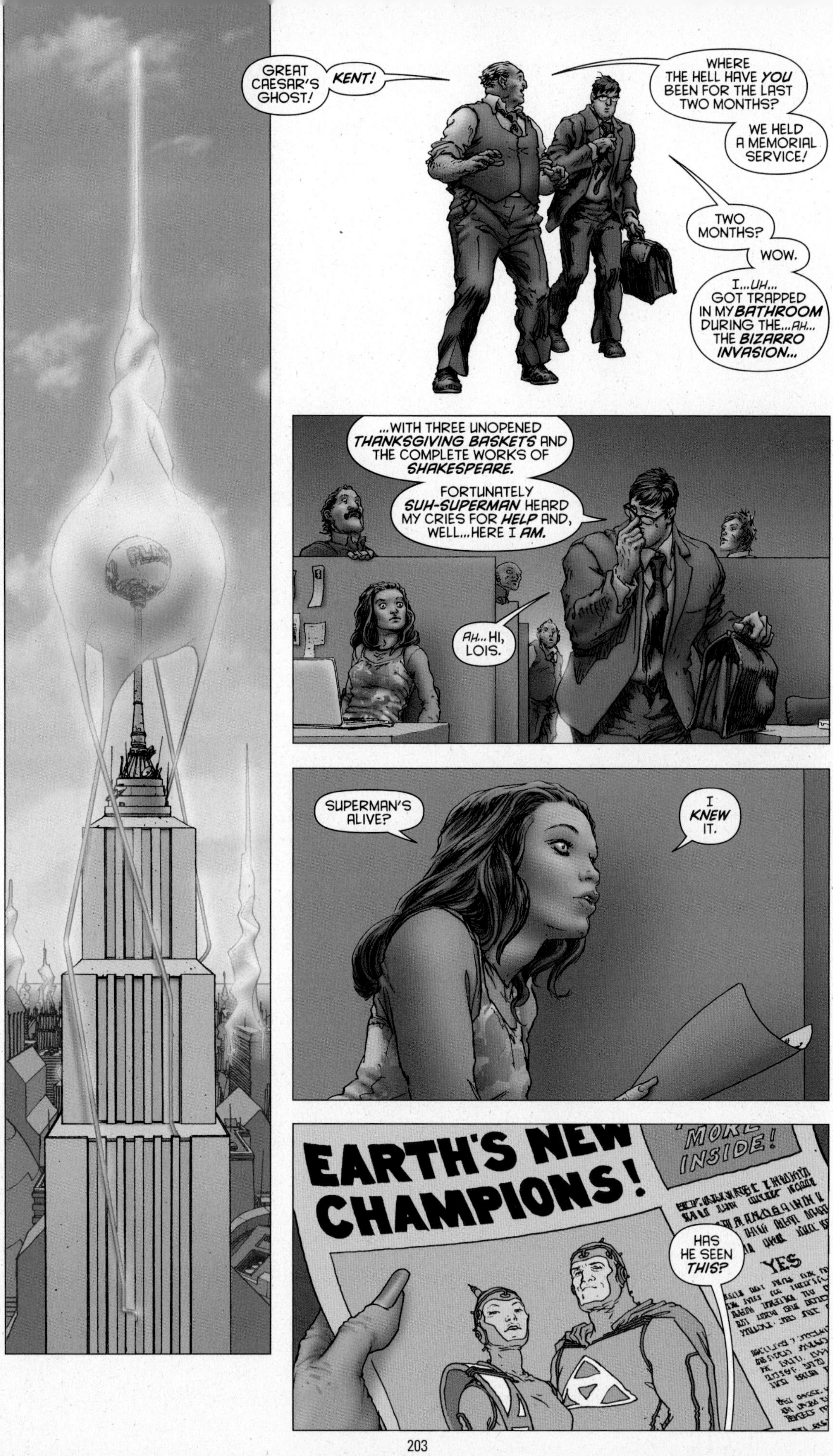
GREAT CAESAR'S GHOST!
KENT!
WHERE THE HELL HAVE YOU BEEN FOR THE LAST TWO MONTHS?
WE HELD A MEMORIAL SERVICE!
TWO MONTHS?
WOW.
I...UH... GOT TRAPPED IN MY BATHROOM DURING THE...AH... THE BIZARRO INVASION...
...WITH THREE UNOPENED THANKSGIVING BASKETS AND THE COMPLETE WORKS OF SHAKESPEARE.
FORTUNATELY SUH-SUPERMAN HEARD MY CRIES FOR HELP AND, WELL...HERE I AM.
AH... HI, LOIS.
SUPERMAN'S ALIVE?
I KNEW IT.
EARTH'S NEW CHAMPIONS!
MORE INSIDE!
YES
HAS HE SEEN THIS?

THAT SHOULD DO IT.

THE NETWORK OF TUNNELS WE'VE DRILLED WILL CAUSE THE WHOLE VOLCANO TO *COLLAPSE.*

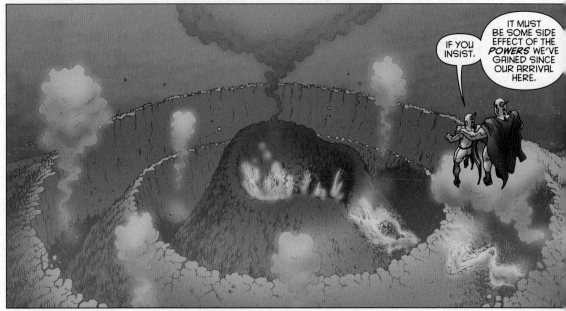

IT MUST BE SOME SIDE EFFECT OF THE *POWERS* WE'VE GAINED SINCE OUR ARRIVAL HERE.

IF YOU INSIST.

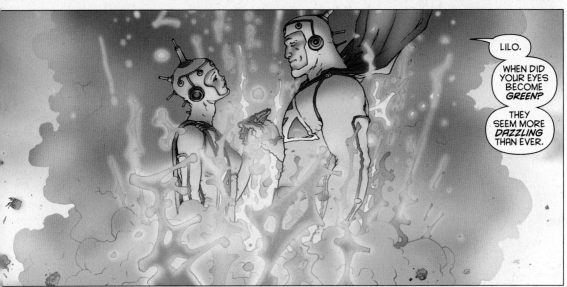

LILO.

WHEN DID YOUR EYES BECOME *GREEN*?

THEY SEEM MORE *DAZZLING* THAN EVER.

HOW ABOUT *THIS* VERY SPOT?

THE CAPITAL OF *NEW KRYPTON* COULD RISE HERE, COULD IT NOT?

MMM.

I THINK WE COULD JUST AS EASILY CLEAR THE APES OUT OF *METROPOLIS* AND BUILD *THERE.*

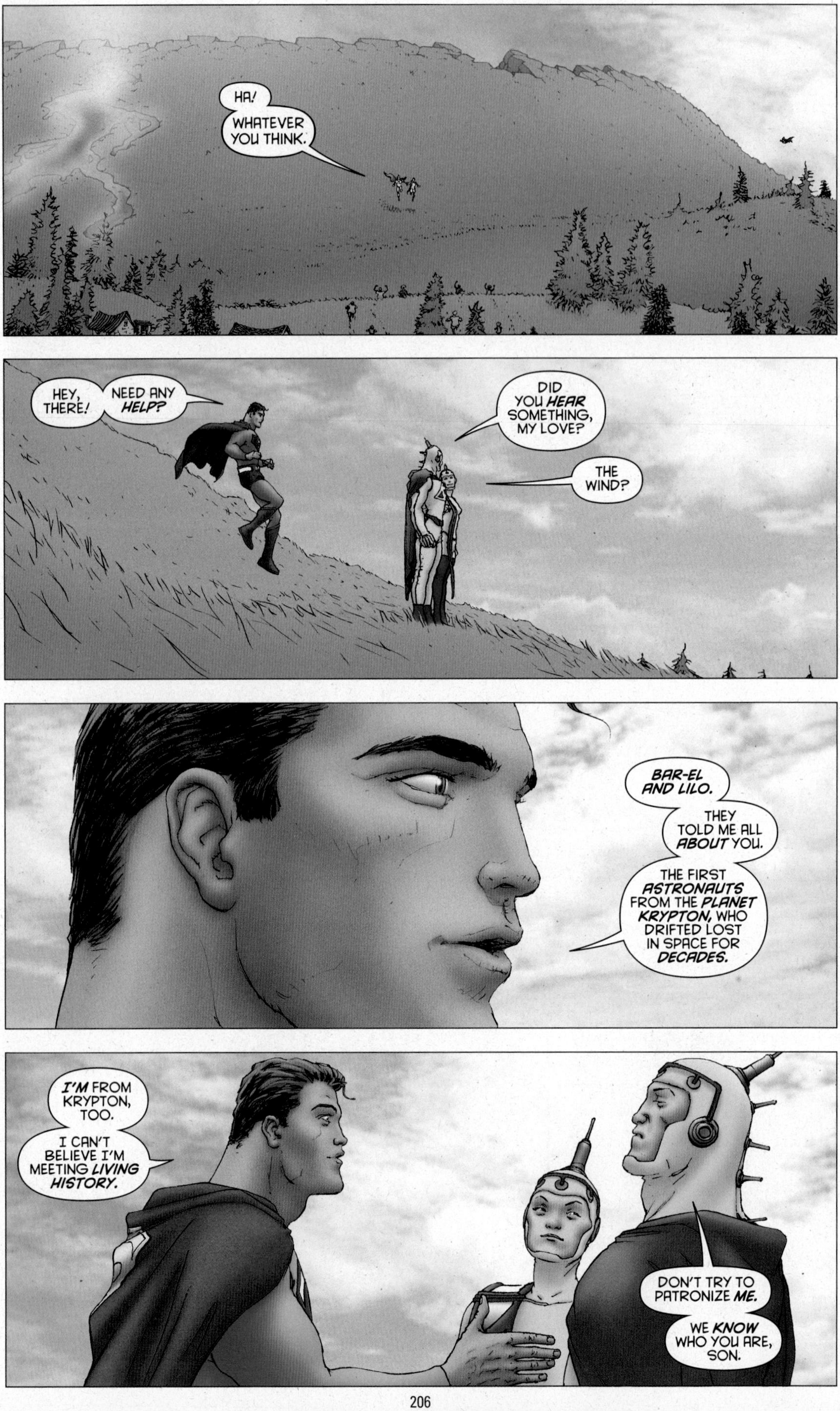
HA!
WHATEVER YOU THINK.
HEY, THERE!
NEED ANY HELP?
DID YOU HEAR SOMETHING, MY LOVE?
THE WIND?
BAR-EL AND LILO.
THEY TOLD ME ALL ABOUT YOU.
THE FIRST ASTRONAUTS FROM THE PLANET KRYPTON, WHO DRIFTED LOST IN SPACE FOR DECADES.
I'M FROM KRYPTON, TOO.
I CAN'T BELIEVE I'M MEETING LIVING HISTORY.
DON'T TRY TO PATRONIZE ME.
WE KNOW WHO YOU ARE, SON.

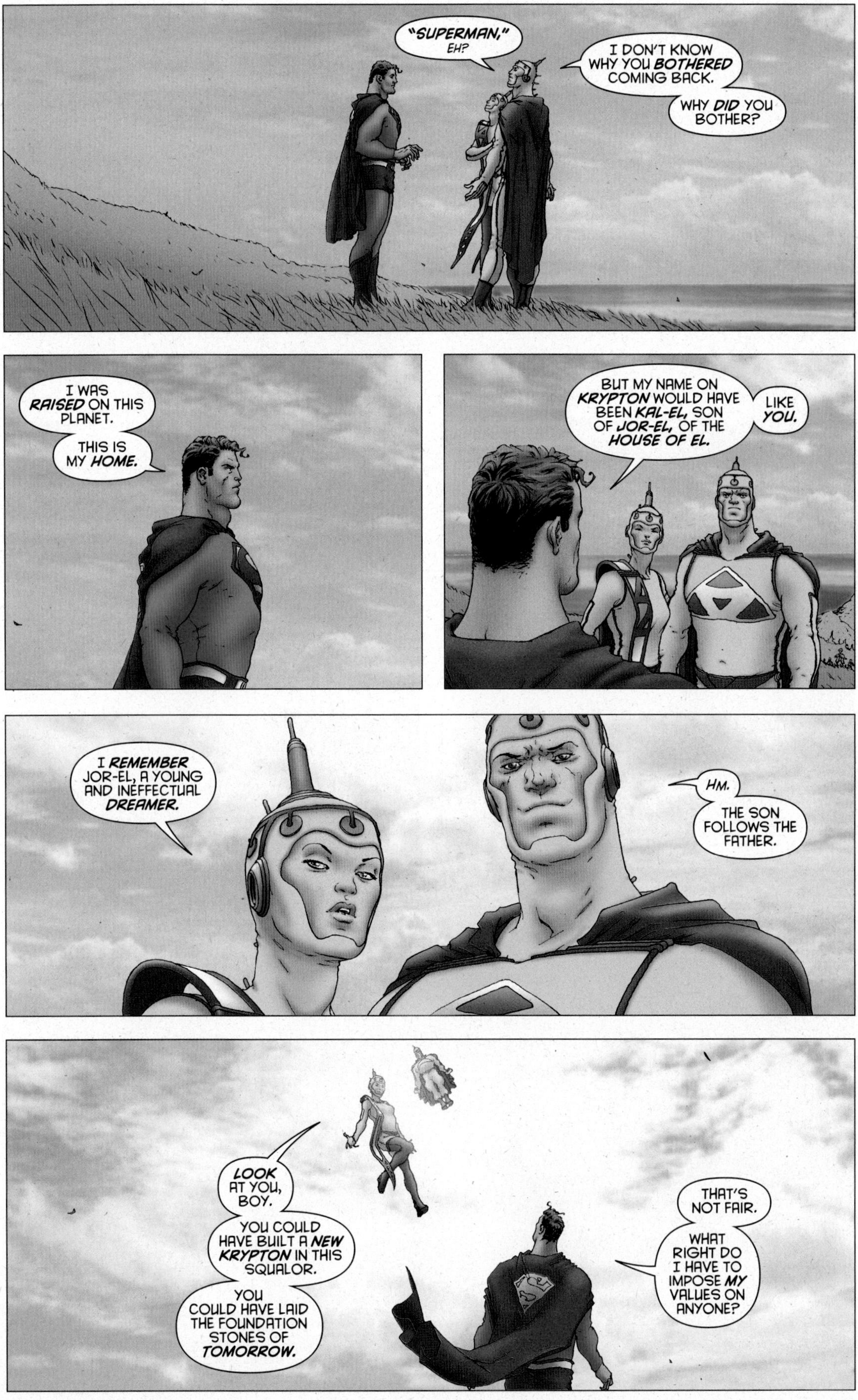

"SUPERMAN," EH?
I DON'T KNOW WHY YOU BOTHERED COMING BACK.
WHY DID YOU BOTHER?
I WAS RAISED ON THIS PLANET.
THIS IS MY HOME.
BUT MY NAME ON KRYPTON WOULD HAVE BEEN KAL-EL, SON OF JOR-EL, OF THE HOUSE OF EL.
LIKE YOU.
I REMEMBER JOR-EL, A YOUNG AND INEFFECTUAL DREAMER.
HM.
THE SON FOLLOWS THE FATHER.
LOOK AT YOU, BOY.
YOU COULD HAVE BUILT A NEW KRYPTON IN THIS SQUALOR.
YOU COULD HAVE LAID THE FOUNDATION STONES OF TOMORROW.
THAT'S NOT FAIR.
WHAT RIGHT DO I HAVE TO IMPOSE MY VALUES ON ANYONE?

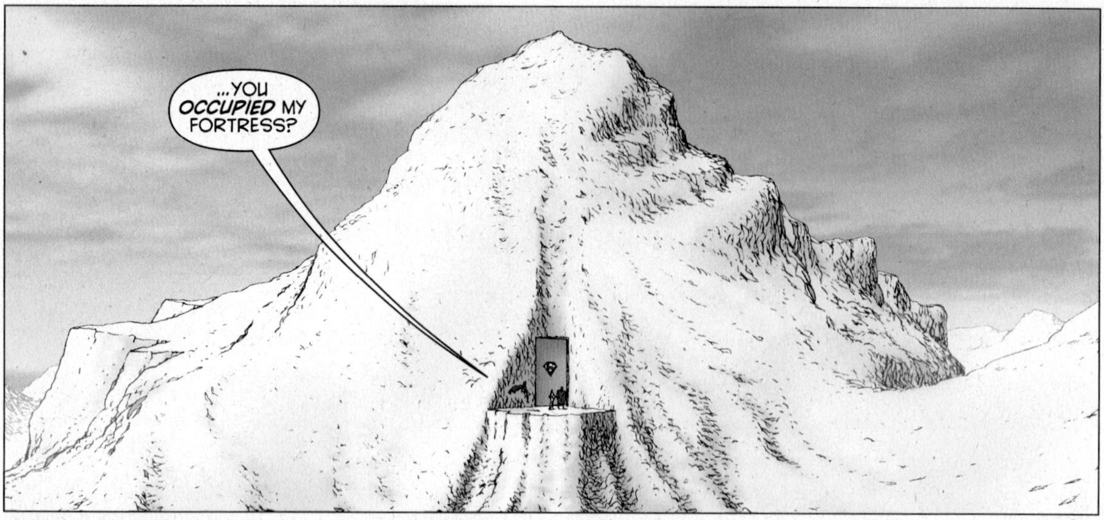
...YOU OCCUPIED MY FORTRESS?

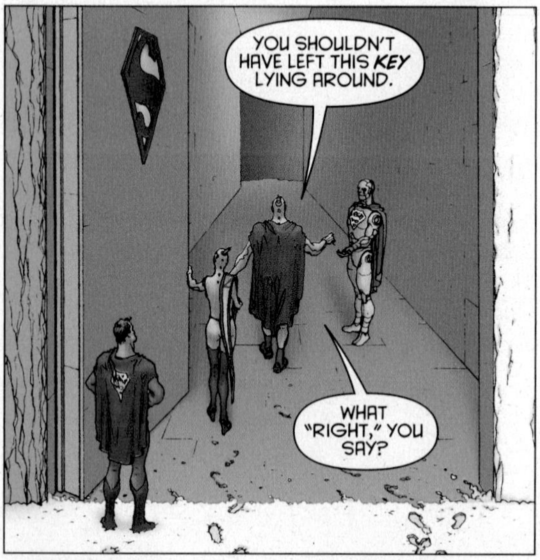
YOU SHOULDN'T HAVE LEFT THIS KEY LYING AROUND.
WHAT "RIGHT," YOU SAY?

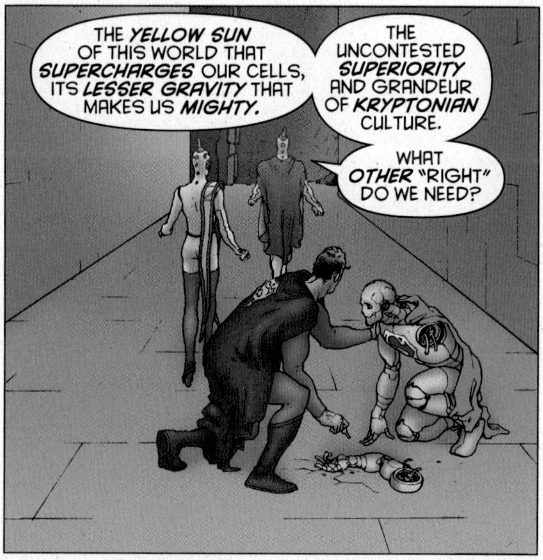
THE YELLOW SUN OF THIS WORLD THAT SUPERCHARGES OUR CELLS, ITS LESSER GRAVITY THAT MAKES US MIGHTY.
THE UNCONTESTED SUPERIORITY AND GRANDEUR OF KRYPTONIAN CULTURE.
WHAT OTHER "RIGHT" DO WE NEED?

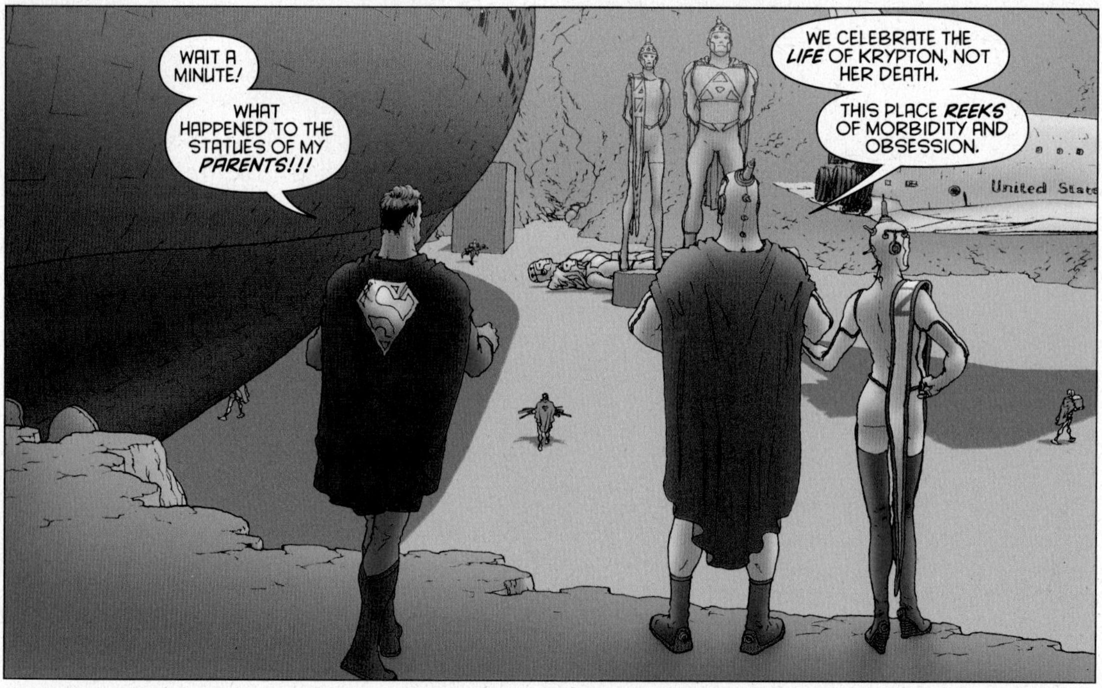
WAIT A MINUTE!
WHAT HAPPENED TO THE STATUES OF MY PARENTS!!!
WE CELEBRATE THE LIFE OF KRYPTON, NOT HER DEATH.
THIS PLACE REEKS OF MORBIDITY AND OBSESSION.
United Stat

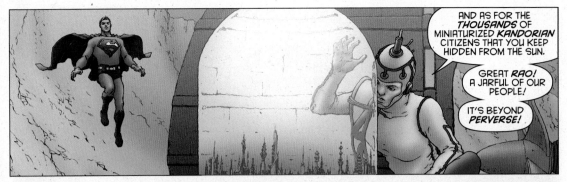

AND AS FOR THE *THOUSANDS* OF MINIATURIZED *KANDORIAN* CITIZENS THAT YOU KEEP HIDDEN FROM THE SUN.

GREAT *RAO!* A JARFUL OF OUR PEOPLE!

IT'S BEYOND *PERVERSE!*

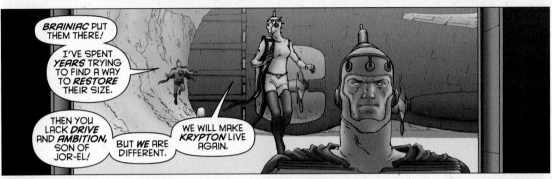

BRAINIAC PUT THEM THERE!

I'VE SPENT *YEARS* TRYING TO FIND A WAY TO *RESTORE* THEIR SIZE.

THEN YOU LACK *DRIVE* AND *AMBITION,* SON OF JOR-EL!

BUT *WE* ARE DIFFERENT.

WE WILL MAKE *KRYPTON* LIVE AGAIN.

OUR PLANET WAS *DEVASTATED,* YOU SAY, *YET* YOU PRESERVE HER SURVIVORS UNDER STIFLING *GLASS!*

GENIUSES, PRODIGIES, *EVERY ONE*--EACH WORTH MORE THAN ANY *THOUSAND* EARTH BARBARIANS.

EVEN INSANE *CRIMINALS,* LIKE THESE IN THE *PHANTOM ZONE,* EVIDENCE MORE *NATURAL* NOBILITY THAN THE *GREATEST* OF THE HUMAN APES.

YOU SHOULD BE *ASHAMED!*

I'M SORRY YOU BOTH FEEL THIS WAY.

I'D HOPED MAYBE YOU COULD *REPLACE* ME IF...IF ANYTHING *HAPPENED* TO ME...

BUT I DON'T THINK YOU HAVE THE BEST INTERESTS OF THIS PLANET AT HEART, DO YOU?

AND THIS IS YOU PUFFING UP YOUR CHEST AT ME NOW, IS IT?

YOU BETRAYED YOUR *HERITAGE.*

YOU WENT *NATIVE.*

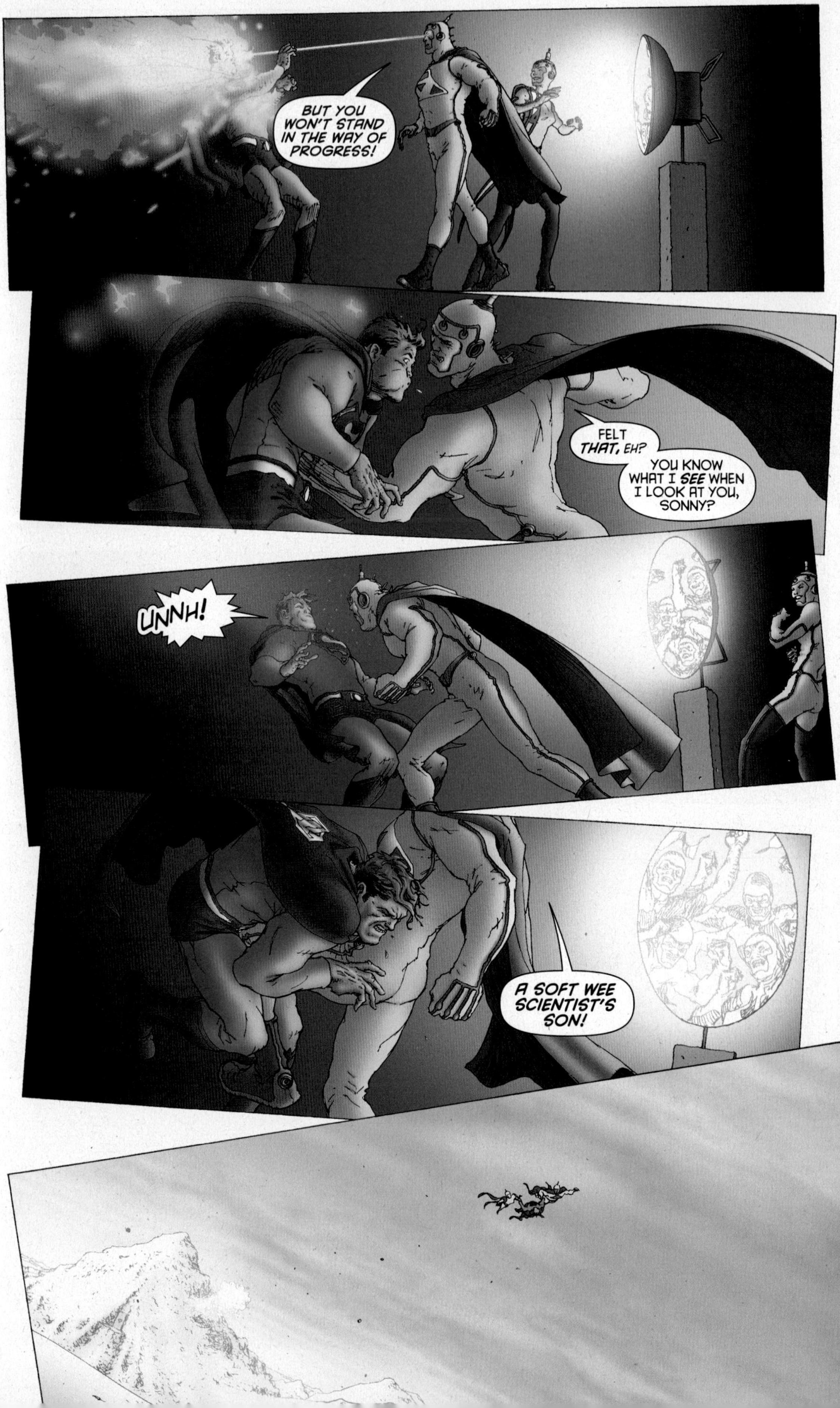
BUT YOU WON'T STAND IN THE WAY OF PROGRESS!
FELT THAT, EH?
YOU KNOW WHAT I SEE WHEN I LOOK AT YOU, SONNY?
UNNH!
A SOFT WEE SCIENTIST'S SON!

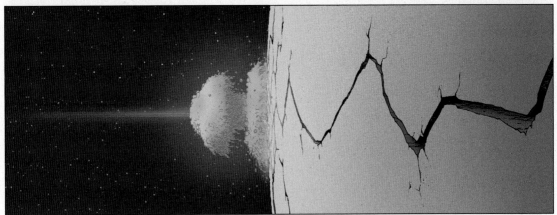

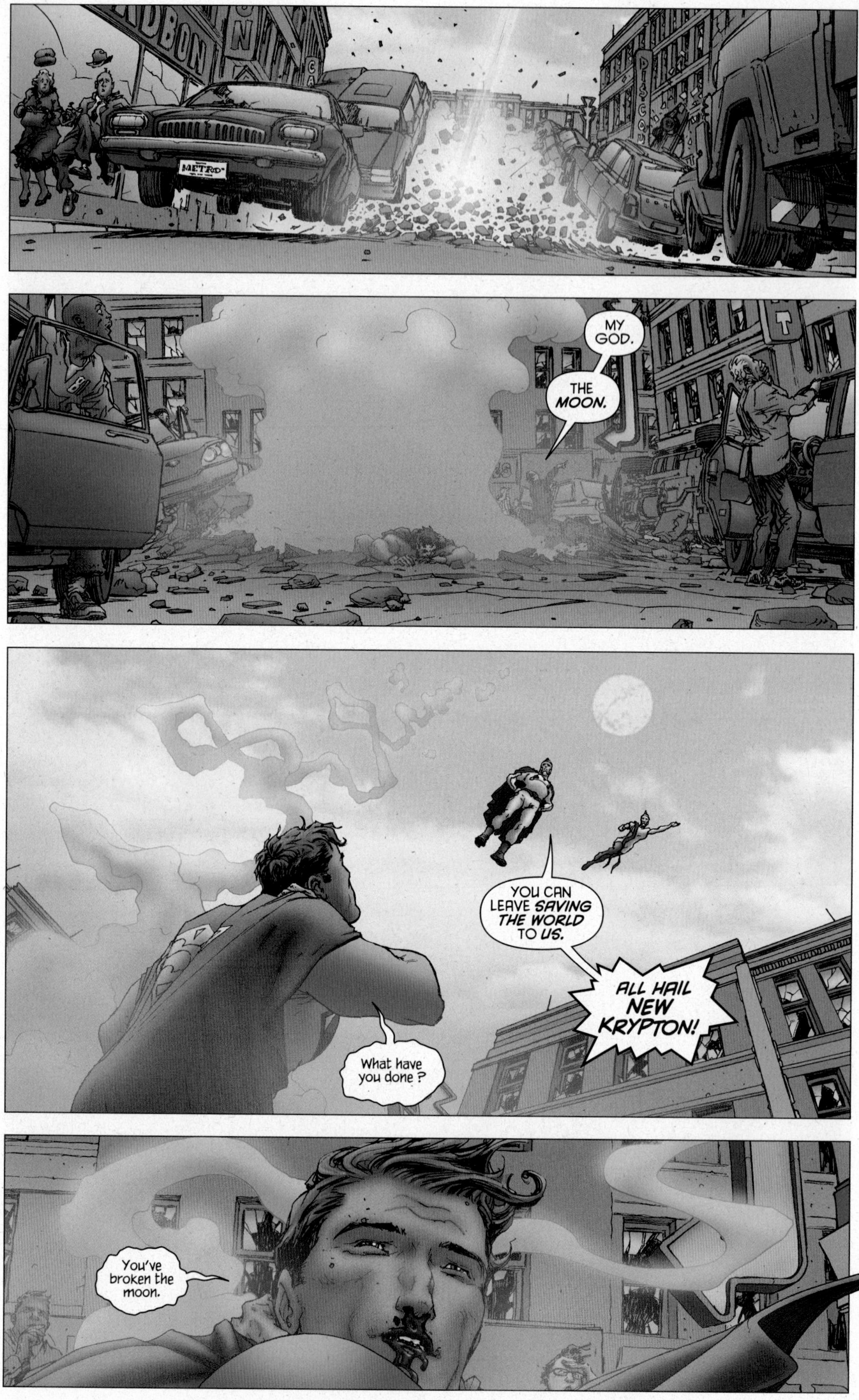
MY GOD.
THE MOON.
YOU CAN LEAVE SAVING THE WORLD TO US.
ALL HAIL NEW KRYPTON!
What have you done ?
You've broken the moon.

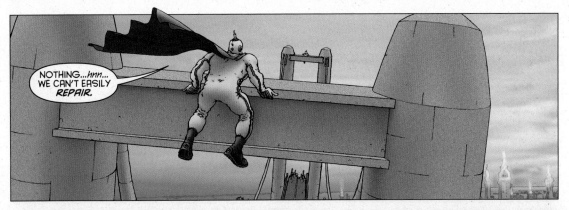

NOTING...*hnn*... WE CAN'T EASILY *REPAIR.*

AFTER TWO WHOLE *MONTHS* OF LISTENING TO THEM TALK ABOUT HOW AMAZING LIFE ON *KRYPTON* WAS, I *FINALLY* CAVED IN...

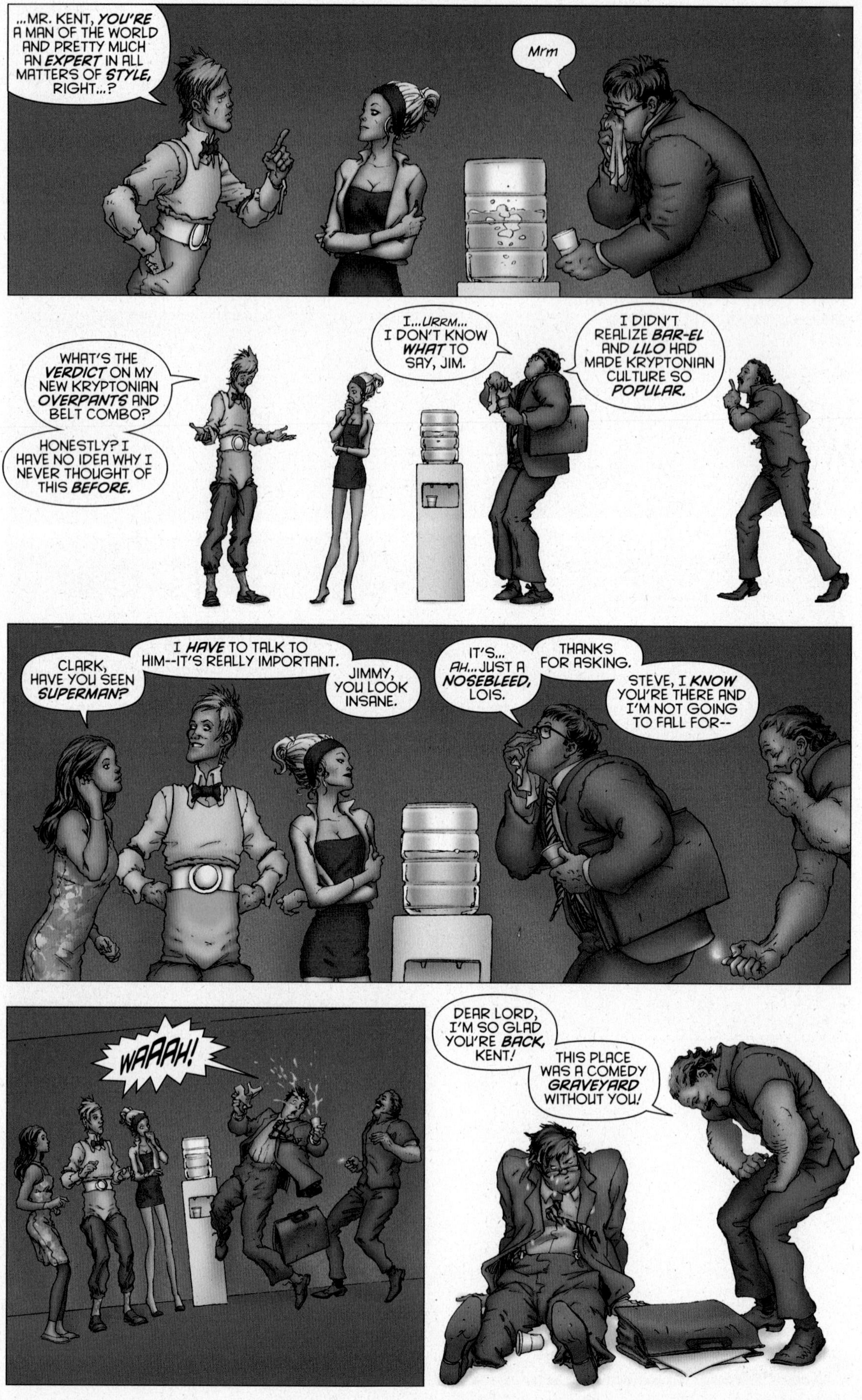
...MR. KENT, YOU'RE A MAN OF THE WORLD AND PRETTY MUCH AN EXPERT IN ALL MATTERS OF STYLE, RIGHT...?
Mrm
WHAT'S THE VERDICT ON MY NEW KRYPTONIAN OVERPANTS AND BELT COMBO?
HONESTLY? I HAVE NO IDEA WHY I NEVER THOUGHT OF THIS BEFORE.
I...URRM... I DON'T KNOW WHAT TO SAY, JIM.
I DIDN'T REALIZE BAR-EL AND LILO HAD MADE KRYPTONIAN CULTURE SO POPULAR.
CLARK, HAVE YOU SEEN SUPERMAN?
I HAVE TO TALK TO HIM--IT'S REALLY IMPORTANT.
JIMMY, YOU LOOK INSANE.
IT'S... AH...JUST A NOSEBLEED, LOIS.
THANKS FOR ASKING.
STEVE, I KNOW YOU'RE THERE AND I'M NOT GOING TO FALL FOR--
WAAAH!
DEAR LORD, I'M SO GLAD YOU'RE BACK, KENT!
THIS PLACE WAS A COMEDY GRAVEYARD WITHOUT YOU!

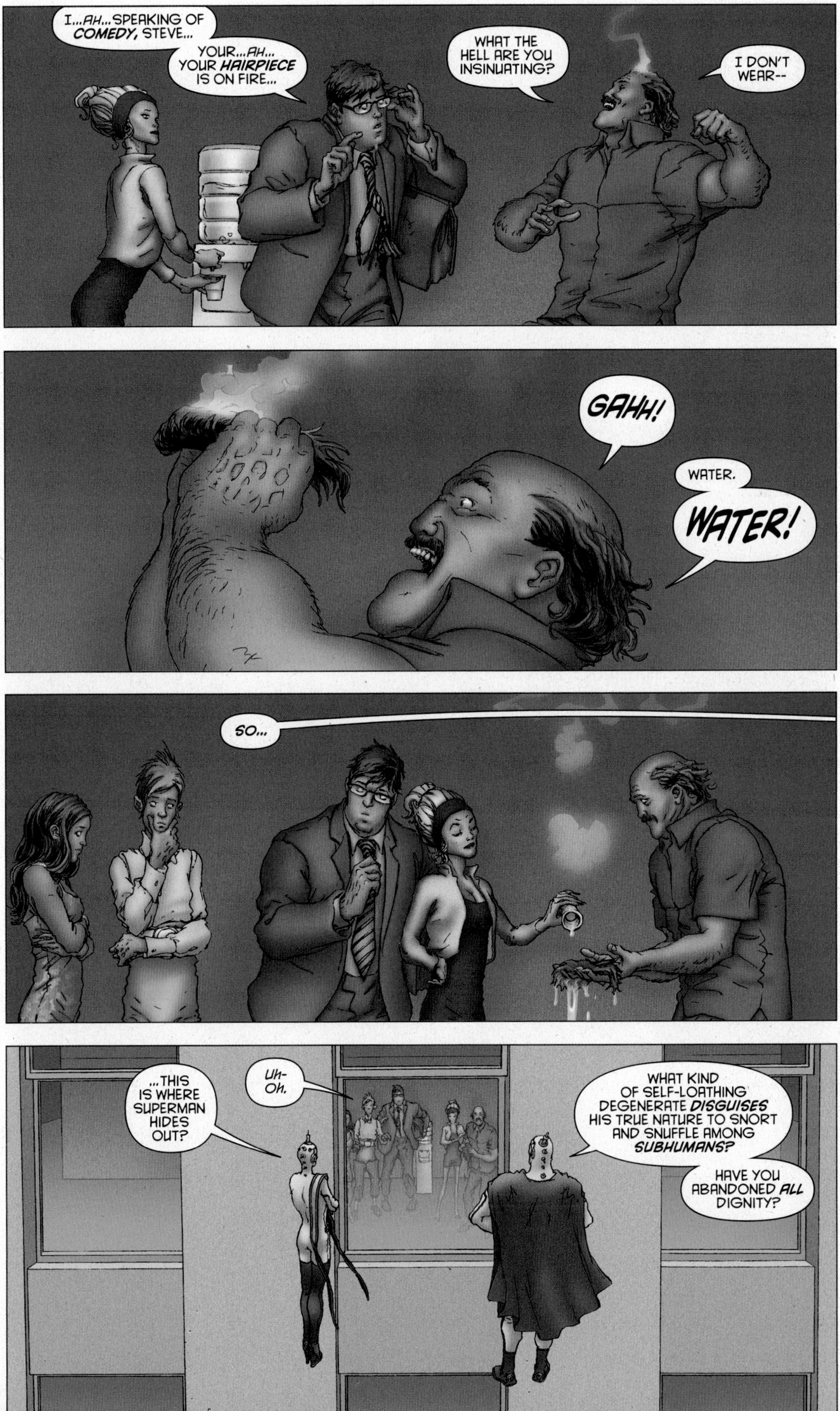

I...AH...SPEAKING OF COMEDY, STEVE...
YOUR...AH... YOUR HAIRPIECE IS ON FIRE...
WHAT THE HELL ARE YOU INSINUATING?
I DON'T WEAR--
GAHH!
WATER.
WATER!
SO...
...THIS IS WHERE SUPERMAN HIDES OUT?
Uh-Oh.
WHAT KIND OF SELF-LOATHING DEGENERATE DISGUISES HIS TRUE NATURE TO SNORT AND SNUFFLE AMONG SUBHUMANS?
HAVE YOU ABANDONED ALL DIGNITY?

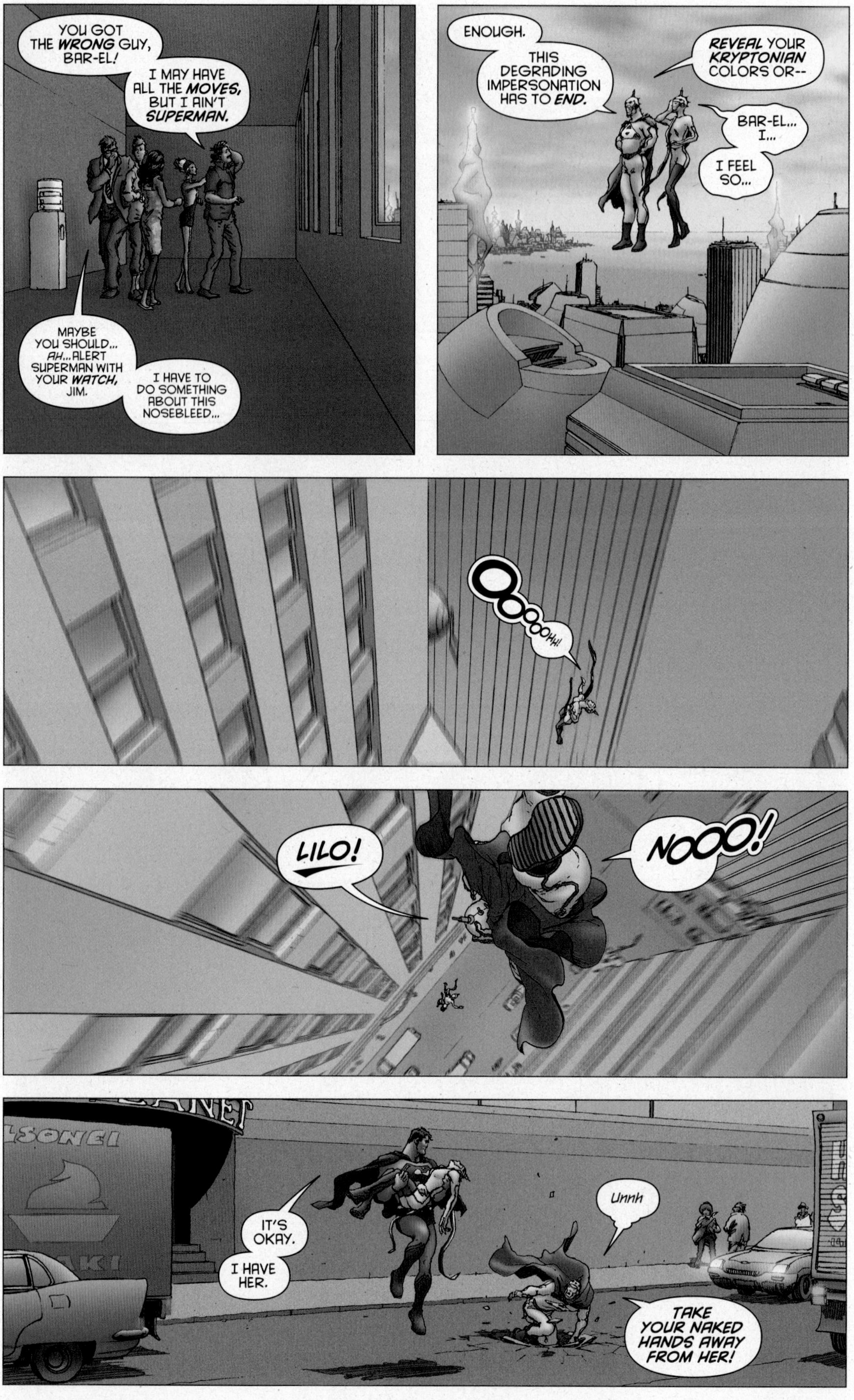
YOU GOT THE WRONG GUY, BAR-EL!
I MAY HAVE ALL THE MOVES, BUT I AIN'T SUPERMAN.
MAYBE YOU SHOULD... AH...ALERT SUPERMAN WITH YOUR WATCH, JIM.
I HAVE TO DO SOMETHING ABOUT THIS NOSEBLEED...
ENOUGH.
THIS DEGRADING IMPERSONATION HAS TO END.
REVEAL YOUR KRYPTONIAN COLORS OR--
BAR-EL... I...
I FEEL SO...
OOOOOHH!
LILO!
NOOO!
IT'S OKAY.
I HAVE HER.
Unnh
TAKE YOUR NAKED HANDS AWAY FROM HER!

I'M *WARNING* YOU...I'LL... I'LL....

I CAN'T *FLY*.

WHY DO I FEEL SO *WEAK*?

AS FAR AS I CAN GUESS, YOU PASSED THROUGH A CERTAIN *RADIOACTIVE CLOUD* IN SPACE-- WHICH CAUSED THE *MINERALS* IN YOUR BODIES TO TURN TO TOXIC *KRYPTONITE*.

IT CAN'T KILL *ME* ANYMORE BUT IT WAS *WEAKENING* ME. AS FOR YOU...

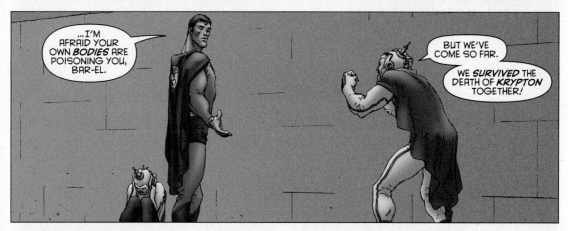

...I'M AFRAID YOUR OWN *BODIES* ARE POISONING YOU, BAR-EL.

BUT WE'VE COME SO FAR.

WE *SURVIVED* THE DEATH OF *KRYPTON* TOGETHER!

I KNOW.

LET ME HELP.

THERE'S ALWAYS A WAY.

LIKE YOU HELPED KANDOR?

URRR

I DON'T *NEED* YOUR KIND OF HELP!

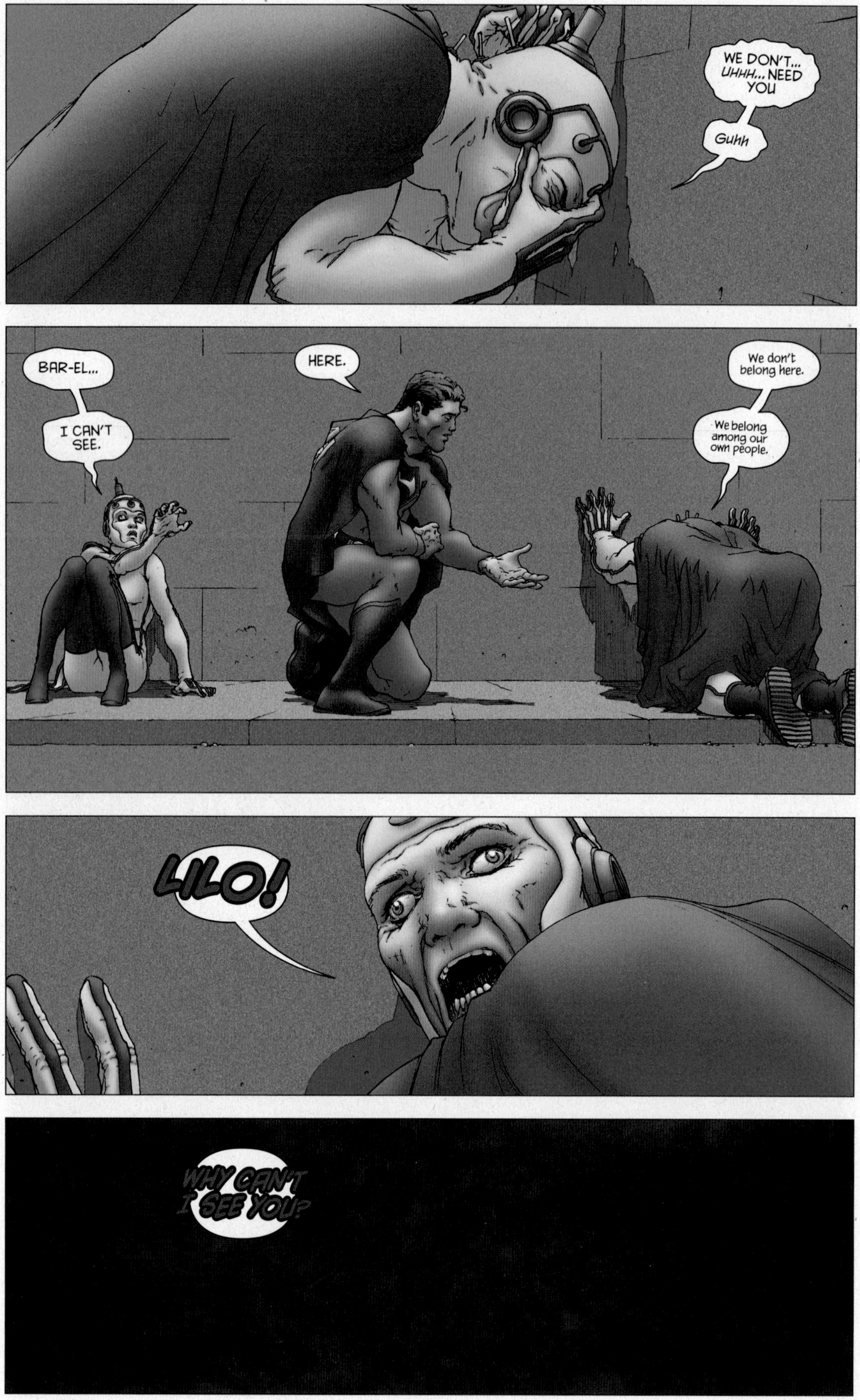
WE DON'T... UHHH... NEED YOU
Guhh
BAR-EL...
I CAN'T SEE.
HERE.
We don't belong here.
We belong among our own people.
LILO!
WHY CAN'T I SEE YOU?

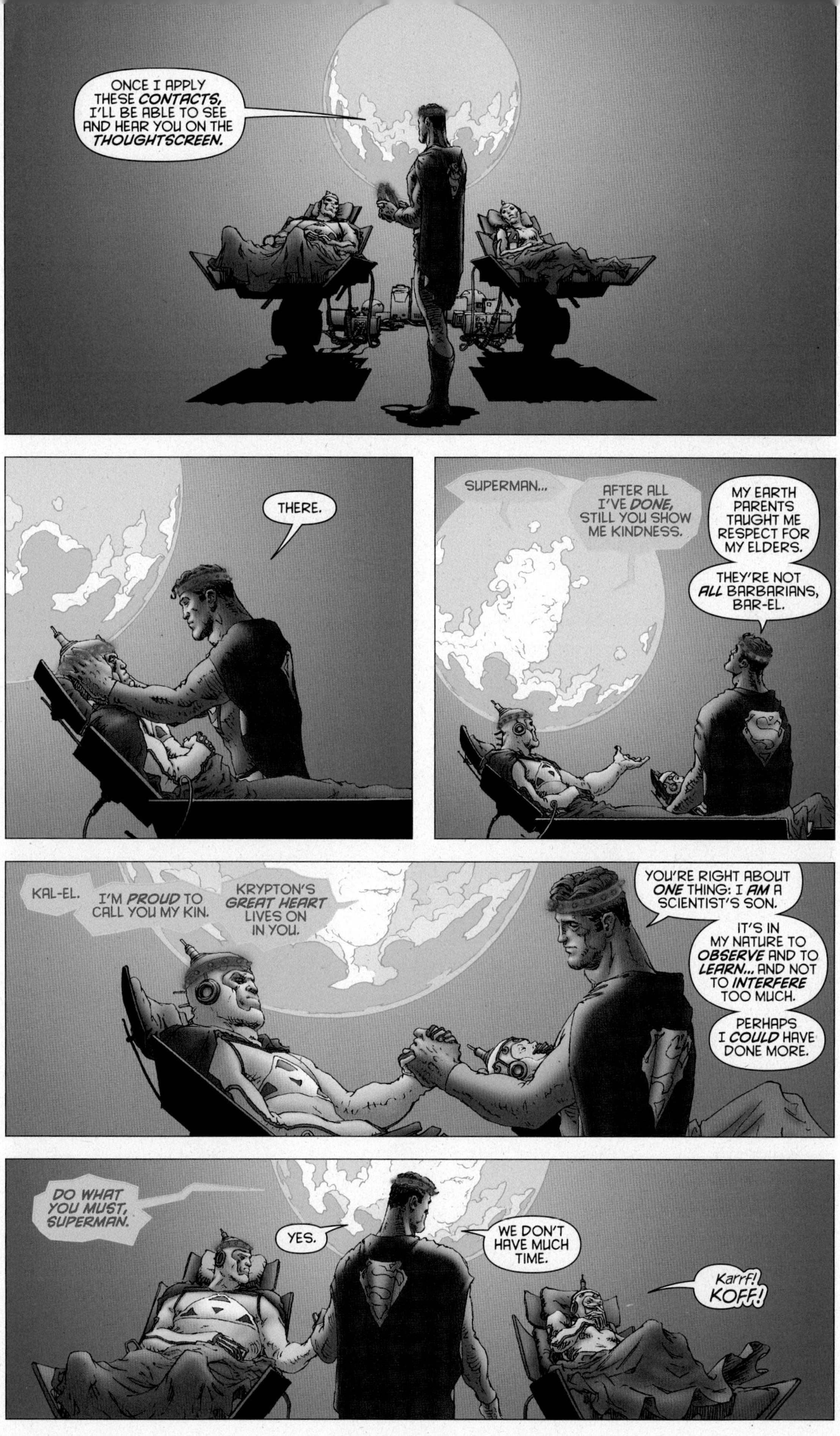
ONCE I APPLY THESE CONTACTS, I'LL BE ABLE TO SEE AND HEAR YOU ON THE THOUGHTSCREEN.
THERE.
SUPERMAN...
AFTER ALL I'VE DONE, STILL YOU SHOW ME KINDNESS.
MY EARTH PARENTS TAUGHT ME RESPECT FOR MY ELDERS.
THEY'RE NOT ALL BARBARIANS, BAR-EL.
KAL-EL.
I'M PROUD TO CALL YOU MY KIN.
KRYPTON'S GREAT HEART LIVES ON IN YOU.
YOU'RE RIGHT ABOUT ONE THING: I AM A SCIENTIST'S SON.
IT'S IN MY NATURE TO OBSERVE AND TO LEARN... AND NOT TO INTERFERE TOO MUCH.
PERHAPS I COULD HAVE DONE MORE.
DO WHAT YOU MUST, SUPERMAN.
YES.
WE DON'T HAVE MUCH TIME.
Karrf! KOFF!

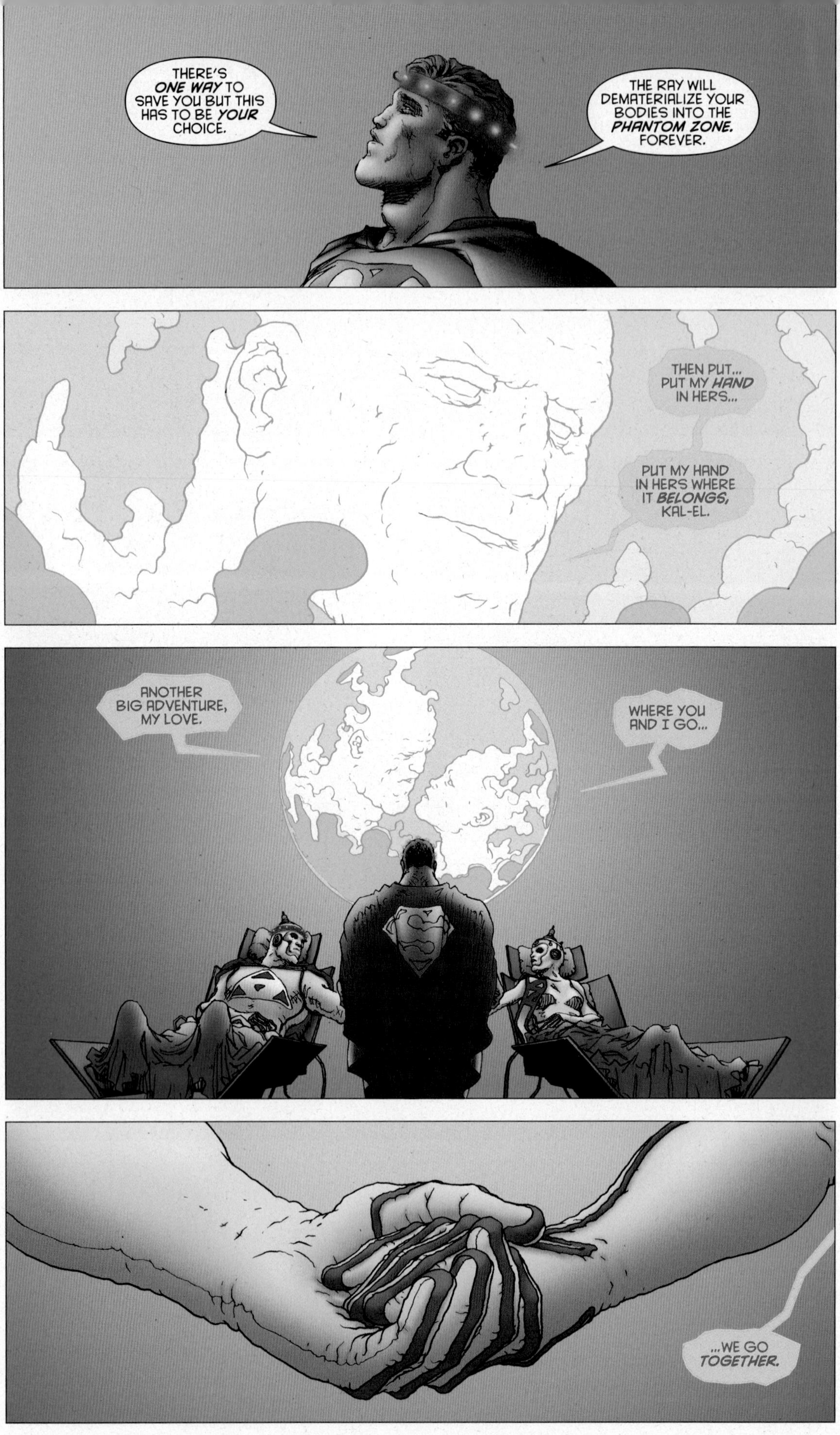
THERE'S ONE WAY TO SAVE YOU BUT THIS HAS TO BE YOUR CHOICE.
THE RAY WILL DEMATERIALIZE YOUR BODIES INTO THE PHANTOM ZONE. FOREVER.
THEN PUT... PUT MY HAND IN HERS...
PUT MY HAND IN HERS WHERE IT BELONGS, KAL-EL.
ANOTHER BIG ADVENTURE, MY LOVE.
WHERE YOU AND I GO...
...WE GO TOGETHER.

IF I CAN, IF I STILL HAVE TIME, I PROMISE I'LL FIND A WAY TO *RESTORE* YOU BOTH.
UNTIL THEN...
...THE PHANTOM ZONE WILL HAVE SOME *LAW AND ORDER* AT LAST.

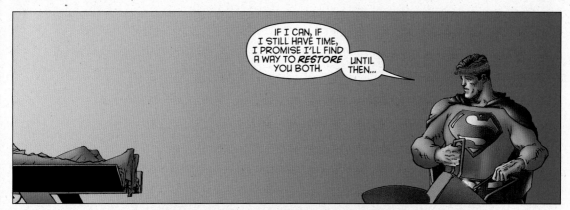

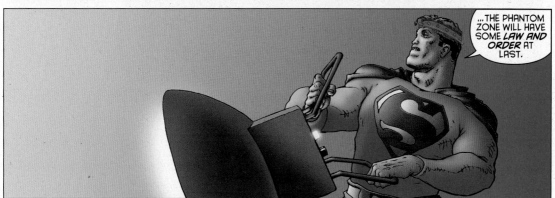

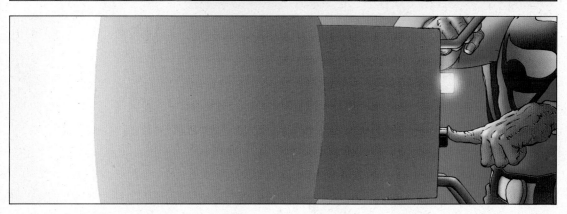

CURSE OF THE REPLACEMENT SUPERMEN

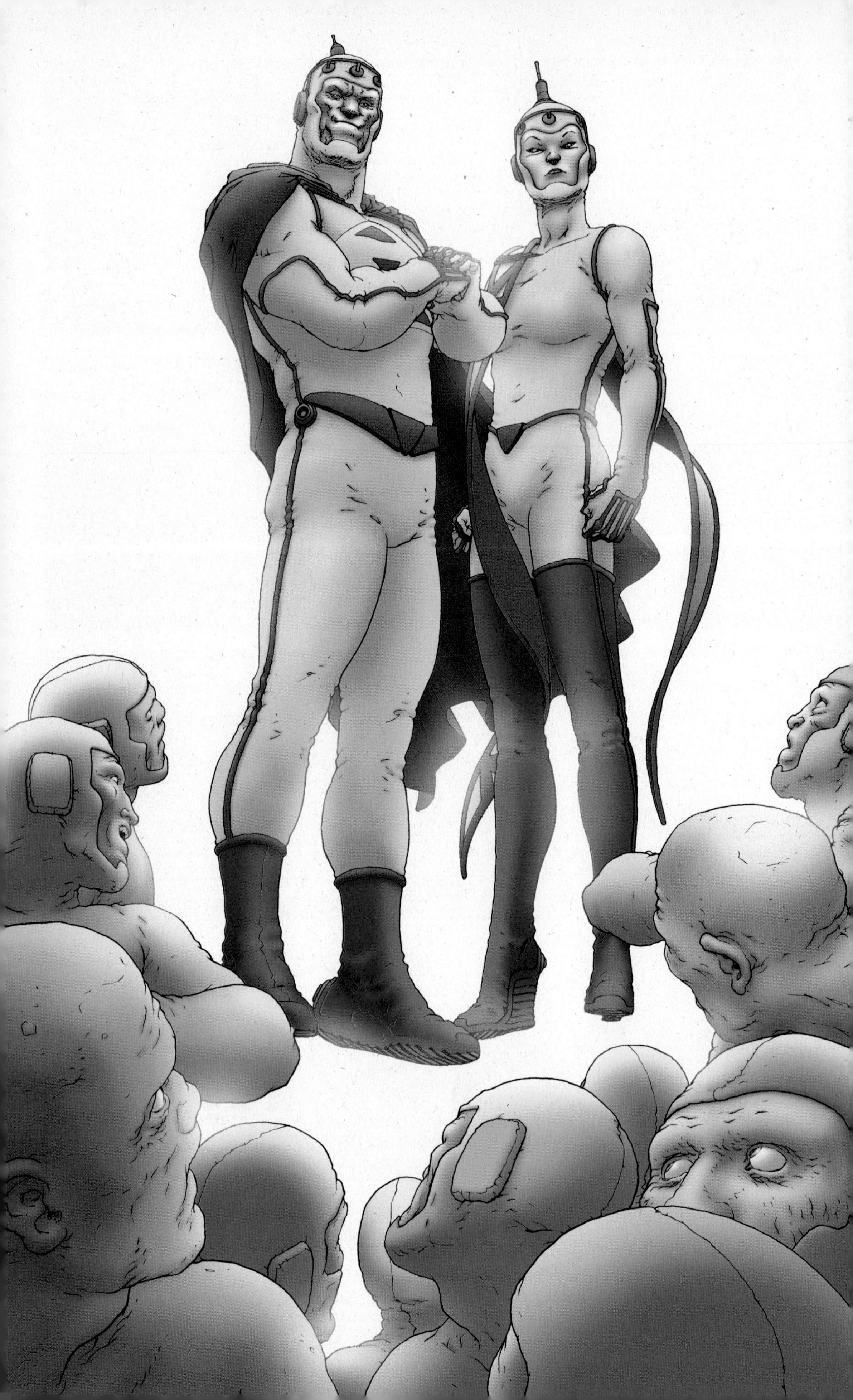

Episode 10

NEVERENDING

Cover FRANK QUITELY with JAMIE GRANT

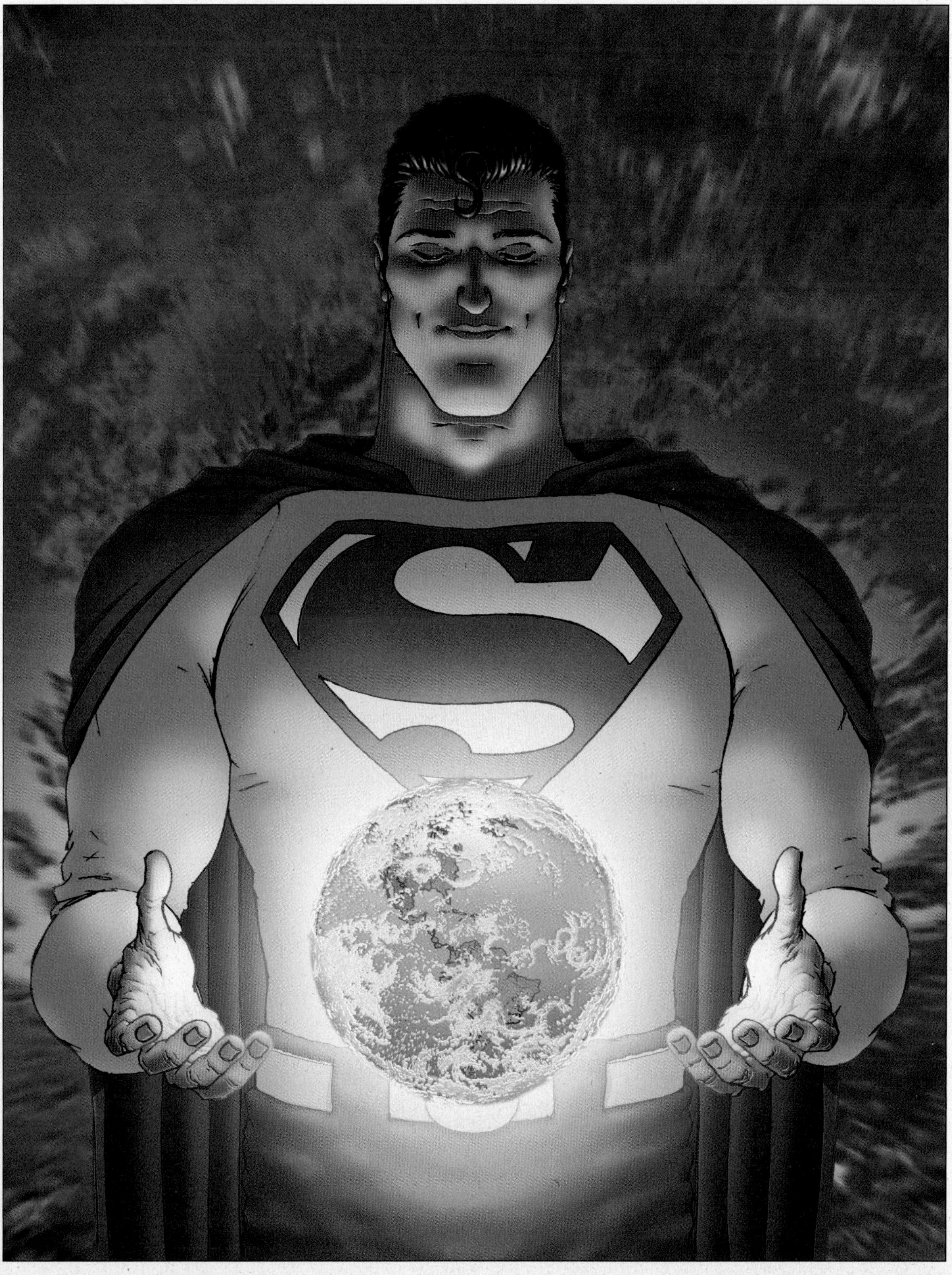

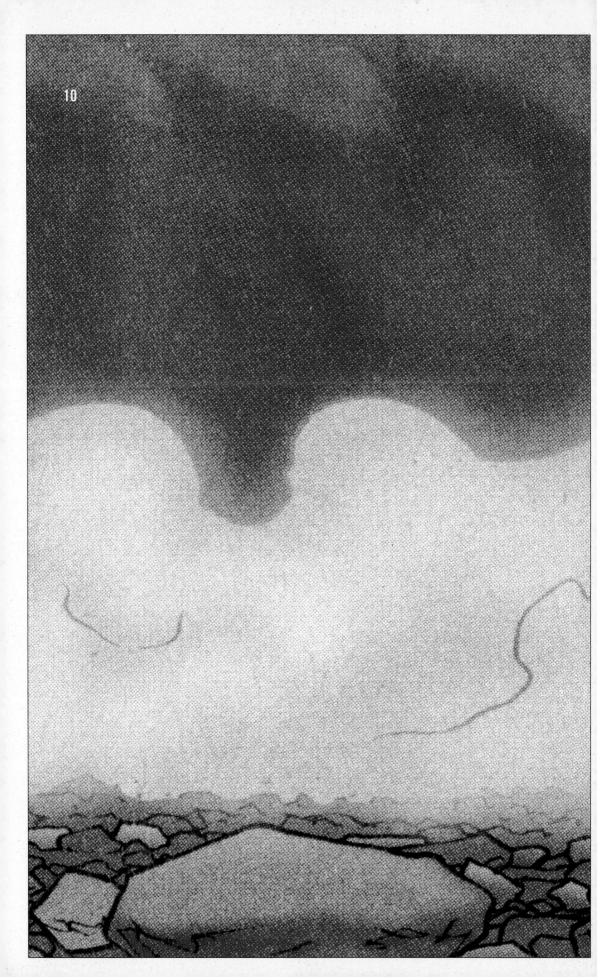

7:02 AM
I'VE NEVER SEEN THEM SO EXCITED.
GOD BLESS YOU, SUPERMAN.
YOUR VISITS ARE ALL SOME OF THEM HAVE TO LOOK FORWARD TO.
IT'S THE LEAST I CAN DO.
11:25 PM
RECORDING:
I, KAL-EL OF KRYPTON, BEING OF SOUND MIND...DECLARE THIS TO BE MY FINAL DISPENSATION...

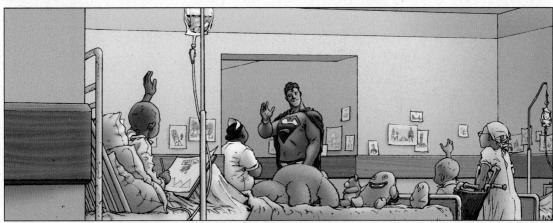

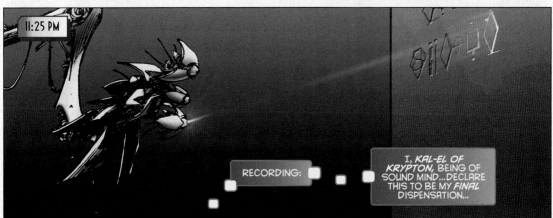

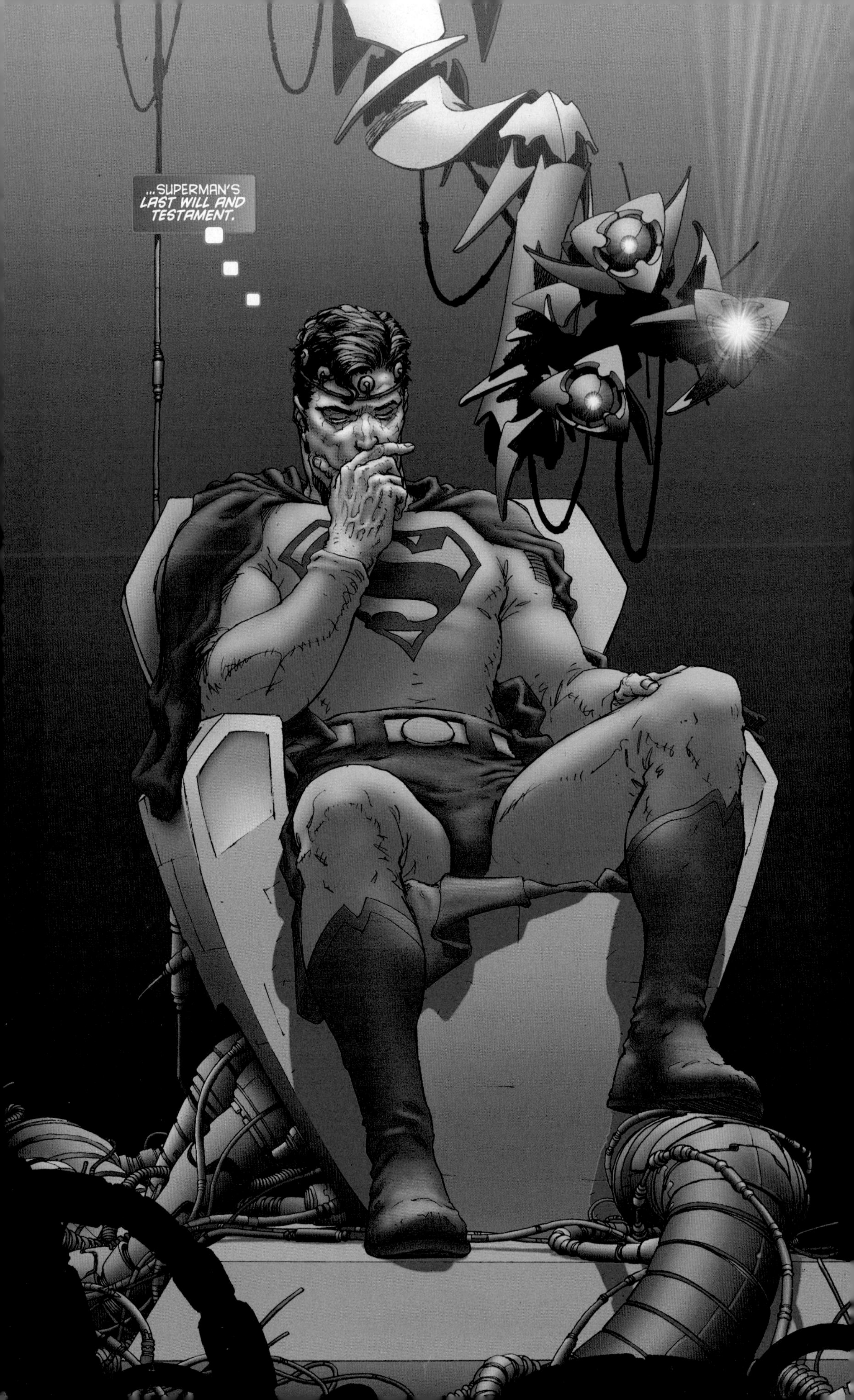
...SUPERMAN'S LAST WILL AND TESTAMENT.

THERE'S SO LITTLE TIME *LEFT* NOW.

THE END IS GETTING *CLOSER* AND THERE ARE STILL SO MANY THINGS I'VE YET TO ACHIEVE.

THE TIME-TRAVELER *SAMSON* TOLD ME I'D COMPLETE *TWELVE* LEGENDARY *SUPER* CHALLENGES BEFORE MY DEATH.

I WOULD *ANSWER* THE UNANSWERABLE QUESTION, OVERCOME THE TYRANT SUN, *SOLARIS*...

...EVEN CREATE LIFE...

EACH CHALLENGE, OF COURSE, BRINGS ME *CLOSER* TO MY DEATH.

AND BY MY RECKONING I'VE ACCOMPLISHED *SEVEN* SO FAR.

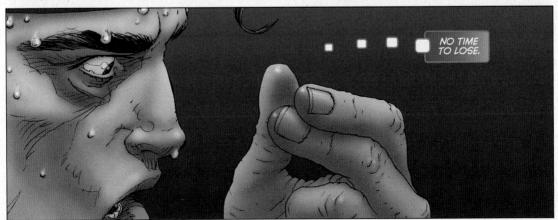

NO TIME TO LOSE.

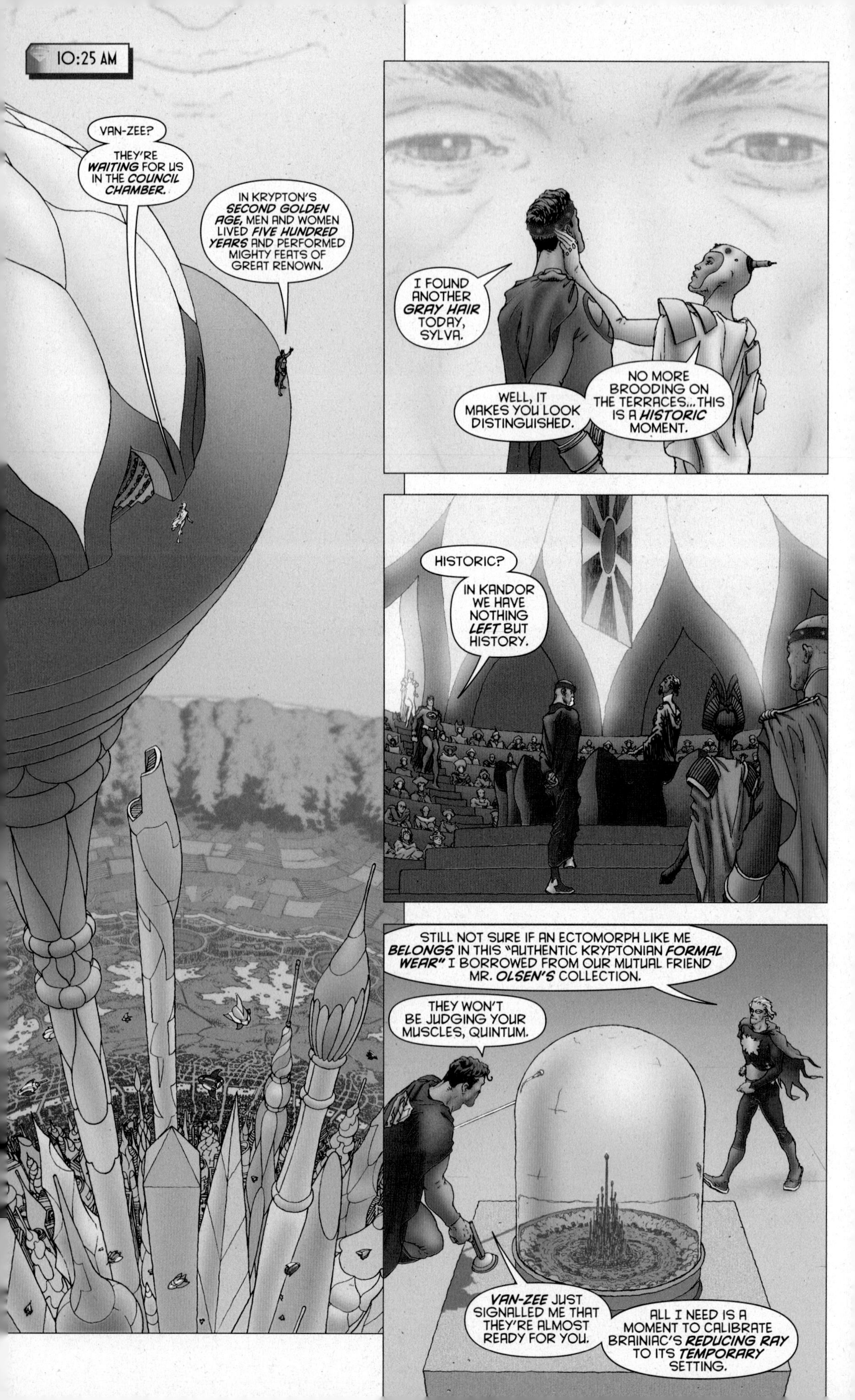
10:25 AM
VAN-ZEE?
THEY'RE WAITING FOR US IN THE COUNCIL CHAMBER.
IN KRYPTON'S SECOND GOLDEN AGE, MEN AND WOMEN LIVED FIVE HUNDRED YEARS AND PERFORMED MIGHTY FEATS OF GREAT RENOWN.
I FOUND ANOTHER GRAY HAIR TODAY, SYLVA.
WELL, IT MAKES YOU LOOK DISTINGUISHED.
NO MORE BROODING ON THE TERRACES...THIS IS A HISTORIC MOMENT.
HISTORIC?
IN KANDOR WE HAVE NOTHING LEFT BUT HISTORY.
STILL NOT SURE IF AN ECTOMORPH LIKE ME BELONGS IN THIS "AUTHENTIC KRYPTONIAN FORMAL WEAR" I BORROWED FROM OUR MUTUAL FRIEND MR. OLSEN'S COLLECTION.
THEY WON'T BE JUDGING YOUR MUSCLES, QUINTUM.
VAN-ZEE JUST SIGNALLED ME THAT THEY'RE ALMOST READY FOR YOU.
ALL I NEED IS A MOMENT TO CALIBRATE BRAINIAC'S REDUCING RAY TO ITS TEMPORARY SETTING.

THE GRAVITATIONAL PULL IN KANDOR WILL FEEL *EIGHT* TIMES STRONGER THAN EARTH'S, AND THE ATMOSPHERE'S MUCH *THINNER.*

YOU'LL NEED *THIS.*

WISH ME LUCK IN THE *BOTTLE CITY,* SUPERMAN.

IT'S *TRADITIONAL* IN KANDOR TO LEAVE *OPEN* THE *SEVENTH CHAIR* AT OUR COUNCIL CIRCLE, BUT THIS...

THIS IS THE *FIRST* TIME AN...*EARTH* ALIEN HAS VENTURED TO MAKE HIS VOICE HEARD IN OUR AFFAIRS.

IF OUR SYNTHETIC GRAVITY MAKES YOU *UNCOMFORTABLE,* FEEL FREE TO DELIVER YOUR PROPOSALS FROM A *SEATED* POSITION, *PROFESSOR QUIN-TUM.*

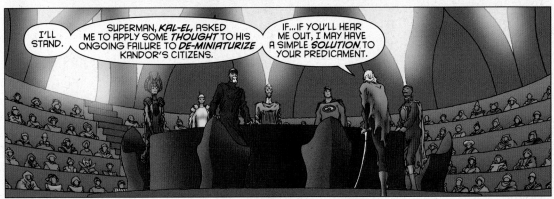

I'LL STAND.

SUPERMAN, *KAL-EL,* ASKED ME TO APPLY SOME *THOUGHT* TO HIS ONGOING FAILURE TO *DE-MINIATURIZE* KANDOR'S CITIZENS.

IF...IF YOU'LL HEAR ME OUT, I MAY HAVE A SIMPLE *SOLUTION* TO YOUR PREDICAMENT.

12:01 AM

SO WHEN I'M GONE...

...WHEN I'M NOT AROUND ANYMORE TO PROTECT THEM FROM THE MAD SCIENTISTS, AND MONSTERS, AND THEMSELVES...

...CAN THEY SURVIVE THEIR OWN SELF-DESTRUCTIVE URGES?

THERE WAS ONLY ONE WAY TO STUDY A WORLD WITHOUT SUPERMAN.

I HAD TO MAKE ONE.

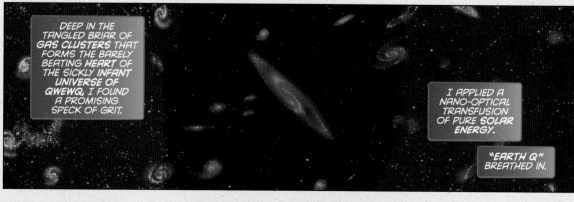

DEEP IN THE TANGLED BRIAR OF GAS CLUSTERS THAT FORMS THE BARELY BEATING HEART OF THE SICKLY INFANT UNIVERSE OF QWEWQ, I FOUND A PROMISING SPECK OF GRIT.

I APPLIED A NANO-OPTICAL TRANSFUSION OF PURE SOLAR ENERGY.

"EARTH Q" BREATHED IN.

THERE ON THE HOSTILE SHORES OF INFINITESIMAL OCEANS...

...LIFE SEIZED ITS MOMENT.

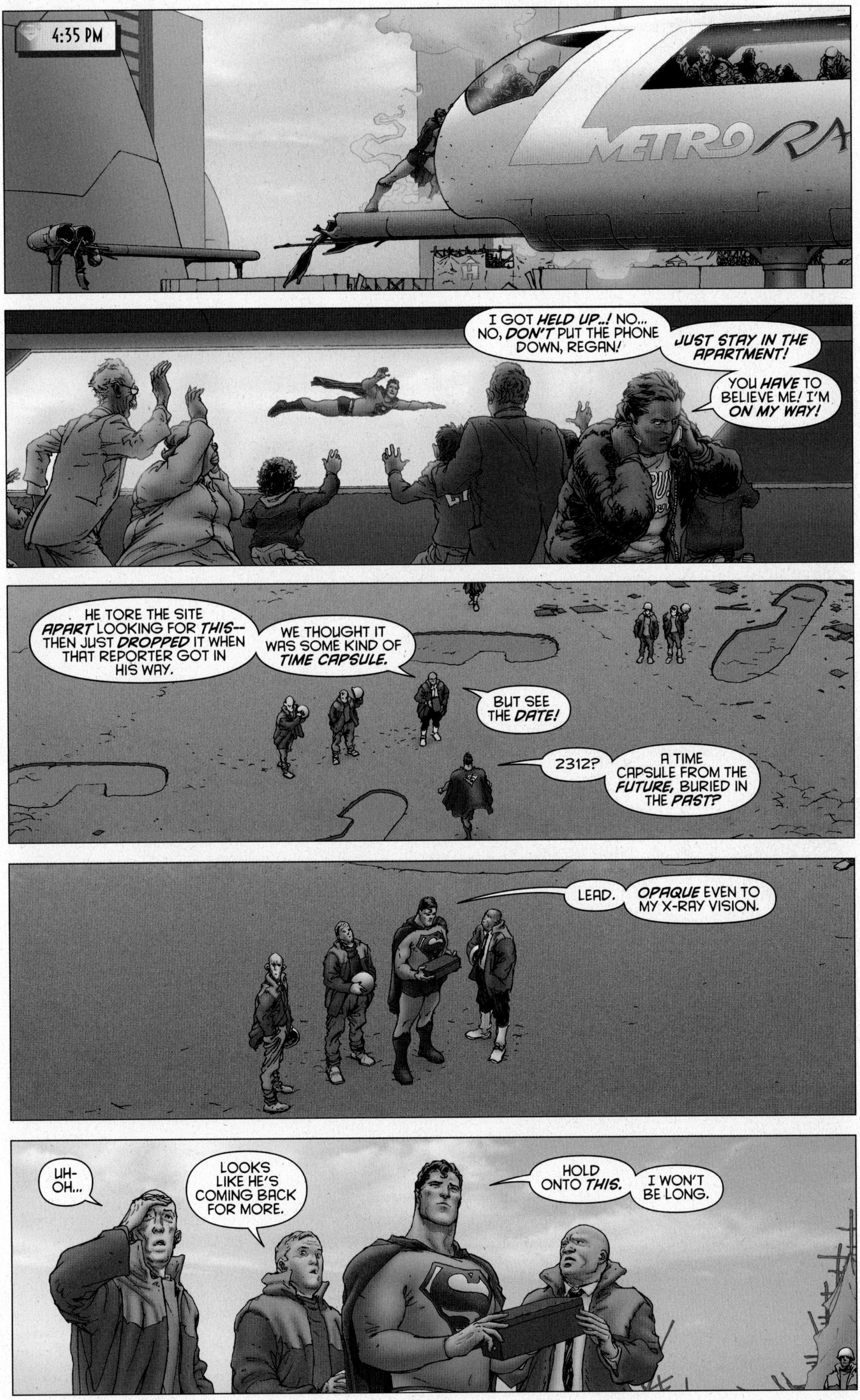
4:35 PM
METRO RA
I GOT HELD UP..! NO... NO, DON'T PUT THE PHONE DOWN, REGAN!
JUST STAY IN THE APARTMENT!
YOU HAVE TO BELIEVE ME! I'M ON MY WAY!
HE TORE THE SITE APART LOOKING FOR THIS-- THEN JUST DROPPED IT WHEN THAT REPORTER GOT IN HIS WAY.
WE THOUGHT IT WAS SOME KIND OF TIME CAPSULE.
BUT SEE THE DATE!
2312?
A TIME CAPSULE FROM THE FUTURE, BURIED IN THE PAST?
LEAD.
OPAQUE EVEN TO MY X-RAY VISION.
UH-OH...
LOOKS LIKE HE'S COMING BACK FOR MORE.
HOLD ONTO THIS.
I WON'T BE LONG.

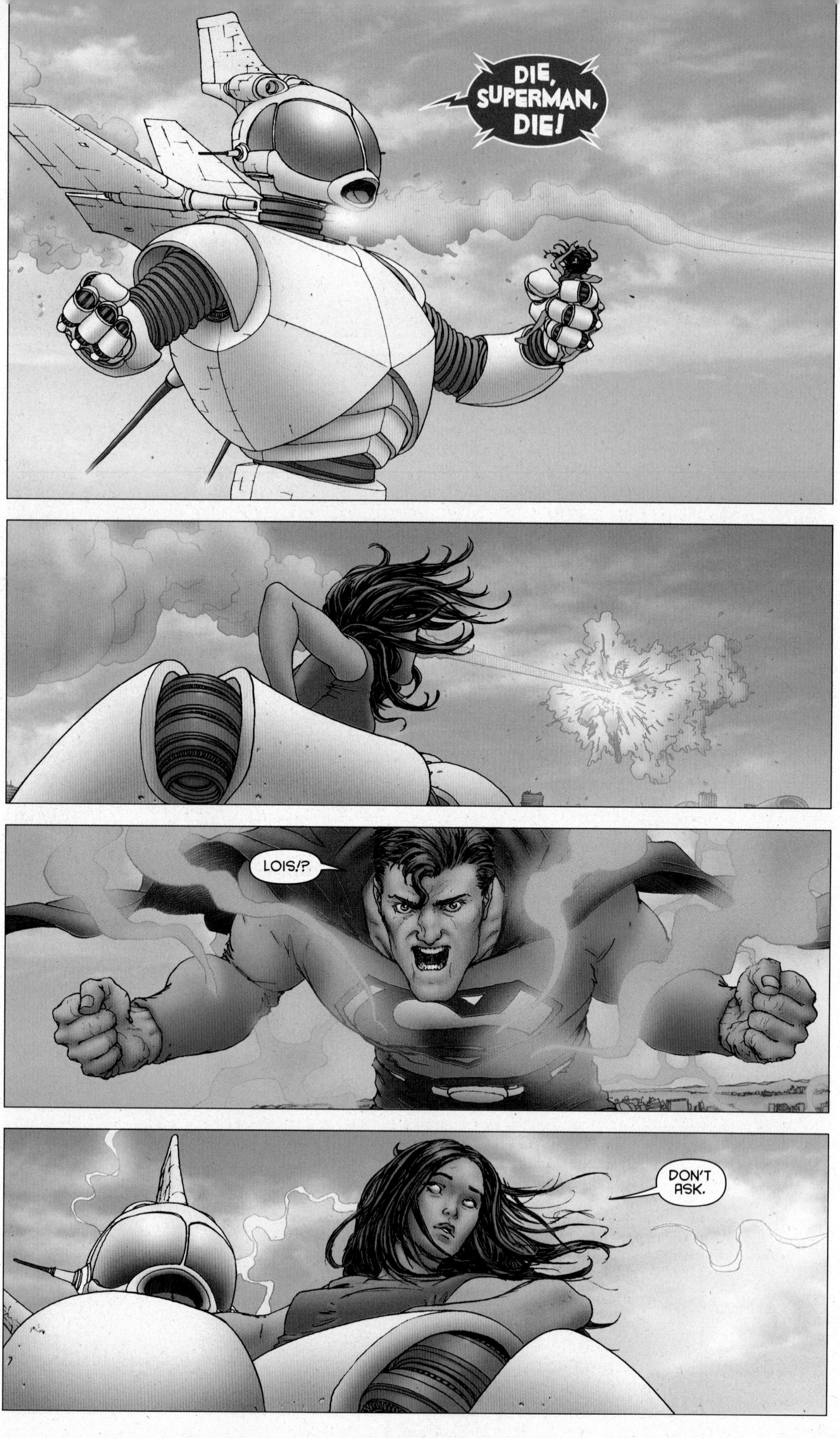
DIE, SUPERMAN, DIE!
LOIS!?
DON'T ASK.

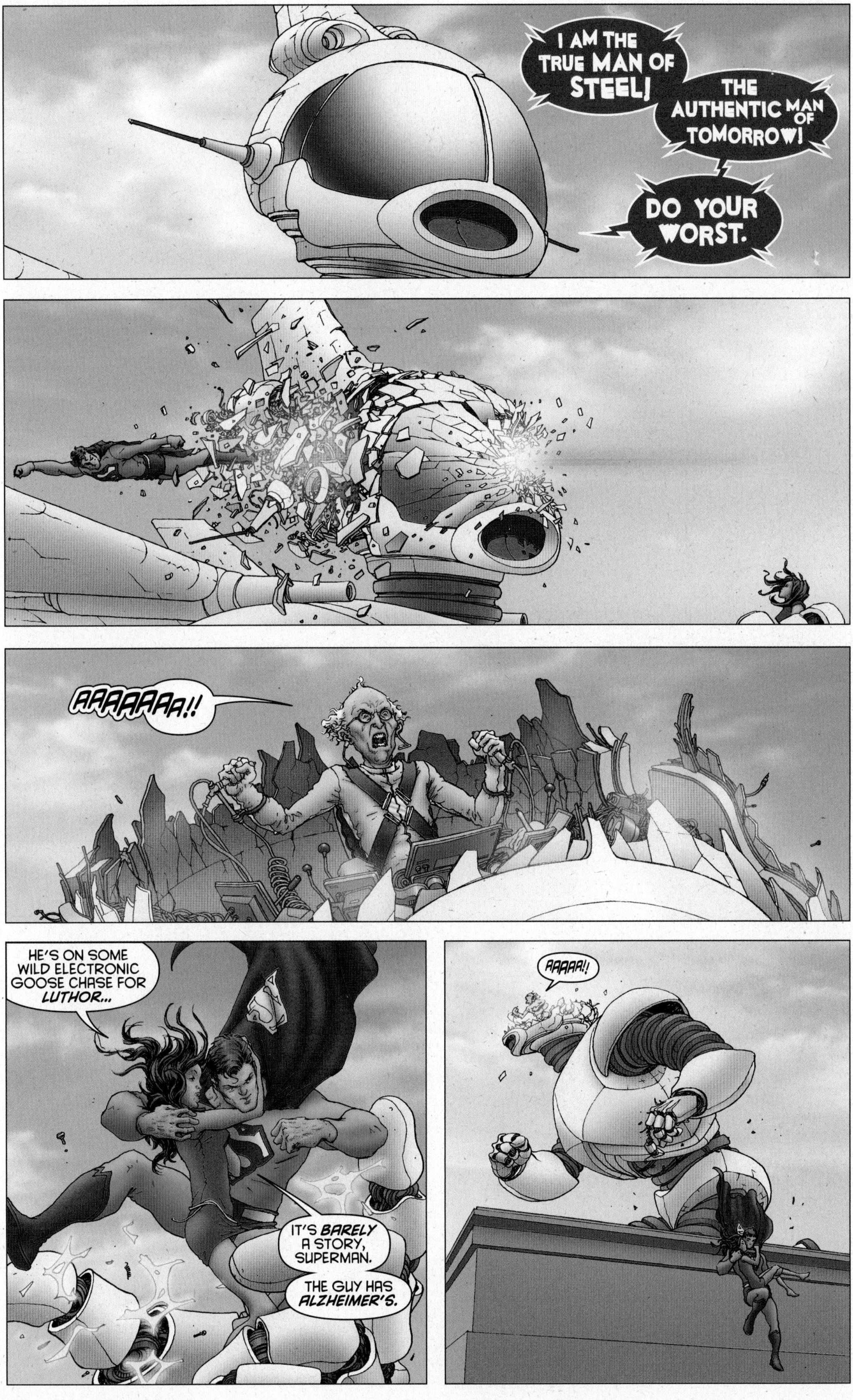
I AM THE TRUE MAN OF STEEL!
THE AUTHENTIC MAN OF TOMORROW!
DO YOUR WORST.
AAAAAAA!!
HE'S ON SOME WILD ELECTRONIC GOOSE CHASE FOR LUTHOR...
IT'S BARELY A STORY, SUPERMAN.
THE GUY HAS ALZHEIMER'S.
AAAAA!!

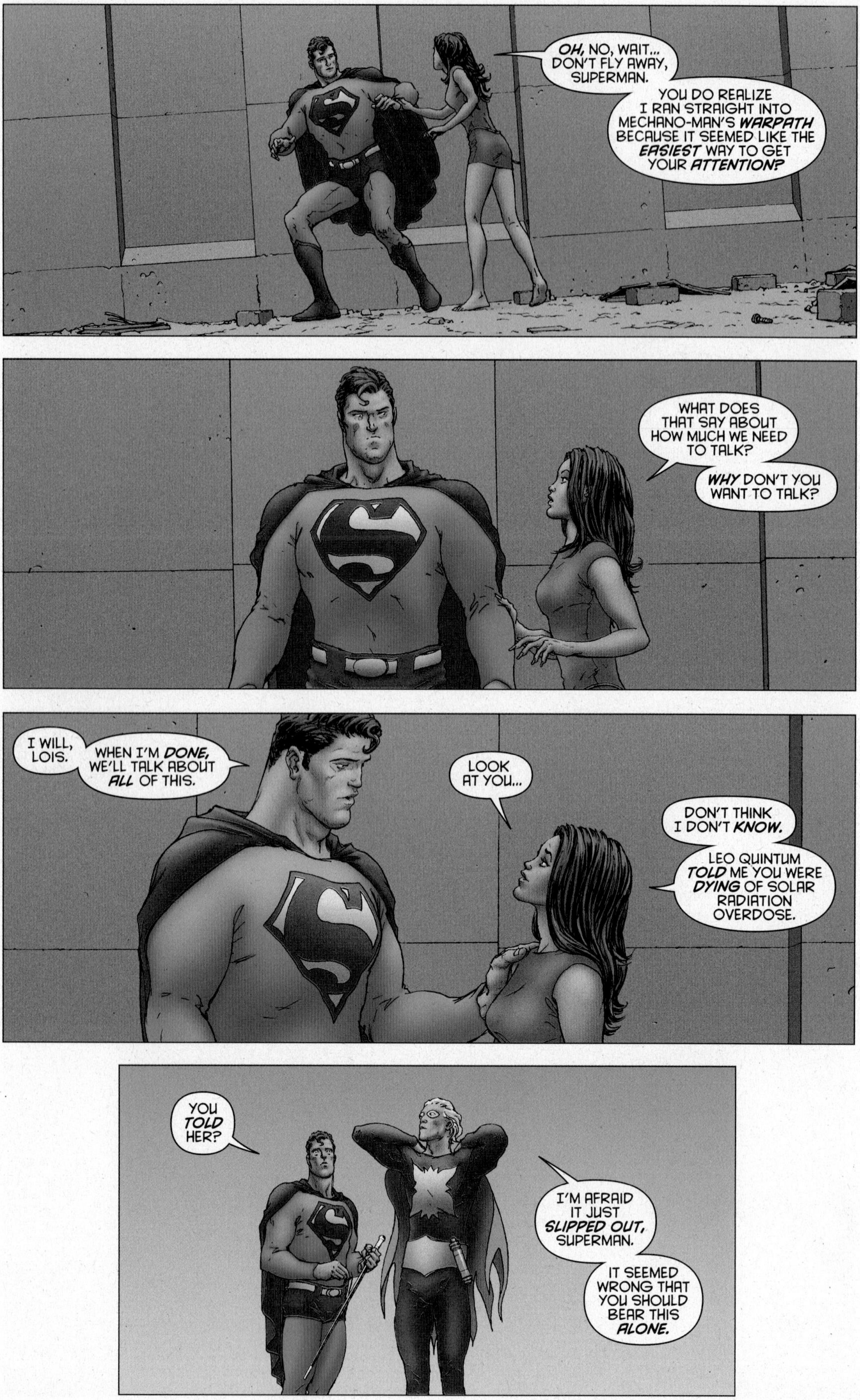

OH, NO, WAIT... DON'T FLY AWAY, SUPERMAN.
YOU DO REALIZE I RAN STRAIGHT INTO MECHANO-MAN'S WARPATH BECAUSE IT SEEMED LIKE THE EASIEST WAY TO GET YOUR ATTENTION?
WHAT DOES THAT SAY ABOUT HOW MUCH WE NEED TO TALK?
WHY DON'T YOU WANT TO TALK?
I WILL, LOIS.
WHEN I'M DONE, WE'LL TALK ABOUT ALL OF THIS.
LOOK AT YOU...
DON'T THINK I DON'T KNOW.
LEO QUINTUM TOLD ME YOU WERE DYING OF SOLAR RADIATION OVERDOSE.
YOU TOLD HER?
I'M AFRAID IT JUST SLIPPED OUT, SUPERMAN.
IT SEEMED WRONG THAT YOU SHOULD BEAR THIS ALONE.

YOU CAN'T DIE.

I KNOW YOU'LL FIND A WAY OUT OF THIS.

PROMISE ME YOU'LL FIND A WAY.

AS SHE *SPOKE,* I WATCHED 35,000 DEAD SKIN CELLS SCATTERING LIKE CONFETTI... LIKE PROMISES...

...LIKE THE DUST OF DEAD STARS.

OUR BIOLOGY IS COMPLETELY INCOMPATIBLE.

NEVER HAVE MORE THAN *THIS.*

WE COULD NEVER HAVE CHILDREN.

THERE'S ALWAYS A WAY.

THAT'S WHAT YOU *ALWAYS* SAY.

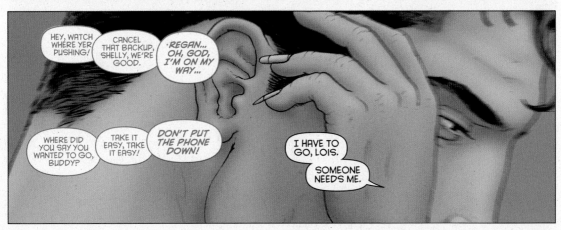

HEY, WATCH WHERE YER PUSHING!

CANCEL THAT BACKUP, SHELLY, WE'RE GOOD.

REGAN... OH, GOD, I'M ON MY WAY...

WHERE DID YOU SAY YOU WANTED TO GO, BUDDY?

TAKE IT EASY, TAKE IT EASY!

DON'T PUT THE PHONE DOWN!

I HAVE TO GO, LOIS.

SOMEONE NEEDS ME.

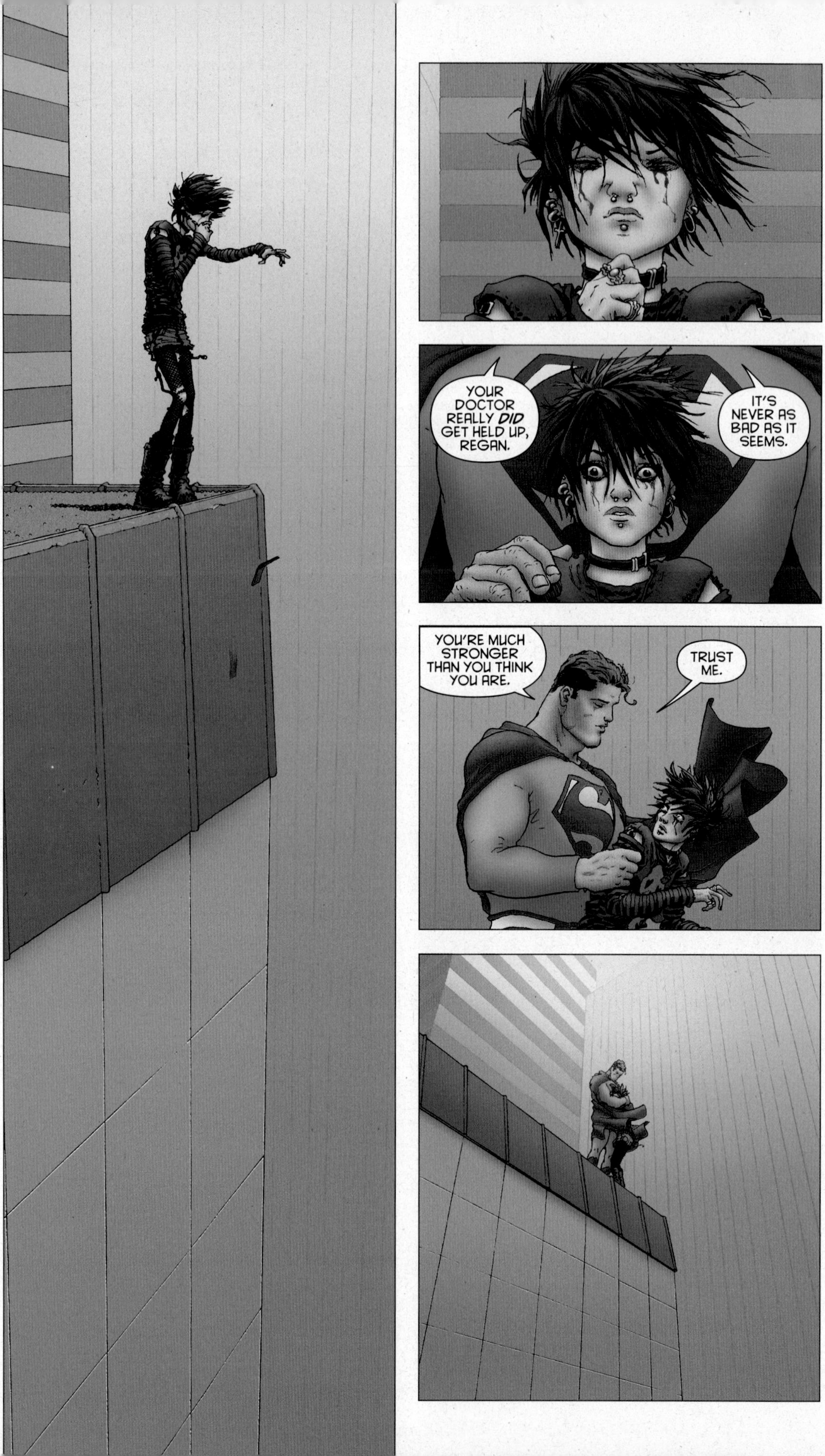
YOUR DOCTOR REALLY DID GET HELD UP, REGAN.
IT'S NEVER AS BAD AS IT SEEMS.
YOU'RE MUCH STRONGER THAN YOU THINK YOU ARE.
TRUST ME.

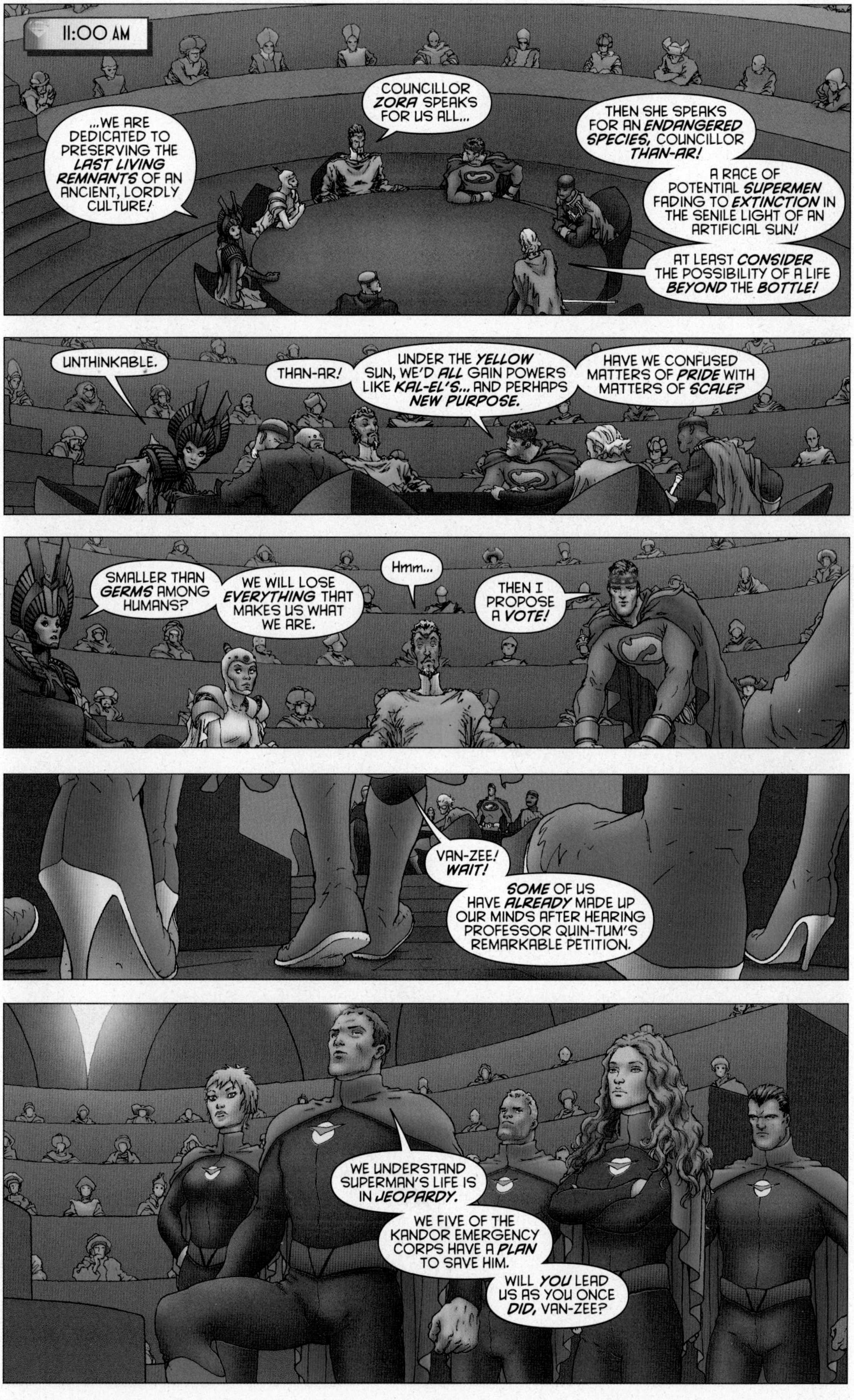
11:00 AM
...WE ARE DEDICATED TO PRESERVING THE LAST LIVING REMNANTS OF AN ANCIENT, LORDLY CULTURE!
COUNCILLOR ZORA SPEAKS FOR US ALL...
THEN SHE SPEAKS FOR AN ENDANGERED SPECIES, COUNCILLOR THAN-AR!
A RACE OF POTENTIAL SUPERMEN FADING TO EXTINCTION IN THE SENILE LIGHT OF AN ARTIFICIAL SUN!
AT LEAST CONSIDER THE POSSIBILITY OF A LIFE BEYOND THE BOTTLE!
UNTHINKABLE.
THAN-AR!
UNDER THE YELLOW SUN, WE'D ALL GAIN POWERS LIKE KAL-EL'S... AND PERHAPS NEW PURPOSE.
HAVE WE CONFUSED MATTERS OF PRIDE WITH MATTERS OF SCALE?
SMALLER THAN GERMS AMONG HUMANS?
WE WILL LOSE EVERYTHING THAT MAKES US WHAT WE ARE.
Hmm...
THEN I PROPOSE A VOTE!
VAN-ZEE! WAIT!
SOME OF US HAVE ALREADY MADE UP OUR MINDS AFTER HEARING PROFESSOR QUIN-TUM'S REMARKABLE PETITION.
WE UNDERSTAND SUPERMAN'S LIFE IS IN JEOPARDY.
WE FIVE OF THE KANDOR EMERGENCY CORPS HAVE A PLAN TO SAVE HIM.
WILL YOU LEAD US AS YOU ONCE DID, VAN-ZEE?

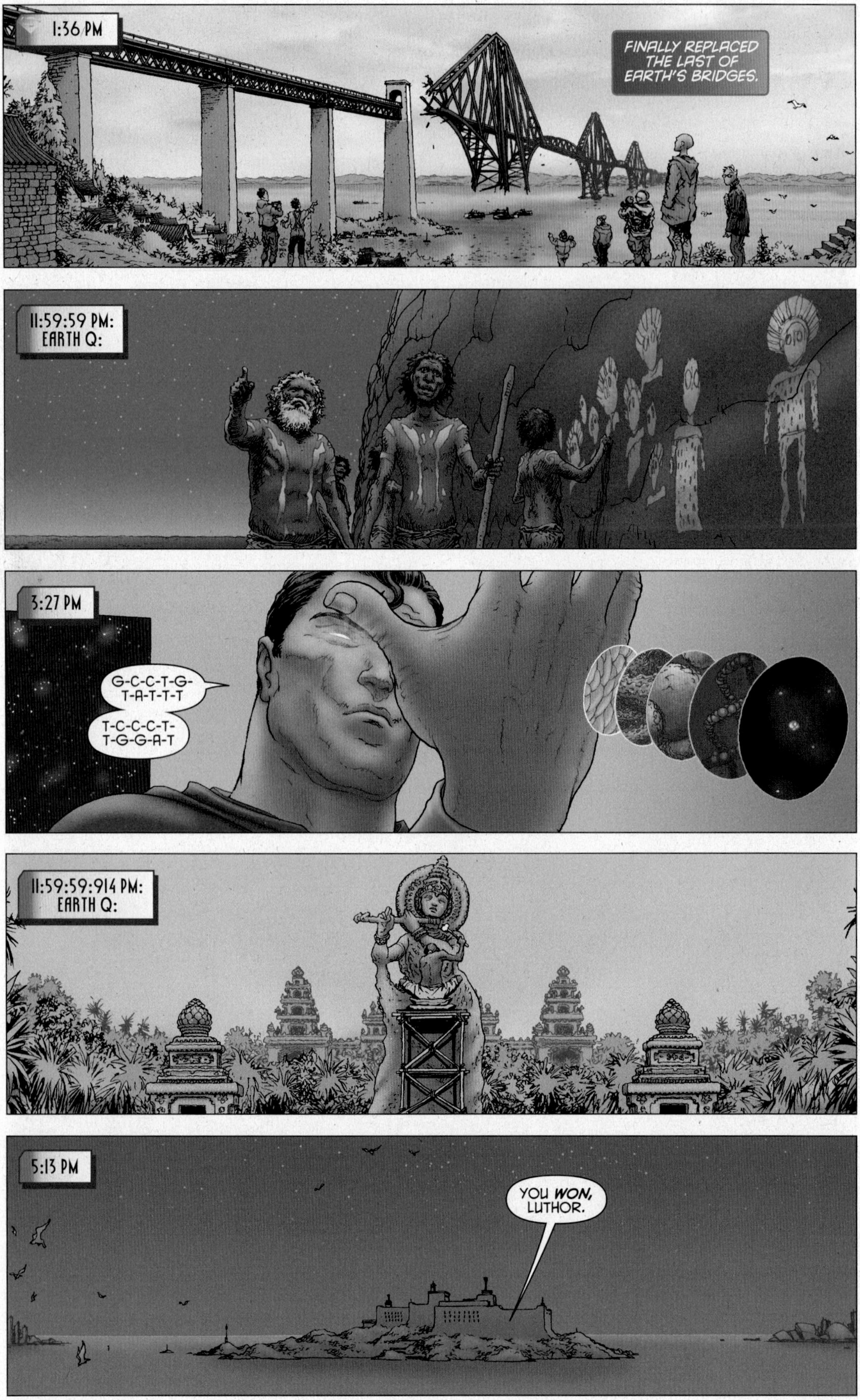
1:36 PM
FINALLY REPLACED THE LAST OF EARTH'S BRIDGES.
11:59:59 PM: EARTH Q:
3:27 PM
G-C-C-T-G-T-A-T-T-T
T-C-C-C-T-T-G-G-A-T
11:59:59:914 PM: EARTH Q:
5:13 PM
YOU *WON,* LUTHOR.

MIXING THE PERFECT COCKTAIL
I'M DYING.
THE WORLD IS YOURS, AT LEAST FOR THE THREE WEEKS YOU HAVE LEFT BEFORE THEY EXECUTE YOU.
THREE WEEKS, LEX; I CHALLENGE YOU...
ALL THOSE THINGS YOU ALWAYS SAID YOU WOULD HAVE DONE TO BENEFIT HUMANITY IF I HADN'T BEEN IN YOUR WAY.
IT'S NOT TOO LATE TO PUT THAT BRILLIANT MIND TO WORK.
LEX, I KNOW THERE'S GOOD IN YOU.

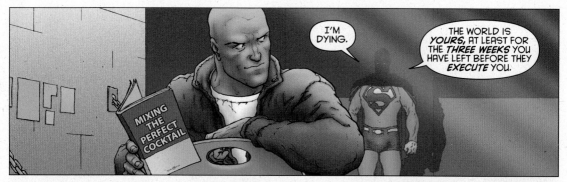

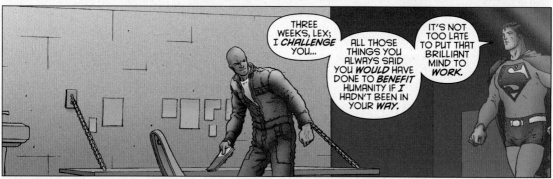

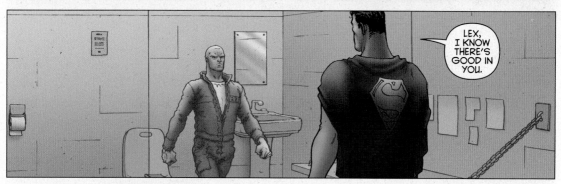

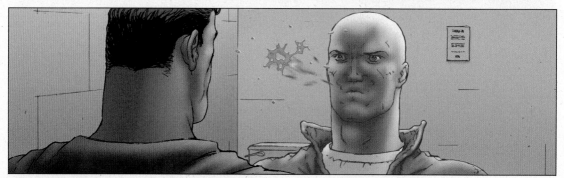

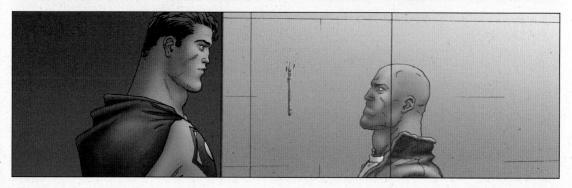

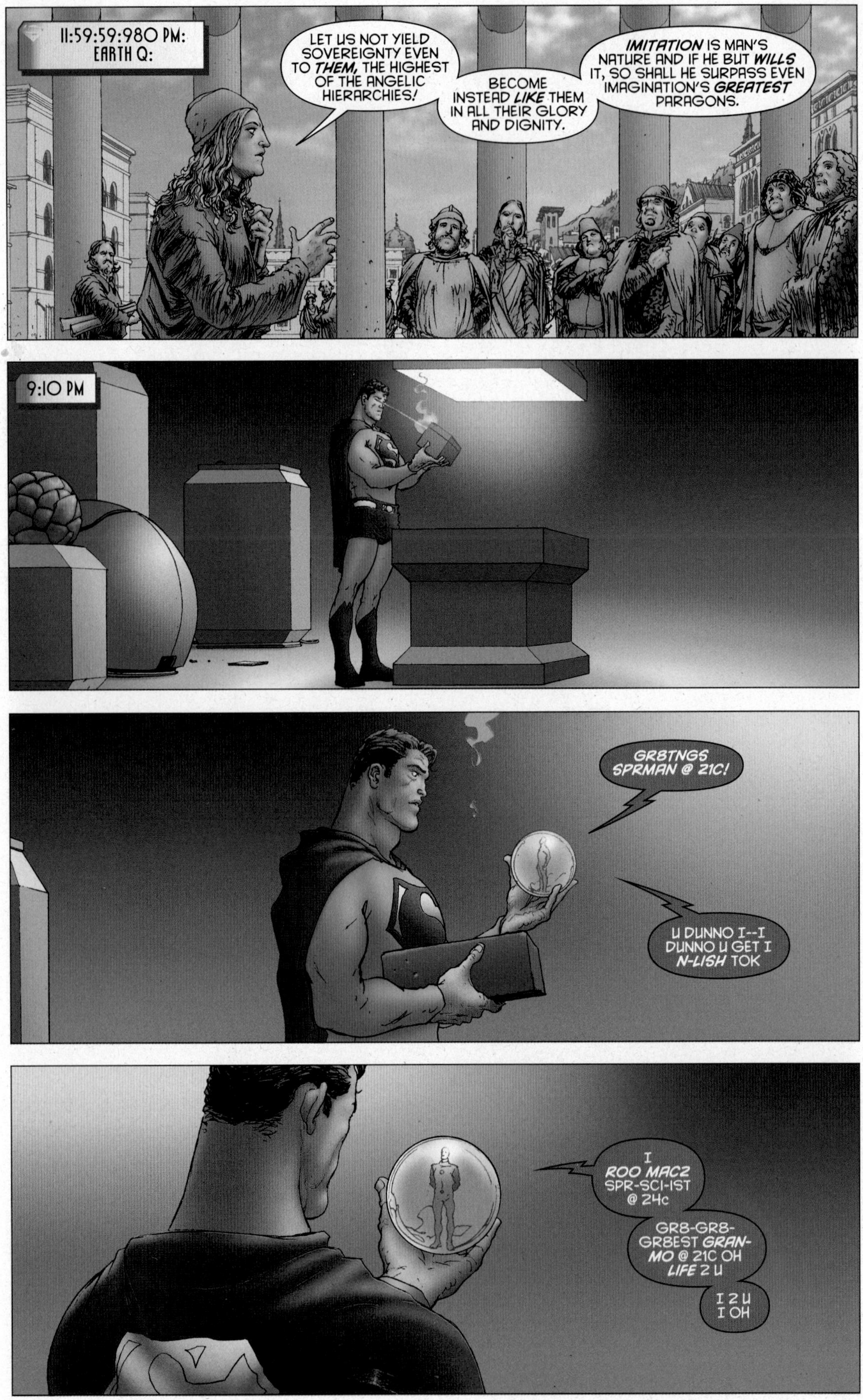
11:59:59:980 PM:
EARTH Q:
LET US NOT YIELD SOVEREIGNTY EVEN TO *THEM,* THE HIGHEST OF THE ANGELIC HIERARCHIES!
BECOME INSTEAD *LIKE* THEM IN ALL THEIR GLORY AND DIGNITY.
IMITATION IS MAN'S NATURE AND IF HE BUT *WILLS* IT, SO SHALL HE SURPASS EVEN IMAGINATION'S *GREATEST* PARAGONS.
9:10 PM
GR8TNGS SPRMAN @ 21C!
U DUNNO I--I DUNNO U GET I *N-LISH* TOK
I *ROO MACZ* SPR-SCI-IST @ 24c
GR8-GR8-GR8EST *GRAN-MO* @ 21C OH *LIFE* 2 U
I 2 U I OH

4-BID 2 SINK INFO 2 U-NOW BUT OH I LIFE.
+ HOPE 4 U C WORNING
GR8TNGS @ I-NOW 24c, SPRMAN!
N-TIME GR8TNGS MADE @ SOLAR N-TEL-SYS/ I-WARE.
SOLAR INTELLIGENCE SYSTEMS.
11:20 PM
MY 8TH CHALLENGE IS ON HIS WAY.
ALMOST COMPLETED MY NEW COSTUME.

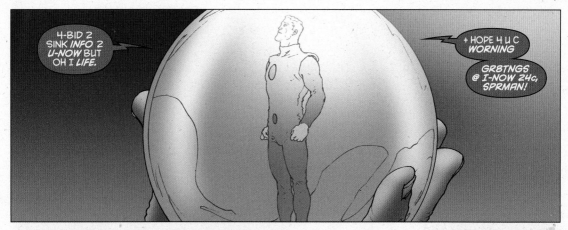

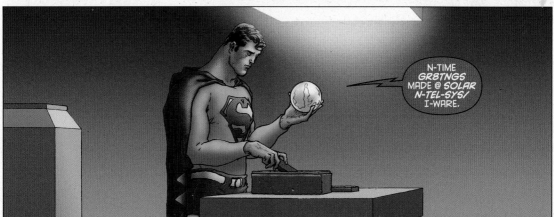

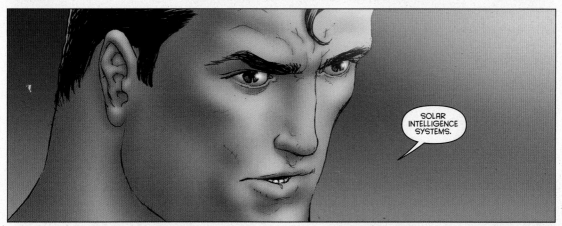

4:30 PM

TO THE PROUD SURVIVORS OF *KANDOR*, MY KIN, I LEAVE A *THIRD GOLDEN AGE*.

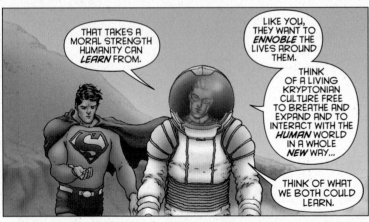

THAT TAKES A MORAL STRENGTH HUMANITY CAN *LEARN* FROM.

LIKE YOU, THEY WANT TO *ENNOBLE* THE LIVES AROUND THEM.

THINK OF A LIVING KRYPTONIAN CULTURE FREE TO BREATHE AND EXPAND AND TO INTERACT WITH THE *HUMAN* WORLD IN A WHOLE *NEW* WAY...

THINK OF WHAT WE BOTH COULD LEARN.

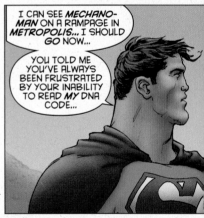

I CAN SEE *MECHANO-MAN* ON A RAMPAGE IN *METROPOLIS*... I SHOULD *GO* NOW...

YOU TOLD ME YOU'VE ALWAYS BEEN FRUSTRATED BY YOUR INABILITY TO READ *MY* DNA CODE...

ARE YOU SAYING YOU'D ENTRUST THE RESPONSIBILITY OF YOUR *GENOME* TO *ME?*

I COULD BE THE DEVIL *HIMSELF* FOR ALL YOU KNOW, SUPERMAN.

I'D LIKE TO THINK I'M A BETTER JUDGE OF CHARACTER THAN *THAT*, PROFESSOR.

I FINALLY COPIED THE ENTIRE EIGHT BILLION LETTER *SEQUENCE* INTO A *BOOK*.

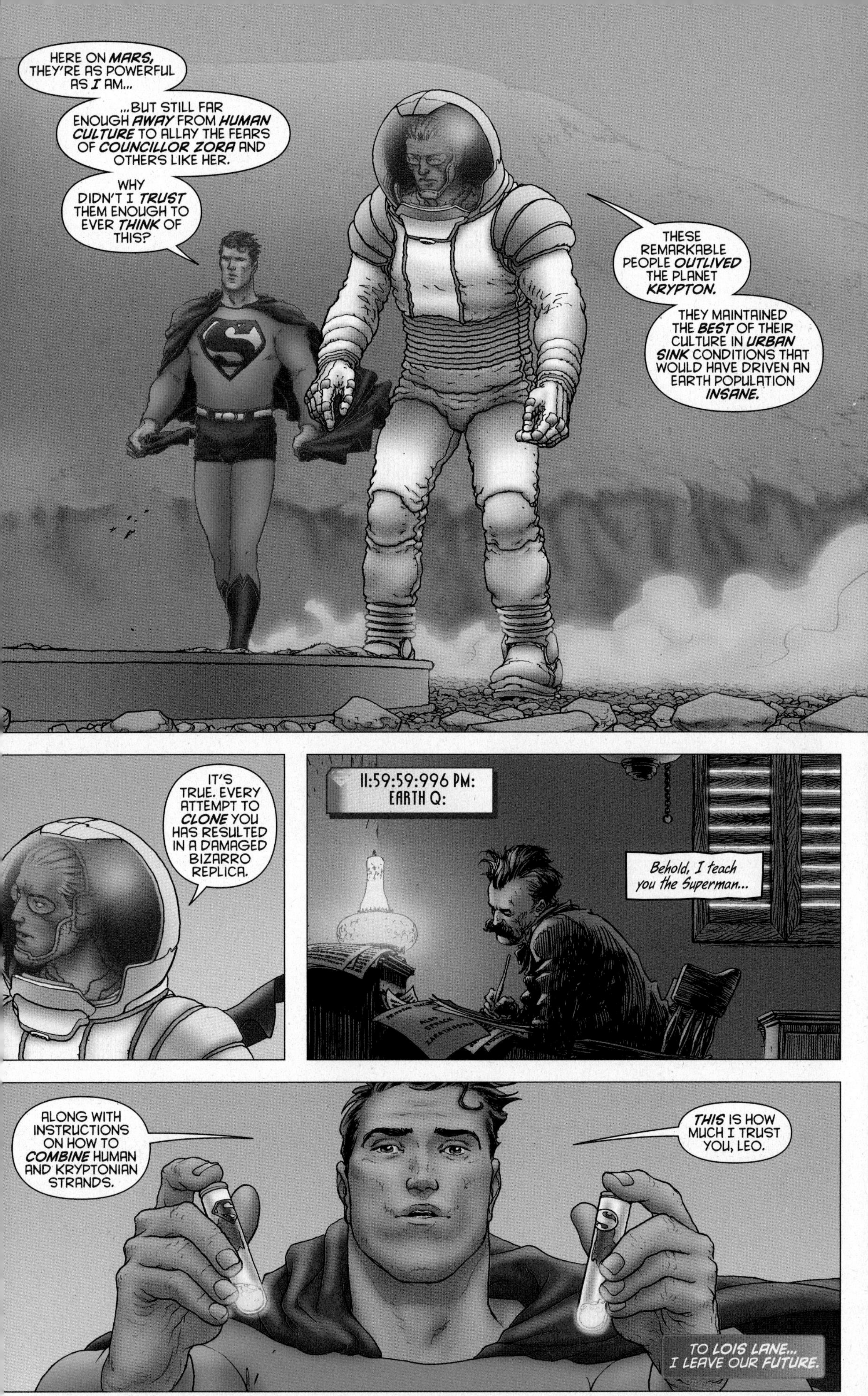
HERE ON MARS, THEY'RE AS POWERFUL AS I AM...
...BUT STILL FAR ENOUGH AWAY FROM HUMAN CULTURE TO ALLAY THE FEARS OF COUNCILLOR ZORA AND OTHERS LIKE HER.
WHY DIDN'T I TRUST THEM ENOUGH TO EVER THINK OF THIS?
THESE REMARKABLE PEOPLE OUTLIVED THE PLANET KRYPTON.
THEY MAINTAINED THE BEST OF THEIR CULTURE IN URBAN SINK CONDITIONS THAT WOULD HAVE DRIVEN AN EARTH POPULATION INSANE.
IT'S TRUE. EVERY ATTEMPT TO CLONE YOU HAS RESULTED IN A DAMAGED BIZARRO REPLICA.
11:59:59:996 PM: EARTH Q:
Behold, I teach you the Superman...
ALONG WITH INSTRUCTIONS ON HOW TO COMBINE HUMAN AND KRYPTONIAN STRANDS.
THIS IS HOW MUCH I TRUST YOU, LEO.
TO LOIS LANE... I LEAVE OUR FUTURE.

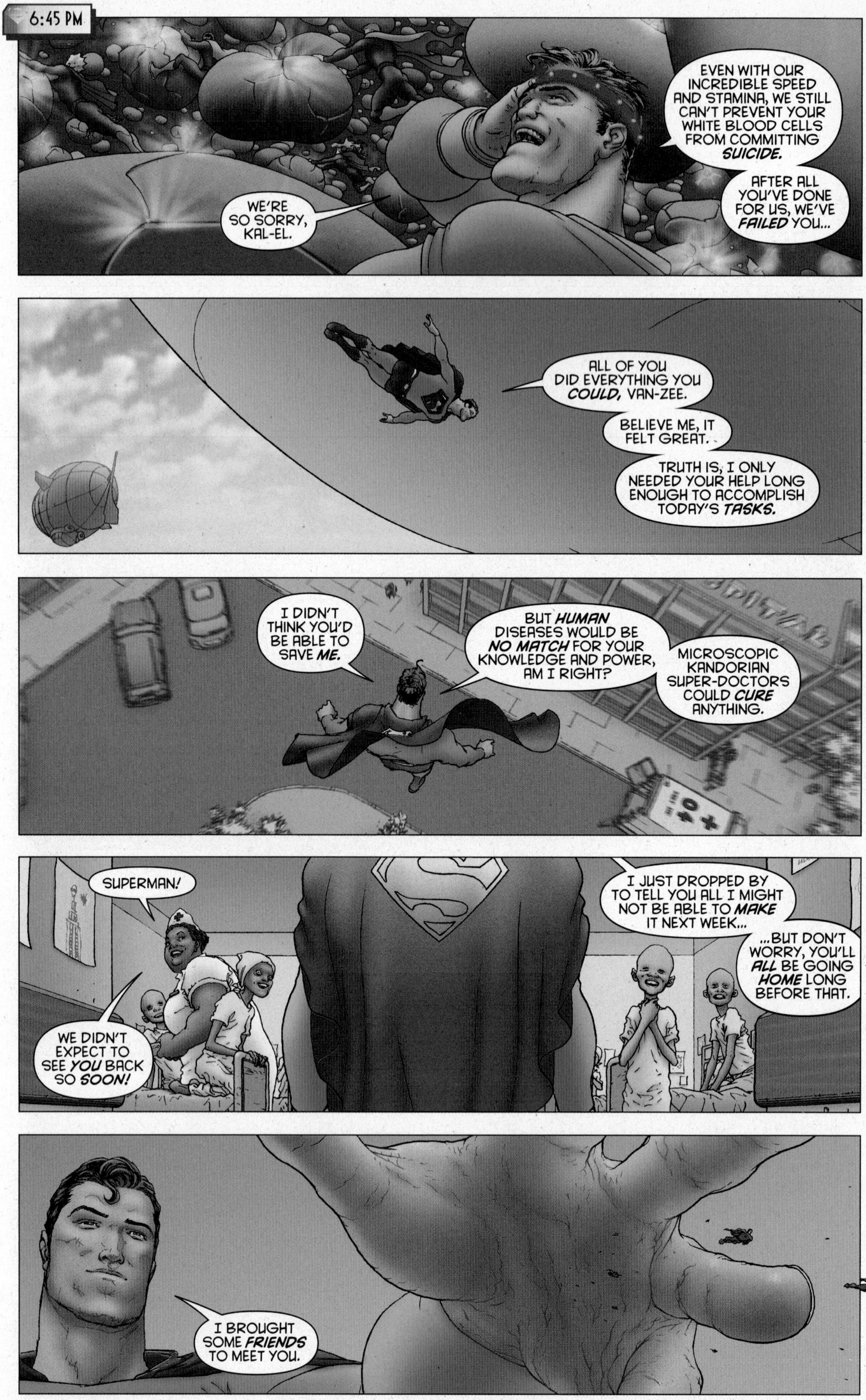
6:45 PM
EVEN WITH OUR INCREDIBLE SPEED AND STAMINA, WE STILL CAN'T PREVENT YOUR WHITE BLOOD CELLS FROM COMMITTING SUICIDE.
AFTER ALL YOU'VE DONE FOR US, WE'VE FAILED YOU...
WE'RE SO SORRY, KAL-EL.
ALL OF YOU DID EVERYTHING YOU COULD, VAN-ZEE.
BELIEVE ME, IT FELT GREAT.
TRUTH IS, I ONLY NEEDED YOUR HELP LONG ENOUGH TO ACCOMPLISH TODAY'S TASKS.
I DIDN'T THINK YOU'D BE ABLE TO SAVE ME.
BUT HUMAN DISEASES WOULD BE NO MATCH FOR YOUR KNOWLEDGE AND POWER, AM I RIGHT?
MICROSCOPIC KANDORIAN SUPER-DOCTORS COULD CURE ANYTHING.
SUPERMAN!
WE DIDN'T EXPECT TO SEE YOU BACK SO SOON!
I JUST DROPPED BY TO TELL YOU ALL I MIGHT NOT BE ABLE TO MAKE IT NEXT WEEK...
...BUT DON'T WORRY, YOU'LL ALL BE GOING HOME LONG BEFORE THAT.
I BROUGHT SOME FRIENDS TO MEET YOU.

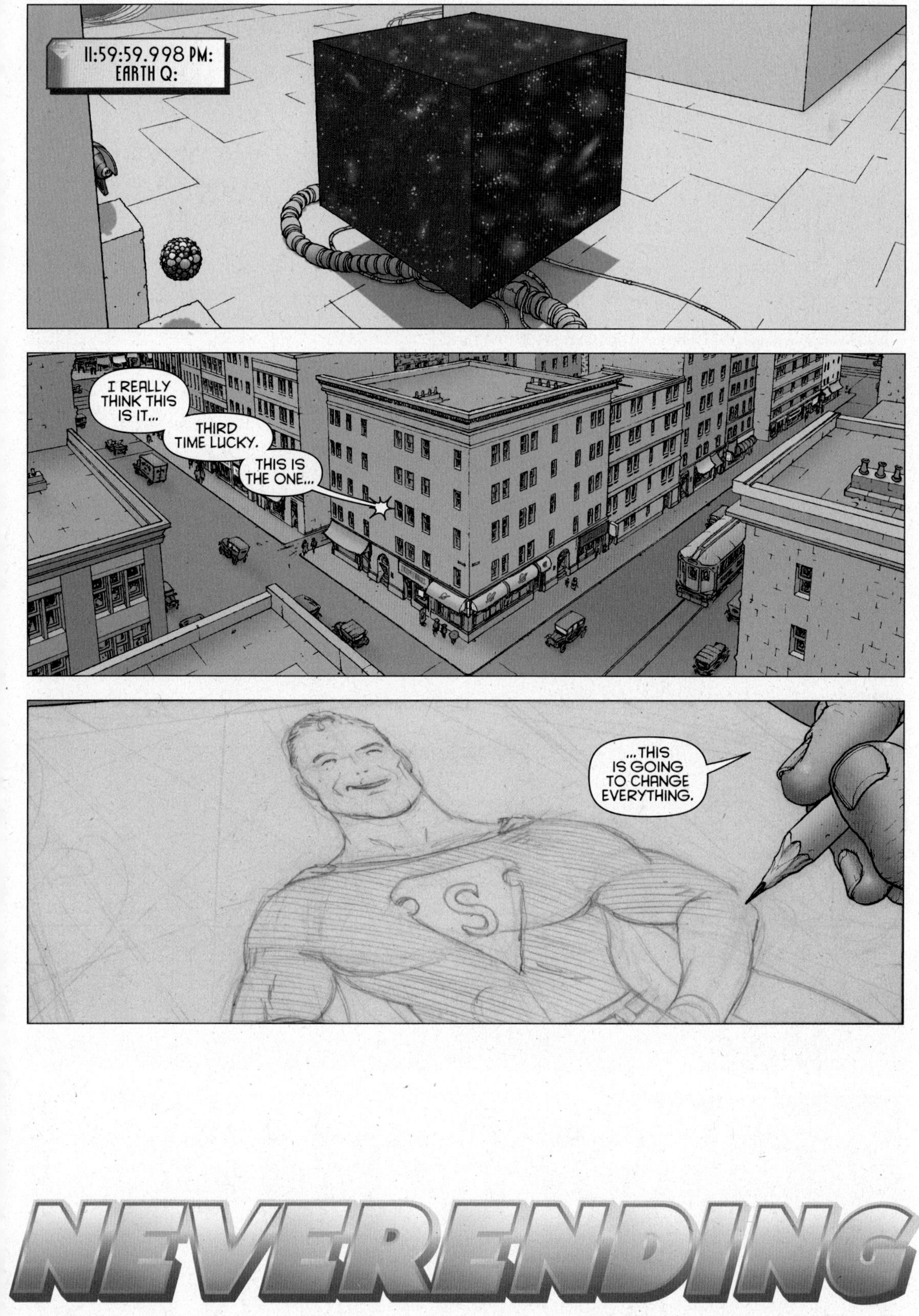
11:59:59.998 PM:
EARTH Q:
I REALLY THINK THIS IS IT...
THIRD TIME LUCKY.
THIS IS THE ONE...
...THIS IS GOING TO CHANGE EVERYTHING.

NEVERENDING

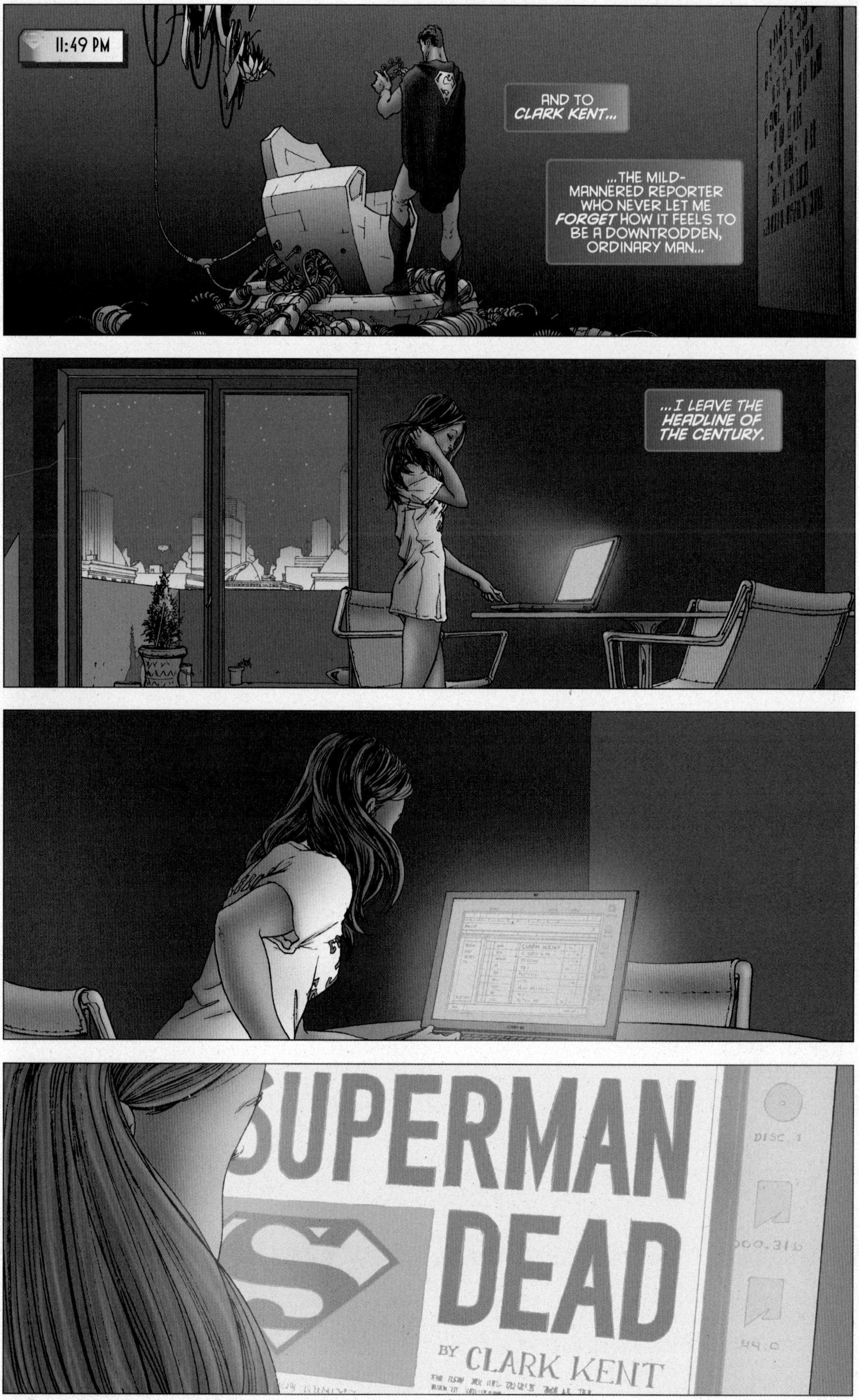
11:49 PM
AND TO CLARK KENT...
...THE MILD-MANNERED REPORTER WHO NEVER LET ME FORGET HOW IT FEELS TO BE A DOWNTRODDEN, ORDINARY MAN...
...I LEAVE THE HEADLINE OF THE CENTURY.
SUPERMAN DEAD
BY CLARK KENT
DISC 1

Episode 11

RED SUN DAY

Cover FRANK QUITELY with JAMIE GRANT

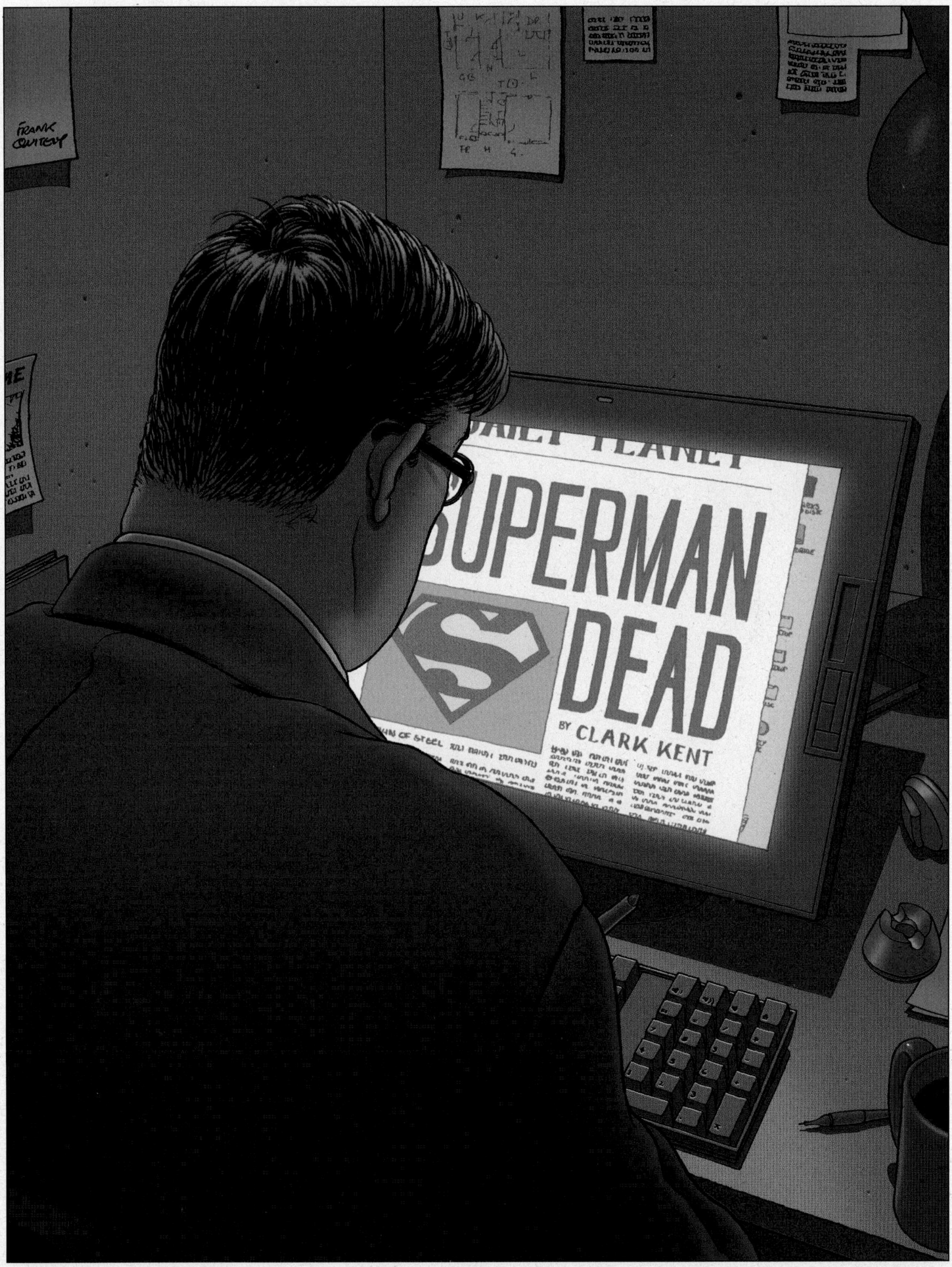

FRANK QUITELY
SUPERMAN DEAD
BY CLARK KENT

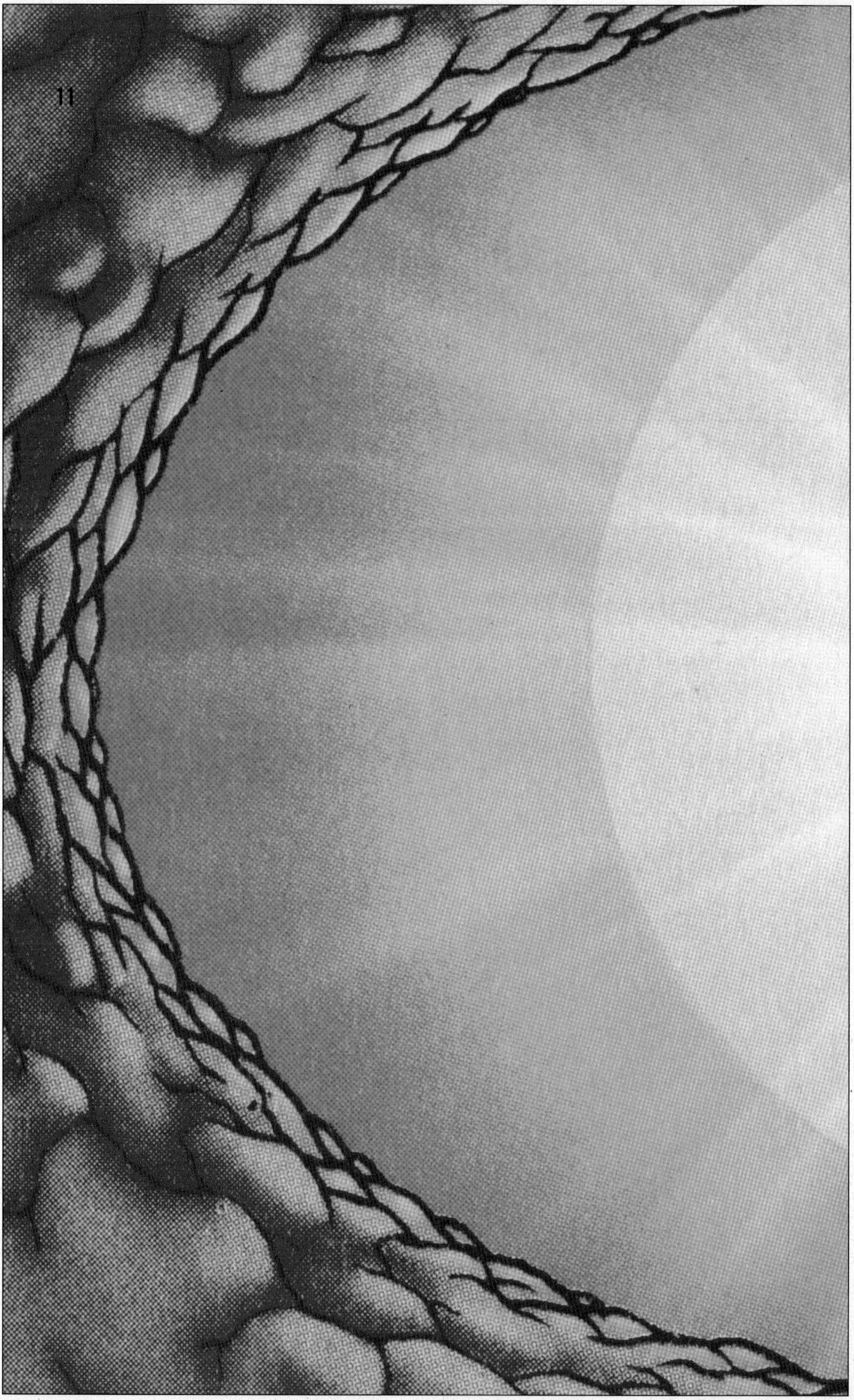
11

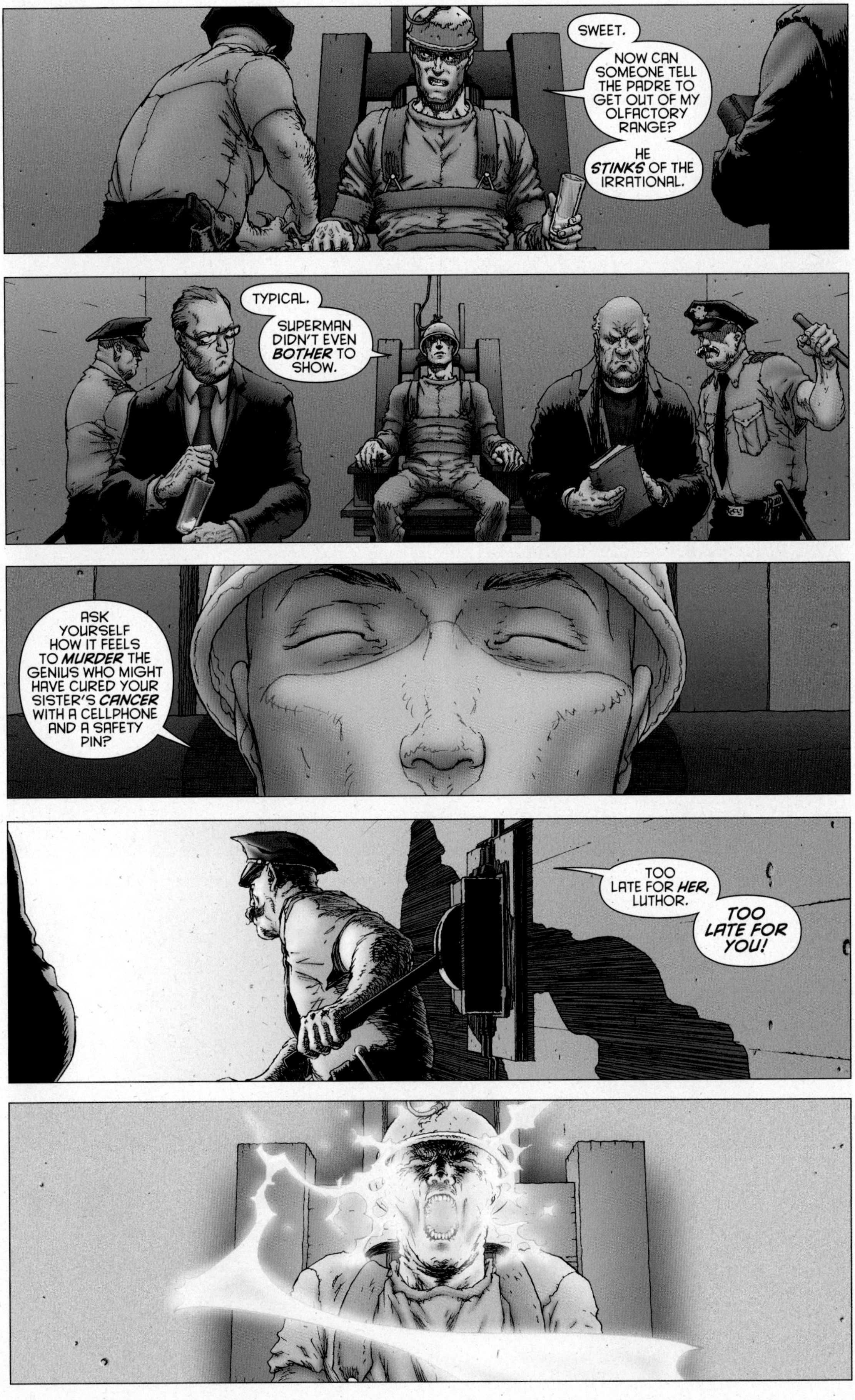
SWEET.
NOW CAN SOMEONE TELL THE PADRE TO GET OUT OF MY OLFACTORY RANGE?
HE STINKS OF THE IRRATIONAL.
TYPICAL.
SUPERMAN DIDN'T EVEN BOTHER TO SHOW.
ASK YOURSELF HOW IT FEELS TO MURDER THE GENIUS WHO MIGHT HAVE CURED YOUR SISTER'S CANCER WITH A CELLPHONE AND A SAFETY PIN?
TOO LATE FOR HER, LUTHOR.
TOO LATE FOR YOU!

...kkᵏ... ha! Kkh!

OH...YOU *MORONS*... YOU KNUCKLE-DRAGGING *NEANDERTHALS.*

THAT "LAST PERFECT COCKTAIL" YOU ALLOWED ME TO MIX...?

...CONTAINED A HIDDEN... PREPROGRAMMED... SHAPESHIFTING MOLECULE I DESIGNED...

...I JUST DRANK... A 24-HOUR... *SUPERPOWER*... SERUM.

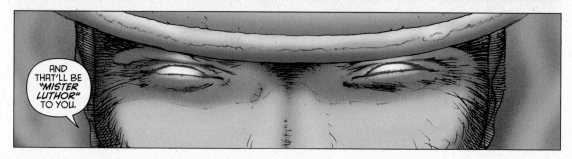

AND THAT'LL BE *"MISTER LUTHOR"* TO YOU.

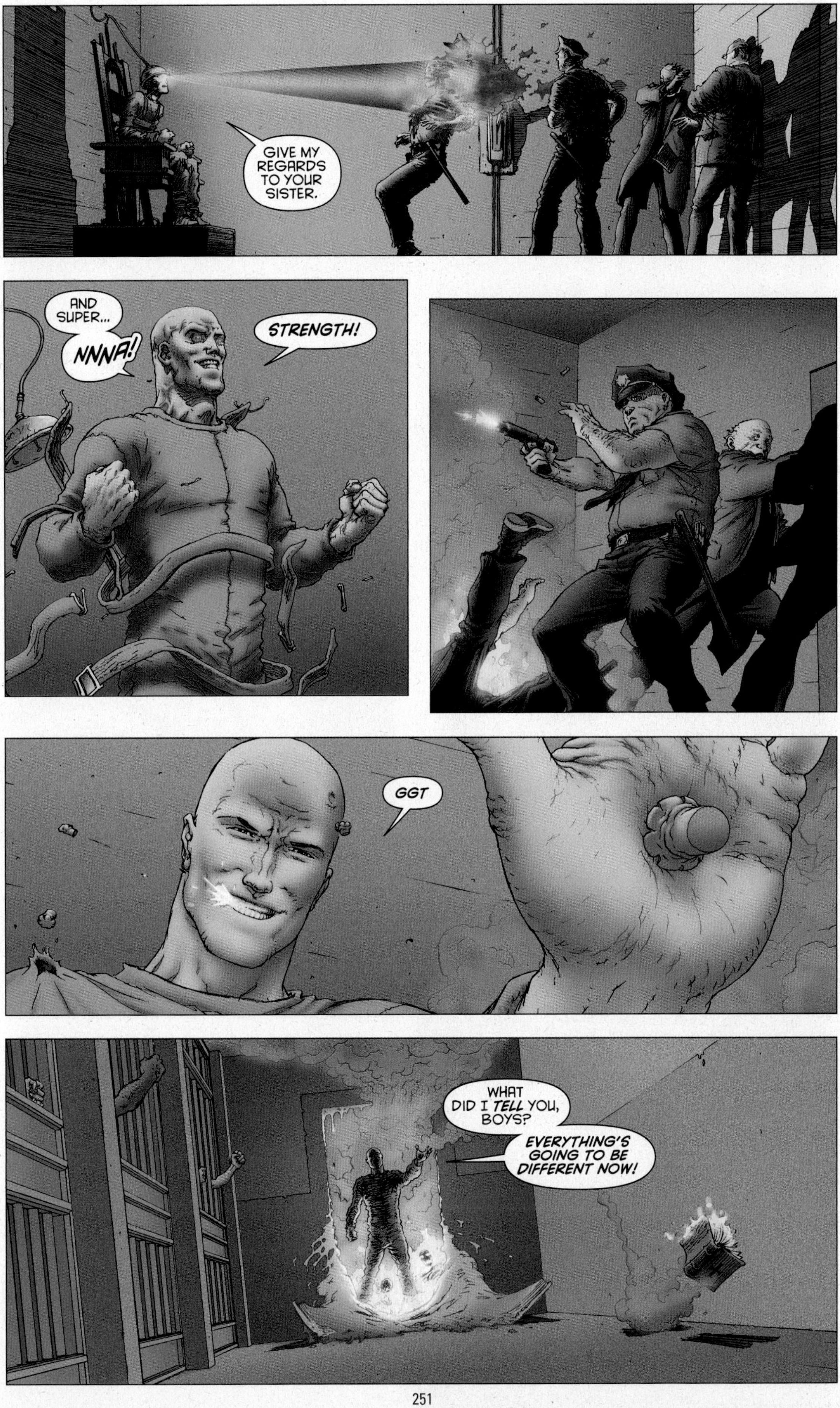
GIVE MY REGARDS TO YOUR SISTER.
AND SUPER...
NNNA!
STRENGTH!
GGT
WHAT DID I TELL YOU, BOYS?
EVERYTHING'S GOING TO BE DIFFERENT NOW!

YOU CAN LEAVE THE GRAVITY STABLE TO ME, SUPERMAN.

IF YOU WISH...

THIS IS JUST MY WAY OF SAYING GOODBYE, ROBOT 7.

IT WAS ONE OF THE MOST DANGEROUS CREATURES IN THE UNIVERSE, BUT I'VE MISSED HAVING OUR LITTLE SUN-EATER AROUND.

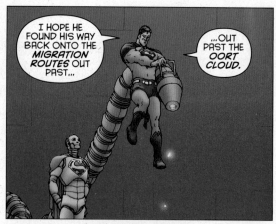

I HOPE HE FOUND HIS WAY BACK ONTO THE MIGRATION ROUTES OUT PAST...

...OUT PAST THE OORT CLOUD.

SUPERMAN...

YOU SEEM UNSTEADY.

MAYBE.

JUST A LITTLE.

CELLULAR BREAKDOWN'S HAPPENING FASTER AND FASTER NOW.

THE END'S NEAR.

AND I HAVE TO STAY ALIVE LONG ENOUGH TO COMPLETE MY FINAL TASKS FOR HUMANITY.

THAT'S WHY I NEED YOUR HELP.

YOU ROBOTS WILL HAVE TO MAINTAIN AREAS OF THE FORTRESS LIKE THE *BIZARRO ZOO.*

THESE POOR CREATURES, DISTORTED DURING THE INVASION FROM THE *CUBE EARTH,* REQUIRE SPECIAL CARE AND ATTENTION.

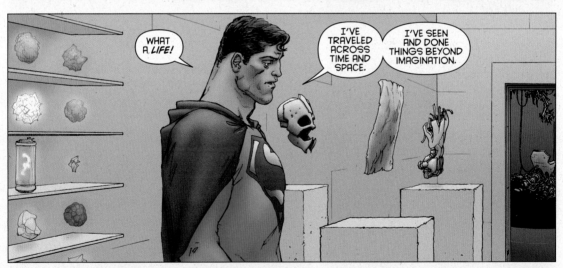

AND THIS...

YOU ASKED FOR THIS TO BE PRESERVED IN SUPERLAMINATE.

ZIBARRO'S POETRY.

...THAT LONELY, SANE VOICE OF A SUNKEN, DARK AND MARVELOUS WORLD.

WHAT A *LIFE!*

I'VE TRAVELED ACROSS TIME AND SPACE.

I'VE SEEN AND DONE THINGS BEYOND IMAGINATION.

BLESSED WITH FRIENDS LIKE *PETE* AND *LANA* AND *JIMMY.*

AND *BATMAN...* WHAT INCREDIBLE ADVENTURES WE'VE SHARED.

WHAT AMAZING PEOPLE I'VE KNOWN.

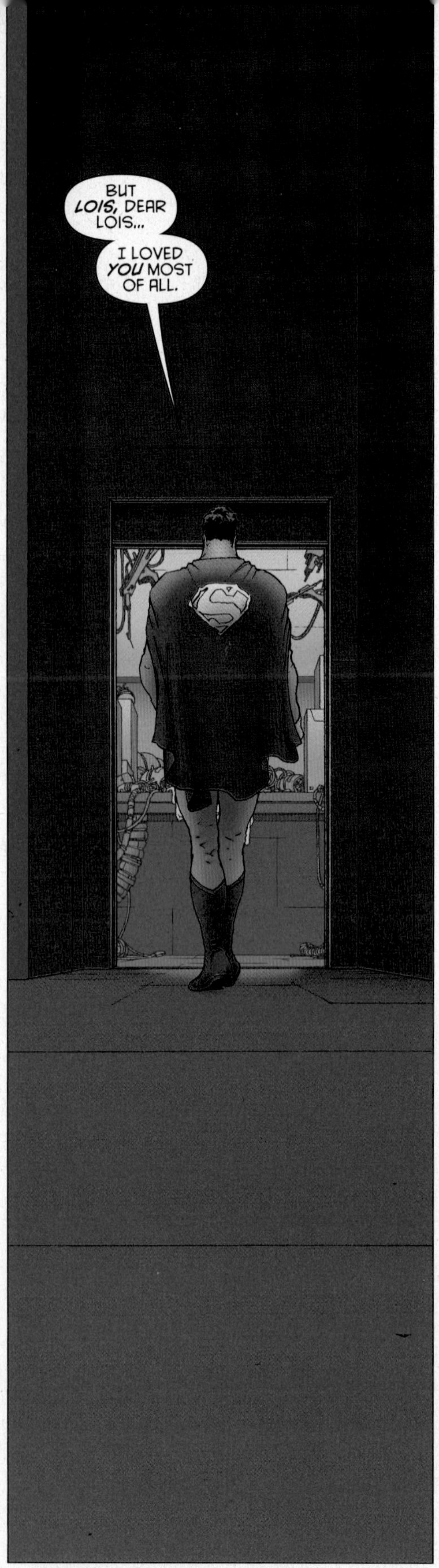
BUT LOIS, DEAR LOIS...
I LOVED YOU MOST OF ALL.

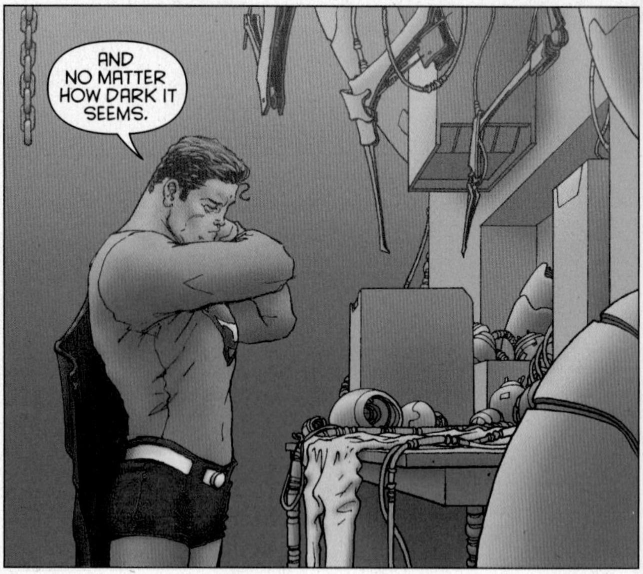
AND NO MATTER HOW DARK IT SEEMS.

RED SUN DAY

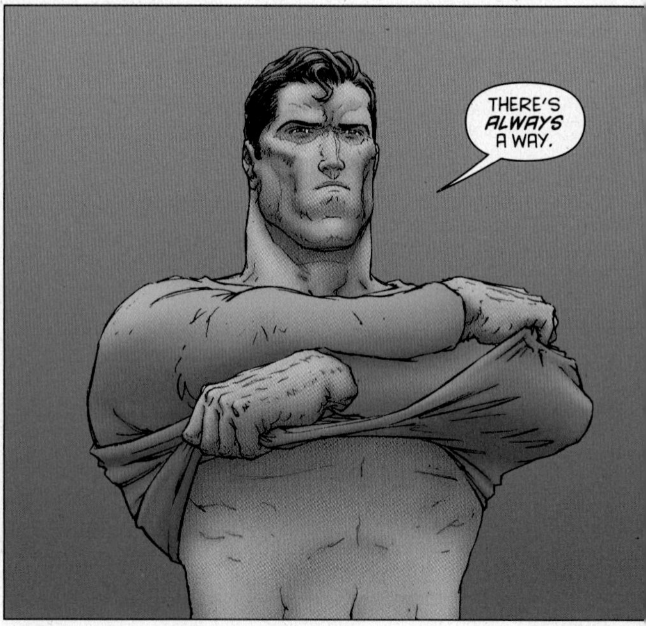
THERE'S ALWAYS A WAY.

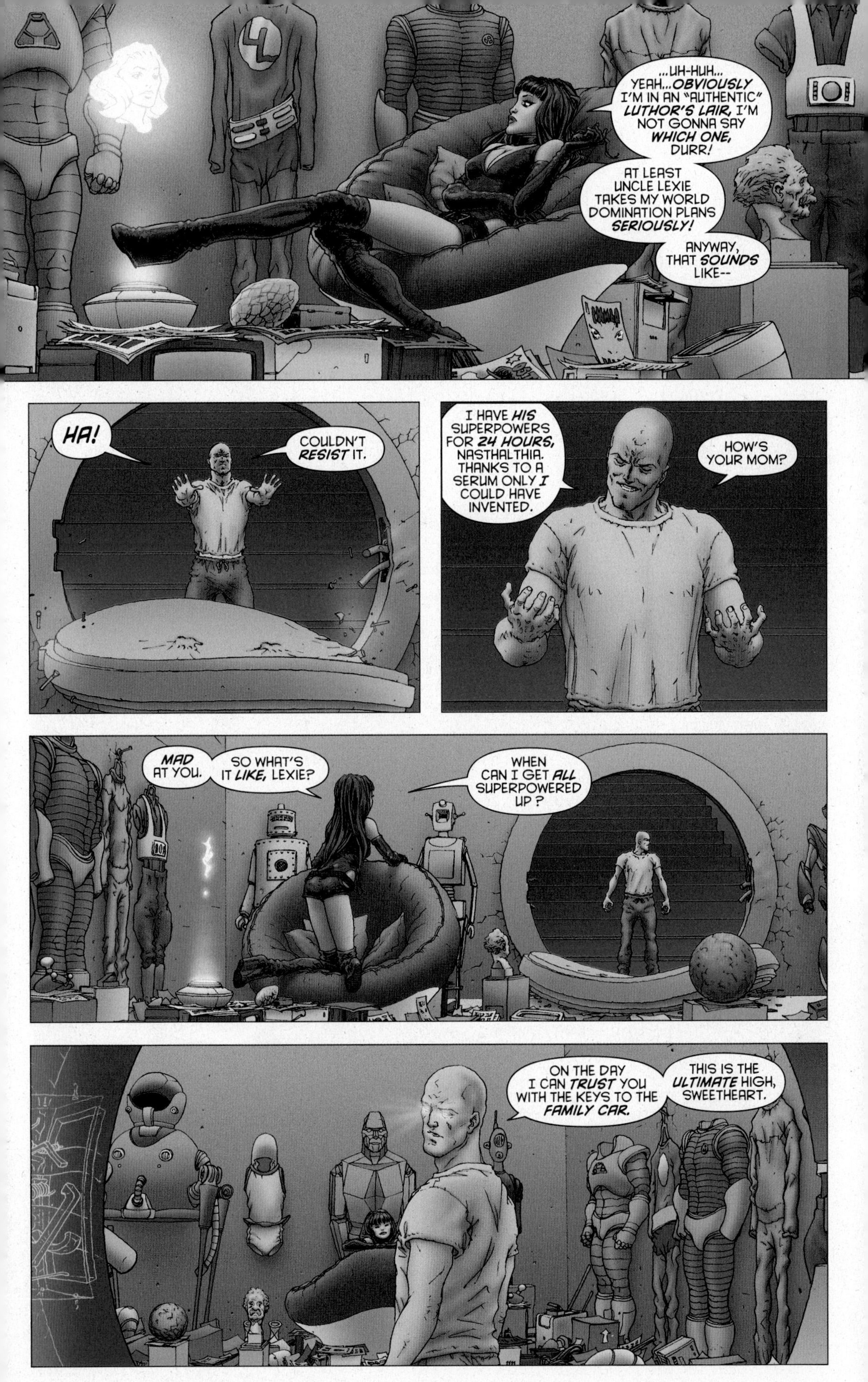
...UH-HUH... YEAH...OBVIOUSLY I'M IN AN "AUTHENTIC" LUTHOR'S LAIR, I'M NOT GONNA SAY WHICH ONE, DURR!
AT LEAST UNCLE LEXIE TAKES MY WORLD DOMINATION PLANS SERIOUSLY!
ANYWAY, THAT SOUNDS LIKE--
HA!
COULDN'T RESIST IT.
I HAVE HIS SUPERPOWERS FOR 24 HOURS, NASTHALTHIA. THANKS TO A SERUM ONLY I COULD HAVE INVENTED.
HOW'S YOUR MOM?
MAD AT YOU.
SO WHAT'S IT LIKE, LEXIE?
WHEN CAN I GET ALL SUPERPOWERED UP?
THIS IS THE ULTIMATE HIGH, SWEETHEART.
ON THE DAY I CAN TRUST YOU WITH THE KEYS TO THE FAMILY CAR.

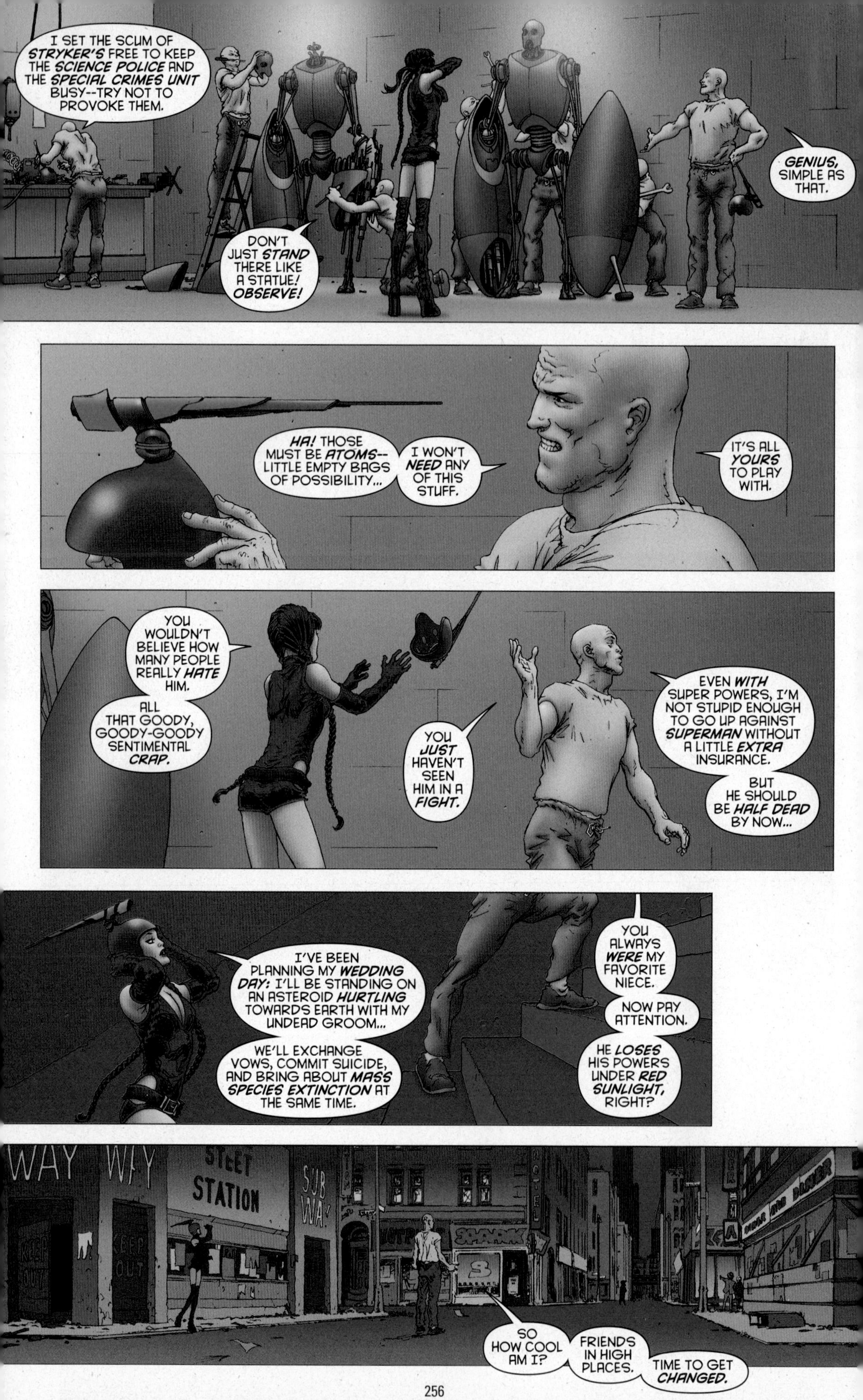
I SET THE SCUM OF STRYKER'S FREE TO KEEP THE SCIENCE POLICE AND THE SPECIAL CRIMES UNIT BUSY--TRY NOT TO PROVOKE THEM.
DON'T JUST STAND THERE LIKE A STATUE! OBSERVE!
GENIUS, SIMPLE AS THAT.
HA! THOSE MUST BE ATOMS-- LITTLE EMPTY BAGS OF POSSIBILITY...
I WON'T NEED ANY OF THIS STUFF.
IT'S ALL YOURS TO PLAY WITH.
YOU WOULDN'T BELIEVE HOW MANY PEOPLE REALLY HATE HIM.
ALL THAT GOODY, GOODY-GOODY SENTIMENTAL CRAP.
YOU JUST HAVEN'T SEEN HIM IN A FIGHT.
EVEN WITH SUPER POWERS, I'M NOT STUPID ENOUGH TO GO UP AGAINST SUPERMAN WITHOUT A LITTLE EXTRA INSURANCE.
BUT HE SHOULD BE HALF DEAD BY NOW...
I'VE BEEN PLANNING MY WEDDING DAY: I'LL BE STANDING ON AN ASTEROID HURTLING TOWARDS EARTH WITH MY UNDEAD GROOM...
WE'LL EXCHANGE VOWS, COMMIT SUICIDE, AND BRING ABOUT MASS SPECIES EXTINCTION AT THE SAME TIME.
YOU ALWAYS WERE MY FAVORITE NIECE.
NOW PAY ATTENTION.
HE LOSES HIS POWERS UNDER RED SUNLIGHT, RIGHT?
STATION
KEEP OUT
SO HOW COOL AM I?
FRIENDS IN HIGH PLACES.
TIME TO GET CHANGED.

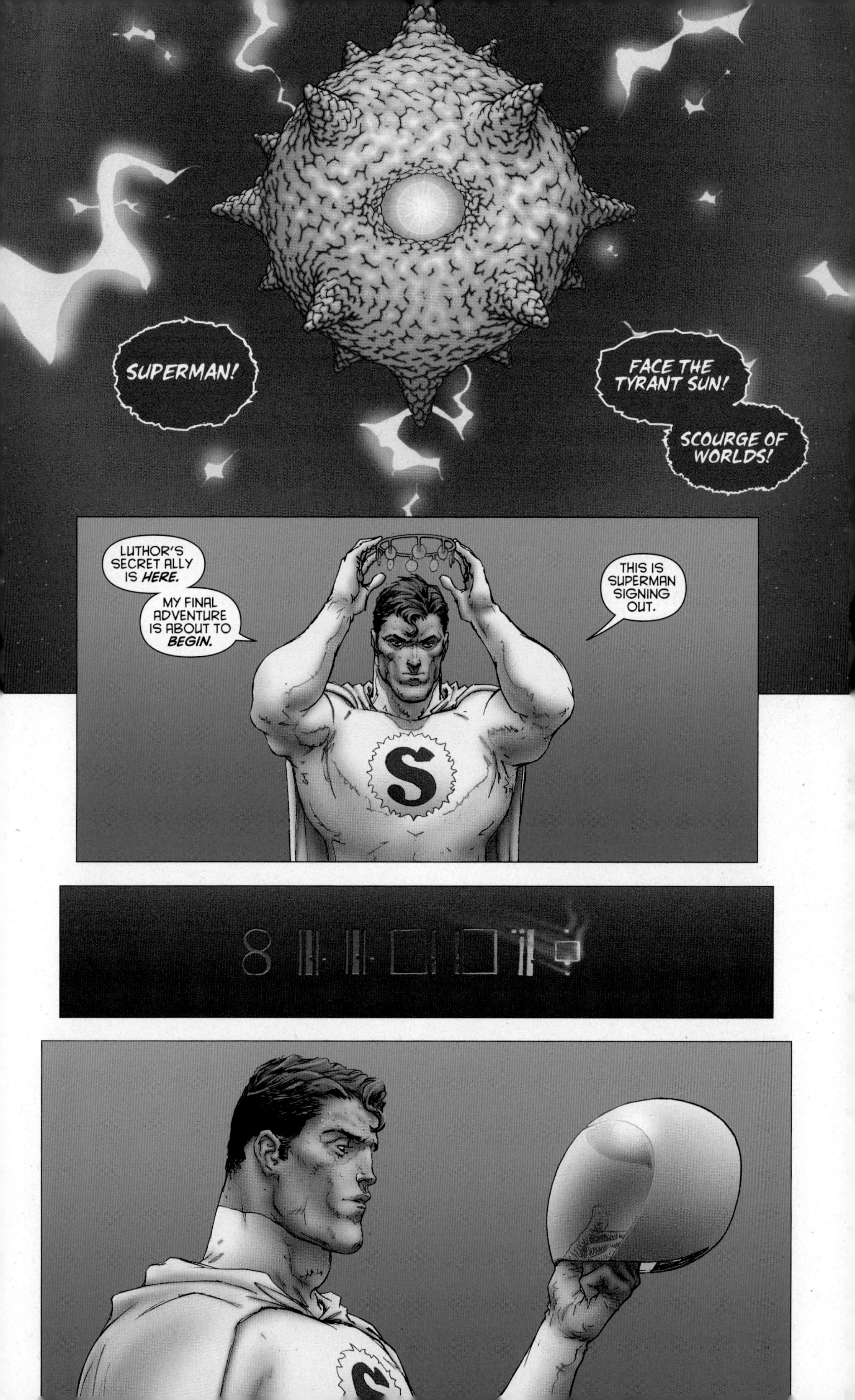
SUPERMAN!
FACE THE TYRANT SUN!
SCOURGE OF WORLDS!
LUTHOR'S SECRET ALLY IS *HERE.*
MY FINAL ADVENTURE IS ABOUT TO *BEGIN.*
THIS IS SUPERMAN SIGNING OUT.

SUPERMAN.

YOU CANNOT STAND ALONE.

I WILL REMAIN TO GUARD THE FORTRESS OF SOLITUDE.

THE REST OF US WILL FIGHT BY YOUR SIDE.

I...I COULDN'T ASK FOR GREATER LOYALTY.

FORT SUPERMAN IS CLOSING DOWN.

SEAL THE FORTRESS!

WELCOME

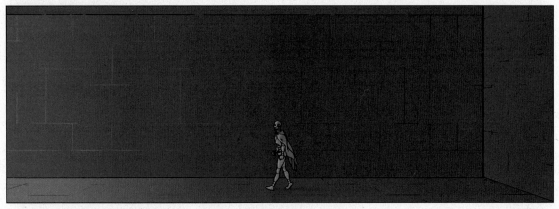

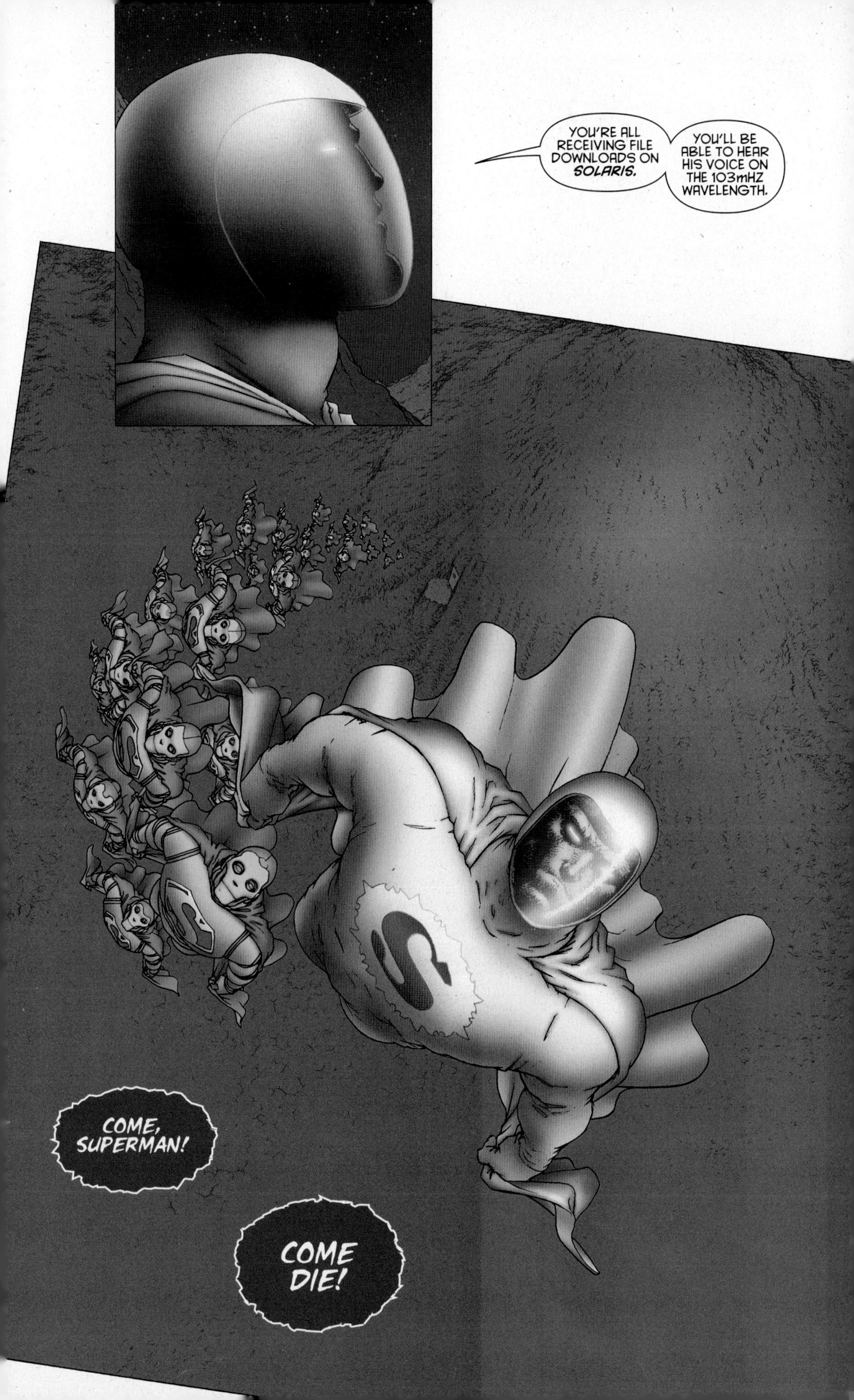
YOU'RE ALL RECEIVING FILE DOWNLOADS ON SOLARIS.
YOU'LL BE ABLE TO HEAR HIS VOICE ON THE 103mHZ WAVELENGTH.
COME, SUPERMAN!
COME DIE!

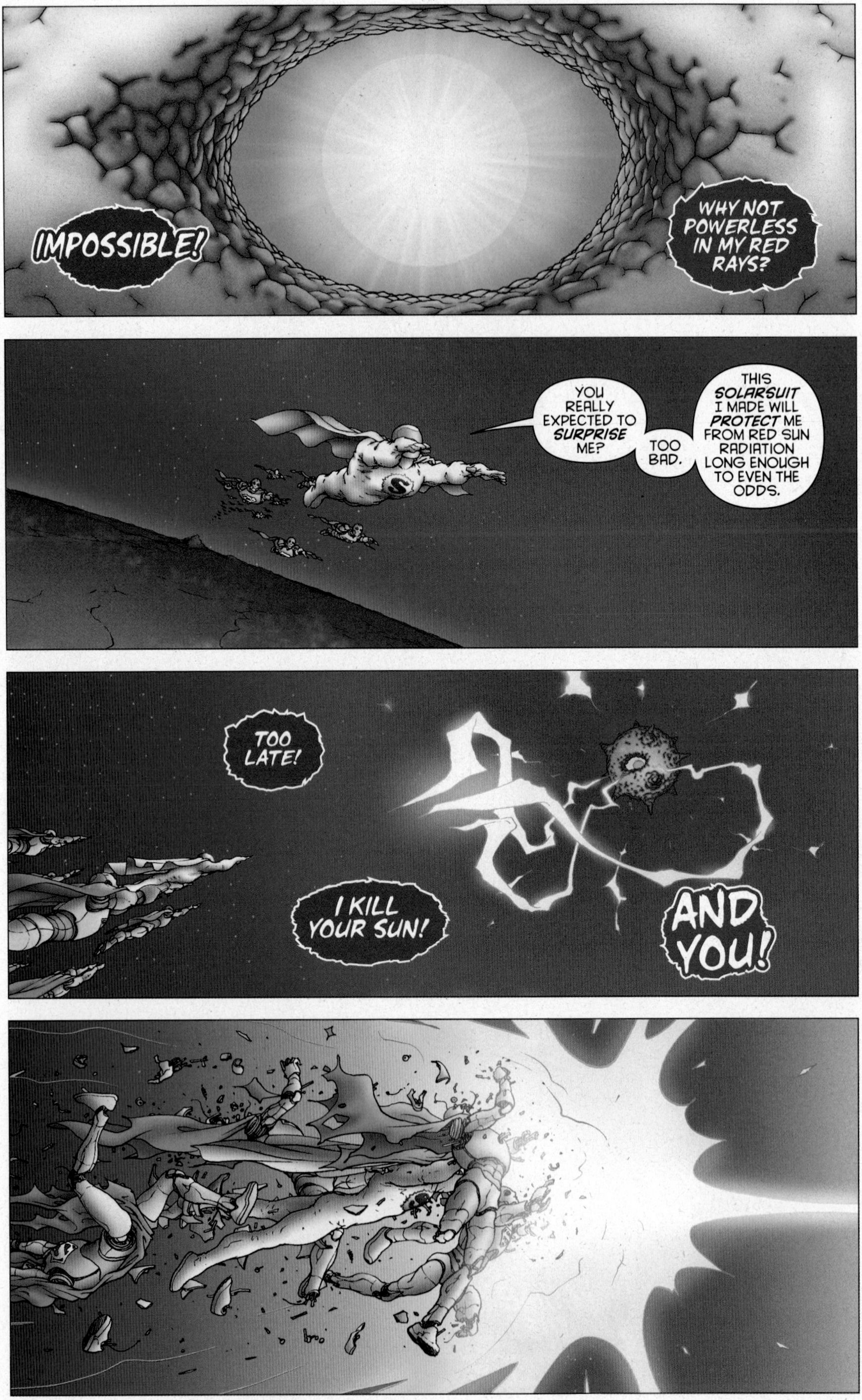
IMPOSSIBLE!
WHY NOT POWERLESS IN MY RED RAYS?
YOU REALLY EXPECTED TO SURPRISE ME?
TOO BAD.
THIS SOLARSUIT I MADE WILL PROTECT ME FROM RED SUN RADIATION LONG ENOUGH TO EVEN THE ODDS.
TOO LATE!
I KILL YOUR SUN!
AND YOU!

GNN!
NEW POWERS? GZZZNN11010010
WHEN YOU ARE DEAD!
I WILL REPLACE!
THE SUN IN THE SKY!

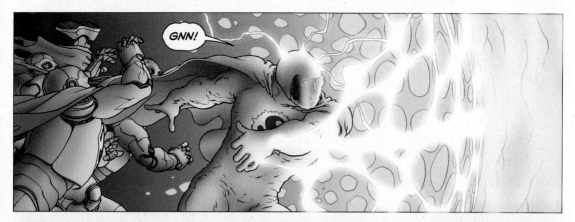

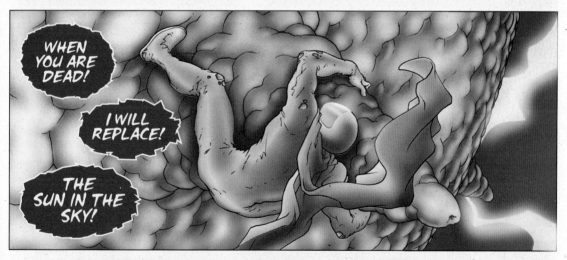

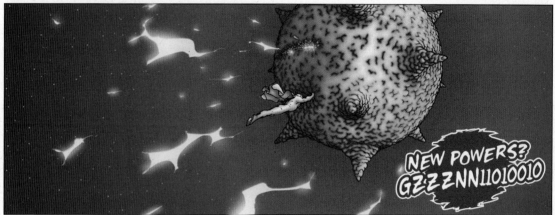

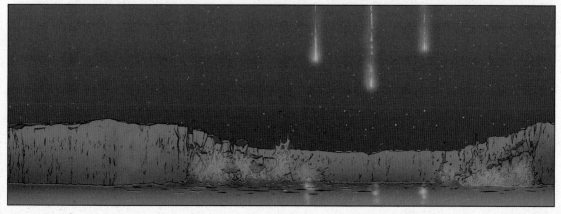

YOUR PEOPLE WILL BOW!
+PRAY TO ME!
OR DIE IN DARKNESS!
HE'LL WIPE YOUR FILES!
SAVE YOURSELVES!
ROBOT 7...MUST ATONE...SOLARIS INVADED NEURAL NET...
GGAAAA!
...SOLARIS STOLE FORMULA...SKKZZKK... SOLARIS STOLE FROM ROBOT 7...STOLE FORMULA...
...STOLE FOR LUTHOR...ROBOT 7... MUST...ATONE...
...FOR...
...GIVE...
...7...
SZZZZAAAARKK
GREAT KRYPTON!

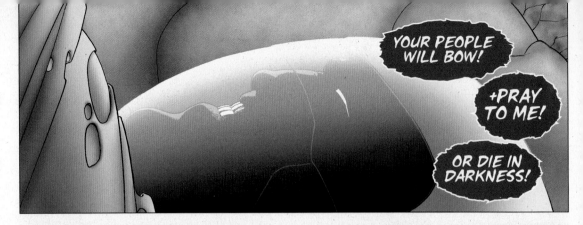

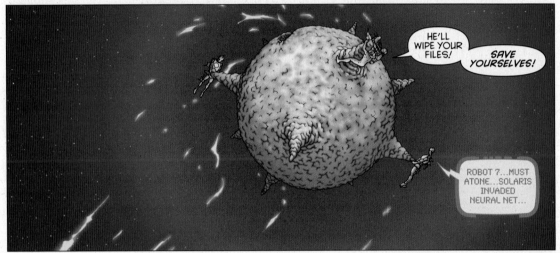

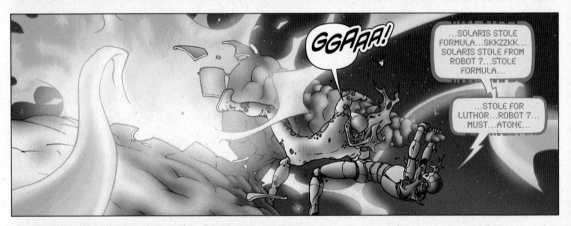

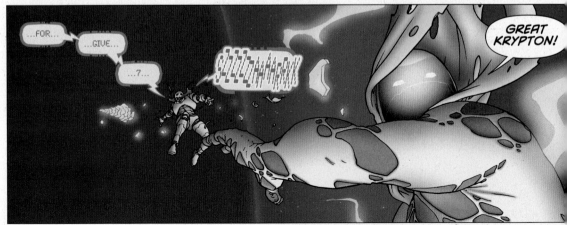

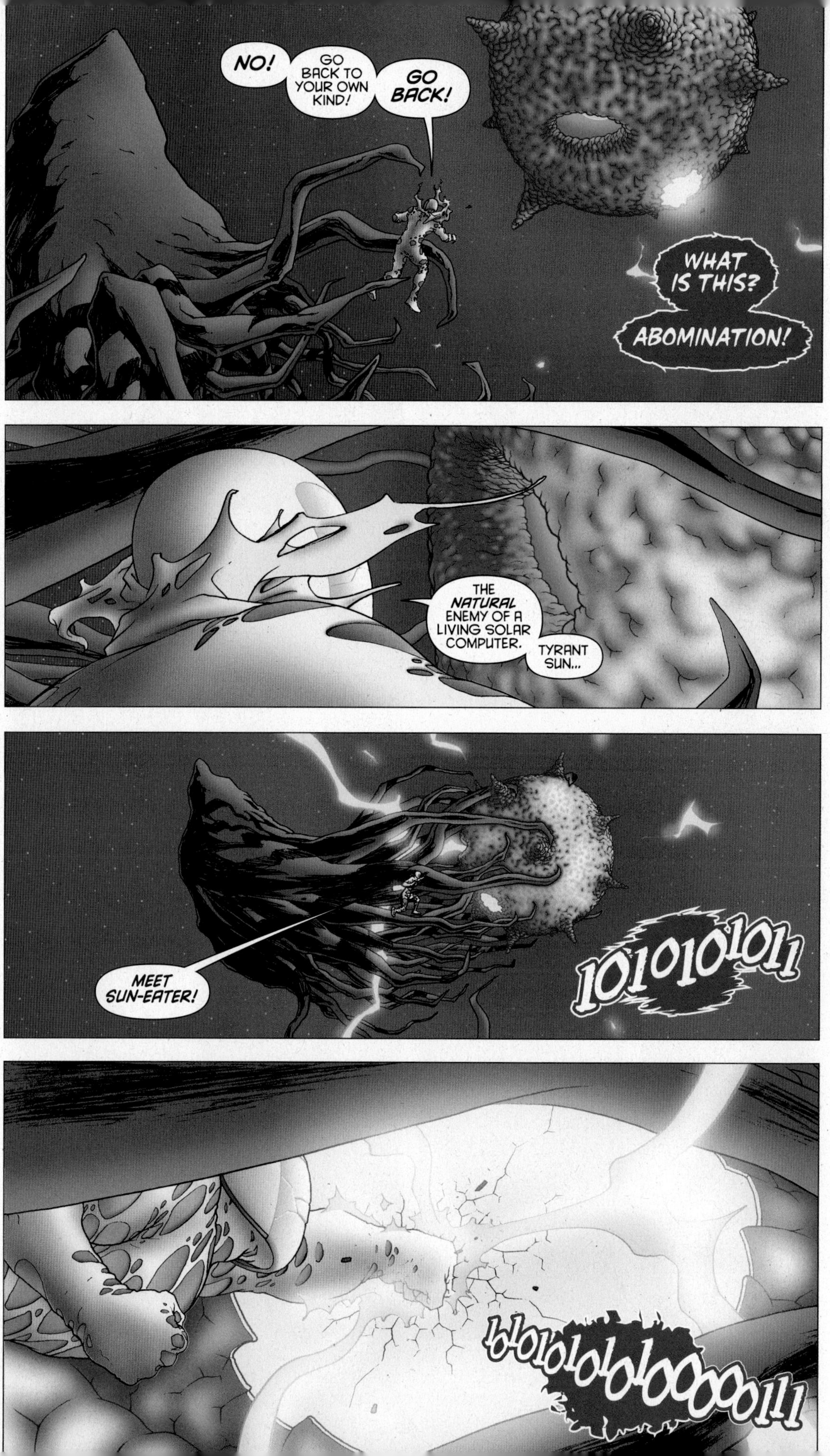
NO!
GO BACK TO YOUR OWN KIND!
GO BACK!
WHAT IS THIS?
ABOMINATION!
THE NATURAL ENEMY OF A LIVING SOLAR COMPUTER.
TYRANT SUN...
MEET SUN-EATER!
1010101011
101010101010000111

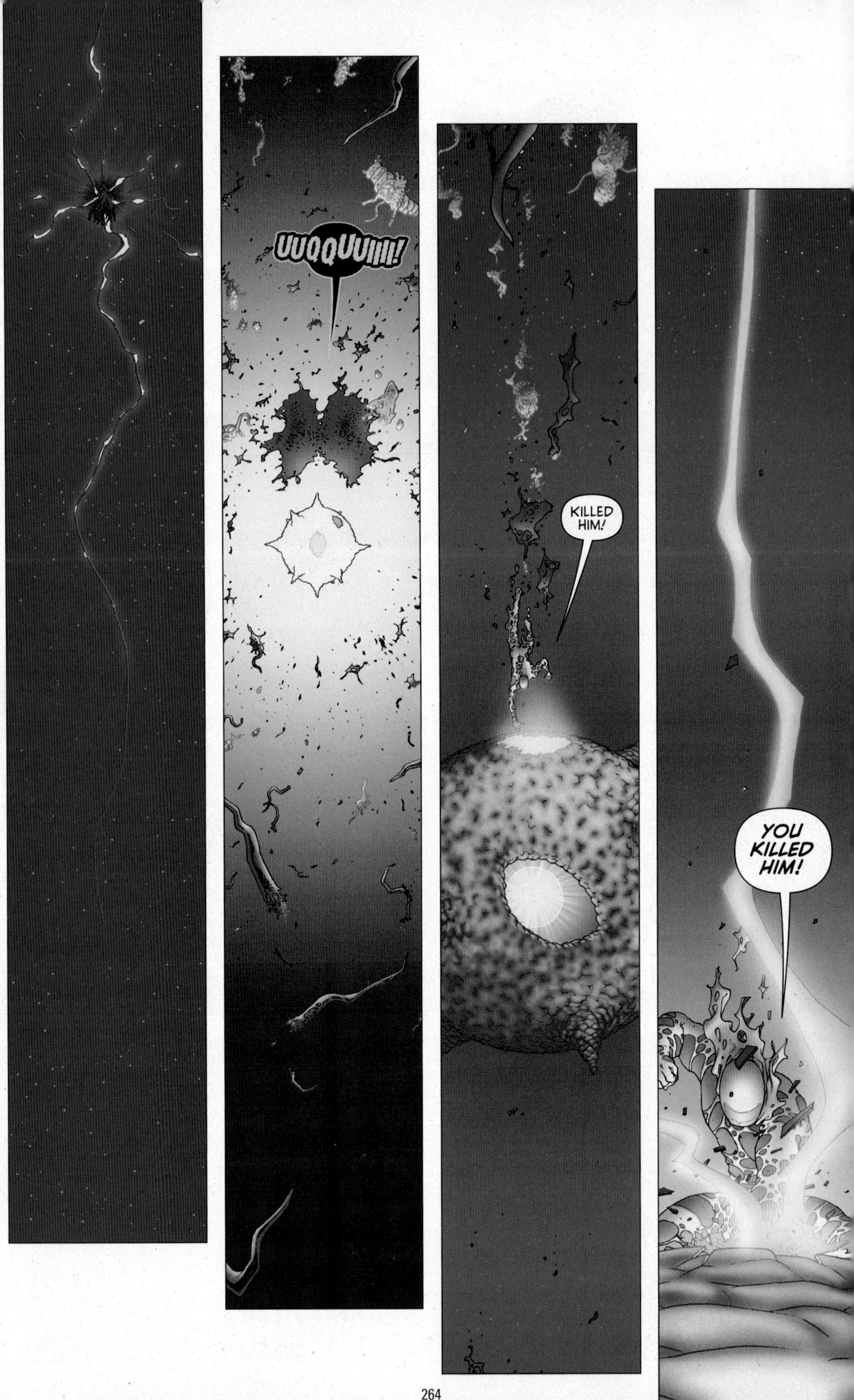
UUQQUUIIII!
KILLED HIM!
YOU KILLED HIM!

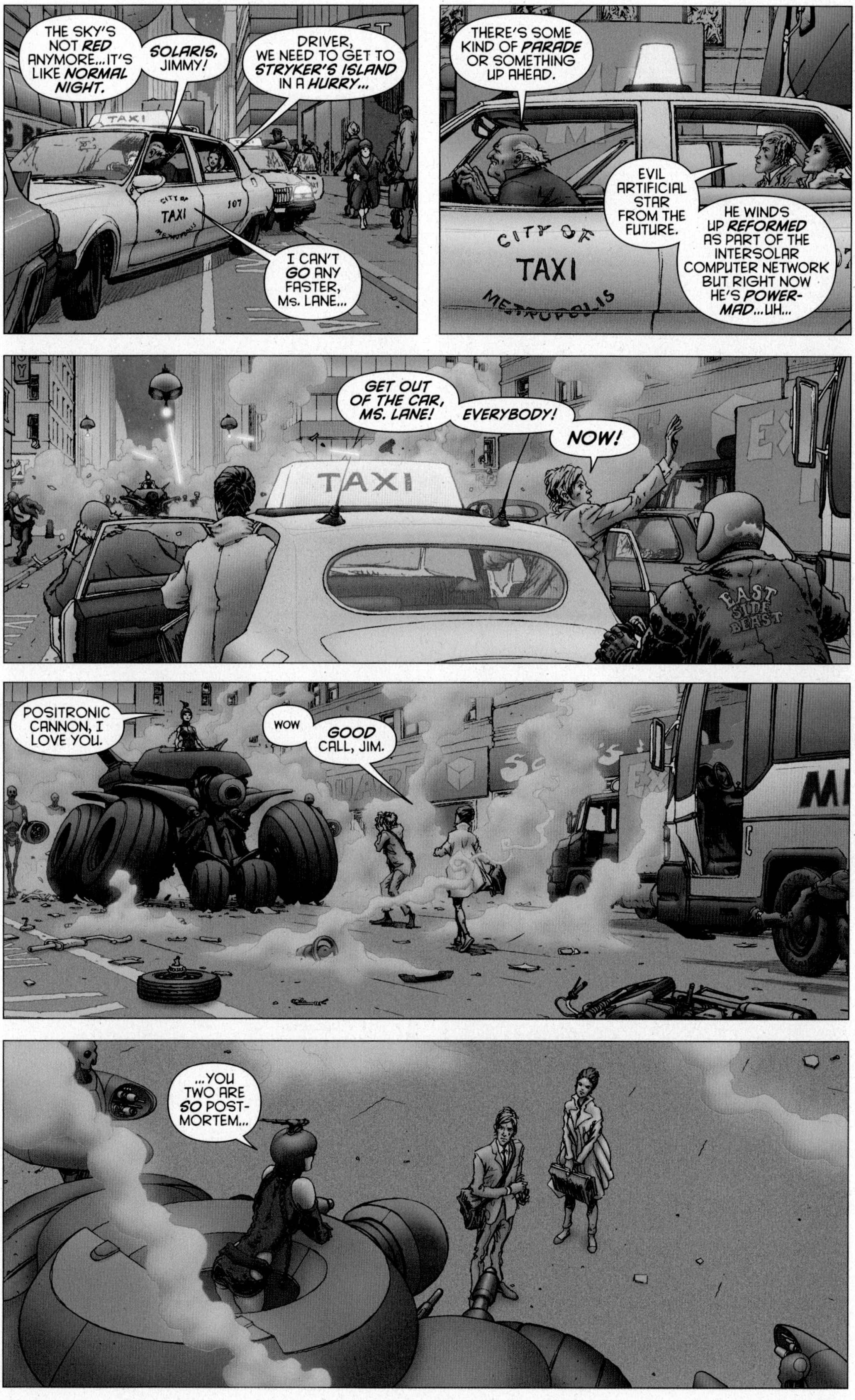
THE SKY'S NOT RED ANYMORE...IT'S LIKE NORMAL NIGHT.
SOLARIS, JIMMY!
DRIVER, WE NEED TO GET TO STRYKER'S ISLAND IN A HURRY...
I CAN'T GO ANY FASTER, Ms. LANE...
TAXI
THERE'S SOME KIND OF PARADE OR SOMETHING UP AHEAD.
EVIL ARTIFICIAL STAR FROM THE FUTURE.
HE WINDS UP REFORMED AS PART OF THE INTERSOLAR COMPUTER NETWORK BUT RIGHT NOW HE'S POWER-MAD...UH...
CITY OF TAXI METROPOLIS
GET OUT OF THE CAR, MS. LANE!
EVERYBODY!
NOW!
TAXI
EAST SIDE BEAST
POSITRONIC CANNON, I LOVE YOU.
WOW
GOOD CALL, JIM.
...YOU TWO ARE SO POST-MORTEM...

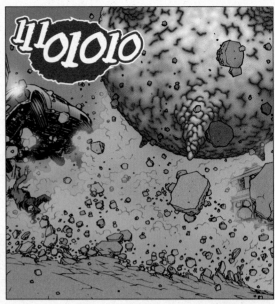

1110I0I0

1110010OPOISONEDOIOSUN1110

I NEED EVERYONE TO TAKE COVER!

NOW!

BY THE 24th CENTURY, I'M TOLD, YOU'LL HAVE BEEN *REHABILITATED* TO WORK *WITH* HUMANITY INSTEAD OF *AGAINST* THEM.

REHABILITATION BEGINS *HERE*. SOLARIS.

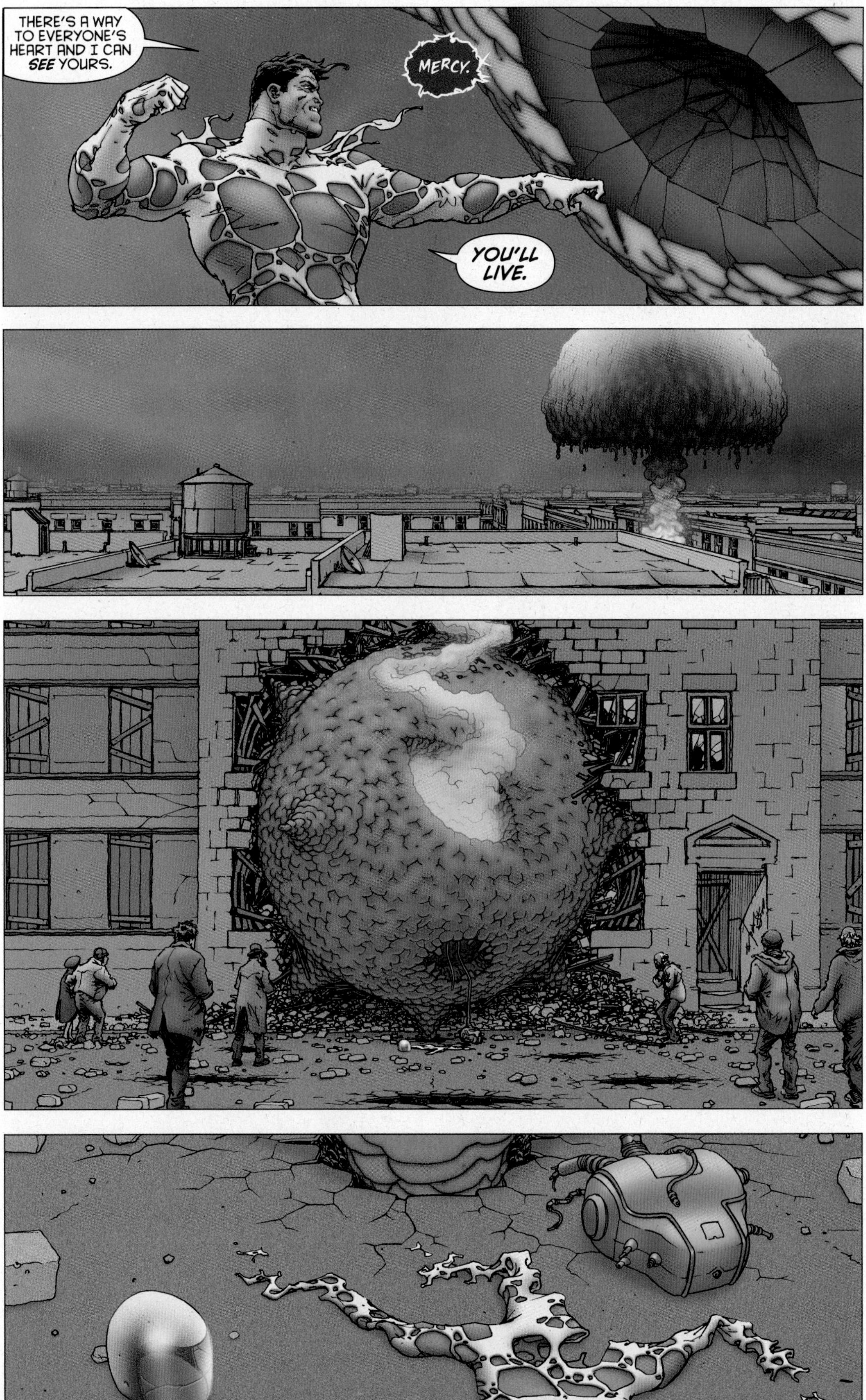
THERE'S A WAY TO EVERYONE'S HEART AND I CAN SEE YOURS.
MERCY.
YOU'LL LIVE.

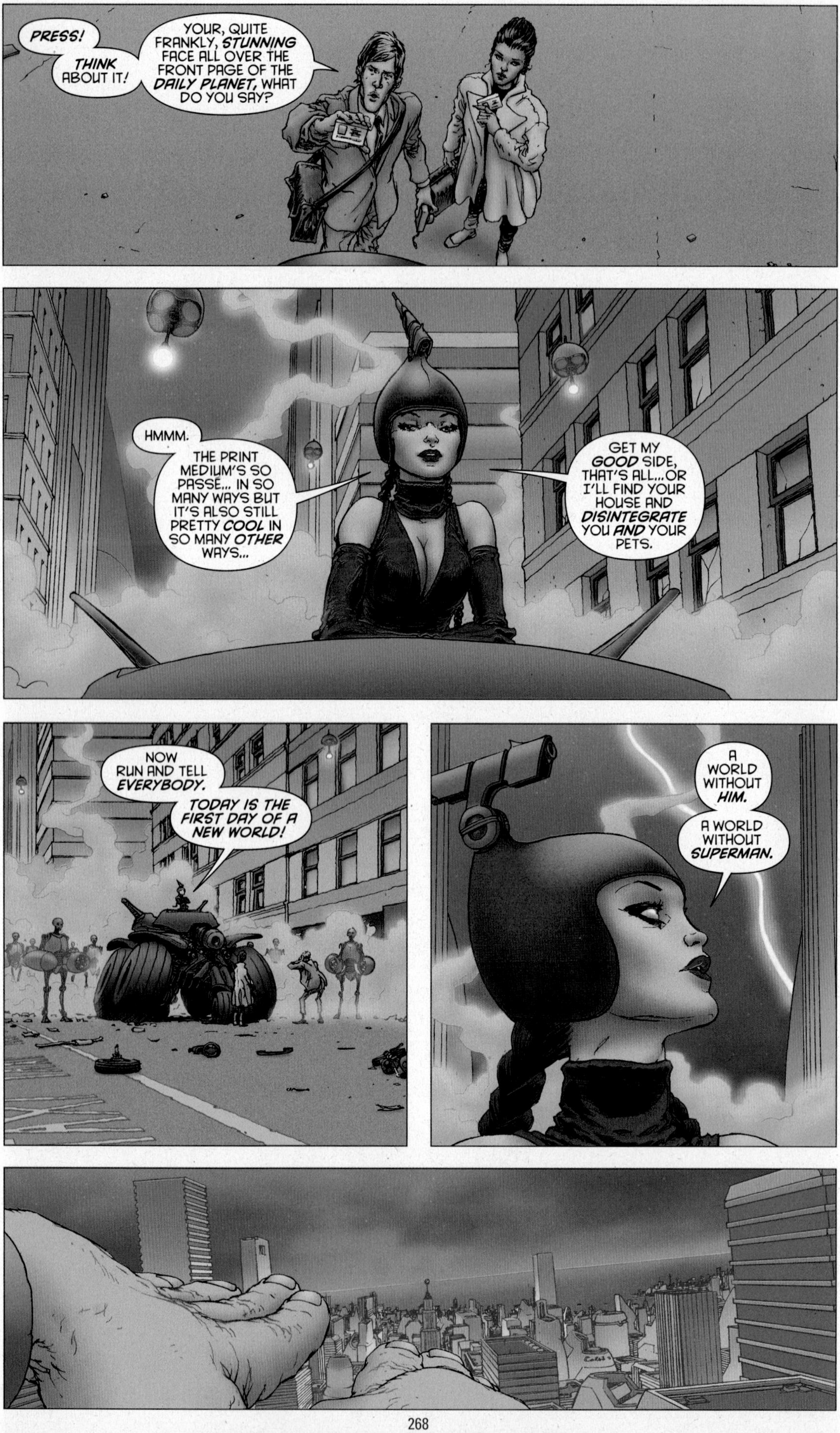
PRESS!
THINK ABOUT IT!
YOUR, QUITE FRANKLY, STUNNING FACE ALL OVER THE FRONT PAGE OF THE DAILY PLANET, WHAT DO YOU SAY?
HMMM.
THE PRINT MEDIUM'S SO PASSÉ... IN SO MANY WAYS BUT IT'S ALSO STILL PRETTY COOL IN SO MANY OTHER WAYS...
GET MY GOOD SIDE, THAT'S ALL...OR I'LL FIND YOUR HOUSE AND DISINTEGRATE YOU AND YOUR PETS.
NOW RUN AND TELL EVERYBODY.
TODAY IS THE FIRST DAY OF A NEW WORLD!
A WORLD WITHOUT HIM.
A WORLD WITHOUT SUPERMAN.

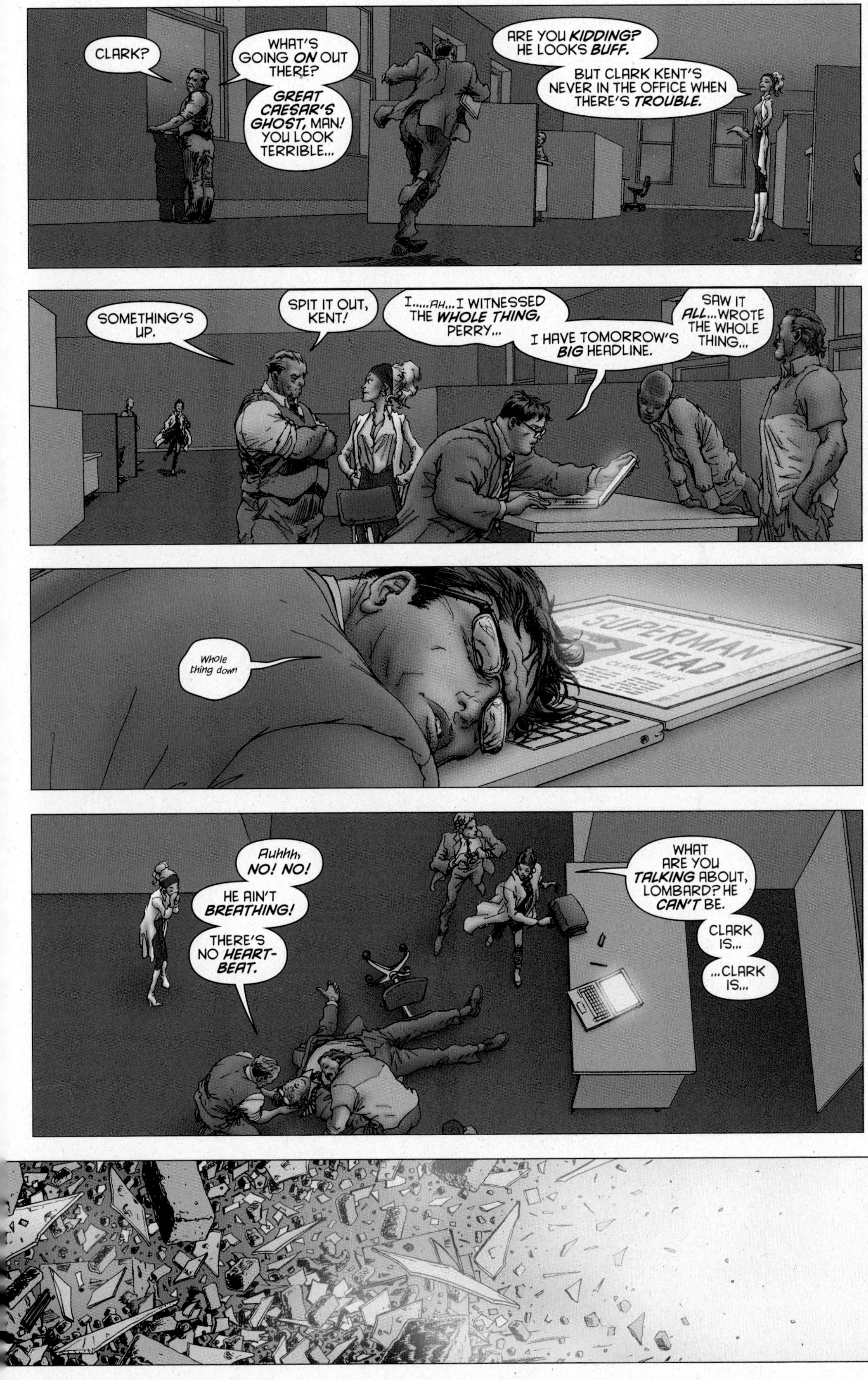
CLARK?
WHAT'S GOING ON OUT THERE?
GREAT CAESAR'S GHOST, MAN! YOU LOOK TERRIBLE...
ARE YOU KIDDING? HE LOOKS BUFF.
BUT CLARK KENT'S NEVER IN THE OFFICE WHEN THERE'S TROUBLE.
SOMETHING'S UP.
SPIT IT OUT, KENT!
I....AH...I WITNESSED THE WHOLE THING, PERRY...
I HAVE TOMORROW'S BIG HEADLINE.
SAW IT ALL...WROTE THE WHOLE THING...
Whole thing down
SUPERMAN DEAD
CLARK KENT
Auhhh, NO! NO!
HE AIN'T BREATHING!
THERE'S NO HEART-BEAT.
WHAT ARE YOU TALKING ABOUT, LOMBARD? HE CAN'T BE.
CLARK IS...
...CLARK IS...

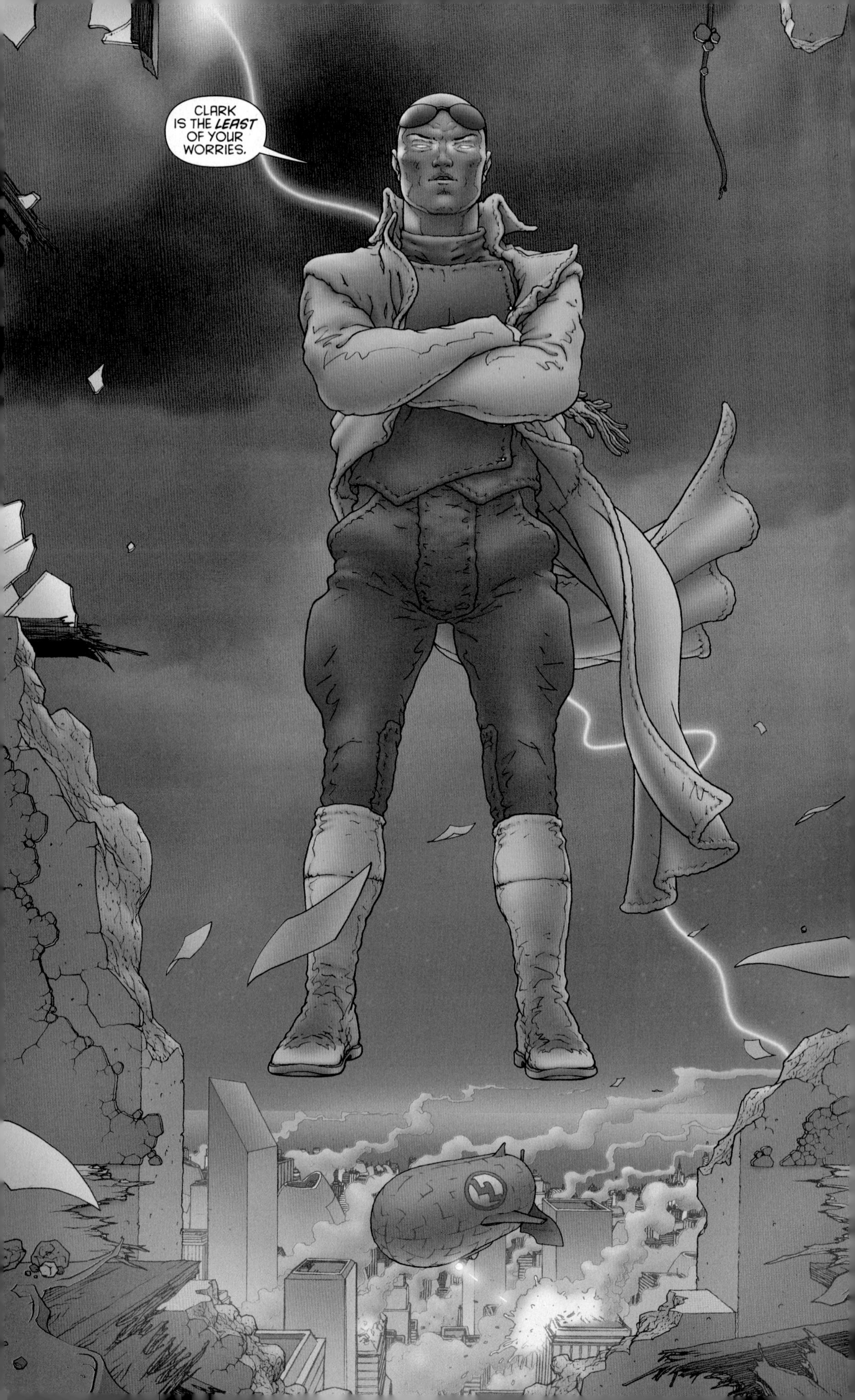
CLARK IS THE LEAST OF YOUR WORRIES.

Episode 12

SUPERMAN IN EXCELSIS

Cover FRANK QUITELY

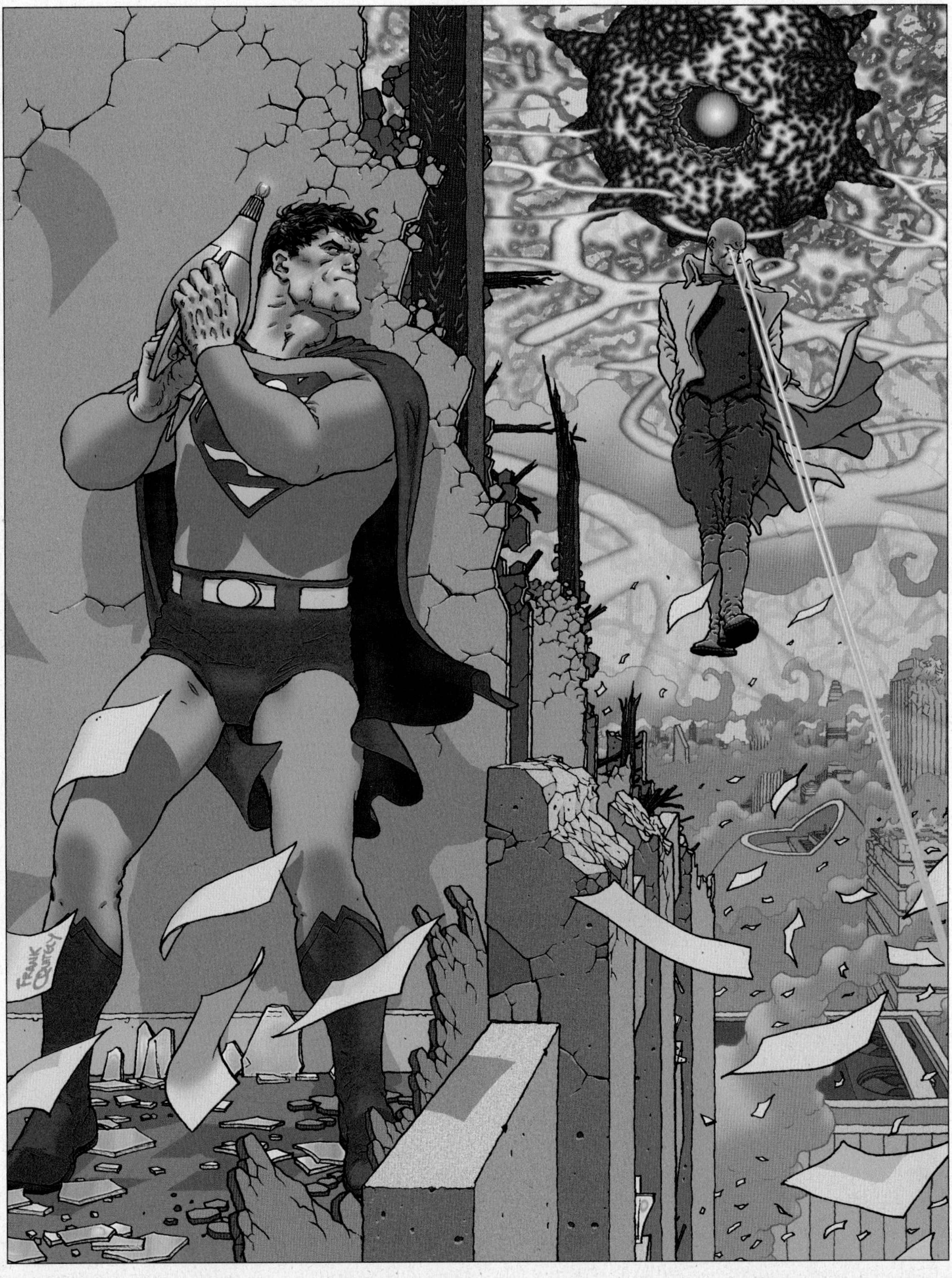
FRANK QUITELY

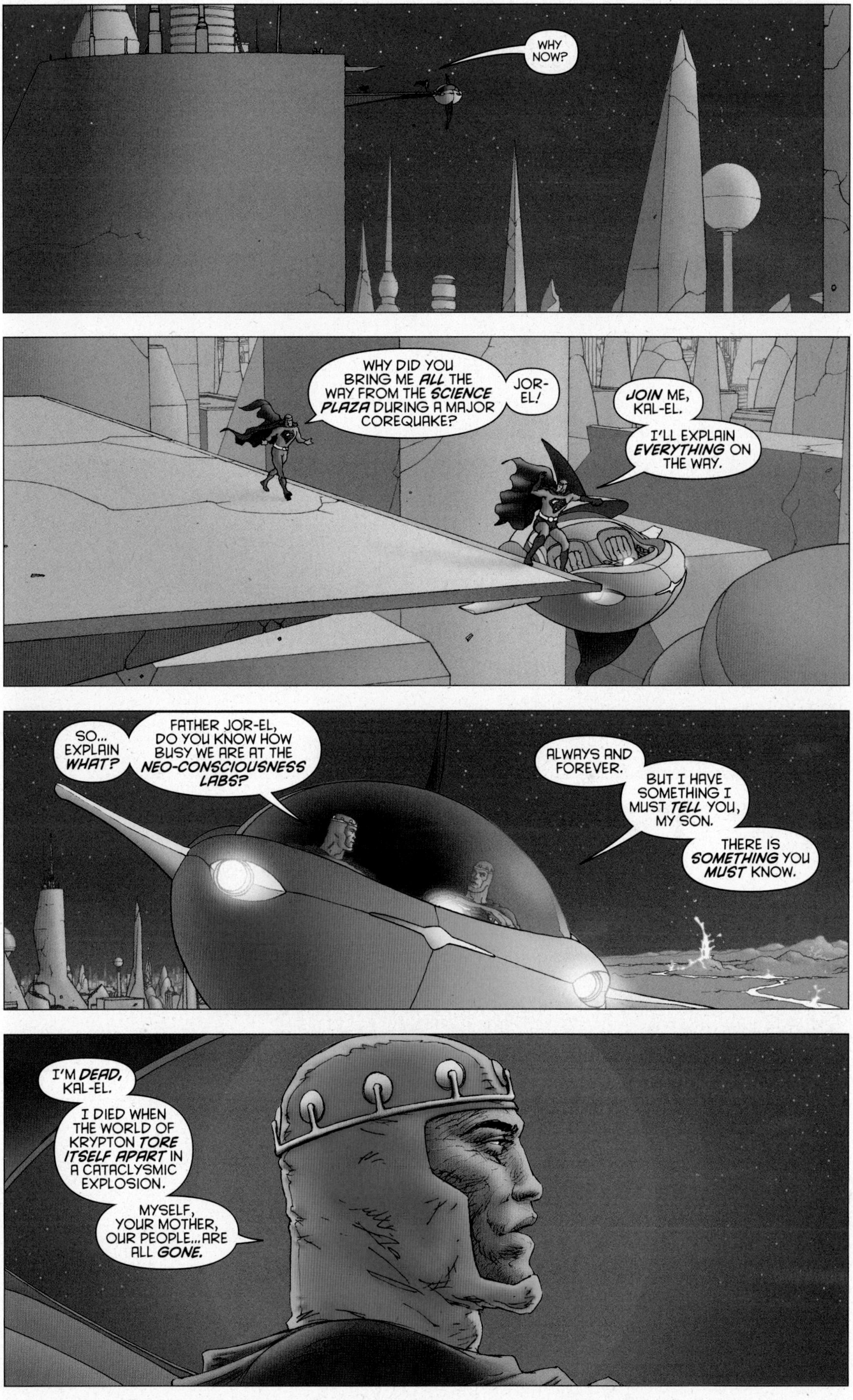
WHY NOW?
WHY DID YOU BRING ME ALL THE WAY FROM THE SCIENCE PLAZA DURING A MAJOR COREQUAKE?
JOR-EL!
JOIN ME, KAL-EL.
I'LL EXPLAIN EVERYTHING ON THE WAY.
SO... EXPLAIN WHAT?
FATHER JOR-EL, DO YOU KNOW HOW BUSY WE ARE AT THE NEO-CONSCIOUSNESS LABS?
ALWAYS AND FOREVER.
BUT I HAVE SOMETHING I MUST TELL YOU, MY SON.
THERE IS SOMETHING YOU MUST KNOW.
I'M DEAD, KAL-EL.
I DIED WHEN THE WORLD OF KRYPTON TORE ITSELF APART IN A CATACLYSMIC EXPLOSION.
MYSELF, YOUR MOTHER, OUR PEOPLE...ARE ALL GONE.

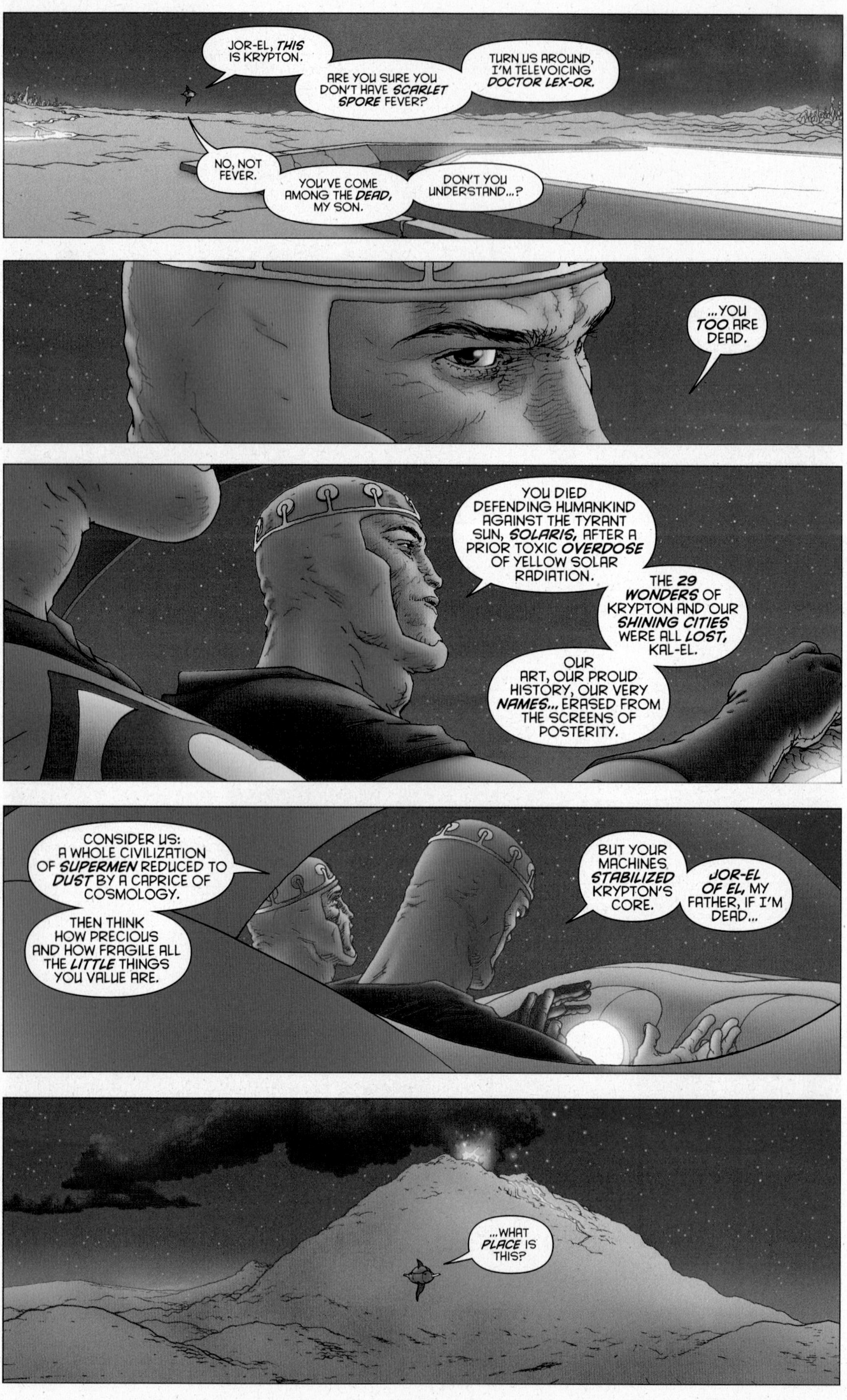
JOR-EL, THIS IS KRYPTON.
ARE YOU SURE YOU DON'T HAVE SCARLET SPORE FEVER?
TURN US AROUND, I'M TELEVOICING DOCTOR LEX-OR.
NO, NOT FEVER.
YOU'VE COME AMONG THE DEAD, MY SON.
DON'T YOU UNDERSTAND...?
...YOU TOO ARE DEAD.
YOU DIED DEFENDING HUMANKIND AGAINST THE TYRANT SUN, SOLARIS, AFTER A PRIOR TOXIC OVERDOSE OF YELLOW SOLAR RADIATION.
THE 29 WONDERS OF KRYPTON AND OUR SHINING CITIES WERE ALL LOST, KAL-EL.
OUR ART, OUR PROUD HISTORY, OUR VERY NAMES... ERASED FROM THE SCREENS OF POSTERITY.
CONSIDER US: A WHOLE CIVILIZATION OF SUPERMEN REDUCED TO DUST BY A CAPRICE OF COSMOLOGY.
THEN THINK HOW PRECIOUS AND HOW FRAGILE ALL THE LITTLE THINGS YOU VALUE ARE.
BUT YOUR MACHINES STABILIZED KRYPTON'S CORE.
JOR-EL OF EL, MY FATHER, IF I'M DEAD...
...WHAT PLACE IS THIS?

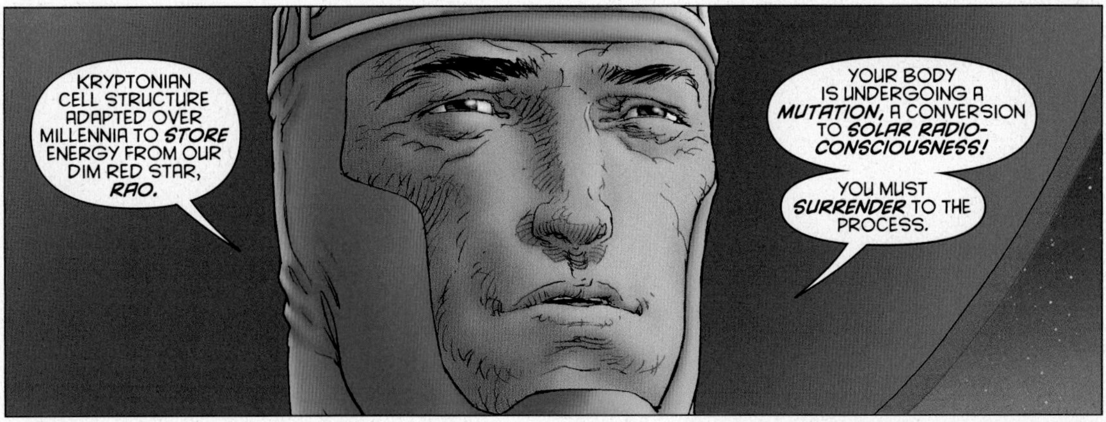
KRYPTONIAN CELL STRUCTURE ADAPTED OVER MILLENNIA TO STORE ENERGY FROM OUR DIM RED STAR, RAO.
YOUR BODY IS UNDERGOING A MUTATION, A CONVERSION TO SOLAR RADIO-CONSCIOUSNESS!
YOU MUST SURRENDER TO THE PROCESS.

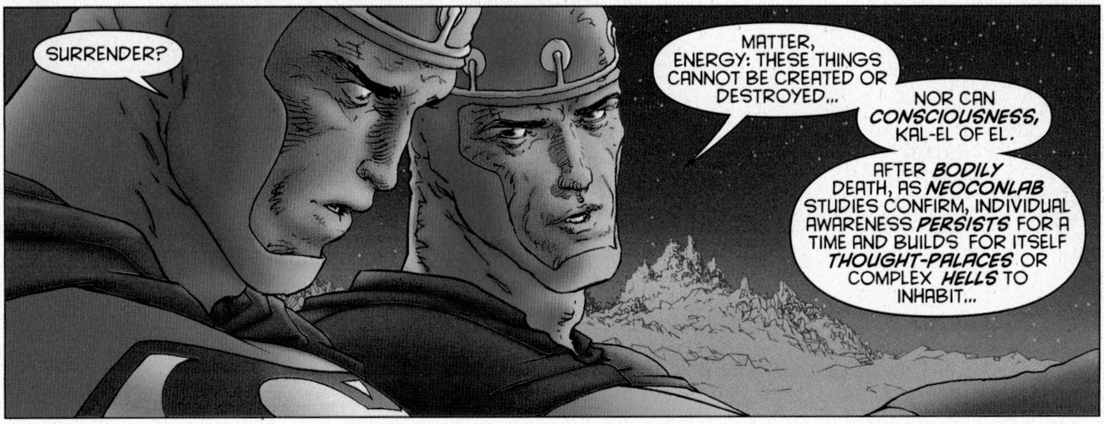
SURRENDER?
MATTER, ENERGY: THESE THINGS CANNOT BE CREATED OR DESTROYED...
NOR CAN CONSCIOUSNESS, KAL-EL OF EL.
AFTER BODILY DEATH, AS NEOCONLAB STUDIES CONFIRM, INDIVIDUAL AWARENESS PERSISTS FOR A TIME AND BUILDS FOR ITSELF THOUGHT-PALACES OR COMPLEX HELLS TO INHABIT...

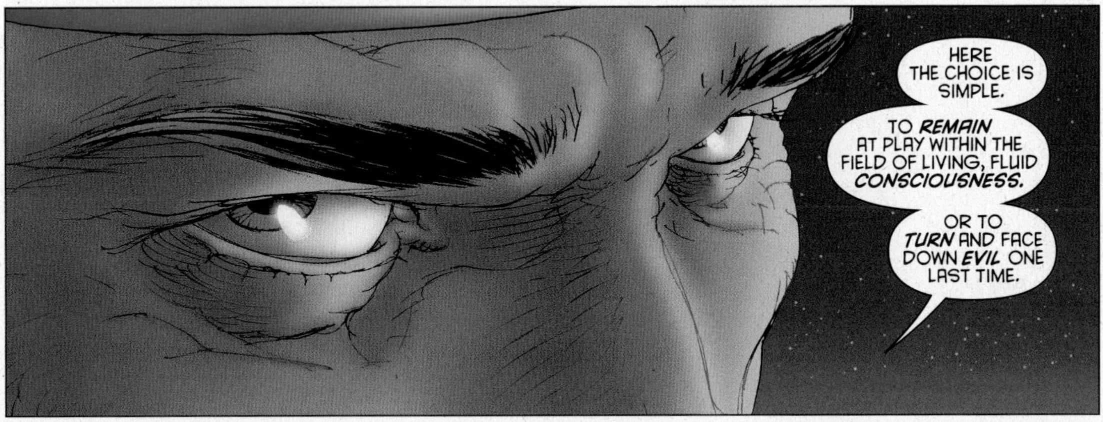
HERE THE CHOICE IS SIMPLE.
TO REMAIN AT PLAY WITHIN THE FIELD OF LIVING, FLUID CONSCIOUSNESS.
OR TO TURN AND FACE DOWN EVIL ONE LAST TIME.

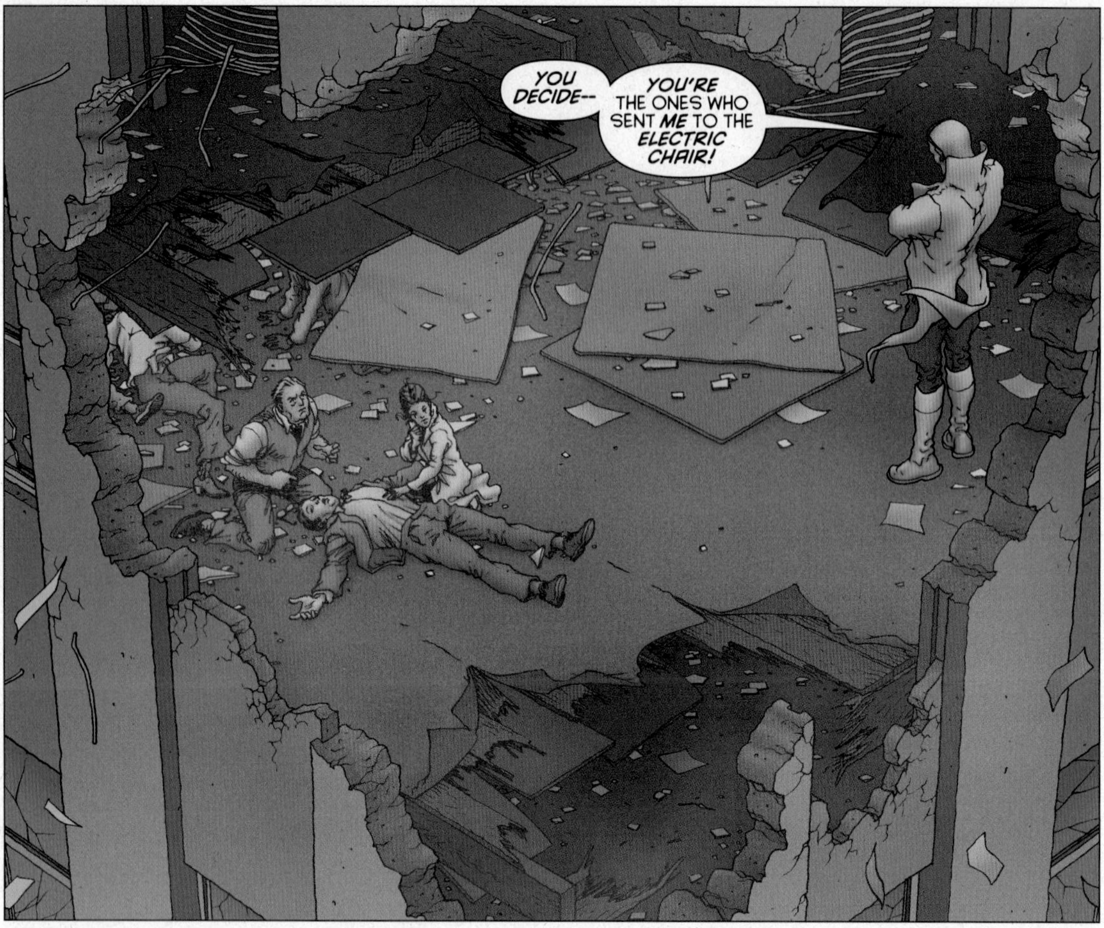
YOU DECIDE--
YOU'RE THE ONES WHO SENT ME TO THE ELECTRIC CHAIR!

SUPERMAN IN EXCELSIS

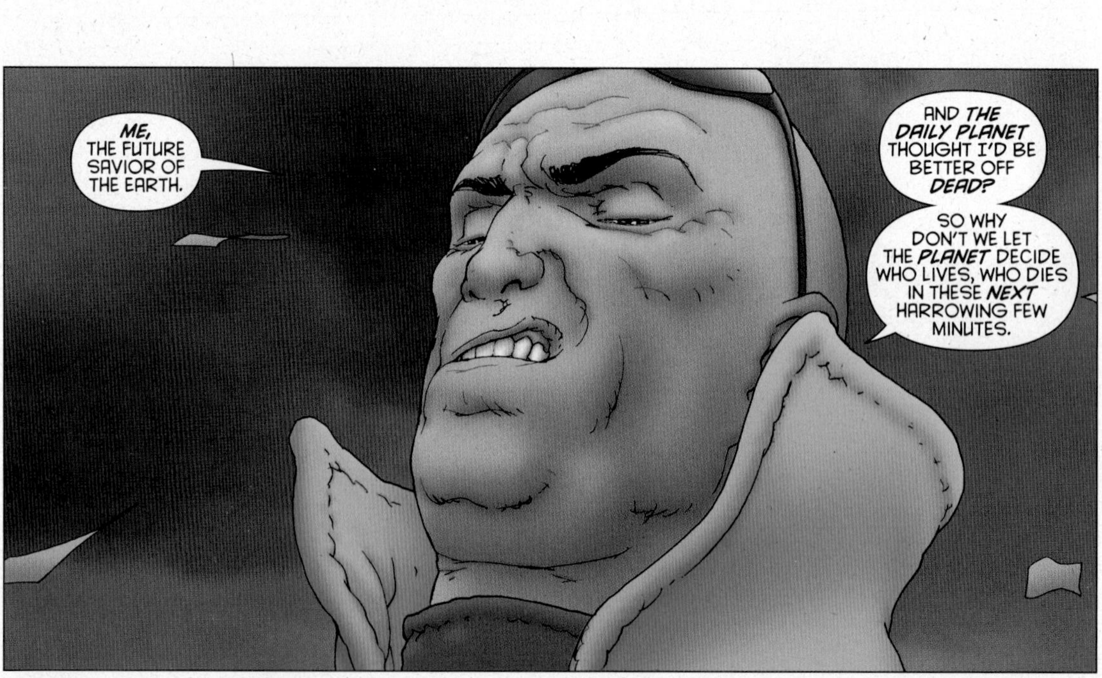
ME, THE FUTURE SAVIOR OF THE EARTH.
AND THE DAILY PLANET THOUGHT I'D BE BETTER OFF DEAD?
SO WHY DON'T WE LET THE PLANET DECIDE WHO LIVES, WHO DIES IN THESE NEXT HARROWING FEW MINUTES.

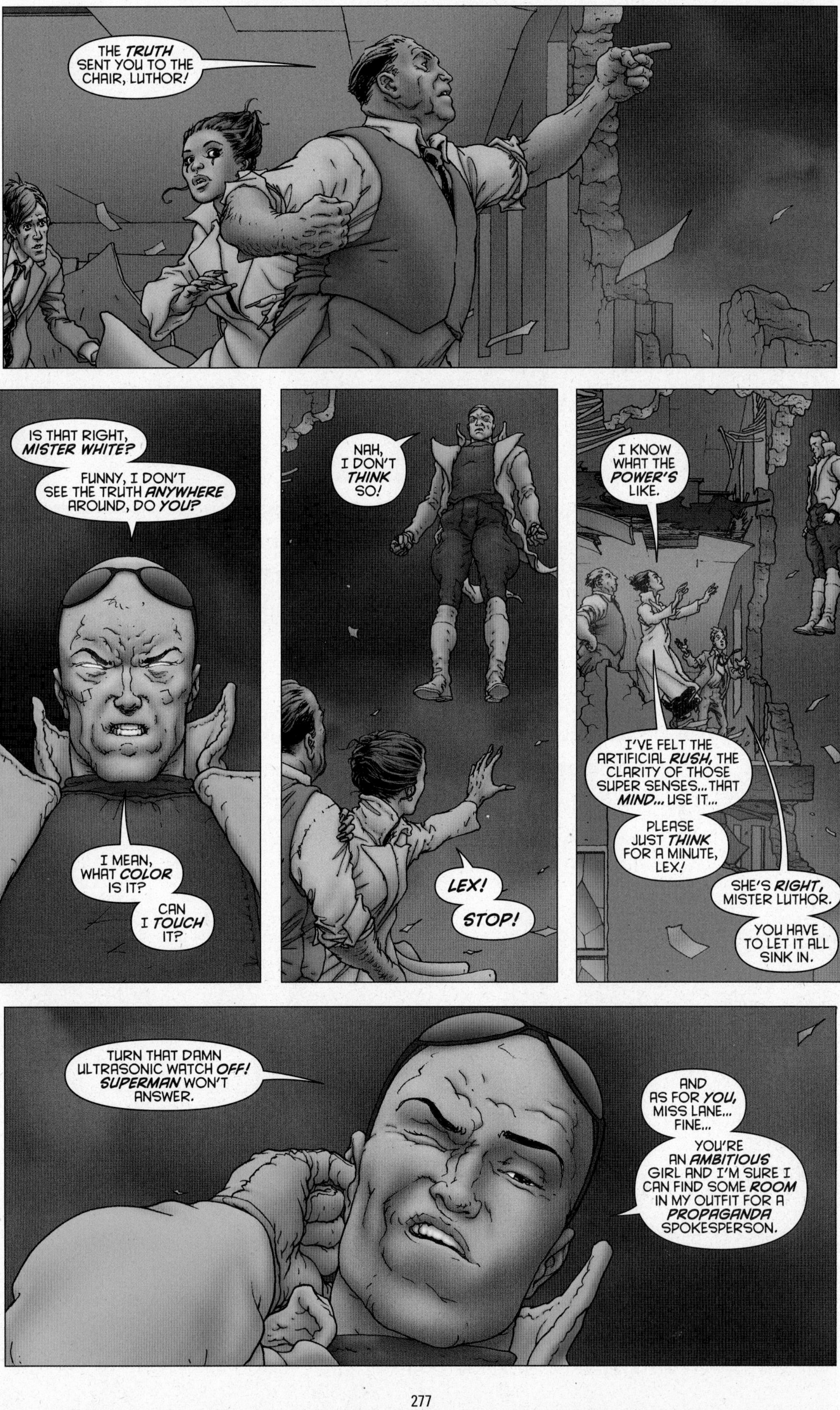
THE TRUTH SENT YOU TO THE CHAIR, LUTHOR!
IS THAT RIGHT, MISTER WHITE?
FUNNY, I DON'T SEE THE TRUTH ANYWHERE AROUND, DO YOU?
I MEAN, WHAT COLOR IS IT?
CAN I TOUCH IT?
NAH, I DON'T THINK SO!
LEX!
STOP!
I KNOW WHAT THE POWER'S LIKE.
I'VE FELT THE ARTIFICIAL RUSH, THE CLARITY OF THOSE SUPER SENSES...THAT MIND... USE IT...
PLEASE JUST THINK FOR A MINUTE, LEX!
SHE'S RIGHT, MISTER LUTHOR.
YOU HAVE TO LET IT ALL SINK IN.
TURN THAT DAMN ULTRASONIC WATCH OFF! SUPERMAN WON'T ANSWER.
AND AS FOR YOU, MISS LANE... FINE...
YOU'RE AN AMBITIOUS GIRL AND I'M SURE I CAN FIND SOME ROOM IN MY OUTFIT FOR A PROPAGANDA SPOKESPERSON.

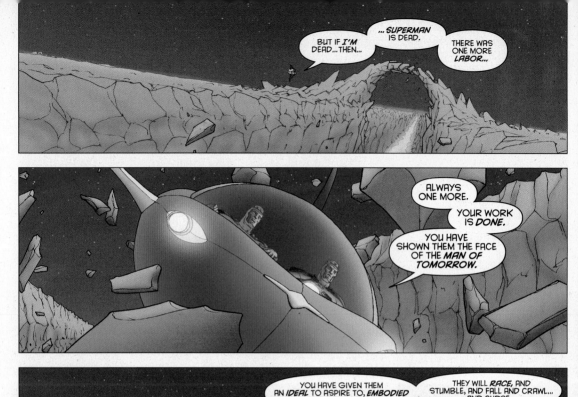

BUT IF *I'M* DEAD...THEN...

...*SUPERMAN* IS DEAD.

THERE WAS ONE MORE *LABOR*...

ALWAYS ONE MORE.

YOUR WORK IS *DONE.*

YOU HAVE SHOWN THEM THE FACE OF THE *MAN OF TOMORROW.*

YOU HAVE GIVEN THEM AN *IDEAL* TO ASPIRE TO, *EMBODIED* THEIR HIGHEST ASPIRATIONS.

THEY WILL *RACE,* AND STUMBLE, AND FALL AND CRAWL... AND CURSE...

...AND *FINALLY*...

...THEY WILL *JOIN* YOU IN THE SUN, KAL-EL.

IN *TIME* YOU WILL NO LONGER BE *ALONE.*

BUT MY LIFE!

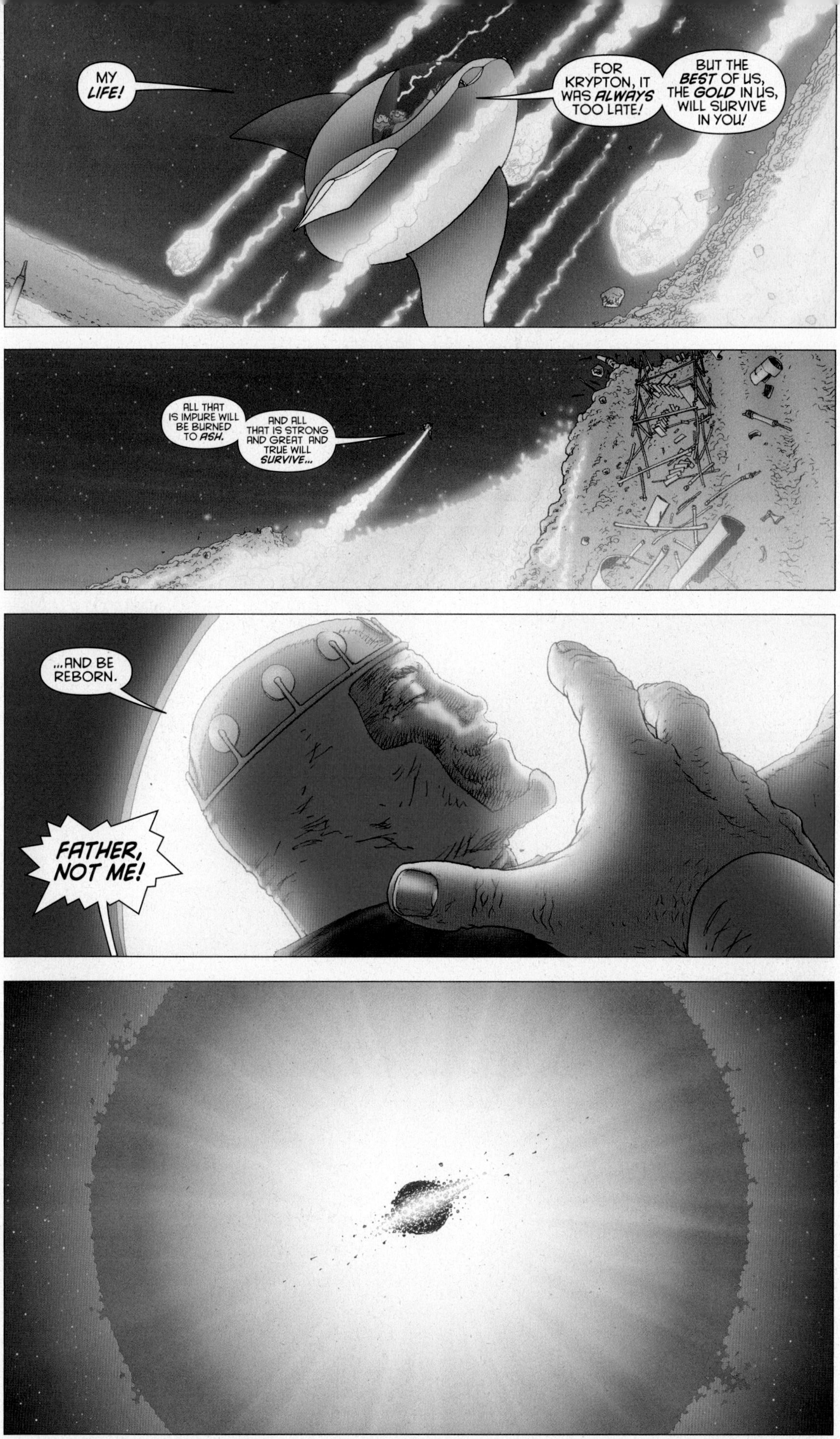
MY LIFE!
FOR KRYPTON, IT WAS ALWAYS TOO LATE!
BUT THE BEST OF US, THE GOLD IN US, WILL SURVIVE IN YOU!
ALL THAT IS IMPURE WILL BE BURNED TO ASH.
AND ALL THAT IS STRONG AND GREAT AND TRUE WILL SURVIVE...
...AND BE REBORN.
FATHER, NOT ME!

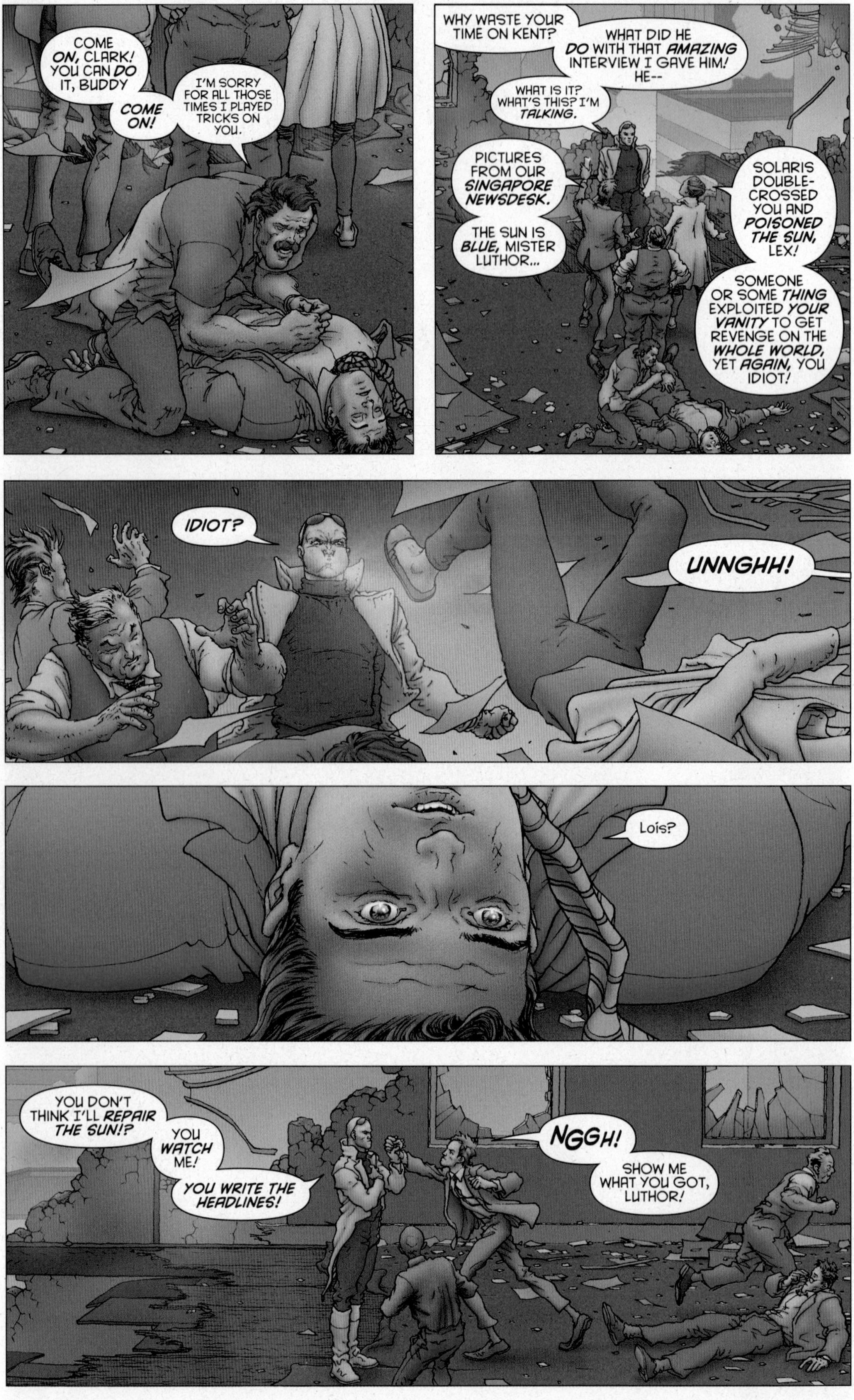
COME ON, CLARK! YOU CAN DO IT, BUDDY
COME ON!
I'M SORRY FOR ALL THOSE TIMES I PLAYED TRICKS ON YOU.
WHY WASTE YOUR TIME ON KENT?
WHAT DID HE DO WITH THAT AMAZING INTERVIEW I GAVE HIM! HE--
WHAT IS IT? WHAT'S THIS? I'M TALKING.
PICTURES FROM OUR SINGAPORE NEWSDESK.
THE SUN IS BLUE, MISTER LUTHOR...
SOLARIS DOUBLE-CROSSED YOU AND POISONED THE SUN, LEX!
SOMEONE OR SOME THING EXPLOITED YOUR VANITY TO GET REVENGE ON THE WHOLE WORLD, YET AGAIN, YOU IDIOT!
IDIOT?
UNNGHH!
Lois?
YOU DON'T THINK I'LL REPAIR THE SUN!?
YOU WATCH ME!
YOU WRITE THE HEADLINES!
NGGH!
SHOW ME WHAT YOU GOT, LUTHOR!

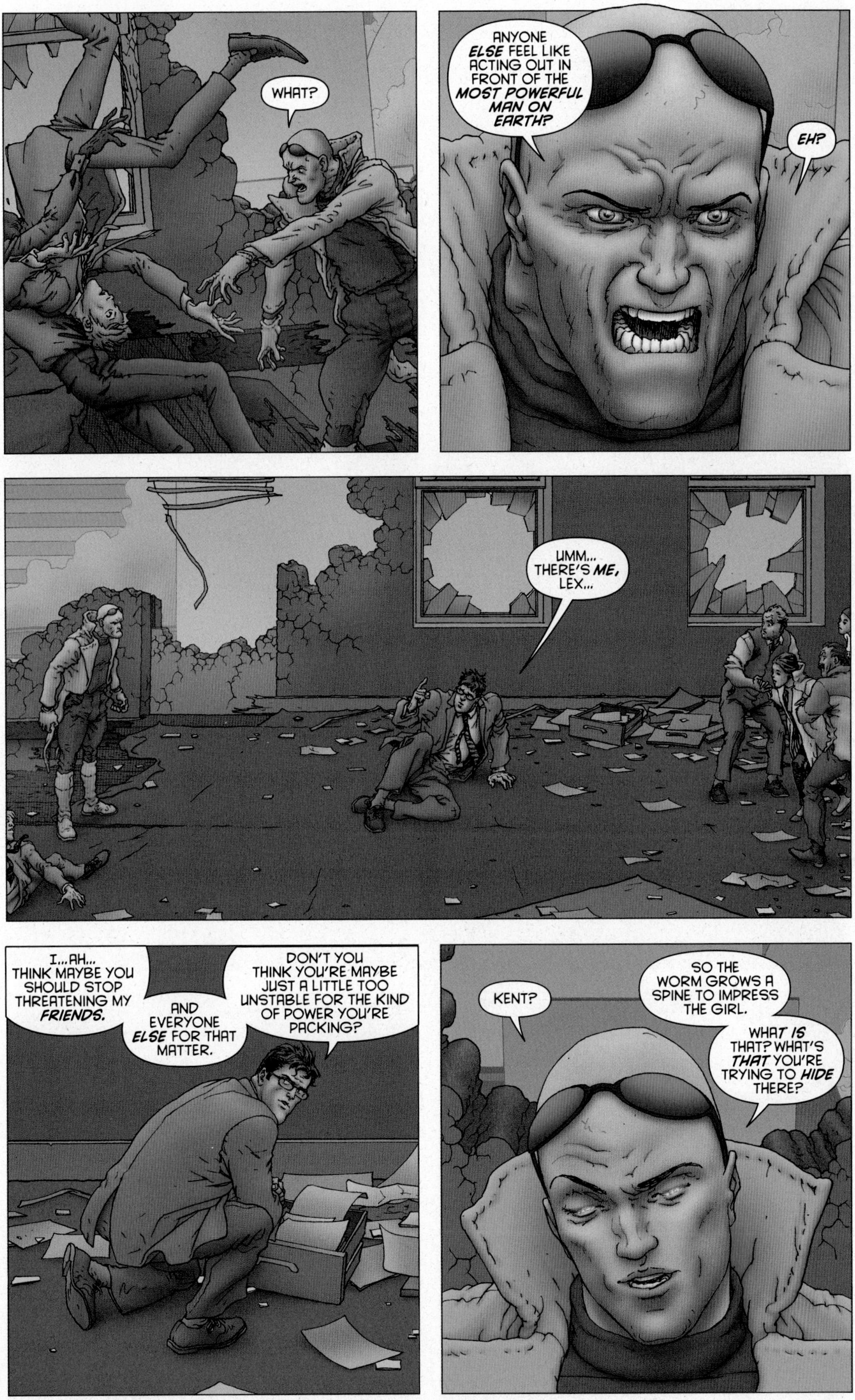
WHAT?
ANYONE ELSE FEEL LIKE ACTING OUT IN FRONT OF THE MOST POWERFUL MAN ON EARTH?
EH?
UMM... THERE'S ME, LEX...
I...AH... THINK MAYBE YOU SHOULD STOP THREATENING MY FRIENDS.
AND EVERYONE ELSE FOR THAT MATTER.
DON'T YOU THINK YOU'RE MAYBE JUST A LITTLE TOO UNSTABLE FOR THE KIND OF POWER YOU'RE PACKING?
KENT?
SO THE WORM GROWS A SPINE TO IMPRESS THE GIRL.
WHAT IS THAT? WHAT'S THAT YOU'RE TRYING TO HIDE THERE?

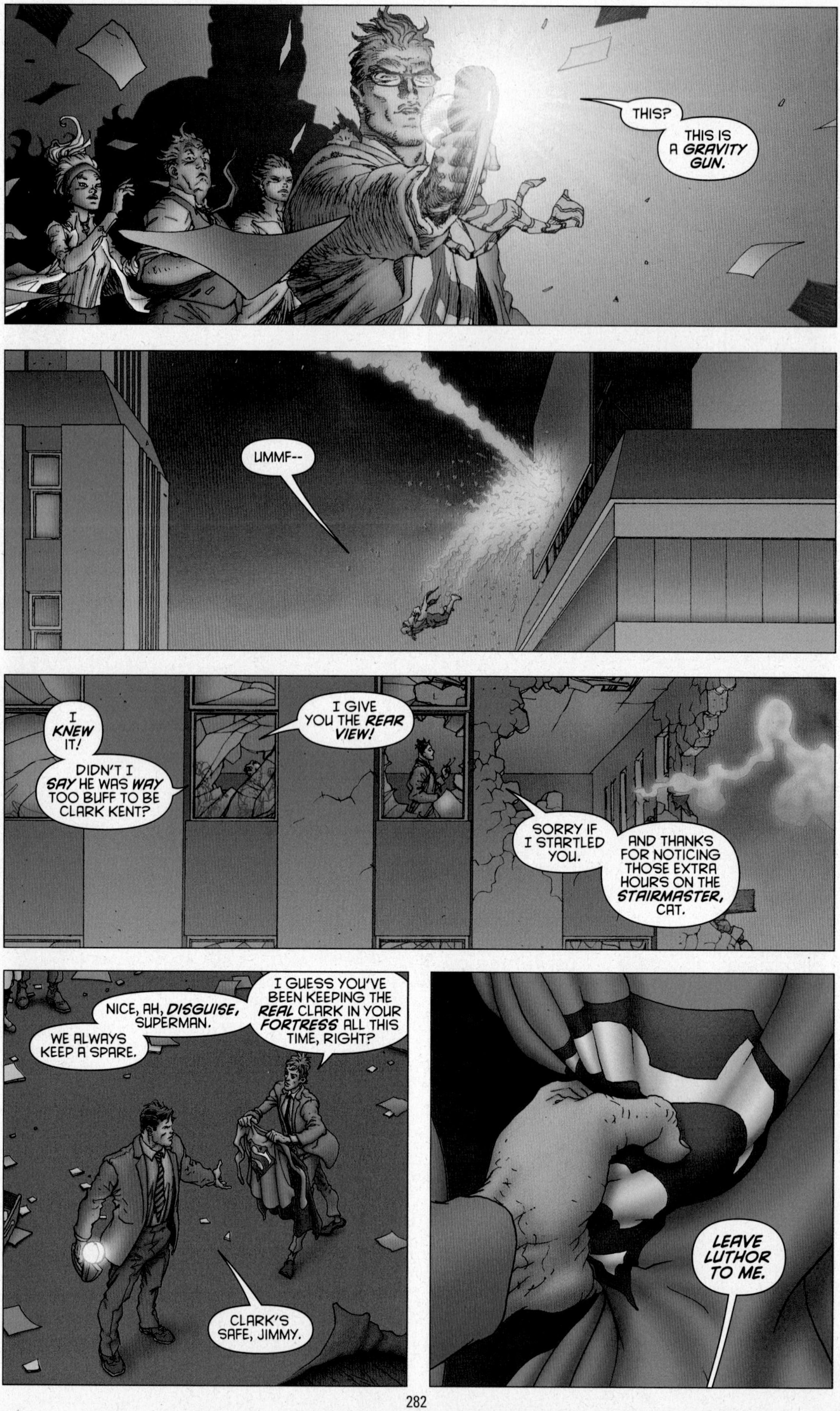
THIS?
THIS IS A GRAVITY GUN.
UMMF--
I KNEW IT!
DIDN'T I SAY HE WAS WAY TOO BUFF TO BE CLARK KENT?
I GIVE YOU THE REAR VIEW!
SORRY IF I STARTLED YOU.
AND THANKS FOR NOTICING THOSE EXTRA HOURS ON THE STAIRMASTER, CAT.
NICE, AH, DISGUISE, SUPERMAN.
WE ALWAYS KEEP A SPARE.
I GUESS YOU'VE BEEN KEEPING THE REAL CLARK IN YOUR FORTRESS ALL THIS TIME, RIGHT?
CLARK'S SAFE, JIMMY.
LEAVE LUTHOR TO ME.

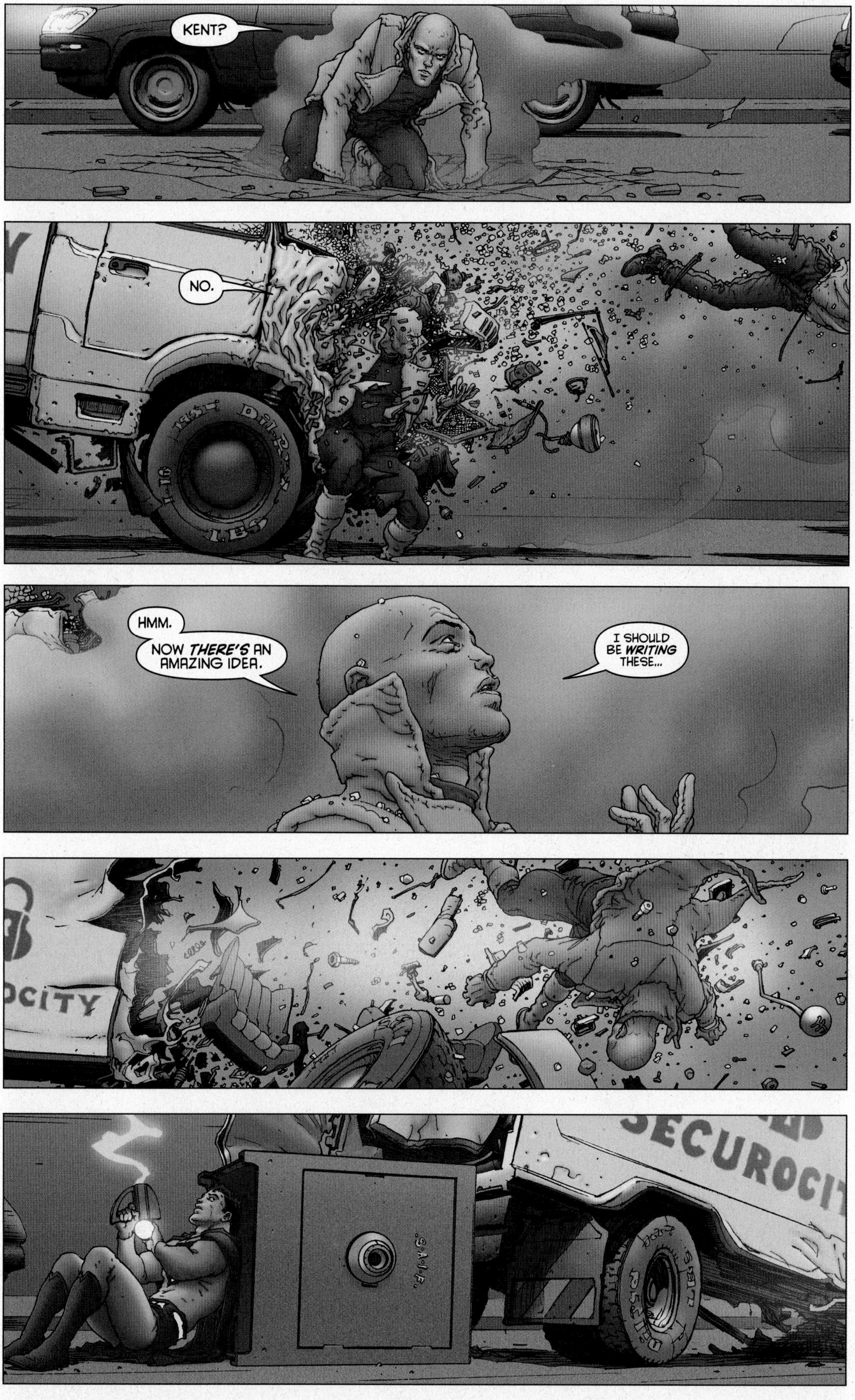
KENT?
NO.
HMM. NOW *THERE'S* AN AMAZING IDEA.
I SHOULD BE *WRITING* THESE...
SECUROCIT

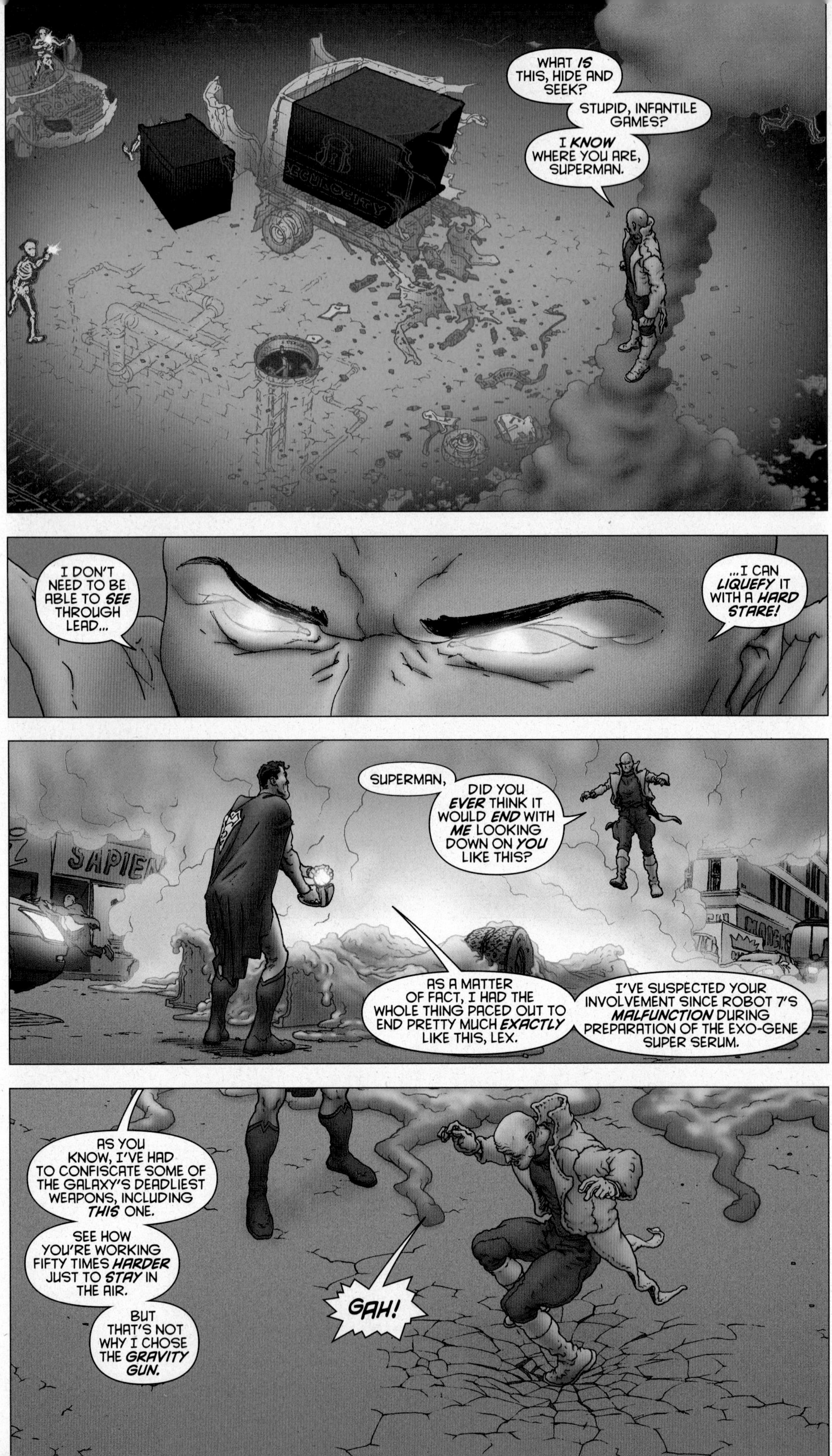

WHAT *IS* THIS, HIDE AND SEEK?
STUPID, INFANTILE GAMES?
I *KNOW* WHERE YOU ARE, SUPERMAN.
I DON'T NEED TO BE ABLE TO *SEE* THROUGH LEAD...
...I CAN *LIQUEFY* IT WITH A *HARD STARE!*
SAPIEN
SUPERMAN,
DID YOU *EVER* THINK IT WOULD *END* WITH *ME* LOOKING DOWN ON *YOU* LIKE THIS?
AS A MATTER OF FACT, I HAD THE WHOLE THING PACED OUT TO END PRETTY MUCH *EXACTLY* LIKE THIS, LEX.
I'VE SUSPECTED YOUR INVOLVEMENT SINCE ROBOT 7'S *MALFUNCTION* DURING PREPARATION OF THE EXO-GENE SUPER SERUM.
AS YOU KNOW, I'VE HAD TO CONFISCATE SOME OF THE GALAXY'S DEADLIEST WEAPONS, INCLUDING *THIS* ONE.
SEE HOW YOU'RE WORKING FIFTY TIMES *HARDER* JUST TO *STAY* IN THE AIR.
BUT THAT'S NOT WHY I CHOSE THE *GRAVITY GUN.*
GAH!

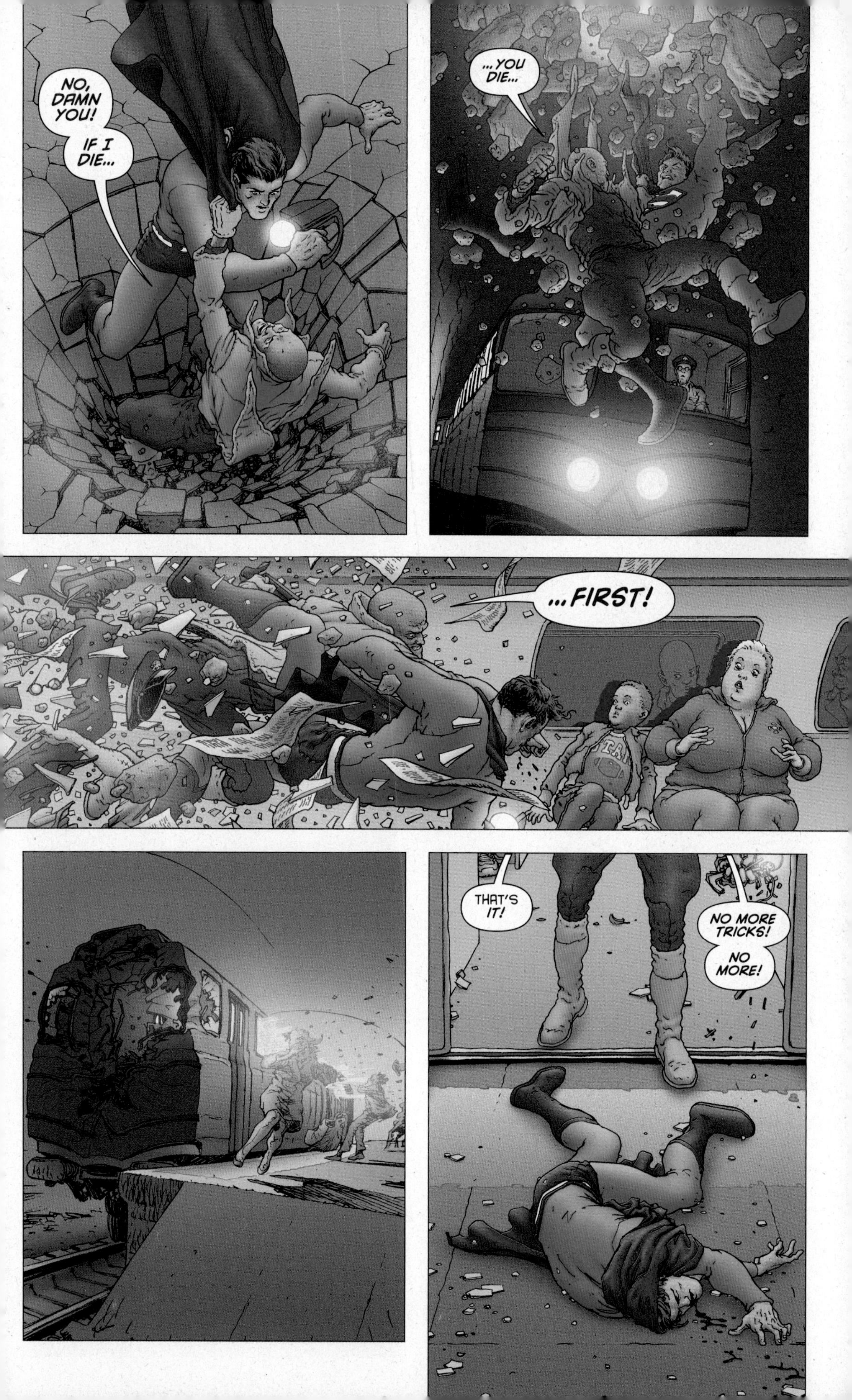
NO, DAMN YOU!
IF I DIE...
...YOU DIE...
...FIRST!
THAT'S IT!
NO MORE TRICKS!
NO MORE!

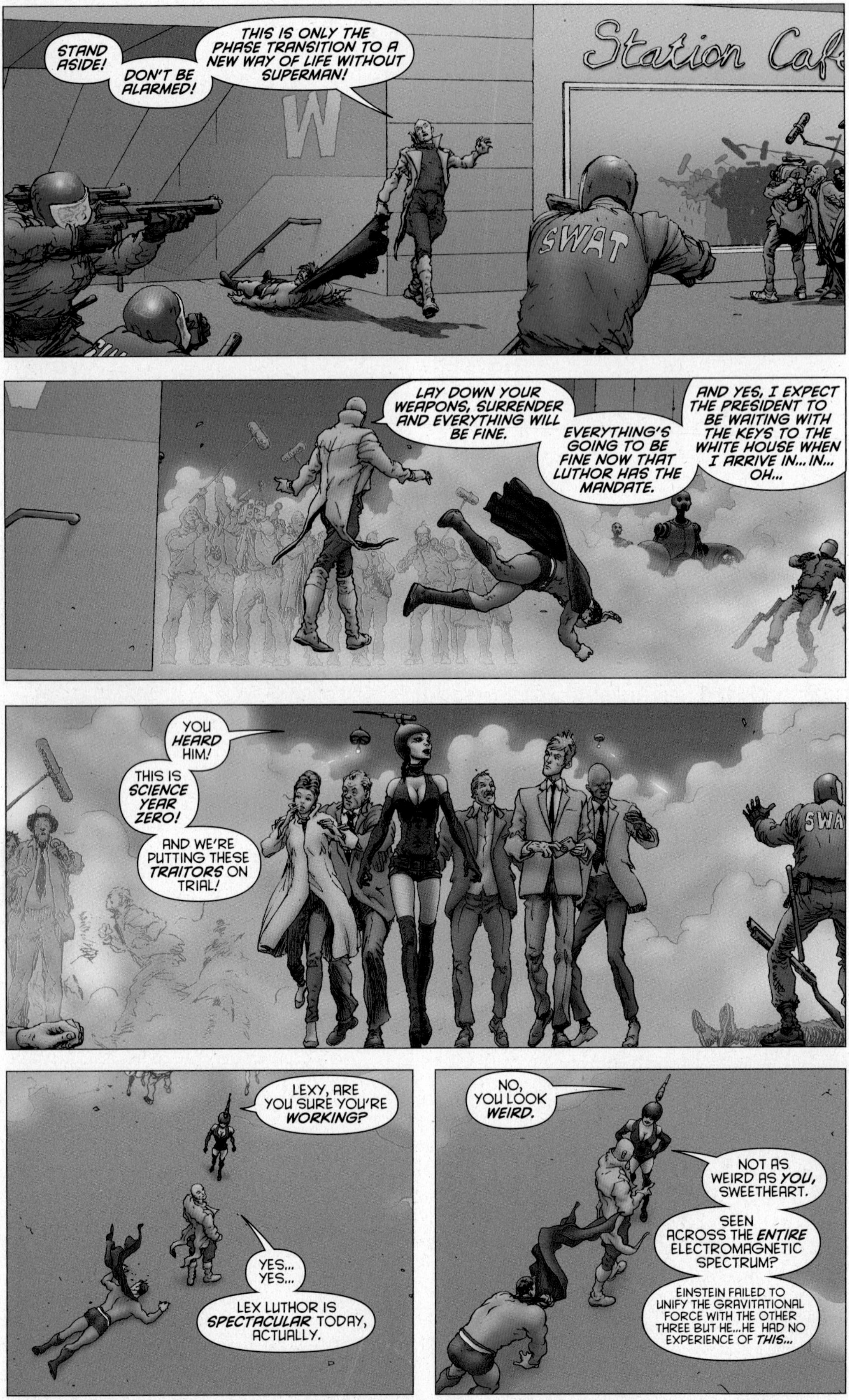
Station Cafe
STAND ASIDE!
DON'T BE ALARMED!
THIS IS ONLY THE PHASE TRANSITION TO A NEW WAY OF LIFE WITHOUT SUPERMAN!
W
SWAT
LAY DOWN YOUR WEAPONS, SURRENDER AND EVERYTHING WILL BE FINE.
EVERYTHING'S GOING TO BE FINE NOW THAT LUTHOR HAS THE MANDATE.
AND YES, I EXPECT THE PRESIDENT TO BE WAITING WITH THE KEYS TO THE WHITE HOUSE WHEN I ARRIVE IN... IN... OH...
YOU HEARD HIM!
THIS IS SCIENCE YEAR ZERO!
AND WE'RE PUTTING THESE TRAITORS ON TRIAL!
SWAT
LEXY, ARE YOU SURE YOU'RE WORKING?
YES... YES...
LEX LUTHOR IS SPECTACULAR TODAY, ACTUALLY.
NO, YOU LOOK WEIRD.
NOT AS WEIRD AS YOU, SWEETHEART.
SEEN ACROSS THE ENTIRE ELECTROMAGNETIC SPECTRUM?
EINSTEIN FAILED TO UNIFY THE GRAVITATIONAL FORCE WITH THE OTHER THREE BUT HE...HE HAD NO EXPERIENCE OF THIS...

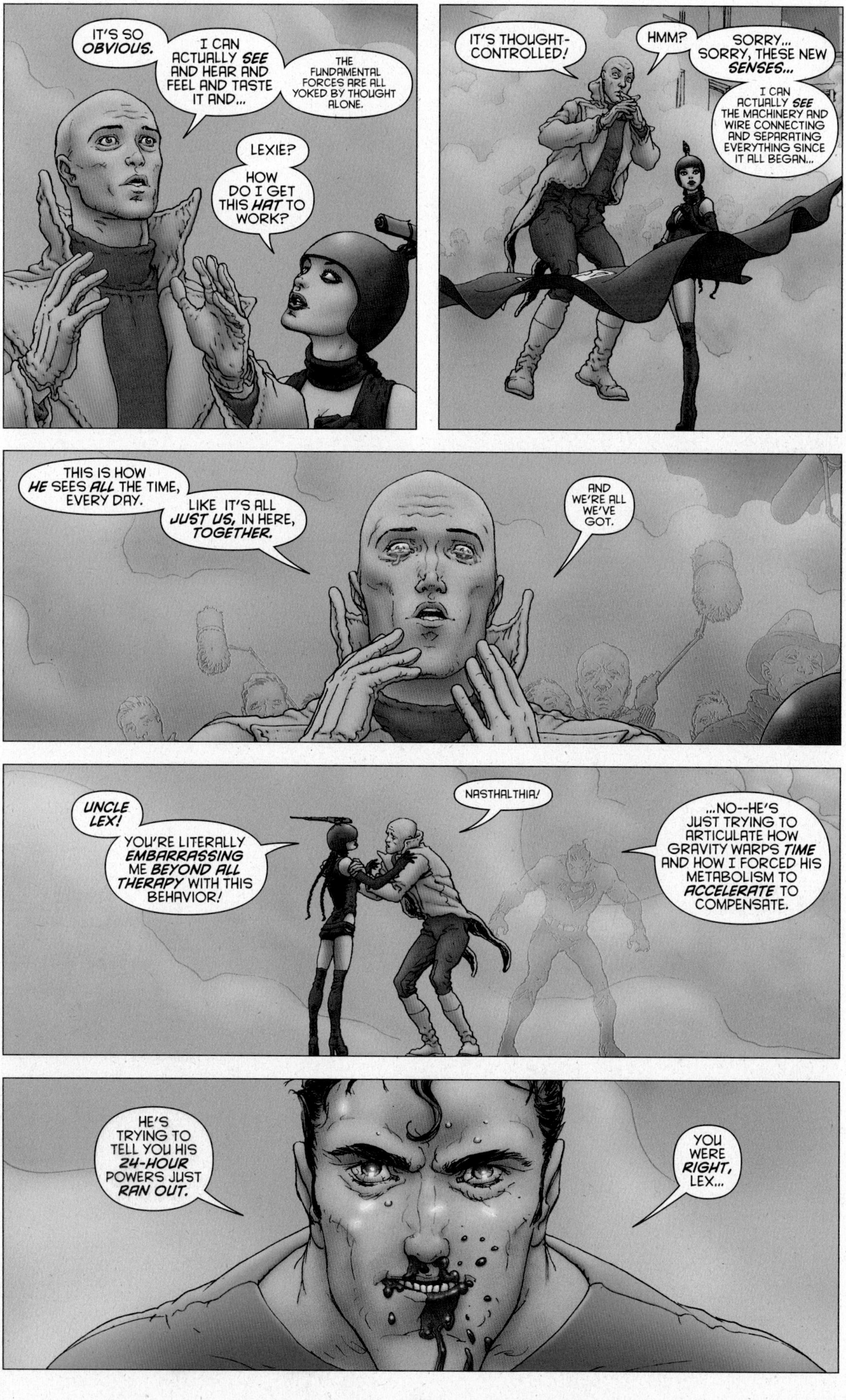
IT'S SO OBVIOUS.
I CAN ACTUALLY SEE AND HEAR AND FEEL AND TASTE IT AND...
THE FUNDAMENTAL FORCES ARE ALL YOKED BY THOUGHT ALONE.
LEXIE?
HOW DO I GET THIS HAT TO WORK?
IT'S THOUGHT-CONTROLLED!
HMM?
SORRY... SORRY, THESE NEW SENSES...
I CAN ACTUALLY SEE THE MACHINERY AND WIRE CONNECTING AND SEPARATING EVERYTHING SINCE IT ALL BEGAN...
THIS IS HOW HE SEES ALL THE TIME, EVERY DAY.
LIKE IT'S ALL JUST US, IN HERE, TOGETHER.
AND WE'RE ALL WE'VE GOT.
UNCLE LEX!
YOU'RE LITERALLY EMBARRASSING ME BEYOND ALL THERAPY WITH THIS BEHAVIOR!
NASTHALTHIA!
...NO--HE'S JUST TRYING TO ARTICULATE HOW GRAVITY WARPS TIME AND HOW I FORCED HIS METABOLISM TO ACCELERATE TO COMPENSATE.
HE'S TRYING TO TELL YOU HIS 24-HOUR POWERS JUST RAN OUT.
YOU WERE RIGHT, LEX...

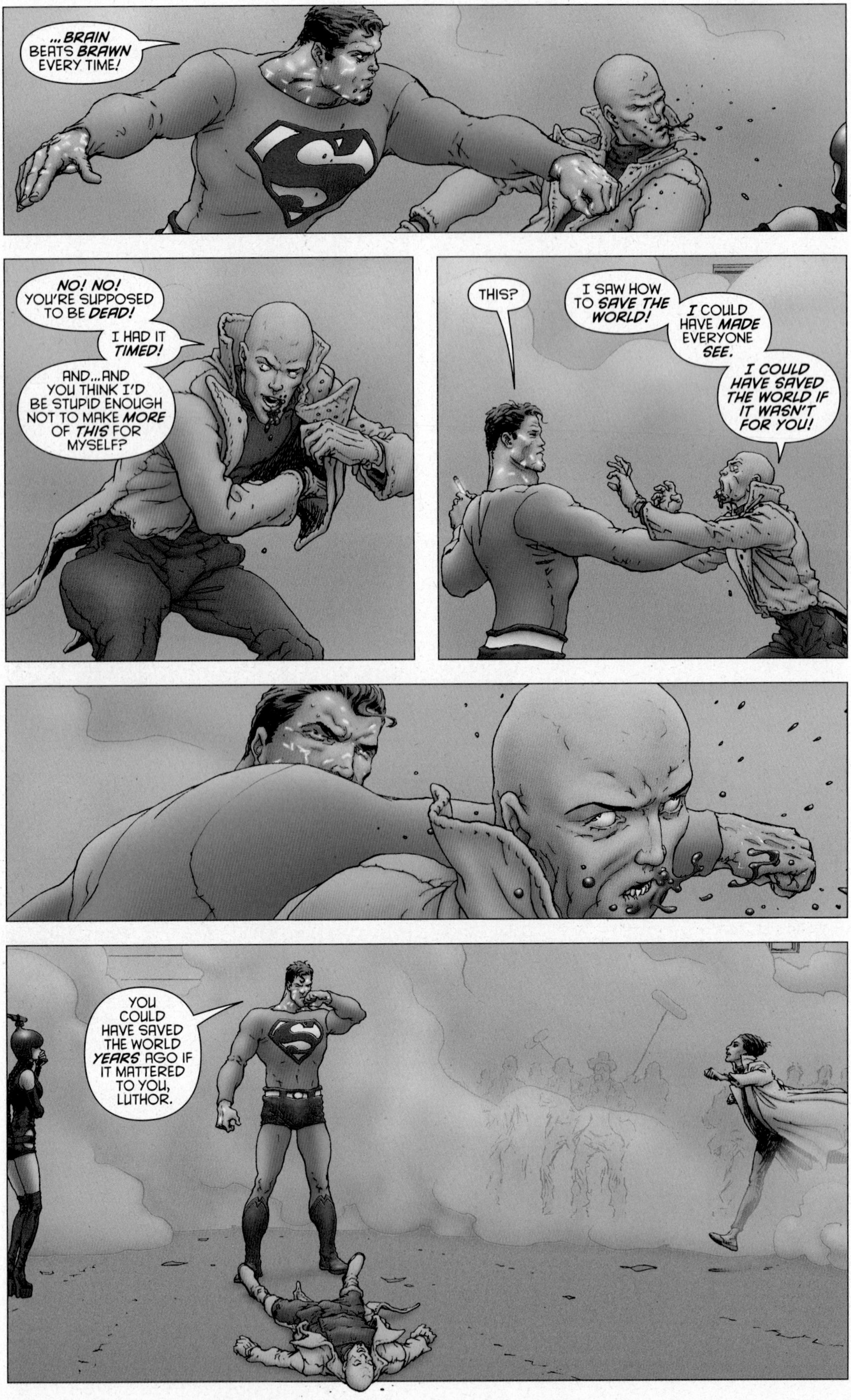
...BRAIN BEATS BRAWN EVERY TIME!
NO! NO! YOU'RE SUPPOSED TO BE DEAD!
I HAD IT TIMED!
AND...AND YOU THINK I'D BE STUPID ENOUGH NOT TO MAKE MORE OF THIS FOR MYSELF?
THIS?
I SAW HOW TO SAVE THE WORLD!
I COULD HAVE MADE EVERYONE SEE.
I COULD HAVE SAVED THE WORLD IF IT WASN'T FOR YOU!
YOU COULD HAVE SAVED THE WORLD YEARS AGO IF IT MATTERED TO YOU, LUTHOR.

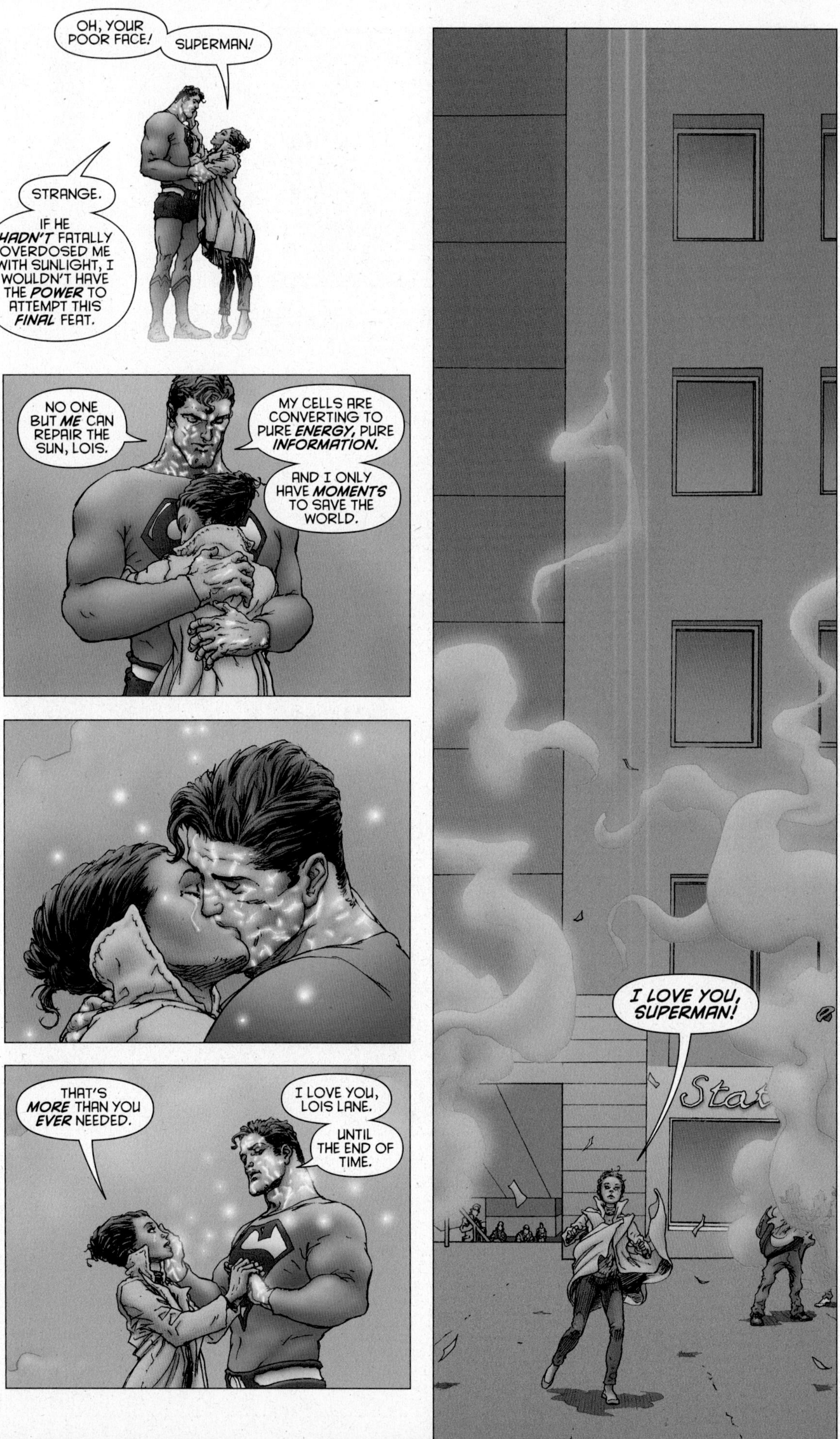
OH, YOUR POOR FACE!
SUPERMAN!
STRANGE.
IF HE HADN'T FATALLY OVERDOSED ME WITH SUNLIGHT, I WOULDN'T HAVE THE POWER TO ATTEMPT THIS FINAL FEAT.
NO ONE BUT ME CAN REPAIR THE SUN, LOIS.
MY CELLS ARE CONVERTING TO PURE ENERGY, PURE INFORMATION.
AND I ONLY HAVE MOMENTS TO SAVE THE WORLD.
THAT'S MORE THAN YOU EVER NEEDED.
I LOVE YOU, LOIS LANE.
UNTIL THE END OF TIME.
I LOVE YOU, SUPERMAN!

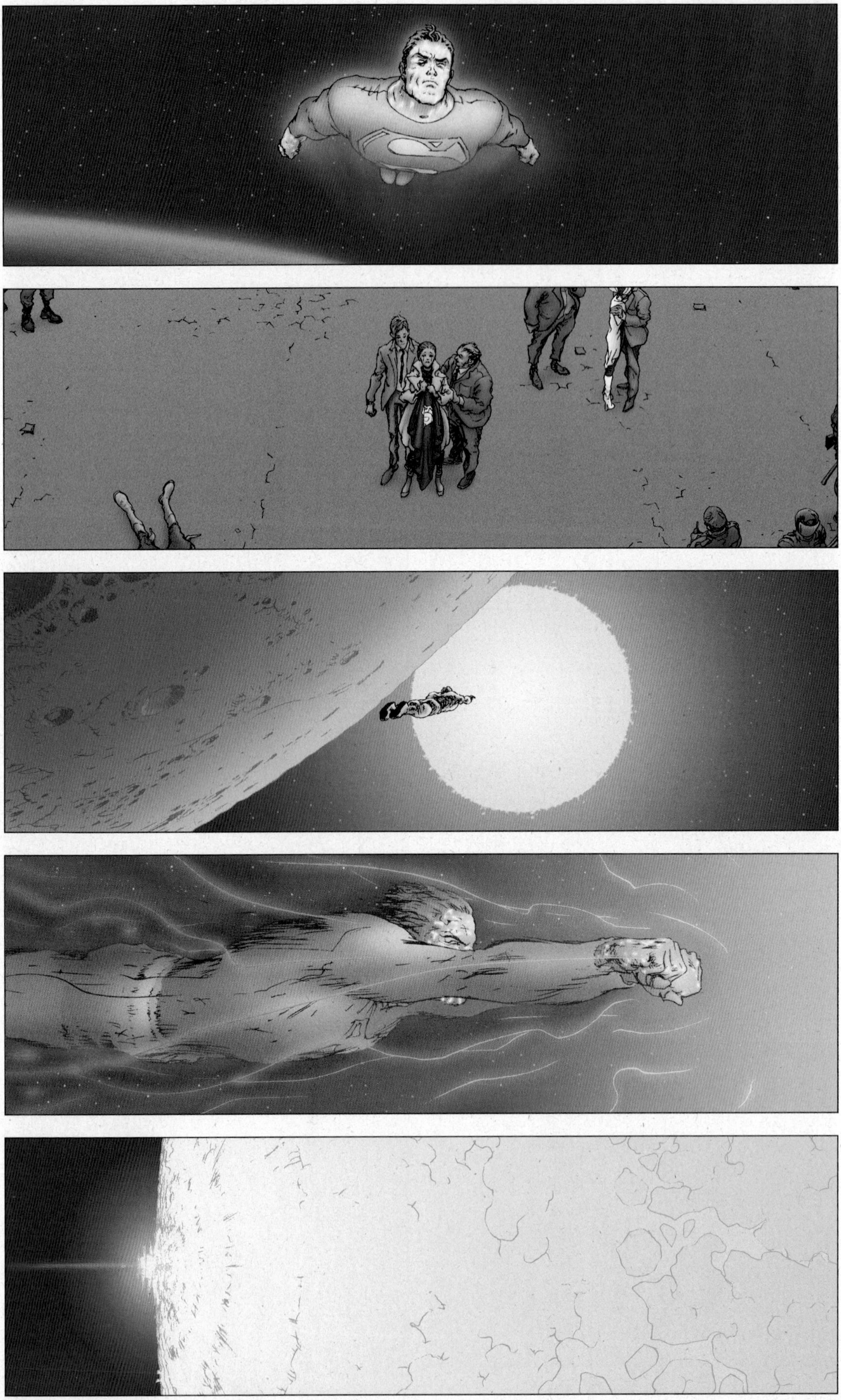

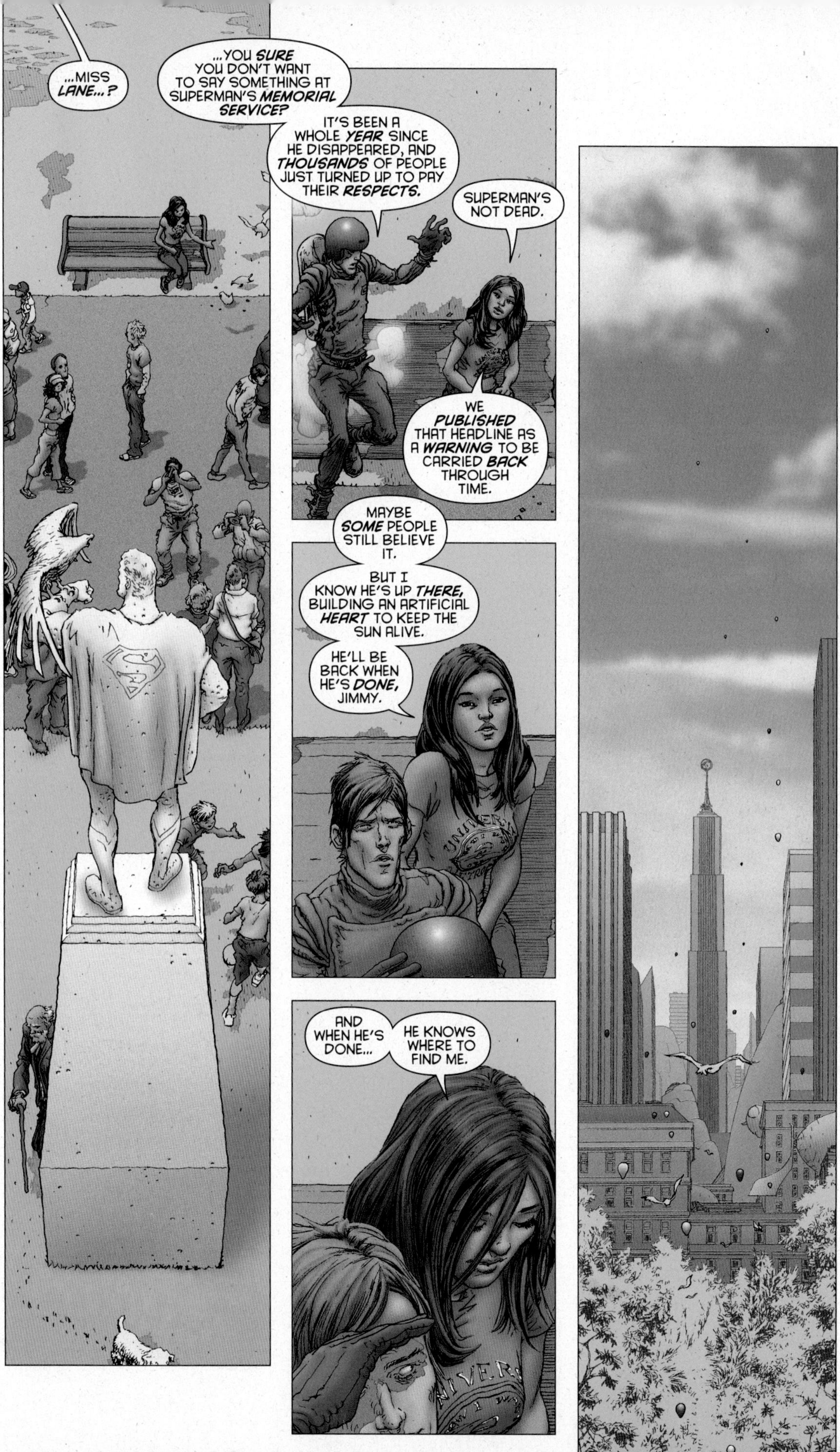

...MISS LANE...?
...YOU SURE YOU DON'T WANT TO SAY SOMETHING AT SUPERMAN'S MEMORIAL SERVICE?
IT'S BEEN A WHOLE YEAR SINCE HE DISAPPEARED, AND THOUSANDS OF PEOPLE JUST TURNED UP TO PAY THEIR RESPECTS.
SUPERMAN'S NOT DEAD.
WE PUBLISHED THAT HEADLINE AS A WARNING TO BE CARRIED BACK THROUGH TIME.
MAYBE SOME PEOPLE STILL BELIEVE IT.
BUT I KNOW HE'S UP THERE, BUILDING AN ARTIFICIAL HEART TO KEEP THE SUN ALIVE.
HE'LL BE BACK WHEN HE'S DONE, JIMMY.
AND WHEN HE'S DONE...
HE KNOWS WHERE TO FIND ME.

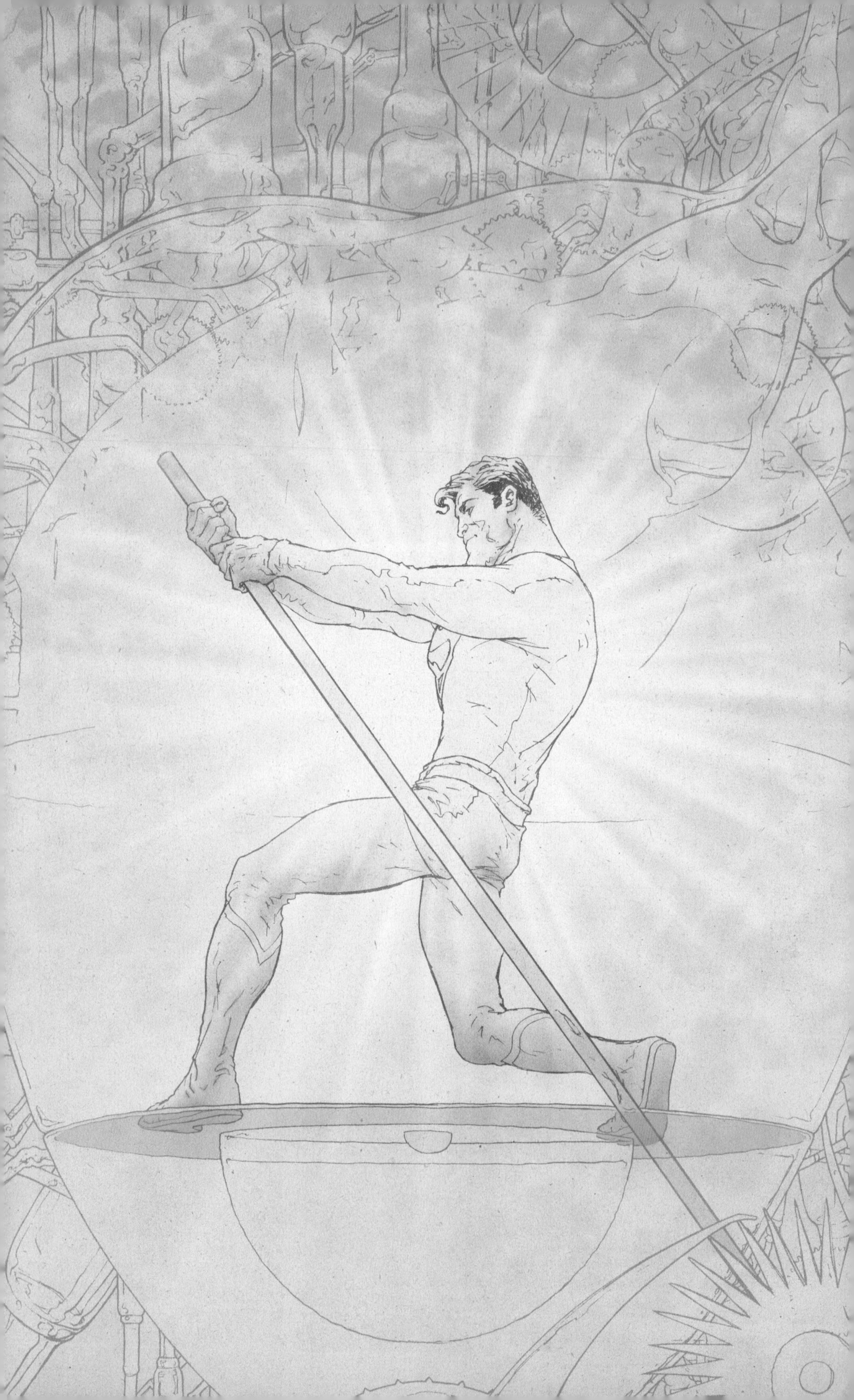

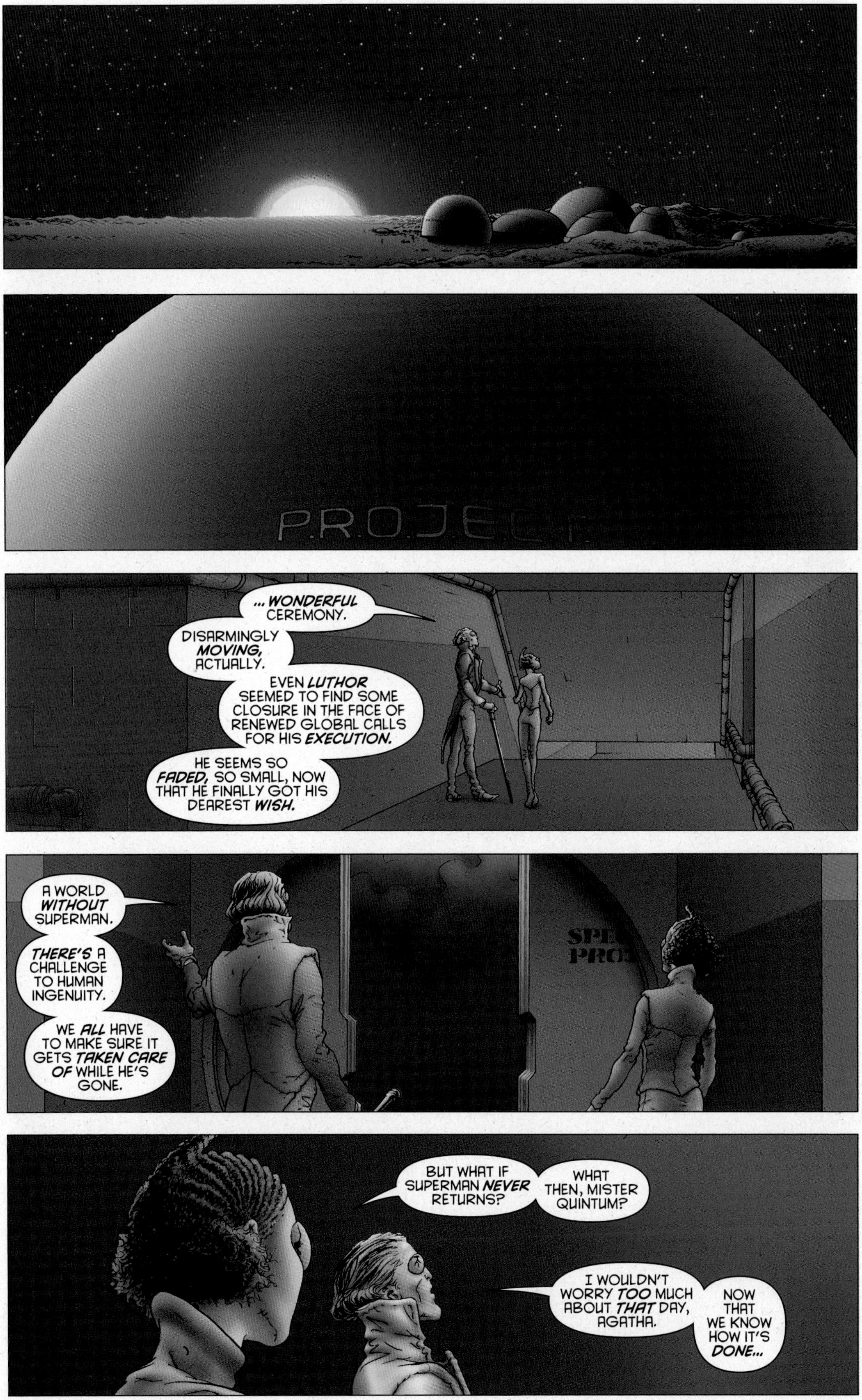
P.R.O.J.E.C.T.
...WONDERFUL CEREMONY.
DISARMINGLY MOVING, ACTUALLY.
EVEN LUTHOR SEEMED TO FIND SOME CLOSURE IN THE FACE OF RENEWED GLOBAL CALLS FOR HIS EXECUTION.
HE SEEMS SO FADED, SO SMALL, NOW THAT HE FINALLY GOT HIS DEAREST WISH.
A WORLD WITHOUT SUPERMAN.
THERE'S A CHALLENGE TO HUMAN INGENUITY.
WE ALL HAVE TO MAKE SURE IT GETS TAKEN CARE OF WHILE HE'S GONE.
BUT WHAT IF SUPERMAN NEVER RETURNS?
WHAT THEN, MISTER QUINTUM?
I WOULDN'T WORRY TOO MUCH ABOUT THAT DAY, AGATHA.
NOW THAT WE KNOW HOW IT'S DONE...

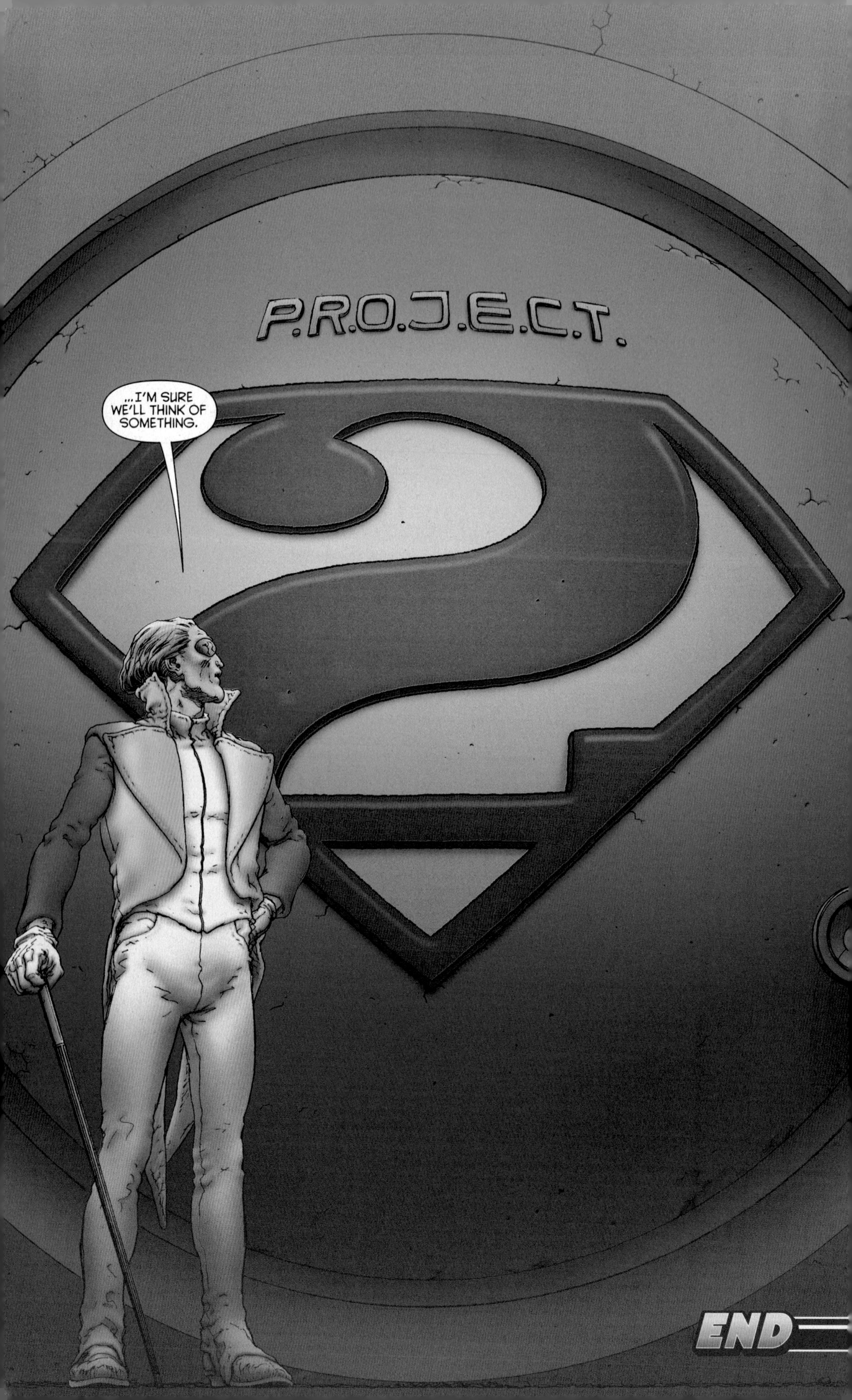
P.R.O.J.E.C.T.
...I'M SURE WE'LL THINK OF SOMETHING.
END

ALL-STAR SUPERMAN

Words by Grant Morrison *Art by* Frank Quitely

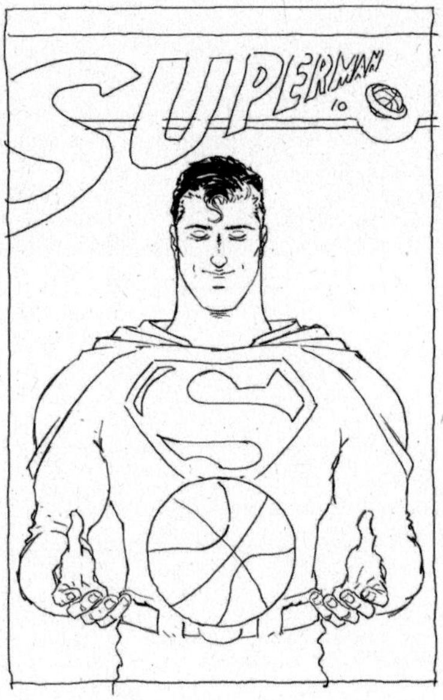
SUPERMAN
10

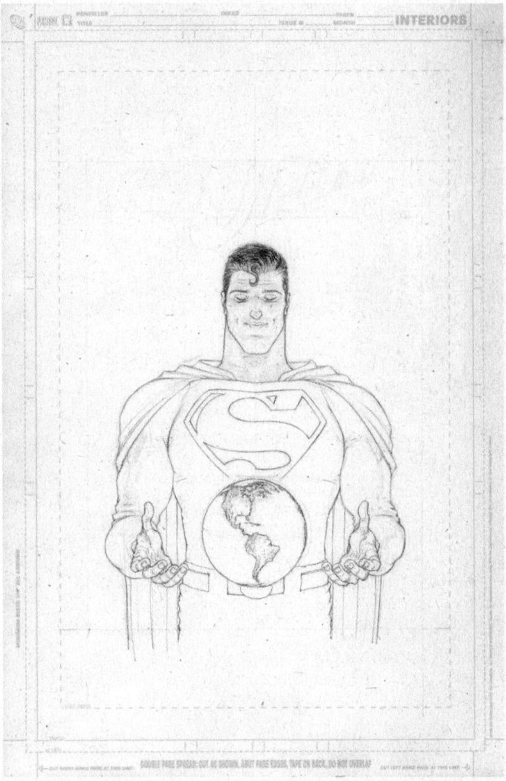
INTERIORS

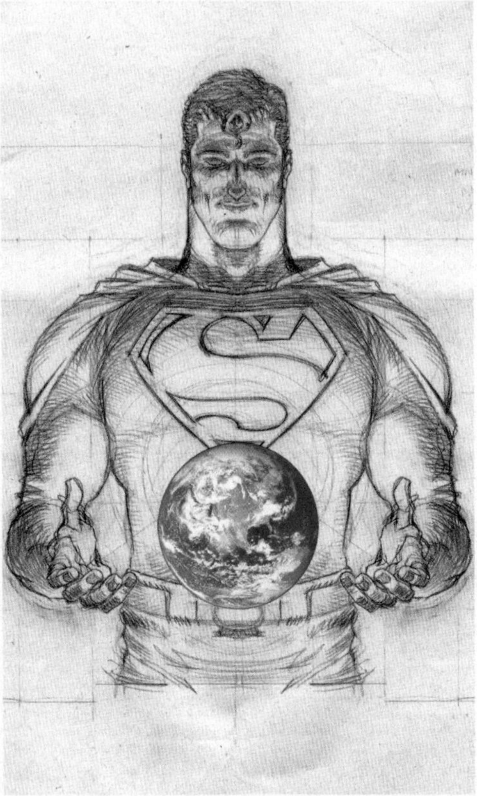

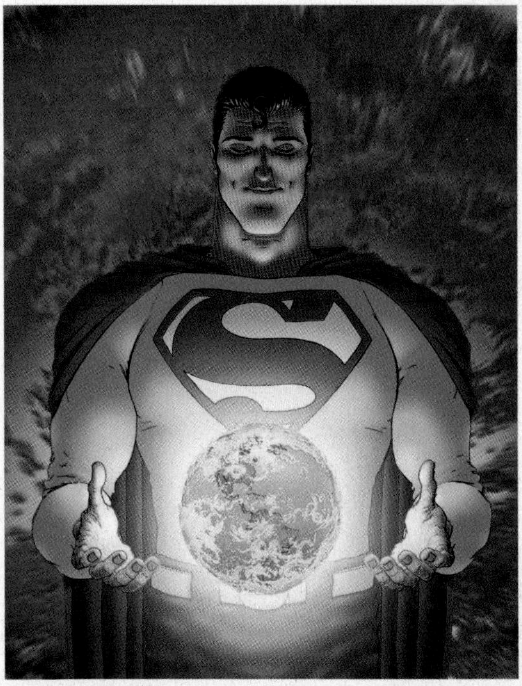

The title ALL-STAR SUPERMAN was DC Co-Publisher Dan DiDio's idea. ALL-STAR COMICS was published by DC in 1940 and introduced to the world the first great superheroine, Wonder Woman, as well as the prototype super-team, The Justice Society of America. Dan revived the All-Star trademark for a play-on-words imprint, established as a playground for "big name" comic book creators to cut loose on non-continuity, "definitive" and personal visions of DC's top characters.

In the end, only two All-Star books were published; this one and the brilliant, controversial ALL-STAR BATMAN & ROBIN, THE BOY WONDER by Frank Miller and Jim Lee.

And so, ALL-STAR SUPERMAN. Saddled with this slightly odd and archaic title, Quitely and I decided to make it literal and to tell the story of Superman as star, or solar "deity," hence our opening shot of Superman framed by solar flares and the structure of the story which traverses one epic "day" — dipping below the horizon in issue six so that Superman, like all good solar myth heroes, can journey through midwinter's longest night and the upside-down underworld before rising again in issue nine, revitalized.

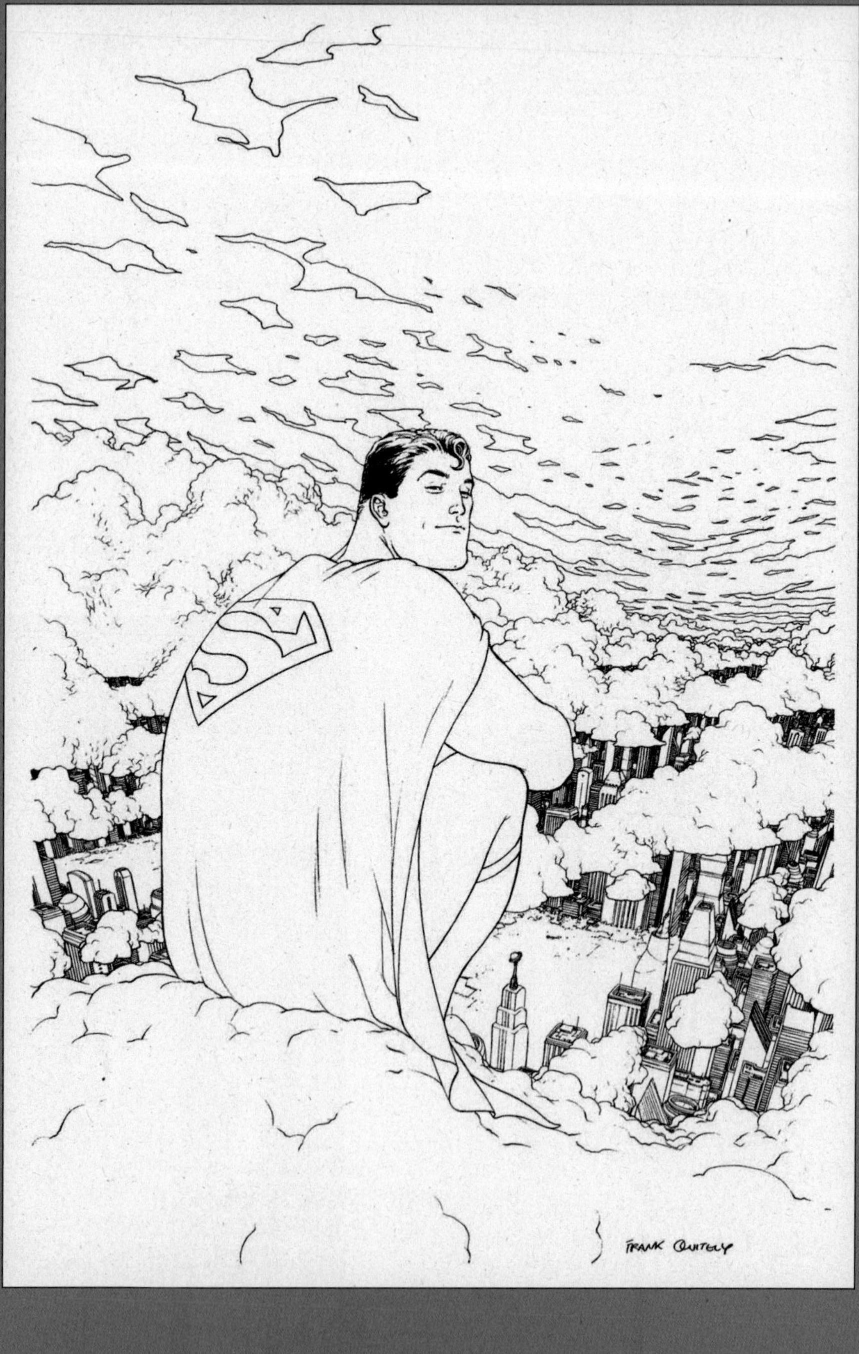
FRANK QUITELY

SUPERMAN

We wanted to present Superman, in this series, as an Enlightenment figure, a Renaissance idea of the ideal man, perfect in mind, body and intention, and I wanted a storytelling style that would reflect that, so we chose a formal approach to layout and storytelling. Some of the original ideas were created for an aborted series entitled SUPERMAN NOW in 1999.

In these primary sketches, you can see a simplified "S" logo. I'd hoped we could do a new Superman insignia that would set the "All-Star Superman" version apart from others and declare our commitment to modernity, but the powers-that-be asked us to stick with the traditional trademark version and we did.

In the end, the idea of the updated logo was developed to a better conclusion and was used as the final image in the book where it was much more powerful and effective than it might have been up front.

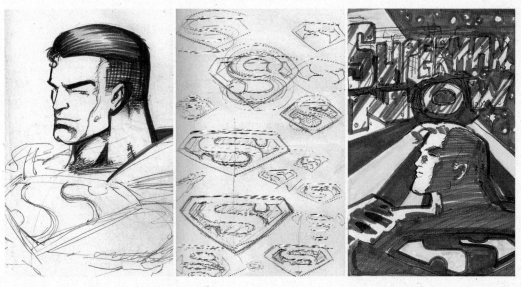

SUPERMAN NOW concept sketches from Grant Morrison's Sketchbook.

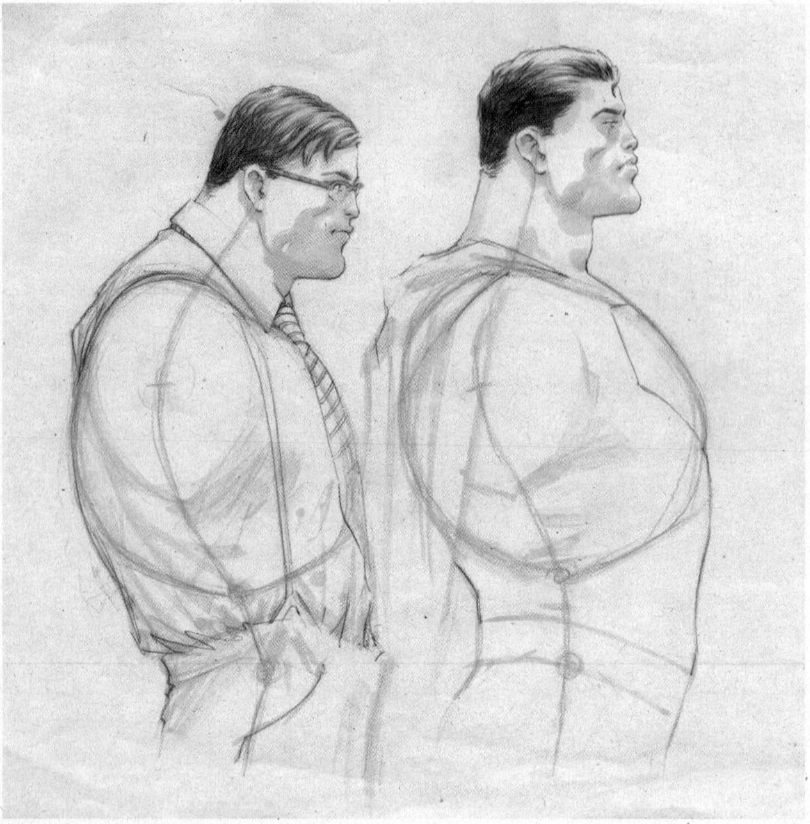
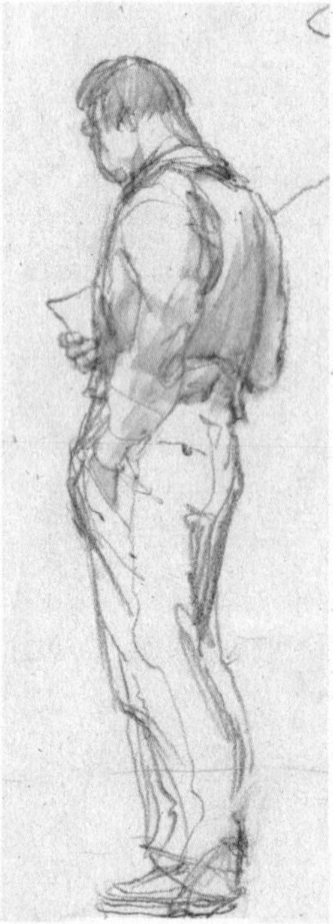
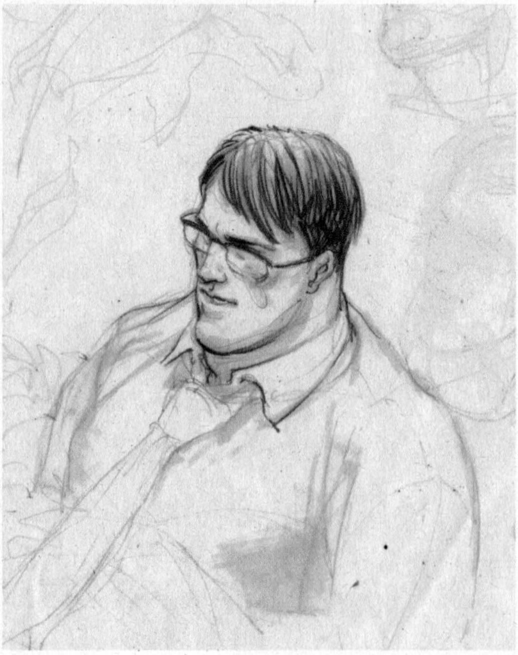
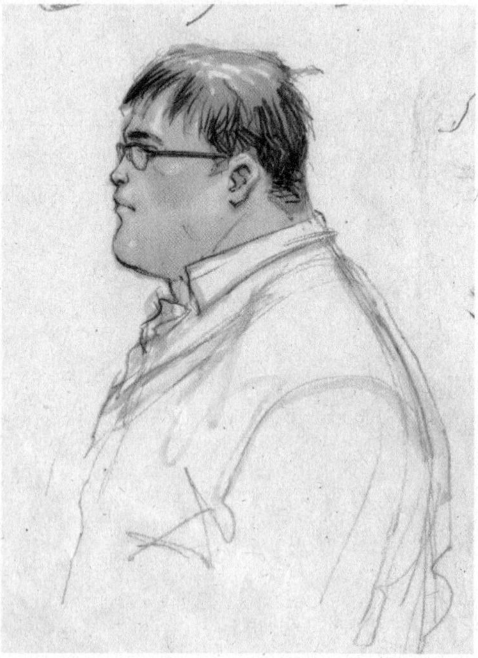

CLARK KENT

It's rare for an artist to really emphasize the difference in physicality between Superman and Kent, but we wanted to make a feature of it. One of my first ideas for Superman was to connect him to his Jewish roots by bringing to All-Star Superman the dramatic, hand-wringing gestures of Yiddish theatre. Frank and I wondered what it might have looked like if Will Eisner had drawn Superman in the 1940s, and from these roots we evolved the contrasting physicality of Kent and Superman.

We wanted his disguise to seem plausible. Generally, Clark Kent is shown as a tall, well-built man whose only real difference from Superman is his slicked-back hair and bottle top glasses.

We decided Superman could release his posture so that his shoulders slumped, his spine curved and his belly stuck out. He could give himself pigeon toes.

Rather than a cowardly, sickly *milquetoast*, we decided instead to make Clark too BIG for his environment. He's playing the part of a hulking farmboy who's used to wide open spaces and can't help bumping into things or tripping over people in the big city.

We also decided that each time Clark did something clumsy, he would actually be saving someone's life. Even as Kent, Superman is never off-duty.

Frank Quitely's mastery of anatomy and body language sold this transformation in a way I'd never seen it before.

LOIS LANE

Lois Lane was an older, wiser amalgamation of all her previous appearances and we really wanted to show why Superman would fall in love with this human woman.

Apart from her obvious beauty, our Lois had to be clever, witty, compassionate, understanding, suspicious, cynical, insulting, courageous and even reckless.

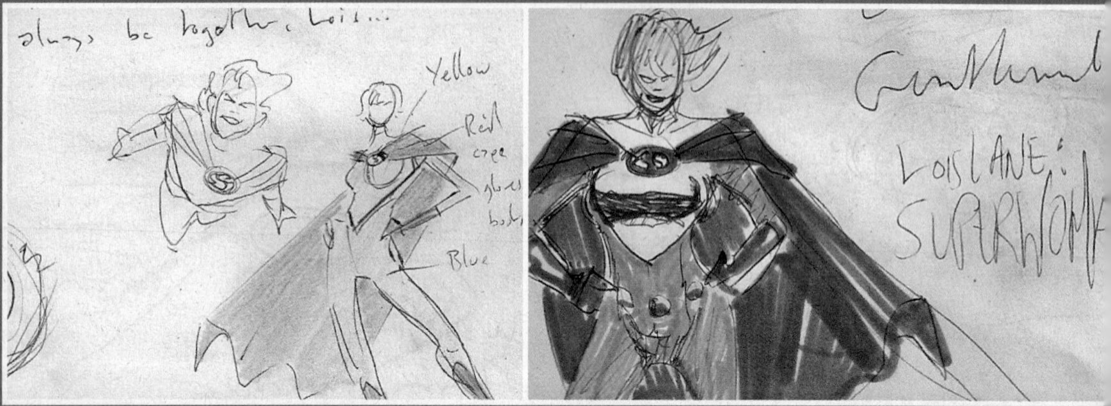
Yellow
Blue
LOIS LANE:
SUPERWOM

Superwoman sketches from Grant Morrison's SUPERMAN NOW sketchbook.

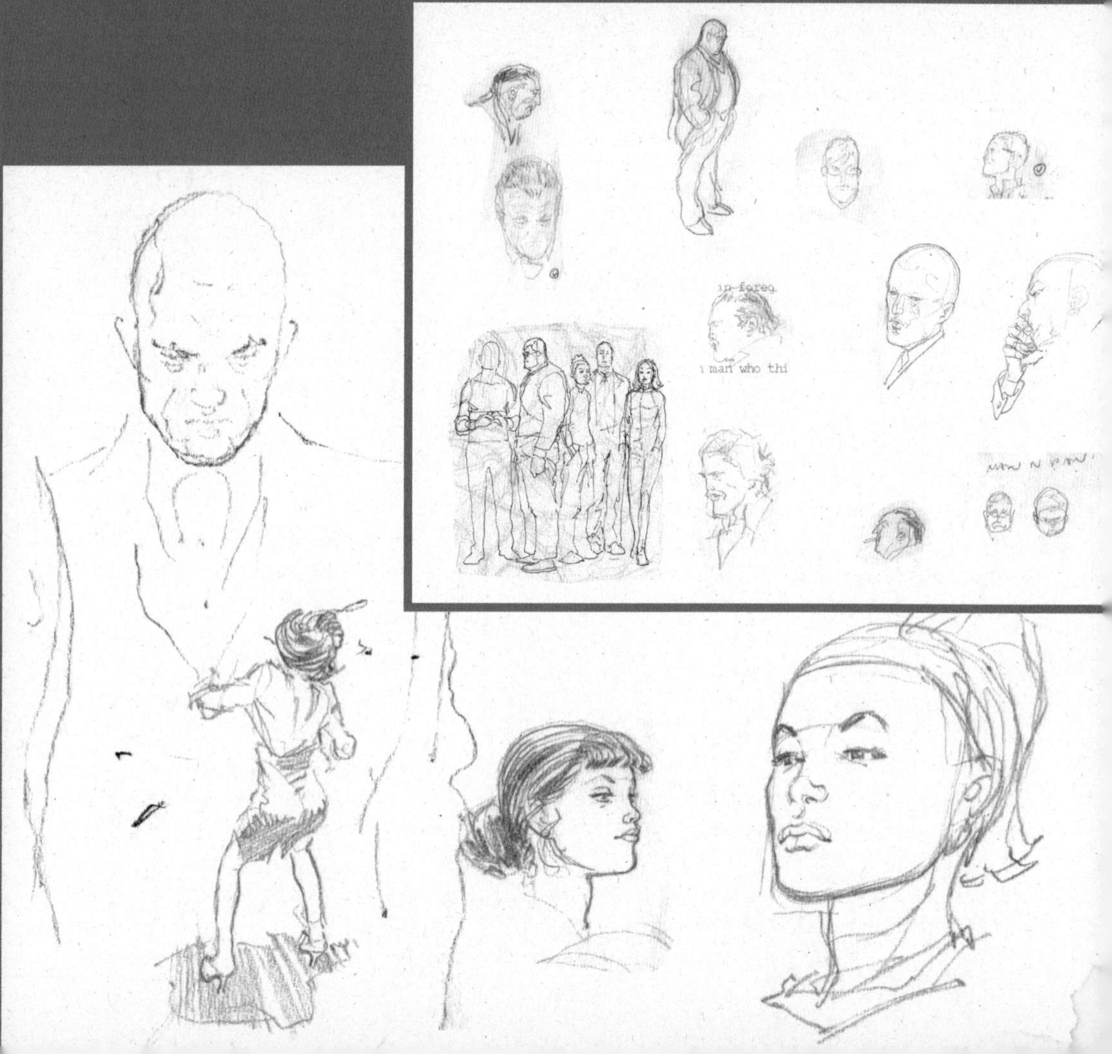

JIMMY OLSEN

Our Jimmy Olsen was a total rethink based on the aspects of Olsen we both liked while playing down the whole wet-behind-the-ears "cub reporter" portrayal, which often cast Jimmy in the role of buffoon.

I borrowed a little from Jack Kirby's "Mr. Action" idea of a more daredevil, pro-active Jimmy, added a little bit of TV comedy character Nathan Barley, some Abercrombie & Fitch preppy style, a dash of Tin-Tin, and a cool Quitely haircut. At the request of the singer Robbie Williams, Frank included the hints of his features that you may still be able to see in these sketches.

Jimmy was renowned for his "disguises" and bizarre transformations (my favorite is the transvestite Olsen epic "Miss Jimmy Olsen" from SUPERMAN'S PAL JIMMY OLSEN #95, in 1966) which gets a nod on the first page of our Jimmy story.

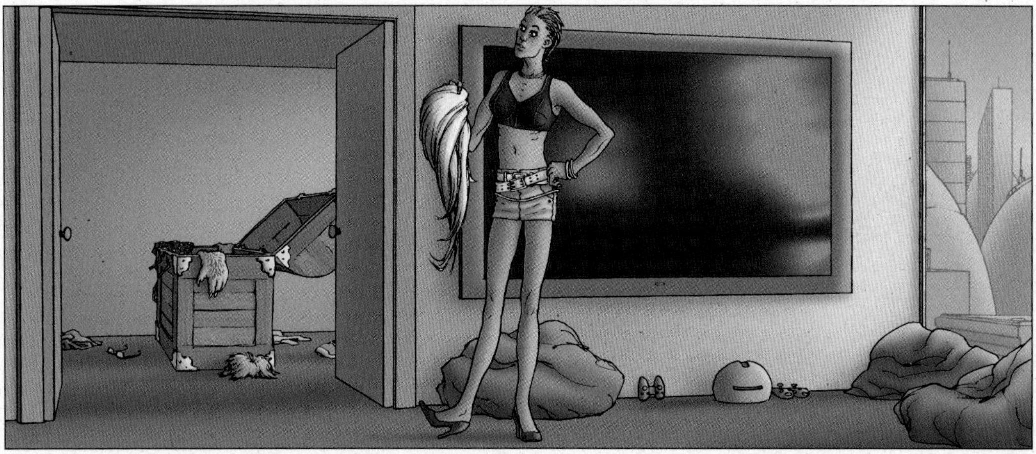

So I wanted to take that aspect of his appeal and make it part of his job.

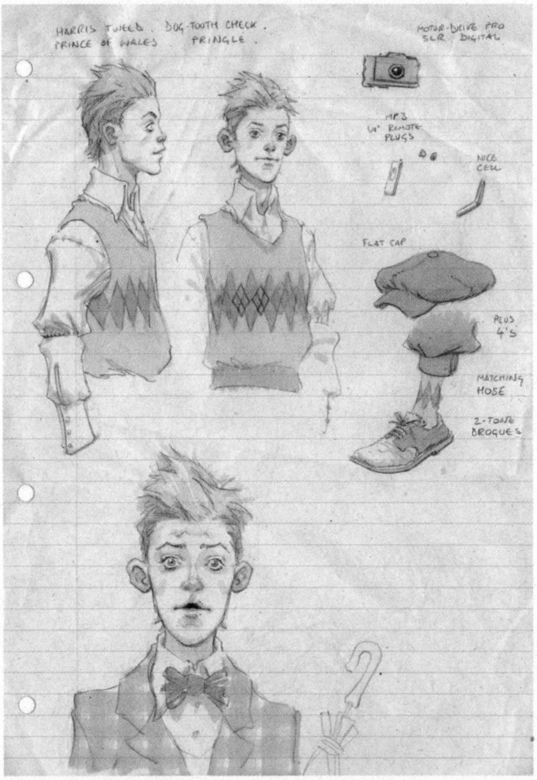
HARRIS TWEED. DOG-TOOTH CHECK.
PRINCE OF WALES. PRINGLE.
MOTOR-DRIVE PRO SLR DIGITAL
MP3
W' REMOTE PLUGS
NICE CELL
FLAT CAP
PLUS 4'S
MATCHING HOSE
2-TONE BROGUES

I don't like victim Jimmy or dumb Jimmy, because those takes on the character don't make any sense in their context. It seemed more interesting to see what a young man would be like who could convincingly be Superman's "pal." Someone whose company a Superman might actually enjoy. That meant making Jimmy a much bigger character: swaggering but disingenuous, innocent yet worldly, enthusiastic but not stupid.

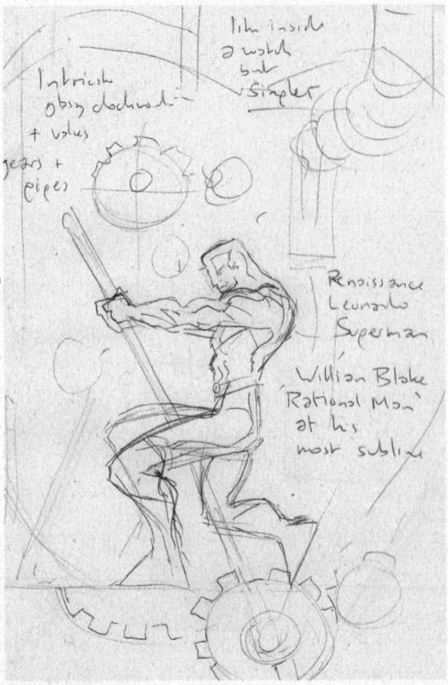
like inside
a watch
but
simpler
Intricate
glassy clockwork
+ valves
gears +
pipes
Renaissance
Leonardo
Superman
William Blake
'Rational Man'
at his
most sublime

Machine from Grant Morrison's sketchbook.

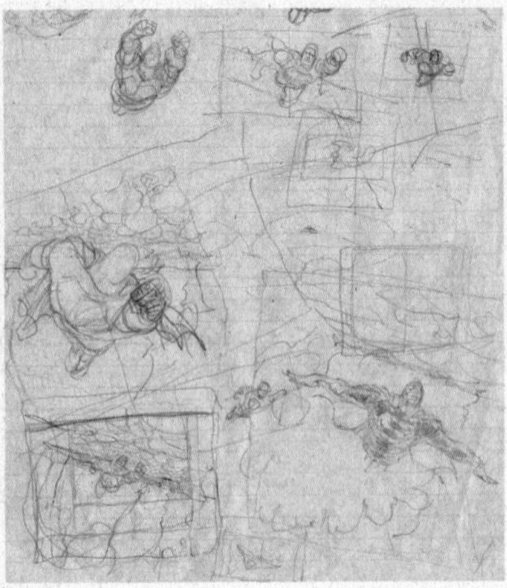

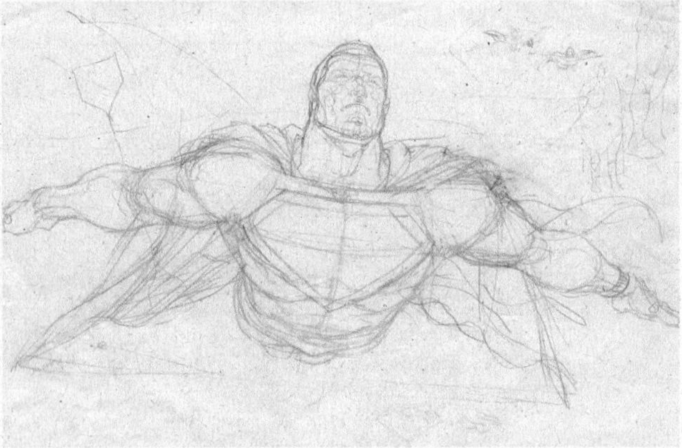

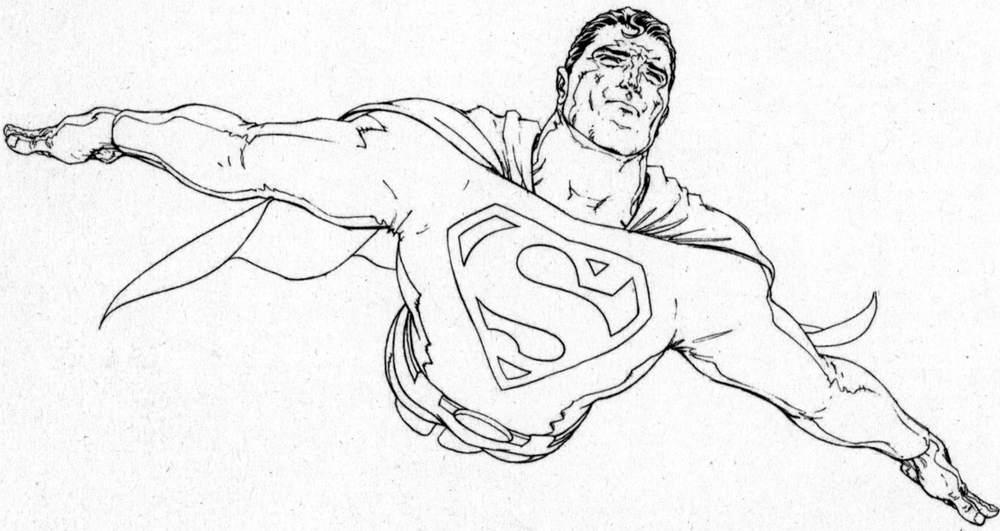

Episode 1

ALTERNATE COVER

Art by NEAL ADAMS and JAMIE GRANT

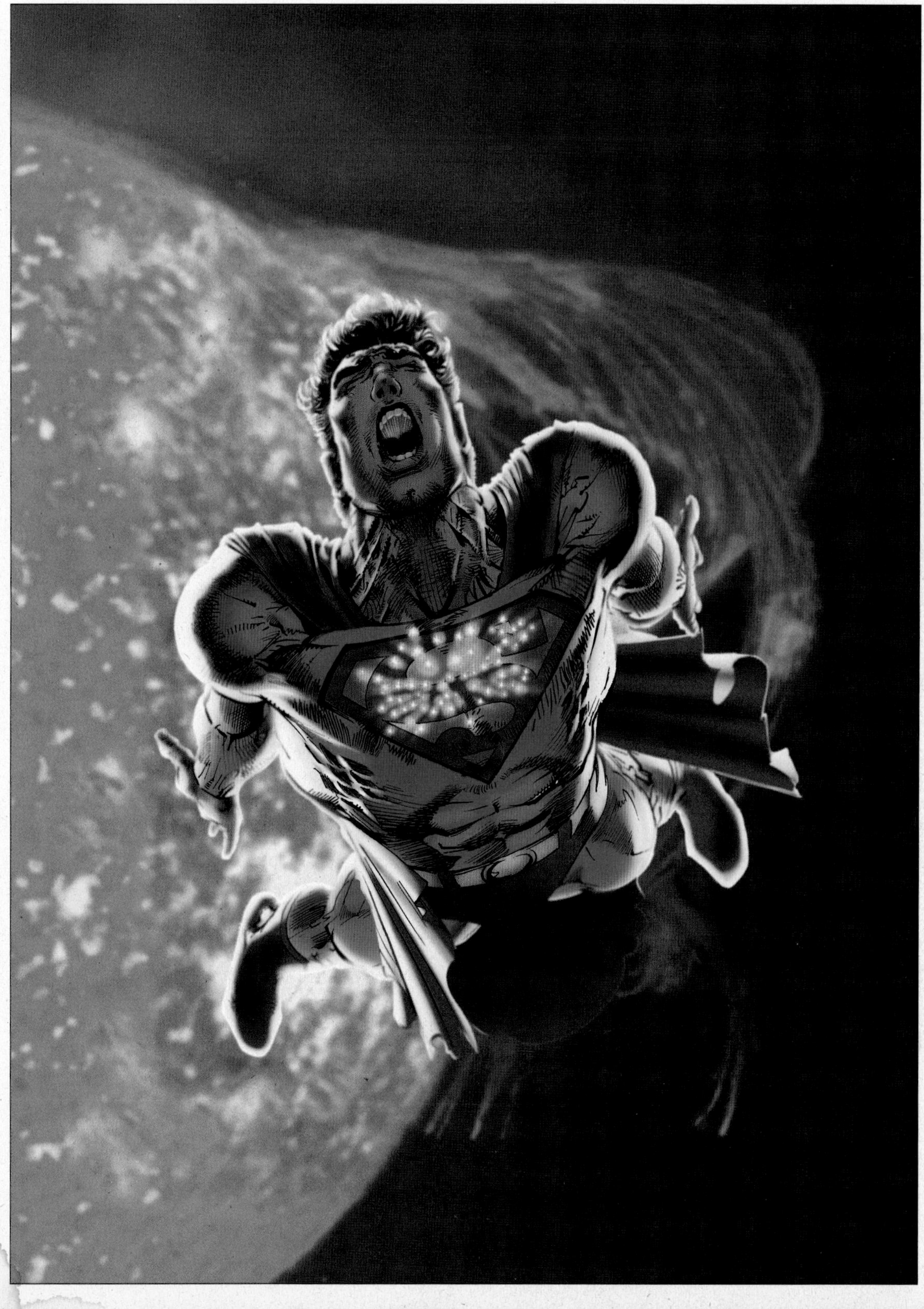

BIOGRAPHIES

GRANT MORRISON

GRANT MORRISON has been working with DC Comics for twenty years, after beginning his American comics career with acclaimed runs on ANIMAL MAN and DOOM PATROL. Since then he has written such best-selling series as JLA, BATMAN and *New X-Men*, as well as such creator-owned titles as THE INVISIBLES, SEAGUY, THE FILTH and WE3. In recent years Morrison has been hard at work expanding the DC Universe in titles ranging from the Eisner Award-winning titles SEVEN SOLDIERS and ALL STAR SUPERMAN to the weekly 52 to the reality-shattering, multiverse-spanning epic that is FINAL CRISIS. In his secret identity, Morrison is a "counterculture" spokesperson, a musician, an award-winning playwright and a chaos magician. He divides his time between Los Angeles and his homes in Scotland.

FRANK QUITELY

FRANK QUITELY was born in Glasgow in 1968. Since 1988 he's drawn *The Greens* (self-published), *Blackheart, Missionary Man, Shimura, Inaba,* ten shorts for Paradox Press, six shorts for Vertigo, FLEX MENTALLO, 20/20 VISIONS, BATMAN: THE SCOTTISH CONNECTION, THE KINGDOM: OFFSPRING, JLA: EARTH 2, THE INVISIBLES, TRANSMETROPOLITAN, THE AUTHORITY, *Captain America, New X-Men,* THE SANDMAN: ENDLESS NIGHTS, WE3, ALL-STAR SUPERMAN and BATMAN AND ROBIN. He has also created covers for *Negative Burn, Judge Dredd Megazine, Classic 2000 AD*, JONAH HEX, BOOKS OF MAGICK: LIFE DURING WARTIME, BITE CLUB, AMERICAN VIRGIN and ALL-STAR BATMAN. He lives in Glasgow with his wife and three children. He used to design his own hats and clothing. Currently his favorite hobby is cooking.

JAMIE GRANT

JAMIE GRANT first appeared in 1968 in Dunfermline, Scotland. As he grew to reading size he began to read *a lot* of comics. Later (when bigger) he penned *Blank Expression* (self-published) and painted *Missionary Man* for the *Judge Dredd Megazine* while performing many other demeaning commercial art services in exchange for money (which he spent on comics). Since 1999 he's lived and got thoroughly wasted in Glasgow while publishing many issues of *Northern Lightz*, an underground anthology comic. He also founded Hope Street Studios (a true comic den) where he crafted the digital inking and coloring techniques applied to Vertigo's WE3 before tackling ALL-STAR SUPERMAN. His favorite music to color comic book super-spandex to is Devo, The Mothers of Invention and Frank Black. Jamie's personal coat of arms: "It doesn't take me long to work half an hour. No job too dangerous!"